LEEDS PALS

*This new edition is dedicated to my beloved wife Lynda who
has changed my life more than I could have imagined.*

LEEDS PALS

A HISTORY OF THE 15TH (SERVICE) BATTALION (1ST LEEDS) THE PRINCE OF WALES'S OWN (WEST YORKSHIRE REGIMENT) 1914–1918

Laurie Milner

Pen & Sword
MILITARY

First published in Great Britain in 1991
This edition published in 2015 by
Pen & Sword Military
an imprint of
Pen & Sword Books Ltd
47 Church Street
Barnsley
South Yorkshire
S70 2AS

ISBN 978 1 47384 181 9

Typeset in Palatino by
Mac Style Ltd, Bridlington, East Yorkshire
Printed and bound in Malta by Gutenberg Press Ltd

Pen & Sword Books Ltd incorporates the imprints of Pen & Sword Archaeology,
Atlas, Aviation, Battleground, Discovery, Family History, History, Maritime,
Military, Naval, Politics, Railways, Select, Transport, True Crime, and Fiction,
Frontline Books, Leo Cooper, Praetorian Press, Seaforth Publishing and
Wharncliffe.

For a complete list of Pen & Sword titles please contact
PEN & SWORD BOOKS LIMITED
47 Church Street, Barnsley, South Yorkshire, S70 2AS, England
E-mail: enquiries@pen-and-sword.co.uk
Website: www.pen-and-sword.co.uk

Contents

INTRODUCTION

My interest in the Leeds Pals – properly, the 15th (Service) Battalion (1st Leeds) The Prince of Wales's Own (West Yorkshire Regiment) – was first aroused in 1982 when, as a collector of First World War souvenirs, I was offered a frame containing the badges and a visiting card of Tom Willey, an officer in the Leeds Pals who was killed on the first day of the Battle of the Somme. The following year, in my efforts to find out more about this man and the manner in which he met his death, I visited Serre, and in a cemetery there I came across the grave of John

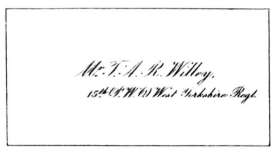

Tom Willey's visiting card.

William Milner, a Leeds Pal who had died on the Somme, aged 36, my age at that time. My late father was convinced that this man was related to his father. However, the subsequent release of the 1911 Census, a decade after this book was first published has revealed he that he was not, and that my father's forbears were from Bradford and not from Leeds.

I had been studying the history of the Leeds Pals for some time with a possible publication in mind, when I saw the first two Pals books published by Wharncliffe. I mentioned them to Bob Reed, a fellow Leeds Pals enthusiast, and on contacting the publishers in order to find out where he could obtain copies of the *Barnsley Pals* and *Accrington Pals* books, Bob enquired whether they would be interested in publishing anything on the Leeds Pals. The reply was that they would certainly give it some consideration, would he like to do it? Bob said, 'No, but I know a man who can!' The result you hold in your hands.

The Leeds Pals' story is one of great patriotism and optimism but also one of great tragedy. During my work on this book I often pondered on the question, 'were they good soldiers?' This is unanswerable, for the tasks they were set, especially on 1 July 1916, were impossible to achieve in the face of the resistance they were to encounter and the tactics they were to use. Perhaps the best answer is that they were certainly brave men, for they left their trenches without hesitation in two major offensives, in 1916 and 1917, and held the line against overwhelming odds when the Germans attacked in March and again in April 1918, even though on one occasion they were isolated and holding the entire Divisional front.

Another question I have tried to answer is 'what exactly constitutes the Leeds Pals?' Is it the men who joined at the Town Hall between 3rd and 5th September 1914? Yet not all of them passed the medical. Is it the men who went up to Colsterdale on 25 September 1914? Yet some of those had, by then, applied for commissions in other battalions. Is it the men who travelled to Egypt in December 1915? Yet by that time many of the men who had trained at Colsterdale had left to take commissions and some had been sent to the 19th Battalion to train the Reservists. Is it the men who went 'over the top' on 1 July 1916?

Although it can be argued that, whatever criterion one applies, the battalion ceased to be the 'Leeds Pals' on 1 July 1916, some of the original 1914 volunteers survived, and served with the 15th, and later the 15/17th, Battalion throughout the war. I therefore decided to write the entire history of the battalion, including its later additions up to its disbandment at the end of the war.

Because I have found so many excellent first-hand accounts of almost every aspect of the Pals' story, I have included as many quotations as possible. I feel that they give the book a unique flavour of the time, which my words alone could not provide. I have also tried to set the Pals' story against a broad historical background in an endeavour both to give the non-specialist reader some idea of the Pals' part in the First World War, and generally to preserve some measure of historical balance.

It has often been said that no book is the work of one person, and this one is certainly no exception. One of the most rewarding aspects of my task was the kindness, interest and enthusiasm shown to me by complete strangers, who often trusted me with photographs, letters and diaries of their relatives, without hesitation. I am indebted too, to the few surviving members of the Leeds Pals I was fortunate enough to meet, for their patience in answering my many and endless questions, and their willingness to pore over photographs of their long lost 'Pals', despite failing eyesight and sad memories in an effort to put a name to a face.

The Leeds Pals' guard at Colsterdale, 1914. Front row second from right is Arthur Dalby.

Acknowledgements

My sincerest thanks, then, to:

(15/259 Private) Arthur Dalby, and his sons Arthur and Douglas. Arthur Dalby (senior) died in 1992.

(15/471 Sergeant) Clifford Hollingworth, and to his wife Blanche and his niece Jackie Lowley. Clifford Hollingworth died in November 1989. Blanche Hollingworth died in September 1990.

(15/1110 Private) Cyril Charles Cryer. Charles Cryer died in 1993.

(15/1767 Private) Herbert Bradbourne, and to his daughter Mrs A. B. A. Hinton. Herbert Bradbourne died in February 1990.

(20733, Private) Percy Barlow, who joined the 15th West Yorkshire Regiment in 1916, and to his niece Elizabeth Beadle. Percy Barlow died in 1989.

(37468, Private) Walter Hare, who joined the 15/17th West Yorkshire Regiment from the Bradford Pals in February 1918. Walter Hare died in 1996.

To the relatives of the following Leeds Pals, respectively:

Kathleen Baker	15/424 Private Walter Hands
Margaret Barstow	15/1238 Private Bernard Gill
Norman H. Bell	15/158 Private Charles Henry Bell
Edna Bews	5/1781 Private Horace Iles
Edward Bickersteth	Lieutant Stanley Morris Bickersteth
Cecilia Brown	15/81 Private Cyril N. Brown
Joan Coates	15/582 Private Alfred Lee
Celia O'Mally Collins	15/400 Sergeant Harold Green
John Collinson	15/217 Private Joe Collinson
Trevor Cosby	15/231 Private George W. Cosby
Dorothy Crabtree	15/1918 Lance-Corporal Walter Wild
Mrs G. Cunningham	15/1951 Private John Jackson Shaw
Mr G. Fenton	15/323 Private Alan James Fenton
Ronald Garner & Harold Nixon	15/686 Private Fred Nixon
Mary Gray	15/396 Lance-Corporal James Grey
Florence K. Groves	15/120 Private Harry Brown
Jeanne and John Kennington	15/825 Herbert Smith
David Hargreaves	15/1082 Private Herbert Hargreaves
Harvey Hirst	15/464 Private Lewis Hirst

Elizabeth Jackson	15/1040 Private Harold L. Jackson
Grace Kemp & Leslie Kemp	15/1906, Private Tom Newton
Gerald Lyons	15/606 Private William Lyons
Eric Maguire	15/1246 Private P. C. Maguire
Ann Marsden	15/497 C. S. M. Arthur Ibbotson
Mary Mawson	41661 Private Arthur B. Beatty
Mrs S. Pellow	15/393 Private George Grant
Mr E. Pickup	15/1094 Private Fred H. Pickup
Mr J. W. Place	15/1101 Private Tom Place, MSM
Dr A. Reeves	15/903 Private Harry Tomalin
Margaret and Philip Sudol	15/672 Corporal Fred Naylor
Mary Wainman	15/944 Private Wilfred Wainman
Charles & Norma Wallace	15/1099 Private Fred Wild
Jeanne M. Waterfield	15/706 Private John W. Parkinson
Margaret Willetts	15/500 Sergeant Alfred E. Ingle
Sheila Yeadon	15/1024, Private John Yeadon

To my two 'Super Sleuths', Paul Laycock of Huddersfield and Bob Reed of York who helped me to track down some of the relatives of Leeds Pals, and who also put me in touch with collectors who had photographs, often using the slimmest of leads. I would also like to thank Bob for his suggestions and help with the nominal roll, and for allowing me to use the diaries of Eddie Woffenden from his collection.

To my army of unpaid researchers and fellow First World War enthusiasts throughout England:
Peter Hawkins formerly of BBC Radio Leeds
Dr Pat Morris and Kathleen Beales of Leeds
Don Jackson of York
Derek Smith and Nigel Hornby of Halifax
Paul Reed of Crawley, West Sussex
Dr Jim Hagerty, author of *Leeds at War*
Susan Cunliffe-Lister author of *Days of Yore – A history of Masham*
John Davies, Head of the History Department of Leeds Grammar School
Jon Cooksey, author of the volume on the Barnsley Pals
David Raw, who has written the volume on the Bradford Pals, and who very kindly shared much of his research with me
Dennis Walsh of Chameleon Television Ltd
Andrew Sheldon and Angela Ewart of Yorkshire TV's *Calendar* programme.

To the custodians of the archival material I have consulted:
Public Record Office
British Library
British Museum Newspaper Library
Westminster Reference Library
Christopher Bye and Kathleen Rainford of the *Yorkshire Evening Post*
Mrs Nichols of Leeds Parish Church
Mr Harry Rayner custodian of Bramwell Methodist Church Cemetery

Mrs Ann Heap of Leeds Local History Library
Peter Brears Curator of Leeds City Museum
Brigadier J. M. Cubiss, CBE, MC, Curator of the Prince of Wales's Own Regiment of Yorkshire
    Museum, York
Stephen Green, Curator of the Cricket Memorial Gallery at Lord's Cricket Ground
J. H. Rumsby, Senior Curator of the Tolson Memorial Museum, West Kirklees
Brian Haigh, Curator of the Bagshaw Museum at Otley

To my former colleagues at the Imperial War Museum:
Professor Peter Simkins (now president of the Western Front Association), Mark Seaman and
    Catherine Moriarty in the Research and Information Office, for sharing my enthusiasm, and
    acting as unpaid sounding boards.
Rod Suddaby, Keeper of the Department of Documents, Philip Reed, Ann Commander and
    Nigel Steel for their help in bringing documents held by the Museum to my notice.
Jane Carmichael, Keeper of the Department of Photographs, for permission to publish
    photographs from the Museum's collection.
Margaret Brooks, Keeper of the Department of Sound Records, for the loan of sound recording
    equipment, Peter Hart for his advice on recording the reminiscences of First World War
    veterans, and Alan Morrow for his expert help with the sound recording and some of the
    photography.
Mike Hibberd for providing information about the Battalion's cloth insignia, and Chris
    McCarthy whose knowledge of the Somme battlefields is encyclopaedic.

To John Harding of the Army Historical Branch of the Ministry of Defence for his support and
friendship.

To Toby Buchan and Roni Wilkinson of Wharncliffe Publishing for their help and encouragement.

Of course, any errors of fact or interpretation are my own.

The best account I have read of the events leading to the outbreak of the First World War is in
Professor Gary Sheffield's *Forgotten Victory*. This book is also, in my opinion, the best single
volume history of an often greatly misunderstood war.

PROLOGUE

In June 1914 the Archduke Franz Ferdinand, heir to the throne of Austria-Hungary, accompanied by his wife Sophia, made a routine state visit to Sarajevo, the capital of the newly annexed state of Bosnia. There they were assassinated by Gavrilo Princip, a hitherto unknown Bosnian nationalist whose action so upset the delicate balance of power that, like falling dominoes, the countries of Europe collapsed into war.

Austria blamed Serbia for harbouring political extremists (a secret Serbian group called the 'Black Hand' had provided Princip with weapons), and her aggressive stance caused Russia, Serbia's ally, to enter the political squabble. Austria in turn invoked her ally Germany whose sabre rattling had been heard throughout Europe for more than a decade. Russia then looked to her ally, France, for support. Still smarting from her defeat at the hands of the Prussians in 1870, France joined the fray.

Von Schlieffen's plan for Germany in the event of war in Europe, depended upon a holding action in the East while the main attack was directed against France. In order to enter France by the route suggested

Gavrilo Princip, the man who fired the shots that started the First World War. He died of tuberculosis in prison during the war.

Archduke Franz Ferdinand and his wife set off on their final journey, Sarajevo, 28 June 1914.

Arrest of one of the assassins, thought to be Cabrinovitz. (Imperial War Museum)

in von Schlieffen's plan, the Germans would have to violate Belgian neutrality unless, of course, Belgium allowed the invading force free passage. Britain, concerned about her Belgian ally, asked France and Germany for assurances that Belgian neutrality would be respected. France reassured Britain that it would, but Germany was evasive. On 1 August 1914, France, Germany and Belgium mobilised. The following day Germany demanded unrestricted passage of her armies through Belgium. On 3 August France and Germany declared war on each other, and on the 4th Germany declared war on Belgium and her armies crossed the border. The same day Britain mobilised, and issued an ultimatum to Germany that unless Belgian neutrality was guaranteed within

German proclamation issued by the GOC, the Army of the Meuse, justifying the Germans' invasion of Belgian neutrality. This was issued as a postcard in Britain accompanied by an English translation. (Author's collection)

AU PEUPLE BELGE

C'est à mon plus grand regret que les troupes allemandes se voient forcées de franchir la frontière de Belgique. Elles agissent sous la contrainte d'une nécessité inévitable. La neutralité de la Belgique ayant été violée par des officiers, français qui, sous un déguisement, ont traversé le territoire belge en automobile pour pénétrer en Allemagne.

BELGES !

C'est mon plus grand désir qu'il y ait encore moyen d'éviter un combat entre deux peuples qui étaient amis jusqu'à présent, jadis même alliés. Souvenez-vous des glorieux jours de Waterloo où c'étaient les armes allemandes qui ont contribué à fonder et à établir l'indépendance et la prospérité de votre Patrie.

Mais il nous faut le chemin libre. Des destructions de ponts, de tunnels, de voies ferrées, devront être regardées comme des actions hostiles.

BELGES !

Vous avez à choisir ! J'espère que l'armée allemande de la Meuse ne sera pas contrainte de vous combattre. Un chemin libre pour attaquer, c'est tout ce que nous désirons.

Je donne des garanties formelles à la population belge qu'elle n'aura rien à souffrir des horreurs de la guerre, que nous payerons en or-monnaie les vivres qu'il faudra prendre au pays, que nos soldats se montreront les meilleurs amis d'un peuple pour lequel nous éprouvons la plus haute estime, la plus grande sympathie.

C'est de votre sagesse et d'un patriotisme bien compris qu'il dépend d'éviter à votre pays les horreurs de la guerre.

Le Général Commandant en Chef l'Armée de la Meuse.

Von EMMICH

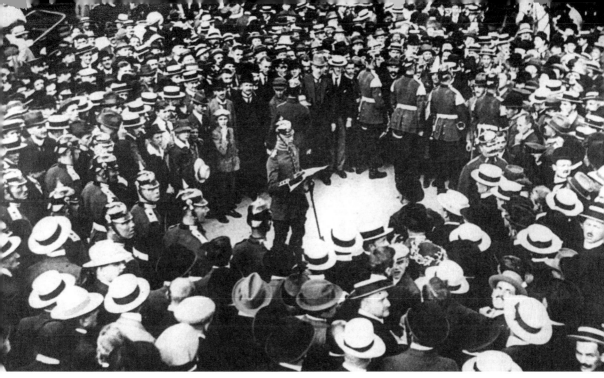

*The Declaration of **Kriegsgefahr** (danger of war) is read out in Berlin, 31 July 1914.*

German infantrymen don their equipment and get ready to go to war.

Optimistic German soldiers on their way to Paris.

Soldiers of the German 47th Infantry Regiment advance, 26 November 1914.

Field-Marshal Lord Kitchener, Secretary of State for War, leaving the War Office to address Parliament on 2 June 1916. Three days later he sailed for Russia and was lost at sea when HMS Hampshire struck a mine off the Orkney Isles.

twelve hours, Britain would declare war on the invader. The ultimatum expired, unfulfilled at midnight, and Britain was at war.[1]

War requires soldiers, and while Britain's small Regular Army was sufficient to police the Empire, it was no match in size for the vast Continental armies of 1914. Britain had traditionally relied upon the Royal Navy as its first line of defence, and its small standing army could be used in conjunction with locally raised forces to protect its colonies. However, the Haldane reforms, between 1906 and 1912, which came at a time when war in Europe seemed a possibility, resulted in the War Office accepting a Continental commitment for the British Army in the event of war.

Britain's second line was also reorganised by Haldane. Raised in the nineteenth century to defend Britain against an invasion by the French, the Rifle Volunteers and Yeomanry Cavalry, became the Territorial Force in 1908. Although the Territorials could not be compelled to serve abroad, the troops who had volunteered for 'Imperial Service' in South Africa during the Boer War had established an important precedent. Field Marshal Lord Kitchener, the Secretary of State for War[2] did not, even in the earliest days of the war, subscribe to the common theory that the armies would be 'home before the leaves fall', or that it would all be 'over by Christmas'. He foresaw that Britain's commitment to her allies, and the vast size of the forces engaged, would require a mass army.

When the war started, therefore, Kitchener immediately proposed to increase the Army's establishment by raising 'Service Battalions', and by doubling the number of Territorial battalions attached to each regiment.

NOTES

1. The best account I have read of the events leading to the outbreak of the First World War is in Professor Gary Sheffield's *Forgotten Victory*. This book is also, in my opinion, the best single volume history of an often greatly misunderstood war.
2. Kitchener succeeded Haldane as Secretary of State for War on 5 August 1914, and was the first serving officer to hold the post.

Chapter One

A 'Friends' Battalion for Leeds

Something that Leeds may do. Why not a 'Friends Battalion'?
Yorkshire Evening Post, *31 August 1914*

RECRUITING IN LEEDS AND RAISING THE PALS, AUGUST–SEPTEMBER 1914

During the Bank Holiday weekend at the end of July 1914, the people of Britain watched the crisis in Europe intensify. British children at school in Germany were being ordered out of the country, and travellers bound for the Continent were being turned back in mid-Channel. On Sunday 2 August prayers for peace were offered in churches and chapels, and in Leeds the Leeds Rifles, the Territorial battalion of the West Yorkshire Regiment, about to entrain for Scarborough for their annual camp on the racecourse, hesitated awaiting confirmation of a rumour that they were to be embodied and mobilised at once. The rumour proved unfounded, so they stuck to their original programme. Almost as soon as they had arrived at Scarborough, however, they were returned from camp to Carlton Barracks and embodied.[1]

Leeds in 1908, a patriotic display in Briggate on 7 July, to celebrate the royal visit of King Edward VII and Queen Alexandra. (Author's collection)

Meanwhile crowds gathered in Leeds City Square, Briggate and Boar Lane. On Bank Holiday Monday, the excursions offered by the railway companies were cancelled and the holidaymakers returned home to the bleak prospect of war. Some men rushed home in order to join up. Fred Nixon, and some of his pals cut short their cycling tour of the Lake District, anxious that they might miss the war that was to be over by Christmas.[2] Further afield Stanley Morris Bickersteth (Morris to his friends and family), fifth of six sons of the Vicar of Leeds, was in Southern Rhodesia. He had been on a long holiday, which had included a visit to his brother in Australia, on the advice of his doctor, following an appendix operation. He travelled through three days and nights from Salisbury to Cape Town and boarded a ship for Britain.[3]

Uncertain of the economic implications of war, some people began panic-buying food and prices rose accordingly. On 4 August, however, the day war was declared, the City of Leeds General Purposes Committee assembled at the request of its Chairman Alderman Charles Wilson and a special meeting of the City Council was convened to assess the situation and bring some measure of control to the panic. It was also at this meeting that the Lord Mayor, Edward Brotherton, made the generous offer of half his capital and the whole of his income to be at the disposal of his country. [4]

A prize-winning team of the Leeds Rifles, the Territorial battalion of the West Yorkshire Regiment, pose with their shooting trophy circa 1910. On the far left is Alfred Ibbotson, who was to be an early volunteer for the Leeds Pals in September 1914. (A. Marsden)

The Reverend Samuel Bickersteth, DD, TD, Vicar of Leeds. Although Honorary Chaplain to the Leeds Rifles, he was an active member of the Leeds Pals Raising Committee.

Although business as usual was advocated, the banks had not reopened after the holiday on Monday, and they remained closed until Friday 7 August.

That same Friday, just three days after the declaration of war, Lord Kitchener's first 'Call to Arms' was published in the local press in Leeds, calling for 100,000 men between the ages of 19 and 30 years to enlist for a period of three years or the duration of the war.[5] It was followed on 10 August by an appeal for 2,000 unmarried junior officers between the ages of 17 and 30 years to take Temporary Commissions in the Army, 'until the war is concluded'.[6]

Throughout the month, a series of public meetings in Leeds produced a good response, and created the momentum needed to bring the Territorials up to full strength, and to provide a significant number of recruits for what rapidly

Above: Edward A. Brotherton, Lord Mayor of Leeds 1913–1914.

Stanley Morris Bickersteth at Rugby School in 1908.

came to be called 'Kitchener's Army'. The Lord Mayor held a mass meeting at the Town Hall, where he appealed for 5,000 recruits, a total that would be achieved and surpassed within a matter of weeks. Another meeting held by the Earl of Harewood, Lord Lieutenant of West Riding, attracted such a crowd that an overflow meeting had to be held. Among the speakers was Alderman Charles H. Wilson, who was to make a significant contribution to the recruitment of the Leeds Pals.

Dr Samuel Bickersteth, Vicar of Leeds, preaching at his Parish Church on 29 August, made an impassioned plea for the young men of Leeds to respond to Lord Kitchener's appeal with patriotism, and offer their services to the armed forces. This plea was echoed by Canon Brameld in St Matthew's, Chapel Allerton, and in St Georges' Church close to Leeds Union Infirmary.

Thus, within days Leeds was already responding to Kitchener's appeal. Nearly 2,000 men enlisted almost at once and by mid-morning on 31 August the recruiting office in Hanover Square was besieged by a crowd of some 300 more applicants. Although adequate for the slow trickle of volunteers before the war, the Hanover Square recruiting office was too small; it was also difficult to find, tucked away as it was in a narrow side street near the University.

Because of the massive crowd, many applicants were told to use the rear entrance to the building in the basement, where they had to 'pass through some unoccupied dungeon-like cellaring thick with filth'.[7]

Undeterred, the men waited patiently as four were admitted at a time, but when the recruiting officer announced at half-past twelve that no more would be admitted until half-past two, there was an angry outburst. 'I have been waiting here since nine o'clock this morning and

General Sir Robert Baden Powell, the Chief Scout (centre in shorts), outside Leeds Town Hall after reviewing his Scouts on Friday, 5 June 1914.

have not been able to get a turn yet,' complained one of the men, 'they talk about the young men of Leeds wanting skirts, but when we come here they won't take us!' and he and several others gave up and left. Inside the recruiting office Captain Kelly and his staff assured a representative of the *Yorkshire Evening Post* that they were doing all they could to process

Leeds Town Hall in 1911.

4

Your King and Your Country Need You.

A Call to Arms.

An addition of 100,000 men to His Majesty's Regular Army is immediately necessary in the present grave national emergency.

Lord Kitchener is confident that this appeal will be at once responded to by all those who have the safety of the Empire at heart.

TERMS OF SERVICE.

General Service for a period of 3 years or until the war is concluded.

Age of enlistment between 19 and 30.

HOW TO JOIN.

Full information can be obtained at any Post Office in the Kingdom, or at any Military Depot.

God Save the King.

Temporary Commissions in His Majesty's Army.

2,000 Junior Officers (unmarried) are immediately required in consequence of the increase of the Regular Army.

TERMS OF SERVICE.

To serve with the Regular Army until the war is concluded. Age 17 to 30.

An allowance of £20 will be made for uniform and of £5 15s. for equipment.

HOW TO OBTAIN HIS MAJESTY'S COMMISSION.

Cadets or ex-Cadets of the University Training Corps or Members of a University should apply to their Commanding Officers or to the authorities of their University. Other Young Men of good general education should apply in person to the Officer commanding the nearest Depot. Full information can be obtained by written application to the Secretary, War Office.

God Save the King.

Lord Kitchener's 'Call to Arms' which appeared in the Yorkshire Evening Post *on Friday, 7 August 1914.*

Lord Kitchener's appeal for officers, published in the Yorkshire Evening Post *on Monday, 10 August 1914. (Leeds Library)*

the applications. Over 100 men had been seen that morning, and the rest of the queuing men would be dealt with by nightfall.[8] Despite suggestions to the contrary, many young men from the Jewish community in Leeds had turned up to join the army but after waiting for hours at the Hanover Square office some had given up. One group, out of work because the clothing industry was slack, had walked to Halifax and been accepted there.[9]

Clearly this state of affairs could not be allowed to last, and when it came to the notice of the Lord Mayor he quickly persuaded the Tramways Committee to allow the army to use the new Tram Depot at Swinegate as a recruiting centre.[10] Meanwhile, the crush at Hanover Square was to continue until 3 September, and a recruiting team went off to tour the football grounds to search for even more recruits.

The Earl of Harewood, Lord Lieutenant of West Riding.

Stirring scenes were witnessed on the Leeds City Football Club's ground last evening at the end of the match with Fulham. The Lord Mayor of Leeds (Mr E A Brotherton), Mr Rowland Barran MP, and Mr W Middlebrook MP addressed in turn a crowd of about 4,000 spectators, and in exactly half an hour 200 recruits were obtained for Kitchener's Army. This was the inspiring outcome of an invitation given to the comptroller of the club, Mr Tom Coombs. The Lord Mayor accompanied by the Lady Mayoress (Mrs Charles Ratcliffe)[11] and Mr Charles Ratcliffe, appeared on the stand towards the close of the game. As soon as the end was reached there was a spirited rush across the field, and rousing cheers greeted the Lord Mayor as he stepped forward to address the gathering. Midway through his speech. Mr Brotherton used a suggestion of the Lady Mayoress that prospective recruits should come up on to the stand. The response was wonderful. Up the steps sturdy young fellows came to receive the immediate guerdon of an armlet of ribbon in the national colours which the Lady Mayoress tied round the left coat sleeve, and to win, perchance with their comrades an imperishable glory on the battlefield. The Lord Mayor shook hands with each recruit, while the crowd contributed encouraging cheers. When the rush subsided it was found that the number of volunteers was 149.

Prospective recruits crowd the entrance to the Leeds Recruiting Office in Hanover Square, Monday, 31 August 1914. (Leeds Library)

THE IDLE, THE IDOL, AND THE IDEAL.

Cartoon from the **Sportsman** *reproduced in the* **Yorkshire Evening Post** *on Thursday, 3 September 1914. (Leeds Library)*

Fred Wilson, the wounded hero, with his wife and family. (Leeds Library, Leeds Mercury 9.9.1914)

The Lady Mayoress called for a further 51. Another dash was made; another round of prolonged cheering. When 21 were required there was a brief pause. An avenue was made through the people, and to the chorus of 'IPs a long way to Tipperary the margin was quickly filled. Captain Kelly, from the Leeds Recruiting Office registered the applicants.[12]

The first day at the Tramway Depot at Swinegate produced 320 recruits, the highest daily total so far. Captain Kelly's staff, now numbering twenty, as well as half-a-dozen doctors, spent a busy day filling in attestation forms and weeding out those unfit for service. Despite an offer of free dental treatment for recruits, men were still being rejected because of the condition of their teeth.

On the second day, the number was in the region of 350 including many boys offering themselves as drummers or buglers, and a veteran of the Crimean War[13] who was regretfully turned down.

Mrs Marjorie Took, 1989.

The illuminated tram used for recruiting in Leeds in September 1914. It is often erroneously described as the Leeds Pals' recruiting car. (Author's collection)

The recruiting campaign was given fresh impetus by running an illuminated tram through the streets. On its first journey it passed along Roundhay Road.

It was just at the bottom here, you see the road wasn't wide like this, it's been widened. At the bottom of the park, just there it came, and I was only a school girl, and we all went down to see this lovely tram. There was a big military man, he stood upstairs like on the top deck, that was open, and he was going with his arms pleading with them, 'We need you, we need you!' All the crowds were watching, and when he'd finished all the young men that were watching got on that tram went inside and enlisted, and I often wondered whether any of them got killed you know.

Marjorie Tooke[14]

The tram was manned by the Lord Mayor and Lady Mayoress accompanied by Aldermen and Councillors of the City, whose speeches were followed by a medley of patriotic songs. Musical accompaniment was provided by the Leeds Tramways Band playing on the upper deck.

On 8 September the recruiting party was joined by Trooper Fred Wilson a Reservist from the 5th (Royal Irish) Lancers who had been called up into the British Expeditionary Force (BEF) and severely wounded at Mons, the army's first major engagement with the Germans on 23 August. Alderman Charles Wilson introduced the wounded man and said:

… his anxiety to get back to the front should act as a stimulus to every young man of Leeds to enlist and seek to follow his glorious example. The 5th Lancers charged five times through the enemy, and the wounded Wilson was now only waiting for his wounds to heal before he would be at the enemy again.

It was in this spirit that the British soldier had got the Germans on the run and having got them on the run would keep them at it. But in order that the German defeat might be made certain

Lieutenant-Colonel J. Walter Stead, CO of the Leeds Pals August 1914–May 1915.

more men were needed for the British force, and he hoped that Leeds would do its share in providing the Army that Lord Kitchener had called for.[15]

While the men of Leeds were making their way to Hanover Square and to Swinegate, another rather different recruiting campaign was gathering momentum.

The idea of Pals battalions has been credited to the 17th Earl of Derby. Certainly he coined the phrase in his speech at St Anne's Street Drill Hall in Liverpool on 28 August 1914, but it seems that Major-General Henry Rawlinson, during his brief service as Director-General of Recruiting at the War Office, had actually come up with a similar concept before Lord Derby put his proposal to Kitchener. The idea was that local authorities be allowed to raise battalions of Pals in which potential recruits could be assured of serving with their friends, neighbours, former workmates or members of the same club or society.[17]

On 31 August 1914 a correspondent signing himself 'Willing' wrote to the Editor of the *Yorkshire Observer*:

Sir, Is there no influential citizen of Leeds who will come forward and call a meeting re the Earl of Derby's scheme for a battalion of 'pals' for this district? The amazing success of the Liverpool meeting is most gratifying, and there must be a great number of young men to whom the scheme appeals. Surely the sooner the matter is put on a definitive footing the more use the battalion will be.

That same day, the *Yorkshire Evening Post* reported the raising of the Liverpool Pals by Lord Derby and suggested a 'Friends Battalion' for Leeds.

… perhaps composed of the vast and, as yet, untapped recruiting ground of the middle class population engaged in commercial pursuits. Young men from the factories, warehouses and offices of the city who desire to go to the front, but hesitate about enlisting lest they should be sent to join a regiment in which they will not have kindred spirits … In these days when the cult of the open air flourishes and men spend their leisure in the cricket and football fields, the golf course, the lawn tennis courts and the weekend camp, office work has no debilitating effect worth speaking of … A Leeds commercial battalion would yield fine fighting material. Its members would be partially trained in advance by reason of the discipline given them in the playing fields, and they would gain immeasurably as men and citizens for the experience of the training camp and of the battlefield. Will nobody come forth and organise them?

Neither party had long to wait, for the following morning the *Yorkshire Post* reported that Lieutenant-Colonel J. Walter Stead, a Leeds solicitor and former Commanding Officer of the 7th Battalion (Leeds Rifles), The Prince of Wales's Own (West Yorkshire Regiment), TF, had

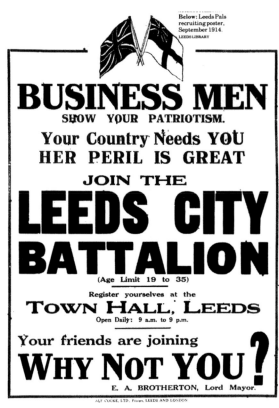

BUSINESS MEN

SHOW YOUR PATRIOTISM.

Your Country Needs YOU
HER PERIL IS GREAT

JOIN THE

LEEDS CITY
BATTALION

(Age Limit 19 to 35)

Register yourselves at the

TOWN HALL, LEEDS

Open Daily: 9 a.m. to 9 p.m.

Your friends are joining
WHY NOT YOU?

E. A. BROTHERTON, Lord Mayor.

ALF COOKE, LTD. Printer, LEEDS AND LONDON

Leeds Pals recruiting poster, September 1914.
(Leeds Library)

Silver cap-badge given to Tom Willey when commissioned in 1914. (Author's collection)

already applied to the West Riding of Yorkshire Territorial Association for permission to raise a battalion of 1,000 men from the City of Leeds, for Lord Kitchener's Army, and that his application had been forwarded to the War Office for approval. Furthermore, the Lord Mayor of Leeds, Edward Brotherton, had sent a telegram to Lord Kitchener, endorsing Stead's proposal. The article invited would-be members to write to Colonel Stead at his office at 3, Cookridge Street, giving name, address, age, occupation, name of present employer, and stating whether the applicant was married or single. The article also confirmed that 'in the event of a number of friends volunteering at the same time for service, the utmost endeavours will be made to attach them to the same company and section so that as chums they may be able to serve together'.

At the next monthly meeting of the Leeds City Council on 2 September, Edward Brotherton proudly announced that he had received a telegram from the War Office, which read: 'The Army Council thank the City of Leeds for their patriotic offer to raise a new battalion'. He continued:

> You have the thanks of Lord Kitchener; I offered it in the name of the City of Leeds, and it has been accepted by the War Office, and I know it will be supported readily by the young men who are anxious to join. I desire that this battalion shall be nearly twelve hundred strong. I know it will be a battalion which we of the City of Leeds will be proud of, and I put this request to you that the names of the men who enrol should be kept in our archives. With regard to the expense, I am not here to ask the Council or the people of Leeds to pay anything towards the cost of raising the

Alderman Charles Wilson, Acting Quartermaster and an energetic member of the Leeds Pals Raising Committee.

battalion. Your Lord Mayor desires to bear the cost out of his own pocket. I propose nominating a committee to meet me in my rooms at eleven o'clock tomorrow morning to complete the scheme.[18]

In the event, it transpired that his generous offer included providing the clothing and personal equipment of the battalion. Each man would be given a cap-badge emblazoned with the coat of arms of the City of Leeds and officers commissioned in 1914 were to have a silver cap-badge[19]. The War Office was to supply all the military hardware such as rifles, bayonets, transport wagons and two Maxim guns. The cost of the Lord Mayor's grand gesture was estimated by Alderman Charles Wilson to be in the region of £6,000, a small fortune in 1914.

Alderman Wilson, seconded by Alderman George Ratcliffe, moved the following resolution:

That the Council learns with great satisfaction that the offer of Colonel Stead to raise a Battalion of Leeds business men, 1,000 strong, to form part of Lord Kitchener's second Army, which offer having been strongly supported by the Lord Mayor of Leeds, Mr E A Brotherton, has now received the official sanction of the Army Council, and desires to thank the Lord Mayor for his patriotic offer to provide the necessary personal equipment and to assure Colonel Stead that the Council will heartily support the efforts he is making.

Councillor George H. Pearson, said that his party (the Labour Party) stood for worldwide peace, and in associating himself with the vote of thanks to the Lord Mayor he did not want it to be forgotten that workmen in the city were making sacrifices by contributions and by answering the calls of duty, and their only assistance was from their fellow men. He expressed his disapproval of the new battalion being confined to businessmen. In reply Alderman Arthur Willey remarked that up to the present Leeds had been rather dormant in its attitude towards the war, but the lead of the Lord Mayor would be a great spur to exertion and enthusiasm. The resolution was carried unanimously.[20]

Brotherton's Committee to administer the raising of the new battalion was composed of the following city dignitaries: the Hon Rupert Beckett, Mr William Nicholson, Dr Bickersteth (the Vicar of Leeds), Mr J. H. Wickstead, Alderman F. M. Lupton, Mr F. J. Kitson (Chairman of the Leeds Chamber of Commerce), Mr M. E. Sadler (Vice-Chancellor of the University of Leeds), Lieutenant-Colonel J. W. Stead, Alderman C. F. Tetley, Mr John Gordon, the Hon F. S. Jackson, Mr Henry Barran, Mr Arthur G. Lupton, Mr A. W. Bain, the Bishop of Leeds (Dr Cowgill), the President of the Leeds Free Church Council (the Rev John Anderson), and Mr Charles Ratcliffe.

At the first meeting the Lord Mayor was able to announce that he had received a telegram from Lieutenant-General Herbert Plumer, GOC Northern Command, congratulating him on the steps he had taken to initiate the raising of a Leeds Pals battalion.[21]

By nine o'clock on the morning of 3 September, when the Victoria Hall in Leeds Town Hall first opened its doors to the recruits for the Pals Battalion, some 200 men had already sent in their names. The linen banners proudly stretched across the busy thoroughfares of Leeds announced in huge letters, 'Business men of Leeds. Your King and Country need you. Join the Leeds City Battalion, Headquarters, Town Hall; 9am to 9pm.' The conditions of enrolment published in the local press stated that only non-manual workers between the ages of 19 and 35 should apply, and that single men were preferred. Ex-soldiers up to 45 years, ex-NCOs up to 46 years and selected ex-NCOs up to 50 years would be accepted. Enlistment would be for the period of the war or for three years and the rate of pay the same as that of the Regular Army.

One man who answered the 'Call to Arms' that day was E. Robinson of Yarnley:

Horace Iles in 1914, aged 14 years; he convinced the Leeds Pals Raising Committee that he was old enough to join the battalion.

> *On September 31 went down to Leeds Town Hall to join the local branch – ie Leeds Pals – of the West Yorks Regiment … The main hall of the Town Hall had about 60 young fellows arguing rather excitedly, but I and a fellow whom I had told my intention to and was joining me, went up to the table at the top of the room where two or three well dressed, prosperous looking gents were seated. I was asked what my father did for a living, much to my surprise, and I suggested I wanted to join and not my father. I said I was a clerk, but they insisted I should say what my father did. It was curiouser and curiouser, but eventually I said he was a farm worker. Very politely, very firmly it was told to me that only professional men's sons, or whose fathers had businesses, could join for a day or two – it was exclusive.*
>
> *My friend promptly nudged me and said he was going about his job, he never did join up … well, my patriotism wasn't very deep, and Belgian atrocities[22] didn't cut much ice, but I was fearfully sick of a humdrum life that led nowhere and promised nothing, so I went to another recruiting depot and was enlisted as a Gunner in the RA.[23]*

By nine o' clock the first evening over 500 men had volunteered, nearly half Colonel Stead's required 1,200. The list included solicitors, schoolmasters, university students, clothing manufacturers, warehousemen, leather merchants, mechanical engineers, mill managers, Board of Trade insurance officers, assistant collectors of taxes, articled clerks and even some 'retired gentlemen'[24] and it was anticipated that the Teachers' Training College would supply a whole company.[25]

The men were described as being 'of the right type – eager, intelligent and of fine physique'.

At a special meeting of the Leeds Chamber of Commerce Mr J. F. Kitson JP, the president, proposed a resolution approving the raising of a Leeds City battalion and commending the movement for consideration by all employers of the city, who would, the members were convinced, afford every facility in their power for members of their staffs and others in their employ to join up.[26]

Clifford Hollingworth in 1911. He gave this photograph to Blanche, his childhood sweetheart, when he joined the Pals.

> *It was quite a common sight to see three or four men from one office walk into the Victoria Hall together, and two or three batches said they had been given special permission by their employers to leave their desks in order to get their names down without delay.*

Said one trio 'Our boss told us to get out of the office and put our names down at once or he would kick us out!'

Yorkshire Evening Post, *Thursday 3 September 1914*

Then I found myself in the awesome town hall, the first time I had ever been there. I had never reason or desire to enter that stone temple of city law and order, yet here I was together with several more fellows who appeared to be at ease, as though they had been in and out of the town hall all their lives in fact. Later I discovered that they had! They were mostly officials and clerks in the city's administration offices.

Arthur Valentine Pearson[27]

On 4 September Edward Brotherton received a telegram from Lord Kitchener:

On behalf of His Majesty's Government, I accept with gratitude your munificent offer to be responsible for the equipment of the Leeds Battalion. This example of generous patriotism will, I am persuaded, have a far reaching effect. I wish the battalion every success, and shall be glad to see you if you wish to discuss matters at any time.[28]

Recruits continued to flock to Leeds Town Hall, and by the end of the second busy day some 800 men had registered. The following day the Incorporated Leeds Law Society added their support to the raising of the battalion, and requested that the Master of the Rolls make a regulation permitting service with the armed forces, for any period of time, to count as service by an articled clerk under articles.

Thomas Arthur Robert Raymond Ellicott Willy, circa 1910. He joined the Leeds Pals as a private in 1914, but was soon commissioned. He was one of the first to die on 1 July 1916.

I had just come from the Carlton Hill Barracks and I had seen the Territorials lined up ready for going away and of course the urge got in you, war was declared and England was in danger and everybody did the same. We were in the first 500,000 the Leeds Pals which was a big thing in the country… and there was a big rush. When I went in I thought I was going to be the only one but it was full…

Clifford Hollingworth[29]

I saw this lot in the paper and it said it was all Leeds people, and I joined up, I didn't know what a soldier [did] … I didn't even know that infantry walked, to be quite truthful with you, I didn't know anything about soldiers. I ought to have joined the cavalry lot, being brought up with horses, but it appealed to me and I went and I've never regret[ted] a moment of it really, because I never met a finer lot of fellows in my life. Lots of them were really well educated and I wasn't because my father made me leave school quite early to drive a ruddy horse!

Arthur Dalby[30]

Everyone rushing to get in, thinking it was a Pals army, they were all full of sportsmanship and that sort of thing. One of the chaps in the office there Lewis Hirst, he lost his legs [on 1 July 1916], he were a pal of mine, we were all footballers together. I went down, I think I was one of six.

Morrison Fleming[31]

Fred Wild (second from right wearing trilby) with some pals before the war. It is not known whether any of the others in this photograph joined the battalion. (N. Wallace)

Morris Fleming and his pals were not the only footballers to join up. When the Northern Foxes Football team of Leeds held their annual meeting to discuss fixtures for the forthcoming season, Arthur Ibbotson suggested that the whole club should enlist in the Leeds Pals. After some discussion this was put to the vote and carried almost unanimously, the only exemption being one member who was a Quaker.[32]

At about the same time, the battalion was also joined by Evelyn Lintott, a famous Leeds City and International half back. In an interview with the *Yorkshire Evening Post*, Lintott said that he believed himself to be the only professional Association player so far who had decided to go on active service. He further stated that there had been a great deal of talk about players not enlisting, but he was of the opinion that, with some encouragement from clubs, about half-a-dozen players from each club would enlist.

Clearly under the impression that footballers were somehow different from their fellow men, Lintott concluded with the observations that 'when professional footballers were criticised for not enlisting it was not remembered that football was, generally speaking, the men's only livelihood, and a wound in the leg would in all probability throw a professional footballer out of work, and as he was often not

Morrison Fleming in 1977.

Cyril Brown, a solicitor's clerk, another of the first volunteers.

trained in any other work, it would be a very serious matter for him. It was perhaps a more serious matter for a footballer than for anybody else.'

Lintott, however, was trained in another profession, and received an income from his other employment, for he was a teacher at Dudley Hill Council School in Bradford. He had also been a sergeant in a Territorial battalion of the Royal West Kent Regiment and would soon receive his sergeant's stripes and, later, a commission in the Leeds Pals.[33]

As one would expect in Yorkshire, cricket was also represented in the battalion. Three prominent Yorkshire players, Major Booth, Arthur Dolphin and Roy Kilner had offered their services and had been accepted, as had other good, if less well-known, local cricketers such as John Yeadon. Among the other sporting celebrities who presented themselves at Leeds Town Hall were the Yorkshire athletes Albert Gutteridge and George Colcroft, and the wrestler

The Yorkshire Cricket Team, 1911. Booth is third from the left, back row, Kilner and Dolphin are seated at the front.

Joseph Jones. Two unexpected recruits to the battalion were the Reverend E. A. Cartwright, former Minister at Camp Road Baptist Chapel, Leeds, who was known for his 'sturdy, muscular Christianity,[34] and Mr Jogendra Sen, a Calcutta-born engineering student at Leeds University who lived in Blackman Lane.

The Reverend E. A. Cartwright.

> *We had a Hindu in our hut, called Jon Sen, he was the best-educated man in the battalion and he spoke about seven languages. But he was never allowed to be even a lance-corporal because in those days they would never let a coloured fellow be over a white man, not in England. But he was the best educated … he was at university when he joined up.*
>
> Arthur Dalby[35]

In response to a request from Colonel Stead, a number of would-be buglers turned up, and the Victoria Hall rang with the sounds of bugle calls from 'Reveille' to 'Lights Out', although the battalion still had no bugles of its own, nor even all the tents and blankets it would need before training could commence.

By noon on Monday, 7 September the total number of recruits had reached 1,100, only 100 short of Stead's required total. He anticipated that a number of men might not pass the medical and so was quite prepared to sign on more than were needed initially. He also announced that any man rejected would receive a certificate signed by the mayor to show that he had responded to the call to arms.

During the week the Battalion's Raising Committee had accepted the generous gift of a set of drums from Mr W. Powell Bowman of Messrs Goodall Backhouse and Company; Mr Ben Wade, a Leeds pipe manufacturer, had promised a pipe decorated with the city's coat of arms for each man, and Messrs Tetley and Sons, tobacconists of Boar Lane, would provide every soldier with a packet of tobacco.[36]

The enthusiastic reports in the local press about the raising and equipping of the Leeds Pals inevitably brought forth some critical response.

One correspondent signing himself 'Hunslet' wrote:

> *When our lads enlist on their own without fuss or bribery, they have to go where and with whom they are sent … May I suggest that when the Lord Mayor equips his Feather Bed Battalion that he be sure and not forget dressing gowns, slippers, eiderdowns, whiskeys and sodas, and, if he can manage it, to throw in a few billiard tables. I have no doubt the battalion will greatly distinguish itself.*

In the Pals' defence, the editor of the *Yorkshire Evening Post* replied:

> *We publish this letter so that, if comment of the kind is being made in the city, it can be answered effectively. 'Hunslet' takes a mean and narrow-minded view of the battalion. It will be equipped exactly like all other battalions of Lord Kitchener's Army, and will serve alongside any other battalion, no matter how or where recruited, and under exactly the same conditions. If 'Hunslet' is qualified to enlist, doubtless he will prefer to serve alongside his friends. This is just what the young men in business prefer to do, and doing it, they will enjoy exactly the same privileges given all other soldiers in Lord Kitchener's Army, and none other. We have already said that the labourer who enlists gives more than some of the business young men, because he gives the whole of his capital, but that is no reason for deriding the public spirit of these young men. When the labourer and the junior partner find themselves in the field together (as they will*

do if they have any luck) we venture to say they will be the best of friends, and find in each other qualities that they had, perhaps, little suspected.

Yorkshire Evening Post, 8 September 1914

On 8 September the battalion was declared to be complete, and a list of 1,275 men who had volunteered was published in four parts in the *Yorkshire Post* between 5 and 9 September.

I went by myself, volunteered… The name and address was taken and it was published in the Yorkshire Post, *not the* Evening Post, *the morning paper, and of course everybody bought that paper the next morning to see your name and address …*

Clifford Hollingworth[37]

Arrangements were soon made for the men to be attested and medically examined. An appeal for doctors resulted in some twenty to thirty offering their services, and a notice in the Yorkshire press called for the newly enlisted Pals to return to the Town Hall on 10 and 11 September, depending on the initial letter of their surnames.

On 11 September we were called to the town hall and we were attested. Eleven, nine, fourteen, and on my discharge paper it said, 'Date of attestation, age nineteen and eleven twelfths', so you can see how near I was to being twenty. We were all about the same age, twenty or twenty-one, and of course there were one or two elderly [older] people got in and that was it.

Clifford Hollingworth[38]

There were forms to sign and vows to vow. We swore to be true and loyal soldiers, to serve King and Country (which somehow seemed to include Alderman Charles Wilson) until death did us part!

Arthur V. Pearson[39]

He looked at me and he says, 'Sallow complexion, prominent nose, mole on the right cheek', before he'd done with me I felt a bit like Frankenstein! Then he says, 'Initials?' I says, 'F-A'. He says, 'You're going to have some trouble with that!' He said, 'F-A in the army doesn't stand for your initials.'

[Fewster] Arthur Dalby[40]

On entering the examination room for their medical, the men, clad only in trousers and socks, first had their height measured.

The height then was five foot six and a half. I was five foot six and was worried stiff so I filled my shoes with paper and fastened big rubber heels on the soles and heels. When I went down they asked me my height and I told them, they hummed and hahed about it so he says 'Well take your shoes off,' well that jiggered it! Anyway.

I says, 'well there's all my pals joining,' and there was six of us all joining, all footballers, so they says, 'Oh, go on, let him go in, so I was one of the midgets.

Morrison Fleming[41]

A cartoon drawn by Cyril Brown and sent to his aunt and uncle in August 1914.

Leeds Pals take the oath of allegiance in the Victoria Hall, Leeds Town Hall, September 1914. Colonel J. Walter Stead, VD, is still wearing his Leeds Rifles uniform, and next to him stands the Lady Mayoress, Dorothy Una Ratcliffe. (Imperial War Museum)

They were then made to stand against a wall and asked to read the letters on an optician's card from a distance of about 20 feet. It was this part of the medical that caused the most rejections – understandably so, for it is impossible to attain an adequate standard of marksmanship without reasonably good eyesight. Next the recruits came under the 'kindly but critical' gaze of the doctor. They were required to have an expanded chest measurement of 34 inches, and were told to whirl their arms around before they were measured in order to bring themselves up to their full girth. After this came the teeth inspection, another cause of many of the rejections. Each man was expected to have at least four opposing molars in good condition, though these could be anywhere on the jaw. A physical examination followed, which included the doctor sounding the recruit's chest, a 'short arm inspection', and a rather bizarre ritual in which the applicant was required to hop along a piece of baize, laid on the floor, to show that he was not flat-footed.[42]

> ... *you went for a medical to see if you could pass, and it's rather funny that half a dozen of us went down together, we went to the same Sunday School, one lived opposite here [Royal Park Avenue], Walter Jowett, and I was the only one of the six that passed. Rather funny was that.*
>
> Clifford Hollingworth[43]

I was AI, I was an athlete because I had my own gymnasium, I mean to say, I had a big hay-loft over the horse thing, and I made half of it … I had punch balls, boxing gloves, wrestling mats, weight-lifting things. I were as fit as a fiddle when I went, because I had my own gymnasium.

Two brothers came, Harold Hartley and his brother. Harold Hartley was an ordinary fellow, put it that way, but his brother was a really big athlete, and his brother says he had no bother about it. He said, 'I can do this, I can do that!' Anyway they turned his brother down, the athlete, and they took Harold. Because, they said, 'Your heart's affected, you're doing too much athletics, your heart's affected.'

Arthur Dalby[44]

In all, about 8 per cent of the men who had presented themselves failed the medical. Those who had been accepted were next measured for their uniforms, which they hoped would soon be supplied. Some of them made appointments with one of the studios in Leeds, where they could have a portrait photograph taken in an army uniform, and even web equipment, provided for the occasion by the photographer.

I was called to put on my first ever tunic and cap at a first class photographers in the city! A pin or two here, a tuck or two there and, from the camera's eye, the tunic was a perfect fit. The cap ($6^7/_8$) had a badge. The City's coat-of-arms, and that was when I first adorned my brow with the badge which I was very proud to wear and serve under for four arduous years. The badge of comradeship, danger, mud, sweat and blood.

Arthur V. Pearson[45]

Although many of the men who had enlisted in the Leeds Pals were potential officers, and some of them were subsequently commissioned from the ranks, Colonel Stead had made his own arrangements about recruiting the battalion's junior officers. Some of these were former members of the Leeds University and Leeds Grammar School Officers' Training Corps, others were the sons of prominent families. Morris Bickersteth, son of the Vicar of Leeds, and who had rushed home from Southern Rhodesia to join up, arrived in Leeds at the end of August 1914 and offered his services to Colonel Stead. He was nominated for a commission although it was to be Stead himself who nearly caused him to fail the medical:

Saturday September 12th 1914 – Morris, by the exercise of a little cunning, has managed to pass the medical preparatory to getting a commission in Colonel Stead's Leeds Battalion. The only difficulty was his eyesight. He went down to the optician, Aitchison's in the morning and took the precaution of learning by heart the card of alphabetical letters which are used as tests. In the afternoon Dr Mayo telephoned him to come down to the Town Hall. He nearly spoilt matters by getting into the clutch of the wrong doctor, whom, however, he left with some abruptness to seek Dr Mayo. The latter he fortunately found in an adjacent room and proceeded at once to have his eyes tested. Of the two cards of letters displayed, he naturally selected the one which he already knew by heart, and entirely satisfied Dr Mayo that even his left eye (which is half blind) was a remarkably long-sighted optic. In a subsequent interview with Colonel Stead, the cat was nearly let out of the bag owing to the stupidity (possibly well-meant) of that officer, who took it into his head to test Morris's eyes himself, this time of course with a fresh set of letters. However, it seems that Morris managed to satisfy requirements, and we now confidently hope that his nomination to a commission will follow in due course.

Bickersteth Family War Diary

On 14 September the General Purposes Committee of Leeds City Council met again and passed a further resolution:

(a) That such of the Corporation lands in the Ure Valley (Colsterdale) as may be required for training purposes be set aside for the use of the War Office in connection with the Leeds City Battalion.

(b) That such of the huts and dwellings as can be reasonably spared at the Breary Bank Village be set aside for their use, having regard to requirements for the construction of the Leighton Reservoir.

(c) That the Waterworks Committee be instructed to proceed at once with the construction either by contract or direct labour, of all the necessary buildings and works in accordance with the requirements of the War Office.[46]

The Waterworks Committee did not need asking twice, for its chairman was Arthur Willey, a prominent Leeds solicitor whose son, Tom, one of his articled clerks, had joined the Pals. The General Purposes Committee resolution was duly minuted by the Waterworks Committee, and the chairman, together with his deputy Alderman Ellis Midgeley and Councillor Frank Fountain, were empowered to make the necessary arrangements.

On 16 September Colonel Stead announced to the press that the Pals were to be trained at Colsterdale, on the Yorkshire Dales, about five miles from Masham. Although the situation was isolated, there was fresh water in the nearby reservoirs, and the site was served by a light railway built in 1901 to take materials up to the Roundhill reservoir, and taken over and extended by Leeds in 1910 to bring men and materials up for the new reservoir at Leighton.[47]

The Pals are measured for their uniforms, September 1914.

Douglas Parker poses in a borrowed uniform and web equipment at James Bacon & Sons' photographic studio in Leeds, September 1914. He was wounded on 1 July 1916. (N. Hornby)

The former recruiting office in Hangover Square, now divided into private flats. (Author's collection)

The basement of the former recruiting office in 1989, apparently unchanged since 1914. (Author's collection)

Some of the men could be housed in the navvies' huts, which would be vacated since work on the reservoir was to be suspended while the Pals were in training,[48] but the rest of the men would have to be accommodated in tents until additional huts could be provided, which would certainly be before the winter set in.

Colonel Stead and his Raising Committee now concentrated their attention on amassing the equipment they would need for training. Their appeal for tents had not been very productive, but at the last minute the War Office was able to provide a hundred tents on loan for the first couple of months until the huts could be built. The first bugle was given by Mr Richard Firth, and subscriptions were sought to provide the other fifteen necessary. An appeal for blankets had brought forth nearly half of the 2,000 required, and sixteen rifles and 50,000 rounds of ammunition had been given to the battalion by members of the Raising Committee. A Leeds cutlery manufacturer supplied a knife, fork and spoon for each man, and a further appeal was made for the loan of field-glasses, which produced fifteen of the forty pairs required. The owners were optimistically advised to scratch their names on them so that they could be returned after the war.[49]

Meanwhile the men returned to their homes, to await the summons to go off to camp.

NOTES

1. Under the Territorial and Reserve Forces Act of 1907 the Territorial Force could be 'embodied' by the Army Council, with the permission of the King and the agreement of Parliament, in the case of national danger or great emergency. This effectively meant that members of the Territorial Force lost their part-time status and became full-time soldiers, although they were still not automatically liable for overseas service.

2. Author's correspondence and conversations with Ronald Garner and Harold Nixon (nephew and brother respectively of 15/686 Private Fred Nixon).

3. Bickersteth Family War Diary. This unpublished diary, consisting of ten volumes, was compiled during the First World War by Dr Samuel Bickersteth, Vicar of Leeds, his wife, Ella, and their six sons, Monier, Geoffrey, Julian, Burgon, Stanley Morris, and Ralph. It contains transcripts of many of the soldier sons' letters home, and a linking narrative written by various members of the family. At the time of writing it was still in the possession of the family, but is now at Churchill College, Cambridge.

4. Scott, W. H., *Leeds in the Great War, 1914–1918,* Libraries and Arts Committee, Leeds 1923, pp 10–11.

5. *Yorkshire Evening Post,* 7 August 1914.

6. Ibid, 10 August 1914.

7. Ibid, 31 August 1914. The former recruiting office building is now a private residence. It has been divided into two houses, which have been converted into flats. The basement is unoccupied and dilapidated, and matches the description given in 1914. The rear yard where the men queued in 1914 can still be seen and, apart from a wall dividing it in two, it too remains apparently unchanged.

8. *Yorkshire Evening Post,* 31 August 1914.

9. Ibid, 31 August 1914. In 1914 Leeds had a substantial Jewish population, mostly Russian emigrants who had fled the anti-Jewish pogroms of the 1880s. Although immigration was restricted from 1905, it has been estimated that by 1911 some 12 per cent of the population of Leeds township was Jewish. See Frazer, D., (ed.), *A History of Modern Leeds,* Manchester University Press, 1980.

10. *Yorkshire Evening Post,* 1 September 1914. *Yorkshire Post,* 4 September 1914.

11. Because the Lord Mayor, Mr Edward A. Brotherton, was unmarried, the duties of Lady Mayoress were taken on by his niece, Mrs Dorothy Una Ratcliffe, the well-known Yorkshire poet.

12. *Yorkshire Post,* 3 September 1914.

13. The Crimean War lasted from 1853–56. This gentleman would therefore have to have been well into his seventies.

14. Recorded interview with Mrs Marjorie Tooke by Dennis Walsh of Chameleon TV, Leeds, October 1989.

15. *Leeds Mercury,* 9 September 1914. Trooper Wilson was no relation to Alderman Charles Wilson whose only son was a member of the Royal Flying Corps.

16. Who, as General Sir Henry Rawlinson, commanded the Fourth Army on the Somme in 1916, and thus has a prominent place in the history of Pals battalions. Lord Derby became Director-General of Recruiting in 1915, the year in which the 'Derby Scheme' came into operation.

17. At a lunch with Major the Hon Robert White at the Travellers Club in Pall Mall, London, Rawlinson asked White to raise a battalion from the firms based in the City of London, and White approached the Chairman of the Stock Exchange and wrote to many city firms including Lloyds and the Baltic Exchange. Although the battalion was complete by 27 August, on the 31st the Yorkshire press carried advertisements for businessmen to join a battalion of city employees, quoting the text of a notice posted at the Stock Exchange in London. See Simkins, Peter, *Kitchener's Army, The Raising of the New Armies 1914–16,* Manchester University Press, 1988, pp 83–4.

18. *Yorkshire Post,* 3 September 1914.
19. *Yorkshire Evening Post,* 3 September 1914. *Yorkshire Post,* 4 September 1914. Record of British Infantry Uniforms and Insignia 1914–1918 a series of questionnaires sent by the National (now Imperial) War Museum to each infantry battalion and cavalry regiment in late 1920 and early 1921. A bound photocopy of these questionnaires is available in the Imperial War Museum, London.
20. *Leeds and District Weekly Citizen,* 4 September 1914.
21. *Yorkshire Post,* 4 September 1914.
22. In the early months of the war, newspapers had often, and luridly, reported supposed German atrocities against Belgian civilians, notably women and children.
23. Undated letter from E. Robinson of Yarnley, Leeds, BBC TV *Great War* Series correspondence, Imperial War Museum, London.
24. *Yorkshire Post,* 3 September 1914.
25. Although the press reported the raising of a company of teachers (see, for instance, *Yorkshire Post,* 3 September 1914), there is no evidence that this was achieved, and Messrs Dalby and Hollingworth were both adamant that there was no such thing (author's recorded interview, May 1988).
26. Minutes of the Leeds Incorporated Chamber of Commerce 1914, *Yorkshire Post,* 4 September 1914.
27. Pearson, Arthur Valentine, *A Leeds Pal Looks Back,* unpublished manuscript in Leeds Local History Library, circa 1961.
28. *Yorkshire Post,* 5 September 1914.
29. Author's recorded interview with Clifford Hollingworth, May 1988.
30. Author's recorded interview with Arthur Dalby, May 1988.
31. Recorded interview with Morris Fleming by Peter Hawkins of BBC Radio Leeds, circa 1986.
32. Brown, Malcolm, *Tommy Goes to War,* Dent, London, 1978.
33. *Yorkshire Evening Post,* 3 September 1914 and 23 September 1914.
34. Ibid, 7 September 1914.
35. Author's recorded interview with Arthur Dalby and Clifford Hollingworth, May 1988.
36. *Yorkshire Observer,* 8 September 1914.
37. Author's recorded interview with Clifford Hollingworth, May 1988.
38. Ibid.
39. Pearson, op.cit.
40. Author's recorded interview with Arthur Dalby, May 1988. Although he was christened Fewster Arthur Dalby, he has always been called Arthur by his friends and family.
41. Recorded interview with Morris Fleming by Peter Hawkins of BBC Radio Leeds, circa 1986. His recollection of the minimum height seems to be inaccurate as it was reported in the *Yorkshire Post* on 4 September 1914 as being 5 feet 3 inches.
42. *Yorkshire Post,* 11 September 1914.
43. Author's recorded interview with Clifford Hollingworth, May 1988.
44. Author's recorded interview with Arthur Dalby, May 1988.
45. Pearson, op.cit.
46. TS copy of the City of Leeds General Purposes Committee resolution, loosely inserted into the Minute books of the Leeds Pals' Association.
47. Cunliffe-Lister, Susan, *Days of Yore – a History of Masham,* privately published, Masham, 1978.
48. Soon after the Pals moved up to Colsterdale there was a rumour of a fissure in Leighton Reservoir. This was reported by the left-wing press apparently to discredit Arthur Willey, Chairman of the Leeds Waterworks Committee. The existence of a fissure was vehemently denied and never proven. See *Leeds and District Weekly Citizen,* 8 January 1915.
49. *Yorkshire Post,* 10 September 1914.

Chapter Two

The Roof of Yorkshire

*The Battalion left Leeds on September 25th, a thousand strong, for
Colsterdale near Masham, on what might be called 'the Roof of Yorkshire'![1]*

TRAINING IN BRITAIN, SEPTEMBER 1914 – DECEMBER 1915

An advance party, of 105 men under Sergeant-Major Yates, accompanied by Evelyn Lintott, now a sergeant, and Quartermaster-Sergeant Touman, assembled at Leeds Station at 7.30am on Wednesday, 23 September, to board the 7.51am train to Masham via Harrogate. They completed their journey on the light railway previously used to take materials and supplies up to the men who were working on the new reservoir. An eyewitness account of their arrival appeared in the local press:

The Leeds "Pals'" Battalion left Leeds this morning to
practise eagle-shooting.

Cartoon published in the Yorkshire
Evening Post, *25 September 1914.*

> *Swank was entirely absent; everybody did his share, and did it willingly, and no one ventured to assert that he knew how to do any particular job better than another. They were Pals in every sense of the word.*
>
> *Whilst the trucks containing the fatigue party's stores were shunted to the narrow gauge railway along which are carried the Leeds Corporation reservoir contractor's stores, the Pals were photographed in three groups.*
>
> *The eagerness and quick despatch of transferring the stores to the small trucks could not have been excelled by trained troops. In fact, but for the lack of uniforms one could have imagined that the men were such.*
>
> *Half the men made the journey to the camp in two waggons behind those containing the stores, the remaining members of the advance party, in charge of Sergeant-Major Yates, making the journey of five miles on foot.*
>
> *An hour's ride over pasture and turnip fields, with here and there a halt to allow stray cattle and sheep to get off the line, brought the train party to their destination, where no time was lost in removing the stores.[2]*

The rest of the Pals were instructed to report to the Town Hall that evening, where each man was issued with a kitbag onto which was fastened a card showing which company he was to join.

The Pals' camp at Colsterdale. The navvies' huts on the left were used by D Company while the rest of the men were accommodated in tents.

The advance party accompanies stores on the light railway from Masham to Colsterdale. (Leeds Library)

The Pals arrive at Masham. Cyril Brown is marked by an X. (Cecilia Brown)

On 25 September 1914 the main body of the Pals set off from the new railway station in Leeds city centre. They were waved off by a crowd of about 20,000, which included Dr Samuel Bickersteth, Vicar of Leeds, Councillor E. F. Lawson, Chairman of the Watch Committee, and Alderman Arthur Willey, Chairman of the Waterworks Committee, whose sons, all members of the battalion, would soon receive commissions.

Friday September 25th 1914 – We all rose at 6.30 in order to have an early breakfast and see Morris off to Colsterdale with the City of Leeds 'Pals' Battalion. Fortunately his uniform arrived the night before. He looked extremely smart in it and was the only officer not in mufti in the whole regiment. Father and Morris went on ahead to the station, Mother, Aunt Alice, Burgon and myself followed a little later. The crowd was tremendous, about 20,000 people altogether, surging and heaving around the iron gates at the entrance to the station, one of which they broke in their efforts to push through. We managed to conduct Mother and Aunt Alice successfully through the press and found Morris and Father looking for the officers' carriage. This, a First Class compartment near the end of the train, we eventually discovered, and we had some time before starting to see some of Morris' brother officers. Young Lawson, who was married a week before, was there, as well as the Doctor. The train moved out of the station amid tremendous cheers from the packed platforms and the Leeds 'Pals' certainly enjoyed an enthusiastic send off.

Bickersteth Family War Diary

Orders for Camp had been issued advising the Pals on what to take with them, and every man carried his kit and a stout walking stick.

So we were given a kitbag to take what you wanted with you and we emerged at the station that morning, and all the girls in all the clothing factories, and all the offices, in Leeds were

26

late because they had come to see the young men off. Their sweethearts and suchlike, and that concourse leading up to the city square station was packed each side.

There was no parade, everyone just simply walked up to the platform and reported and you were told to go there, go there, go there, and by the time you got there you were partly sorted out into companies. Now when we got to Masham, we disembarked at Masham, then they started sorting you out properly.

15/471 Private Clifford Hollingworth, D Company[3]

The North Eastern Railway had made all the arrangements to move the Pals from Leeds to Masham, but not all the men made it onto the train.

The second special train arrived [at Masham] shortly after ten o'clock, but even then all the 'Pals' were not on the spot. Half-a-dozen were so intent on bidding goodbye to their friends at the Leeds New Station that they were left behind. They managed however to get an ordinary train to Ripon and then it cost them a few shillings for a taxi cab to Masham.[4]

At Masham, the men loaded their baggage onto the light railway and formed fours to march the 6 miles up to Colsterdale. They were preceded by their Corps of Drums and Bugles, and by Colonel Stead, who rode at the head of the column on horseback.

Out of the station yard onto the road, over Masham bridge through the village up and out onto the road to Colsterdale. Past the Church, chapels, pubs, small farms and houses. The Dale lay spread out before our eyes. Many of us had our first sight of Druid's Plantation and other scenery with which we got all too familiar on marches and cross country runs.

When we reached the foot of the hill someone had opened the gate and we began to climb up to Breary Banks. At the top a large field had rows and rows of tents erected, and behind them rows and rows of dark-looking huts, the dwellings of the labourers and families who had worked on the Leeds City waterworks project.

15/711 Private Arthur V. Pearson, C Company[5]

At 12.30, shortly after their arrival, the Pals were paraded and addressed by their Commanding Officer, Colonel J. Walter Stead. He reminded them that they were associated with the West Yorkshire Regiment, which had a fine record and he thought that they would not need urging to uphold it. He asked the men to practice punctuality, particularly on early morning parades.

When the bugle sounds Reveille, I want you to get up at once, so that you will have plenty of time to get ready. I want you each morning to be out of the lines before the actual time of parade, and I may tell you that coffee will be served to you each morning before going on parade.[6]

NCOs were chosen, and the various groups of Pals who wanted to be together sorted themselves into sections.

When we went there, we had no NCOs, no lance-corporals and corporals. They'd sergeants, Reserve men 40 or 50 years of age you see, but they knew the job. So we'd find some NCOs. Mind you, it didn't just happen to the Leeds Pals, it happened all over because they'd a million men in no time, you know, and it takes some working. Anyway, if they'd gone through a teacher's course and got their diploma as being a teacher of Swedish Drill, then they were promoted to unpaid Lance-Corporal, which after three months was made paid Lance-Corporal – they got another threepence a day, or something like that. But that was the nucleus of the NCOs of our battalion. Bobby Bland – he was a school teacher, Waterhouse 'Bucket' – he was a school teacher, Spencer – he was a school teacher. All these teachers, they knew how to give orders for Swedish Drill – leg, neck, arm, trunk, leg, [it] was most important to get people fit.

15/471 Private Clifford Hollingworth, D Company[7]

The Leeds Battalion.
The Prince of Wales's Own West Yorkshire Regiment.

ORDERS FOR CAMP
BY
Lieut.-Colonel J. WALTER STEAD, V.D.

Town Hall, Leeds, *September 21st, 1914.*

1. CAMP.
The Battalion will encamp at Colsterdale on **Friday, September 25th, 1914.**

2. ADVANCE PARTY.
Men who have given in their names will attend at Headquarters, on **Tuesday, September 22nd,** between 6 p.m. and 8 p.m., to draw kitbags. It is recommended that those who can do so should bring in a pair of Blankets in a paper parcel for their own use. These will have a label attached with name and number and will be issued on arrival at Camp. Each man will receive a card showing the Company to which he has been posted, and on presenting this to the Quartermaster-Sergeant will receive his kitbag, to which the card will be affixed.
The advance party, under Sergeant-Major Yates, will parade with overcoats, sticks and kitbags, at the North Eastern Railway Station, Leeds, on **Wednesday, September 23rd.** 7.30 a.m., and proceed by train to Masham for Colsterdale Camp.

3. ISSUE OF KITBAGS.
The remainder of the Battalion will attend at Headquarters, on **Wednesday, September 23rd,** between 4 p.m. and 8 p.m., to draw kitbags. During the scarcity of Camp equipment, it is recommended that those who can do so should then bring a pair of Blankets in paper parcel for own use. These will have a label attached with name and regimental number, and will be issued on arrival at Camp. Each man will receive a card showing the Company to which he has been posted, and will receive from the Quartermaster-Sergeant his kitbag with the card affixed.

4. ARTICLES TO BE BROUGHT.
Men will attend in plain clothes, with caps, sticks and overcoats, and each man is recommended to be in possession of the following articles in his kitbag :—Two pairs of socks, one shirt, pair of pants, hair brush and comb, tooth brush, clothes brush, small dubbin brush, razor and shaving brush, two towels, pair of strong leather laces, pair of shoes (canvas preferred) to wear in camp after drill. No unauthorized bags or boxes will be taken to Camp. Hair should be cut short.

5. OFFICERS' BAGGAGE.
Officers should arrange to have their baggage ready packed and labelled at Headquarters, not later than 8 p.m. on **September 24th.**

6. BATTALION PARADE, SEPTEMBER 25th.
The Battalion will parade in plain clothes, with overcoats, sticks and kitbags, at the North Eastern Railway Station, Leeds, on **Friday, September 25th.** Men will fall in by Companies on the platform at 8.30 a.m., and afterwards proceed by rail to Masham for Colsterdale. On arrival at Masham kitbags will be collected and transported to the Camp.

7. ENTRAINING.
When entraining perfect silence must be maintained as far as possible by all ranks to ensure expedition in the work. Men must not entrain until ordered.

8. HOURS OF REVEILLE, &c.
The Buglers will sound the following calls at the hours stated :—

Reveille	5.45 a.m.
Dress for parade	6.15 a.m.
Parade	6.30 a.m.
Retreat	7.0 p.m.
Tattoo, First Post	9.0 p.m.
Tattoo, Last Post	9.30 p.m.
Lights Out	9.45 p.m.

Absolute silence is to be maintained in Camp between the hours of Lights Out and Reveille.

9. SATURDAY'S PARADE.
The Battalion will parade as strong as possible on **September 26th.** at 6.30 a.m., for check roll-call. All N.C.O.'s no matter how employed, must attend this parade. Employed men will be allowed to go back to their work when permission has been obtained. Pay Sergeants will attend with their pay lists to check the names.

10. CAMP ORDERLY DUTIES.

BATTALION ORDERLY OFFICER.
The duties of the Orderly Officer will commence at *Reveille.* He will remain in Camp during his tour of duty, and cannot exchange duties without the permission of the Adjutant. Officers on duty will invariably wear belts. The Battalion Orderly Sergeant and Corporal assist the Orderly Officer in his duties. Orderly Officer's Reports should be made to the Adjutant by 9 a.m. daily.

BATTALION ORDERLY SERGEANT.
Tour of Duty.—His duties will commence at *Reveille,* reporting himself to the Captain and Subaltern of the day.
Reveille.—Go round the Camp after *Reveille* sounding, and see that the curtains of the men's tents are rolled up (weather permitting), reporting to the Orderly Officer.
Sick.—Parade all N.C. Officers and men reported sick, receiving the Companies' Sick Reports from Orderly Corporals of Companies, and march them to the Hospital. After the Sick have been examined, march all men not detained in Hospital back to Camp, reporting to the Orderly Corporals of Companies any men detained in Hospital, &c.
Rations.—Parade the Orderly Corporals and Orderly Men to draw Rations, seeing that they are in clean fatigue dress.
Meals.—Accompany the Orderly Officer at the meal hours.
Orders.—Show the daily Orders to the Field and Staff Officers, receiving the book from the Sergeant-Major after the Orders have been given out.
Tattoo.—Parade at Tattoo, reporting to the Sergeant-Major that the Orders have been shown.
Lights out.—See that all lights are extinguished on *Lights out* sounding, reporting to the Orderly Officer when this is done.
Quitting Camp.—He will on no account quit Camp during his tour of duty except when permission has been granted (under exceptional circumstances) by the Officer commanding his Company ; a substitute appointed, and the same notified to the Sergeant-Major.

BATTALION ORDERLY CORPORAL.
Tour of Duty.—His duties will commence at *Reveille,* reporting himself to the Battalion Orderly Sergeant for instructions.
Reveille.—Assist the Battalion Orderly Sergeant in seeing that the curtains of the men's tents are rolled up.
Sick.—Assist in parading the men reported Sick.
Rations.—Be present when the Orderly Corporals and Orderly Men parade to draw Rations.
Meals.—Accompany the Orderly Officer at the meal hours.
Tattoo.—Parade at Tattoo with the Battalion Orderly Sergeant, and assist in seeing the lights out in the men's tents.
Quitting Camp.—As above.

COMPANY ORDERLY SERGEANT.
Tour of Duty.—His duties will commence at *Reveille.*
Reveille.—On *Reveille* sounding, see that the men have risen, and that the beds have been placed outside, and tent flies rolled up (weather permitting).
Parades.—Be ready to fall in immediately on Orderly Sergeants sounding previous to parade. Directly the Company is formed up, call the roll of his Company, reporting to the Sergeant-Major any absentees throughout the day. Parade all men punctually for Guards and Fatigues, warning all men personally for duties immediately on receiving the details from the Sergeant-Major.
Meals.—Accompany the Orderly Officer at the meal hours.
Orders.—When the bugle sounds for *Orders* take his Company Order Book, pen and ink, to place appointed, and copy the Regimental Orders.
Parade State.—Make out the Parade State, Crimes, Passes, &c. ; have them signed by the Colour-Sergeant and Officer Commanding the Company, and sent to the Orderly Room not late than 8.30 a.m.
Tattoo.—Call the roll ten minutes *before Tattoo,* and report to the Sergeant-Major, on *Last Post* sounding, the names of absentees, the Absent Report being made out in duplicate.
Lights out.—See that all the lights of his Company are extinguished on the bugle sounding.
Quitting Camp.—As above.

COMPANY ORDERLY CORPORAL.
Tour of Duty.—His duties will commence at *Reveille.*
Reveille.—Assist the Orderly Sergeant in seeing that the men have risen, taking the names of men reporting themselves sick.
Rations.—Parade the Orderly Men of tents on the bugle sounding for *Rations,* seeing that each Tent Orderly receives his proper quantity of bread and meat. Draw the Ration Tickets for Beer and Ginger Beer from the Quartermaster, and hand them over to *the Orderly Men* of Tents.
Sick.—Parade the men reported Sick, and hand them over to the Battalion Orderly Sergeant.
Documents.—Obtain the State, Passes, Crimes, &c., from the Company Orderly Sergeant, and take them to the Captain of his Company for signature ; then hand them over to the Orderly-Room Clerk *not later than* 8.30 a.m. Receive the *Order Book* from the Orderly Sergeant, and take it to the Colour-Sergeant, then to the Officers of his Company.
Guards' Meals.—Parade the Orderly Men with the Guards' Meals, and see them handed over to the men on Guard.
Prisoners.—See that the Greatcoat and Two Blankets belonging to men confined in the Guard Tent are sent to them after *Retreat* sounding ; and towels, soap, brushes, razors, &c. ; *immediately after Reveille,* so that they may appear clean at Office hour.
Tattoo.—Assist the Orderly Sergeant in calling the roll at Tattoo.
Quitting Camp.—As above.

11. TENTS.
The Senior N.C.O. or Private of a Tent is responsible for the good order, arrangement and cleanliness of that tent, and he should report his tent present, or otherwise, to the Orderly Sergeant at Tattoo.
If rain or heavy dew is likely, the tent ropes must be slackened.
The Tent Orderly is responsible that no refuse of any sort is allowed to remain either in or near to the tent. The senior N.C.O. of the tent must see this duty carried out so that the lines may be at all times tidy.
All tents, and the ground around, are to be cleaned up first thing in the morning, and all rubbish to be placed in a small heap outside by the Orderly Man before going on parade. No rubbish must be placed outside again until next morning, but must be taken by the Orderly Man to the Refuse Pit. On no account should bottles be left lying about, these must be returned to the Canteen as soon as done with.
Paper and straw must not be scattered about the Camp. No dirty water must be thrown out, except at places provided for the purpose.
It must be distinctly understood that any damage or loss of public property (tents, blankets, ground sheets, etc.) occurring, will be chargeable to the men occupying the tent in which the loss or damage occurs.

Lieutenant-Colonel Stead's 'Orders for Camp'. A copy was given to every man. (Leeds Library)

Men who had any experience of drill and discipline in Boys Brigades, Boy Scouts etc. were asked to step forward and see what sort of Army NCOs they were likely to make. I had been recognised somewhere during the day by some old school friends who were one man short of their tent complement of eight, so I was invited to make up the party and the survivors of that happy tent have stuck together ever since.

15/711 Private Arthur V Pearson, C Company[8]

The Pals were shown where they would sleep, and set about making themselves comfortable in their new homes. The men of D Company were assigned to the few navvies' huts available, while A, B and C Companies were put into the rows of bell tents that had been erected by the advance party.

28

12. OBJECT OF TRAINING.

The object of all training is the preparation of the individual officer and man for the duties he will have to carry out in war. Hardly less important than the training and education of the officers and N.C.O.'s is the adequate physical and intellectual training of the private soldier, who must not only be taught to march, use his eyes, judge distance, shoot, scout, etc., but must also be so instructed that he may be able to comprehend the meaning and object of every movement he is directed to carry out.

His individual intelligence will thus be called into play and he will gradually be induced to take a personal interest in his own fighting efficiency (extracts from sec. 158, *Combined Training*).

13. THE COMPANY, THE UNIT FOR TRAINING.

The Company in the Infantry is the unit for training purposes. The ideal perfection in the Company as a fighting unit is having that mutual confidence between all ranks inspired by the feeling that each man knows his duty thoroughly, and by the habit of constantly working together. This aim once attained we have a sound basis upon which to build up a discipline second to none.

14. THE IMPORTANCE OF "OBEDIENCE."

First, men must be taught instinctive *obedience* to the command of their superiors; in the performance of all military exercises and duties, this important aim should never be lost sight of, and it should be the object of all officers and N.C.O.'s to instil into their men's minds gradually and surely. Men cannot be handy in action unless they have been thoroughly well-drilled. He who overlooks the slightest tendency on the part of his men under him to unpunctuality, or to slackness in obeying an order, is doing his men and the corps incalculable harm. All work done on parade must be smartly done, work so done is practical and useful; nothing is useful if performed in a slovenly manner.

15. SMARTNESS ON PARADE.

The preliminary foundation of discipline can be acquired only on the drill ground, drill training makes men individually braver than they would be without it, and collectively far braver than the individual can ever be. The object of Field Training is to make men efficient for war, and smartness is the visible sign of willingness and ability to give prompt obedience—the very foundation of everything.

16. DISCIPLINE ON THE MARCH.

The smartness shown on the parade ground cannot possibly be retained at manœuvres or in active service, yet the smarter the drill and the more perfect the discipline displayed in the ranks during peace training, the more efficient a corps will prove itself in the field, because it will carry these higher ideals and will therefore deteriorate far less than a slovenly battalion; it will never be seen straggling on the line of march, breaking out of the ranks for water, or slow to fall in after a halt, and any sudden order will always find it alert to obey. The importance of march discipline can scarcely be exaggerated, and it is very certain that good drill is the mainspring of it. March discipline carefully taught and enforced. Properly maintained it keeps men handy and alert just as parade ground drill has made them so when they were recruits.

17. SALUTING.

There is perhaps no more useful assistance to the foundation and maintenance of discipline than the system of paying compliments to officers. The officer holds the King's commission, and so long as he holds it, whether serving in this battalion or in some other, is entitled to the salute, because he represents the great bond which unites all ranks, viz., discipline. The soldier therefore who smartly salutes his officer, pays respect to the sovereign who is the individual representative of the entire nation, and thus shows respect not only for the officer and for the sovereign, but also for himself. Whenever an officer approaches a group of men, it is the business of the first soldier who sees him to call the remainder to attention, all should spring up smartly and face the officer while the senior salutes.

18. TRESPASS.

(*a*), (*b*), (*c*), (*d*) and (*f*) to be read out on three successive Parades.

(*a*) All ranks are warned that trespass either in pursuit of game or otherwise is illegal.

(*b*) On Field Days care must be taken not to break down fences or leave gates open.

Any damage, whether unavoidable or not, must be reported to the Adjutant on return to Camp.

(*c*) Smoking in the vicinity of ricks or farm buildings is forbidden.

(*d*) Glass bottles and paper in which refreshments are taken must not be left lying about. The paper in which ammunition is wrapped must not be thrown away, but burnt.

(*e*) The greatest care must be taken by all ranks to control fire when horses or any stock might be frightened and come to harm. This is especially the case near roads, and men will cease fire while stock of any kind is passing. They should also cease fire if stock begins running in a field, and if working in extended order they should open out and let the animals come through the lines.

To a great extent the fences consist of walls in many instances made of loose stone, which easily falls off. In getting over these walls every care must be taken to prevent this. Gaps made in walls will not only be the cause of claim for damage, but will also let the stock through and give trouble to the farmers. If the wall is at the side of a hill, there is also the danger of dislodged stones rolling down the slope and causing serious damage to men who may be below.

(*f*) The greatest care should be taken to prevent heather or long grass getting on fire.

Matches must not be thrown carelessly away, but must be put out. If cooking is done in the open, bare patches of ground will be chosen for places for the fires, and the Company Officers will be responsible that the fires are properly put out before leaving.

Especial care must be taken in peaty soil, which will smoulder almost invisibly and break out afterwards.

19. FIRE.

A light is never to be left burning in an unoccupied tent.

In the event of fire in a Tent, efforts must be made to beat it out with blankets, great coats, tent bags, &c. If it has gone too far, the tent must be let down by breaking the pole if necessary. All tents in the immediate vicinity will be struck at once.

20. ALARM POSTS.

In case of fire or any other alarm Companies will fall in on their private Company parade ground, and will then be marched to the Battalion parade ground, form up in quarter column, and await orders.

21. SICK.

The ordinary hour for inspection of the sick will be at 7 a.m., when men will parade at the Orderly Room under the Battalion Orderly Sergeant.

Serious cases should be reported to the Medical Officer in charge without delay.

22. PASSES.

No man is allowed to leave Camp except on duty until after the Afternoon Parade. Every man must be in Camp by 9 p.m., and answer his name to the Orderly Sergeant of his Company. Men requiring leave of absence must send in a Pass, recommended by the Officer Commanding the Company, so as to reach the Orderly Room by 9 a.m. daily. A limited number of Passes only will be granted.

23. INSTITUTIONS.

All Institutions open to rank and file will be closed a quarter-of-an-hour before all Parades, and will remain so until Parades are dismissed. They will close at 9 p.m.

24. AMUSEMENTS.

A Battalion Amusement Committee will be formed, consisting of two men per Company.

25. HAWKERS.

No hawkers are permitted to enter the Camp.

26. WATER.

Great care should be taken to economize water in the Camp as much as possible. Taps should on no account be left running.

27. HINTS ON MARCHING.

(*a*) Boots should be an easy fit, as the foot increases in size on the march. **New boots should never be worn on a march.**

(*b*) Socks should be of wool, *free from darns*, and should be worn inside out.

(*c*) If the feet are soft, they should be washed in alum and water, or soap and water.

(*d*) If the feet are inclined to be sore, soap the socks on the side worn next to the feet. Blisters should be at once reported on return to Camp.

(*e*) Men are reminded that smoking—especially cigarettes—is detrimental to good marching, and that they will carry out their work more comfortably and efficiently if they refrain from doing so until a meal of some duration occurs or until they have had a meal. At any time pipes are preferable and less harmful than cigarettes.

(*f*) **Never drink on the march without eating at the same time.** Always carry a biscuit or a piece of bread in the haversack.

If men once commence to drink on an empty stomach their thirst becomes worse and their bodies slack, and their power of endurance is greatly diminished. They should therefore get into the habit of doing without water on the march altogether.

28. NOTEBOOKS.

Officers should at all times carry with them a Notebook, a map of the district and a copy of Standing Orders.

N.C.O.'s should provide themselves with a good Notebook, which should be carried on all parades.

29. STANDING ORDERS.

These Standing Orders must be carefully studied and remembered by all ranks. Officers Commanding Companies are to explain to their Companies on two or three of the first parades those paragraphs which affect their men—particularly the paragraph on **trespass.**

30. LETTERS.

Letters for Camp should be addressed as follows:—

Rank and Name,
—— Company, Leeds Battalion,
West Yorkshire Regiment,
Colsterdale Camp,
North Yorks.

The first evening was spent by some of the men in the canteen, which had until then been run for the reservoir workers. From the day the Pals arrived half the canteen was set aside for their use, and the place was packed to suffocation with 200 to 300 Pals, each with a pint mug, and all singing the latest popular songs and the old favourites. Some men, already missing their loved ones made use of the comparative peace of the navvies' main room to write their first letters home.

The next day saw the start of the difficult job of turning 1,100 city businessmen into a battalion of soldiers.

North Eastern Railway

Telegraphic Address:
"NOBLE, NORTHEASTERN, LEEDS."
TELEPHONE 2197.

District Superintendent's Office

Leeds

Advice R.S. 82.   Sept 22nd, 1914.

ENCAMPMENT OF LEEDS CITY BATTALION . THE PRINCE OF
WALES'S OWN WEST YORKSHIRE REGIMENT at Masham.

WEDNESDAY 23RD SEPTEMBER 1914.

The Advance Party of about 120 men in 3 thirds and van (for
mens kits etc) will travel by ordinary trains as under :-

		a.m.
Leeds	dep	7-51
Harrogate	arr	8-32
"	dep	8-53
Masham	arr	9-30

The carriages and the van to be placed at No 8 platform by
7-0 a.m. and afterwards attached on rear of the 7-51 a.m. train
ex Leeds.

FRIDAY 25TH SEPTEMBER 1914.

LEEDS TO MASHAM - Special Trains.
(Main body 950 Officers & men)

		a.m.	a.m.
Neville Hill Carr Sdgs	dep	7-35	7-40
Leeds (No 7 platform)	arr	7-50	7-55
"	dep	8-35	8-45
Arthington	pass	8-54	9-4
Starbeck	"	9-12	9-20
Ripon	"	9-27	9-37
Melmerby	X "	9-32	9-42
Tanfield	X "	9-40	9-51
Masham	arr	9-50	10-1

THESE TRAINS SHOULD RUN PUNCTUALLY

Masham to Neville Hill Car Sdgs - Empty Trains.

		a.m.	a.m.
Masham	dep	10-30	10-55
Tanfield	pass	10-37	11-2
Ripon	"	10-50	11-15
Harrogate	"	11-12	11-38
Wetherby West Jct	"	11-27	11-53
Cross Gates	"	11-52	12-18
Neville Hill Carr Sidgs	arr	11-58	12-24

Stock 1 C. (treble) 9 (5 compt) T. 2 (3 compt) B. each.

R.S. 82 (ctd)

GENERAL ARRANGEMENTS.

LEEDS NEW STATION.

The trains will be dealt with at No 7 platform
the station to be closed to the public except for intending
passengers and others having business on the station, from 7-45 am
Mr Nicholson, to arrange.

IT IS IMPORTANT THAT THE TRAINS SHOULD LEAVE
PUNCTUALLY AND EVERY EFFORT MUST BE MADE TO ENSURE THIS BEING
DONE.

MASHAM.

The 8-53 a.m. ord train from Harrogate to Masham
to be arrived at Masham at the excursion platform from which
platform it will also depart at 10-10 a.m.

The first special train will be run direct into the
Goods Yard where the men will de-train. The second train to be run
to the ordinary platform. All necessary points into the Goods Yard
to be clamped or wedged. The District Engineer will arrange for
platelayers to be in attendance for this purpose.

INSPECTOR GROVES to be in attendance.

8-53 a.m. ord Harrogate to Masham
10-30 a.m. ord Masham to Ripon.

It is essential that these trains should run to time
and all concerned must see to this.

Horse Boxes & carriage trucks must not be accepted
for these trains on this date.

If, however, the 10-10 a.m. ex Masham is delayed by
the specials to such an extent as to jeopardise the connection with
the 10-22 a.m. ex Harrogate at Ripon, the latter train must be stopped
specially at Melmerby to make the connection. The Masham Station
Master to wire Ripon and Melmerby departure time of the 10-10 a.m.
train and the station Masters at Ripon and Melmerby to arrange as
necessary for the stopping of the 10-22 a.m. ex Harrogate at Melmerby.

PROVISION TRAFFIC.

Commencing on Thursday 24th inst, and until further
notice, a van for the conveyance of provision etc traffic, will
travel from Leeds daily by the 11-0 a.m. train to Ripon and forward
from Ripon to Masham by the 1-53 p.m. Goods train. The van to be
available for loading in No 4. platform, Leeds New Station, from
7-0 a.m. each day.

ADVISE ALL CONCERNED AND ACKNOWLEDGE RECEIPT BY RETURN.

[signature] W. Noble

---

*The detailed instructions issued by the North Eastern Railway, for the 'Encampment of
Leeds City Battalion', 22 September 1914. (Regimental Museum)*

---

*Shall we ever forget that first morning? Seven men all trying to shave, and all using cut-
throat razors. The wonder was that we all turned up on parade with features complete, except
perhaps for a wee gash here and there.*

15/711 Private Arthur V Pearson, C Company[9]

They were woken at 5.45am by Sergeant Macaulay, an ex-Regular with twelve years' service
in the Scottish Rifles. True to his word, Colonel Stead had arranged for coffee to be served to
all but the two or three who, despite his comments about punctuality, had overslept. The men
then went on parade for their introduction to Swedish Drill.

The Pals parade with their kitbags. The officer is Philip Mellor.

Colonel Stead addresses his battalion at Colsterdale. The chapel to the left of this picture is now used as a store by the Forestry Commission.

Hopping around a field, first on one leg and then on another, may seem almost a ridiculous procedure and one very far remote from the supreme object of killing Germans, but it has a very real place in the long preparation of the true soldier and the Leeds men are taking it up with enthusiasm, as a course of training which they recognise is good for them.

Yorkshire Post, *28 September 1914*

Later they were given a hearty breakfast of bread, bacon and coffee, the catering being under the supervision of Charles Wilson, Acting Quartermaster. At 9.30am the Pals paraded once more and marched in companies up to the windswept heights above the camp, where

Right: Some of No.14 Section, No.4 Platoon, A Company, outside their tent. Harold Green is centre of the back row (with pip), and Arthur Thomas is second from left, front row.

The tents needed constant attention on the windswept Yorkshire Dales. A working party pauses to have a photo taken.

they formed up into sections of ten or a dozen to learn the rudiments of marching and squad drill. After a traditional roast beef lunch, they continued with their training until they were dismissed at 4.45pm for tea. They were then free until supper at 6.45, and turned in at about nine o'clock.

That night, their second in camp, was a chilly ordeal for the men in the tents, particularly after their strenuous day in the gale-force winds that blew across the Yorkshire Dales.

> *Getting out of warm blankets at two o'clock in the morning may be all right on a nice summer morning, but when it is pitch dark – so dark in fact that you cannot see a hand in front of you – and with the wind blowing at 70 to 80 miles an hour, ugh! It's a cold job. In two or three cases the bell tents collapsed and fell about the ears of the slumbering occupants, who had a sorry time extricating themselves and getting the tent up again.*[10]

Men of No.15 Platoon, D Company, outside their hut. Joe Collinson is fourth from left, back row (wearing a cap). Clifford Hollingworth is seated in the front row (wearing his cap back to front).

The officers were accommodated in bungalows built for the managers of the Waterworks Committee. Although they were sheltered from the ravages of the high winds, they could not escape the freezing cold at night when the temperature plummeted.

Colsterdale Camp Masham September 26th 1914

My dear Father and Mother, It is already fairly cold at night – and we are told this is a very cold part of Yorkshire, and we had better be prepared, as frequently when it is a beautiful day in Leeds, there has been heavy snow here.

Last night, of course we slept in rooms, it was very cold underneath as of course I was not sleeping on a mattress, so I had actually to get up and wear my greatcoat (of which I was very glad) before I could get warm.

I will now tell you all we have done so far. Certainly we had quite a cheery send-off— but it seemed as if most of the audience thought we were going straight to the front and certainly

MARCHING AND RUNNING

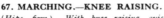

66. MARCHING.—HEELS RAISED.

Quick—march. On the toes—march. . . .
Quick—march.

March on the toes with a light, springy step ; cadence as in marching but step a little shortened ; trunk and head well stretched upward, knees braced back.

67. MARCHING.—KNEE RAISING.

(Hips—firm.) *With knee raising, quick—march. . . . Class—halt.*

March on the toes, raising the knees high at each step ; cadence slower and step shorter than usual. Avoid stamping by keeping the heels up ; trunk and head erect, lower leg and toes straight downward.

68. MARCHING.—HOPPING.

(Hips—firm.) *On alternate feet—hop. . . . Class—halt.*

This exercise consists of alternate step and hop. Step forward with the left foot, then spring upward, at the same time stretching out the knee and ankle of the rear leg. Swing the right leg forward and hop, and so on, on alternate feet. Keep the trunk and head erect.

On *Halt,* make one more hop and then bring up the rear foot.

69. RUNNING.

Double—march. . . . Quick—march.

Run lightly on the toes, arms moving freely, knees well raised, body slightly inclined forward.

On *Quick—march,* run two more steps, and change to the march on the third.

Progression : *(a) Running with knee raising.* Commands as in 67.

Swedish Drill – designed to get the men into peak physical condition. (Author's Collection)

the Yorkshire Post *talked a lot of rot. We arrived at Masham about 10 o'clock and formed up in a field nearby. I have been attached for the present to B Company. There are to be four subalterns to each company of 250 men, and each subaltern will be in command of a Platoon of about 75 men.*

The men certainly seem quite an intelligent lot, and I should think that at least one in every three has done some training before. We have some pretty good athletes – in my Platoon, I have Booth and Kilner, two of Yorkshire's first class cricketplayers, and Lindot [Lintott] who is one of the halves in the Leeds City Football team.

Another man we discovered, had just been seven years in the Regular Army and therefore knows all the drill. Why he has enlisted in this, I cannot think. So I do not think it will take us so long to train as we thought, if and a very large if, we get some really efficient officers of which there are none at present, except the Colonel and a Grammar School master called Kirk, who really is a very decent fellow.

Directly we got here we had lunch. Three companies of the men are in tents and the fourth in huts. They are building huts for the remainder as soon as possible, as of course they cannot sleep in the tents much longer, as it is mighty cold for them – but they have all been given three blankets.

We spent most of the afternoon in getting them fixed up in companies and tents arranging for particular friends to be together etc. After four o'clock they were free. We are really extremely comfortable. We have taken the Corporation house here for the officers' mess. The Corporation are building waterworks here and therefore have built themselves an extremely comfortable house here – where some member of the Corporation apparently sleeps a night or so every week to see all is going well with the works. Here at present, the Colonel, Wilson and Kirk sleep, and there will be room for two or three Majors and Captains when they have been sent by the War Office.

Here also of course is our smoking room and dining room. They always have three or four permanent servants here, and an extremely good cook (you can bet the Corporation would have that) and we have simply taken these on. So at present, the food has been as plentiful and as well cooked and as good as you, Mother, provide for us at home, and therefore it is exactly like staying in an extremely comfortable private house. It is about five minutes walk below the camp.

Men of No.16 Platoon, D Company. On the far right is Jogendra Sen, from Calcutta.

The 'Feather-bed Battalion' gets its palliasses ready for another night under canvas. (James Hagerty Collection)

We (the subalterns) sleep in some huts about three minutes from the camp. Why they are called huts, I don't know – it is more like a bungalow. The rooms are quite clean and dry, all have fireplaces, two bathrooms and decent sanitary arrangements. There is no hot water although there is a hot water system, because of course we are having no fires.

I must stop now and finish this tomorrow, as the post is just going and I think if I post now, you may get it tomorrow.

The other subalterns are almost without exception dreadful – all good-hearted, but none of them gentlemen

I feared as much – but the Doctor is a nice fellow.

September 27th 1914

… I was just going to tell you about the officers. Kirk, a Grammar School master is at present acting Adjutant until the War Office sends a Regular. He is an old St John's Oxford man – and really very charming. The Doctor is also nice but not quite a gentleman. There are two subalterns whom I like quite and who are more or less gentlemen – but as for the rest they are all I feared they would be. This sounds vilely snobbish, but when one throws in one's lot with a small community for perhaps two or three years, one may be pardoned I think for being slightly disappointed.

… I only hope the War Office sends down some good fellows, but the Colonel doesn't expect them to do this for a month or so yet until the recruiting stage of the men is over. Friend Lawson whom Ralph and I so heartily detest is the most trying, he bores me to tears. The others are mostly very Yorkshire – and most have a broad Yorkshire accent.

None of us have yet been commissioned, and except for the Colonel, the Doctor and myself, none of them wear officer's uniform. The majority know even less about matters than myself – and so very often on parade we have had some pretty amusing scenes, though thank Heaven I do not think I have made many blunders myself yet.

… Well I suppose we shall muddle through somehow – though I think it is very bad for the men to have so very few efficient officers – and officers who are not gentlemen, and being very pleased with their new and in some cases I should think rather unexpected position, behave in many cases to say the least of it without much tact. Of course the bottom of the matter is, Stead is not a gentleman himself; if he had been, I feel sure he would have left some of these officers behind with no small profit to the ultimate good of the Battalion.

… Of course we have no Captain to our Company simply because at present there are no Captains on the staff and so there are five subalterns in our B Company, myself among them. We have decided to take the Company in turns to get as much practice as possible. I took it this morning and got on all right I think. The other officer in my bedroom is a Swede, a nice fellow, a man of about thirty-five he has just been naturalised and he is here principally to organise Swedish Drill, which we always have from six-thirty to seven-thirty.

… This brings Burgon the very best of luck, I do hope he will have a good time, I should very much like him to come over here if he could some time, I would like to show off a smart cavalry officer to some of these men…

Ever your loving son, Morris[11]

Now that the Pals had arrived in camp and started training, the officers came under close scrutiny, not only from the men but, as Morris Bickersteth wrote in his first letters home, from their brother officers. Bickersteth's hasty judgement that none of them were gentlemen was perhaps unfair, while a criticism from the local press in Leeds that preference had been given to the sons of aldermen of the city seems to have been unfounded.[12]

We have already briefly met Colonel Stead, a 'dugout'[13], who had once had command of a Leeds Territorial battalion, as well as his honorary quartermaster, Alderman Charles Wilson, and Stanley Morris Bickersteth, the well-educated, if somewhat unworldly, son of the Vicar of Leeds. Let us now take a brief look at all the embryo officers of the battalion and their apparent qualifications to command the Pals.[14]

Charles Henry Wilson, a member of the 2nd Yorkshire (Leeds) Royal Engineers Volunteer Corps for eleven years and a member of the National Reserve, he was also the first Captain of Leeds Rifle Club. Wilson was an accountant by profession, had been a Councillor and later an Alderman of the City, and was head of municipal finances for ten years prior to joining the Pals. He took a leading part in settling the Leeds Corporation strike in 1913, was a Justice of the Peace, a former President of the Incorporated Society of Accountants and Auditors, and a Freemason.

James Alan Ross Armitage had formerly been employed for two years at the family business, Farnley Crab and Iron Company Ltd of Leeds, of which his father, Dr J. A. Armitage, was Chairman. Educated at Oundle, he served his time as an engineer in the shops of the London and North-Western Railway Company at Crewe.

Edward Karl Maur de Pledge was the son of Mr W. T. de Pledge, a Leeds timber merchant.

Lacey Bathurst, Royal Army Medical Corps, attached to the Leeds Pals.

The guard at Colsterdale, armed with old 'drill purpose' rifles. Fifth from the right is Arthur Topham. (K. Topham)

The Pals' first officers outside their bungalow at Colsterdale, September 1914. Many of them still wear their old OTC uniforms. The light-coloured armbands show they are to be commissioned officers in the Leeds Pals (see text for their names).

Axel Jonas Alfred Poignant, had served for twelve years in the Royal Swedish Navy.

Lieutenant-Colonel J. Walter Stead, VD[15], formerly in command of the 7th Battalion (Leeds Rifles), The Prince of Wales's Own (West Yorkshire Regiment), began his service in the ranks, reached sergeant and was offered a commission. He was a keen rifle shot and served as Honorary Secretary of the Yorkshire Territorial Team Association; he was also involved with the National Reserve.

Richard Morris Stanley Blease was the son of Ellwood H. Blease of Liverpool. Born in Queensland, Australia, he graduated from Leeds University with a BA (Hons) in Classics.

Thomas George Gibson, the son of Dr Charles Gibson of Harrogate, was educated at Epsom College, where he was a member of the Rifle Corps, and Pembroke College Cambridge. He was articled to a firm of Leeds solicitors, and on being admitted as a solicitor was appointed prosecuting solicitor to HM Customs and Excise in Leeds.

John Thornton Dufton was the grandson of Mr John Thornton, Clerk of the Leeds Magistrates, and a member of Leeds University OTC.

Unidentified member of Leeds University OTC.

Lionel Hall Lawson was the son of ex-Alderman Fred Lawson, a former Lord Mayor of Leeds, and a member of Leeds University OTC.

Stanley Morris Bickersteth was the fifth of the six sons of Dr Samuel Bickersteth, Vicar of Leeds. He was educated at St David's Reigate, and at Rugby School, where he was a member of the OTC, and lastly at Christ Church College, Oxford.

Leslie Christian Kirk was Language Master at Leeds Grammar School (French and German) for three years, and a Second Lieutenant in the School OTC. He was educated at King Edward School, Sheffield and St John's College, Oxford.

George Clifford Whitaker, the son of Mr Matthew Whitaker, a railway contractor of Horsforth, was educated at Ilkley Grammar School, and served for two years with the 5th Battalion, The King's Own Yorkshire Light Infantry. He was a member of the Headingley football team and an engineer by profession.

John (Jackie) Gilbert Vause, the son of Mr F. W. Vause of the firm Thomas Vause and Sons Ltd was educated at Leeds Grammar School and at Leeds University. He was a member of both the Leeds University and the Leeds Grammar School OTCs.

Philip Horace Leyland Mellor was a grandson of the late Judge Mellor. He was well known in Yorkshire cricket circles, being a product of school cricket at King William's College, Isle of Man. He was also a good gymnast, and helped in the instruction of Swedish Drill at Colsterdale.

Roy Balfour Hodgson Rayner was educated at Leeds Grammar School and was a student in the Textiles Department of Leeds University when war broke out. He was also a member of Leeds University OTC.

David Brian Gill, the son of Mr Joseph Gill, a bleacher, was a member of Leeds University OTC.

Stretcher-bearers training. Harold Hartley is in the foreground (in a dark suit). (Leeds Library)

George Stephen Ward was a member of Leeds University OTC.
Norman Evers was a member of Leeds University OTC.
Henry Samuel Bridel was a member of Leeds University OTC.
Unidentified member of Leeds University OTC.

As we have already seen, the qualifications required of men applying for Temporary Commissions in Kitchener's New Armies were that they should be unmarried, aged between 17 and 30, and of good education. Cadets and ex-cadets of the University Officers' Training Corps or members of a university were especially welcomed and were advised to apply to their commanding officers or the university authority.

Of the twenty-two men in that first photograph of the Leeds Pals officers, eighteen had previous military or naval service, including twelve who were members of a university or school Officer Training Corps. Of the remaining four, one was a university graduate, and therefore qualified in the eyes of the War Office, while another excelled at sports and yet another was a trained engineer, experience which could be considered relevant to military training.

On the first Sunday, a Church Parade was held at a local church on the road to Masham.

One man said he was Plymouth Brethren, he was told, 'Well you can clean the toilets while the others are at church.' The next Sunday he joined the others at Church Parade. An officer said, 'I thought you said you were Plymouth Brethren.' He said, I was, but I don't like their place of worship!'

15/259 Private Arthur Dalby, D Company[16]

Once the men had settled into the routine, they were sorted according to any previous experience they had, which might be put to good use.

They started picking specialists out. We had a man called Summersgill, he was a plumber, well he was put on to the water. We had a man who was a butcher, he was put into the butcher's department. A man who was a tailor was put into the tailoring department to patch up the clothes, and men who had served behind counters were put into quartermaster stores. By the time we got organised after six months, you see, they'd moulded us into a unit, and from the colonel right down to the junior private you've got to have some kind of a building.

15/471 Private Clifford Hollingworth, D Company[17]

The high spirits of the Pals in camp, and the enthusiastic press reports of the progress of their training, were tempered by an article which appeared in the *Leeds and District Weekly Citizen* on 2 October. It read:

Why Recruiting Stopped
The Pals Battalion and Others
Leeds and Snobbery

The departure of the Pals Battalion to be known in the New Army as the City of Leeds Battalion of Business Men, was marked by the presence of a huge crowd at the new station last Friday morning. It is estimated that twenty thousand people were gathered in the precincts of the station to see the last of the young men who were leaving the city to go into training close by Colsterdale. There were cheers outside the station and inside the station, and there were songs and Boy Scouts and Territorials. What a contrast the animated scene made to some of the other departures! Ninety per cent of the recruits in Leeds have gone away to the war, or to training in preparation for the war without a cheer and without a song, except the song that sprang up amongst the men on the journey. There were no cheers, no crowds, no recognition of any kind. They just went in silence, entraining their horses and guns amid glances of curiosity, but nothing more. With their khaki and their equipment they made a more soldier-like appearance than the 'Pals', but the people are all too familiar with khaki and soldiers' equipment. So the Artillery and Infantry regiments went away without any demonstration or message of goodwill. They didn't mind that, for they were only eager to get across the sea and to face the troops of the modern Napoleon.

Snobbery and Recruiting

It was the cheering that killed recruiting in Leeds. There has been no public protest, no outspoken contempt, but just silence and a huge drop in the rate of recruiting. Alderman Wilson started two 'Workers' battalions, as distinct from the 'Pals' and he promptly yoked himself to the 'Pals' and left the workers to recruit as they liked. Artisans able to earn three or four pounds weekly by their skilled labour offered themselves for the 'Pals' battalion, and their names and other details were taken. Then they got postcards informing them that their services would not be required. Clerks and budding travellers with smaller physiques and smaller pay were accepted. Why? They belong to the clan, the class of the special elect, and the Workers could form battalions of their own. There is a supreme compliment in the word 'workers' as distinct from somebody else. When the workers see that they really are the producers, and that they are a back number every time, they will change things. The boom over the 'Pals' was all very nice and full of esteem and goodwill, but it froze the stream of recruits right off. It was the sharp contrast that did it, and potential recruits felt something they could not express and stayed at their work. Yet the men who got no cheers, and no presents, and no electrically lighted huts are soldiers of the King, as good as the next and better than some. Fair play for the recruits, please.

These young men may yet have to stand shoulder to shoulder against a rain of bullets, and class differences sink then, when all are comrades in arms. We at home must sink them too, and learn a lesson in war that shall be useful in times of peace.

While the comments about the Pals' send off seem justified,[18] the decline in recruiting in Leeds cannot wholly be blamed on the Pals' selective recruiting policy, nor even on Charles Wilson's apparent abandonment of the proposed 'Workers' battalions. By October 1914 the number of recruits offering their services was declining nationally. Although there was a brief recovery in January 1915, possibly as a result of the War Office's decision to raise Reserve companies for many of the Pals battalions, the recruiting figures generally continued to decline steadily. One contributing factor was the placing of War Office contracts, which regenerated the manufacturing industries in Leeds, creating many new jobs which were eagerly filled.[19]

Back in Colsterdale, meanwhile, the battalion cooks set to work, after a shaky start due to a last-minute delay in installing the kitchen equipment, and to the high winds, which had prevented them from lighting some of the fires. Under the watchful eye of Charles Wilson, they soon began to satisfy the hearty appetites of the Pals, appetites increased by hard physical exercise in the Yorkshire Dales. The cooks' day began between three and four in the morning when they got up to light the stoves and boilers on which they would prepare the early morning hot drinks and, later, breakfast. The main meal was served in the middle of the day, and the men had a light supper in the evening. Those who were still hungry could supplement their rations from a shop set up on the roadside, or could visit the canteen for some liquid refreshment.

An idea of the quantity of food consumed by 1,100 hungry men undergoing military training can be gathered from the following list of some of the rations for two days, published in the local press:

Sunday
6.00am, 150 gallons Coffee;
7.45am, 200 gallons Coffee, 500lb Sausage;
12.30pm, 1,000lb Beef, 400lb Puddings, 9 sacks Potatoes;
4.30pm, 200 gallons Tea;

Monday
6.00am, 150 gallons Cocoa;
7.45am, 200 gallons Cocoa, 500lb Haddocks;
12.30pm, 1,000lb Beef 120lb Peas, 9 sacks Potatoes;
4.30pm, 200 gallons Tea.[20]

Alfred E. Ingle, Battalion Cook. (Margaret Willets)

Although the provisions were still supplied at the Lord Mayor's expense, the *Leeds and District Weekly Citizen* felt obliged to accuse the 'devoted Conservative butcher' who provided the Pals with their meat of 'overcharging or something that calls for a stronger word'. No mention was made of the quality of the meat offered by the 'shocked Leeds butchers' who had submitted cheaper tenders.[21]

Mainstay of the Pals' midday meal was stew:

Dixie after dixie was emptied of its stew. Everything was rough and ready, but we were healthy youths with healthy appetites and even if it was not the stew that mother used to make we still tucked in with gusto, and when the QM came round there were 'no complaints'.

15/711 Private Arthur V. Pearson[22]

Recipe for Plain Stew
Ingredients for 100 men
60lb of meat 3lb onions
7lb vegetables 3lb flour
pepper and salt to taste
stock

Method of making
Separate the meat from the bone, cut up into small cubes.
Clean and cut up the mixed vegetables, peel clean and cut up the onions finely. Place a little stock in the bottom of a camp kettle, place in the ingredients, and mix up well together, season with pepper and salt, barely cover with stock.
Then place on the fire and bring to the boil, and allow to simmer 2 hours. In the meantime make a thickening of flour, salt and water, and pepper, bring the stew to the boil again, add the thickening and allow to simmer for ten minutes stirring it all the time.

15/500 Private (later Sergeant) Alfred Ernest Ingle, Battalion Cook[23]

A variation in the Pals' diet led to an unfortunate misunderstanding when, on Saturday, 31 October, the North Eastern Railway thoughtfully laid on a special train for friends and relatives to visit the Leeds Pals in camp at Colsterdale. Colonel Stead had other ideas, however. He took the battalion on a route march, and the hundreds of people who had made their way up to Colsterdale waited vainly in the pouring rain for a glimpse of their Pals.

There was one Saturday we shall never forget. The day we were marched to Swinton Castle to thank Lord Masham for the rabbits. Our loved ones at home, wives sisters, mothers and

The battalion cooks set to work. (Author's collection)

sweethearts thought it was time they came to see how their menfolk were faring out in the wild country … The 'Powers that be' had got wind of this excursion and had decided that this was the opportunity to show what Army discipline (and awkwardness) meant. We were on parade cheering like mad (and how mad we were!) for the addition to the menu, rabbits which we had been presented with.

15/711, Private Arthur V Pearson, C Company[24]

Cyril Brown's card to his family warning them that he may not be in camp if they visit on 31 October. (C. Brown)

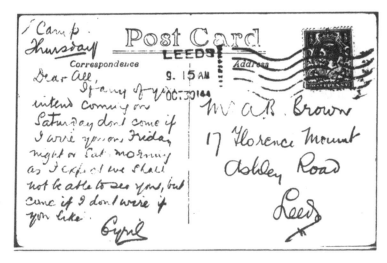

Leeds Pals on the march.

My brother came, and he brought my young lady. I didn't see them, they went before I got back.
15/259 Private Arthur Dalby, D Company[25]

... [It was] idle to deny that last Saturday's experience was a bitter disappointment both to the few hundred visitors who had made the journey from Leeds with the object of seeing their friends in the Battalion, and to those men who were looking forward to a brief reunion with their 'ain folk'. In a final effort to snatch a word with friends, visitors tramping the six miles back

to Masham, hailed the returning Battalion with shouts of 'What Company? 'Is Bill Smith near?' and the like; and some peered into the faces of the outside men of the fours' in the faint hope of recognizing the looked-for 'Pal'. What is needed to obviate a similar contretemps in the future is an official intimation one way or the other as to the Battalion's movements on Saturdays. Lieutenant-Colonel J W Stead, the commanding officer, I happen to know, is anxious to do all he can, commensurate with his duties, to meet the desires of the men. He holds the view that Saturday is the most opportune day for arduous tasks, preceding as it does the only day of rest. Incidentally, it would be to the point, and an act of courtesy, if the North Eastern Railway Company were to inform him of their intention to run excursions, and I have no doubt he would, if at all practicable, fit it into his programme.

Yorkshire Evening Post, 6 November 1914

It seems that the 'arduous task' the colonel had in mind for his men that day was a cheer for Lord Masham, owner of the Swinton Estate, to thank him for rabbits he had kindly given the battalion.

… Three cheers for Lord Masham, I wouldn't say exactly what everyone said, it wasn't cheers anyway! Although it wasn't his fault really, it was our old colonel, he did it on purpose, I think really because he was invited to stay there for dinner.

15/259 Private Arthur Dalby. D Company[26]

Although they had been prevented from meeting their visitors, this did not mean that the Pals had no time for recreation.

The North Eastern Railway poster announcing its special excursion. (Leeds Library)

We'd been up [at Colsterdale] about a month or five weeks and it was a lovely summer's day. We said we'd have a walk over the moors and this would be perhaps beginning of November. We walked on and we came across a little croft, a little farm – a shepherd's place, and that chap didn't know the war had broken out! He didn't know anything about the war! But you see parts of the country like that, they go to town twice or three times a year. They buy the bulk of their food for the year. Because they live off the land normally. He'd only been the week before the war broke out, down to town, him and his three children and his wife, they didn't know the war had broken out.

15/471 Private Clifford Hollingworth, D Company[27]

By the end of October the new huts were complete, and A, B and C Companies were able to move from their draughty tents to the comparative comfort of their new homes.

Some of the battalion's athletes pose outside Metcalfe's store at Colsterdale.

New huts were rapidly being built across the road, and soon we were under a roof of our own, a platoon to a hut with a sergeant in his own 'bed-sitter' at one end. We were as snug as we could be by the time winter crept up on us. The stoves in each hut were stoked up, and at night, after work and parades were over, there were arguments and discussions, hotter even than the stove! All subjects under the sun were discussed and youth, in all its confidence, settled the problems of the world. How long the war would last! Would it be over before we got overseas?

We made our own fun off parade. One member of our platoon had his gramophone sent up from home and we sat around imagining ourselves back in Leeds Grand Theatre once again listening to 'Our Miss Gibbs', 'The Quaker Girl', 'Maid of the Mountains' and Gilbert and Sullivan operas. We spent many happy hours sitting around that gramophone until some unmusical Philistine began cutting bread on it and gummed up the works!

15/711 Private Arthur V Pearson, C Company[28]

A sports and recreation committee was set up, and its membership included the well-known sportsmen in the battalion. In addition to the cricketing and football celebrities who had joined, it soon became apparent that the Leeds Pals numbered several good cross-country runners among its ranks. It was with great sadness, therefore, that they received news of the death of the former Yorkshire Cross-Country Champion, 15/216 Private George Colcroft, on 19 November. Colcroft, aged 29, had been taken into Seacroft Hospital a week earlier where, according to a local paper, he had died

Colcroft's grave in Bramley Methodist Church cemetery, 1988. (Author's photographs)

A Pal has his hair cut. On the right is Roland Barrett.

A battalion working party. Left foreground (leaning on a spade) is Harold Child, next to him (kneeling) is George Ferrand.

Trench digging on the Yorkshire Dales, excellent practice for what was to come. (Cecila Brown)

The battalion guard.

of complications arising from rheumatism.[29] He was buried at Bramley Baptist Church on 22 November 1914, the first Leeds Pal to die during military service.

Route marches and fieldcraft were soon added to the Pals' repertoire and they became intimately acquainted with the local countryside.

One day we marched into Middleham and were delighted at being' dismissed' for half an hour, and it was there that I tasted beer for the first time. How I enjoyed that shandy! Plus the two slices of dry currant bread we were issued with as 'rations'. Later when we were in the desert, my thoughts often went back to that drink when we were hot, thirsty and always short of water. We strolled under the shadow of the castle and some enterprising spirits even had a look round the racing stables. The turf on those gallops was soft and springy like walking on a carpet with six [under]felts underneath, it put new life and energy into tired limbs and aching feet for the return march.

15/711 Private Arthur V Pearson, C Company[30]

Their uniforms had still not arrived, but the War Office was paying an allowance to men who were training in 'civvies',[31] and even if the men did not look like soldiers, some of them were beginning to feel the effects of their robust outdoor life.

Heads up and shoulders back, cold water washes, cold water shaves and plenty of good food, we were soon fit as fiddles. The natty gent's suiting in which we lived and moved and had our being

The Corps of Bugles and Drums. George Grant is forth from the right (wearing a muffler). Walter Wild (with moustache) is kneeling to the left of the bass drum.

soon began to show that they had not been made to stand the rough wear that they were getting. We looked more like tramps every day as we bust our jackets and tore our trousers. Scarves began to take the place of collars and ties, even though some of these collars were made of celluloid which would wash with a lick.

15/711 Private Arthur V Pearson, C Company[32]

During November, the results of a competition to write a marching song for the Pals were announced. The winner, selected by a committee of Leeds journalists who were also members of the Pals, under the paternal guidance of Walter Stead, was Miss Ellen Rose of George Street, York. Her song, written to the tune of 'The Boys of the Old Brigade' went as follows:[33]

Gaily we'll march to war my lads,
March with ringing cheer,
March with rifles and bayonets fixed,
Never a thought of fear!
No room for cowards within our ranks,
Bravely we'll meet the foe.
True we will be to our dear old Flag,
As in the long ago.

Refrain:

Then cheerily marching to battle,
Cheerily singing our song,
Leeds boys are we gallant and free,
In duty and daring strong.
Sad though we be to leave Britain's shores,
Hear we our country's call,

The Pals on the march once more, but with musical accompaniment.

Ready to help in her sorest need,
Ready to win or fall!
Proudly our banners we'll wave aloft,
Leaving the City's hum,
Onward we'll go with our swinging tramp,
On to the sound of the drum.

Soon we'll be far from Leeds, my lads,
Goodbye to England dear!
Though there's a lump in our throats, my lads,
'Pals' should not shed a tear!
Conquer we will or we'll die, my lads;
All hearts beating as one;
Steadily marching side by side,
Steadily tramping on.

A marching song begs the support of a band, and although the Pals had a Corps of Drums and Bugles, other more melodious instruments were needed.

A working party under the command of Sergeant Easy (far left); next to him (holding a spade) is Harold Child. Harry Brown (circled) sent this photograph to his family. (F. Groves)

A similar group, this time with uniforms. Pioneer Corporal Harold Child on the left and pioneer Sergeant George Easy on the far right. In the centre of the photo Joe Collinson (shading his eyes) poses with his pal, Arthur 'Snowy" Howard (still in civilian clothes). (J. Collinson)

> *When they were marching at ease he [George Grant] was usually called upon to play the mouth organ, as this helped to pass away the time and the miles, the men joined in the singing, I understand one of their favourites was 'Cock of the North'. The men were singing and my father playing, along came an officer on horseback, and he rode alongside them for some time, my father at this time was not sure whether he should continue playing or not, but he decided that having seen and heard what was going on and quite satisfied to ride alongside them he would continue to play. The officer moved on, nothing was said about the episode, but shortly after, the surprise came when a notice posted on the notice-board read, Anyone who could play a mouth organ if they would present themselves at the stores would be issued with a mouth organ. The order was signed by the officer who had ridden alongside them and obviously approved.*

> *Sarah Pellow (neé Grant)[34]*

Towards the end of November, the Pals received their first issue of boots, part of the uniform paid for by Edward Brotherton. But some of the boots did not stand up to the rigours of military training.

> *Our first issue of service boots turned out to be very poor stuff. They could not stand up to ordinary wear and tear let alone the rough country we worked over. The boots were not made by a Leeds firm or the heels would have stayed on once they were put on instead of falling off as happened scores of times. Many a chap has lost his heel miles away from camp and had to make*

his own way back sometimes arriving in the early hours of the next morning somewhat the worse for calling at the village hostelries on his way, as closing time was not very rigidly adhered to in those parts.

15/711 Private Arthur V. Pearson, C Company[35]

The poor quality of the Pals' first boots was seized upon by the ever-watchful *Leeds and District Weekly Citizen*, which wasted no time in reporting the scandal. A representative of the newspaper met with Councillor John Buckle, President of the Boot and Shoe Operatives' Union, and was shown an example of the boot in question. The heel had been ripped off revealing a thick pad of paper pulp – hardly suitable for military use. Among those complaining vociferously about this apparent scandal were the Leeds boot manufacturers Messrs T Malbane, who had been in correspondence with Brotherton, Colonel Stead, and the Battalion Quartermaster, Charles Wilson, early in September, and had offered to fit each man with a pair of boots 'at an almost record low price of 14s 6d [72½p] per pair'.

The contract had, however, been given to another Leeds firm, Messrs Midgeley & Sons who were merchants and not manufacturers. They had quoted a price of 10s [50p] per pair, a difference of £137.50 on the total order of 1,100 pairs, and had submitted a sample for approval. The boots were made by a company in the Midlands, and were to be delivered in batches direct to the battalion up at Colsterdale. No sooner had the first consignment of 250 pairs been delivered and issued, to C Company, than the faults became apparent.

Colonel Stead immediately contacted the contractors and manufacturers whose representatives hurried to Colsterdale for a meeting. The outcome was that although the manufacturers admitted that they were at fault, the use of this type of boot, which did not have flexible soles, for Swedish Drill had contributed to the damage. It was clear, however, that the boots were simply not sturdy enough, and so a compromise was reached. The entire order of 1,100 was returned, and a better-quality boot was to be provided at a cost of 11s 6d [57½p] a pair, with delivery of the first consignment on 20 December. In the meantime, Colonel Stead made arrangements to purchase a further 1,100 pairs of boots from another manufacturer, at a higher price, so that each man would eventually have a spare pair, and he also undertook to ensure that the men were provided with flexible footwear for Swedish Drill.[36]

Soon the Pals' uniforms began to arrive. They were made by Joseph May and Sons of Leeds, and the contract had been placed in September, but the shortage of khaki serge had led to a delay in fulfilling the order.

One day at last the uniforms arrived in the stores, and some members of the battalion began to get a 'new look'. Men at drill were ordered to fall out' of the squads and report to the Quartermaster's Stores. Perhaps they took a size 6⁷/₈ in caps and a cargo of 6⁷/₈ had arrived or perhaps they measured 38 inches around the chest and a consignment of 38 inches had arrived. Off they were marched as 'ragged elbowed civilians' and lo and behold, they returned as 'semi-soldiers'. One chap would have a cap and a pair of puttees, the next man would be blushingly adorned with a tunic and a pair of civilian trousers. In these days of transition, No 11 Platoon was a proper piebald platoon. However the uniform contractors were catching up with the job in spite of many difficulties, and the powers behind the Leeds hub of the battalion (Alderman Arthur Willey for one) got things moving and soon we were all clad in our full rig-out, and what a difference that uniform made.

15/711 Private Arthur V. Pearson, C Company[37]

Early in December the officers' commissions were published in the *London Gazette*, and included three recent promotions from the ranks – Sergeant Pope-Smith (more popularly

Part of No.7 Platoon, B Company. Herbert Smith is seated in the centre of the first row, next to the Bass beer bottle.

known as 'Pip'-Smith), and Privates Hummel and Willey were gazetted as second-lieutenants. On 18 December it was announced that Sergeant Evelyn Lintott, the footballer, was also to be commissioned.[38]

As Christmas approached, the officers and men began to speculate about the likelihood of leave. Obviously not all of them would spend Christmas at home, for they were now in the army and war had been declared.

'Christmas! Don't mention that word to me', was the exclamation of Lieutenant-Colonel Walter Stead, the Commanding Officer of the Leeds Battalion when I ventured to ask him of the prospects of leave for the season which in normal times is the season of Peace and Goodwill.

The fact is our CO has been pestered with such persistence on the matter that the word is becoming almost as banal to him as it was to poor old Scrooge before his conversion, but the Colonel has more humane feelings towards us than Dickens's immortal character respecting Bob Cratchit, and if only the War Office grant him the necessary permission, he will, he assures me, do the very best to ensure a big percentage of the 'Pals' eating their Christmas dinner of turkey – if they feel inclined to dine off a bird of such forbidding cognomen – in the luxury of their own homes.

'Yorkshire Post *member of the Pals'*[39]

On 13 December Colonel Stead had issued his orders concerning Christmas leave. Each man would have four nights off, and 25 per cent of the battalion would go off on each of the following dates: 26–30 December, 30 December–3 January, and 3–7 January.

These groups overlapped in Leeds, and on Saturday 26 December two of the contingents met up in the city and marched from the North Eastern Railway station via Boar Lane, Briggate and Upperhead Row, to Victoria Square, where they were inspected by the Lord Mayor, James E. Bedford, accompanied by his predecessor, Edward A. Brotherton, the battalion's Honorary Colonel, and other civic dignitaries. It was the first time the people of Leeds had seen the Pals en masse in their smart new uniforms and fully equipped with rifles and fixed bayonets, and they could not help but be impressed by their soldierly bearing.

Saturday 26 December 1914–At 12.30 I went down in a cab with mother and Geoffrey to see half of the Leeds Battalion, who were in the City on leave, march through the streets to Victoria Square, headed

Cyril Brown (second from left) with his Pals.

Arthur Dalby (centre with hand in pocket) out for a stroll with some of his comrades. Although he is wearing riding breeches he still has his puttees tied infantry-fashion.

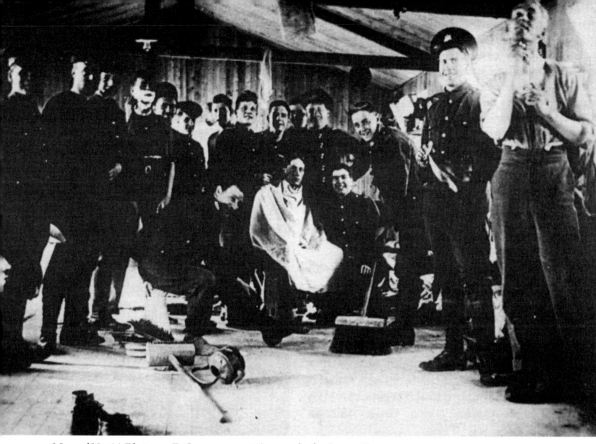

Men of No.14 Platoon, D Company, getting ready for inspection.

The new huts at Colsterdale.

COLSTERDALE CAMP,

Christmas, 1914.

O Come, all ye Faithful.

O COME, all ye faithful,
  Joyful and triumphant,
O come ye, O come ye to Bethleham ;
  Come and behold Him
  Born, the King of Angels ;
  O come, let us adore Him,
  O come, let us adore Him,
O Come, let us adore Him, Christ the Lord.

  God of God,
  Light of Light,
Lo ! He abhors not the Virgin's womb ;
  Very God,
  Begotten, not created ;
  O come, let us adore Him, &c.

  Sing, choirs of Angels,
  Sing in exultation,
Sing, all ye citizens of Heav'n above :
  " Glory to God
  In the highest ;"
  O come, let us adore Him, &c.

  Yea, Lord, we greet Thee,
  Born this happy morning ;
Jesu, to Thee be glory given ;
  Word of the Father,
  Now in flesh appearing ;
  O come, let us adore Him,
  O come, let us adore Him,
O come, let us adore Him, Christ the Lord.   Amen.

Hark ! the Herald-Angels Sing.

HARK ! the herald-angels sing
  Glory to the new-born King,
Peace on earth, and mercy mild,
God and sinners reconciled.
Joyful, all ye nations, rise,
Join the triumph of the skies ;
With the Angelic host proclaim,
" Christ is born in Bethlehem "
  Hark ! the herald-angels sing
  Glory to the new-born King.

Christ, by highest Heav'n ador'd,
Christ, the Everlasting Lord,
Late in time behold Him come,
Offspring of a Virgin's womb.
Veil'd in flesh the Godhead see !
Hail, the Incarnate Deity !
Pleased as Man with man to dwell,
Jesus, our Emmanuel.
  Hark ! the herald-angels sing
  Glory to the new-born King.

Hail, the heaven-born Prince of peace !
Hail, the Sun of righteousness !
Light and life to all He brings,
Risen with healing in His wings.
Mild He lays His glory by,
Born that man no more may die,
Born to raise the sons of earth,
Born to give them second birth.
  Hark ! the herald-angels sing
  Glory to the new-born King.   Amen.

Christians, Awake.

CHRISTIANS, awake, salute the happy morn,
  Whereon the Saviour of the world was born ;
Rise to adore the mystery of love,
Which hosts of Angels chanted from above ;
With them the joyful tidings first begun
Of God Incarnate and the Virgin's Son.

Then to the watchful shepherds it was told,
Who heard the Angelic herald's voice, " Behold,
I bring good tidings of a Saviour's birth
To you and all the nations upon earth :
This day hath God fulfill'd His promised word,
This day is born a Saviour, Christ the Lord."

He spake ; and straightway the celestial choir
In hymns of joy, unknown before, conspire :
The praises of redeeming love they sang,
And Heav'n's whole orb with Alleluias rang :
God's highest glory was their anthem still,
Peace upon earth, and unto men goodwill.

Then may we hope, the Angelic hosts among,
To sing, redeem'd, a glad triumphal song :
He that was born upon this joyful day
Around us all His glory shall display ;
Saved by His love, incessant we shall sing
Eternal praise to Heav'n's Almighty King.   Amen.

While Shepherds Watch'd.

WHILE shepherds watch'd their flocks by night
  All seated on the ground,
The Angel of the Lord came down,
  And glory shone around.

" Fear not," said he ; for mighty dread
  Had seized their troubled mind ;
" Glad tidings of great joy I bring
  To you and all mankind.

" To you in David's town this day
  Is born of David's line
A Saviour, Who is Christ the Lord ;
  And this shall be the sign :

" All glory be to God on high,
  And to the earth be peace ;
Good will henceforth from Heav'n to men
  Begin and never cease." Amen.

Christmas carol sheet. (Sarah Fellow)

Colonel Stead (left) with his staff: (left to right) Howard (adjutant), Captain Wilson (Quartermaster) and Lieutenant de Pledge.

by Colonel Stead and a local band. Morris led his Company, the men marched with fixed bayonets and looked extremely soldier-like and smart. They received with considerable enthusiasm, the Lord Mayor and ex-Lord Mayor who has largely financed the scheme. Both made speeches on the Town Hall steps and the surrounding streets were crowded with interested onlookers. Morris marched straight back to the station and returned to Colsterdale that afternoon, after four days' leave.[40]

The unlucky members of the battalion who had stayed at Colsterdale during Christmas had their share of festivity, even if they could not be with their families.

On Christmas Eve we were taken down to the officers' quarters by a warrant officer and sung the good old carols. WOs and NCOs were invited in (they couldn't have the lot of us in or they wouldn't have enough drinks to last them over the festive season). However, officers came out to us and handed out gifts of boxes of cigarettes. We sang more carols and then went back to our hut to our 'Miss Gibbs' and the 'Quaker Girl' (gramophone records of course). On Christmas

A group of men from No9. Platoon, C Company. (Back row, left to right) Jim Lunham, Edric Longfield, John Ratcliffe, Willie Earnshaw; (front row) Joe Prince, Walter Withell, Bert Sunderland, and Percy Earnshaw.

59

morning, the usual church parades were held. The 'sheep' were addressed by the Padre while the 'goats' went down to the Wesleyan Chapel on the side of the compound. Back to camp for our Christmas dinner and what a gargantuan meal it turned out to be. Turkeys, geese and poultry galore, followed by Christmas pudding and rum sauce – the lot! Fruit and nuts and two bottles of beer for each man, our genius of a QM had certainly 'done us proud'. The orderly men had the whale of a time clearing away and washing up. Then the dining room was cleared and we had a rousing concert given by our own battalion's talented artists. Brilliant some of them. They had moved in the highest musical circles in Leeds and the surrounding district.

15/711 Private Arthur V. Pearson, C Company[41]

The New Year was also celebrated in the traditional manner by the men up at Colsterdale, for only a quarter of the battalion had been allowed home on leave.

Colsterdale 1 January 1915

My darling Father and Mother, just a line to tell you that we had quite an amusing evening last night. I rang you up to wish you all good wishes for the new year and then I believe I forgot all about it. But as usual I had to say goodbye rather quickly as somebody wanted to use the telephone. We had a battalion concert in the big dining hall at 9 o'clock, this lasted till 11.30, and some very good turns there were as we really have a good deal of talent in this regiment. Of course the Colonel and all the officers were there and to begin with the CO made a short speech and amongst other things he mentioned his visit to the War Office at the beginning of the week and he said the general opinion was that Kitchener would send out a huge army in April to the front, but equally certain it was that he would not send out anyone who was not able to go. I wondered if he realised how much this applied to himself. Before the concert began he asked all the officers to distribute two ounce packets of tobacco which someone had sent, this we did, of course all the men were very cheery and in an extremely happy mood, so that the whole thing went well, but I fear that some of them were not quite sober.

At 11.30 we went out into a field in front where a large bonfire had been prepared and a good number of fireworks. At 12 o'clock the Sergeant of the band struck a drum twelve times, we then all of us formed a huge circle round the fire, crossed hands and sang 'Auld Lang Syne', really quite a moving experience. Then there was a tremendous cheering and we all went about wishing each other a Happy New Year. Of course all my own men came up and shook hands and wished me the best of luck, but besides that I must have shaken hands with hundreds of men.

By this time the fire was burning merrily. I was standing fairly close looking at it and getting warm because it was a jolly cold and frosty night, when suddenly from behind I heard a rush and a tremendous yell of 'B Company come along!' I was hoisted off my legs onto the shoulders of half-a-dozen men and I was rushed round the fire three times in the middle of the yelling mob of men all shouting 'Hurrah for Mr Bickersteth!', and then when they had put me down they gave me three cheers. I really was quite overcome, but they certainly are an awfully nice set of men, and we seem to get on pretty well together. Of course do not show this letter beyond the immediate family. They chaired Charlie Wilson too and two other officers.

More snow today and tomorrow the Brigadier comes to inspect, and I am in command of B, it ought to be rather funny. I must fly to mess. Your loving son, Morris[42]

Early in January 1915 the War Office instructed Colonel Stead to raise a Depot Company of 300 men, to be held in reserve when the battalion went overseas. This reserve was nominated E Company, and its men were given '15' prefixes to their regimental numbers just as in the other four companies. Because so many men had left, or were leaving to take commissions, however, the battalion required a considerable intake to bring it up to strength before a reserve company could be formed.

Our ranks began to thin as men who had applied for commissions left us for higher spheres. We must have had officers who obtained commissions out of the battalion in every British regiment throughout the world. Some climbed the giddy heights and commanded battalions and brigades. Some returned to the battalion and became leaders amongst their old crowd, to fall during trench duties or 'over the top'.

When on leave we always congregated at the good old Mitre, it became more or less the Leeds Pals' club. You were pretty sure to meet a crowd in there. Men who had left the battalion for commissions were there in all their glory of Sam Browne belts and Fox's puttees.

15/711 Private Arthur V. Pearson, C Company[43]

The number of men that got commissions was amazing. All of a sudden you'd hear about Bill So and So, then you heard about him that he'd got a commission at the Durhams or the Bradford Pals or suchlike. Of course the two Bradford Pals, 18th and 16th West Yorks, they wanted men, they wanted officers like they wanted men in when the war broke out in 1914. It's all right

Battalion transport – several members of the Raising Committee sent their cars up to Colsterdale for the battalion's use. This 1912 Crossley was driven by Wilf Wainman.

Battalion transport – Harold Brown on one of the battalion's horses; in the background is one of the battalion's motor cars, perhaps the Crossley on the other photograph.

starting a shop or a factory you can get 500 employees but you've got to have people to manage the 500 and they're scarce.

15/471 Private Clifford Hollingworth, D Company[44]

Towards the end of January the battalion was engaged on the construction of two open-air miniature rifle ranges, and by the middle of February the men had also built an indoor range, so that they could practice their musketry in all weathers. Weapons were still in short supply, with only 400 obsolete Lee-Metford[45] rifles available, but at least the general principles could be learned.

Early in February the Pals adopted a mascot, Reuben Henry Larcombe, the 7-year-old son of Fred Larcombe, a 'Navvy Digger', who had been employed on excavating the new reservoir. Reuben was a friendly young lad and the Pals kitted him out with a uniform, pack and wooden rifle. His mother who lived with her husband and three sons in married quarters up at Colsterdale, became great friends with many of the Leeds Pals, helping out with their washing and mending and generally mothering them, for some of them had never been away from home before.[46]

In the same month, the battalion was joined by two ex-Regular officers, Major L. P. Baker, a Canadian-born veteran of the South African War, and Temporary Captain R. B. Shepherd. Training for night operations started and on 18 February the men were inspected by Brigadier-General Molesworth, General Officer Commanding 93 Brigade, as they skirmished across the Yorkshire Dales around Jervaulx Abbey in the pouring rain.

The Brigadier came up in the middle of the week and spent all afternoon with us at a Battalion Field Day. He had all the officers up and told them that he was very pleased with what he had seen. Of course he made a few criticisms and suggestions but that is exactly what we wanted from him. But his last words to us were that he had nothing to grouse at and that he was very pleased with our progress. He told the Adjutant afterwards that we were far and away the best battalion that he had seen yet.

The Colonel has been pretty hopeless again this week and has at once got on the wrong side of the Major with whom he has had a good many rows. I only hope it means that he has put another nail in his coffin.

Lieutenant S. Morris Bickersteth, B Company[47]

Reuben Larcombe guards the Pals' camp, spring 1915.

Throughout February and March the training was stepped up, with field work and route marches on alternate days. Sporting activity also continued with 15 Platoon emerging victorious in the inter-platoon rugby competition after beating 14 Platoon in the final on 13 March.

On 14 April, the pals were again inspected, this time by Major-General Lawson, General Officer Commanding, Northern Command.

As the men's fitness and stamina increased so too did the length of their route marches, and on 29 April they left for a two-day return march to Ripon, staying overnight at No 1 Camp, which would soon be their new home.

> *We marched the twelve miles to Ripon. It was a hot day and we welcomed a long halt by the roadside to be lectured by an officer who had been in the thick of the fighting in France. He tried to give us a picture of what the conditions were like for the infantry but I suppose we took some of it in and discarded what we thought sounded too much like war. After these 'tips for the fighting man' we fell in and set off to finish the march to Ripon. Arriving at the Town Hall we stood in ranks to attention while the civic dignitaries made speeches of welcome. We were standing only a yard or two from the crowd and we were smiled at, winked at and generally given the 'glad eye' by the young females, and it was rather a strain to stand to attention in a soldier-like manner. Then we got 'slope arms, right turn' and we were off to the new camp.*
>
> 15/711 Private Arthur V. Pearson, C Company[48]

> *We had an excellent march to Ripon and back. We started yesterday at 2 o'clock and arrived in Ripon at 8. You may have seen something about it in the* Yorkshire Post. *We would not have been so late only the Brigadier stopped us on the way as he had got a captain with him who had just returned from the Front, and he gave us a lecture in a field which delayed us nearly an hour.*
>
> *Of course the whole show in Ripon was too absurd for words. We were met by the town band which played us into the market square, where we all formed up and received a civic welcome and an address from the Mayor. The Army Service Corps of Kitchener's 5th Army, billeted there, also turned out with their officers as a guard of honour. It was too ludicrous for words, and we were all frightfully sick about it, but of course the Colonel and Quartermaster simply live for such things. The only thing that pleased us all was that after the Captain lectured, the Colonel had to ride for two miles, trotting beside the Brigadier's carriage and as he is not accustomed to riding, we all enjoyed the sight. We slept in some of the new huts last night. It was a vile night and I hardly slept a wink, of course we had to lie on the bare boards and it was beastly cold. Reveille went at 4.30am and we were away by 6 o'clock. We turned into camp about 11.30 so we did thirty-five miles in just over twenty-two hours which is fairly good going, the men carrying packs of course and all their rations with them. We also of course wore packs and my shoulders are pretty stiff now, but I am not at all too tired.*
>
> Lieutenant S. Morris Bickersteth, B Company[49]

The men, now looing more like soldiers, are reviewed by visiting 'bigwig', including Brigadier-General Molesworth and Major-General Lawson.

The winning team of the inter-platoon rugby match. Clifford Hollingworth is front row left and his childhood friend, Fred Naylor, is front row right.

Spot the Ball! A crucial moment in the match, judging from the men's expressions. Evelyn Lintott, the footballer (centre), appears to be shouting in dismay. Third from right is young Horace Iles.

Members of the losing team scowl at the camera – including Horace Iles, (back row second from right), Evelyn Lintott (centre row second from right) and Harold Jackson (front row extreme right).

On 12 May Battalion Sports were held at Colsterdale, and on the next day the Pals received confirmation of a rumour that Colonel Stead was to be replaced, exchanging command with Lieutenant-Colonel Taylor of the 11th King's Own Yorkshire Light Infantry, based at Halifax. This was music to the ears of Morris Bickersteth, who so disliked his commanding officer, and at first most of his brother officers, that he had tried to get a transfer to another regiment, but had been prevented by Stead himself.[50]

Colsterdale Camp Masham May 4 1915

The Brigadier came up yesterday and was very pleased with our field day. He said it was the best he'd seen us do yet. In the afternoon he and the Brigade Major and the Colonel and Captain Howard all motored over to Richmond. Today we went (on)

Each member of the winning team received a silver and enamel medal. This one was awarded to15/1060 Private C. Wood.

C Company trench digging.

Attacking Hill 650 at Colsterdale. The barbed wire in France would not be so easy to negotiate.

Lighting fires to cook their food, an essential part of the Pals' fieldcraft.

A route march to Middleham – few of the men have rifles.

A steep hill 'somewhere in Yorkshire'.

A pause for a photograph during field exercise.

The Pals parade in on of the local villages on a wet day.

B Company marching at ease, led by Major Baker.

another route march and when talking to the Major he told us he knew for certain that a Regular colonel was coming up here soon to take command. A man who had only left the Army two months before the war broke out. I do hope this may be true, but I shall never believe anything until it really happens.

Morris Bickersteth

Colsterdale Camp Masham May 5 1915

It has happened at last, the Colonel has been transferred to the Reserve Battalion of the 11th Battalion of the KOYLI, Kitchener's Army, their Colonel, Colonel Taylor, comes to us. The transfer is to take place as soon as possible, isn't it splendid?

When the CO actually goes I cannot tell, but it cannot be long now. What Colonel Taylor is like I don't know, but he cannot very well be worse. He's an old Regular and commanded somewhere in East Africa I believe and has not long left the Army so I hope now all will go well.

Morris[51]

Syd Walton relaxes after a hard day.

Battalion sports at Colsterdale, the final of the 100 yards.

Programme of Events.

COMPANY CHAMPIONSHIP.

Colonel E. A. Brotherton will present a silver cup to the Company obtaining the most points, which will remain in the custody of the Officer Commanding that Company.

Points will be awarded as follows :—

4 points for the 1st.
2 " " 2nd.
1 point " 3rd.

With the exception of the following events :—

Tug-of-War, Company Team Race, Officers' Race, Sergeants' Race, Obstacle Race. In the Tug-of-War and Company Team Race 12 points will be awarded the Winners and 6 points to the Runners-up.

A Special Cup, presented by the Adjutant (Captain L. M. Howard), will be given to the competitor obtaining the highest number of points.

COLOURS.

A	Company	Blue and White.
B	"	Black and Gold.
C	"	Red and White.
D	"	Black and White.
E	"	Purple and White.

Item 1.—100 Yards Flat Race (Semi-Finals).

1st Heat.	2nd Heat.
Ashworth No. 32 C Coy.	Rhodes No. 757 B Coy.
Hey No. 1208 E Coy.	Corpl. Butterfield A Coy.
L. Corpl. Bean B Coy.	Nettleton No. 678 A Coy.
Hartley No. 436 A Coy.	Bywater No. 98 A Coy.
Lawrence No. 570 A Coy.	Newlands No. 681 D Coy.
Dimmery No. 279 B Coy.	Hill No. 459 D Coy.
Garbutt No. 357 D Coy.	Sowden No. 835 D Coy.
Lieut. Bridel E Coy.	Shipp No. 81 D Coy.

Item 2.—Tug-of-War (First Round).

D Company v. E Company.
A, B and C Companies byes.

Item 3.—120 Yards Hurdles (Semi-Finals).

1st Heat.	2nd Heat.	3rd Heat.
Hill No. 459 D Coy.	Lawrence No. 570 A Coy.	Lieut Bridel E Coy.
Napper No. 1222 E Coy.	Roper No. 774 B Coy.	Ellis No. 307 D Coy.
Smithson No. 830 D Coy.	Newlands No. 681 D Coy.	Beard No. 91 C Coy.
Lieut. Oldham B Coy.	Laxton No 576 B Coy.	Thompson No.889 D Coy
1st.	1st.	1st.
2nd.	2nd.	2nd.

Item 4.—Throwing Cricket Ball.

1st, 4 points.	2nd, 2 points.	3rd, 1 point.
1st.	2nd.	3rd.

Distance—

Item 5.—100 Yards Flat Race (Final).

1st Prize Silver Cup (Presented by Lt.-Colonel J. W. Stead, V.D.)
2nd Prize Small Silver Cup.

1st, 4 points.	2nd, 2 points.	3rd, 1 point.
1st.	2nd.	3rd.

Time—

Item 6.—Tug-of-War (Semi-Finals).

(a) Winner of Item 2 v. C Company.
(b) A Company v. B Company.

Item 7.—Half Mile Flat Race.

1st Prize Silver Cup.

1st, 4 points.	2nd, 2 points.	3rd, 1 point.
Beard No. 91 C Coy.	Howard No. 480 D Coy.	
Napper No. 1222 E Coy.	Newlands No. 681 D Coy.	
Mellor No. 1164 A Coy.	Althorp No. 8 A Coy.	
Nettleton No. 678 A Coy.	Rimmer No. 765 A Coy.	
Sgt. Gutteridge A Coy.	Stockwell No. 1171 E Coy.	
Gilbert No. 372 D Coy.	Cryer No. 1110 D Coy.	
1st.	2nd.	3rd.

Time—

Item 8.—Putting the Weight.

1st, 4 points.	2nd, 2 points.	3rd, 1 point.
1st.	2nd.	3rd.

Distance—

Item 9.—120 Yards Hurdles (Final).

Silver Cup presented by Mrs. Ratcliffe.

1st, 4 points.	2nd, 2 points.	3rd, 1 point.
1st.	2nd.	3rd.

Time—

Item 10.—Long Jump.

1st, 4 points.	2nd, 2 points.	3rd, 1 point.
Cooper 227 D Coy.	Flynn 342 A Coy.	Thompson 896 D Coy.
Smithson 830 D Coy.	Cpl. Jackson E Coy.	Boyd
March 613 A Coy.	Lt. Oldham B Coy.	Lt. Bridel E Coy.
Hill 459 D Coy.	Gray 396 B Coy.	Napper 1222 E Coy.
Hawley 436		
1st.	2nd.	3rd.

Distance—

Item 11.—Sergeants' Race (Quarter Mile Handicap).

No points awarded.

1st.	2nd.	3rd.

Item 12.—Quarter Mile Flat Race.

1st Prize Silver Cup.

1st, 4 points.	2nd, 2 points.	3rd, 1 point.
Nettleton No. 678 A Coy.	Dimmery No.279 B Coy.	
Rimmer No. 765 A Coy.	Lawrence No. 570 A Coy.	
Sergt. Gutteridge A Coy.	Bywater No. 98 A Coy.	
1st.	2nd.	3rd.

Time—

Item 13.—Tug-of-War (Final).

Medals will be presented to the Winning Team.

1st, 12 points.	2nd, 6 points.
Winner of A. v. Winner of B. (See Item 6).	
1st.	2nd.

Item 14.—Officers' Race.

1st.	2nd.	3rd.

Item 15.—Mile Flat Race.

1st Prize Silver Plated Cup. 2nd Prize Small Silver Cup.

1st, 4 points.	2nd, 2 points.	3rd, 1 point.
Nettleton No 678 A Coy.	Rimmer No 765 A Coy.	
Sergt. Gutteridge, A Coy.	Stockwell 1171 E Coy.	
Napper 1222 E Coy.	Bywater 98 A Coy.	
1st.	2nd.	3rd.

Time—

Item 16.—High Jump.

1st Prize Silver Cup.

1st, 4 points.	2nd, 2 points.	3rd, 1 point.
Lt. Oldham B Coy.	Cpl. Bradley E Coy.	L.-Cpl. Laxton B Coy.
Flynn No. 342 A Coy.	Shepherd No.1096A Coy.	Armitage No. 24 C Coy.
Pontefract No.726 C Coy.	Cpl. Mossop D Coy.	Napper 1222 E Coy.
Sgt. Gutteridge A Coy.		
1st.	2nd.	3rd.

Height—

Item 17.—Company Team Race.

1st Relay, 220 yds. 2nd Relay, 220 yds. 3rd Relay, 440 yds. 4th Relay, 880 yds

First Prize a Special Silver Cup, presented by the Officers of the Battalion and 4 cups in miniature to the members of the winning team The cup to be competed for every month by the Companies and cups in miniature to be presented to the winners each month.

After the Battalion is disbanded the cup becomes the property of the Leeds Corporation.

1st, 12 points.		2nd, 6 points.		
A Company	B Company	C Company	D Company	E Company
	1st		2nd	

Item 18.—Obstacle Race

No points awarded.

1st.	2nd.	3rd.

A Silver Cup, presented by Major L. P. Baker, will be awarded Sergt. Jones in recognition of his work in providing Sports for the men of the Battalion.

PRESENTATION OF PRIZES BY MRS. RATCLIFFE.

COMPANY CHAMPIONSHIP.

SUMMARY OF POINTS.

EVENT.	COMPANIES.				
	A	B	C	D	E
100 yds. Flat Race					
Half Mile					
Hurdles					
Putting the Weight					
Long Jump					
Quarter Mile					
Tug-of-War					
Throwing the Cricket Ball					
Mile Flat Race					
High Jump					
Company Team Race					

Winner of Company Championship ....

No. of Points.....................

Winner of Adjutant's Cup.....................

No. of Points.....................

The prize giving.

Lieutenant-Colonel Stuart Campbell Taylor was indeed an old soldier, and had seen active service on the North-West Frontier of India, and in South Africa with the King's Own Yorkshire Light Infantry. Although he had retired from the army in 1911 to take an administrative post in Nigeria, he was still, at 41, young enough and fit enough to lead the Pals to war.[52]

> *One never-to-be-forgotten morning onto the parade ground trotted a new figure. This was our new Commanding Officer, Stuart C. Taylor. He sat on his horse giving us all the 'once over', believe me! Then he dismounted, his groom taking his horse, and he walked up and down the ranks inspecting us.*
>
> *Of course we were inspecting him at the same time, we saw a rather stocky figure, very florid of face, reddened by campaigns all over the globe judging by the dazzling array of ribbons on his tunic. In our ignorance of military decorations, his ribbons seemed to take him back to the Battle of Hastings. Cropped military moustache and a cropped manner of speaking. We were to realise that this Colonel was a martinet but fair. A thorough soldier with a habit of speaking his thoughts out loud. Years later after the battalion had sustained heavy losses and we were being reinforced by new drafts, I heard him mutter as he passed me in the ranks, I wish I had my old boys back again.*
>
> *15/1113 Private Arthur V. Pearson, C Company*[53]

Captain Louis Meredith Howard, who had been the battalion's Adjutant from December 1914, was promoted major and became second-in-command. He too had seen active service, as a corporal in the Cape Mounted Rifles, and had been commissioned for an act of gallantry during the South African War. He was especially popular with the men, having risen from the

74

Battalion cooks. Alfred Ingle is third from right, back row.

Battalion signallers with their semaphore flags.

Battalion scouts resting by the light railway. The Army scouts' badge (fleur de lys) can be clearly seen on some of the men's sleeves.

J Walter Stead poses for a last photograph with his Quartermaster, Charles Wilson and Adjutant, Louis M Howard (right) before his departure to the 11 KOYLI.

Stuart C. Taylor, the Pals' new Colonel.

James Gray's silver medal.

ranks. The position of Adjutant was taken over by Captain de Pledge.

On 29 May the Pals won yet more sports trophies when they sent a team to the Northern Command Cross Country Championship at Gosforth Park, Newcastle.

Recruiting continued all the while, and in an attempt to attract the right sort of men, a cricket match was held at Headingley ground on 1 June, the Leeds Pals versus Yorkshire County. Nearly the whole battalion was present, having travelled down on a special train from Masham and then marched through the city. The result not surprisingly, was a win for Yorkshire by eighty-one runs, although the Pals had some top-class players among their ranks.[54]

On the next evening Colonel Stead took the stage at the Empire Theatre, Leeds, accompanied by his recruiting party and the cross-country team, which had returned from its victory at Gosforth Park. Appeals were also made at the Hippodrome and a special recruiting rally was planned to continue throughout the next week. Charles Wilson was among the speakers, and was in fine form.

Cyrill Cryer's bronze medal.

Major Howard and Captain Anderson spoke, and they were followed at the second house by Captain and Quartermaster C. H. Wilson, who said we were now at death grips with the enemy; it was a life-or-death struggle for our very existence. The Pals Battalion had been able to send 100 men to other regiments – many as officers. Men were wanted to step into the breaches. It was for everyone to do his bit. (Applause) 'I began at five this morning, and I shall be going until two o'clock tomorrow morning.' (Applause) Referring to the German barbarities, Captain Wilson said that if it were left to him he should do more in the way of reprisals than was being done. It was necessary for every man in the country to prove his manhood.[55]

At last the days at Colsterdale were coming to an end. The Leeds Pals were to move to Ripon for brigade training, where they would join the other three battalions which made up 93 Brigade of 31st Division.[56] Their companion units were the 16th (Service) Battalion (1st Bradford), The Prince of Wales's Own (West Yorkshire Regiment), the 18th (Service) Battalion (2nd Bradford), The Prince of Wales's Own (West Yorkshire Regiment), and the 18th (Service) Battalion (1st County), The Durham Light Infantry.

The Pals really were part of the British Army now, and noticed the difference.

77

The Pals' athletics team's triumphant return from Gosforth park.

The two cricket teams pose for a photograph. John Yeadon is in the front row, extreme left.

The cricketers make their way onto the pitch.

The Pals enjoy a mug of tea and a 'wad' at the cricket match, Headingley, 1 June 1915. The man on the right (stooping) is Clifford Hollingworth.

Some of the NCOs of the 19th Battalion at Clipstone Camp. In the centre is Company Sergeant-Major Alfred Ibbotson.

> We left Breary Banks to make our home in North Camp, Ripon – Now we were really and truly caught up in the military machine. 'Red Caps'[57] all over the place, no slouching about, heads up, no tunic buttons undone, and night ops two or three times a week, crawling round the undergrowth miles from camp, while other units of the Brigade were 'all dressed up and nowhere to go', standing on the pavements and grinning at us as we passed going on 'nightshift and night exercises'.

> *15/711 Private Arthur V. Pearson, C Company*[58]

Not all the men went to Ripon with the battalion, however, E Company, which was soon to be combined with the Reserve Company of the Leeds Bantams[59] (17th Battalion West Yorks) to form the 19th Reserve Battalion, was to remain at Colsterdale to continue training, as were the men who were awaiting news of their commissions.

> A certain number of men in Morris' Platoon have applied for commissions and are likely to get them, they are splendid men and officers are wanted.

> Colonel Taylor decided therefore to leave these behind at Colsterdale in Reserve. These men came to Morris before they left to ask if he would come to a dinner at Masham which they wanted to give him. Of course he said that he would come and they made very nice speeches saying how sorry they were to leave him.

> Besides that, when the regiment marched out of Colsterdale to go to Ripon, the Reserves stood and watched them go and cheered the Colonel who led the Regiment. Then when Morris marched past in about the middle of the Regiment they cheered him also. He was the only one cheered besides the Colonel.

> *Bickersteth Family War Diary*

Alfred Lee who served with E Company at Colsterdale, and the sketch he was issued so that he could lay out his kit for inspection.

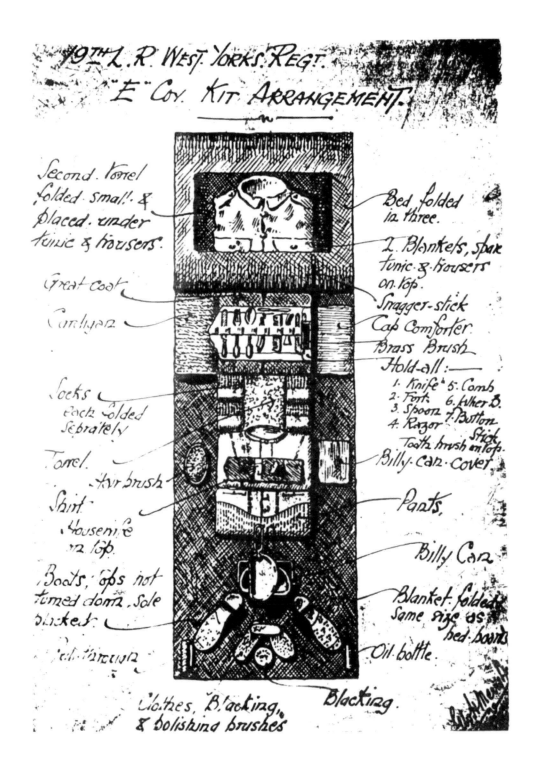

49TH L.R. WEST YORKS REGT.
"E" Coy. KIT ARRANGEMENT.

Second. Towel. folded. small. & placed. under tunic & trousers.

Great coat

Cardigan

Socks each folded separately

Towel.

Hair brush

Shirt.

Housewife on top.

Boots. tops not turned down. Sole outside.

Razor

Clothes. Blacking, & polishing brushes

Bed folded in three.

2. Blankets, spare tunic & trousers on top.

Swagger-stick

Cap Comforter.

Brass Brush

Hold-all :—
1. Knife   5. Comb
2. Fork   6. Other B.
3. Spoon   7. Button
4. Razor   Stick
  Tooth brush on top.

Billy. Can. Cover.

Pants,

Billy Can

Blanket folded same size as bed boards

Oil. bottle.

Blacking.

Some of the men who were courting, uncertain of the future, decided to get married before the battalion went on active service. Three Pals who had joined together, Alan Fenton, Fred Parkinson and Herbert Harvey, became related when Fenton and Parkinson married Harvey's two sisters.[60]

Harry Brown's desire to be with his childhood sweetheart, Annie Schofield, caused him some problems. Stationed at Ripon, his home town, he saw his bride-to-be, out with his sister, while he was marching up to Ripon Cathedral for Church Parade, and he broke ranks to have a chat to them. He was confined to barracks for this breach of discipline, but as he was attached to the Battalion Transport and regularly took a cart into Ripon to pick up rations, his punishment was merely a formality. What did cause him great annoyance, however, was the unrealistic attitude of the officials at the Registrar's Office who, because of a minor irregularity in their application, refused to grant him a licence to marry. Eventually they were married by special licence in June 1915.[61]

Not so lucky was Morris Fleming, who lost his girl when he joined up.

> *Me joining the Pals, we had a row on it. 'Well,' I said, 'I've joined now, I can't do any more.' 'Well,' she said, ' You can either have me or the Pals.' I said' Well, its got to be the Pals.' 'Oh,' she said, 'That's done it then!' So I didn't see her then for about oh, a month or so, and I had the key of the house and everything and didn't know what the Dickens to do, so anyhow, me going away and leaving her to it, she married my pal and I married her pal.*
>
> *15/339 Morrison Fleming, D Company[62]*

Arthur Dalby's motives for marrying his fiancée before he went overseas were more practical.

> *I'd been engaged about a year, we were both 21. We waited until we were 22. I said, We'd better get married now before I go abroad, because if I get killed, you'll get twelve shillings a week for life.*
>
> *15/259 Private Arthur Dalby, Battalion transport[63]*

The battalion's stay at Ripon was quite brief, and the training intensive, but the Pals still managed to find some pleasure, and even humour, in army life.

> *There is one incident that stands out a mile in my recollections of our stay at Ripon. As we fell in for what*

Herbert Bradbourne (in uniform) who joined the Pals in June 1915 and completed his training with the 19th Battalion. Next to him, sporting a Leeds Pals badge in his lapel, is his cousin Johnny Brittain, who was in a reserved occupation so did not join the army.

Alan James Fenton with his bride Amy Harvey, 29 June 1915.

Harry Brown with his sweetheart Annie Schofield.

Herbert Harvey.

appeared to be an ordinary afternoon parade – it was a Ripon market day – a party of us were detailed off and marched under a sergeant to Ripon railway sidings. There, from standing lines and lines of railway horse-boxes, came heavy thuds as hooves banged the thick, wooden sides. Snorts of temper and fear which sounded murderous to us who were mostly a non-equestrian party.

Why we had been selected for this job was beyond our comprehension. We were all scared to death of anything on four legs bigger than a dog. It was another of those subtle army jokes who generally worked on the line of 'square pegs in round holes' and made army tailors out of life-long electricians. However, here we were, but no one was really anxious to open one of those box doors. Then the sergeant, a very plucky man that sergeant, unfastened the many bolts, clamps and catches and the lower part of the door flew out with a

Most of the officers attended a course of instruction before the battalion went overseas. Here a Leeds pals officer, thought to be Lionel Lawson, is among those receiving instruction on a Lewis gun.

The battalion guard at Ripon. Compare this to the photograph on page 38.

Men of B Company with their pet goat at Ripon. In the forground in shirt sleeves (with broom) is George W. Cosby.

bang, followed by a flurry of flying hooves. Those horse-boxes were packed with mules. Great hairy brutes who had only just arrived from their port of debarkation and the roaming prairies where they had been brought up. They all appeared to be stark raving mad, and we poor mutts had to go in and untie them. What a pantomime in those sidings! Mules plunging high into the air with a scared foot-soldier hanging on to his halter. Those boxes were eventually emptied and we set off back to camp. As aforementioned it was market day in Ripon. It is not a roomy place at best, and with stalls cluttering up the streets, it was no place to be leading untamed 'hairies'. I set off with a mule in each hand, but this trio hadn't gone far before there were only two of us. I let one mule go, one was quite enough for me to tackle! What a relief to turn into camp and hand our charges over to the transport staff, who could only stand and grin. There were mules running loose all over the countryside for days. They were adopted by all manner of regiments who were not supposed to own them and were not included on their 'strength'.

15/711 Private Arthur V. Pearson, C Company[64]

21 June 1915. Today we have been drilling in delightful and ideal surroundings, and if only we had had no pack and rifle and could have gone about and done just as we liked it would have

been fine. We went for the day to Studley Park, the weather was blazing hot and as we had a lot of 'doubling' to do we didn't half sweat.

I wish Eileen could see a little goat which wanders about our lines. It is particularly attached to one of the cooks and the way it knows him and rubs up against him like a cat is very peculiar. He causes many a laugh by running about and jumping and the goat runs after him and jumps and kicks when he does. You'd almost die with laughing to see its absurd antics. Its funny.

A bit of fun was caused in the lines tonight by a chap illustrating the best way of carrying the pack [in] this hot weather. He strutted about in a bathing costume and rubber shoes, with his pack on, and the figure he cut was ludicrous in the extreme.

15/470 Lance-Corporal W. Arthur Hollings, D Company[65]
(Although the goat remained at Ripon when the Pals departed, they were accompanied by an unofficial mascot, a dog named Belgie who had attached himself to the battalion and was smuggled aboard the troopship when the Pals went overseas.[66])

Recruiting rosette worn by Alan Hey. (Bagshaw Museum)

In order to bring the battalion up to full strength, a Leeds tram, decorated with recruiting posters and with the Leeds City Tramways Band on board, toured the suburbs of the city. It was manned by Colonel Taylor accompanied by some of his officers and men, and Mr J. B. Hamilton, General Manager of the Tramways.

Each prospective recruit was attested on the spot, then rushed by car to the Tramways Depot, in the city centre, where he was medically examined and fitted out with a uniform.

Company Sergeant-Major Alfred Ibbotson displays his magnificent waxed moustache. His recruiting rosette can be seen on the left side of his cap.

The recruiting party. Front row: (left to right) Private Kilner, Sergeant Booth, Captain Whitaker, Sergeant Jones, Private Dolphin and Dr Wainman. Second row: Privates Smithson, Armitage and Hartley. Back row: Private Howarth, Corporal Child, Lance-Corporal Hemingway, Private Watson and Lance-Corporal Hudson.

When the recruiting tram visited Bramley, everyone was surprised when one of the speakers, Mr James Thompson, a Labour member of the City Council for the Bramley Ward and well-known for his pacifist views, announced his intention of enlisting in the Pals. After attesting, he addressed the crowd inviting the men in the audience to follow his example – fifteen men came forward immediately, to cheers. Thompson was later interviewed by the local press and said that at first he had strongly disapproved of the war.

But, he added, I have had to change my views as a result of reflection and reading of incidents like the Lusitania[67] and the Report of the Bryce Commission[68] and other evidence which convinces me that

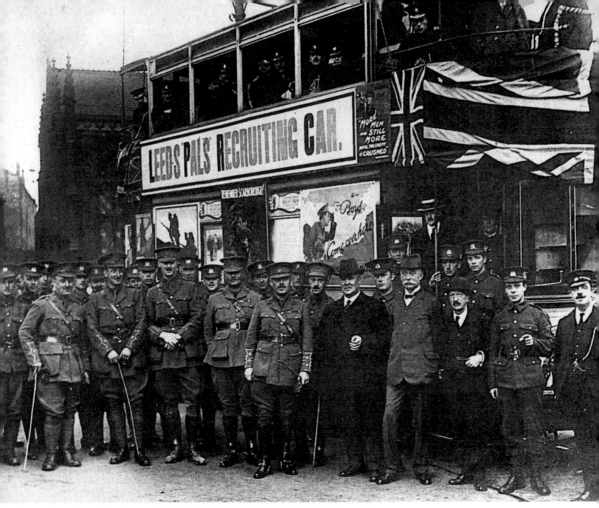

The Leeds Pals' recruiting tram, manned by Lieutenant-Colonel Taylor (centre), Major Howard (to his right), and Mr J. B. Hamilton, General Manager of the Tramways (in civilian clothes to Taylor's left). On the upper deck is the Leeds Tramways band.

the Germans before the war must have studied a system of scientific cruelty which they are deliberately carrying out now. German 'culture' has been educating their people up to the idea of world power, and their record of shameful treatment of women and children and the civil non-combatants generally and wounded soldiers, is such that would turn, I think, the weakest pacifist into an indignant and manly soldier.

There are times for criticism, but it now seems to me now is not the time. Everything worth living for is in the melting pot – representative government, liberty, freedom of speech, Trade Unionism, religious or ethical ideas and the hopes of democracy, and with them is Prussianism. I say deliberately, that any man of military age who now stands aside is assisting the Prussian Attitude.[69]

The Leeds Pals on their marathon march from Ripon to Leeds, 25 June 1915.

Towards the end of June, the brigade was inspected by Lieutenant-General Sir Archibald Murray, Chief of the General Staff, GHQ France. Surely this meant that their departure was imminent? But the Leeds Pals were still not up to full strength, and so the recruiting campaign continued with a march from Ripon to Leeds on 25 June.

Lieutenant-Colonel Taylor is greeted by the Lord Mayor, Mr J. E. Bedford, on the Town Hall steps.

Monday, June 28 1915 – At 95 Westbourne Terrace, Morris arrived on Saturday at noon having slept out all night and marched 28 miles from Ripon with his pack on his back. I was out at the Solemn Eucharist at the Parish Church but Morris had to go at once to lunch with the Lord Mayor. All the evening he was out recruiting and secured several men himself. He spoke to about a hundred men on the steps of the Corn Exchange, answering questions. He was very tired and slept late on Sunday. On Sunday afternoon he helped me pack as we had decided to go to Ralph at Treport. And then at seven o'clock the whole Battalion left Leeds to march back to Ripon. They secured eighty men. I believe they slept on the Stray at Harrogate. Morris goes south somewhere soon for a Company Commander's course.

Bickersteth Family War Diary

At last, on 5 July, the battalion was at full strength and recruiting was closed. The Raising Committee expressed their particular thanks to everyone who had assisted and special mention was made of Mr J. Wardle, whose son, James, had been commissioned into the battalion in December 1914.

Brigade Sports were held on Ripon racecourse on 10 July and the Leeds Pals were able to show their new comrades-in-arms their sporting prowess. They won the meeting, with second prize going to the 18th Battalion, the Durham Light Infantry, and third to the 1st Bradford Pals. Towards the end of the month the camp was visited by a photographer who took group pictures of each platoon, and the entire brigade was inspected on Ripon racecourse by the Raising Committee.

On 30 July 1915, Colonel Taylor went to France to view the situation. Meanwhile, some of his officers and men attended course of instructions.

> *NCOs who by this time had got used to the sound of their own voices giving commands, were sent off to various army schools on course to return with an extra stripe and glistening crossed flags as signallers, or crossed flags as pioneers, or crossed swords as physical training instructors, plus a new 'aldershot accent', which was far removed from the Yorkshire twang that they went away with.*
>
> 15/711 Private Arthur V. Pearson, C Company[70]

HRH The Grand Duchess George of Russia presents prizes on Ripon Racecourse, 10 July 1915.

The Leeds Pals Band. Bandmaster James Garside poses behind the Bass drum.

The end of August saw the departure of the battalion second-in-command, Major Howard, who left to take command of the 2th (service) Battalion (1st Tyneside Irish), The Northumberland Fusiliers. This left a vacancy which was not filled until the eve of the Pals' departure on active service.[71]

During the first weeks of September the men fired Parts I and II of their Musketry Course at Wormald Green range. The Pals now looked and felt like real soldiers. The only thing missing was a band, an omission remedied in mid-September when a contingent of former members of Leeds Tramways Band formed the Leeds Pals Band, under the direction of their old conductor, now Bandmaster, James Garside.

On 19 September, an advance party under Second-Lieutenants G. S. Ward and E. Lintott travelled to Fovant, near Salisbury Plain in Wiltshire.[72] They where joined by the rest of the battalion on the 24th, and now that the division was all together speculation that the Pals would soon be going overseas increased. Training continued, with much emphasis on getting the men through the final part of their Musketry Course, and teaching them effective use of the bayonet and how to throw hand grenades.

The division was inspected by Lieutenant-General Sir Arthur Paget, GOC Southern Training Centre, on 5 October, and a week later the Pals said farewell to another of their original officers, Charles Wilson. As the result of injuries sustained when he fell off his horse in July, Wilson retired from the battalion on health grounds. He exchanged a four-legged steed for a more placid four-wheeled one on his return to Leeds, where he raised a unit of the National Motor Reserve.[73] Meanwhile the Pals, continuing their record of sporting success, while at Fovant, entered and won the Southern Counties Cross Country Championship on 1 November.

Edric Longfield (right) and his Pals show off their newly issued 'Pattern 1914 Leather Infantry Equipment'.

Battalion parade. The officers appear to be struggling to keep their mounts under control while the men wait patiently.

The officers of the battalion at Fovant just before they left to embark for Egypt. Back row
(left to right): Lt J. G. Vause, 2/Lt T. A. R. R. E. Willey, Lt G S Ward, Lt R. B. H. Tolson,
Capt R. Atkinson, Lt H Smith, Sec Lt A. Liversedge. Middle row: 2/Lt M. Booth, 2/Lt L
Foster, Lt R. M Blease, 2/Lt A. N. Hutton, Lt J. S. Pope-Smith, Lt S. M Bickersteth, 2/Lt J. P.
Everitt, Capt J. L. Armitage, Lt N. Evers, Lt E. Lintott. Front row: Capt F. H. Boardall, Revd
C. Chappell (chaplain), Hon Lt and Quartermaster R. J. Anderson, Capt P. H. Mellor, Major
L. P. Baker, Lt-Col S. C. Tayor, Capt and Adjutant E. K. M. de Pledge, Capt T. G. Gibson,
Capt G. C. Whitaker, Capt L. Bathurst (RAMC), Capt S. T. A. Neil.

Rumours that the battalion would soon be off to France continued to circulate and were
fuelled, on 9 November, by the issue of new equipment to the men who were to go overseas.

> Today it has been pouring down with rain and we have been getting our new equipment which
> is of green leather, very similar to the old. I believe I told you that webbing equipment has been
> condemned for active service because it shrinks when wet.
>
> Those registered for munition work and those who are staying behind as first Reserve Detail
> have not drawn this new equipment.[74]
>
> 10 November 1915. While we were on the range this morning I had a Register to keep of a
> certain number at the firing point and during the time I was on this Lieutenant Wardle came
> along and I had a heart-to-heart chat with him. I think I told you that the Colonel had chosen him
> to be left in charge of those who are to stay here as first reserve. Well! When he first got to know, he
> sent for our Sergeant (Scholes) to the officers' quarters as they have worked together for so many
> months and I understand that he had tears in his eyes when he told the sergeant that he could not go
> with his platoon overseas. This morning he asked me how I was going on as Lance Corporal and

An aerial view of the Pals' camp at Colsterdale, taken in 1966; the layout of the camp can still be seen quite clearly.

Layout of the Pals' camp.
1. Memorial Cairn (built in 1930s).
2. Orderly Room.
3. Old huts (September to December 1914).
4. Canteen.
5. New huts (December 1914 to May 1915).
6. Guardroom.
7. Sergenant's Mess.
8. Dining Hall.
9. Ablutions.
10. Bath-houses.
11. Parade ground.

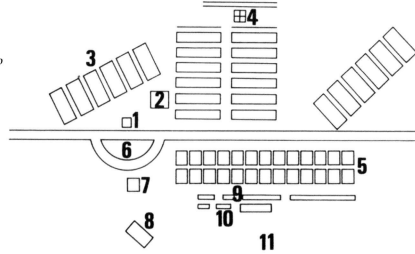

all about it. He said 'Hollings I've tried a long time to get you promotion as I wanted you for one of my corporals, I should have liked to have gone with my platoon but it's been decided otherwise. I wish you the best of luck.' In his interview with Sergeant Scholes he said 'You'll look well after the boys won't you?' He then went on to talk to me about the departure and said he thought we should go out about Christmas and everything pointed to our destination being France.

15/470 Lance Corporal W. Arthur Hollings, D Company[75]

On 11 November 1915 the battalion was ordered to hold itself ready to go to France. The Pals were paraded on 1 December and each man was issued with an identity disc and 120 rounds of ammunition, but on the following day the orders for France were cancelled. The destination was to be Egypt.[76]

NOTES

1. Bickersteth, The Rev. Samuel, *Morris Bickersteth 1891–1916*, privately published, Cambridge, 1931, p. 69.
2. *Yorkshire Evening Post*, 24 September 1914.
3. Author's recorded interview with Clifford Hollingworth, May 1988.
4. *Yorkshire Evening Post*, 25 September 1914.
5. Pearson, Arthur Valentine, *A Leeds Pal Looks Back*, unpublished manuscript in Leeds Local History Library, circa 1961.
6. *Yorkshire Evening Post*, 25 September 1914.
7. Author's recorded interview with Clifford Hollingworth, May 1988.
8. Pearson, op.cit.
9. Ibid.
10. *Yorkshire Evening Post*, 28 September 1914.
11. TS copies of letters from Lieutenant S. Morris Bickersteth to his family, 26 and 27 September 1914, Bickersteth Family War Diary.
12. *Leeds and District Weekly Citizen*, 24 December 1914. Of the twenty-two original officers, one, Charles Wilson, was an Alderman and another, Lionel Lawson, was the son of a former Alderman. Tom Willey's commission, announced on 4 December, seems to be the first to the son of an Alderman.
13. A word used in the Great War for retired officers who returned to service, that is, were 'dug out' of retirement.
14. *Yorkshire Post*, 29 October 1914. The officers in the photograph were identified by Clifford Hollingworth, assisted by pencil notes on the back of an original print kept by Edric Longfield, and by careful comparison with contemporary newspaper photographs.
15. In this context, the initials VD stand for Volunteer Decoration. The award was changed to the Territorial Decoration (TD) on the creation of the Territorial Force in 1908, but recipients prior to the change continued to use the initials of the original award after their names.
16. Conversation with Arthur Dalby, 11 March 1989.
17. Author's recorded interview with Arthur Dalby and Clifford Hollingworth, May 1988.
18. See Bickersteth's letter of 26 September 1914.
19. Leeds, a major industrial city by 1914, had a considerable manufacturing capacity. As well as the clothing contracts one would expect to be given to a city noted for its textile products, Leeds factories eventually were engaged in manufacturing a large variety of munitions, and even locomotives for use on the railways of the Western Front. Scott, W. H., *Leeds in the Great War, 1914–1918*, Libraries and Arts Committee, Leeds 1923. *Yorkshire Evening Post*, 9 November 1914. *Yorkshire Evening News*, 17 November 1914. *Yorkshire Post*, 2 December 1914.
20. *Yorkshire Evening Post*, 4 December 1914.
21. *Leeds and District Weekly Citizen*, 11 December 1914.

22. Pearson, op.cit.
23. Extract from a notebook kept by Alfred Ernest Ingle, Battalion Cook.
24. Pearson, op.cit.
25. Author's recorded interview with Arthur Dalby, July 1988.
26. Ibid.
27. Recorded interview with Clifford Hollingworth and Arthur Dalby by Dennis Walsh of Chameleon TV, Colsterdale, 30 September 1989.
28. Pearson, op.cit.
29. Undated and unidentified newscutting in Leeds Local History Library. *Soldiers Died in the Great War 1914–1919, Part 19, The Prince of Wales's Own (West Yorkshire Regiment)*, HMSO, London, 1921. In 1896, and even as recently as 1986, 'rheumatism' was a generic term for a number of conditions, including rheumatic fever. It seems to have fallen into disuse for it is seldom used to describe anything more serious than the acute local pain that we generally associate with the term nowadays. See Thomson, Spencer, *A Dictionary of Domestic Medicine*, Charles Griffin, London, 1896, and Walton, J., Beeson, P. B., and Scott, R. B., The Oxford Companion to Medicine, Oxford University Press, 1986.
30. Pearson, op.cit.
31. 'Owing to the very satisfactory response to Lord Kitchener's appeal for recruits some time must necessarily elapse before uniform can be issued to all. Recruits should therefore, wherever possible, join with odd suits of clothes, good boots, and with greatcoats if they possess them.' 'An allowance of 10s will be paid to each man who produces greatcoat, suit of clothes and boots in serviceable conditions.' Army Council Instructions No.176, 12 September 1914.
32. Pearson, op.cit.
33. *Leeds and District Weekly Citizen*, 20 November 1914.
34. Author's correspondence with Mrs Sarah Pellow, daughter of 15/393 Private George Grant, D Company, 1988.
35. Pearson, op.cit.
36. *Leeds and District Weekly Citizen*, 27 November 1914. *Yorkshire Evening News*, 2 December 1914.
37. Pearson, op cit.
38. *Yorkshire Evening Post*, 4 December 1914. *Yorkshire Evening News*, 18 December 1914.
39. *Yorkshire Evening Post*, 4 December 1914.
40. Bickersteth Family War Diary, main narrative for 26 December 1914.
41. Pearson, op.cit.
42. TS copy of a letter from Lieutenant S. Morris Bickersteth to his family, 1 January 1915, Bickersteth Family War Diary.
43. Pearson, op.cit.
44. Author's recorded interview with Clifford Hollingworth, May 1988.
45. The forerunner of the Short Magazine Lee Enfield, which was the standard British infantry weapon of the First World War, and indeed of the Second.
46. Author's correspondence with Mrs Irene Larcombe, February 1989.
47. TS copy of a letter from Lieutenant S. Morris Bickersteth to his family, 21 February 1915, Bickersteth Family War Diary.
48. Pearson, op.cit.
49. Undated TS copy of a letter from Lieutenant S. Morris Bickersteth to his family, received 3 May 1915, Bickersteth Family War Diary.
50. Main narrative and TS copies of letters from Lieutenant S. Morris Bickersteth to his family, 23 October 1914–15 May 1916, Bickersteth Family War Diary.
51. TS copies of letters from Lieutenant S.Morris Bickersteth to his family, 4 and 5 May 1915, Bickersteth Family War Diary.
52. *Quarterly Army List*, HMSO, London, January 1916 and July 1918.

53. Pearson, op.cit.
54. *Yorkshire Post*, 4 June 1915.
55. Ibid.
56. Becke, Major A. F., *History of the Great War: Order of Battle Divisions*, HMSO, London, 1935–45.
57. Military Police were called 'Red Caps' because of the red tops to their peaked caps.
58. Pearson, op.cit.
59. 'Bantam' battalions were raised from men who were below average height. The Leeds Bantams joined the Leeds Pals in 1917 to form the 15/17th Battalion, (see Chapter 6). In August 1915 the Depot Company of the Leeds Pals joined the the Depot Company of the 17th Battalion, The West Yorkshire Regiment at Clipstone Camp to form the 19th Reserve Battalion. The Depot Companies of the 16th and 18th Battalions formed the 20th Reserve Battalion, also at Clipstone. On 1 September 1916 the 19th and 20th Battalions became the 88th and 89th Training Reserve Battalions. See James, Brigadier E. A., *British Regiments 1914–18*, Samson Books Ltd, London, 1978.
60. Author's correspondence with Mr G. H. Fenton, July/August 1988.
61. Author's correspondence with Mrs Florence Groves, March/April 1988, and family correspondence loaned for copying.
62. Recorded interview with Morris Fleming by Peter Hawkins of BBC Radio Leeds, circa 1966.
63. Recorded interview with Clifford Hollingworth and Arthur Dalby by Dennis Walsh of Chameleon TV, Colsterdale, 30 September 1989.
64. Pearson, op.cit.
65. Letter from Arthur Hollings to his father, 21 June 1915.
66. Belgie was humanely destroyed by the Battalion Medical Officer just before the Pals sailed for France in March 1916. Author's recorded interview with Clifford Hollingworth, May 1988.
67. On 7 May 1915, the Cunard liner RMS *Lusitania* was sunk off the coast of Ireland by a German submarine. The Germans claimed that she was carrying munitions. Among the 1,198 passengers lost were 128 Americans.
68. In December 1914 the British Government appointed a committee of lawyers and historians chaired by Lord Bryce, a respected diplomat and former Ambassador to Washington. Among the many honours he received before the war was the Pour le Merite, Germany's highest decoration. The Committee's report, published by HMSO in 1915, appears to have been based largely on hearsay evidence offered by Belgian refugees. It contained numerous gruesome accounts of German 'frightfulness', but the veracity of these stories has since been challenged.
69. Unidentified newscutting in Leeds Local History Library, circa June 1915.
70. Pearson, op.cit.
71. Lieutenant-Colonel Howard died of wounds on 10 July 1916.
72. Battalion War Diary, Public Record Office, London: WO95/4590.
73. Ibid.; Scott, op.cit.
74. Letter from Arthur Hollings to his father, 9/10 November 1915. Hollings was misinformed about the equipment. The Pattern 1914 Leather Infantry Equipment was issued as a stop-gap measure because there were only two companies in Britain capable of producing web equipment at that time. A 'release' scheme was operated by the Army Council, from early in 1915, to allow skilled men to return to factories for essential munitions work. See Simkins, Peter, *Kitchener's Army*, Manchester University Press, 1988.
75. Letter from Arthur Hollings to his father, 9/10 November 1915.
76. Battalion War Diary, op.cit.

No.9 Platoon, C Company. In the centre of the front row is Sergeant Evelyn Lintott.

No.3 Platoon, A Company. The officers are (left to right) Lieutenant R. M. S. Blease and Captain S. T. A. Neil.

No.13 Platoon, D Company. The officers are (left to right) Captains Dufton and Gibson and Lieutenant Wardle. Arthur Hollings is in the third row to Wardle's left.

Lieutenany Roy Rayner with some of No.7 Platoon, B Company. Front row (seated with cane) is William 'Tiny' Demaine.

No.14 Platoon, D Company. The officers are Captains Gibson and Dufton. Third from left fifth row is Clifford Hollingworth.

No.12 Platoon. The officer on the right is Lieutenant Norman Evers.

No.16 Platoon, D Company. The officers are Captains Dufton and Gibson, and Lieutenant Vause. Arthur Dalby is fifth from right, fourth row. In the forground is 'Belgie', the battalion pet.

Roy Rayner poses with No.5 Platton, B Company. George Cosby is 4th from the left, third row, John Parkinson is fourth from right.

Captain Armitage (officer on the left) with some of B Company.

No.9 Platoon, C Company. The lance-corporal seated second from the left, second row is Fred Naylor.

Chapter Three

'Three Huts, Two Sheds and a Toilet'

… We went on to Port Said, then we went up the [Suez] Canal, past Kantara.
Kantara was three huts, two sheds and a toilet.
15/471 Private Clifford Hollingworth, D Company[1]

GUARDING THE SUEZ CANAL, DECEMBER 1915–MARCH 1916

When Europe went to war in August 1914, Turkey remained neutral, for although she had signed a treaty with Germany and had mobilised her army, she resisted Germany's attempts to draw her into the war.

Out on the Mediterranean, two German cruisers, SMS *Goeben* and SMS *Breslau* were being hunted by the Royal Navy. After shelling Algerian ports on 4 August, then stopping to take on coal in Italian territorial waters, the two ships fled through the Dardanelles to Constantinople, arriving on 11 August. Giving refuge to the *Goeben* and *Breslau* was a threat to Turkey's neutral status, but the Germans provided a solution by offering to sell the two cruisers. They would replace the two ships that were under construction in Britain for the Turkish government, but which had been requisitioned by the Royal Navy.

The Turks renamed the ships *Yavuz Sultan Selim* and *Midilli* and made their former commander, Vice-Admiral Wilhelm Souchon, C-in-C of the Turkish Fleet. Souchon's first action was to take his two ships and bombard Russia's Black Sea ports. Germany's compromise of her ally's neutrality was complete, and on 5 November 1914 Britain, France and Russia declared war on Turkey.

Kantara West. (D. Hargreaves)

Kantara East. (D. Hargreaves)

SMS Goeben, Genoa 1914.

SMS **Breslau.** *(Imperial War Museum)*

Vice-Admiral Wilhelm Souchon.
(Author's collection)

This increase in their enemies complicated matters for the Allies. Turkey closed the Dardanelles, preventing access to Russia's only warm-water port; threatened British oil interests in Mesopotamia; and threatened the Suez Canal, a vital sea link connecting Britain with her empire.

Britain responded to the latter threat by sending a force from India to protect the Canal. Led by Lieutenant General Sir John Maxwell, this consisted of two infantry divisions entirely composed of Indian troops, and supported by three mountain artillery batteries, and a brigade of cavalry. Two field artillery brigades were soon added, but the warships on the Canal were to provide the main artillery for its defence.

The Suez Canal was no easy target. Any land attack would have to be made across the Sinai Desert, a distance of about 100 miles. A march along the coast was out of the question since Allied warships were on constant patrol, and a naval attack depended on enemy vessels entering the well-defended Port Said, or Suez, ports, again in the face of the powerful Allied navies.

The main land defences were therefore concentrated along the banks of the Canal facing the Sinai Desert, while warships protected the ports and could, if necessary, be brought into the Canal to oppose a land attack. In order to reduce the frontage, a cutting was made in the Canal bank and part of the desert was flooded.

In January 1915 intelligence reports confirmed that a large Turkish force was massing, ready to cross the Sinai Desert.

It was a daunting task for the Turks, and required an expeditionary force said to number 20,000 men,[2] complete with artillery, metal pontoons and rafts with which to cross the Canal and 5,000 camels just to carry water. Although some stretches of the desert were quite passable, much of it consisted of large sand dunes or deep shifting sand, which the invaders would have to find their way through, often constructing brushwood tracks for their columns.

Djemal Pasha, the Turkish commander, hoped that the appearance of a large hostile force on the Canal would be followed by an uprising of the Egyptian nationalists opposed to British rule, but in any case, his main goal was 'to force his way suddenly astride the Canal, hold the crossing for a few days, and in that time close the Canal permanently.'[3] While his estimation of Egyptian sympathy for the Turks was probably exaggerated, his plan to make the Suez Canal impassable was at least feasible as there were ships moored in the Timsah, which could be sunk in order to block the waterway.

TURKISH ARMY CORPS ORDERS [Translation]

All the detachments of the enemy have been pushed back to the west bank of the Canal. A part of the east bank of the Canal, between Ismailia and Large Bitter Lake, is occupied by a few sentinels of the enemy. The enemy's warships are in Timsah and Large Bitter Lake.

By the Grace of Allah we shall attack the enemy on the night of the 2nd-3rd February, and seize the Canal. Simultaneously with us the 78th Column will attack Suez, and one Company Kantara. The 66th Regiment will attack at El Ferdan and Ismailia. The Lieutenant-Colonel will

HMS Jupiter, *one of the warships sent to defend the Suez Canal. (N. Longfield)*

attack Suez, and one Company from 10th Division will attack Shaluja. The Champions of Islam (Mujahid) from Tripoli in Africa from the left wing will advance to Serapeum and South of Serapeum to act as reserve. During the attack the 10th Division will take up a position in advance of the present camp.

As soon as it is dark the heavy artillery battery with the 75th Regiment will take up its position in the vicinity of Bir Fuad and Bir Murffa. A battalion of the 10th Division will be assigned to the heavy battery to assist it during the march. Its task is to destroy the enemy's warships in Lake Timsah. If it gets the opportunity it is to sink a ship at the entrance of the Canal. After executing this task it will immediately move south and subject the enemy's warships in the Large Bitter Lake to its fire.

The infantry regiments are to be ready to march at 6 o'clock this evening, formed up and facing the west.

The order of the regiments is thus 73rd and 74th.

Bir el Kurra, 1st February 1915

1. During today's and tomorrow's advance on the Canal absolute silence must be preserved by both officers and men. There must be no coughing, and orders are not to be given in a loud voice. Fortifying [entrenching] tools and water flasks are to be tied in such a way that they will make no sound during the march. There is to be no cigarette smoking. On the eastern bank of the canal no rifles are to be loaded. On the west bank of the canal rifles are to be loaded, at the orders of the officers. Before the advance begins, the Company Commanders will personally inspect the rifles, and make

Turkish troops prepare to cross the Sinai Desert, February 1915.

themselves certain that they are not loaded. Later, a squad officer will again examine the rifles to see that they are not loaded. The embarkation and disembarkation from the rafts and pontoons is to be carried out noiselessly and speedily. Soldiers must be told off to man rafts and pontoons. Disembarkation on the opposite bank is to be accomplished without noise.

2. The ammunition in the war baggage will be distributed to the soldiers in the forenoon, and is to be carried by them in their bread sacks and packets. Empty ammunition boxes and cases are to be handed over to the soldier's supply column. It is to be explained to the soldiers that the ammunition is sufficient for requirements, and further that they are to [take] ammunition off any soldiers who may be killed. Haversacks and overcoats are to be left at the camp.

3. The soldiers (from the weak and ill) from each company are to be left with the baggage.

4. Communication and company baggage will be collected by the regiment and left at the camp in the care of an officer until further orders (presumably field telephones and such like materials). The cases, boxes and stretchers of the sanitary corps are to be conveyed by soldiers of their corps. Before leaving the camp soldiers will have their water flasks filled.

5. If the detachment which crosses the Canal meets the enemy in the vicinity of the Canal they are to attack and disperse him.

6. On the day of attack provisions will not be sent to the soldiers accordingly I allow them one day's rations.

7. All officers and men will attach a white band to the upper part of their arm as a distinguishing mark.

8. On the night of the attack the pass word will be 'The Sacred Standard'. The password 'Sacred Standard' is given in order that friends of detachments may be able to recognise one another in the dark.

9. One pontoon and two rafts will be given to each full company, and designated to the attack. Rafts will also be given to the two weak companies, according to the number of rafts available. Eighteen soldiers must be detailed to carry each pontoon, and twelve soldiers to carry each raft. These soldiers must be changed every half hour. To-morrow at 6.00pm the squads of bridge makers are to present themselves at the supply column. Their rifles will be carried by other soldiers. A few engineer soldiers are to be assigned to each raft and pontoon.

The Army Corps Commander Jehac[4]

On 1 and 2 February 1915 there were some skirmishes, but the main Turkish force had still not revealed itself, and the defending force was still not certain where the main attack would take place. On the afternoon of the 2nd a high wind whipped up the desert and the ensuing sandstorm lasted through the night. As the moon rose, the main attack came at last. Indian sentries peering through the blinding sandstorm, their faces protected with their puggarees and their rifles wrapped in oiled rags, could barely make out dark shapes moving down the gullies on the east bank towards the water, carrying pontoons and rafts. They opened fire and most of the Turks abandoned their craft. Some of the pontoons that were in the water were holed and sunk, but three got across to the west bank of the Canal. The occupants were met by a bayonet charge from the 62nd Punjabis and 128th Pioneers, and were all killed, wounded or captured.

At dawn on 3 February the Turks tried to renew the attack from entrenched positions in the desert, but again they were beaten back by the Indian soldiers, who succeeded in enfilading one party with a machine-gun. Sporadic fighting continued until 5 February when it was discovered that the Turks had evacuated their trenches. Maxwell's force was ordered not to pursue the enemy for more than 10 miles as there was a possibility that the Turks would be

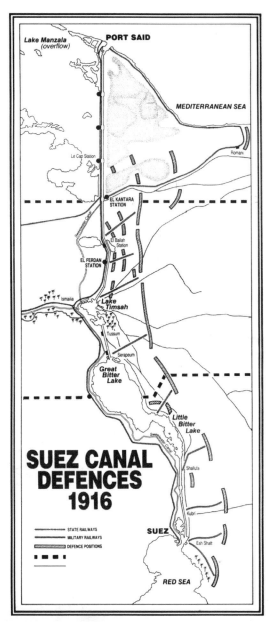

SUEZ CANAL DEFENCES 1916

Lake Manzala (overflow)

PORT SAID

MEDITERRANEAN SEA

Le Cap Station

Romani

EL KANTARA STATION

El Ballah Station

EL FERDAN STATION

Ismailia

Lake Timsah

Tussum

Serapeum

Great Bitter Lake

Little Bitter Lake

Shallufa

Kubri

SUEZ

Esh Shatt

RED SEA

STATE RAILWAYS
MILITARY RAILWAYS
DEFENCE POSITIONS

reinforced, but in fact they were in full retreat.

The Allies then turned their attention to the Dardanelles as Russia, hard-pressed by German and Austro-Hungarian forces on its western borders, was in a desperate plight. If the Navy could reopen the Dardanelles and threaten Constantinople, Turkey might capitulate, depriving Germany of an ally and opening the way for an outflanking move against Germany and Austria through the Balkans. This would relieve the pressure upon Russia as well as allowing her Black Sea ports to be used once again. The attempt, in March 1915, to force the Narrows 'by ships alone' with an Anglo-French naval force failed, as did two attempts to secure the Gallipoli Peninsula by landing Allied troops there which, if successful, would have allowed ships to get through to Constantinople. In December 1915 the decision was made to evacuate the Peninsula, and this was successfully completed by January 1916. But the Allied withdrawal would release the Turkish troops who had been committed to defending Gallipoli, and consequently Suez would be at risk once again.

The Leeds Pals sailed for Suez early in December 1915. The Transport Section, accompanied by Captain Boardall and Second-Lieutenants Smith and Everitt with 102 men, sailed from Devonport aboard the Shropshire on 6 December and had a relatively uneventful, if rough, voyage.

We lost three men, didn't find them for five days because they were sick …

We passed Gibraltar and all of a sudden 'Becky' [1511674 Private John Beckton] appeared. You never saw a walking corpse in all your life. He'd had nothing to eat and he said 'I don't want nothing to drink!' He could hardly walk …

We had rations for fifteen men, six of us … I was only sick once, two or three minutes and I just got it off my chest… of course they said if you are sick go down amongst the horses, the mules, and talk to them, they'll do you good, but the stench of them made it worse too!

15/471 Private Clifford Holtingworth, D Company[5]

For the horses and mules the journey was terrifying. Unable to take any exercise, and frequently slipping in their own vomit and excrement, many were seriously injured and had to be destroyed.

> *… Going to Egypt, we threw a lot overboard with sickness and illness. At least twenty-nine horses and mules. In the Bay of Biscay it was rather rough, it was December and do you see, they were stood up for three weeks, they couldn't lie down, they were in between planks. I think they were dying of fatigue as well really.*
>
> *… Horses can't stand sickness you see, they choke, mules and horses, … For three weeks they were stood, and the smell was terrific. You pulled them out and tried to sweep all the manure, but what happened, you see, with the urine and what have you, it got slippery and they kept falling down, with the roll of the boat as well.*
>
> *… We took about 50 or 60 mules but there must have been hundreds of horses and mules on the ship that I went on, the Shropshire.*
>
> *15/259 Private Arthur Dalby, Battalion Transport*[6]

During the voyage a close watch was kept for German submarines, although none were sighted.

> *We had an officer in charge and he had us a yard apart all round the boat … anything suspicious you saw was reported … we got one fright once, we spotted something in the dim light and we said that the chap that spotted it should have kept his mouth shut, we'd have got to bed earlier. However we circled round this thing twice to make sure that it was alright, so when we were coming away we fired four shots from the 4.7[-inch] gun. The gunner reported that he'd got a direct hit, so we made sure that it was alright.*
>
> *15/471 Private Clifford Hollingworth, D Company*[7]

After passing through the Straits of Gibraltar, the ship made for Valetta Harbour.

> *Then we arrived at Malta which was a great time. We weren't allowed ashore, but the sailors were. So 'Stiffy' [15/226 Private George A. Cooper] and I got dressed up as sailors and went ashore with these sailors for a leg-stretch and a drink …*
>
> *… They lent us this blue uniform, oh, we went off with a scarf round our necks and he said 'Don't put your cap on straight, put it over here.' Mind you if they'd have looked, the army boots would have given us away, but anyway we risked that. Coming back we'd to climb a vertical ladder up the side of the ship out of a boat. That were an experience, and all! He said 'Now don't forget that you've always three holds on an upright ladder… never leave go, always have two feet and one hand on, you move your foot so you've one foot and two hands.' Common sense… We came back with them, went down and changed into our uniforms and came back upstairs. 'Where have you been, we've been looking all over?' 'Oh, just had a walk round!'*
>
> *15/471 Private Clifford Hollingworth, D Company*[8]

The *Shropshire* sailed on to Alexandria, where the men were allowed ashore for some exercise, and then to Port Said, docking on 20 December 1915.

> *We went ashore when we got to Alexandria. They took us for a walk round Alexandria to get our legs loose. Then we went on to Port Said, then we went up the [Suez] Canal, past Kantara. Kantara was three huts, two sheds and a toilet.*
>
> *15/471 Private Clifford Hollingworth, D Company*[9]

The main body of the battalion, together with the Divisional Pioneers, 12th King's Own Yorkshire Light Infantry, and some Army Service Corps troops, joined the rest of 93 Brigade aboard the *Empress of Britain*. Just before they sailed, the Leeds battalion was joined by a new second-in-command, Major Eric C. Norman, who had come straight from the 9th Buffs (East Kent Regiment) at Shoreham-by-Sea in Sussex.[10] Although the brigade was bound for a 'destination unknown', the boxes of pith helmets that arrived just as the ship was about to cast off must have given the men some inkling of their likely course. The pith helmets were loaded aboard by No. 11 Platoon and at 10.15 on 7 December 1915, the troopship steamed out of Liverpool.

What a pandemonium broke out as we moved slowly from our moorings. Every boat that had a whistle or a hooter gave us 'all they had'. What an ear-splitting racket! I should say that foreign spies for miles around would know what the row meant, and made a note that the Empress of Britain *was on its way out East with the pride of Kitchener's Army aboard, as new members of the BEF.*

15/711 Private Arthur Pearson, C Company[11]

On board, conditions were hardly ideal, with some 6,000 troops crowded between the decks – where there had once been cabins – and in the cargo holds.

All today has been spent in getting the men on board, and a dreadful business it has been, poor fellows, I really can hardly bear to think of the hardships they are bound to go through during this voyage. They are packed absolutely like sardines right away below where on ordinary occasions, cargo and the steerage are. The place is now divided up into Messes, eighteen to a Mess. At night time they sleep in hammocks hung from hooks above the tables where they eat and sit all day. If it is rough, as it is sure to be, I shudder to think of the results. They will be sick all night onto what they eat off all day. I'm sure that we will need at least a fortnight or three weeks for them to recuperate after it all. I am very comfortable in a first class cabin with Armitage and a fellow called Hutton, this cabin is just the same as it always is except they have put in an extra berth, and taken away the wardrobe so you must admit we are pretty lucky.

As I told you in my last letter, the men's quarters are very rough, just what one is always led to expect on a troopship. I suppose it is necessary to pack men like sardines, as the fewer transports they use the less likely they are to be submarined …

I have kept pretty well myself in fact I am, of course, quite alright while I keep upstairs, but the moment I go below to the men's quarters it is about all I can do to manage it. The smell is dreadful especially in the early morning just after they get up. But it is a thousand times worse for them, poor fellows, so one has absolutely nothing to grouse about.

Lieutenant S. Morris Bickersteth, Commander No.6 Platoon, B Company[12]

For many of the Pals it was their first voyage and, although the sea was fairly kind, some men suffered from a combination of the effects of seasickness and the cholera inoculation they had received shortly after setting sail.

8th December 1915 – 6am-10am. Trying to spew but unable. 10am Parade. Felt bad all day. Slept on deck. No meals.

15/1003 Private Edward Woffenden. C Company[13]

The food on offer did little to ease the men's suffering.

The food served up to us on that ship was most unappetising and most of it uneatable. Boiled mutton day after day. We swore we got the same piece of mutton day after day, too, as we couldn't touch the stuff.

15/711 Private Arthur V. Pearson, C Company[14]

The men have their dinner at 11.30, they get fairly good food, excellent bread and butter and the meat too is alright but it is always boiled and so for anyone who is feeling a bit off colour I can imagine it is not exactly appetising. For the rest of the day there is not much to do except for issuing beer at three o'clock to the men which they are allowed if they pay 4d.

Lieutenants S. Morris Bickersteth, Commander No.6 Platoon, B Company[15]

HMT **Empress of Britain.**

On 11 December, four days after setting off, the Pals passed through the Straits of Gibraltar.

At midnight on 13 December, sailing on a zig-zag course without lights, the *Empress of Britain* collided with the French steamship *Dajurjura*,[16] carrying mail from Salonika and Malta. The French ship was almost cut in half and sank within half an hour. Two French seamen were lost, one of them washed through the hole made by the *Empress of Britain's* bow.

After we had passed through the Straits of Gibraltar and were heading towards Malta we were all suddenly awakened about midnight to the obvious fact that the ship had come into violent collision with something pretty solid. Almost simultaneously with the impact came the noise of the sudden stoppage and presumably reversal of the engines. For a moment the vessel rocked from side to side causing hundreds of enamel plates piled on the mess tables to slide to the deck adding to the alarming effect of the collision. The silence that followed was only broken by the shuffling sound of hundreds of men sliding out of their hammocks and feeling around for their life jackets in the almost total darkness. So far, of course, no-one had any idea as to what had happened; the possibility of a torpedo strike was uppermost in everyone's mind, on the other hand the thud which must have roused everyone on board did not sound like an explosion. However, after a short while our Company Commander [Major Baker] came down the companion [way] and in his well-known confident tones addressed us 'Its all right men, we have only run into a fishing smack'.

15/1233 *Private Robert Norman Bell, B Company*[17]

The most penetrating sound is the continual throb of the engines, suddenly it stops and one realises something must be wrong. That sudden silence and the slight bump we felt awakened the heaviest sleeper. Hammocks were empty in a flash and everyone was making for the stairways to the upper decks.

15/711 Private Arthur V. Pearson, C Company[18]

… Suddenly there was a report, and our siren screamed the alarm signal in shrill blasts. I jumped out of bed quicker than I have ever done before, put on a pair of shoes, my fleece-lined tunic, stuck all my money in my pockets with a pair of spectacles, put on my life-belt, and took my place on deck at the alarm post. The men were already falling in perfectly orderly … The only thing I remember one of the men saying was 'More Headlines for the Harmsworth Press Sir!'…

…A troop ship is not allowed to stop for anything, so we started to get along, leaving this unfortunate French boat to its own devices. It seems a very hard plan, but one cannot risk 6,000 men's lives by remaining stationary picking up people out of the water. Suddenly about 500 yards away there flashed a signal lamp, which said in code, 'No danger, stand to, and pick up survivors'. So we again stopped and turned in a tremendous circle round the now rapidly sinking ship.

… The lamp which had signalled to us belonged to a Destroyer which had suddenly appeared out of nowhere. It is extraordinary really how every bit of water is patrolled by some ship or other. We had to take the survivors on board; luckily it was quite calm, and they were able to climb up the rope ladders with fair ease. While we were doing this they shewed a bright electric light on the boats in which the men had come. The whole thing reminded me of a Cinematograph film. Everything was pitch dark except for the circle of bright light in which one could see the men swarming up the side of the ship … We picked up three boatloads – about 70 or 80 of them, and two ladies, one of whom turned out to be the wife of the French Ambassador at Athens. The whole thing delayed us about one and a half hours. Of course we did a certain amount of damage to our bows, and sprung some plates, but not nearly so much as I thought we should have done.

Lieutenant S. Morris Bickersteth, Commander No.6 Platoon, B Company[19]

The *Empress of Britain* restarted her engines at about 1.20am and resumed her voyage. The next morning Arthur Pearson had an opportunity to observe the sailors who had been rescued.

… A more cut-throat lot of brigands we never saw. Long John Silver would have been proud of such a crew. They wore striped jerseys of all colours, berets, oilskins and all had bare feet. They were of all shades and shapes of humanity. They smiled looking none the worse for their adventurous night.

15/711 Private Arthur V. Pearson, C Company[20]

At 4.30pm on the 14th the troopship put into Valletta Harbour for repairs, supplies and coaling, with the Leeds Pals' band playing on deck.

14 December 1915 – Still safe and sound & expect to sight Malta any moment. Arrived Sliema 4.30pm. Unnatural sight. Band played for first time. Boat undergoing repairs. Natives. Several war vessels in harbour.

15/1082 Private Herbert Hargreaves, A Company[21]

15 December 1915, 7.30–11am. Baggage fatigue. Moving sacks of potatoes. Watched Maltese 'coaling the boat. Low type of man – like big children. Disgusting habits. Band played on deck. Slept below.

15/1003 Private Edward Woffenden, C Company[22]

It may be that the three-day stay in Malta enabled the enemy to gather some information about the troopship, for it was attacked by a German submarine soon after leaving Valletta Harbour.

Edward Woffenden.

The entry in Herbert Smith's paybook to show he had been inoculated against Cholera, 7 and 17 December 1915. (Jean Kennington)

We had a brush with submarines. They had a shot at us but the torpedo missed us, the wash from our propellers helping to turn it away. I was orderly officer, one of our duties being to see that beer was issued to men who wanted it at 3 o'clock. During the proceedings I noticed men pointing to something astern, on the starboard side, and suddenly our six-inch gun fired. The first shot was fired at a range of six thousand yards. The second at nine thousand. The gun had not time to fire a third before she dived. We were in sight of St Paul's Island at the time, and they say that these

Port Said.

waters are infested with submarines. There was no confusion on board, and we didn't stop issuing beer though perhaps one or two got rather more than the regulation pint.

Lieutenants S. Morris Bickersteth, CommanderNo.6 Platoon, B Company[23]

The *Empress of Britain* docked at Port Said shortly after 8 o'clock on the morning of Tuesday, 21 December 1915.[24] As the ship steamed into the harbour the Pals on deck caught their first sight of the statue of Ferdinand de Lesseps, architect of the Suez Canal, on the quayside, and a French warship played 'Tipperary' to greet them. The rest of the day was spent packing up and clearing the ship, and early the next morning the Pals disembarked. They were marched to No. 8 Camp at Port Said, near the railway station, where they had to pitch their own tents, although some men who had not been detailed for fatigues went into town for a look-around.

22 December 1915 – Got up at 4.30am. Breakfast at 5.30am. Drew rifles and disembarked at about 8.30am. Pitched tents on sands. Near sea, Suez Canal and Port Said. Half of a ship's loaf for dinner. Tea – same. Boiled our own tea. Went into Port Said. Hawkers everywhere. Strolled around.

15/1003 Private Edward Woffenden, C Company[25]

When we arrived there was nothing but bare sand and desert. In about one and a half hours we had the whole camp pitched drawing on an average a tent for every ten men … 7 sleep in an ordinary bell tent with a double lining with two other subalterns of B Company, Foster and Rayner. I simply hollow a place in the sand, put my waterproof sheet down and sleep on top in my sleeping bag. I have slept like a log each night so far. The only thing troubling me so far being

The statue of Ferdinand de Lesseps, Port Said.

the the sandbugs which, like all bugs, seem to enjoy biting me. My right knee was a tremendous size yesterday.

Lieutenant S. Morris Bickersteth, Commander No.6 Platoon, B Company[26]

For the next two days the massive quantity of stores needed by an infantry brigade were unloaded from the *Empress of Britain* as she lay at anchor.

After often being unable to stomach the food offered to them on their voyage from Liverpool, the Pals were disappointed with the bully beef and biscuits, which was to be their staple diet for some time to come, and some of them sought an alternative.

23 December 1915 – Tent Orderly. Breakfast – Ship's biscuits. Dinner – same. Tea – same. On Inlying Picquet. Only Battalion represented. Went into town with S. Redshaw and Cpl Sharpes and had a good tea. Walk round town.

15/1003 Private Edward Woffenden, C Company[27]

23 December 1915 – Relieved from guard 10am. Went into town at night. Had a substantial feed for first time since leaving England.

15/1024 Private John Yeadon, B Company[28]

While they were at Port Said, the officers' food, if not very hygienically prepared, was at least more varied than that on offer to the men.

The Officers' Mess here consists of a small wooden shed covered over with some reeds. We are fed by a native caterer who rejoices in the name of 'Jim Irish', and pay him three shillings a day for his pains. The whole thing is typically Eastern as they have a tiny little stove and most marvellous dishes are produced, but it is no good to watch them cook or one would never eat anything. For instance the other night we had some barley soup and one of the officers had seen a native with very dirty hands picking the barley out of the soup and pinching it in order to make it soft. But what the eye doesn't see the heart does not grieve over so why worry to go and look at them.

Lieutenant S. Morris Bickersteth Commander No.6 Platoon, B Company[29]

On Christmas Eve Brigadier-General Kirk issued orders for 93 Brigade detailing which Battalions were to be on duty for the following week.[30] The Leeds Pals were dismayed to hear that they would be on duty on Christmas Day.

George W. Cosby.

25 December 1915 — Xmas Day! On fatigue and Picquet all day.

15/231 Private George W. Cosby, B Company[31]

Despite orders forbidding the men to go into Arabtown[32], some of the Pals, drawn by curiosity, decided to take the risk.

You weren't allowed to go into Arabtown, that was out of bounds, but of course I went in.

There were six of us went in, we went in just for excitement and we saw some dancing girls and we had a drink of wine and we ate one or two nasty dates. Then, I forget now who it was, he was a big lad, he said, 'I think we'd best be going lads, I think we ought to be getting out of this place.' He says, 'Come on.' [Someone replied] 'Well we're going to be early in', he said. 'Never mind, if we're early in we'll go in canteen and have a drink, anyway', he said, 'I'm getting out'.

You felt as if they'd started watching you then, you see. We got out, and as we were going out there were one or two moved as if they were going to try to stop us. When 'Taffy' Jones, he was a big rugby union forward, [said]'Look out lads!', so we just simply stiffened ourselves and walked through the door because we weren't armed, we just had our bayonets, so we just put our hands on our bayonets like that.

15/471 Private Clifford Hollingworth, D Company[33]

The orders placing the Arab quarter of Port Said out of bounds to British soldiers were given for good reason; the troops were not welcome there and some of them had been attacked. On Christmas Day a picquet composed of men from B and C Companies was sent in.

25 December 1915 – Town picquet & around Port Said at night. Native wedding in Arabtown. Soldiers attacked by natives. Man on barrow.

15/231 Private George W. Cosby, B Company[34]

We were fallen in at the double and marched into Arabtown, 'belt and bayonet' as a company to clear the 'low dives' of Arabtown of all troops. A British soldier had been fished out of the Canal with his eye gouged out. He had been set upon by Arabs in some back alley in the Kasbah.'

15/711 Private Arthur V. Pearson, C Company[35]

Because the Pals were on duty, most of them had no opportunity to avail themselves of the Christmas dinner on offer at the Casino Palace Hotel, where the meal was accompanied by a concert performed by the bands of the Leeds and Bradford Pals. But all the men were given a Christmas gift, from Colonel Taylor, consisting of biscuits, an orange, and some cigarettes.[36]

On Boxing Day the Pals were issued with their pith helmets and later in the day had to parade in full marching order to ensure that their puggarees had been fitted properly, and that none of their kit had been lost on the journey from Britain.

We had a bit of fun putting the puggaree around. I was used to materials being in the clothing trade you see, so what I'd done when I was on the boat, there was a Lascar and he was putting a puggaree on for one of our officers. I watched him, and what you wanted was some pins, and of course it's about six inches wide, something like that, and you fold it into three and using your button stick, you know, you get it even, like that, and by the time you finish you've got it an inch and a half wide you see. Now you start, you start with a pin, pin it at the back, then you go round, and as you go round you go round twice level to make, give it a foundation, then as you go round again, you lift it an eighth of an inch at the middle and then go back again. At the end, you give it a twist and by the time you get to the finish you've an inch at the front and at the back, and you've two inches at the side to cover your temples.

Mind you, then when we come to show them on parade, there were some halfway up the helmet like that, you know, anyway they had to take them off, and it's rather funny, we had a corporal and he was instructed to teach everybody, and he looked at mine and he says 'Who put yours on?', I says 'Me'. 'Well' he says, 'Show me.' I said 'No, you're the Corporal in charge, you're getting paid for this.' And he'd boasted that he'd done it in India so that's why he got the job. You should keep your mouth shut you know!

So anyway, I helped my pals in our platoon and all our section had very smart puggarees, I can say that because I corrected them and our officer congratulated us.

15/471 Private Clifford Hollingworth, D Company[37]

That night a second Christmas dinner was laid on at the Casino Palace, and another was served at the Continental Hotel.[38]

The menu from the Continental Hotel, Port Said, Boxing Day 1915.

26 December 1915 —Xmas dinner at Continental Hotel. Attack of Cholic sickness. Ill all night.

15/231 Private George W. Cosby, B Company[33]

On the next day the battalion marched through the town and down to the Canal for a bathe, but, in the afternoon, lest they had forgotten that they were soldiers on active service, they returned to camp for company drill and rapid loading and aiming.

The whole Battalion parades as strong as possible and marches down to the beach, there they divest themselves of all clothes and bathe. The water is beautifully warm and by 11 o'clock the sun is really hot. Except for the crowd of a thousand naked extraordinarily fit young men I was

118

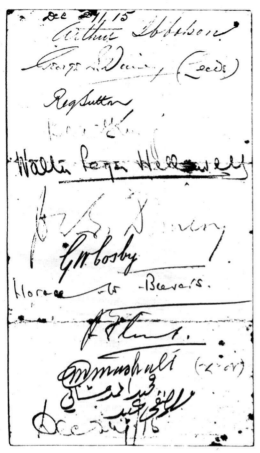

reminded very much of our bathes in Brittany. This afternoon we have a short parade for close order drill, rifle drill etc. to keep them smart.

Lieutenant S. Morris Bickersteth, Commander
No.6 Platoon, B Company[40]

I well remember the whole Battalion undressing on the beach at Port Said, bang in front of the hospital and not half a dozen swimming costumes amongst us. The Colonel and the nursing staff sat on the balcony, interested spectators, though they couldn't tell an officer from any other rank without a stitch on him.

15/711 Private Arthur V. Pearson[41]

The second day in Egypt, we stripped off, it were that hot we stripped off … and there was a big spider creeping up George Cooper's back. I said, 'There's a hell of a big spider on your back, George'. ' Knock it off!' I said, 'Wait a minute, I've never seen one as big as this,' and a fellow passed, he had a stick and he went like that, onto [the] floor and put his foot on it. He said, 'Don't you know a scorpion, you silly bugger, when you see one!' I said, 'No, never seen a scorpion!'

15/259 Private Arthur Dalby[42]

Early in the morning on Tuesday 28 December J. advance parties were sent along the Canal to El Kab, Kantara, and Ballah, to prepare for the Pals' takeover, while the rest of the men took the opportunity of having another swim in the Canal. At 5pm on 29 December the camp was struck in readiness for the next day's move, and the men slept out in the open under the starry sky. At 8.25 on the following morning the battalion left Port Said to take up its new defensive positions along the Canal. C Company went to El Kab; A Company went to Spit Post; 15 and 16 Platoons, D Company went to Bridge Head; 13 and 14 Platoons, D Company went to 50.8 Post; and B Company went to Ballah. These posts were situated about 20, 22, 28, 31 and 32 miles, respectively, from Port Said. Battalion Headquarters was moved to Kantara, about 27½ miles from Port Said.[43]

The Canal was to be guarded and patrolled by day and night, to protect it from 'evilly disposed persons'. Detailed instructions were issued by Brigade Headquarters:

The following system of patrolling will be followed throughout the section:

I. By day (a) Look out sentries provided with glasses will be posted at every permanent post on the Canal. At the posts which are at the Canal Company's Stations a sentry on the roof or in the crow's nest can see to a great distance.

(b) A path will be swept daily, before dark, along the East bank from the right of the section as far North as TINA in such a way that anyone crossing it during the night will leave a track. The apparatus for making this swept path and the necessary camels will be arranged for by sub-section commanders. Orders will be issued to prevent the swept path being crossed or walked on unnecessarily.

A view of the Pals' camp and the Sweetwater Canal at Suez, from the observation mast at El Kab. Another photograph taken by Edric Longfield.

Picquet leaving camp to take up its post for the night.

(c) As soon after daylight as it is possible to see, patrols will be sent out from each post to examine the swept path and to follow up and investigate any tracks found. The morning report which has to be rendered by headquarters of sub-sections to Corps Headquarters, will to a great extent be based on the result of the examination of the swept path.

II. By night, (a) Patrols will be sent out along the West bank simultaneously from neighbouring posts, so as to meet halfway, by mutual agreement between officers commanding, not less frequently than every two hours during the night. The actual hours of starting will be constantly changed, also the intervals of time between patrols.

(b) The above procedure will be varied from time to time by putting out a line of standing picquets every mile and patrolling between them at frequent intervals; such variations being arranged between officers commanding posts. The picquet system is more suitable for moonlight than for dark nights.[44]

In addition, the railway which ran along the west bank of the Suez and the Sweetwater Canal also had to be protected, and soon after their arrival the Pals fired their first shots in anger.

We went to Fifty-Point-Eight, a post at fifty-point-eight, and I'll tell you an amusing incident there. There was a railway ran on the side of the Canal and we was told that they didn't run after dark, owing to the enemy, the other side of the Canal. Well 'Taffy' Jones and Denton Rogers were on sentry duty and you used to walk fifty yards in front of the post on the railway and this train come, and it wouldn't stop at midnight, and they fired on it.

Of course we all got out and the train didn't stop it went on. The train kept going, anyway a report came back about it and of course they were making a report to our officer He said, 'You shouldn't have done that. Taffy Jones said 'They shouldn't have ruddy well come sir'. Taffy Jones came straight out with it, he said, 'We were on duty and our orders were to stop everything.' And of course the train wouldn't stop.

15/471 Private Clifford Hollingworth, D Company[45]

30 December 1915 – 4pm paraded for Railway patrol with Harry Clapham. Went to C Company at 8pm with a lamp. Lamp went out on the way back. Heard noise & saw someone, he got running. So fired but missed.

15/158 Private Charles H. Bell, A Company[46]

On New Year's Eve the Pals relieved the 2/3rd Gurkhas who had served in France, before coming out to Suez, and were to move to an outlying post in the Sinai Desert.[47]

When we took over from the Gurkhas at Fifty-Point-Eight, well the Gurkhas had pigeons, pigeons flying all over, and they left bags of food to feed the pigeons. We wanted to get rid of them because pigeons bring lice, anyway we had to keep them … He found a kukri, a Gurkha knife, did Agutter [15/7 Private Frank Agutter], he was boasting about it 'Look at this lads!' Anyway one of them went up to him, he pulled it from his hand, made him cut his finger. He said 'You've cut my ruddy finger, look, blood' and a Sergeant said 'You were lucky he didn't cut your ruddy throat'. He said, 'Them's sacred weapons, you want to be careful if you find owt like that, either hand it in or keep quiet.'

15/471 Private Clifford Hollingworth, D Company[48]

B Company, furthest from Port Said, had an Australian unit on their right flank. The Leeds men were assigned to their duties, some of them guarding fixed installations such as water tanks, while others were marched to outposts on the east side of the Canal.

1st January 1916 – New Year Night. Spent on Picquet Duty on desert & fatigue duty all day. Paraded for Inlying Picquet at 5pm. Spent night in trenches.

15/231 Private George W. Cosby, B Company[49]

Walter Withell, and John Ratcliffe pause to watch a Dutch steamer pass through the Suez Canal, while Bert Sunderland washes his clothes. (N. Longfield)

The Pals stood to on 2 January when the Australians reported a Turkish camel corps about eighty strong only a few miles from the Canal, but the Turks did not venture any closer and were not engaged.[50]

I think there is little danger of our being attacked in this small position, the only thing being that they might send a small body just to break through, damage the Canal and get away. Well let them try here, they'll never get away! We tracked a party eighty strong on camels about six miles off a day or two ago, but they came no nearer.

Lieutenant S. Morris Bickersteth Commander No.6 Platoon, B Company[51]

The soldiers' food still consisted of bully and biscuits and, occasionally, bread, and some of the men received short rations when it was discovered that some of the bread was mouldy.

1 January 1916 – Relieved from Guard 9.30am. Smashed a tooth with eating Army Biscuit … Rotten grub – Only Biscuits & Bully. Had this since leaving Port Said.

15/1024 Private John Yeadon, B Company[52]

Teddy Webster, Bert Sunderland and Edric Longfield on the bank of the Suez Canal, December 1915. (N. Longfield)

For tea we drew lots for bread as some was mouldy. One slice per man which was rations.

15/158 Private Charles H. Bell, A Company[53]

Coincidentally, at the time that the food was at its worst, the new scale of rations for the men of the Egyptian Expeditionary Force was published in Section Orders.

19 – SCALE OF RATIONS.

For all European Troops in Egypt with effect from 1-1-16 will be as follows:-

Meat 1lb; Vegetables ½lb; Salt oz; Bread 1lb; Potatoes ¼lb; Pepper $^1/_{36}$oz; Tea $^5/_8$oz; Sugar 3oz; Mustard $^1/_{50}$oz; Bacon 4oz; Cheese 3oz; Jam lb

Scale of equivalents
1lb meat – 1lb nominal preserved meat; 1lb bread – 1lb biscuits or ¾lb flour; $^1/_{50}$oz mustard— $^1/_8$oz curry powder; 4oz fresh vegetables – 2oz rice – 3oz potatoes – 4oz onions. Condensed milk at the rate of 1 tin per 16 men in lieu of the cheese ration

C. A. Howard, Major, Brigade Major, 93rd Infantry Brigade.[54]

On 7 January a Court of Enquiry was established to look into the question of the quantity and the quality of the rations on issue to the brigade and although there had been a temporary improvement, after the publication of the scale of issue, the men's food was still poor. In the attempts to effect an improvement it seems that some unusual sources of supply were tapped.

Some men were told to go down to Headquarters and get some tins of food that had been sent up by the commanding officer, and it had come from Gibraltar.

The desert railway that ran from Kantara to Romani. (Imperial War Museum)

Indian transport at El Kab. (N. Longfield)

When it came, there were tins of food without labels! So of course you took the luck of the draw, one tin per man. So we thought oh, good! So you'll be surprised when I tell you what I drew. I drew tripe and onions! Tripe and onions! In onion sauce. And these tins were reported to be about forty years old! They'd been in the dungeons at Gibraltar. Of course, they were rusty outside but they were alright inside, so there was only one thing to do. Well we opened them out, and one chap got a rabbit pie in it, another chap got steak and onions and sausage and such like that. So anyway, we warmed them up, we made one fire and we took the lids off and just put them on the edge to warm them up. Well we'd a bit of a laugh about it and one chap says, 'Here, give us a spoonful of your tripe and onions, kid, and I'll give you a drop of my soup', so we swapped spoonsful like that. But it was rather funny that I should get tripe and onions, I told a tripe dresser in town, Benjamin Enns. 'Well', he said, 'It might have been our tripe.' I said, 'Anyway, it had travelled a bit whether it was your tripe or not.'

15/471 Private Clifford Hollingworth, D Company[55]

14 January 1916 – Curious meals. Sardines for breakfast – (rotten), cooked bully & dates & rice for dinner (good), Bully for tea (rotten).

15/1024 Private John Yeadon, B Company[56]

John Yeadon.

An improvised cooking range for the Officers' Mess at Point 80, with Private Catterick in charge.

Field kitchens at Point 80.

Cavalry on the way to water their horses at point 40.

Out on the Canal, guards and patrols continued, while those men not on duty took part in the nightly mouse hunt.

Among other things we are absolutely overrun with rats and mice. Of course we sleep on the ground on our valises and they simply run over one all night. I now sleep with my head in a pillow case to avoid being bitten.

Lieutenant S Morris Bickersteth CommanderNo.6 Platoon, B Company[57]

On 19 January the Pals were recalled to Kantara where they repitched their tents and awaited further instructions. The following day the entire battalion was paraded to hear sentence passed on Private Frederick Brennan of A Company, who had fallen asleep on guard duty in the desert. Brennan, who was present under guard, was given fifty-six days' detention. Then the Colonel addressed the men, reminding them that they must not have letters published in the newspapers, by which he was probably referring to the account of the collision at sea which had been sent to the *Yorkshire Evening Post* by a soldier from B Company.[58]

You ask me if we really did run down a French ship, I wrote you an account of it perhaps you did not get the letter, anyway you will have seen the most exaggerated account of it in the Yorkshire Evening Post. The man who wrote that I do not think will write another letter of that kind for a long time, unfortunately he is a Corporal in my platoon. I have given him absolute hell on account of it.

Lieutenant S. Morris Bickersteth, Commander No.6 Platoon, B Company[59]

Privates Robinson and Burton making a dugout.

Filling sandbags in the desert.

An advance party had meanwhile been despatched to Point 80, which was to be the Pals' next base camp. By 23 January the whole of A and D Companies had arrived while the rest of the battalion remained temporarily at Kantara. Setting up the new camp was quite a task, for the desert first had to be cleared of all scrub and brushwood and, when the tents had been pitched, work commenced on dugouts for the battalion's Orderly Room, Guard Room, Officers' Mess, Signal Post, and so on.

January 1916 – Fatigues all day. Digging Surgery underground.

January 1916 – Fatigues all day. Digging Guard Room and Ammunition Room.

15/158 Private Charles H. Bell, A Company[60]

No sooner had the Pals had got their tents pitched and some semblance of order in their camp, than a storm blew up on the night of 24 January and several of their tents, including Colonel Taylor's, were blown down.

The weather was extremely boisterous. It blew hard last night and this morning most of the camp was down. The ordinary regulation tent peg is unsuitable for sandy soil as it does not take a sufficient grip of the ground.

93rd Field Ambulance War Diary, 25 January 1915[61]

… Mine was amongst the six tents that didn't blow down, even the Colonel's marquee tent blew down. He was out in his pyjamas and one thing and another … anyway, we laughed about it, but it was a serious job, you know, because when you're putting tent poles up in the Army, you don't put them as you like, everybody is lined up like that. Number three, this way, number two, that way, until they're all in a straight line see, both ways. When we pitched our tent, Foster said 'Try and find us a big tin'. Well we found an old tin … so we made a hole and we put the tin and put the pole in then we filled it full of sand and rammed it in and then rammed it round the tin to cover it. Now then, when we got the guy ropes on we'd got something to pull against and we'd a good tent. We laughed at some of our chaps running around in their shirts, some were sleeping in their shirts, some of them slept semi-nude, on the desert and this wind and the sand was hitting you know. A fright if anybody hadn't anything on.

15/471 Private Clifford Hollingworth, D Company[62]

Also at about this time, the men's attempts to hold a football match were also complicated by a sandstorm.

When we got out in the desert we said that we would have a football match, so the Regimental Sergeant-Major got every man-jack out, and he flagged it out, the four corners, and we walked across a foot at a time. When I say a foot, a boot, stamping, to get it flat, and then we'd come that way, by the time we'd finished we'd nearly got it like a billiard table. Anyway we got it nice and flat for the match [on the next day]. That night we had a wind, and when a wind comes down the desert there's nowt to stop it. On our football field was a mountain, and a mountain over here had disappeared, you know, a little hillock, it was just like snow.

15/471 Private Clifford Hollingworth, D Company[63]

While the men were out in the desert, they had an ideal opportunity for them to carry out field firing practice with Mark VI ammunition. Ranges were built using sandbags – which, not surprisingly, were in plentiful supply – and targets were improvised from paper discs, biscuit-tin lids, and bottles. Such practice was doubly useful, as it also gave the company and platoon commanders experience in giving fire orders and controlling the fire.[64]

One serious disadvantage of the Pals' new camp was that water, which had never been plentiful, in any case, was now in very short supply, and had to be brought in by camels.

Our daily ration of drinking water was one mess tin per man per day. With that we had to wash and shave, wash our clothes and have a weekend tub. The occupants of a tent would pool their supply, dig a hole in the sand, spread a waterproof groundsheet in the hole and pour in the water, then toss up for who had the first tub. By the time the last man got his turn the water was a grey puddle.

15/711 Private Arthur V Pearson[65]

A football match in the desert.

Herbert Hargreaves (second from right, back row) with some of his pals. (D. Hargreaves)

We got a pint of water per day. With that pint of water you made your breakfast, you washed and shaved in it and it was your drinking water for the day. So when six of you'd been in one tin of water to shave, you can imagine the thickness of the mud at the bottom!

I'll tell you what I used to chew on [in] the desert, I had a button and a pebble. When I'd chewed my button until I'd got tired of it, I'd take it out and put the pebble in my mouth. The main thing was you created a slight saliva which kept you from wanting a drink. Your mouth got dry with the sun, but you created a slight saliva that kept your throat [from getting] dry. Just for that time it helped considerably and was very important.

15/471 Private Clifford Hollingworth, D Company[66]

Of course the main thing is water. It is not so bad here [Kantara] or actually on the Canal, but out in front there is only just enough for drinking and cooking purposes and an officer is lucky if he can get a glassful to shave with in the morning. As for washing, well we don't, that is what it comes to, and when it get a bit hotter it will not be very pleasant. What a lot of Kaiser will have to answer for when the war is over.

Lieutenant S Morris Bickersteth, Commander No.6 Platoon, B Company[67]

A camel driver in conversation with a Leeds Pal appears wary. (N Longfield)

The battalion water tanks, the only means of storing water in the desert.

Soon the men were called upon to get started on their real work, digging trenches to establish a defensive network deep in the desert that would prevent the Turks from getting anywhere near the Suez Canal. The digging parties made an early start each morning, and were given a daily quota. Once they had completed their allotted tasks they were finished for the day. This proved real incentive, and the Pals set to work with a will.

The camp was guarded around the clock, especially at night, with picquets being sent out into the desert each evening at dusk. The Turks weren't the only problem, however, for thieving by local Arabs was difficult to prevent.

You slept with your rifle. You wrapped it round with your overcoat and slept with it. That was the idea and the last thing you did, when you got into camp, you unloaded your rifle and you stood it in its place in the post till you got to bed, and then you got it and wrapped it in your overcoat and that was your bedmate. Because, you see, they could move about in the stillness of the night, and we also have labourers, camp labourers, that were Arabs, and take the refuse and burn it, they used to burn the camel dung as well. And, you didn't know who they were, so of course all these precautions, you can smile about it now.

15/471 Private Clifford Holingworth, D Company[68]

The Medical Officer inspects a patient on the battalion sick parade.

It must be said that the British soldiers' treatment of the Arabs did nothing to improve relations between the two sides.

Every Medical unit should have an interpreter at hand. It is impossible to deal satisfactorily with Arab Camel drivers unless this is done.[69]

The personnel of section forbidden to bent Arab Coolies under any pretext whatsoever.[70]

Every pair of camels has a native driver, they are supposed to know all about loading, this is seldom the case, so one has to do all the work one's self. All they do is to jabber at the top of their voices, so now I always start proceedings by kicking the man as hard as I possibly can behind, generally lifting him two or three yards. This of course makes him furious but obedient.

Lieutenant S. Morris Bickersteth, Commander No.6 Platoon, B Company[71]

On 8 February B Company arrived at Point 80 from Kantara to join the rest of the battalion in their trench digging. That night a tragedy occurred. A party of men from No.9 Platoon, C Company, had just returned from guard duty at Point 80 and were cleaning their weapons when Joe Prince accidentally shot Edward Wintle. Private Wintle was fatally wounded. He died later that night before the Battalion Medical Officer could reach him, and Private Prince was put on a charge to await a Court Martial.[72]

We had an unfortunate accident at the beginning of the week, a fellow while unloading his rifle, he'd been out on outpost duty all night, by some mistake or other fired a round and killed his best Pal who was standing two yards off. The case is all the more pathetic as the fellow who fired had persuaded his friend to join and promised his parents he would look after him as best as he could. Chappell preached his sermon on this incident and was quite effective.

Lieutenant S. Morris Bickersteth, Commander No.6 Platoon, B Company[73]

This was not the first time a rifle was accidentally fired while the Pals were in Egypt. Private Bell of A Company had fired his rifle while cleaning it a month previously, fortunately without hitting anyone.[74]

Private Wintle's body was carried across the desert by his comrades, while the buzzards circled overhead, and his funeral was held at Kantara on 9 February. Clifford Hollingworth was one of the buglers in attendance.

Wintle's grave at Kantara.

Church Parade in the desert.

 I marched down from Point Eighty to attend the funeral. I had my bugle with me and I remember the Colonel was in tears.

 When we got there, there were about four officers and a firing party [to fire a volley over the grave], and we were walking along the side of the trench. Sand is very queer stuff unless it is boarded up, revetted. You've only to touch the side of the trench and you're down, and two of us slipped in. The Colonel said 'Oh my poor boys, my poor boys!' Poor old chap, he thought a lot of us and he had tears in his eyes as he lifted me out, 'Come on, my boy,' everybody was boys, if you were thirty you were a boy.

 Then we got into line and we sounded the Last Post, but he [Private Wintle] wanted to lay on his face. He wasn't on his back, we'd to turn him over, and as fast as we turned him over he went back again, because the sides of the trench would be so lopsided. So one of our lads says, 'Put him this way,' and as he brought him that way he put his foot down and put a pile of sand under his back and said, 'Now you stay there.'

 Anyway we got the poor old lad laid down and we blew the Last Post. We marched back to camp and we didn't feel so very cheerful, there was the firing party and us, and when we got back they'd put on a high tea for us, so we couldn't complain.'

    15/471 Private Clifford Hollingworth, D Company[75]

Clifford Hollingworth with his bugle. (J. Lowley)

Joe Prince. (N. Longfield)

Edward Wintle. (N. Longfield)

On the day of the funeral, a Brigade Order was published which read, 'In order to prevent accidents in future, no man is to clean his rifle without first taking the bolt out and the MAGAZINE. When cleaned, the bolt is to be replaced and closed before replacing the magazine.'[76]

Poor Prince's Court Martial took place at Point 80 on 18 February. It was presided over by Major Kennedy of the 2nd Bradford Pals (18th West Yorkshire Regiment). The outcome is not known, but it seems likely that the charges were dropped and a verdict of accidental death recorded.

> There was an enquiry, but there was no charge, it was an accident, but it was an accident that could have been avoided because you should not clean your rifle when you've one in the slot. Your rifle should be clean empty.
>
> *15/471 Private Clifford Hollingworth, D Company*[77]

A moonlight memorial service for Edward Wintle was held at Point 80 on the following Sunday, attended by the men who were unable to be present at his funeral in Kantara.[78]

Despite the lesson provided by this unfortunate episode, and the order from Brigade Headquarters, on the very day of Prince's Court Martial, Corporal Child of B Company, preparing for picquet duty out in the desert, accidentally fired his rifle. He was taken immediately to the Guard Tent, but was released in time to go out with the picquet. The next morning Colonel Taylor reduced him to the ranks and gave him twenty-eight days' Field Punishment No.2[79], the maximum sentence, while the whole of B Company was to be punished with company drill for an hour every day until further notice. This punishment was later reduced to seven days, but in fact only lasted for four days as it was interrupted when the battalion moved to Point 40 on 23 February.[80]

Wintle was not the only casualty of the careless handling of firearms by members of the battalion. Two more Pals from C Company were injured in an accident with a privately-bought

The officers' smoke room, Point 80. Left to right, Captains Gibson and Boardall, Second-Lieutenant Willey, Lieutenants Vause and Rayner.

automatic pistol just five days after Private Prince's Court Martial, one of them from the same section as Wintle and Prince. A press report early in March led the people of Leeds to believe that the Pals had been in action, but it was later admitted that the two casualties listed, Privates John Ramsden Whiteley (who was shot in the leg), and Frank L. Pontefract, had been accidentally wounded when one of the Pals had been showing his comrades a pistol.[81]

In mid-February the trenches were inspected by General Sir Archibald Murray, now Commander-in-Chief of the Mediterranean Expeditionary Force, who was accompanied by an entourage, which included his standard bearer, a Sikh sergeant. The battalion's work was almost finished and Murray congratulated the men on their efforts.

John Ramsden Whiteley, wounded by accident.

> *Inspection of trenches by GOC the Defence of Suez – Gen Murray. Magnificent sight — native Hindoo carrying Union Jack – very fine.*
> *15/1024 Private John Yeadon, B Company*[82]

While the trench lines were being completed, an advance party of two platoons from A Company went off to Point 40, about 3 miles away, on 19 February.

> *Returned from Picquet at 7am. Breakfast 7.30am. Parade at 8.30am for trenches. Awful job carrying barbed wire from point mile away – did 5 journeys = 7 miles. B Coy paraded from 3pm to 4pm as a punishment for Corporal Child firing his rifle. This parade to last for 7 days – rotten.*
> *15/1024 Private John Yeadon, B Company*[83]

On 23 February the rest of the battalion assembled at Point 40, where they were given a welcome rest after their hard work in the desert. They joined Brigade Headquarters and 12th KOYLI there, and rumours that they would soon be in France abounded. There was still some military activity, however, for two days later D Company, with two machine-guns, was sent to establish an outpost and protect a well at Bir-el-Druidar, about 8 miles east of Point 40[84]

Camel transport with an armed escort.

During the night of 27/28 February, the news broke that the expected move was on. Some of the men had packed their kit in anticipation on the day before, and the battalion transport set off before daylight. The rest of the battalion were awoken at 4am and by 8.30 the camp had been cleared and the Leeds Pals were on their way to Kantara. On the next day they had their last bathe in the Suez Canal, and on 1 March took the train to Port Said, where they boarded the troopship that was to take them to France.

Weather has been excellent this month. Have had abundant correspondence. Battn styled the 'Nomads' – [always] moving from place to place on desert. Have had plenty of hard work but on the whole not had a bad time. Great movement of troops during the last two or three days of the month. Those from Dardanelles relieving 31st Division which is going to France.

15/231 Private George W. Cosby, B Company[85]

Regimental signallers, Lance-Corporals Firth and Sheppard, in their dugout in the desert.

Captain Lacy Bathurst, the Battalion Medical Officer.

NOTES

1. Author's recorded interview with Clifford Hollingworth, May 1988.
2. MacMunn, Lieutenant-General Sir George, KCB, KCSI, DSO, and Falls, Captain Cyril, *Military Operations Egypt and Palestine*, HMSO, London, 1928.
3. Ibid.
4. Translation of the Turkish Orders for the Attack on the Suez Canal, 1 February 1915, papers of Lieutenant-Commander (later Commander) H.V. Coates RN, Department of Documents, Imperial War Museum, London.
5. Author's recorded interviews with Clifford Hollingworth, May 1988 and July 1988.
6. Author's recorded interview with Arthur Dalby, May 1988.
7. Hollingworth, op.cit., May 1988.
8. Hollingworth, op.cit, July 1988.
9. Hollingworth, op.cit, May 1988.
10. Battalion War Diary, 6 December 1915, Public Record Office, London: WO95/4590.
11. Pearson, Arthur Valentine, *A Leeds Pal Looks Back,* unpublished manuscript in Leeds Reference Library, circa 1961.
12. TS copy of a letter from Lieutenant S. Morris Bickersteth to his father, 10 December 1915, Bickersteth Family War Diary.
13. Diary of 15/1003 Private Edward Woffenden, 8 December 1915, in the possession of Bob Reed, York.
14. Pearson, op.cit.
15. Bickersteth, op.cit. above.
16. Battalion War Diary, op.cit., 13 December 1915.
17. Letter from Robert Norman Bell of Farnham, Surrey, to the Producer of *The Great War*, 6 July 1963, BBC TV Great War Series correspondence, Imperial War Museum, London.
18. Pearson, op.cit.
19. Bickersteth, op.cit, 16 December 1915.
20. Pearson, op.cit.
21. Diary of 15/1082 Private Herbert Hargreaves, 14 December 1915.
22. Woffenden, op.cit, 15 December 1915.
23. Bickersteth, op.cit, 18 December 1915.
24. Battalion War Diary, op.cit, 21 December 1915.
25. Woffenden, op.cit, 22 December 1915.
26. Bickersteth, op.cit, 25 December 1915.
27. Woffenden, op.cit, 23 December 1915.
28. Diary of 1571024 Private John Yeadon, 23 December 1915.
29. Bickersteth, op.cit, 25 December 1915.
30. 93 Brigade Orders, 24 December 1915, in 93 Brigade War Diary, Public Record Office, London: W095/2353.
31. MS copy of the diary of 15/231 Private George William Cosby, 25 December 1915.
32. Hollingworth, op.cit., 9 May 1988.
33. The Arab quarter of cosmopolitan Port Said.
34. Cosby, op.cit, 25 December 1915.
35. Pearson, op.cit.
36. Woffenden, op.cit, 25 December 1915.
37. Hollingworth, op.cit, May 1988.
38. 93 Brigade Orders, 24 December 1915, in 93 Brigade War Diary, op.cit.
39. Cosby, op.cit, 26 December 1915.
40. Bickersteth, op.cit, 29 December 1915.
41. Pearson, op.cit

42. Author's recorded interview with Arthur Dalby, June 1990.
43. Battalion War Diary, op.cit, 30 December 1915.
44. Appendix 14, Instructions for the Safeguarding of the Suez Canal in No. 3 Section, 93 Brigade War Diary, op.cit
45. Hollingworth, op.cit, May 1988.
46. Diary of 15/158 Private Charles Henry Bell, 30 December 1915.
47. The 2/3rd Gurkhas were mobilised on 9 August 1914 and arrived in France on 12/13 October, where they suffered heavy casualties from German shell fire, and from sickness due to the severe winter. They took part in the attack at Neuve Chapelle on 10 March 1915, spent the next five months in and out of the trenches, and were in action again near Loos in September 1915, when Rifleman Kulbir Thapa won the battalion's first VC. In November 1915 they went to Suez and were then sent out into the Sinai Desert, and they eventually took part in the campaign in Palestine.
48. Hollingworth, op.cit, May 1988.
49. Cosby, G. W., op.cit., 1 January 1916.
50. Diary of 15/1238 Private (later Sergeant) Bernard Gill, 2 January 1916.
51. Bickersteth, op.cit, 3 January 1916
52. Yeadon, op.cit, 1 January 1916.
53. Bell, op.cit, 2 January 1916.
54. Section Orders, No. III Section Canal Defence Force, 3 January 1916, 93 Brigade War Diary, op.cit
55. Hollingworth, op.cit, May 1988.
56. Yeadon, op.cit, 14 January 1916.
57. Bickersteth, op.cit, 3 January 1916.
58. Diary of 15/1951 Private John Jackson Shaw, 20 January 1916. Bell, op.cit, 20 January 1916. Cosby, op.cit, 20 January 1916. Yeadon, op.cit, 20 January 1916. *Yorkshire Evening Post*, 28 December 1915. Section Orders, No. III Section, Canal Defence Force 14 January 1916, 93 Brigade War Diary, op.cit.
59. Bickersteth, op.cit, 23 January 1916.
60. Bell, op.cit., 23/24 January 1916.
61. 93rd Field Ambulance, RAMC, War Diary, 25 January 1916, Public Record Office, London: W095/2354.
62. Hollingworth, op.cit, May 1988.
63. Ibid.
64. Battalion War Diary, op.cit, 31 January 1916.
65. Pearson, op.cit.
66. Hollingworth, op.cit, May 1988.
67. Bickersteth, op.cit, 23 January 1916.
68. Hollingworth, op.cit., May 1988.
69. 93rd Field Ambulance, RAMC, War Diary, op.cit., 3 January 1916.
70. 71st Sanitary Section, RAMC, War Diary, 10 January 1916, Public Record Office, London: W095/2355.
71. Bickersteth, op.cit, 20 February 1916.
72. Wintle's death was recorded in the diaries of Bell, Cosby, Woffenden and Yeadon, op.cit, 8 February 1916. Prince's Court Martial (93 Brigade Orders, 16 February 1916, 93rd Brigade War Diary, op. cit), and the information that he was in the same section as Wintle (Roll of 15th [Service] Battalion [1st Leeds] Prince of Wales's Own [West Yorkshire Regiment]) 1915, printed by John Turner, Pontefract), led the author to ask Messrs Dalby and Hollingworth whether they knew who shot Wintle. They confirmed that it was Prince. Author's interview with Arthur Dalby and Clifford Hollingworth, May 1988.

73. Bickersteth, op.cit, 12 February 1916.
74. Bell, op.cit, 10 January 1916.
75. Hollingworth, op.cit, May 1988.
76. 93 Brigade Orders, 93 Brigade War Diary, op.cit.
77. Hollingworth, op.cit, May 1988.
78. Cosby, op.cit, 13 February 1916.
79. There were two types of Field Punishment; No. 1 consisted of tying the offender to a fixed object such as a tree or waggon wheel (this was discontinued towards the end of the war); No.2 consisted of varying periods of drill, with full pack, often carried out 'at the double'.
80. Yeadon, op.cit, 18 February 1916.
81. Unidentified newscutting in Leeds Reference Library, dated 23 February 1916
82. Yeadon, op.cit, 12 February 1916.
83. Yeadon, op.cit, 19 February 1916.
84. Battalion War Diary, op.cit, 25 February 1916.
85. Cosby, op.cit, 29 February 1916.

Chapter Four

'Sheer Misery!' – Trench Warfare

Rifle grenades pour into our sector 1st line. Very trying. Raining off and on.
Condition most miserable. Raining most of the night. Sheer misery!
15/231 Private George W. Cosby, B Company[1]

FRANCE, MARCH–JUNE 1916

By March 1916, the threat to the Suez Canal had lessened. Although Turkey now had at its disposal a large contingent of men who had been released from Gallipoli after the Allied evacuation, so too had Britain. The British troops in Suez had pushed their defences deep into the desert and the trenches, including those dug by the Leeds Pals, would prevent the Turks from reaching the Suez Canal. As the weather in the Sinai Desert became hotter and the wells dried up, the likelihood of a Turkish force crossing the desert became less. The failure of the campaign in Gallipoli gave the 'Westerners' (those political, military and other figures who were convinced that the war could only be won on the Western Front) the impetus they needed. A major offensive on the Western Front was now inevitable. It had been decided, at a conference

Haig greets Joffre at his chateau. (Imperial War Museum)

Haig's minute to his Adjutant-General. (Imperial War Museum)

in Chantilly early in December 1915, that a joint Anglo-French offensive would be mounted in the new year. Soon after this, General Sir Douglas Haig, an ardent 'Westerner', had replaced Sir John French as Commander of the British Expeditionary Force.

Haig, as commander of First Army, had been involved in the planning of the Neuve Chapelle attack in 1915, and he was now keen to begin planning his summer campaign for 1916. He favoured a late offensive in Flanders which – apart from driving the Germans back and perhaps allowing an outflanking movement, reversing the 'race to the sea'[2] – would regain British control of the Belgian coast and prevent German U-boat operations from the Belgian ports. Chasing the Germans out of Belgium was, after all, one of the reasons why Britain had entered the war.

On the Western Front in France and Belgium, meanwhile, British troops had by this time taken over yet more of the line from the French, so that their sector now extended from near

142

A direct hit on Fort Douaumont, Verdun, 1916.

The shell-torn landscape of Verdun.

the Channel coast south to the River Somme. At the insistence of General Joffre, the French Commander, it was therefore decided that a joint Anglo-French offensive should naturally take place where the British and French armies met – on the Somme.

Meanwhile, in February 1916 the Germans, perhaps sensing the inevitable, mounted an attack on Verdun – France's historic fortress, but soon reduced to a useless salient in the line, but one which the French would defend at all cost. This new development made the Somme offensive a necessity in order to relieve pressure on the French, although France's involvement in the joint offensive would, naturally, be reduced.

Since the creation of the trench lines, the Germans had mainly fought a defensive war in France, making great efforts to take and hold the high ground dominating the Allies' trenches. The chalk soil of the Somme was particularly suitable for the construction, by the German troops, of well-fortified trenches, machine-gun posts and deep dugouts, some of them 40 feet underground and complete with electric lighting.

The British High Command had a different attitude, however – the trench lines were only temporary, and constant aggression with the emphasis on killing the enemy was the answer.

It was an attitude which merely caused the Germans to fortify their trenches. So it came about that in the spring of 1916, the British Army massed its forces on the Western Front. Kitchener's Army was ready for its baptism of fire.

The Leeds Pals, released from their 'Eastern' obligation, embarked on HMT *Ascania*, bound for Marseilles, at 6.30am on 1 March 1916. At last the Pals were about to do the job for which they had joined the army – they were going to push the Germans right back to Berlin.

> *Oh, we were all sure we were going on to Berlin. We were going to have a happy time in Berlin, that sort of talk. At that time everyone was all thrilled with it.*
>
> 15/399 Private Morrison Fleming, D Company[3]

*Programmes for the entertainments laid on for the Pals onboard HMT **Ascania**.*

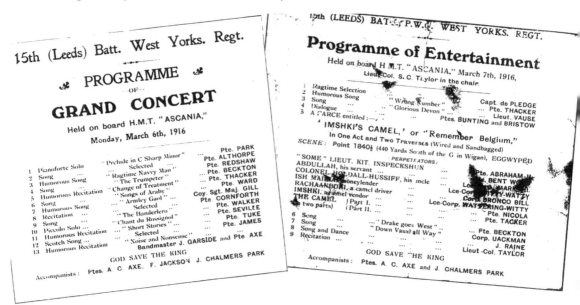

The Pals' journey to France was rather better than their maiden voyage. Aboard the *Ascania* they found themselves in unaccustomed luxury, especially after their spartan existence in the desert.

We started from Port Said last Wednesday week, March 1st and landed yesterday at Marseilles. We had an excellent voyage in a very comfortable Cunard liner. Only our regiment and Brigade Headquarters being on board. There was plenty of room for the men and it was different altogether from the Empress of Britain, *the food for the men was excellent and the accommodation also, every man getting a bunk and not those vile hammocks as before. Another great boon was that the men ate in different places to where they slept, so if any were sick it did not affect the others, but as I say, the weather was excellent and nearly everyone was quite well.*

We called nowhere, simply stopping outside Malta for orders. We had no excitements I'm glad to say, as before, although the submarines are still at work, a French auxiliary cruiser being sunk while escorting a troopship while we were still at sea, but nothing came our way.

Lieutenant S. Morris Bickersteth, Commander No.6 Platoon, B Company[4]

Left [Kantara] March 1st 6.45am. Embarked at Port
Said, set sail at 4.00[pm] on HMT Ascania.
March 3rd Band played on deck.
March 4th Boxing, wrestling – comic sketch.
March 5th Church service. Band played when passing
through Malta.
March 6th Passed some rocks.
March 7th Passed Sardinia.
Arrived Marseilles March 8th at 7.30[am].

15/1951 Private John Jackson Shaw, Bandsman[5]

Watching the entertainments, en route to France.

145

HMT Ascania.

A comic boxing match performed by members of the battalion.

The Leeds Pals' band performs on deck.

Once more we boarded an army transport, this time a converted liner HMT Ascania. *The conditions on this voyage were quite different to our trip out from England on the* Empress of Britain. *The* Ascania *was a much smaller and only carried our battalion and a few 'spares'. The whole voyage was a pleasure cruise, we didn't have the same feeling of dread and apprehension, although we were on the sea, we didn't seem to worry about German submarines. Life was jollier, the food was better and we slept below. The days got colder as the sun lost its power. We had evidently acquired a little of the old campaigner's unconcern. Our band gave concerts on deck and played their loudest as though they didn't care for all the submarines that were probably prowling about. Bandmaster Garside, Jim Park and Arthur Axe were amongst the artists we listened to. We had a good time on that and an eventful voyage. As we sailed towards France we crowded the rails as we passed the Balearic Isles, looking dark and foreboding in the dusk.*

Coming into Marseilles Harbour, we were thrilled to see the sinister looking Chateau d'If and to imagine Monte Cristo being thrown into the sea in his escape sack. The first French words as we tied up at the docks was 'Doughnuts' which sounded English enough to me. Small boys were selling doughnuts and they did a roaring trade, as anything was regarded as a luxury that was not on the army menu. Of course No. 11 Platoon were baggage party! We loaded trucks and travelled from ship to railhead, through the streets, but we didn't see very much of the city.

15/711 Private Arthur V. Pearson, C Company[6]

The Pals disembarked from the *Ascania* at 11am on 8 March and formed up to follow their kit to the railhead to begin the journey north. It proved to be a very long journey.

We landed yesterday about 10am and were all entrained by 2pm, when we started on our long and I fear it will be somewhat tedious journey. The men are nearly all in the ordinary cattle trucks, thirty to thirty five in a truck, but the journey is scheduled to take 53 hours. As I am writing to you we are now four hours late (1 pm) so I do not suppose we will reach our destination until the early hours of Saturday morning. Why the journey should take so long I cannot make out. Of course we stop pretty continually on the way, sometimes for half an hour or more to allow the ordinary trains to pass. We have also had two halts of two hours to get the men hot tea and to

Nominal Roll of Officers disembarked per H.T.

"ASCANIA" on the 8th March 1916.

Brig Genl: H.B.Kirk.	93rd Inf'try Brigade.
Major C.A.Howard.	do.
Captain J.P.Kayll	do.
Lieut H.J.Clark.	do.
Lieut F.O'Carroll	do.
Major E.C.Norman.	15th W.Yorks: Regt.
Lieut Col: S.C.Taylor.	do.
Major L.P.Baker	do.
Captain T.G.Gibson.	do.
Captain E.K. de Sledge	do.
Captain G.C.Whitaker	do.
Captain F.H.Boardall.	do.
Captain P.H.L.Mellor.	do.
Captain S.T.A.Neil	do.
Captain J.R.Atkinson.	do.
Lieut S.M.Birkersteth	do.
Lieut R.B.H.Rayner	do.
Lieut J.G.Tause	do.
Lieut R.M.S.Blease	do.
Lieut G.S.Ward.	do.
Lieut N.Eden.	do.
Lieut E.H.Lintott	do.
Lieut J.S.D.Smith.	do.
2Lieut T.A.R.R.E.Willey.	do.
2Lieut A.N.Hutten.	do.
2Lieut J.S.Everett	do.
2Lieut R.H.Tolson.	do.
2Lieut E.St.A.Brooksbaut.	do.
2Lieut A.Liversidge.	do.
2Lieut M.W.Booth.	do.
2Lieut L.Foster	do.
Lieut R.J.Anderson.	do.
Captain L.Bathurst. RAMC.	do. attd.
Rev: C.K.Cheppell (Chaplain)	do. attd:

The nominal roll of the officers who went to France. The surnames of de Pledge, Bickersteth, Vause, Evers, Hutton, Brooksbank and Chappell have been misspelt.

serve out rations, one last night about 10pm and again this morning. Of course this kind of thing delays us, but 53 hours is tremendous for the distance.

We know where we are going for the present but I feel I cannot mention it by name. At any rate, it is a base, a good distance behind the firing line, but not the same as Burgon went to, to start with. Of course how long we are likely to be there no-one knows. I am in a carriage with five other officers, the Doctor [Bathurst], Chappell, Gibson, Neil and the Brigadier's ADC, a fellow called Clark, a very decent fellow. Chappell has a Primus stove and we have great rags preparing our food. We have the ordinary army Maconochie ration which boiled up makes extraordinarily good stew. Then we buy eggs, bread butter etc at different stations and I can tell you we manage to do ourselves quite fairly well.

Lieutenant S. Morris Bickersteth, Commander No.6 Platoon, B Company[7]

… in the railway sidings, were long trains made up of horse-box trucks, '40 Hommes and 10 Chevaux'. This was the Southern terminus of the Paris, Lyon, Marseilles railway, and we were to travel nearly into Paris in these horse-boxes. Forty men, no blankets, no bedding, no nothing – just 40 'hommes'! I suppose the novelty of a situation puts a keener edge on it, and also, what made changing situations so tolerable was the fact that we were with our pals who had shared all this for two years. Now we had a mobile home for a few days. We settled down on our floor space, about the width of our packs, we joked as the guard blew his little, squeaky tin trumpet and we were off

The Leeds Pals board their train for Pont Remy. This photograph was taken by Edric Longflied, who managed to take his camera to France.

once more on the move, this time on a two day journey up to Paris. On the rear of each truck was a platform with an iron ladder leading up to a box built on top of the coach about the size of a small pigeon loft with windows, and in our turns, we spent hours up there observing the world as we travelled slowly along.

15/711 Private Arthur V. Pearson, C Company[8]

We have had the usual kind of procession through France which I imagine every British troop train has. All along the line the countryside turns out to meet us and wave flags shouting 'Vive les Anglais!' and ask for souvenirs. The latter we find it very difficult to prevent the men from giving. For instance, yesterday afternoon in Dijon station there were crowds of people of every description and French soldiers brought the men hot water in their billy cans and working girls walked along the footplates shaking hands and if possible, kissing any available Tommy whose attention they could attract, and in some cases you may imagine this was not difficult. The result was that many buttons and badges etc were lost and as the train steamed out of the station everyone held up what they had managed to get hold of, a curious conglomeration of things, hat badges, shoulder titles, buttons, picture postcards, army ration biscuits, bully beef and in one or two cases even New Testaments.

When we got to Dijon it began to snow and ever since we left there we have travelled through snow-clad country. You can imagine the change from Egyptian weather is somewhat great. A fortnight ago we were sitting in a desert not even expecting a change of any kind. I can tell you I have been extremely glad of my fleece lined Burberry and Julian's fur waistcoat will now come in extremely useful; I keep fairly warm at nights except for my feet, which have been absolutely icy. This morning we passed Versailles but of course we have not gone into Paris, but skirted round it. All along the line we have seen many German prisoners working in the fields. At Marseilles we tied up almost alongside two ships full of them. All of them being pretty fair specimens.

Lieutenant S. Morris Bickersteth, Commander No.6 Platoon, B Company[9]

Walter Wild with his family.

Walter Wild, a trombonist with the band, did not accompany his fellow musicians to France. A member of the Leeds City Tramways Band, Wild was 41 when he joined the Leeds Pals. Although he had lost an eye in a firework accident when he was a child, he was accepted as a member of the Leeds Pals, along with most of the Tramways Band, and went with the battalion to Egypt. However, the desert sand had irritated his eye socket and caused it to become infected, so he was left in hospital in Egypt when the Pals – and his kitbag – departed for France. His army days were over, and he was eventually repatriated to Britain and discharged on medical grounds.[10]

On the afternoon of 10 March the Pals arrived at Pont Remy where they left the train that had been their home for nearly three days. It took them two hours to unload their kit and, after a break for some tea, they fell in for the 12-mile march to their new quarters. A and D Companies were to be in Neuville-au-Bois and B and C Companies in Forceville[11] and officers were sent on ahead to arrange billets. As the men rested on the roadside during a break in the march, they heard the sound of the guns for the first time, a sound that would become all too familiar to them.

After we had gone about three miles, the CO ordered me to go on and see about the billets for B and C Companies. The regiment is divided up in two villages. He also told me to get the C Company Commander's horse, which I did. I rode on as fast as I could and found some difficulty in finding the way, as I had no map. It was quite dark and my directions were not very clear, but still with the help of my small stock of French, I arrived at this village about 7.45pm.

Knowing that the half-battalion would come in under the hour, I rode straight up to the Chateau in the centre of the village and asked where the Mayor lived, was directed to his house but found when I got there that he was away from the village, but fortunately his son who spoke a little English had been told to expect our arrival, but only three hundred men, not nearly five hundred which I had following me. But still I went round the village with him with a lantern and he showed me every available place where men could be put. A few houses but mostly barns. Of course I had to decide how many each place would hold.

I had not quite finished when the two companies rolled up, all pretty tired as twelve miles in full packs, when we have done no marching for at least three months, is a fairly large order. Still, I only kept them waiting a quarter of an hour and I then handed to each Company Commander a list of his billets, names of the owners and how many men each would hold, and all the men were under cover and most of them asleep within an hour of them entering billets.

Lieutenant S. Morris Bickersteth, Commander No.6 Platoon, B Company[12]

10 March 1916 – … Pont Remy 2.30. Got off train 3pm. Had tea and bully [beef]. Marched 12 miles with full pack to Forceville. Absolutely jiggered. Slept in a barn on straw.

15/1003 Private Edward Woffenden, C Company[13]

10 March 1916 – … arrived Pont Remy, then had to march ten miles to Neuville au Bois where we had to sleep in a barn. Next morning had to find a well for water.

15/1951 Private John Jackson Shaw, Bandsman[14]

10 March 1916 – … arrived Pont Remy at 4.0pm, marched 12 miles full pack and blanket. Billeted in small barn, lights out at midnight.

11 March 1916 – Removed billets to large barn, better accommodation. 6.0 walked to the nearest village.

15/158 Private H. Bell, A Company, attached HQ[15]

In France at last, some of the linguists tried out their French in the local shops, with varying degrees of success.

11 March 1916 – Wash and shave. Very cold. Bought bread. Large piece 5d. Cleaned rifles and billets. Rifle inspection. Tried my French on some natives with slight success. Changed 10/- note at French Mill. 13 Francs for 10/- owing to depreciation in value of Franc. Cliff in billet next to ours so visited his billet and went inside the house. Had a stroll.

15/1003 Private Edward Woffenden, C Company[16]

A chop called Sewell, he made a fool of himself when we were coming from Egypt, he said 'When we get to France, I shall be alright, I can speak French.' Well Sergeant Jackson, he was a schoolteacher, could speak French. We were going down the street and we went into a shop as Sewell was coming out, and he was looking red-faced, and the two ladies of the shop were laughing

'Oh', he says, 'I don't know what they're talking about.'

So we went up and 'parlayed' what they were talking about and of course he [Sergeant Jackson] laughed and said, 'Well, you damned idiot!'

[Sewell] had gone in and said, 'Bonjour Madame', she said, 'Bonjour Monsieur'. He said, Je suis un oeuf s'il vous plait'.

Not have you got an egg, I am an egg!

Well of course the lasses laughed. So he [Jackson] said, 'You just simply told them you were an egg, and you're a bad egg. Now go and apologise and tell them what you want.' He said, 'No'. He said, 'You'll go there and don't be so damned silly, they're two nice ladies there.'

15/471 Private Clifford Hollingworth, D Company[17]

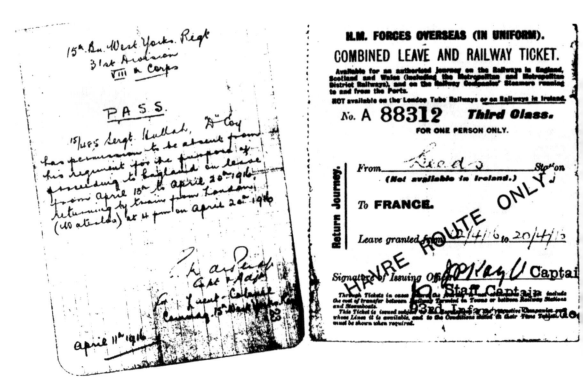

11 March 1916 – Acted as interpreter purchase of straw etc and to the Battalion in general. Very cold damp wintry day.

Our billet at this period was in the barn of a farm at Forceville-en-Vimeu-par-Oisement, Somme. Chez Mme Farsy Morel. This is a small village of 260 (population) inhabitants 50 of whom gone to war.

15/231 Private George W. Cosby, B Company[18]

The next day, Sunday, while they were at Church Parade, the Pals again heard the guns firing.

Now their work began again in earnest. Worn-out or damaged clothing, equipment and boots were replaced, and rifles were inspected frequently. On 13 March, as if to remind them of the new dangers they would have to face, they were paraded and every man was issued with a gas helmet.

Company drill, Swedish drill, bayonet fighting, rapid loading and regular route marches got the men back into peak condition after the enforced idleness of their long journey from Suez. Many of the men, having done little in the way of marching on the desert sands of Egypt, suffered terribly because their feet had softened, especially those who had new boots to break in.

Sergeant Hullah of D company was among those lucky enough to get home on leave when the Pals arrived in France. (Regimental Archive)

The Leeds Pals with their first anti-gas helmets. The last of Edric Longfileds photographs in France. (N. Longfield)

153

14 March 1916 – … Route march. Battalion went about nine or ten miles, sore feet.

15/1003 Private Edward Woftenden, C Company[19]

Although the men were working very hard they had the opportunity to visit the local estaminet[20] when they were off duty, and, in contrast to the dull and repetitive bully and biscuits of their brief stint in the desert, they were able to indulge themselves there.

13 March 1916 – Fine meal again prepared by French lady, Pork Chop & Chips – Coffee & Grenadine.

15/1024 Private John Yeadon, B Company[21]

16 March 1916 – Spent evening at Cafe. Purchased bottle of Dubonnet.

15/231 Private George W. Cosby, B Company[22]

The men also received a large delivery of mail, and rumours about leave began to circulate. On the 20th five men were granted seven days' leave and were sent home the next day. Arthur Dalby was among the lucky ones.

When I was in Egypt, he [Captain Gibson] said, 'You've got a telegram to say you've had an increase in your family, Dalby.' I said, 'I know, I've been expecting it for a week', and when we got back to France he said, 'When leave comes round, Dalby, I'll try and get you on the first batch that ever goes, so you can see your new baby,' and he did. I was one of the first fellows in the Leeds Pals ever to have a leave.

15/259 Private Arthur Dalby, D Company[23]

Arthur Pearson was not so fortunate.

Leave had begun, and the lucky ones went off to the railhead and down to the port, across the Channel and home. I never got home on leave. I know I spoilt my chances by protesting to higher authority that the man chosen for leave was a newcomer to our platoon and had not been long on active service with the battalion. After all, fair's fair. My name was duly removed from the leave roster and placed at the bottom.

15/711 Private Arthur V. Pearson, C Company[24]

On 23 March eleven officers and forty-one men went up to visit the trenches, while the remainder of the battalion packed up to move. On the next day there were six inches of snow to greet the Pals when they awoke, and it continued to snow all day as the men packed their kit. On the 25th, they took to the road in full marching order once again for a four-day march to new billets at Mailly-Maillet, prior to their first tour of duty in the trenches.

Saturday 25th March – Reveille 5am. Everything cleared away and billets cleaned up. Parade at 9am – pack very heavy. Left Forceville 9.30pm Passed thro' Worrel [Woirel], Wery [Wiry-au-Mont], Allery. Arrived Arraines about 12.30pm 8 miles. Market town. Allowed out to 8pm. Feet very sore with new boots. 16th Bfds[25] also here. Beautiful day.

Sunday 26th March —… Feet terribly sore and having a very bad time – murder marching. Passed thro' Hangest. Raining. Arrived Vignacourt at 2pm – demanded desperate effort to last out. Distance 15 miles. Billeted in stable – very comfortable. Attended to my feet. Bed very early and slept well.

Monday 27th March – Reveille 5am. No rations therefore very little breakfast. Feet very bad to start off and became gradually worse. Absolute torture. Passed thro' Flesselles, Talmas. Feet horribly bad – after great effort compelled to fall out. Completed journey in motor lorry. Billeted in broken down barn at Rubempre. Bought some bread and eggs. Went to see doctor— bed very early.

Tuesday 28th March – Mr Rayner tried his best to arrange for a vehicle but couldn't manage it. Rested as much as possible. Parade 2.30pm – in agony. Stuck it till 6.30pm – rum and tea served out. Completed journey without pack. Lads of No. 9 Section carried my pack. Arrived at Mailly 9pm absolutely exhausted – chocolate and beer given us by Mr Rayner.

15/1024 Private John Yeadon, B Company[26]

Tuesday 28th March – Reveille 6.30am Marched off at 3pm. Stopped at 6pm for tea and rum (¾ hour) 11 miles. Had to keep quiet as we were in danger of artillery fire. Marched for 2 hours and 5 minutes without rest – absolutely jiggered! Heard guns very plainly and saw starlights. Am at Mailly Maillet about 1 mile from trenches at 8.55pm. Slept in a house.

15/1003 Private Edward Woffenden, C Company[27]

The Pals went into the trenches for the first time on the following day, 29 March. They were met by guides from the unit they were to relieve, 'Orangemen' of the 8th Battalion, The Royal Irish Rifles, and taken to the sector they were to hold, opposite the enemy lines between Hawthorn Redoubt and the Redan. The relief commenced at 7pm, with C and D Companies going into the front line, B Company in support, and A Company in reserve in Auchonvillers.[28] By 9.25pm the changeover had been completed and the Leeds Pals began their first night in the trenches.

Wednesday night we came right in and took over this section of the trench exactly three weeks after arriving in France. The trenches were dug originally by the French and there is a tremendous amount of work to be done on them.

I have got quite a good dugout in the side of a hill where it would be difficult for shellfire to reach, that is to say except for steep-angle fire such as howitzer fire. In it I have a bed that we pinched from some cottage nearby, looking glasses etc so I am quite comfortable.

The only thing that really bothers me is the rats and they are legion. I thought they were bad enough at Ballah but here the trenches are simply alive with them at night. But I believe the whole line is the same.

I am extremely glad to have got over the first time of being under fire and I must admit that it was quite different to what I had expected.

We started marching off at 7pm from the village where we'd slept the night before, after we'd gone half a mile or so we were met by guides from the regiment whom we were relieving. All around us we could see the flare lights and the star shells going up till the shells began to burst fairly near us and the zirrr of the sniper's bullets made me think of the Ripon rifle range …

We got to a small village about 1,000 yards from the front line. There was hardly a house standing here and the guide hurried us through as there were many unhealthy corners and crossings. But luckily all went well. Friend Bosche never expected anything extraordinary going on so left us alone.

We soon arrived at the head of a communication trench and we all silently filed in, some of us not at all sorry to get under cover without any casualties. The trench was in fairly good condition but it now began to snow heavily and it is wonderful how soon a trench becomes slushy. Here bullets began to increase in numbers but we all felt quite safe in the friendly trench, and I must admit that the rifle fire under such circumstances is no more extraordinary and no more frightening than if one is in a rifle butt.

We took over from an Irish Territorial Regiment[29], *a lot of very nice fellows. They had been here since October last and were now going to a rest billet for a change. They left in one officer per company and one NCO per platoon for 24 hours after we had relieved to give us any help we needed. This really is an excellent tip as we learned a lot of useful information from them which otherwise might have had to buy at a serious expense.*

The weather since we've been here has been glorious by day and night but extremely cold at night and I can tell you that fur waistcoat of Julian's has been of the greatest use. We have not

3rd Army.

Panorama No. 3   made on 4/8/15   from Sheet 57.D.(..74. b. 9.7)

including a field of view of 55 from about E.N.E. to E. by S.

Approximate Scale of Degrees (1 degree equals 1 1/13th inch).

0   1   2   3   4   5   6

Above and Below: The view from the trenches opposite Serre in August 1915. A panorama issued by Third Army. (Imperial War Museum)

brought packs into the trenches but I managed to carry a waterproof sheet, blanket, change of underclothes, socks, collars, handkerchiefs etc. and various other small items.

What I feel most is the lack of sleep. There is practically no sleep in the night at all except perhaps between two and four. When we are not on watch, we are probably in charge of a working party mending the parapet or wire and there is a great deal of work to be done. We do at night what it is impossible to do in the day.

In my opinion there is a good deal of sniping here. Too much in fact and last night I spent four fairly strenuous hours strengthening the corner of a trench which had become extremely unhealthy because of a sniper. This morning he was very annoyed and I had an idea that he might become a trifle incautious so one of my marksmen was on the lookout and sure enough a head appeared out of a large shellhole where I suspected he might be. He'll never lift it again.

We generally have a hymn of hate at stand-to in the morning and evening. Last night friend Bosche put twelve whizz-bangs into our front line and blew a sniper's position and a machine-gun emplacement into nothing. I was not far off and saw every shell burst. Of course their effect is very local, which I was glad of at the time. Well I'm told I really must end this off as the post is going by. I am extremely well, we have six days in and six days out altogether.

Lieutenant S. Morris Bickersteth, Commander No.6 Platoon, B Company[30]

It snowed on our first night in the front line, and what a slow and freezing relief of battalions it was. Our company had to take over the sentry's posts in the sector from the Irishmen. We seemed to be hours getting into position. We lay in snow at the roadside, then moved a bit nearer until we did get into the communication trench and down to our posts in the front line. Gingerly we got onto the firestep and peeped over the parapet, having our first view of no man's land, which was a jumble of barbed wire, ours and the Germans'.

The Irish boys had told us that this was a quiet sector, but before the night was over our chaps had livened it up somewhat! Every wiring post and mound of earth was, to our unaccustomed

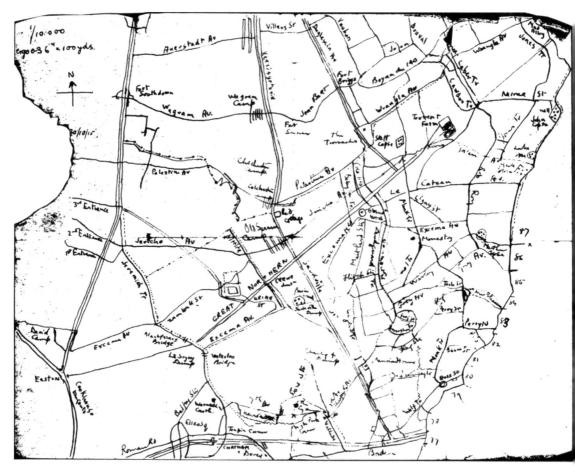

A sketch map of the British trenches opposite Serre, 30 October 1915. The jumping-off trenches for the 1 July attack were added by the 31st Division. (Author's collection)

eyes, a moving German, and all along our battalion front we let go round after round. The German troops in front wouldn't need telling that fresh troops were the new tenants opposite.

> *15/711 Private Arthur V. Pearson, C Company*[31]

Pearson, a bomber, also had the dubious pleasure of being among the first of the Leeds Pals to go out into no man's land on patrol.

Later in the night I was 'warned' for patrol in no man's land. It was the first patrol that C Company had done in France and I can't say that I felt highly honoured to be chosen.

I was strapped into a canvas jacket with ten pockets each holding a Mills bomb. When the time came for the patrol to go out, we were assembled at a point shown to us by one of the Irish officers, where a passage could be made through our wire. We followed our guide over the sandbag parapet

B.E.F.
c/o G.P.O.   Mar. 11th/1916.

Dear Father,

I little guessed when writing my last letter that we should write our next so soon after from "Somewhere in France." For some things we were rather disappointed to leave Egypt so without seeing more of it, the towns, I mean. We have not even been to Cairo – that mecca of tourists. As for sand & wilderness – well, we've seen enough, & the Sinai Peninsular is not a very hospitable spot I can assure you.

Compared with our voyage out, our return sea-voyage was a pleasure trip. We were able to have big canvas baths rigged up & sports of various kinds on deck.

The weather soon got colder however & we left the sunny skies behind. We expected calling at Malta & had prepared for it, but just outside the harbour we received orders to proceed on our journey. Arrived Marseilles we marched straight off the quay to the railway, packed into cattle trucks, thirty in each & for over fifty hours this was our home & we were not permitted to leave it except at rare intervals & then only for a few minutes. We spent two nights en route & had to sleep as best we could on top of each other. Coming straight from Egypt we found it extremely cold travelling & as we came north we found the country covered with snow & flooded fields with a coating of ice. We have come right across France & are now

in billets, mostly barns. After our experience in the cattle truck & the subsequent twelve mile march, it was a distinct pleasure to arrive at last at our billet a good lofty barn with plenty of straw for a bed. We are in a small country village & the bit of French we have learnt has already stood us in good stead & we are rapidly adding to our vocabulary. Although we did not travel first class & in spite of the cold, we managed to derive some pleasure from the scenery on the way & we were given a good reception at most places we passed through. Compared with England the country of France seems deserted & old men & women are the only ones working

in the fields. – I suppose all the young men are at the front & the girls are in the towns & cities doing their work. We passed through the capital during the second night.

We took some mails on the train at Marseilles & they were given out at one of the stops we had. I got two letters, one from Albert & one from Mr Peace. I suppose we shall get our mails earlier now. Although it is plenty far enough even now, yet we feel a lot nearer home here.

Best Love
Arthur.

I'll write more when I get acclimatized. I've not been warm since I got into France.

Arthur Hollings's letter to his father, 11 March 1916.

with our hearts in our mouths expecting every second to be shot at, but the enemy just ignored us, we didn't get a single shot fired at us.

Our own men had been warned that a patrol was out in front. What an unearthly din we seemed to kick up, as wherever we stepped there were empty bully beef tins, jam tins and Woodbine [cigarette] tins, it was just like the town tin dump, and try as we would, we couldn't help kicking them, and the noise, to our fearful ears, sounded like bedlam. However, we gradually got braver and braver. I picked some sort of flower out of no man's land and sent it home as a souvenir in one of my many letters home.

Back in the trench I was glad to strip off my load of destruction, as round the bay came one of our company with a dixie of tea strapped to his back. How very good that 'petrol' tea tasted.

15/711 Private Arthur Pearson, C Company[32]

Next day the Pals suffered their first casualty in France – and their second accidental death since leaving Britain – when Corporal Frank Bygott of D Company was shot through the main artery in his thigh from which he died soon afterwards.[33]

During the next two days there was an artillery duel, the Pals' trenches were shelled, and snipers were very active, but fortunately there were no further casualties. Then on 3 April, after stand-to at 3.15am, the Pals cleaned the trenches and packed up ready for their relief in the evening by the 1st Battalion, The King's Own Scottish Borderers. By 11.30pm they were back in their billets in Mailly-Maillet, and early the next morning were marched to Bus-les-Artois.

The pals in their billets 'somewhere in France' are joined by a signaller from the Divisional Royal Engineers, and a soldier from the 18th Durham Light Infantry. The Leeds Pal standing on the left is Harold Jackson.

At about this time the battalion started to receive its first issue of steel helmets, and some men were issued with the new soft cap, which could be folded up and put into the haversack.[34]

I think it was at Bus that we were first issued with tin hats. It was strange at first trying to balance a steel bowl on your head, but like other Army ways we got used to them and felt that nothing could harm us now. One night, soon after we got them, I went out in front as a covering party to a wiring job. As I lay outstretched, I took my tin hat off and propped it up, stuck it in the earth in front of me, got behind it and felt as safe as houses.

15/711 Private Arthur V. Pearson, C Company[35]

93rd Light Trench Mortar Battery; this photograph was probably taken at a training school in France. The men were drawn from the infantry battalions in 93 Brigade including the Leeds Pals.

> *6 April 1916 — Got a new trench cop, don't care for it.*
>> *15/1024 Private John Yeadon, B Company*[36]

Now that they were 'out on rest' the work began again. Route marches, Swedish drill, company drill, and some new delights—trench-digging and testing their newly issued anti-gashelmets.

> *Friday 7 April 1916 – Lecture on gas at 9am. Tested gas-helmets by going into room full of poisonous gas. Awful stuff— smelt it immediately.*
>> *15/1024 Private John Yeadon, B Company*[37]

During the month there were some changes among the officers in the battalion. On 7 April Lieutenant Norman Evers and ten soldiers were struck off the strength of the battalion and sent to form the nucleus of 93 Brigade Trench Mortar Battery. Evers was placed in charge of the battery and training was commenced.[38]

On the same day, Major Norman, the battalion second-in-command, appeared before a General Court Martial. A veteran of the South African War and the North-West Frontier, he had joined the battalion from the 9th Buffs, just before the Pals set sail for Egypt.

> *We had a Major Norman, who had been in France, been slightly wounded and then they sent him out to join us, and he says to me, he says 'You know, Dalby, I'm not going back there', he said I don't give a so-and-so if I get cashiered, he said I'm not going back to France I've had enough. [Of] course he was a regular, he'd had trench warfare and he'd had as much as he wanted.*

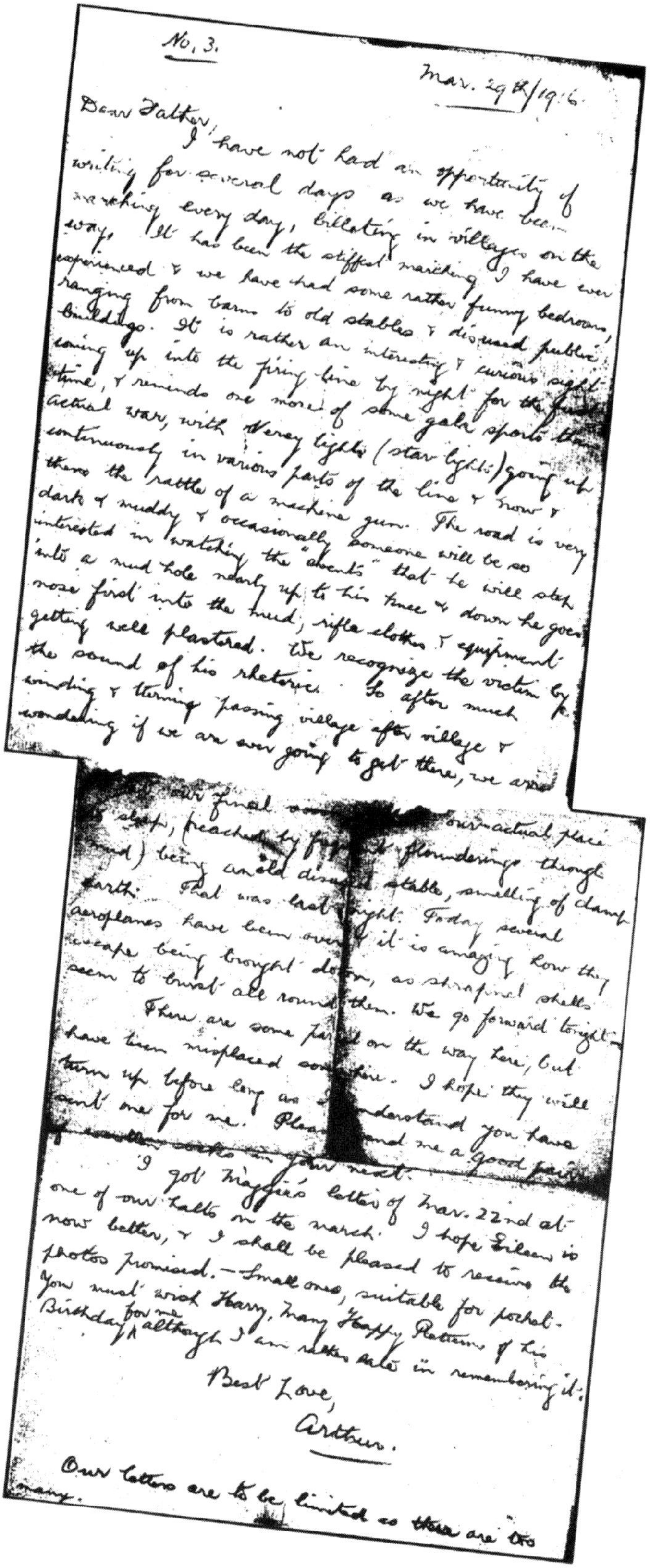

No. 3.

Mar. 29th/1916

Dear Father,

I have not had an opportunity of writing for several days as we have been marching every day, billeting in villages on the way. It has been the stiffest marching I have ever experienced & we have had some rather funny bedrooms, ranging from barns to old stables & disused public buildings. It is rather an interesting & curious sight coming up into the firing line by night for the first time, & reminds one more of some gala sports than actual war, with Verey lights (star lights) going up continuously in various parts of the line & now & then the rattle of a machine gun. The road is very dark & muddy & occasionally someone will be so interested in watching the "events" that he will step into a mud hole nearly up to his knee & down he goes nose first into the mud, rifle clothes & equipment getting well plastered. We recognize the victim by the sound of his rhetoric. So after much winding & turning passing village after village & wondering if we are ever going to get there, we arrive [illegible] our final [illegible] our actual place to sleep, reached by [illegible] floundering through mud) being an old disused stable, smelling of damp earth. That was last night. Today several aeroplanes have been over & it is amazing how they escape being brought down, as shrapnel shells seem to burst all round them. We go forward tonight.

There are some parcels on the way here, but have been misplaced somewhere. I hope they will turn up before long as I understand you have sent one for me. Please send me a good pair of woollen socks in your next.

I got Maggie's letter of Mar. 22nd at one of our halts on the march. I hope Eileen is now better, & I shall be pleased to receive the photos promised. — Small ones, suitable for pocket. You must wish Harry, Many Happy Returns of his Birthday for me, although I am rather late in remembering it.

Best Love,

Arthur.

Our letters are to be limited as there are too many.

Arthur Holling's letter to his father, 29 March 1916, in which he describes his first time in the trenches, and his billets.

He got cashiered, he got drunk and fell into Sweetwater Canal that runs alongside the Suez Canal. He told me himself, he said 'I'm not going back, if I get cashiered I'm not going back.' I don't know what happened to him, he disappeared, that's all I know about him.

15/259 Private Arthur Dalby, D Company[39]

Major Norman was Dismissed the Service on 23 April 1916. His subsequent fate is not known. He received his full medal entitlement at the end of the war, but the available records give no further information.[40]

While they were 'out on rest' the Pals continued their training and were also called upon for such tasks as burying telephone cables, improving trenches, and even helping to unload lorries.

12 April 1916 – Swedish [Drill] at 7am. Called in one blanket – healthy sign? 11am – Parade for trench digging. Raining heavily when we started out and never abated till after we returned 7pm. Absolutely soaked to the skin.

15/1024 Private John Yeadon, B Company[41]

18 April 1916 – 7am. Marched to Colincamps. Laying grass on parados. Pouring with rain. Back about 2.30pm absolutely wet through. Liberal Rum Ration. Watched the mice running along the walls.

15/1003 Private Edward Woffenden, C Company[42]

18 April 1916 – Wet miserable cold day. Warned for Motor Bus digging fatigue but at last moment sent to RE Headquarters Courcelles. A very rotten miserable time unloading motor lorries.

An Easter card sent to Edric Longfield.

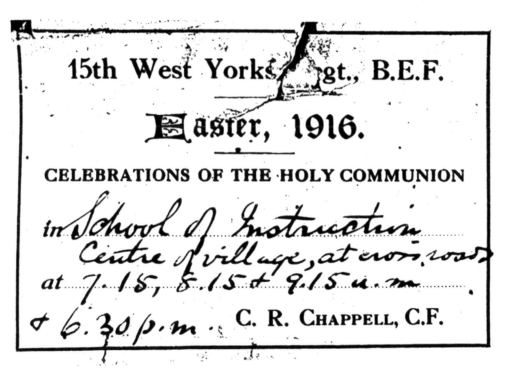

Holy Communion card issued to Wilferd Wainman by the Reverend C. R. Chappell, Battalion Chaplain.

19 April 1916 – RE Camp again … very miserable time moving logs etc. Afternoon free. Digging party at night, trench for cable – returned 11.15pm.

April 1916 (Good Friday) – Wet miserable day. Working parties sent to trenches each day. Returned in sorry plight—everyone very miserable due to discomfort.

April 1916 – Wet miserable day. Inside parade for MG Section. Returning working parties wet to skin & miserable. Worried by rats in night. Fed up generally.

15/231 Private George W. Cosby, B Company[43]

I have been up in the trenches all day right up to the firing line with a working party … We have had the most awful weather lately, and the trenches are in pretty rotten condition. There is about two feet of water in the front line trench and the communication trenches are not much better. Nearly all the trenches have floorboards down, these are, of course in nearly every case, floating, and one can not tell what depth the water is underneath as every twenty yards or so there are sumps, that is to say holes, for the water to drain into under ordinary conditions. Therefore, what generally happens is for one to step on the front portion of a board, the far end of it to rise up and hit you in the face and then to find one's self sitting down in a hole about four feet deep full of water. I saw a fellow go right in up to his chest and this is no exaggeration. His only remark then was 'Good God, bloody lucky I wasn't torpedoed!'

Lieutenant S. Morris Bickersteth Commander No.6 Platoon, B Company[44]

On Easter Sunday, 23 April, Morris Bickersteth and about forty of the Pals attended a Communion Service held by the Chaplain, the Reverend Claude R. Chappell, at the Divisional School of Instruction in Courcelles.

I think I have seldom spent a more queer Easter Sunday. I went at 8.15 to the Holy Communion which Chappell held in the disused schoolroom in our village. He had about forty men and one officer. We could hear the guns going all the time of course, and sometimes the anti-aircraft guns almost drowned what he was saying.

Lieutenant S. Morris Bickersteth Commander No.6 Platoon, B Company[45]

In the late evening Bickersteth took another working party of a hundred men up to the trenches while the rest of the battalion prepared for their second spell in the lines, which was to begin on the next day. While the Pals were getting ready to go into the trenches, they were joined by Lieutenant James K. Wardle and Second-Lieutenant R. M. Davy, who had been left behind to clear up when the battalion sailed for Egypt.[46] Lieutenant David B. Gill, one of the Pals' original officers from 1914, also rejoined from the Reserve Battalion, and Major C. Dewhurst was attached from the Lancashire Hussars as second-in-command to replace Major Norman.

On 24 April the battalion went into the trenches to relieve the Bradford Pals. This time A, B and C Companies went into the front line and D Company was in reserve.[47] By 11.10pm the relief had been completed and once more the Pals posted sentries and prepared themselves for a busy night in the trenches.

24 April 1916 – Paraded 6.30pm and marched to trenches. Very muddy. Got to position in firing line about 10.45pm. On Sentry Post 2017. Lovely weather.

15/1003 Private Edward Woffenden, C Company[48]

Went out on patrol amongst barbed wire at 11.30pm – inspected the wire. Returned to trench at 2am.

15/1024 Private John Yeadon, B Company[49]

The second day was uneventful apart from an exchange of rifle fire during stand-to at dawn, which caught a working party out in no man's land, fortunately without casualties, and smashed a periscope in the trenches.

The weather had changed, bringing days of bright sunshine, which at least improved conditions slightly, although the trenches were still far from dry.

So far we've been most awfully lucky as regards the weather, it has been absolutely perfect ever since we came in. Cloudless skies and delightfully warm sun. It simply makes the whole difference and the trenches are drying up splendidly.

Lieutenant S. Morris Bickersteth Commander No.6 Platoon, B Company[50]

9am Paraded to clear mud and water out of front line trench – terribly hard work – All day job.

15/1024 Private John Yeadon, B Company[51]

On 26 April, their third day in the line, the Pals suffered their first casualty from enemy action when Sergeant Clifford Brooke of No.5 Platoon, B Company, was hit in the bottom lip by a sniper's bullet.[52] Both sides had patrols out during the night of 27/28 April, and in the early hours of the morning a clash in no man's land resulted in more casualties. A party of the Leeds Pals, under the command of Lieutenant Elphinstone, threw bombs at a German patrol, and the Pals also opened fire from their trenches with a machine gun. The enemy retaliated with an artillery bombardment, which killed two men (Privates Power and Beard) and wounded nine, including Lieutenants Wardle and Gill. One of the wounded men, Corporal George Stanley Fairburn-Hart, died of his injuries soon after he had been brought in.[53]

9pm–12pm out in front of our barbed wire acting as a screen [covering party] for wiring party – a most exciting time – spotted by aid of starlights. Heavy bombardment all night.

Bombing Party smash German Party between lines, midnight – 2am – under Lieut Elphinstone. Throw a number of bombs – several casualties amongst enemy party.

15/1024 Private John Yeadon, B Company[54]

Our machine-gun started in front of our position. Germans sent big shrapnel and high-explosive shells. Awful concussion. Beard killed. Part of his skull blown in. Foxton and Capes wounded. Power (A Coy) killed. About 15 wounded. Lt D.B. Gill and Lt Wardle wounded. Sgt Barker wounded.

15/1003 Private Edward Woffenden, C Company[55]

Very hot fire at night. Worst experience so far about 1am. Alan Power killed, very trying time.

15/231 Private George W. Cosby, B Company[56]

The battalion was relieved in the afternoon of 28 April by the 14th York and Lancaster Regiment (Barnsley Pals)[57] and marched by

Private Harold Beard, killed by German artillery fire during the night of 27/28 April 1916.

FATE OF FOUR MISSING YORKSHIRE SOLDIERS.

MEN NOW REPORTED DEAD.

Corporal G. Stanley Fairburn-Hart was the only son of Mr. W. FairburnHart, patent agent, of Leeds and Newlay, and, as announced in "The Yorkshire Evening Post," yesterday, he died from wounds received on Thursday last. Before joining the Leeds "Pals" Battalion he was a textile designer with Messrs. Learoyd Bros. and Co., Huddersfield.

Private Geo. H. (Harty) Hannam, reported wounded and missing in October, 1914, and now officially reported killed, was a Leeds man, well-known in the Beckett Street and Wortley districts. He was 31 years of age, single, and lived with his parents, who reside at 1, Sixth Avenue, New Wortley. Before re-joining the colours as a reservist on the outbreak of war Private Hannam was employed at Messrs. Hickman's, hairdressers, Boar Lane.

(cs.) FAIRBURN-HART   Private HANNAM

FIRST OFFICER OF THE LEEDS "PALS" TO FALL.

LIEUT WARDLE DIES FROM WOUNDS.

The first officer of the Leeds "Pals" Battalion to fall is Lieutenant James Kenneth Wardle, the only son of Mr. James Wardle, of Moor Cottage, Far Headingley. His parents first received word that he had been wounded last Friday, and yesterday they received a message from the War Office that he had died.

The only child of Mr. Wardle, who was formerly a major in the Leeds Engineers, Lieutenant Wardle joined the Leeds "Pals" in the early stages of the war, but only went to the front a fortnight ago, on his

Lieut. J. K. WARDLE.
Photo: Hoskins.

26th birthday. He was educated at Filey and at Bradfield College, and before the war was stationed at Derby for the Liverpool, London, and Globe Insurance Company.

Mr. James Wardle will be remembered as one of the officers who actively assisted in the promotion of the Leeds "Pals" Battalion, and much sympathy will be extended to him in his loss.

sections to Bertrancourt via Colincamps and Courcelles. As they arrived in their billets they heard that Lieutenant Wardle had died of his wounds, the first officer of the battalion to die on active service. He had only been in France for five days, and had arrived on his 26th birthday.

Relieved by Y & L about 3pm. Shelled on leaving. Marched in to Bertrancourt. Large Marquees. 5 day's growth on chin. Lt Wardle died of wounds.

15/1003 Private Edward Woffenden,
C Company[58]

Reached Bertrancourt about 5pm. Very thankful. Everyone arrived worn out and thankful to reach a comparatively safe spot.

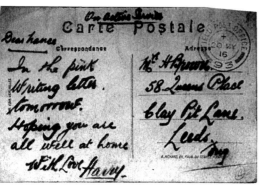

A postcard from Harold Brown to his Nancy.

15/231 Private George W. Cosby, B Company[60]

Their second tour of duty in the trenches, had been a salutary experience for the Pals. Gone forever were the comparatively carefree days of Colsterdale and Suez. The battalion was now at war, and the steady toll of casualties had begun.

Early in May they moved to billets in Bus-les-Artois. Colonel Taylor went home on leave, and there were some further changes of personnel when Second-Lieutenants Sormani, Leek, Oland and Macdougald joined from the 14th (Reserve) Battalion in Britain, and Second-Lieutenant Davy, who had arrived in France with Lieutenant Wardle, transferred to the Bradford Pals. Lieutenant Bickersteth was appointed acting second-in-command of C Company, and a draft of three NCOs and seventeen soldiers joined from the base at Etaples to replace the recent casualties and the men who had been transferred to the Trench Mortar Battery.

Herbert Hargreaves.   *Major-General Sir Wanless O'Gowan, GOC 31st Division.*

It was at about this time that the Battalion Medical Officer, Captain Bathurst, sent a report to Brigade Headquarters to the effect that, owing to the men being employed continuously on working parties, their physical fitness was not as it should be, and suggesting that a day's holiday should be given occasionally. This provoked a response from none other than Major-General Sir Wanless O'Gowan, the Divisional Commander, who lectured the Battalion's officers and NCOs on the need to push forward with work in the trenches, and to organise working parties so that the maximum of work could be done. This was followed by a Divisional Order forbidding troops to buy or receive alcoholic drinks.[60]

13 May 1916 – About 90 men in hospital at this time generally done up. MO (Dr) reports Batn not fit to go into trenches at present.

15/231 Private George W. Cosby, B Company[61]

On 14 May the Pals moved to Courcelles and the next day to Bus-les-Artois. This seemingly random and endless series of movements, in rapid succession, from one billet to another while the Pals were out of the trenches was actually in accordance with another Divisional Order, which set out how each battalion and brigade was to be rotated, moving from Brigade Reserve to Divisional Reserve and into Corps Reserve before returning to the trenches for a five-day stint.[62] The battalion remained in Corps Reserve at Bus-les-Artois awaiting the order to go into the trenches once more.

During the night of 15/16 May the men were roused and ordered to stand-to at 1.45am, because the neighbouring 48th Division was under heavy bombardment and an enemy attack seemed likely. But by 2.35am the situation was under control and the Pals were stood down.

At 9.40am on 19 May, the battalion paraded for the trenches. It was a hot day, which made the march along the communication trenches all the harder. A and D Companies went into the firing line on the left and right respectively, with A Company in Monk Trench and D Company in the Catacombs. B Company went into the support trenches while C Company was left in reserve at Basin Wood. They arrived in the trenches once more at about 1pm, to relieve the Bradford Pals.[63]

After marching 7 miles we take our place, relieving 16th W Y. The Germans proceed [to] shell our communication trenches & the first line. We suffer no damage however. A hot day passes with rifle fire and a few rifle grenades. At night the rifle fire becomes more intense, but no damage is done whatever. The following day, Fritz puts out of action our periscope. Then Lieutenant Oland takes it into his head to strafe with rifle grenades, but fails utterly. Of course we get them returned. The Bosche have our range to perfection, with the result that 1 r & f [rank-and-file] killed [Private Walter Brown, D Company] & 2 wounded. Also Arthur Thomas slightly wounded. They send over about 10 and then thank God they stop. Then starts the rifle fire again. Whizz-bangs are unchanged. No damage.

15/1082 Private Herbert Hargreaves, A Company[64]

Stand-to on 20 May was from 2.30am till 4am, and soon the sun rose on another scorching day. The men of B and C Companies were hard at work on fatigues for most of the day, while the men in the front line rested to prepare themselves for a busy night.

In the early evening the fatigue parties carried barbed wire and stakes up to the front line. That night a wiring party from A Company went out into no man's land accompanied, as usual, by a covering party. While they were out of the trench, they were attacked by a German patrol, and in the ensuing fight Privates J. W. Ackroyd and William Wilkinson were wounded. When the wiring party got back to their trench it was discovered that three men, Privates Hargreaves, Hewson and Rawnsley, all from No.4 Platoon, A Company, were missing. Search parties were immediately sent out, but failed to find them.

Meanwhile, probably as a result of the clash in no man's land, the German artillery had opened up and sent a few 'whizz-bangs' over to the British lines. One of them caught Colonel Taylor in Legend Trench, where he was inspecting the B Company Headquarters dugout, and wounded him in the leg. He was immediately taken to the Regimental Aid Post and Major Dewhurst took over command.

On the following day the hot weather continued. Down at Euston Dump soldiers of C Company were busy bringing up screw pickets and coils of barbed wire, as well as water rations for the men in the front lines.

Went to Euston dump twice carrying pickets and barbed wire coils. Water fatigue. Two of us carried 6 cans of water in two journeys. Terribly hot. Sweat poured out of system.

15/1003 Private Edward Woffenden, C Company[65]

The fatigues continued until 11pm, and during the night an officers' patrol went out into no man's land to look for any sign of the missing men. They found Frank Hewson's rifle and some of his equipment, and one of the officers picked up a German hand grenade.

Monday 22 May was cooler. It rained a little towards the end of the afternoon, and in the evening work on the barbed wire was resumed. Men from Nos.7 and 8 Platoons went out with a covering party and these too were attacked by a German patrol, whose members threw bombs, which killed Corporal Herbert Rhodes and Lance-Corporal Harry Watson, and fatally wounded Privates Ernest Walker and John Sheard. The Germans then tried to get into the Pals' trenches, but were driven off by Lieutenant Valentine Oland, who gathered together a bombing party, rallied the wiring party and counter-attacked, driving the Germans into the sights of one of the battalion's Lewis guns.

22 May 1916 – Set off for wiring at 7.30pm. Got coils of wire and took equipment off. Took bandolier, gas helmet and rifle only. Everything quiet. No firing from enemy as all first part got out. Heard a few bombs burst on A Coy's section, then suddenly was plastered[?] out in bottom of trench … gradually got covered with dirt and then whole sandbags. Heard chap behind me yell out that his arm was off. [66] He crawled over top of us and left trenches. Things quietened down in about 40 minutes so worked myself loose and got up. Got hold of rifle with a fixed bayonet and manned parapet ready for attack. Opened rapid and machine-gun fire.

15/1253 Private Bernard Gill, B Company[67]

At about 10.30pm, shortly after the fight in no man's land, the German artillery opened up again and shrapnel rained down on the men who were trying to rescue the wounded members of the wiring party.

22 May 1916 – A terrible night. Front trenches shelled for over hour. Bat. suffers greatest loss so far – about 50 casualties. Bombardment took place about 10.30. An unforgettable experience.

15/231 Private George W. Cosby, B Company[68]

Day broke, and with it came the full realisation of what had happened. This was the Leeds Pals' first close encounter with the enemy, and although they had responded with speed and courage, they had lost some fifteen men killed, and thirty-four wounded, with another three missing.[69] Among the dead was Sergeant Kerton, whose body could be seen hanging on the barbed wire as day broke. His brother had to be physically restrained from going out to bring him in until it was safe to do so. Also killed was Private Jogendra Sen of D Company, 'the best-educated man in the battalion'.

Lieutenant Roy B. H. Rayner was severely wounded by shrapnel and Gezaincourt, and Second-Lieutenant Elphinstone was shell shocked as a result of the bombardment.[70]

Lieutenant Valentine Oland, who had led the bombing party, which drove the Germans away, was awarded the Military Cross, and Lance-Corporal Joe Clark, although recommended for a Distinguished Conduct Medal, was awarded the Military Medal.

These were the battalion's first gallantry awards.[71]

Although the Pals had suffered many casualties, some Germans had undoubtedly been killed; three bodies and the severed leg from a fourth had been found, and two wounded prisoners had been brought in but had later died. At about 2.00pm on 23 May a German who had been hiding in a shell hole in no man's land gave himself up to A Company, and was sent off to Brigade Head-quarters to be interrogated. He was 21 years old and had arrived in the trenches for the first time on the previous night, just before the patrol action. It turned out that he had only recently completed his training, having been conscripted after rejection on medical grounds on a previous application. He also stated that the troops of his unit, the 121st Reserve Infantry Regiment from Wurttemburg, were well-fed, liked their officers and NCOs, and would win the war. All the men who saw him agreed that he was a fine specimen, and were quite glad that the Leeds Pals had taken a prisoner. Another thing the prisoner was able to confirm was that Privates Hargreaves, Hewson and Rawnsley, who had gone missing on 20 May, had been taken prisoner.[72]

On 24 May 93 Brigade was relieved by 92 Brigade, and the 12th Battalion, The East Yorkshire Regiment took over the trenches held by the Leeds Pals. While the companies that had been in the front lines were waiting to be relieved, some of the men of C Company, who had been in reserve at Basin Wood, were detailed to carry the bodies of their fallen comrades and of the enemy dead to the cemetery.

May 1916 – All the dead brought to Basin Wood. 9 of ours and three Germans. Making temporary stretchers to carry them to Cemetery near Sugar Refinery ...

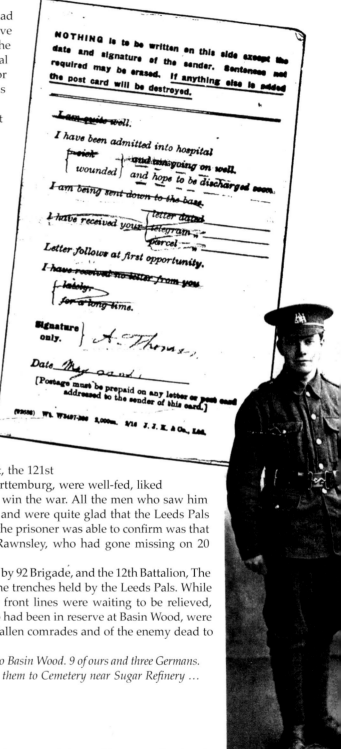

Arthur Thomas and the card he sent to his family.

LEEDS "PAL'S" SAD DEATH.

YOUNG WIFE PREPARING FOR HIS HOMECOMING.

The death in action of Sergt. S. Kerton, of the Leeds "Pals" battalion, is attended by very sad circumstances.

SERGT. AND MRS. KERTON.

Prior to the war Sergt. Kerton was in business as a tailor on his own account in Woodhouse Lane, Leeds, but when the "Pals" battalion was formed, in September, 1914, he disposed of his business and joined their ranks.

Whilst in training at Colsterdale he obtained a week's leave at the beginning of May last year, and was married at St. Mark's Church, Woodhouse. He subsequently returned to his regiment, and up to a month ago his wife had resided with her father-in-law, Mr. George Henry Kerton (a cutter at Messrs. John Barran ad Sons, Ltd., Chorley Lane), at Hall Grove, Hyde Park.

During the last few weeks, however, Sergt. Kerton's wife had been busily preparing a home for her husband, who was expecting to come to Leeds on a short furlough. She had taken a house at 6, Glossop Mount, Delph Lane, Woodhouse and had got it practically finished when she received news that her husband had fallen in action.

Sergt. Kerton, who was 33 years of age, was formerly in the Leeds Rifles, and on joining the "Pals" he was given the rank of Sergeant. A younger brother, also in the Leeds "Pals" has been wounded, but not very seriously.

OST, FRIDAY, JUNE 2.

LEEDS "PALS" LOSE AN INDIAN COMRADE.

PRIVATE SEN KILLED IN ACTION.

Among the casualties in the Leeds "Pals" Battalion one is reported to-day which has a singular interest. A young Indian named J. N. Sen, a native of Chandenagore, Bengal, came to the Leeds University in October, 1910, to study, and after taking an engineering course for three years, graduated as bachelor of science. Soon afterwards he secured a position under the manager of the Leeds Corporation Electric Lighting Station in Whitehall Road, and ultimately was placed on the staff as an assistant engineer. While there he gave much promise of a successful career, and being of a cheerful disposition, was much liked by everybody.

When the "Pals" Battalion was formed in September, 1914, Private Sen, who was then only 27 years of age, became one of its first members. He has been killed.

Several months ago when the "Pals" paraded the City Private Sen came in for much notice because of his evident connection with the East. He was a single man, and his mother resides in India. Prior to joining the colours he lodged in Grosvenor Place, Blackman Lane.

Private SEN.   **Private E. HOPKIN.**

Another of the Leeds "Pals" to lose his life in the recent fighting was Private Edward Hopkin, son of Mr. and Mrs. Hopkin, of 23, Roundhay View, Leeds. He was wounded on May 23rd, and he died on the 30th, his right arm having in the meantime been amputated. Twenty-two years of age, he joined the battalion in September, 1914, prior to which he was engaged as a traveller with Messrs. J. A. France and Son, of Newcastle. He was a well-known member of Trinity Presbyterian Church in Harehills Avenue, being treasurer of the Sunday School and a member of the choir. His two brothers are also in the Army, both being sergeants in the Royal Engineers.

Private R. H. Slater, of the Manchester Regiment, who has been killed in action, was the son of Mr. Ronald Slater, for many years resident in Headingley.

Sgt Kirton [sic] and Pte Harrison 'D' Coy brought in dead. Also 2 German dead. Sgt Newborne died of wounds in hospital making 12 dead.

May 1916 – Went to Euston Dump taking dead men's rifles and equipment. Battalion relieved by E. Yorks. Our Coy about 4pm. Had to stay behind to help carry dead to cemetery. Set off about 7pm. 4 to a stretcher. Full equipment and very treacherous under foot. Machine-gun trained on us between Excema [sic] Trench and roadway, so got into trench. Arrived at cemetery about 9.15pm. Mr Chappell and Mr Martin[73] read burial service for Pte Harrison and Sgt Kirton. Got in motor lorry from Courcelles to Bertrancourt. Tea and buns at YMCA – thanks to Chaplains. Arrived at Bus (Coy HQ) at 12pm. Dead beat.

> *15/1003 Private Edward Woffenden,*
> *C Company*[74]

On 24 May, Lieutenant Rayner died of his wounds, and with the Colonel and Major Baker away from the battalion recovering from wounds, and Gibson on leave, more replacements and some reshuffling of the officers were necessary.

I've changed my duties again today, I am now temporarily commanding B Company. Major Baker as I think I told you in my last letter was slightly wounded, about three weeks ago, in the head, he is now in England. I heard from him today and he tells me that his head is in some way affected and he may have to have a small operation. Anyway he's struck off the strength of the Battalion. Gibson therefore is left in command of B [Company] but he has gone on leave today. Of the two other subalterns, one I am sorry to say died of his wounds two days ago, which he received last time he was in the trenches, and the other has gone home with what they call 'Shell shock'. His nerves having absolutely gone, and I do not think we shall see him again, so there was no-one left who knew the Company well. Five new subalterns arrived from the Reserve Battalion at the beginning of last week and three of them have been posted to B Company, but I suppose it was thought that they were all too new to take command so here I am.

> *Lieutenant S. Morris Bickersteth, B Company*[75]

Out of the line once more the Pals continued with their work, mainly digging trenches and burying telephone cables, although they were given an unaccustomed day off on Sunday 28 May. On 3 June the Pals were ordered to prepare themselves for another spell in the trenches. During the afternoon a German shell landed in Wicker Trench killing Captain de Pledge, the Adjutant, and wounding Major Dewhurst, who was temporarily in command. Lieutenant Pope-Smith was also slightly injured. The relief took place the next afternoon when the battalion took over the centre of the divisional sector with A, B and C Companies in the trenches and D Company in reserve. They were joined on 5 June by two

Joe Clark. He received this letter from the Corps Commander congratulating him on the award of his Military Medal. (Author's collection)

Herbert Hargreave. His diary for 20 May recording his capture, and the identity disc he was wearing at the time. He sent the card to his family from Giessen in 1916. He is on the extreme left of the back row in the group photograph. 'The second the fire stops, out rush 15 or so Germans. Ye Gods, before we know where we are, we are prisoners in the German lines. My thoughts are indescribable. We three fellows look at each other in dismay. We are taken to a fine dugout and questioned by an officer and also searched …'

In Loving Memory

of

LIEUT. ROY B. H. RAYNER,

15th Batt. West Yorkshire Regiment,

Died of Wounds, in France,

May 24th, 1916,

Aged 23 Years.

"Until the day break and
the shadows pass away."

Mr. & Mrs. J. Hodgson Rayner

and Family

return sincere thanks for all

the sympathy and kindness

shewn to them in their great

sorrow.

Oakroyd,
Horsforth.

June, 1916.

Roy Rayner, who died of wounds on 24 May 1916, and the memorial card sent out by his family.

MORE CASUALTIES AMONG THE LEEDS "PALS."

FOUR CITY HEROES WHO HAVE FALLEN IN ACTION.

Further casualties among the Leeds "Pals" are reported to-day.

Corporal Herbert Wilson, who joined the "Pals" in September, 1914, has been killed in action. Thirty-five years of age, the deceased was a son of Mrs. M. J. Wilson, late of Fenton Street, and before enlisting he was employed by Messrs. Wilson Bros., jewellers, Market Street.

CORPL. H. WILSON.   PTE. J. HAYHURST.

Private J. Hayhurst, another member of the "Pals" and late of Pearce's, jewellers, Leeds, has been killed in action. He was 21 years of age, and lived with his parents at The Drive, Roundhay, Leeds.

PTE. J. L. SHEARD.   PTE. H. WILLMAN.

Private John Linley Sheard, whose parents live at 226, Cross Flatts Grove, Beeston, and who was shot in the spine on Wednesday night last, and died from his wounds on Friday, was also a member of the Leeds "Pals" Battalion. Twenty-four years of age, he was before the war a clerk employed by Messrs. Leech Goodall and Co., engineers, Hunslet. He was educated at the Leeds Modern School.

Lance-Corporal H. Watson, who joined the "Pals" when the battalion was formed, has also fallen. He was 25 years of age, and the eldest son of the late Mr. and Mrs. Watson, of 33, Kingston Road. Before joining up he was employed as a cutter by Messrs. David Little and Co.

Private H. Willman, of the K.O.Y.L.I., was wounded whilst attending to a ————

ANOTHER OF THE LEEDS PALS' LOSSES.

The tale of casualties among the Leeds Pals is not yet complete. Another of

those killed in action was Pte. Ernest Walker, the only son of Mr. and Mrs. Walker, of 13, Marshall Street, Crossgates. He was killed by a shell on the evening of May 22, while out with a working party from the front line trenches.

Twenty-three years of age, he was formerly a clerk at the Central Agency (Ltd), North Street, Leeds. His platoon officer was Lt. Roy Rayner, who died from wounds.

PTE. E. WALKER

Pte. C. E. Gaunt, of 84, Louis Street, Leeds, another member of the same battalion, is in hospital suffering from shrapnel wounds in the thigh and foot. A comrade standing beside him was killed by the same shell. Pte. Gaunt has two brothers with the Army and another in the Naval Air Service.

Ernest Walker's grave at the Sucrerie Military Cemetery, Colincamps.

MORE CASUALTIES AMONG THE LEEDS "PALS."

COMMANDER AND OTHER OFFICERS FALL.

Great regret will be felt in Leeds to-day over the announcement which the "Yorkshire Evening Post" has to make relating to more casualties in the Leeds "Pals" Battalion. On Saturday, in a bombardment, Major Dewhirst, who was temporarily appointed commander of the battalion, was killed, along with the popular young adjutant, Captain Depledge. Another officer—Lieutenant Pope Smith—was wounded.

Casualties in the "Pals" Battalion have come with painful frequency since it went into action. Lieutenants Wardle, Hummel, and Raynor were killed some weeks ago, and the Commanding Officer (Lieutenant-Colonel Stuart Taylor) was wounded in the leg. Major Dewhirst, who is stated to be from one of the Lancashire Regiments, was appointed to succeed Colonel Taylor in the command less than a month ago.

News of the death of Captain Depledge was received this morning at his home, Rosehurst, Headingley, in a letter sent by the Brigadier-Major, who wrote that he "was awfully fond of the boy" and keenly regretted his loss. It was only last week that Captain Depledge was home on seven days' leave. He returned to France on Friday, and a postcard has been received from him written on Saturday morning. The postcard stated that they were "going forward sooner than they expected." He was killed by a shell the same night.

Photo:: Bacon.

Captain Depledge was only 22 years of age, and was the only son of Mr. W. T. Depledge, timber merchant, of Headingley. Educated at Uppingham, he went into his father's business, and, whilst living at Harrogate, was a prominent member of the Harrogate Old Boys' Football Club. He gained some distinction as a three-quarter back, and played for Yorkshire against Cumberland on January 13, 1913. He joined the Leeds "Pals" Battalion as a private on its formation, and was given his commission a month later. He was aide-de-camp to Colonel Stead on the "Pals'" Christmas march through Leeds, and in May, 1915, was made adjutant of the battalion, with the rank of captain.

Lieut. Pope Smith, who is wounded, was also a private in the "Pals" Battalion at Colsterdale, and rose gradually in rank until he obtained his commission in January, 1915.

There have been three commanding officers of the Leeds "Pals" Battalion — Lieut.-Colonel J. W. Stead, Lieut.-Colonel Stuart Taylor (wounded), and Major Dewhirst (killed).

LT. POPE SMITH
—Photo. Bacon.

Lance-Corporal Fred Naylor, wounded on 9 June 1916.

Harry Tomalin wounded on 10 June 1916. He was commissioned in August 1917 and transferred to the King's Own Yorkshire Light Infantry. (Dr A. Reeves)

Captain Edward K. M. de Pledge, the Battalion Adjutant, killed by a shell on 3 June 1916.

officers with confusingly similar names. Captain Stanley T. A. Neil, who had been away from the battalion since March, acting as an instructor at the Divisional School, took over as Adjutant, and Major Redmond B. Neill from the 1st Battalion, The Royal Irish Fusiliers, took command until Taylor's return. Neill, a 36-year-old New Zealander, had served in the Boer War and in India.

Although Divisional Orders stipulated that battalions in the trenches would be relieved every five days, on this occasion the Leeds Pals were in the line for eight. During this time the condition of the trenches rapidly deteriorated, as did the men's morale. Enemy action, some of it in retaliation for a 'strafe' on the German lines by 93rd Trench Mortar Battery, increased.

3 June 1916 — Very drab outlook at this period. Nothing to look forward to except a possible 'Blighty'. Off to trenches tomorrow again.

6 June 1916 – … Rained heavily off and on, trenches in unsatisfactory condition. What a misery this life is in trenches!

7 June 1916 – Rifle grenades pour into our sector 1st line. Very trying. Raining off and on. Condition most miserable. Raining most of the night. Sheer misery!

8 June 1916 – Still in trenches. Weather wet and miserable.

15/231 Private George W. Cosby, B Company[76]

9 June 1916 – Wet. Day sentry until 12 Noon. Lovely afternoon. Our trench mortars and Stokes Gun play havoc with their front line. Heavy shelling and rifle grenades in return. Pte J. Garbutt killed, Cpls H. Armitage, F. Naylor and J. Mason wounded at Euston Dump whilst on rations. Fine night.

176

June 14th/1916.
Wednesday

Dear Father,

We have just come back into billets after an eight days spell in the trenches, and the wettest time I have ever known, for we have not had a single fine day. Most of the trenches were up to the knees in liquid clay. I should never have thought that I could have stood being wet through for eight days without catching a severe cold; but I have stood it & feel no worse for it. In fact, I feel as fit as ever I was.

I heard about the Invincible going down, but was hoping against hope that Harry would somehow be amongst the saved. Have they heard from the Admiralty.

Thank Maggie for the chocolates. They were exquisite. The cake etc. were fine. You need not send tobacco, as I smoke my pipe very little. I have had a few letters lately. One from Mr Place & one from Albert's cousin.

How is Alice managing now that Harry has joined up? We have just heard that we have got a D.C.M. & Military Cross in the Battalion. I will let you know definitely later.

I often wonder how you are all going on at home. One of the chaps in our section has just been home on leave & he had to answer thousands of questions when he came back. It seems a long time since I left England.

Albert has told me in his letter that Harry Dixon has been drafted to the 13th West Yorks. Let me know particulars & his address when you can.

Of course I am all ears, listening for news of the wedding.

Before I went into the trenches I had resolved to write asking you not to send any more parcels as they cost so much; but during the time I was in the trenches I received your parcel & was glad I had not so written, as it was a real treat. We had the mail bags to carry from the limber wagons to the various Coy. H.dqrts & it's no easy job with the trenches being so wet & soft; but when there is one included for me, well! it's a pleasure.

I expect you have had a very busy time at home lately with all the various events.

I heard from Albert that Father had given him a beating at billiards. I think I shall be "well amongst the emptys" at billiards when I come back.

We are back in billets again & are on with our regular work.

Best Love to all,
Arthur.

Tell Alice I will write as soon as I can. I should like to write a note to Uncle Harry & Aunt Lizzie, but I did not want to be too previous until they read official news about the Invincible.

Arthur Holling's letter to his father after an eight-day stint in the trenches.

10 June 1916 – Cold. Feet very much so. Our front line is heavily shelled. All not on duty returned to supports. Wet and fine in turn. On 'Listening patrol' at night. In disused trench between two lines. Very heavy bombardment for an hour by both sides. Narrow escapes. Crawled back after 'Strafe' and manned the parapet. Drewry and Pickup killed. Frieder, Mick Wood, Nichol, Tomalin and Tinsdale wounded.

11 June 1916 – Cold. On day post from 12 noon to 'Stand to'. Narrow shave with piece of shrapnel. On night post in next bay. Our 'Listening patrol' bombed by Germans. L/Cpl Wharton and J. Calvert wounded. Manned parapet expecting bombing attack. Nothing doing.

15/1003 Private Edward Woffenden, C Company[77]

12 June 1916— (Whit Monday) Left trenches – relieved by East Yorks Regt. Arrived Bus Billets at 6pm thoroughly wearied out.

15/231 Private George W. Cosby, B Company[78]

NOTES

1. MS copy of the diary of 15/231 Private George William Cosby, 7 June 1916.
2. After the initial battles of 1914, from about mid-September there was a series of attempts by both sides, to outflank the opposing force's lines. As this progressed northwards it became known as the 'Race to the Sea', and ended with the creation of a static line of trenches that reached from the Belgian coast to the Swiss border.
3. Recorded interview with Morris Fleming by Peter Hawkins of BBC Radio Leeds, circa 1986.
4. TS copy of a letter from Lieutenant S. Morris Bickersteth to his family, 9 March 1916, Bickersteth Family War Diary.
5. Diary of 15/1951 Private John Jackson Shaw, 1–8 March 1916.
6. Pearson, Arthur Valentine, *A Leeds Pal Looks Back*, unpublished manuscript in Leeds Reference Library, circa 1961.
7. Bickersteth, op.cit, 9 March 1916
8. Pearson, op.cit.
9. Bickersteth, op.cit, 10 March 1916.
10. Author's correspondence with Dorothy Crabtree (neé Wild), Walter Wild's daughter, April 1988.
11. Battalion War Diary, 10 March 1916, Public Record Office, London: W095/2361.
12. Bickersteth, op.cit, 11 March 1916.
13. Diary of 1571003 Private Edward Woffenden, 10 March 1916, in the possession of Bob Reed, York.
14. Shaw, op.cit, 10 March 1916.
15. Diary of 15/158 Private Charles Harold Bell, 11 March 1916.
16. Woffenden, op.cit., 11 March 1916.
17. Author's recorded interview with Clifford Hollingworth, May 1988.
18. Cosby, op.cit, 11 March 1916.
19. Woffenden, op.cit, 14 March 1916.
20. A cafe or bar, often in a private house, selling food and drink to British soldiers.
21. Diary of 15/1024 Private John Yeadon, 15 March 1916.
22. Cosby, op.cit, 16 March 1916.
23. Author's recorded interview with Arthur Dalby and Clifford Hollingworth, May 1988.
24. Pearson, op.cit
25. The 16th (Service) Battalion, (1st Bradford) The Prince of Wales's Own (West Yorkshire Regiment).
26. Yeadon, op.cit, 25–28 March 1916.

27. Woffenden, E., op.cit, 28 March 1916.
28. Battalion War Diary, op.cit, 29 March 1916.
29. The 8th Royal Irish Fusiliers was a Service battalion raised in Belfast from the Ulster Volunteer Force in September 1914. See James, Brigadier E.A., OBE, TD, *British Regiments 1914–1918*, Samson Books, London, 1978.
30. Bickersteth, op.cit, 30 March 1916.
31. Pearson, op.cit
32. Ibid.
33. *Soldiers Died in the Great War 1914–1919*, Part 19, *The Prince of Wales's Own (West Yorkshire Regiment)*, HMSO, London, 1921. Woffenden, op.cit, 30 March 1916.
34. 31st Division Adjutant General and Quartermaster-General's War Diary, Public Record Office, London: W095/2344.
35. Pearson, op.cit
36. Yeadon, op.cit, 6 April 1916. The new trench cap was approved by the Army Clothing Department on 14 March 1916; see ACD files in the National Army Museum, London.
37. Yeadon, op.cit, 7 April 1916.
38. Battalion War Diary, op.cit, 7 April 1916.
39. Author's recorded interview with Arthur Dalby and Clifford Hollingworth, May 1988. Although Arthur Dalby recalled that Major Norman had told him he had been in France, this seems unlikely. The entry in the Medal Roll Index at the Public Record Office, London, indicates that Major Norman entered a theatre of war for the first time on 21 December 1915, when he arrived in Egypt
40. The entry in George W. Cosby's diary op.cit. for 29 January 1916 mentions 'Major Norman deposed for drunkedness'. The 31st Division Adjutant-General's and Quartermaster-General's War Diary op.cit. 7 April 1916, records 'Gen Court Martial on Major Norman "The Buffs"'. *The London Gazette*, 24 May 1916, records 'E. Kent R. – Major E. C. Norman is dismissed the service by sentence of a General Court Martial. 23rd April 1916'.
41. Yeadon, op.cit, 12 April 1916.
42. Woffenden, op.cit, 18 April 1916.
43. Cosby, op.cit, 18–22 April 1916
44. Bickersteth, op.cit, 21 April 1916.
45. Bickersteth, op.cit, 26 April 1916.
46 Battalion War Diary, op.cit., 6 December 1915.
47. Ibid, 25 April 1916. Although the Battalion War Diary records that the Leeds Pals went into the trenches on 25 April, the private diaries of Gill, Woffenden, Cosby, and Yeadon all give the date as 24 April, as does Bickersteth in his letter home on 26 April. The date that the Pals were relieved is also apparently incorrect in the Battalion War Diary.
48. Woffenden, op.cit., 24 April 1916.
49. Yeadon, op.cit, 24 April 1916. In a letter to the author in June 1988, Miss Sheila Yeadon recounted one of her grandfather's anecdotes: 'One of the stories he used to tell was that he and colleagues used to crawl at night through the wire into no man's land and lob grenades into the enemy trenches. One night because of his deafness, he didn't hear the command to return, and was left on his own in no man's land, having to find his way back at dawn.' John Yeadon's deafness got progressively worse, and in June 1916, after a spell in hospital, he was declared unfit for active service and transferred to the Royal Army Medical Corps where he was given a job as a clerk in a military hospital.
50. Bickersteth, op.cit, 26 April 1916.
51. Yeadon, op.cit, 26 April 1916.
52. Woffenden, op.cit, 26 April 1916. Sergeant Clifford Brooke evidently recovered from his wound and rejoined the battalion. He was killed in action on 1 July 1916.

53. Battalion War Diary, op.cit, 27/28 April 1916.
54. Yeadon, op.cit, 27/28 April 1916.
55. Woffenden, op.cit, 27/28 April 1916.
56. Cosby, op.cit, 27/28 April 1916.
57. Battalion War Diary, op.cit The date recorded in the War Diary for the Pals leaving the trenches on this occasion is inaccurate. See also Note 47 above.
58. Woffenden, op.cit, 28 April 1916.
59. Cosby, op.cit, 28 April 1916.
60. Battalion War Diary, op.cit, 18 May 1916.
61. Cosby, op.cit, 13 May 1916.
62. 31st Divisional Order No. 16,14 May 1916, 31st Division General Staff War Diary, Public Record Office, London: W095/2341.
63. Battalion War Diary, op.cit, 18 May 1916.
64. Diary of 15/1082 Private Herbert Hargreaves, 19 May 1916.
65. Woffenden, op.cit, 21 May 1916
66. This is possibly 15/475 Private Edward Hopkin, who was reported to have died of wounds on 29 May after his arm was amputated. *Yorkshire Evening Post*, 2 June 1916.
67. Diary of 15/1253 Private Bernard Gill, 22 May 1916.
68. Cosby, op.cit, 22 May 1916.
69. Battalion War Diary, op.cit, 22 May 1916.
70. Ibid.
71. Lieutenant Valentine Oland received the ribbon of the Military Cross from the Brigade Commander on 29 June 1916 (Woffenden, op.cit). He was killed on 1 July 1916 so he probably never received the actual award (*Yorkshire Evening Post*, 10 July 1916). Arthur Hollings wrote in a letter to his father on 14 June 1916, 'We have just heard that we have got a DCM and Military Cross in the Battalion, I will let you know definitely later.' Joe Clark was awarded the Military Medal, now in the author's collection (see illustration). The award appeared in the *London Gazette* 10 August 1916. Clark was wounded at Euston Dump on 26 June 1916, so missed both Oland's investiture and the 1 July attack (Woffenden, op.cit).
72. Battalion War Diary, op.cit, 23 May 1916.
73. Hargreaves, op.cit, 20–31 May 1916.
74. The Reverend Claude Chappell was the Church of England Chaplain, and Mr Martin the Wesleyan Minister. Both joined the battalion at Colsterdale. Bickersteth, op.cit, 13 December 1914 and 14 January 1915.
75. Woffenden, op.cit, 23/24 May 1916.
76. Bickersteth, op.cit, 23 May 1916.
77. Cosby, op.cit, 3–8 June 1916.
78. Woffenden, op.cit, 9–11 June 1916.
79. Cosby, op.cit, 12 June 1916.

Chapter Five

'God Help Us If We Lose'

*… Brigadier came round, Brigadier Ingles. Said 'You've done a good job chaps,
you've done a very good job!', and one fellow said, 'We've hell as like, we've lost!'…
He said, 'Don't talk like that, lost, you mustn't speak like that man!' 'Have we won then? Cos if
we've won, God help us if we lose!'*
15/471 Private Clifford Hollingworth, D Company[1]

1 JULY 1916

Early in June, while the Pals were in the trenches, the battalion commanders had received notification from Brigade Headquarters that the long-awaited 'Big Push' was imminent. They were to provide working parties to dig assembly trenches and dugouts for the attacking troops, and for the massive amounts of ammunition and supplies they would need.

Lietenant-General Sir Aylmer Hunter-Western, commander of VII Corps (centre holding map), with his staff. (Imperial War Museum)

An aerial view of the 93 Brigade sector taken early on the morning of 1 July 1916 by a reconnaissance aeroplane of the Royal Flying Corps. (Imperial War Museum)

View from the Pals' trenches, 12 April 1916. (Imperial War Museum)

When the Pals returned to their billets on 12 June, they had only one day to get themselves cleaned up before starting work. In order to give them time to complete their tasks, the clock was advanced by one hour on 14 June, giving the men an extra hour of daylight.

14 June 1916 – Parade to be detailed for digging. YMCA. Parade 5.40pm. Reported at Colincamps and followed wagon to Euston Dump. Carried logs to Flag Avenue. Extra journey from Charing Cross to Flag with corrugated iron. Time put on 1 hour. Arrived back 3.30am.

15/1003 Private Edward Woffenden, C Company[2]

15 June 1916 Paraded at 6am for party to trenches. Helping KOYLIs at sapping work emptying sandbags etc. Returned to Bus at 5.30pm. Tired out very exhausting day.

15/231 Private George W. Cosby, B Company[3]

For weeks at night we'd working parties digging this stepping-off trench to go over the top to no man's land, and Jerry had never put a single shell across at all, and we thought he hadn't noticed it, but by God when the Zero was called they knew exactly where it was.

15/1110 Private Cyril Charles Cryer, Battalion Runner[4]

On 19 June orders were issued that most of 93 Brigade would move to Gezaincourt to receive training for the forthcoming battle, but the Leeds Pals and three companies of the 18th Durham Light Infantry had already received their briefing just behind the lines.[5]

When orders came through for the advance, we had a miniature of the German trenches and points which we were to take in our particular sector. The company officers assembled the NCOs and explained to them from maps the whole position and our objective, and the NCOs passed this information on to every man, so that no casualties should interrupt the progress of the battalion. We had to reach the fourth line of the German trenches and there consolidate, which meant reversing the trench so that the high side becomes the low side.

15/1713 Corporal James Thomson, B Company[6]

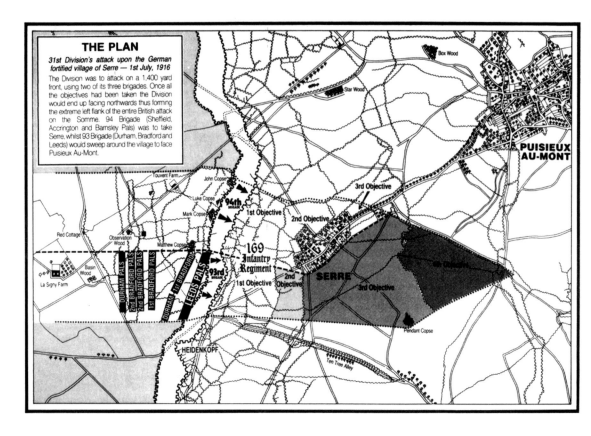

16 June 1916 – Got up at 8am. Parade 9.45am. Demonstration of Great Push. YMCA. Sleep.

15/1003 Private Edward Woffenden, C Company[7]

We knew a bit about it before, because they took us out into the country behind the lines and they had it all threaded out… They had red lines, blue lines, tapes and they drew a map by tapes and pegs of our objective. Now when you get to that red line, wait until the next one. When you get to the blue line wait. This was alright in theory by the headquarters, but when you come to do anything in practice, theory goes out of the window.

15/471 Private Clifford Hollingworth, D Company[8]

Throughout the week work continued, and patrols were sent out to inspect the German wire. On 24 June the artillery began a systematic bombardment of the German trenches and barbed wire, and began searching for the German artillery emplacements. The day of the attack was drawing ever nearer, and on the evening of 27 June the Leeds men held a party in Bus-les-Artois

Our lost evening in the village was like a gala night at Roundhay Park. There was the band on the green; there was the hearty laughter and the insistent burr of the broad West Riding twang; and there was much talk of Briggate and Boar Lane and the Saturday morning Bond Street 'crawl'. But we missed the Yorkshire lasses – and there were no French demoiselles available as partners for the dance. Yet it was a rollicking night – a night that those of us who survive will remember as long as memory lives.

15/1276 Private Lance Grocock, C Company[9]

Two nights before, oh yes, we'd a free-for-all in the market square with a band and one of the privates took the baton from the bandmaster and oh, we'd a real time, the French people brought their beer out, we'd brought [ours], we got them sozzled on our beer and we were up all night with their beer, but I don't know whether it was a good thing because it was supposed to be hush-hush, was this. The Germans knew what was going on. As a matter of fact, when I was taken prisoner-of-war, I met a man who was on that front and he said that they'd been expecting it for a week.

15/471 Private Clifford Hollingworth, D Company[10]

On Friday 28 June the battalion officers were called into a meeting, to be told that Zero hour had been postponed from 29 June to 1 July because of the appalling weather and the condition of the trenches. Otherwise everything was ready, and everyone had been briefed.

The Leeds Pals were to lead 93 Brigade into the attack, followed by the 1st and 2nd Bradford Pals and the 18th Durham Light Infantry. Their objective was to link up with 94 Brigade to create a defensive line north of the village of Serre, and they were to advance on a two-company front in successive waves.

The enemy trenches had been marked in different colours on the briefing maps, and each man was now given a coloured ribbon to tie to his shoulder strap to ensure that he ended up in the right place.[11]

Quite unexpectedly I found I could get over to see Morris [Bickersteth] and hoping he was still at B [Bus-les-Artois] I started off at 6am yesterday morning.

By 9.15 I was at B, found Divisional HQ, then Battalion HQ, then B Company HQ. The latter is a farm, very cramped and uncomfortable, but then so are we here.

Morris with one of his Subalterns(!) was sitting writing, and as I stood in the doorway gave a shout of pleasure. He gave me tea and we talked. He showed me maps and told me his plans. He was himself wearing a red bow on his shoulder straps, which meant that his objective was the red line – one of the Subalterns of another Company was wearing a green one – his meant he had to go to the green line.

All the men wore a coloured bow of some kind – green, red, blue or brown. So if in the attack one saw a man with a blue bow in a red trench, or with a brown in a green and so forth, one turned him out. One could see at a glance in the heat of the battle whether the men were where they should be; white tape had been put out in no-man's-land to show the exact breadth of a Company in extended order – this was to prevent any possibility of overcrowding or over-extension. Morris seemed to know every detail of the attack in his sector and on his flanks – and the whole affair seemed to have been extremely carefully and efficiently worked out.

At 2.45 Morris' Battalion was drawn up in parade and the Divisional General made them a speech. This speech Julian and I heard. Morris commands his Company with the greatest of self-possession, gives his orders to his subordinates clearly and with authority, and yet with all that charm of manner which you know he possesses. I should say he was extremely efficient.

Burgon Bickersteth[12]

Just before marching into the trenches, the Pals paraded for inspection in a courtyard at Bus-les-Artois. Private Robert Henderson, a Gallipoli veteran from South Shields and an expert bomber, was redistributing his deadly load of primed grenades when two of them went off, killing him and wounding fourteen other men of D Company. One of them, 'Peggy' Hewitt, suffered more than fifty wounds and was to spend almost all the rest of the war in hospital. William Spence was another who was wounded and would miss the attack.[13]

Well now, we were in a courtyard in Bus-les-Artois prior to going up. That was your parade ground because we couldn't parade in the village street, and we were all in ranks and Henderson, a chap that had joined us from Gallipoli, he joined us when we were coming from Egypt. He was a nice lad, was Henderson, and from what I can gather, you know them water buckets that horses have. They had grenades and bombs in them and he was taking one out of his, say, right and putting it into the left, when as he put it in it triggered off. Course they were all primed were these. Mills bombs and rifle-grenades, and of course once you trigger one off the whole lot goes. So of course he was killed and all the chaps round about him were thrown on their backs. I was thrown on my back and I was hit on the nose, just bits of shrapnel, and there was blast. So we lost thirty-five men that night before we went up and that was at 5 o'clock approximately. It was 15 Platoon I think that got the worst, part of 14 and 15 Platoon, but I was so far back that I wasn't up with it at all. But in a confined space like this, we had men like that, you see in three tiers, it was a matter of, well, you just simply stood there when this thing crackered off. It was so chaotic [that] just for a few minutes we didn't know who was who and what was what. Then when they got those wounded men out we marched off but every man was examined before he went through that gate. But that was an accident, a proper accident… But understand this much, he was making himself more comfortable and he thought more safe, he perhaps thought that would be more safe in there than in there. He were a complete bomber, he'd been through a course of every bomb of [every] description.

A bomber cleans and primes his Mills grenades. (Imperial War Museum)

15/471 Private Clifford Hollingworth, D Company[14]

At 6pm on the last day of June, still shaken by this devastating accident, the Pals began the long march into the trenches to take up their positions. It was a slow process as the men stumbled along the communication trench loaded down with everything they could conceivably need for the forthcoming offensive.

It was by no means quiet, for there had been wiring parties and patrols out on the previous nights and the Germans, far from being dead or ready to surrender at the sight of a British assault, were sending over a steady salvo of shells.

But at 4am the German artillery fire suddenly intensified, with a heavy barrage directly on to the assembly trenches where the Pals waited for Zero hour.[15]

We went down the line about 4 o'clock, and got our places in the front trench, with C Company in the front trench, and following up was A Company … The ground was just like an upheaval, you could hear nothing for the noise of the shelling.

15/339 Private Morrison Fleming, D Company[16]

Roy Kilner wounded.

Some men became early casualties, one of them well known in the battalion.

> *As we staggered into the trenches I saw Roy Kilnerpass along the top, his hand swathed in bandages.*
>
> 15/711 Private Arthur V. Pearson, C Company[17]

Corporal Kilner was fortunate. His wound was a 'Blighty one', which meant that he would soon be safe in England. He later wrote to the Secretary of the Yorkshire County Cricket Club from a hospital in Birmingham to say that his wound was in the right wrist, which would have been a disaster for many cricketers. Kilner, however, was a left-hand bowler.[18]

> *They were under continual fire, six men of B Company being wounded as they went in. At 1am Morris sent Bristow to inform Company HQ of the casualties, also at his direction he got a rifle and bayonet and bandolier from a wounded man and placed it by Morris, as Morris thought it would be more valuable to him than to use his revolver. Between two and three they tried to rest a bit, but with little success. At three-thirty he sent Bristow again forward, as Battalion HQ were in a dugout in front of the assembly trench, with the casualty report which at that moment, however, was a clean sheet. About five o'clock Morris sent Clarence Parkin, his servant, with Bristow's watch that he might set it exactly the same time as the CO's.*
>
> *About six forty-five, having been very cold in the night as they had no greatcoats, Morris ordered each man to eat a sandwich and the usual tot of rum was served round to them.[19]*

Meanwhile, the British bombardment, which was supposed to save the men in the trenches by pounding the German lines, was adding to their discomfort.

> *… They brought two eighteen-pounder guns forward, they were only twenty yards behind us and they were sending them over five to the minute, eighteen-pounders, and we were nearly deafened with them, and that didn't do your nerves much good, knowing that you might have to face that coming the other way.*
>
> 15/471 Private Clifford Hollingworth, D Company[20]

The artillery stepped up its bombardment for an hour before Zero, and a ten-minute 'hurricane' bombardment from the Stokes mortars of 93rd Trench Mortar Battery, positioned in a sap off the front line, was to make doubly sure that the Pals met no resistance.[21]

Out in no man's land, tapes had been laid to show each wave the extent of its line. At about 7.20, No.10 Platoon under the command of Second-Lieutenant Arthur Hutton, and No. 13 Platoon commanded by Second-Lieutenant Tom Willey, the leading waves of C and D Companies respectively, climbed out of the trenches, spaced themselves out, and lay down on the tapes to await the signal to attack.

> *On that fateful morning of July 1st we all stayed in the front line trench for several hours subjected to a very heavy bombardment. At about 7.15, Mr Willey passed down the order, 'get ready, 13,' as casually as though on an ordinary parade. We then filed out, up the scaling ladder, through the gap in our own wire, and to our place as the first wave (the post of honour) in advance of our wire. Mr Willey said, 'Ten paces interval, boys,' and it was done just as though on manoeuvres.[22]*

The honour of being first 'over the lid' of our Brigade fell to my own platoon (13) and No 10. Not a man hesitated. In broad daylight (7.30am) last Saturday morning our lads had the order to advance. No sooner had the first lot got over the parapet than the Germans opened up a terrific bombardment, big shells and shrapnel, and their parapet was packed with Germans exposing themselves over the top to their waist and opened rapid fire. They had machine-guns every few yards, and it seemed impossible for a square inch of space to be left free from flying metal. Our guns had kept up a hot bombardment for seven days, and for over an hour just preceding our platoon going over the lid, it seemed to us as if nothing could live in their first line trench; individual shells could not be heard, however big they were; it was one continuous scream overhead, and roaring and

What the Pals expected to see, a shattered German trench on the Somme. (Imperial War Museum)

188

ripping of bursting shells just 'across the way', but at the moment of our advance the Germans seemed to be giving us shell for shell.

'Young' Willey led our Platoon. I wish you could make it in your way to see Alderman Willey, and tell him that I but express the feeling of us all when I say that we are absolutely proud of him. He has always shown calm grit and courage in the firing line, and we had every confidence in him, but never has he appeared so noble and courageous as he did at 7.30am last Saturday. At the order every man swarmed out of the front line trench, and doubled out a few yards and extended to 20 paces' interval between each man and laid down for nine minutes. At the end of that time 'Young' Willey jumped up, and waving his revolver, shouted 'Come on 13. Give them Hell!'

He knew what a great responsibility rested on him, for the day before in conversation with our two M-T he said holding up a pencil, that's a spearhead, and see, I'm that point, meaning that our part of the line juts out, and he had to lead his men absolutely on the apex of that part. It depended on the steadiness of this 'first wave' how the other waves followed, but Leeds showed the way. Well he was a Leeds lad and we're proud of him.

We were repeatedly struck by fairly large pieces of spent shrapnel, but when the moment came for the advance, and we saw the calm steady way in which our lads climbed over the trenches on the parapet, and made for their positions in regular order (I have often read the phrase 'as if on parade'. I thought it rather ambiguous, but I am a sceptic no longer, I have seen it done), we felt inspired and stood out of the trench watching them.

15/470 Private W. Arthur Hollings, D Company[23]

Tom Willey with No.13 Platoon. Few would survive the attack on 1 July.

In our sector we were deputed to lead the attack on the German lines. My own platoon (No. 10, C Company) was first 'over the lid'. We got into our trenches about midnight on Friday and then for seven hours had to wait for the signal, all the time being subjected to a hellish and uninterrupted bombardment from every variety of that wide range of powerful ordnance which the enemy have used so well in this war. But the men stood firm through it all, and though, if anything, the storm of fire had increased, there was no flinching when shortly before half past seven in the morning the order came to 'Get over'.

There was neither confusion nor haste when the signal came. The men clambered out from the trenches into the metal-swept open ground, and in a line dead straight and true made steadily forward – as if on parade —for the enemy. Men fell rapidly under the deadly fire, but the remainder swept on, and shortly the second and third lines came over to fill up the gaps.

Joe Collinson wounded.

My hand was badly smashed, and I lay in a shell hole.[24]

Just before zero all hell broke loose, one of the first to be killed was our bombing Sergeant. The two Platoons in advanced trenches had to climb out and lie on a white tape which had been laid during the night, then, just before 7.30am to move forward forming the first waves to move over No Man's Land, followed by wave after wave as each Platoon climbed the parapet and over to spread out in open order. And not a man hesitated.

15/711 Private Arthur V. Pearson, C Company[25]

In their trenches the men of the German 169th Infantry Regiment were waiting. They had survived the bombardment intended to destroy them and their defences, and they were ready to face the Pals' attack.

The most ardent wish that we all cherished was that they would finally come.

… Now everyone knows that the hour of retaliation will soon come. Cartridges and hand-grenade reserves are made ready; everything is ready; and at 8.30 the alarm call 'They are coming!' is screamed in the dugouts.[26]

Faced by a hail of artillery and machine-gun-fire, the two platoons out in no man's land, stood up at the signal and tried to advance. But many of them had been wounded or killed where they lay by the German bombardment.

As Joe [151217 Private Joe Collinson, D Company] lay there, he felt a sudden pain in his thigh. Shrapnel had lodged there. Looking back toward his own trench as the shrill whistles of officers sounded, he recognised several men of that proud battalion being mown down. The severity of enemy firepower was so heavy Joe had to crawl to a nearby shell-hole. Here he was up to his chest in water. Before July 1st there had been a great deal of heavy rainfall, and although the day of the attack dawned to a lovely summer day, the ground was drenched. Hence the bathing pool in which Joe found himself[27]

The following waves tried to scramble out of the trenches, but they too were cut down by the murderous fire coming from the German lines.

The first and second waves stagger and are swept away with the firing. Our artillery strikes in, so that shreds are flying. The others who are coming are finished as they come; they do not once reach their first trench.

190

GERMAN DEFENCE BROKEN ON 16-MILES FRONT.

BRITISH TROOPS' FINE WORK NORTH OF THE SOMME.

FRENCH ATTACK IN CO-OPERATION.

MESSAGE FROM SIR DOUGLAS HAIG.

JOINT PLAN OF CAMPAIGN IN USE.

After a steady bombardment of the German line, lasting a week, followed by a concentrated bombardment of special intensity, the British Army attacked the enemy this morning north of the Somme on a front of 16 miles.

The information comes in an official message from the British Headquarters, and is supplemented by some details from a newspaper correspondent, which we print in an adjoining column. The official message was received at 11.55 a.m., and is as follows:—

Attack launched north of River Somme this morning at 7-30 a.m in conjunction with French.

British troops have broken into German forward system of defences on front of 16 miles.

Fighting is continuing. French attack on our immediate right proceeding equally satisfactorily.

On remainder of British front, raiding parties again succeeded in penetrating enemy's defences at many points, inflicting loss on enemy and taking some prisoners.

There is already a disposition to regard this as the beginning of the "big advance." It may be, and the fact that the attack is a joint one by the Allies shows how the plans for a synchronised plan of campaign have been matured.

But it is impossible for anybody on this side to read the minds of General Joffre and Sir Douglas Haig on the matter, and conjectures as to the extent to which they hope to develop the attack will be in vain.

It may be an attack launched to probe the German lines, find exactly how they are held, and, if they are held lightly, to go through as far as circumstances permit. It may be the prelude to a much bigger attack on a still wider front. Or it may be designed to draw German troops from other fronts where the Allies are ready to take advantage of such diversion.

We have reached a critical stage of the war, when we must be prepared for news of great events, but it were unwise to draw large conclusions from the early news of attacks such as we chronicle this afternoon.

It will be noticed that in the French official report, received this afternoon, there is no reference to the new offensive. Probably it will be described in the report sent from Paris late to-night.

GERMANS AGAIN ENTER THE THIAUMONT WORK.

FRENCH RECOVER ANOTHER WORK TEMPORARILY LOST.

The following French official report was issued this afternoon:—

On both banks of the Meuse the enemy directed repeated and violent offensive actions

THE ATTACK MADE THIS MORNING.

PRECEDED BY A TERRIFIC BOMBARDMENT.

MANY PRISONERS TAKEN BY THE BRITISH.

British Headquarters, France,
Saturday, 9.30 a.m.

At about half-past seven this morning, a vigorous attack was launched by the British Army.

The front extends over about twenty miles, north of the Somme.

The assault was preceded by a terrific bombardment lasting about an hour and a half.

It is too early as yet to give anything but the barest particulars, as the fighting is developing in intensity, but the British troops have already occupied the German front line.

Many prisoners have already fallen into our hands, and, as far as can be ascertained, our casualties have not been heavy.

On Thursday night the Anzacs made a raid on the enemy lines, eighty German soldiers and two officers being killed. Our casualties were very slight. Other raids resulted in numerous prisoners being taken.

—Press Association Special Correspondent.
Friday.

The enemy made an ineffective raid upon our trenches west of the Lille road, after a heavy bombardment, on Wednesday night. Three raids made by our troops in the neighbourhood of Messines accounted for a number of the enemy, and the King's Shropshire Light Infantry, after another of these expeditions into the enemy's line, brought back a batch of a dozen prisoners.

—Press Association.

THE LAST BIG ATTACK.

The last big attack made jointly by French and British troops was that on September 25 last year, after a bombardment of German positions for 25 days.

The British attacked south of La Bassee Canal, and German trenches were captured and lines penetrated to a depth of 4,000 yards. Twenty-six guns and 3,000 prisoners were taken.

In Champagne, the French penetrated the German lines on a front of 15½ miles and depth of 2½ miles. One hundred and twenty-five German guns were captured, and 23,000 prisoners taken.

THE PROLONGED BOMBARDMENT

GERMANS WITHOUT FOOD FOR THREE DAYS.

The British bombardment of the German line, along the entire front of 80 miles, has lasted a week, and the Paris Press experts have come to the conclusion that Sir Douglas Haig is conducting "new style" warfare.

A high French military authority praised enthusiastically the plan adopted by the British. He said the method was new in war, was better studied than the German way at Verdun, and more effective. British raiding parties push right on to the line of German trenches, march along thoroughly till they are convinced that no guns or men remain. As the correspondent of the "Liberte" at the British front says, it is the methodical destruction of the enemy's defensive works. Infantry only come in to clean up and complete the work of the artillery.

It is obvious from the latest reports that the Germans are trying, by far-divided counter-offensives, to find out what is to be the next move.

THE BRITISH HAVE THE "PULL."

There can be no doubt [writes a "Yorkshire Post" correspondent from British Headquarters] that at last we have begun to get the guns and the munitions we have been waiting for, and that we are using them to the fullest extent. Not merely is our artillery equal to the Germans. I believe in many respects we have the "pull" over them—a belief shared by expert artillerists who have had the opportunity of watching the ding-dong big gun duel which has been going on for nearly a week.

The recent raids so brilliantly carried out on the British front against the German trenches have served one very useful purpose. We know exactly what battalions of infantry the enemy has opposed to us from the sea to the Somme. This identification has been established much...

"WE SHALL WANT EVERY MAN."

NEARING HEIGHT OF TREMENDOUS STRUGGLE.

The men who removed themselves, or were somehow removed, into exempted occupations, when the first Military Service measure was brought in are now being combed out, and we understand, the "Saturday Review" says, the yield of them has been satisfactory, on the whole, of late.

But very shortly the demand will once more inevitably be for men and more men and yet more men, just as it will be—and is—for munitions and more munitions and yet more munitions.

The public and the Press have tended somewhat to go to sleep in this matter of late. They will presently wake up with a start and discover that we are really nearing the height of a tremendous struggle, and that "arms and the man" is still, and for a long time must be, the cry.

We have to pile up the men for all sorts and kinds of foreign service with the Army, and for all sorts of home service with the Army, and in the munition factories.

"We shall want," said the Government a great many months ago now, "every man." That saying holds quite as true to-day as it is held then. We write at random, or in any mood of exaggeration. We write of what we know.

The way in which lazy minds and bodies overlook this great, pressing need of more men and more munitions is lamentable indeed.

ENEMY IN FLIGHT AFTER FALL OF KOLOMEA.

AUSTRIAN PRISONERS CONTINUE TO FLOW IN.

The capture of Kolomea is confirmed from Petrograd. A Russian official communication to-hand to-day says:

The troops on the Russian left wing to-day took the town of Kolomea, the most important converging point of the railways of the Bukovina.

The enemy continues to fall back to the west, clinging to previously prepared positions. North-west of Kimpolung the enemy is trying to resume the offensive with larger forces.

The troops of General Lechitsky are carrying out their offensive in extremely difficult conditions, torrential rains having wrought havoc to roads, which were already bad in the sphere of action of these valiant troops. North-west of the confluence of the Lipa and Styr, on the Lutsk-Brody line, the Austrians, supported by fire of heavy and light artillery, took the offensive against the Russian positions, near the villages of Gnenki and Natalin.

Our troops, with imperturbable sang-froid, let the enemy approach our barbed wire entanglements and then shot them point-blank. In the region of the Lipa, the enemy repulsed once in preparing a new attack.

According to the latest reports, the total number of prisoners made in the period from June 4th to 26th amounts to 212,000 men, including officers. Prisoners continue to flow in.—Press Association.

VERDUN AND THE BRITISH FRONT.

FRENCH FORECAST OF A CANNON WAR.

Paris, Saturday.

Referring to the capture of Thiaumont, M. Marcel Hutin, in the "Echo de Paris," says: This marks with a white stone our entrance upon the 24th month of the war. The impression from the British and French fronts alike is very good. It is all right now. With considerable resources of war-powerful material, which can be renewed for many weeks to come, a cannon war is to be waged simultaneously on all the fronts, and will last a long time.

The "Petit Parisien" says the German guns are clearly overpowered, and will have to be reinforced from Verdun, to the great relief of the French. For this reason it is believed the Verdun undertaking is nearing its close. The Crown Prince is making his final effort, and the events in Flanders may compel him to suspend operations.

—Exchange.

AN IRISHMAN IN BERLIN.

German newspapers contain large advertisements announcing a public lecture, by "Dr. Chatteron Hill" at the Philharmonie Hall in Berlin.

The lecturer is described as "the only Irishman working publicly in Germany to enlighten Germany about Ireland and her importance in the world war."

"Every week brings a new pile of regulations, prohibitions, and fasting orders," says Maximilian Harden, of conditions in Germany.

At an exhibition at the Camera Club, Adelphi, a striking portrait of Lord Ripon, with an account vase in his hands, is entitled "The Connoisseur."

LATE NEWS.

THE BRITISH ATTACK

... Towards 9.30am the troops opposing us showed no more desire to attack.[28]

1 July 1916 – Terrible bombardment by both sides from midnight. Almost half the battalion 'out of action' before 'zero' (7.30am). Was hit in left arm by shrapnel 7.15am. 10 Platoon over parapet at 7.20am, 12 Platoon at 7.25am. Lads mown down by machine-gun fire and shrapnel as they advanced. Wound dressed in Basin Wood. Went to Colincamps, then to Bus, then to Acheux. Cliff and I (Cliff, bullet in knee), saw Bert with bullet in knee at Acheux. Slept all night on straw.

15/1003 Private Edward Woffenden, C Company[29]

1 July 1916 – The fatal day. The Big Push Somme Battle.

Went over the top at 7.30am. Wounded about 9am. Left Bus for Acheux at 7pm.

The ring I wore in the advance was made out of a French bullet and is worn as a mascot.

Wounded about 9am. Bandaged myself up best possible and crawled through trenches in search of a dressing station. Wounded in face en route. Progress very difficult. Intense shelling of support trenches. Found 15th W York Dressing dugout and was bound up by Ward the orderly. Afterwards crawled to Basin Wood and had rest, afterwards proceeded to Euston Dump – practically helpless on feet – lucky to meet RAMC men who very kindly pushed 4 of us on truck to Colincamps. Hobbled to Dressing Station which was crowded – waited long time —place crowded— was finally bandaged again and put on Ford Car and sent to Bus Hospital, left equipment here. Arrived at Bus about 6pm greeted by Chaplain. Had a cup of cocoa and left with Cliff Evans on Motor Bus for Acheux about 7pm. Arriving about 8.30. Placed on blanket on ground and placed next to a Seaforth Highlander. Slept out all night.

15/231 Private George W. Cosby, B Company[30]

The whistle blew and over we went.

One or two of our lads had dropped down, they were dropping all round us, and one that had dropped was screaming out, his leg was in a [bad] way. I knelt down to pull his puttees off and his boot, he'd been badly smashed in the leg, and up behind me then come Major Booth, he was the Yorkshire cricketer, he came forward and he said to me 'What are you doing? Come on, it doesn't matter about him, it's onward you go, come on, get hold', and he got hold of me, lifted me up, and the pair of us went forward. The Jerry was up with his machine-guns firing at us from a distance of about fifteen yards ahead of us. There was two shell-holes open, one was on the right, in the wire, and one was on the left. He said 'Come on, make for if. I made for one shell-hole and he made for further on. He'd got about a few yards and there was a shell burst and it was just one mass of bodies and one thing and another flying up in the air.

I dropped myself in a shell-hole ... the memory's terrible ... I got in the shell-hole and thats where I stuck. I'd a spot on my arm it was just cut and a bullet in through my leg, the top of my leg, I was unconscious, laid in that trench and thats where I laid the whole day. I could see the bodies going up in the air. A terrible sight, a sight that I'll never forget, and the ground was just like an upheaval, one mass of flame everywhere.

Anyway the night come along and I managed to get alongside one of our lads, he seemed to be alright, we managed to get back into the line. There was very few of us left, I think about four of us, that was about all and that's where I laid.

15/339 Private Morrison Fleming, D Company[31]

All the battalion officers who went into the attack were killed or injured. Although no more than twenty-two officers were supposed to go in,[32] twenty-four of the Leeds Pals officers went over the top with their men. Perhaps this irregularity was allowed because Colonel Taylor was still in hospital recovering from the leg wound he sustained in June, and the battalion

FOOTBALLER

Lieutenant Lintott, the international footballer, who was killed in the big advance last week.

Lieutenant Major Booth (in sports gear), killed.

was temporarily under the command of Major Barry Neil. The latter was wounded at the commencement of the attack on 1 July but tried to press on. Hit a second time, he managed to get back to the trench and was later evacuated to England.[33]

Second-Lieutenant Major Booth, the Yorkshire cricketer, was killed a few moments after he had pulled Morris Fleming away from his wounded comrade. An eyewitness account in a letter to the *Yorkshire Evening Post* described the last moments of Evelyn Lintott the footballer and Booth the cricketer.

> *Lieutenant Lintott's end was particularly gallant. He led his men with great dash, and when hit the first time declined to take the count. Instead he drew his revolver and called for further effort. Again he was hit but struggled on, but a third shot finally bowled him over. Lieutenant Booth, too, though in sore agony from a shell fragment which penetrated the shoulder and must have touched the heart, tried his utmost to go forward, but pitched forward helplessly after going a few yards. He and Lintott were two gallant sportsmen who knew how to die – but then so did all the boys. They went out to almost certain death with the cry 'Now Leeds!' on their lips.*[34]

Second-Lieutenant Arthur Hutton, commander No. 10 Platoon C Company, wounded.

Tom Willey and Arthur Hutton, the young subalterns whose platoons led the attack, both became casualties. Willey lost his legs when he was hit by a shell, and his body was never recovered, although some of his platoon went out into no man's land that night to try to find him.[35] Hutton was wounded in the right shoulder and evacuated to Britain. He wrote to Tom Willey's family from Whitworth Hospital in Manchester.

> *Dear Mr Willey, I cannot possibly express to you my very deep sorrow and regret at the news of Tom's death. Everyone loved Tom and, as you know, he was more often than not the very life and soul of our mess. He was a great officer and a great man and we shall miss him tremendously. He was always cheerful and full of life. I can't realise what has happened. All the best have gone, I cannot see why I didn't go with them.*
>
> *I hope both Mrs Willey and yourself will accept my most heartfelt sympathy in your great loss, and find consolation in the thought that Tom, like the boy he was, always did his duty. Yours very sincerely, Arthur Hutton[36]*

Willey's childhood friend, Jackie Vause, was also killed.

A private who had been with him recounted Vause's death from his bed in the 3rd Western General Hospital at Newport, Monmouthshire.

> *Lieutenant Vause was first hit in the elbow just as he had led his men over the parapet. He went on, however, and after having his wound bound up, reached the barbed wire entanglements in front of the German trenches which his Platoon had to take. He was hit a second time in the thigh, and, with the only remaining soldier in his Platoon by his side, he lay in a*

Second-Lieutenant Thomas Arthur Robert Raymond Ellicott Willey, commander of No.13 Platoon, D Company, killed.

> *trench under a terrific bombardment. His companion in describing their situation says: 'We lay there talking about Leeds and discussing the possibility of getting home again. Lieutenant Vause told me that he had been recommended for his third star[37] and was very much 'up' about if. Some time later the gallant officer was again hit, first on the chin and then in the back. He made the remark 'This has just about finished me off and died shortly afterwards. His companion lay with two shattered legs for 36 hours before being rescued.[38]*

Morris Bickersteth's brother, Julian, made strenuous efforts to piece together his last moments. He rushed over to the 31st Division area on 3 July, and after making enquiries eventually met one of Morris's men who had been with him at the end.

> *A Private was there who could tell me of how dear Morris died. I went out at once and found a handsome boy of eighteen, very fair and good looking and he immediately gave me more details I so badly wanted to know. He nearly broke down several times poor boy, he was slightly wounded*

A.F.A. 2042.
114/Gen. No./5243.

FIELD SERVICE

POST CARD

The address only to be written on this side. If anything else is added, the post card will be destroyed.

NOTHING is to be written on this side except the date and signature of the sender. Sentences not required may be erased. If anything else is added the post card will be destroyed.

I am quite well.

I have been admitted into hospital

{ sick, } and am going on well.

{ wounded } and hope to be discharged soon.

I am being sent down to the base.

I have received your { letter dated_____

{ telegram „ _____

{ parcel „ _____

Letter follows at first opportunity.

I have received no letter from you

{ lately.

{ for a long time.

Signature only. }

Date_____

[Postage must be prepaid on any letter or post card addressed to the sender of this card.]

(S2309) Wt. W3497-293 2,250m. 4/16 J. J. K. & Co., Ltd.

Arthur Holling's card to his father to let him know that he was safe. Hollings was detailed to carry ammunition on 1 July, so did not go over with the fighting waves.

195

Short Form of Will.

(See instruction 4 on page 1).

If a soldier on active service, or under orders for active service, wishes to make a short will, he may do so on the opposite page. It must be in his own handwriting and must be signed by him and dated. The full names and addresses of the persons whom he desires to benefit, and the sum of money or the articles or property which he desires to leave to them, must be clearly stated.

The following is a specimen of such a will leaving all to one person:—

In the event of my death I give the whole of my property and effects to————

————

(Signature) JOHN SMITH,
Private, No. 1793,
Gloucester Fusrs.

Date————

The following is a speci——— f such a will leaving legacies to more than o——— h I give £10 to

In the event ——— 5 to

and I g——— y proper

Date———

In the event of my death I giv the whole of my property & effects to Mrs Elizabeth Smith (mother) 3 Byres St Stanningley Rd, Armley Leeds.

Signed Herbert Smith Private No 825

Herbert Smith, (front row right) at home in Leeds after recovering from his wound. Tom Willey's death was one of his most painful memories every 1 July. (Jean Kennington)

LEEDS "PALS" AFTER THE BATTLE.

The survivors of No.13 Platoon. They searched no man's land under fire, in a desperate attempt to find Tom Willey's body.

A glimpse of a group of Leeds "Pals" enjoying a well-earned rest not long after the first "push." The men belong to "D" Company, and mostly hail from the Beeston, Holbeck, and Hunslet districts. In the back row (reading left to right) are Private J. Henry, of Beeston Hill, grandson of Mr. Joseph Henry, senior, J.P.; and Private J. Preece, of Hunslet Lake. The figures in the front r x commencing with the second, and reading left right, are Private A. Hollings, son of Councillor W. Hollings, Hunslet, Private Smith, Private Jubb, and Lance-Corporal J. Brown.

196

HE BIG BATTLE DESCRIBED.

RAL SITUATION IS FAVOURABLE.

OUGLAS HAIG'S REPORT.

RT RETAINED AFTER HEAVY FIGHTING.

lowing are the latest official messages mbined British and French offensive rom Sir Douglas Haig:

Sunday, 7.45 p.m.

antial progress has been made in the of Fricourt, which was captured by ops by 2 p.m. to-day.

noon to-day some 800 more prisoners en taken in the operations between re and the Somme, bringing the total ,500, including those captured on arts of the front last night.

Sunday, 10.45 p.m.

fighting has taken place to-day in rea between the Ancre and Somme, ally about Fricourt and La Boiselle. rt, which was captured by our troops 2 p.m., remains in our hands, and progress has been made east of the e.

the neighbourhood of La Boiselle the is offering a stubborn resistance, but roops are making satisfactory progress. onsiderable quantity of war material allen into our hands, but details are t present available.

either side of the valley of the Ancre the tion is unchanged. The general situa- may be regarded as favourable.

er information of the enemy's losses that our first estimates were too low.

terday our aeroplanes were very active -operation with our attack north of the ne, and afforded valuable assistance to operations. Numerous enemy head- ters and railway centres were attacked bombs.

one of these raids our scouting aero- es were attacked by 20 Fokkers, which driven off. Two enemy aeroplanes were to crash to earth, and were destroyed.

me long-distance reconnaissances were ied out in spite of numerous attempts by ny machines to frustrate the enter- es.

hree of our aeroplanes are missing. Our -balloons were in the air the whole day.

W AND METHODICAL PUSH.

OBJECTIVE AND PROSPECTS IN THE ATTACK.

Press Association correspondent at British Head- ters, writes:—

hilst, at the moment, the situation looks promising, well not to carry satisfaction to the point of too expectations. We are fighting a strong, deter- d, and resourceful foe, and although he has now smitten harder than at any time before by the ish Army, it would be very unwise to underrate powers of resistance, particularly in the face a highly menacing position. The present nsive has a definite objective, and if this is attained d it is not unduly sanguine to predict that it will the British Army on the Western front will have factorily fulfilled the role expected of it for the ent.

n the other hand, if, under the pressure now being wn by our Army upon the enemy, and by the ach on our right, the assaulted front crumbles, great events may follow. It is an undeniable fact all those prisoners who were taken in the storming the front line showed a remarkable willingness to render, and complained that they had been virtually hout food for some days, not because of any shortage supplies in the rear, but because the deadly character our almost ceaseless barrage during the past week dered it so difficult to maintain transport. It seems improbable that the comparative feebleness of the rman artillery response was due to a shortage of ailable ammunition from a similar cause.

A French semi-official report contains the following: The first day of the offensive is very satisfactory. ... is not a thunderbolt, as has happened

"THE ATTACK WILL BE MADE AT 7.30."

OUR MEN'S NIGHT OF WAITING.

HOW NORTH-COUNTRY TROOPS MARCHED TO BATTLE.

In the "Daily Telegraph" Mr. Phillip Gibbs thus describes a scene on the British front the night before the attack:—

I could not see the faces of the men, but by the shape of their forms could see that they wore their steel hel- mets and their fighting kit. They were heavily laden with their packs, but they were marching at a smart, swinging pace, and as they came along were singing cheerily. They were singing some music-hall tune, with a lilt in it, as they marched towards the light of all the shells up there in the place of death. Some of them were blowing mouth-organs and others were whistling.

I watched them pass—all three tall boys of a North- country regiment—and something their spirit seemed to come out of the dark mass of their moving bodies and thrill the air. They were going up to those places without faltering, without a backward look—and sing- ing! Dear, splendid men . . .

A Staff officer had whispered a secret to us at mid- night in a little room, when the door was shut and the window closed. Even then they were words which could be only whispered, and to men of trust.

"The attack will be made this morning at 7.30."

During the night there was one curious phenomenon. It was the silence of all the artillery. By some atmo- spheric condition of moisture or wind (though the night was calm), or by the configuration of the ground, which made pockets into which the sound fell, there was no great uproar, such as I have heard score of times in smaller bombardments than this.

It was all muffled. Even our own batteries did not crash out with any startling thunder, though I could hear the rush of big shells like great birds in flight. Now and then there was a series of loud strokes, an urgent knocking at the doors of night. And now and again there was a dull, heavy thunder-clap, followed by a long rumble, which made me think that mines were being blown further up the line. But for the most part it was curiously quiet and low-toned, and somehow the muffled artillery gave one a greater sense of awful- ness and of deadly work.

But now on the morning of battle this phenomenon, which I do not understand, no longer existed. There was one continual roar of guns which beat the air with great waves and shocks of sound, prodigious and over- whelming.

The full power of our artillery was let loose at about six o'clock. Nothing like it has ever been seen or heard upon our front before, and all the preliminary bombardment, great as it was, seemed insignificant to this.

Troops were moving forward to the attack from behind the lines. It was nearly 7.30. All the officers about me kept glancing at their wrist watches. We did not speak much then, but stared silently at the smoke and mist which floated and banked along our lines. There, hidden, were our men. They, too, would be looking at their wrist watches.

The minutes were passing very quickly—as quickly as men's lives pass when they look back upon the years. An officer near me turned away, and there was a look of sharp pain in his eyes. We were only lookers-on. The strong men, our friends, the splendid Youth that we have passed on the roads in France, were about to do this job. Good luck go with them! Men were mut- tering such wishes in their hearts.

It was 7.30. Our watches told us this, but nothing else. The guns had lifted and were firing behind the enemy's first lines, but there was no sudden hush for the moment of attack. The barrage by our guns seemed as great as the first bombardment. For ten minutes or so before this time a new sound had come into the general thunder of artillery.

It was like the "rafale" of the French soixante quinze, very rapid, with distinct and separate strokes, but louder than the noise of the field guns. They were our trench-mortars at work along the whole length of the line before me.

INFANTRY SCREENED BY SMOKE.

It was 7.30. The moment for the attack had come. Clouds of smoke had been liberated to form a screen for the infantry, and hid the whole line. The only men I could see were those in reserve, winding along a road by some trees which led to the attacking points. They had their backs turned, as they marched very slowly and steadily forward.

I could not tell who they were on the road a day or two before. But, whoever they were, English, Irish or Welsh, I watched them until most had disappeared from sight behind a clump of trees. In a little while they would be fighting, and would need all their courage.

At a minute after 7.30 there came through the rolling smoke-clouds a rushing sound. It was the noise of rifle fire and machine guns. The men were out of their trenches, and the attack had begun. The enemy was barraging our lines.

THE FIRST RUSH.

At first, it is certain, there was not much difficulty in taking the enemy's first line trenches along the greater part of the country attacked. Our bombard- ... had done great damage, and had smashed down ... When

PROGRESS WILL BE SLOW BUT SURE.

EVERY GAIN CONSOLIDATED.

MANY GUNS AND MUCH WAR MATERIAL CAPTURED.

Paris, Monday.

The semi-official statement issued last night says:—

The French and British offensive was continued with desperation throughout the day and night of July 1 and the day of July 2. To-day's results were no less en- couraging than yesterday's. We made fresh progress, repulsed all counter-attacks, and took great numbers of prisoners.

In the British sector the struggle is particularly keen between the Ancre and the Somme, round the village of Montauban, which was captured yesterday. Despite violent counter attacks during the night we firmly held Fricourt, and at La Boiselle our Allies are making progress.

On the right wing held by the French the enemy several times made vigorous counter-attacks against our positions on the edge of the village of Hardecourt, but he was routed by our fire. To the south we carried, after violent fighting, the village of Curlu, and a neigh- bouring quarry which had been strongly fortified.

South of the Somme we made further advance, and reached a number of points in the German second position on a front of about seven kilometres, between the Somme and Assevillers. This advance gave us the village of Frise, only eight kilometres from Peronne, and also the Mereaucourt Wood to the east.

In two days over six thousand unwounded prisoners have fallen into the hands of the French, and the British on their side report having taken 2,500. Be- sides this we have captured many guns and consider- able war material.

The opening of battle has been magnificent, and operations are continuing favourably, although the Ger- mans are putting up strong resistance. However, our progress must be expected to be relatively slow but sure, for the tactics employed consist in consolidating every gain before attacking the next objective.

Let us therefore congratulate ourselves on the pre- sent, and await the future with patience. The enemy has just sustained a very hard shock which will be followed by many more. Engaged as he is on two wings on the Somme and the Meuse, and rebuffed before Verdun by our violent attacks, it seems an im- possibility that he should be able to withstand the push which is going to be made against him, without giving way.

In any case the Germans are forced to admit our success in their official communique. They say we gained important advantages, adding:—

"We preferred to withdraw to a position situated midway between the first and second lines. Material, which was permanently fixed in our advanced lines and which, moreover, had been rendered useless, was lost as is usual in such cases." The admission is significant. —Press Association.

DOUBLE-BARRELLED APPEALS.

PROTEST MADE AT A WEST RIDING TRIBUNAL.

The East Central (West Riding) Appeal Tribunal again sat at Wakefield, to-day, Mr. T. Norton presiding.

Mr. J. Atkinson, from the office of Mr. A. Willey, Leeds, appeared in support of an appeal for exemption made on the ground of domestic hardship by a Feather- stone man, aged 32, described as a commission agent. He stated that he had a wife and three young children, and also supported his father-in-law, who was helpless.

Mr. Atkinson added that the applicant had run the Featherstone Main Cigarette Fund for soldiers at the front. He had 327 names of soldiers on his books, which entailed 71 parcels per week on the average.

The report of the Local Tribunal was that they did not consider the man was doing any work of national importance sufficient to justify his exemption, and no serious hardship would be entailed by his joining the Forces.

The appeal was dismissed, and no time allowed.

A firm of colonial meat dealers appealed for the ex- emption of the managers of their shops at Wombwell and Normanton.

It appeared that appeals had also been lodged at Leeds, and Mr. Turner remarked that the firm appeared to want to have two-barrelled shots. He considered this was unfair, as it was prejudicing other butchers, who had only the opportunity of appearing before the local tribunals. It was not fair that these syndicate shops should have such an advantage over private traders, and in his opinion the cases ought all to be dealt with by the local tribunals.

The appeals were dismissed.

A Hoyland insurance agent, aged 36, married, with one child, appealed for exemption and expressed his willingness to work in the mine. He worked 11½ years in the mine, and it was 11 years since he left.

The appeal was dismissed, but one month's grace was granted.

In the case of a Goole tenant farmer, the military representative asked if he had applied to the Labour Exchange for help.

Applicant's solicitor: Oh, it's a farce. I would like to challenge the military representative to prove that one man has been sent by the Labour Exchange to farmers in this district.

POWERFUL PUSH THAT MAY LAST MONTHS.

QUIET CONFIDENCE IN PARIS.

HOW NEW FRENCH GUN WIPED OUT ONE VILLAGE.

Messages from Paris this afternoon show that the French people, while delighted with the success of the Allied offensive, are in no way excited, but remain cool and absolutely confident. They fully realise the tre- mendous task confronting the Allies.

French experts, says a "Star" message this after- noon, are enormously impressed by the colossal artillery with which the British Army is now provided, as well as the profusion of munitions. The new big French gun (says this correspondent) is marvellous, and puts the famous German 16-inch entirely in the shade.

The correspondent of the "Petit Parisien" on the Somme front on Friday, was present while one of these guns demolished a village within the German lines. With each shot a dozen houses disappeared, and pre- sently the village, with the Germans in it, was wiped out.

Just before the French offensive began, the Chief of a Corps put a carnation in his button-hole, shouting to his men: "It will fade among the Boches." There- upon every soldier stuck a flower or sprig in his helmet. Three hours later that general entered Dompierre, at the head of his troops. It was a brilliant feat, for the enemy had turned this important position into a regu- lar fortress. Two regiments carried it with such dash that the Germans had no time to turn their machine guns on them and these guns were captured before they had fired a shot. A furious hand-to-hand strug- ended in complete victory for the French. Of the Ger- man garrison 700 surrendered. The remainder, abo 1,500, had been killed.

Paris, Monday.

The "Petit Parisien" says:—"The news is go and very good. The Franco-British offensive h started under excellent conditions, and important p gress has been realised in the sectors entrusted to French troops, though it is impossible to give f details.

"The villages of Montauban and Mametz, which h been defensively organised by the Germans, have b firmly occupied by the British, and the battle contin very fiercely between La Boiselle and Gommecourt. configuration of the ground aided the Germans betw Contalmaison and Pozieres, but, generally speaking, situation is excellent.

"We must not, however, forget that the offens will last long. It is a question, not of an operat intended to relieve the pressure on Verdun, but of extremely powerful push against the German w which will last several months."

THE BRITISH WITHSTOOD FIERCE ATTAC

The "Petit Journal" says:—The British are e cising a strong pressure on the enemy. They have to sustain several strong counter-attacks, but the man assaults, which were multiplied night and broke against the firm resistance of the British, remained entire masters of the terrain, and infli bloody losses on the enemy. In the northern se the British, after an heroic resistance had, it is to give up some points captured on the previous but altogether the situation of our Allies remains favourable. The ground which they have defin gained is very appreciable.

Colonel Rousset says: Victory is probable this because our preparations were complete, minute precise, because we are both acting in perfect ac and the enemy assailed everywhere at once is b down, and has only very reduced liberty of mover All that the Allies have conquered they are hol These are happy auguries, and their realisation w due to the soldiers whose bravery is admirable to the wise organisation of resources.

The following brief resume of the opening oper in the great offensive is published here:—"Five incessant bombardment of the front between Go court and Chaulnes was followed just after seven o on Saturday morning by a sudden cessation of art action, and simultaneously, the infantry divisions pated for the first assault were launched to the a and seized the whole of the German front lines.

The Germans had left between their first and s lines only weak contingents, which, however, wer reinforced, and attempted to check the rush Allied troops, and a terrific battle then deve along the entire front.

BRILLIANT ASSAULT BY THE FRENC

In the French sector the enemy was overwhe and fell back upon his sector lines, but thro yesterday the battle continued incessantly, alw our advantage, and by the end of the mornin front, which had advanced over the line mencerd at Hardecourt, the point of junction of t Allied armies, and ran southwards through west of the village of Feuilleres, and then t Herbecourt and Assevillers.

The success of the assault was remarkably b One French division stormed the village of Fr the Somme Canal, and then, dashing on, captu Mereaucourt Wood, which had been transformed Germans into an extremely powerful defensive The division then swept to the outskirts of the of Feuilleres.

The British, thanks to their capture of Mam Montauban, were able to carry their new line southern sector almost as far ahead as the new line, but the British troops encountered great ties north of Mametz, at Contalmaison, parts of however, they succeeded in seizing.

"It is noteworthy that all the German new speak to-day of the Allied offensive, and admit defeats; but, as usual, they are extremely vague statements. It is significant, however, that the of having to fall back at certain points, and to a certain amount of material."—Central News.

and had been buried alive but had got out. He was the last man Morris spoke to, his name is Private Bateson No 1218

[He] crawled to his [Bickersteth's] side to obtain permission to go back because he was wounded. Morris in spite of the turmoil and terrible fire coolly wrote him out a chit, signed it, and told him to get back as best as he could.

Directly after Morris handed the piece of paper to the boy he looked round to see if there was any support coming from the trenches behind. At that moment a shrapnel bullet struck him on the back of the head, a second later another bullet passed right through his head coming out through his forehead. He just rolled over without a word or a sound and Bateson was able to see that he was quite dead, killed instantly. This excellent lad who told me this story so simply and bravely went on to say that seeing he couldn't do any more for his officer he managed to let the sergeant know that Morris had been knocked out and so the sergeant took command and then, how he doesn't know, he managed to get back into our trench. Immediately afterwards a shell fell on the parapet and blew it in and he was buried, but fortunately he was dug out in time, though terribly shaken and unnerved he managed to get back to the dressing station. What was left of the Battalion got back to Monk Trench 100 yards behind the front line trench from which the attack was started finding it absolutely impossible to hold our old front line and that is how the situation is at present.

Julian Bickcrsteth[39]

Morris's father, Samuel Bickersteth, traced Private Edmund Bristow, another of his son's men, and interviewed him at Leeds Vicarage.

[Morris] took his own men over. As soon as he got to the tape, he ordered them to get down because the men there before them had only just started on and that order was his last spoken word. Immediately afterwards high-explosive shrapnel burst and a large portion struck the back of his head causing a very bad wound and the impact must have stunned him. It was certain that he would have had no real feeling of dying or of pain although both his legs and arms worked for a minute or two.

Bristow was laying about two yards to the side of him but such was the machine-gun fire that he could only creep round to the side of Morris from behind, when he saw him struck by the high-explosive shrapnel [which] hit him on the head just below where the helmet would have protected him, he said to Mr Jenkinson, Morris's servant, 'Mr Bickersteth has gone west'.

As near as possible he thinks the moment must have been 7.55am, the attack having commenced at 7.30. Bristow was then wounded in the hand and also in the shoulder by high-explosive, which he still has in him, which was not removed in France owing to the pressure of worse cases. After his first wound he greatly wanted to try and get back to see if he could recover the body but he couldn't face the rain of machine-gun bullets without certain death. He was afterwards buried by the high-explosive himself.

With regard to what Bateson told Julian about the bullet through the forehead, I have my doubts although its not exactly consistent with what has been said by Bristow, and Julian may have wished

Lieutenant John Gilbert 'Jackie' Vause, commander of No.15 Platoon, D Company, killed.

to spare us that detail if Bateson had mentioned it to him. Bristow will confirm that our dear lad's face was not mutilated, blood was coming from his nostrils and his face perfectly white but untouched, which is a great comfort to mother and me.[40]

Monier Bickersteth, Morris's eldest brother, rushed to Leeds from London, where he was employed as Secretary of the Jerusalem and the East Mission and the Syrian Relief Fund. With him he brought a letter from Morris, written on his last leave and handed over at Waterloo Station as he departed for France. It was to be opened only in the event of his death, and read:

May 7th 1916, Sunday. In the train from Leeds to London.

My own Darling Mother and Father, In the event of my getting a clean knock-out blow from the Hun, Monier will send you this letter. I just wanted to tell you that I do not fear death except in so far as everyone must fear it, viz. undergoing some experience which one has never had before. But I just want you both to remember this one thing, after all, what is death? Death to my mind is simply a gateway through which one passes into Life, I mean real Life. We merely exist in this world, in the world to come we shall LIVE. We are all bound to come to this gateway called death

Lieutenant (Acting Captain) Stanley Morris Bickersteth, acting commander of B Company, killed.

sooner or later. Whether it is sooner or later can really matter very little to any of us. Simply because in thirty or forty years the whole family will be together for ever in eternal life. And what is thirty or forty years together in this world compared to the endless ages we shall all spend together in the life to come. If you look at it in this light, death has no terror, and really very little sorrow or grief attached to it. At least you should feel none of these things. Both of you will have to die sooner or later. If Mother dies first, you Dad will know that I shall be there waiting at the gate to give her a welcome. And if Dad dies then you, Mother darling, will know that Dad and I are waiting for you; isn't that just splendid? At any rate this is what I believe, and I believe it because you two, by your dear lives, have taught us all to believe in Jesus Christ the Son of God, who died that we might live. Don't forget that I shall be loving you both at the moment that you are reading this, just as dearly as I do now while writing it. Ever your own loving Son, S Morris Bickersteth[41]

Lieutenant Robert Huntries Tolson, commander of No.2 Platoon, A company, Killed.

Mr Whiteley Tolson of Huddersfield, whose son Robert, a lieutenant with the battalion, led No. 2 Platoon into the attack, heard that he was wounded and in hospital in Britain, and made an appeal in the local press for any further information. In the meantime, the Chaplain wrote to Lieutenant Tolson's wife to say that he had been wounded, but could offer no more news. Eventually it was confirmed that Tolson had been killed. He was buried in Serre Road No.1 Cemetery.[42]

Still under heavy fire from the German machine guns and artillery, and without any officers to take the lead, the attack ground to a halt. Those Pals who had not been killed outright took cover in shell-holes. Most of them had been wounded, and their only thought was to get back to their lines, and away from the German shells that were churning up the ground on which they lay.

> *[I] came across some of our company in a shell hole. There would be about eight of us under a sergeant. Here we huddled, sheltered from the bullets but battered by shrapnel. First one man got hit, then another and if they could crawl they struggled back to the trench.*
>
> *15/711 Private Arthur V. Pearson, C Company*[43]

Joe Collinson was about to crawl back to the trench from a shell hole when

> *… someone slithered into it head first. He lifted him right side up and immediately recognised him as a lad in his own Company. He was moaning, and Joe said, 'Where are you hurt, Puss?' – his name was Cathrick [151181 Private Harry Cathrick], hence his nickname. He died in Joe's arms shortly afterwards. He placed him on the side of the shell-hole so he would be found.[44] He then decided he must crawl his way back to his line as best as he could, by way of one hole after another. Joe flung himself into a second shell-hole where his knee hit a bayonet, causing a second wound. Crawling out of there and aiming for the next hole, he came across a ghastly sight. For in front of him lay the lower part of a man's body, and a little further on was the remainder. Turning away, he scrambled into a nearby crater. There sheltering from the overhead threat were two*

Private Fred Tucker, killed.

more Pals, one looking little more than a youth. After a short stay with the two men, Joe decided to make a final bid to reach the comparative safety of the trench, from where he was taken to a field dressing station. Thence to England.[45]

For other Pals, even the shelter they could scramble to gave no guarantee of survival.

Mrs Higginbottom whose husband Private J F Higginbottom was in C Company, Leeds Pals, has received a letter from the Chaplain to the Battalion, who writes that Private Higginbottom was wounded in a trench, 'but I fear that he was killed where he lay, like so many more, before he could be removed … Many men were seen wounded, and then nothing at all was heard of them, many were buried in the trenches owing to the shellfire, and I feel pretty sure that this happened to your poor husband'.[46]

Mr T Axe has received news that his brother Private Arthur Cecil Axe, C Coy, died in action on July 1st. While the War Office has intimated that he is missing, a comrade, Private H Evans who is in hospital in Hants, in a letter to Mr Axe says 'Your noble brother succumbed to a wound in the thigh. I went over the top along with him and he was quite cool. We had got about 20 yards when Arthur received the wound. I tried to bandage his thigh, but I had to press on. A bullet broke my leg when I had got about ten yards from him. I lay there all day and at night, with a great effort, I crawled back to our lines. I passed Arthur on the way back and saw that he was dead.'[47]

Mr C. W. H. Tucker of Harrogate received the following letter from his son's Platoon Sergeant, Eric Jenkyns of A Company:

I can give you all the particulars that you want about Fred Tucker as he was in my Platoon. I saw he had been reported missing, but he was killed halfway across 'No Man's Land' between the English and German lines on that terrible morning we went over. He was one of the best men and was always a chap you could trust to help you in a tight corner anytime. He was killed helping a Pal into a shell-hole who was terribly wounded, everybody seems to have been laid out except Fred, and he lay down and tried to drag this other into a shell-hole for safety. All this was done under an appalling bombardment, the whole world seemed to be on fire. He was killed absolutely instantaneously, as he was lying so peacefully with a beautiful smile on his face. He was laid to rest with all the other boys we left behind there. Tell Mrs Tucker he died as he had lived, a hero and a perfect gentleman and as fine a friend as anybody could have wished for and we all feel his loss keenly.[48]

Crouched in a shell-hole, Arthur Pearson had a narrow escape.

The noise was shattering, as every burst hit you under the tin hat rim and deafened you. By this time the sergeant and I were the only two left alive in the shell-hole, curled up to be as little exposed as possible. During a burst of shellfire I felt two terrific thumps on my back. I couldn't do anything about it then, but when I eventually got the chance to take off my gear, I saw what had caused the

HEROIC SONS OF YORKSHIRE.

HEAVY CASUALTIES IN BIG ADVANCE.

LEEDS "PALS" BATTALION LOSES MANY MEN.

OFFICER IN COMMAND AMONG THE KILLED.

In the fighting in the British offensive last week-end no battalion appears to have suffered more severely than the Leeds " Pals " Battalion. Many more casualties are announced to-day as having occurred on July 1, a date which will long be a fateful memory in Leeds. Yesterday we announced the death of Captain. E. C. Whitaker and Lieut. S. Morris Bickersteth, who had been officers in the battalion since its formation. To-day to the list of killed has to be added the names of Captain S. T. A. Neil, Lieut. J. G. Vause, and Sec.-Lieut. T. Willey.

Capt. Stanley T. A. Neil, who was temporarily in command of the battalion, was the second son of Mr. V. W. Neil, assistant to Mr. Geo. A. Hart, sewerage engineer of the Leeds Corporation. He was 27 years of age and unmarried. A civil engineer by profession, he was, before the war, the resident engineer (under Mr. C. J. Henzell, waterworks engineer to the Leeds Corporation) at New Leighton Reservoir. He also took a large share of the responsibility for the design and erection of the new camp at Colsterdale.

Capt. Neil joined the " Pals " as a ranker when the battalion was formed. He was immediately promoted lieutenant, and given his captaincy just before they left for Egypt last December. He came home on leave last month, returning to France on Saturday, June 3. While in Leeds he visited the homes of most of the Leeds " Pals " who had fallen or had been wounded.

CAPT. S. T. A. NEIL.
(Killed.)

2nd-LIEUT. WILLEY.
(Killed.)

Photos: Hoskins.

Second-Lieut. Willey is the elder son of Mr. Arthur Willey, solicitor, for whom much sympathy has been expressed in Leeds to-day. Mr. Willey has received sympathetic letters from Major Hartley, who now commands the battalion in succession to Capt. (temporary Major) Neil. Another officer of the battalion writes:— " It has been a terrible business for our poor battalion. I have asked several men about poor Tom Willey, and they say he was magnificent. He was the hero of the battalion, both with officers and men. From the bottom of my heart I grieve for you. I cannot write more now. Vause, Whitaker, Bickersteth, Neil, and many more are gone."

The death of Lieut. Tom Willey will cause widespread regret. Only 19 years of age, he was an undoubted favourite wherever he went. Educated at Roscoes College, Harrogate, and at Harrow he was articled to his father, and joined the ' Pals " as a private, being given a commission six months later. At his weight he was the best boxer in the battalion.

Mr. F. W Vause, of 32, Clarendon Road, Leeds, and of the firm of Thomas Vause and Sons (Limited), shoddy manufacturers, Low Road, Hunslet, has been officially informed that his youngest son Lieut. John Gilbert Vause, is among the missing. Lieut. Vause, who was single and 23 years of age, was acting captain

when the big offensive was made. When the war broke out he was an apprentice with the firm of Messrs. Mortimer and Co., woollen manufacturers, Morley.

He was educated at the Leeds Grammar School, and later at the Leeds University.

Among the non-commissioned officers and men reported wounded is Lance-Corporal G. Mawson, youngest son of Mr. Banks Mawson, of The Boundary, Street Lane, Roundhay, who sustained shrapnel wounds in his arm and is now in hospital in England. Private Richard Kitchen, of 35, Emsley Terrace, Beeston Road, Leeds, was wounded in the left hand and right leg.

Three sons of Mr. C. E. Mason, of " The Yorkshire Post," are serving with the Pals, and word has been received that one of them, Private Roy Mason, has been shot through the right calf and is now in a Manchester hospital. He is progressing satisfactorily. Mr. W. Abdy, of the London City and Midland Bank, City Square, Leeds, has also received news that his only son, Lance-Corporal C. W. Abdy, has been wounded and is in a Bristol hospital. Before the commencement of the war Lance-Corporal Abdy, who is 27 years of age, was in the employment of Messrs. T. F. Braime and Co. (Ltd.), engineers, Hunslet.

Lieut. O. S. HYDE.
(Killed.)

Lieut. J. G. VAUSE.
(Missing.)

Private Fred Wild, wounded.

thumps and what a lucky escape I had had. Through my haversack, which had been worn on my back, were four holes – each the size of a half-crown. Two holes were in the front where the shrapnel had entered and struck two tins of bully beef bursting them open and then turned out through the bottom of the haversack. But for those two tins of Fray Bentos', those lumps of steel would have gone right through me!

15/711 Private Arthur V. Pearson, C Company[49]

In the trenches of the British front line, the men who were to follow the fighting waves prepared to go over, although it was clear that the attack had fallen into chaos under the murderous fire pouring from the German lines.

202

A charabanc outing in Britain for some wounded soldiers, among them Fred Wild. (N. Wallace)

I was sent over to find out how the first wave of attack had got on and what advance they'd made, and there was no actual sign of anybody, they'd all been wiped out.

I was hit. I was knocked down, something hit me and I was knocked down and I thought I'd been … my head blown off. Eventually I got up and when the roll call was taken of the survivors after the battle, the officer said 'Have you seen your helmet, Cryer.' I said 'No'. When I took it off and looked there was a bulge in my helmet, steel helmet, that I could get my fist in, and it was a huge piece of shrapnel that had ricocheted off and if I hadn't had my helmet on I would have had my brains blown out!

15/1110 Private Cyril Charles Cryer, Battalion Runner[50]

I didn't go in the first wave, no. Oh, the first wave, they'd been gone ten minutes before I went. When I got over it were too late.

We knew what were happening, we saw the wounded coming back, because they passed us on the Leeds Trench and my friend Fred Wild, passed me wounded. He came home and he told them, 'Don't worry, Cliff didn't go over the top', he says, 'don't worry', but he'd gone when we went you see. He was wounded in the first wave, got a nasty wound. He could walk but only just, mind you he said he fainted when he got to the dressing station. I said 'It served you right, you shouldn't have been in such a big hurry.'

I was picked out with Sergeant Summersgill, he was the water man, I was ready with a pannier at the front, two at the front and one at the back, square petrol cans with the screw top, burnt out so there's no smell of petrol and filled full of water, and my uniform and my kit on. I broke three ladders in getting up. I weighed nearly thirteen stone and then I had those damned things, then they said why hadn't I run? I said 'Run? I couldn't ruddy well walk'.

Stretcher-bearers carry a wounded man along a narrow communication trench on the Somme.

> *Anyway, we went over, we went over to see if we could do anything but no, they were all dead. We were looking for wounded that wanted a drink, but they were all dead.*
>
> *15/471 Private Clifford Hollingworth, D Company[51]*

Seriously wounded and unable to move, some men lay out in no man's land all day and into the night. Lance-Corporal Sydney Hicks of No.2 Platoon, A Company, who had received three or four shrapnel wounds, was hit again by a machine-gun bullet as he made his way back towards the trenches.

> *… This of course crippled me and I had to stop where I was from 8am Saturday to about 10pm Sunday when one of our stretcher-bearers found me. They could not come out until dark. It was*

THE WAR'S TOLL ON YORKSHIRE.

FURTHER LIST OF KILLED AND WOUNDED.

LEEDS PALS' CASUALTIES.

OFFICERS AND MEN WHO FELL IN THE GREAT OFFENSIVE.

A further batch of casualties among officers and men of the Leeds Pals Battalion is to hand to-day, and emphasises how severely the city battalion suffered in leading the attack in their sector last Saturday.

The latest casualties mostly relate to men who have been wounded. One of the Pals, writing from hospital at Manchester, says:—"Our battalion was the first in our division to go over 'the top,' and, of course, we suffered heavily. Lieutenant Dickenteth was killed directly he got over at 7.30, and nearly all the officers were placed 'hors de combat' early on."

Second-Lieutenant Leonard Foster is the latest of the Pals' officers who is announced to have been wounded. He is in hospital in France. Lieutenant Foster, in civil life, was an architect and surveyor, in the service of the Leeds City Council.

One of the Pals who lost his life was Private Frederick Richard Lewis, who lived at Stratford Street, Dewsbury Road, Leeds. He was 21 years of age, and prior to joining up, was a clerk in the Dewsbury Road branch of the Yorkshire Penny Bank. So far as can be ascertained, he died whilst being brought back to England on the hospital ship. He was at one time a member of the Leeds Parish Church choir.

Private Charles Bannister (23), is reported to have died from wounds. He was the only son of Mr. Tom Bannister, organ builder, of Blackman Lane. He was a letterpress machinist, employed at Goodall and Suddick, printers.

The following are some of the non-commissioned officers and men of the battalion, of whom official notification has been received that they are wounded:—

Company Sergeant-Major Gill was wounded early in last Saturday's advance. He took part in the South African war as a colour-sergeant. He was an electrical engineer. His wife lives at 42, Warrender Street, Meanwood Road, Leeds.

Sergeant Lawrence A Hudson, son of Mr. Albert Hudson, 14, St. John's Terrace, Leeds. Now at Northampton Hospital. He was with Collett's (Ltd.), Shaftesbury Avenue, London, before the war.

Sergeant Walter Moorhouse, son of Mr. J. W. Moorhouse, 4, Ridgway Terrace, Hyde Park, was shot through the neck, and is in hospital in France.

Sergeant Edgar Chapman has sent word to his wife, at 75, Mexborough Street, Leeds, that he is wounded in the head, and is in hospital in the Isle of Wight.

Lance-Corporal James Nicol, of Spencer Place, of Messrs. Nicol and Co., electro-typers, is now in hospital in Cheshire.

Sergeant Cyril Sheard, son of Mr. A. Sheard, of Springfield Place, has received a shrapnel wound in the left leg.

Lance-Sergeant Gordon B. Gillatt, son of Mr. S. B. Gillatt, tailor, Allison Place, was wounded in five places, but is doing well.

Lance-Corporal Claud Thornton and Private Cecil Thornton, two brothers, are both reported wounded. The home of the former, who is married, is at 78, Winfield Mount, Leeds.

Lance-Corporal J. Wharton, of Roundhay, who was employed at David Little's, is reported seriously wounded.

Private R. LEWIS.
(Killed.)

Sergeant-Major GILL.
(Wounded.)

Corporal W. A. Hey is back in England, wounded. He is the son of Mr. E. A. Hey, of 16, Airlie Place, Markham Avenue, Leeds.

Corporal W. Marchant, the son of Mr. Joseph Marchant, of 39, Victoria Street, Chapel-Allerton, has been wounded in the head, and is now in a Birmingham Hospital. He was managing clerk at the office of Mr. A. Pettitt, solicitor, of Albion Place.

Lance-Corporal J. Wharton and Private J. W. Calvert were out as a listening post, on June 11th, when they were attacked by a German bombing party and both wounded. They are progressing fairly well at a York hospital.

is a son of Mr. G. W. Jenkinson, of Newstead House, Spencer Place, Leeds.

Private John S. Mahon, of Wentworth Road, Doncaster, was wounded, and is now in hospital near Chester.

Private T. Scholefield is in a Sheffield hospital suffering from wounds in the leg, hand, and shoulder. He lived at 20, Moorfield Place, Beeston Hill.

Private J. Brady, whose parents reside at 37, Caledonian Street, Leeds, is among the wounded.

Private J. Pape, of 129, Cardigan Road, Leeds, has also fallen. He was employed with Messrs. William Pape and Co. (Ltd.), tailors, of Grace Street.

Private Albert Holton, of 321, Kirkstall Road, another victim, was formerly employed by Messrs. Chartons, engineers, Hunslet.

Private W. N. Sutcliffe, of Bristol Road, who was employed at Messrs. Edmondson's clothing warehouse, is in hospital; and Private Sydney Atkinson, of Camberley Street, Dewsbury Road, is injured in the left forearm.

Private W. Limbert, elder son of Mr. J. Limbert, 24, Ellers Road, has been shot through the thigh, and is now in hospital at Bristol.

Private J. E. J. Mason, a member of the staff of the Bradford District Bank, was wounded by shrapnel, and is in hospital at Chichester. He is a son of Mr. Joseph Mason, of Eton Place, Hyde Park.

Private J. Wright, an assistant at the Co-operative Society's Dewsbury Road Branch, was wounded on June 26. His home is at 117, Cemetery Road, Beeston Hill.

Private Basil Storey has been wounded in the arm,

2nd Lieut. D. E. WARD
(Wounded.)

Lieut. G. C. WARD
(Killed.)

and is in Didsbury Hospital. He is the son of Mr. and Mrs. Robert Storey, of Harehills Lane.

Private Esmond A. Wigglesworth, the youngest of three brothers who are serving, and whose address is 8, Hawes Street, Rider Road, Woodhouse, is in hospital in London.

Private John F. C. Park was wounded by a shell, and was assisted to safety by his twin brother, Signaller James Park, of the same company. The wounded soldier, whose home is at 3, Belmont Grove, Clarendon Road, is doing well at Cardiff Hospital.

Private George W. Clarkson, who is wounded, was a student at the Leeds University until he joined the Pals.

Private G. E. Webster, whose mother lives at 47, Ingram Road, Domestic Street, is in a Manchester hospital suffering from a bullet wound in the right leg.

Private W. H. Gibson, son of Mr. M. Gibson, of 15, West View, Beeston Hill, is in Gloucester Hospital, suffering from shrapnel and bullet wounds.

Private C. E. Exley, of 10, Grove Gardens, Headingley, is in Gravesend Hospital.

Private H. Evans, who is wounded, lived at 60, Clifton Mount, Harehills.

Private Walter Metcalf, son of Mr. Richard Metcalf, wholesale confectioner, of Morley, has lost his right leg.

Private Norman Howarth, wounded in the leg by shrapnel, is an only son, and lived at 17, Ayresome Avenue, Roundhay.

Private Douglas Agutter, one of two sons of Mr. E. F. Agutter, 11, Norman Terrace, Street Lane, who are in the "Pals," was wounded in the leg.

Other wounded men of whom very brief messages have been received are:—Private J. W. Collinson (20), of 12, Longwood Grove, Hunslet; Private Harold Carter, whose wife lives at 23, West End Terrace, Hyde Park; Sergeant Tom Crowther, Lance-Corporal G. W. Hinchliffe, and Privates W. Jones, H. Armitage, L. Pontefract, W. Ramsden, and H. Shaw, members of the Pudsey Conservative Club; Private Ralph Turner, of De Lacy Mount, Kirkstall, wounded in face; Private Sydney Redshaw, youngest son of Mr. Harry Redshaw, removing contractor, of Leeds; Private Fred Wild, 49, Rosebank Grove; Lance-Corporal Vernon West, 309, Roundhay Road; and Private J. Raymond Pickard, is in hospital at Liverpool. Others in hospital at Bristol include A. Mann, F. Abrams, E. Major, W. A. Armitage, T. Beecroft, H. Brockbank, A. Richardson, A. Hodgson, A. H. Swetman, W. H. Gibson, E. Spence, F. Stead, and H. Blackwell.

Lance-Corporal Frank Briggs, youngest son of the late Mr. W. J. and Mrs. Briggs, of 53, Mount Preston, has been hit on the jaw-bone.

The Leeds Rifles have also been in heavy fighting.

Mr. and Mrs. W. G. Ward, of Fregmore, Upper Armley, Leeds, have received news that one of their sons has been killed in the big battle and another seriously wounded, and both of them are officers in one of the battalions of the Leeds Rifles. Lieutenant G. C. Ward, their fourth son, who has been killed, and Second-Lieutenant D. E. Ward, their fifth son is wounded. Both casualties occurred on July 2.

One of the rank and file of the Leeds Rifles, Private William Dobson (31), was wounded on Saturday.

Lieutenant Percy C. Bunns, a Leeds man who has been wounded, was in the Miners' Battn. of the K.O.Y.L.I., and in command of a trench mortar battery in *not a nice experience lying there, not being able to move and wondering if they would find me, and the beastly Huns were shelling the whole time. However, I prayed God to help me, and He has answered my prayer.*

15/456 Lance Corporal Sydney Hicks, A Company[52]

Searching no man's land that night was a dangerous job, as it was still being raked by machine-gun and artillery fire; and Private Sydney Rayfield, a battalion stretcher-bearer, was among those killed while looking for the wounded.

Not all who were rescued survived. Wilfred Denison Lumb, seriously wounded in the stomach, lay out in no man's land, calling to his comrades. His cries were heard by Harold Green, who led some of his section out to find Lumb and bring him in. Lumb died of his wounds on 3 July. His parents, who had already suffered the loss of their youngest son the previous year, sent Denison's wristwatch to Harold Green as a keepsake in thanks for his efforts.[53]

Private Cryer and some of his friends helped to bring in a wounded man.

We rescued him from a shell-hole, as we were going over the ground, we heard somebody moaning. He was very badly wounded, he couldn't move and we somehow got him on a temporary stretcher and carried him to a First Aid Station, just a few yards up the line. It was all uneven and blown up, you know. I've lost sight of him since then, how he got on.

Private Cyril Charles Cryer, who rescued Arthur Dobson from no man's land.

15/1110 Private Cyril Charles Cryer, D Company Runner[54]

The man they had rescued was Private Arthur S. Dobson, but it was too late to save him, for he died later that day.[55]

Another Pal who succumbed to his wounds was Sergeant Albert Gutteridge, one of Yorkshire's finest athletes. He suffered a broken leg and five other wounds when he was blown out of one shell-hole into another. Evacuated to England, he died in Bethnal Green Hospital, London, after having his broken leg amputated. Private John Aspinall suffered a similar fate. He was evacuated to Netley Hospital where his left leg was amputated at the knee on 14 July, and he was reported to be doing fairly well. On the next day he died.[56]

Altogether ten Leeds Pals died of wounds received on 1 July, after arriving in Britain. One man, Frederick Lewis, died on a hospital ship on 5 July, while on his way home to Britain.[57]

The 10 per cent who had been held in reserve[58] watched in horror as their wounded Pals staggered back, and were soon employed in bringing out the dead who lay in the assembly trenches.

I were in the transport, I were helping the following day to bring some dead in as well on lorries, we called them limbers not lorries, and we were bringing back what we could and we were burying them. We buried a lot in one hole. It were a case of making a man up, wrapping 'em in a blanket. It was a sickening job really, especially as you knew a lot of them, who weren't recognisable any longer.

15/259 Private Arthur Dalby, Transport Section[59]

At home in Leeds, after reading optimistic reports of a breakthrough on the Somme, the families of the Leeds Pals gradually learned the horrific truth about the disaster at Serre.

*Private (later Sergeant) Harold Green and the
letter he was sent by Wilfred Lumb's parents.*

The columns of the local press were black with the names of those who had been killed or wounded and right into August there were desperate pleas for information from the families of those who were listed as missing.

There were, however, some people who clearly had sensed that all was not well. Grace Newton was helping her mother prepare their regular parcel for Private Tom Newton, her brother, when she had an awful feeling that something was wrong. Tom was killed in the attack, and would no longer worry about being taunted while on leave in Leeds.[60]

*Private Arthur Spencer Dobson,
died of wounds 1 July 1916.*

*Private John Aspinall, died of
wounds 15 July 1916.*

Private Tom Newton, killed.

14 Ashworth Place
Woodhouse Leeds
Yorks
Sunday July 9th

My Dear Horace

Just a line or two to thank you very much for the card which mother gave me yesterday it is very pretty. I am so glad you are alright so far but I need not tell you what an anxious time I am having on your account. You have dropped in for the thick of it and no mistake I only hope you have the good luck to come back safely like your father did. and my dear boy I dont care how soon I should be more than pleased to see you I can tell you. You have no need to feel ashamed that you joined the 'Pals' now for by all accounts they have rendered a good account of themselves no one can call them "Feather-bed soldiers" now. I think Barron's boss has got him off so he will feel a bit easier if it is so. He has not told me himself so I am not sure, but I think it must be right. Bob has not heard yet but is expecting to hear

any day now. We did hear that they were fetched all back from France under 19. for goodness sake Horace tell them how old you are I am sure they will send you back if they know you are only 16 you have had quite enough now just chuck it up and try to get back you wont fare any worse for it if you dont do it now you will come back in bits and we want the whole of you. I dont suppose you can do any letter writing now but just remember that I am always thinking of you and hoping for your safe return so no more this time only my love Bob says you are to hurry up and come back.

Your loving sister Florrie
x x x x x x x x x

P.S. Did you know Roy Mason had been wounded; shot in the leg, he is now in Manchester hospital. F.

Iles's letter from his sister, Florence, written some days after his death on 1 July.

Killed in Action
Pte H Iles 1782
15 West Yorks
31 Division
A. P. O. S.11
B.E.F.

Private Horace Iles poses in a borrowed uniform in 1914. He was 14 years old when this photograph was taken. Killed.

Florence Iles of Woodhouse wrote to her brother, Horace, on 9 July, pleading with him to own up to the fact that he was only 16 years old, as men under 19 were being returned from France. Horace had lied about his age to join the Pals when he was just 14. He had been wounded during the German bombardment on 22 May and had not long returned from a spell in hospital. He was killed on 1 July, and his sister's letter was returned by the Infantry Records Office at York marked 'Killed in Action'. He was probably the youngest Leeds Pal to be killed, but he was not the only one under the age of 19. Private Tom Clarkson, who died of wounds in St Bartholomew's Hospital in London, was only 17. He was buried with full military honours in Holbeck Cemetery on 17 July.[61]

At least one of the Pals seems to have got as far as the German lines, and there been taken prisoner.

Private Arthur 'Snowy' Howard, captured.

> *'Snowy' Howard, you've heard me speak of 'Snowy', he got through to Serre.[62] He was taken with about eight others. He said, 'All I did, Cliff,' he told me after the war, 'I just kept going over the wire like that, going over the wire, kept saying Come on! I turned round,' he said, 'there was twenty of us and I found out there was two of us and went and got into Serre village.' But, he said 'You see that saved our lives, by doing that. If we'd have stopped we should have been killed, but we got clear of the fire.' They got into the clear ground you see, where there was nothing except machine-gun bullets, but then they were taken prisoner. When they were taken prisoner he said 'Cor blimey, I thought we'd won!' He said, 'I was waiting for them to put their hands up and they didn't'*
>
> *15/471 Private Clifford Hollingworth, D Company[63]*

Behind the lines the medical staff at the Casualty Clearing Stations desperately tried to treat the wounded men as they were brought in. Inevitably, some of the less urgent cases had to wait until the following day before they were seen by a doctor.

> *2 July 1916 – Awoke about 5am and soon after formed queue to have name registered etc. Between 6am and noon was inoculated for tetanus and bandaged by the nice doctor – had long wait in queue – big crowds. Started to make for train and in slow stages managed to get on train about 5pm for Gezaincourt – where arrived about 7.30.*
>
> *15/231 Private George W. Cosby, B Company[64]*

The Pals stayed in the line until 5 July. They had been reinforced by forty members of the '10 per cent detail' that had been left behind, and by the 12th King's Own Yorkshire Light Infantry, who were to dig communication trenches from the saps that ran out into no man's land from the front line. While the Pals were still in the trenches, they were also joined by Second-Lieutenant G. S. King from the 9th KOYLI.

Every night, parties continued to go out into no man's land to search for the wounded and to try to bring in the bodies that lay all over the shell-torn battlefield.

When the battalion was relieved on the afternoon of 5 July, an estimated forty-seven of the men who had gone into the attack marched out, and even they weren't entirely unscathed.

> *Twenty-five of us were slightly wounded, a chap with a piece of shrapnel in his arm picked it out, but he was bleeding. So when we got back into the trenches, I said 'Come on, give us your pad', you always used his dressing, not yours. So anyway I bandaged it up with his first-aid [dressing].*

A wounded soldier waits for attention.

> *Well, that's what we did with one another, just tidied ourselves up and then, two days after we got out, a handful of men came. Then a Corporal came with another [lot] of men, he took charge, then gradually we got a unit but only forty-seven of the original came out.*
>
> *15/471 Private Clifford Hollingworth, D Company*[66]

On the following morning all that remained of the battalion was paraded and addressed by Lieutenant-General Sir Aylmer Hunter-Weston, the VIII Corps Commander, and every man received a printed letter of congratulation from him.

The men were then marched to Beauval and, on 7 July, marched to billets at Fienvillers where they were met by a draft of fifty-five reinforcements. On 8 July they continued their journey, marching to Contevilliers where they were put on a train for Burgette. Eventually they marched to Busnes where, on 10 July, they were addressed by their Divisional Commander, Major-General Wanless O'Gowan, who also congratulated them. The men who had survived the attack had also been addressed, soon after their return from the trenches, by their Brigade Commander, Brigadier General Ingles, although his speech was not well received.

GALLANTRY OF OUR MEN IN THE ADVANCE.

TE TO THE LEEDS AND BRADFORD PALS.

OFFICER'S LETTER.

SUALTIES AMONG OFFICERS AND MEN.

ributes to the gallantry of the Leeds and Pals in the British offensive north of the July 1 are paid by officers who witnessed k.

View, Leeds, was employed as a cutter by Messrs. Joseph's, clothiers, Leeds.

Private Clifford E. Evans, of Haigh House, Stourton, severely wounded, in hospital at Chichester, was a draughtsman at Messrs. Kitson's and Company, Hunslet.

Sergeant A. Gattridge is in a London hospital, with a broken leg and five other wounds. He was one of the best athletes in Yorkshire and one of the chief officers of the Leeds Athletic Harriers and a sterling distance runner. He was with Messrs. Russell, printers, Leeds.

Private Eric Mitchell, son of Mr. Fred Mitchell, Fairlea, Wood Lane, Headingley, of the firm of Messrs. Mark Oldroyd and Sons (Ltd.), Dewsbury, is in base hospital in France, slightly wounded in the left temple, back of the neck, and shoulder. He is 1 years of age, and was a student at the Leeds University (Textile Department).

Private F. Boot, of 22, Crockell Street, Holbeck, who was buried twice and then wounded in the side, was employed at Messrs. Rhodes' clothing factory, Marsh Street.

Private W. H. Hewington, of 105, Bayswater Place, Leeds, hit in the left arm, is at the Royal Infirmary, Manchester.

Private Russell Fawbert, son of the late Mr. Henry Fawbert, and Mrs. Fawbert, Castor House, Station Road, Castleford, wounded in the back and left side, is in a Norfolk hospital.

her. At the formation of the Sportsman's Battalion he joined as a private, and was subsequently given a commission. Second-Lieutenant Haigh, who was a Selby lawyer, captained the Selby Mizpah Association Football Club, and was also a well-known cricketer.

Second-Lieutenant Arthur Basil Lee, West Yorkshire Regiment, only son of Mr. C. A. Lee, manager of the Ilkley branch of the Bank of Liverpool, was killed on July 2nd. Before the war Lieutenant Lee was with Messrs. Sutherland, Parker and Co., stuff merchants, Bradford, and was a playing member of the Ilkley Rugby Union Football Club. Captain MacKay, in a letter to Mr. Lee, informing him of his son's death, states that Lieutenant Lee was leading his men along a German trench they had just taken, when a German officer, from a dug-out, shot him with his revolver. Death was instantaneous and painless.

Captain Alan Clough, of the West Yorkshire Regi-

BRIDLINGTON LADY'S ... WITH GERMANS.

PARTING GIFT OF TWO ROSES FROM AN OFFICER.

The Danish steamer Flora, which was stopped in the Cattegat while on her voyage from Copenhagen to England, and taken into Swinemunde by the Germans, reached Hull last night. The vessel was captured on Wednesday by a submarine, in accordance with German Admiralty orders, and taken to Swinemunde in order to find out if she was carrying cargo other than agricultural produce. This was found not to be the case, and the steamer was thereupon released.

The vessel, which is commanded by Captain Petersen, is a regular Hull trader. There were seven passengers on board, only one of whom was a British subject, a young lady, Miss Hermon, of Bridlington, who has been in Denmark for the past 12 months undergoing

t the officers persistently reported killed in the letters from the front appeared the name nant J. G. Vause, and an announcement to t appeared in the Press on Friday. His father, . Vause, of 32, Clarendon Road, Leeds, has,

SEC.-LT. A. B. LEE (Killed). SEC.-LT. J. J. HAIGH (Missing).

rer, on seeking news about him from the War received a telegram in reply, stating: "Lieut. J. G. Vause is reported missing July 1st. This not necessarily mean wounded or killed." to date the casualties of the Leeds Pals officers reported as follow:—

KILLED.	WOUNDED.
. E. C. M. Deplodge.	Lieut.-Col. S. Taylor.
. G. C. Whitaker.	Major R. B. Neill.
. S. T. A. Neil.	Capt. P. H. L. Mellor.
t. J. K. Wardle.	Capt. J. W. Stanley.
t. R. B. H. Rayner.	Lieut. R. M. S. Blease.
t S. M. Bickersteth.	Lieut. B. D. Gill.
t. E. H. Lintott.	Sec.-Lieut. A. N. Hutton.
-Lieut. T. A. Willey.	Sec.-Lieut. Pope Smith.
-Lieut. J. P. Everitt.	Sec.-Lieut. Elphinstone.
-Lieut. V. Oland.	Sec.-Lieut. Leek.
-Lieut. M. W. Booth.	Sec.-Lieut. Wells.
-Lieut. A. Liversedge.	Sec.-Lieut. Jones
MISSING.	Sec.-Lieut. Bayley.
ent. J. G. Vause.	
eut. R. H. Tolson.	

A LONG LIST OF WOUNDED MEN IN HOSPITAL.

Few additional official announcements have as yet been made in regard to men of the Leeds Pals Battalion killed in the big battle.

The death in action of Private A. S. Dobson, whose home is at Meynell Road, Colton, near Leeds, has been announced to relatives by his chum, who is now in hospital. Private Dobson was 28 years of age, and single, and employed by Messrs. Isaac J. Dewhirst, wholesale drapers, Kirkgate, Leeds.

Another of the Pals, Private John Edwin Balme, eldest son of Mr. George P. Balme, of Outwood, has died in Netley Hospital from his wounds. He was 26 years of age.

The following are men of the Pals Battalion who have been wounded:

Private James Pape, son of Mr. W. M. Pape, 129, Cardigan Road, Headingley, Leeds, is wounded and not killed as was first reported. He is in hospital in France, and is doing well.

Lance-Corporal W. Norman Brown is in hospital at West Didsbury. He is the son of Mr. W. Thomas Brown, late of Harehills, and now of York.

Private Fred M. Walton, of 3, Laurel Terrace, Stanks, Cross-

GOOD NEWS OF ARTHUR DOLPHIN.

Much uncertainty has been expressed regarding the welfare of Private Arthur Dolphin, the well-known Yorkshire cricketer, who is in the Leeds Pals Battalion. A postcard received by his wife is reassuring. He states that he is "doing his bit, and is all right." In a letter

Private DOBSON. (Killed) Private F. DALTON (Killed).

received a week ago he stated that bits of shrapnel had struck him on the head, but that his "tin hat" had saved him.

"I am more convinced than ever," he wrote, "that the Germans are getting whacked. While they are getting weaker we are getting stronger." Using a cricket metaphor, he adds: "I thought it was just a bit different from playing for England at Lord's. It is the biggest match of all time, and I have an idea that we are wearing the Hun bowlers out. In the end we shall have ... they will have to get a few to win."

THE DEBIT SIDE OF THE BRITISH OFFENSIVE.

LEEDS TROOPS WHO KNEW HOW TO DIE.

COLONEL TAYLOR'S SORROW.

LAST MOMENTS OF LIEUTENANTS BOOTH AND LINTOTT.

A touching letter deploring the heavy losses in the Leeds Pals Battalion is published to-day from Lieut.-Col. Stuart Taylor, the commanding officer of the battalion, who was wounded some weeks before the attack on July 1st. Col. Taylor, who is now at Queen Alexandra's Hospital for Officers, in London, writes:—

I mourn the loss of tried comrades and dear friends, men with whom I have been closely associated, day and night, in sunshine and storm, for the past fourteen months. But with my sorrow is mingled an immense pride, a great gladness, as I hear from all sources of the magnificent bearing and heroic conduct of our dear lads, who have cheerfully given their lives for their King and country. The tidings of their gallant conduct and courageous deeds causes me no surprise, as I well know how splendidly they would stand the test when the supreme call was made upon them.

To those who are left behind to mourn their loss may God grant consolation in the sure knowledge of their dear ones' valiant death. For the wounded I pray earnestly for a speedy return to health and strength. For myself my only wish is that I had been able to be with the battalion in their great and glorious attack.

In the list of Leeds Pals officers' casualties published in the "Yorkshire Evening Post," yesterday, appeared the names of twelve officers who had been killed, two missing, and thirteen wounded. It now appears that Sec.-Lieut. R. H. Tolson is no longer missing, but is wounded, and in hospital. A telegram to that effect has been received from the War Office by his father, Mr. Whiteley Tolson, of Dalton, Huddersfield. Lieut. Tolson was in Beckett's Bank, Leeds, prior to the war. Joining the Public Schools Battalion as a private, he obtained a commission in the K.O.Y.L.I., and was transferred to the Pals last September.

We reproduce to-day a photograph of Lieut.-Colonel L. M. Howard, lately commanding the Tyneside Irish, and for nearly a year adjutant of the Leeds Pals, who has died of wounds.

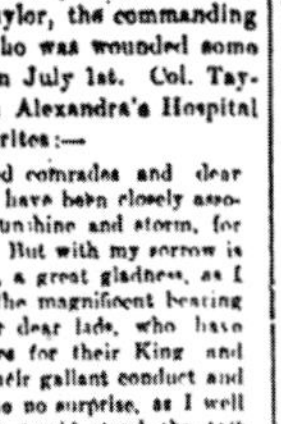

Lieut.-Col. L. M. HOWARD. (Killed). Photo: Bacon.

In a letter which we have received to-day from one of the Pals, the writer says:—"Lieut. Lintott's end was particularly gallant. He led his men with great dash, and when hit the first time declined to take the count. Instead, he drew his revolver and called for a further effort. Again he was hit and still he struggled on, but a third shot finally bowled him over. Lieut. Booth, too, though in sore agony from a shell fragment which penetrated the shoulder, and must have touched the heart, tried his utmost to go forward, but pitched forward helplessly after going a few yards. He and Lintott were two gallant sportsmen who know how to die—but, then, so did all the boys. They went out to almost certain death with just the cry, 'Now Leeds!' on their lips."

There is, after all, sad confirmation of the death of Lieut. J. G. Vause, the son of Mr. F. W. Vause, of 32, Clarendon Road, Leeds. Lieut. Vause was officially reported missing by the War Office, but a private in his platoon, who is now lying wounded in the Third Western General Hospital, at Newport (Mon.), gives particulars of the manner of his death. Lieut. Vause was first hit in the elbow just as he led his men over the parapet. He went on however, and after having his wound bound up, reached the barbed-wire entanglements in front of the German trenches which his platoon had to take. He was hit a second time in the thigh, and, with the only remaining soldier in his platoon by his side, he lay in a trench under a terrible bombardment.

His companion, in describing their situation, says: "We lay there talking about Leeds and discussing the possibilities of getting home again. Lieut. Vause told me that he had been recommended for his third star, and he was very much 'up' about it." Some time has just about finished me off," and died shortly afterwards. His companion lay with two shattered legs for 36 hours before being rescued.

Lieut. J. P. Everitt was in charge of the first platoon of the Leeds Pals to go over the parapet, and he was killed before he had gone more than a few yards. The command then devolved upon a sergeant.

ROY KILNER'S LETTER.

Corporal Roy Kilner, the Yorkshire county cricketer, who is in hospital at Birmingham, has written to Mr. F. C. Toone, the county secretary, stating that his wound is in the right wrist, which he hopes will soon be quite sound again. Referring to the death of his fellow county cricketer, Lieutenant M. Booth, he writes:—"He was always the same old fellow, one of the few who never did get 'swelled head.' I had the pleasure of being in his company on the eve of the 'scrap'—also Dolphin. I cannot say what's become of Dolphin. He is lucky if he has got out. Let's hope he has. He did not go over with the lads, because he was what you would call 'twelfth man.'" After referring to the possibility of getting a bit of cricket with Yorkshire soon, he says, "When I see you I shall be able to give you a better idea of what happened on that awful Saturday morning when poor old Major went west. We can never replace him—in fact Yorkshire will not be Yorkshire for a long time without Major Booth."

Letters of sympathy upon the death of Lieutenant Booth have been received by Mr. Toone, the secretary of the Yorkshire County Cricket Club, from Captain H. D. G. Leveson-Gower, captain of the Surrey Eleven, and Dr. Russell Bencraft, president of the Hampshire County Club. Captain Leveson-Gower writes: "Will you kindly convey to the president of the Yorkshire County Cricket Club and the members of the Committee my very sincere sympathy at the loss sustained by the death of Lieutenant Booth. He died as he lived in the real sense of the word 'playing the game.' Cricket has lost in him not only a great player, but a fine example and type of the professional cricketer." Dr. Bencraft sympathises with Yorkshire in the loss of "not only a brilliant cricketer but a charming fellow."

Lance-Corporal S. C. Hicks, son of Mr. and Mrs. F. J. Hicks, 120, Hyde Park Road, has been wounded. Writing to his wife, who resides at Norwood Road, Leeds, he says he had 3 or 4 slight shrapnel wounds, and just as he was getting back into a bit of trench, he was shot through the hip by a machine-gun bullet. "This, of course, crippled me," he writes, "and I had to stop where I was from 8 a.m. Saturday to about 10 p.m. on Sunday, when our stretcher-bearers found me. They could not come out until dark. It was not a nice experience lying there, not being able to move and wondering if they would find me, and the beastly Huns were shelling the whole time. However, I prayed God to help me, and he has answered my prayer."

THE LEEDS PALS' LOSSES.

SEVERAL OF THE RANK AND FILE DEAD FROM WOUNDS.

Several more of the Leeds Pals' rank and file are reported dead.

We learned to-day that Company Sergeant-Major Harry Gill, who was wounded on July 1st, succumbed to his injuries two days later and was buried in the civil cemetery at Doullens. His wife lives at 42, Warrender Street, Meanwood Road, Leeds. The sergeant-major was nearly drowned on his 21st birthday in the River Vaal, while serving in the Boer War, being rescued by Private Coultate, of the Leeds Rifles.

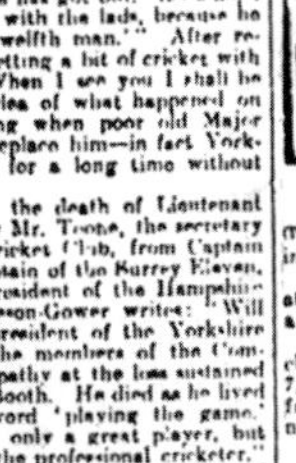

C.S.-M. HARRY GILL. (Died from wounds).

Sergeant-Major Gill formerly served 14 years with the Leeds Rifles, and had the Territorial Medal. He was an electrical engineer at the Leeds Slate and Marble Works. He was a nephew of Mr. Arthur Gill, the well-known Leeds Labour leader.

Private F. R. Lewis has died on board ship of gunshot wounds received in action. He was 22 years of age, and lived with his parents at 95, Stratford Road, Dewsbury Road, Leeds. Prior to the war he was employed at the Dewsbury Road branch of the Yorkshire Penny Bank. The funeral, which will be the first in Leeds of a Leeds Pal, takes place to-morrow afternoon, at Holbeck Cemetery, preceded by a service at the Leeds Parish Church.

Private Harry Dent, of the Leeds Pals, has died in Carlisle Hospital of wounds. Twenty-one years of age, he was the youngest son of the late Mr. Harry Dent, late of the Harrison's Arms, Harrison Street, Leeds. The funeral, which will take place in Leeds, on Thursday, will be of a military character. A service will be held at two o'clock, and the burial will take place at

Private Walter Metcalfe (21), who is dead, was the only son of Mr. Richard Metcalfe, jam and cake manufacturer, of Park Dene, Morley. He succumbed to his wounds on Sunday, at the military hospital, Whalley, Lancashire. Private Metcalfe had had one leg amputated at the knee. Prior to joining the Army, he assisted his father. He was formerly a choir boy at St. Andrew's, Bruntcliffe, Morley. The body will be

Lieut. W. P. TAYLOR. (Killed.) (Photo: Bacon.) Lieut. R. T. CASEBOURNE. (Killed.) (Photo: Bacon.)

interred at Morley Cemetery on Thursday afternoon.

Private J. Kerbetson (killed) lived with his parents at 11, Broadway Street, Beeston Hill. He was killed by a shell on July 3.

Signaller W. R. Priestley is reported by one of his chums to be missing. His mother, Mrs. Priestley, of 7, Broomfield Road, Headingley, who has not heard from him since the big battle began, would welcome news about him.

A LONG LIST OF WOUNDED

Non-commissioned officers and privates of the battalion who are reported wounded include:

Sergeant Victor Richardson, only son of Mr. A. Richardson, 28, Winston Gardens, Headingley, now at a convalescent camp in France with a slight shrapnel wound in the shoulder. He is a member of the staff of the Yorkshire Penny Bank.

Lance-Sergeant ... Naylor, son of Mr. H. R. Naylor, 4, Quarry Mount Street, Leeds, wounded with shrapnel in the right thigh; in hospital at Stockport.

Private Frank Wilson (19), of 13, Cheetham Avenue, Dewsbury Road, wounded in arm; employed by Messrs. J. Fowler and Sons.

Private T. E. Noble (21), son of Mr. W. Noble, Bridlepath Cottages, Seacroft, wounded in left shoulder, now at the Royal Victoria Infirmary, Newcastle.

Mrs. Wathall, of 5, Regent Terrace, Leeds, has been informed that her husband, Private Walter Wathall, is lying, wounded by shrapnel in the thigh, in the Dorset County Hospital, Dorchester.

The two brothers of Mr. F. W. Jones, of 17, Seaforth Grove, Harehills, are injured. Private H. P. Jones is wounded in the left arm, and is in hospital at Sittingbourne, Kent. Private P. M. Jones, who was buried in a front line trench and was injured in the back, is in a French convalescent camp. The latter, prior to enlistment, was employed by Messrs. Ashworth, Brown, and Company.

Another employee of the same firm wounded is Private G. W. Farndale, whose home is at Colton. His wound is in the shoulder. He is in hospital at Tarporley, Cheshire.

Two other brothers who have been wounded are Privates Stanley and Jim Worboys, sons of Mr. and Mrs. Worboys, of Tong Village, late of Burley. The former is in Edmonton Hospital, London, and the latter in hospital at Aldershot. Both worked for Ashworth, Brown, and Co., St. Paul's Street.

Private John Rockliffe, son of Mrs. K. Foster, of 1, Markham Crescent, Haxby Road, York, is in hospital at Orrell, Lancs., suffering from slight wounds and shell shock. He was formerly a clerk in the goods department of the North-Eastern Railway.

Private Thomas Clarke (17) is in St. Bartholomew's Hospital, London, suffering from shrapnel wounds in the head.

Private Ernest Lindley, formerly a cutter with Messrs. J. May and Son, Leeds, is in a Cheshire hospital with a wound in the left arm.

Two former Leeds employees of the National Health Insurance Committee wounded are Private Jack Allsopp, of Chapel Allerton, and Private J. W. Parkinson, of 12, Gipton Mount, Gathorne Terrace. The former, with a shrapnel wound in the thigh, is in a Kent hospital, and the latter in a hospital in France.

Private T. A. Herd, whose parents reside at 65, Clifton Terrace, Leeds, has been wounded for the second time. He is now in hospital in England.

Private J. W. Perkins, who was attached to the Pals R.A.M.C. Field Ambulance, is wounded in back and arms, and lies in Warrington Hospital. He was 21 years of age, and resided with his widowed mother at Woodgrove Street, Kirkstall. He was employed at Messrs. Atkinson's ... Mills, Horsforth.

Private A. Nelson, son of Mr. and Mrs. W. C. Nelson, 44

Rifleman ARTHUR WILSON. (Killed.) Rifleman F. RAWNSLEY. (Killed.)

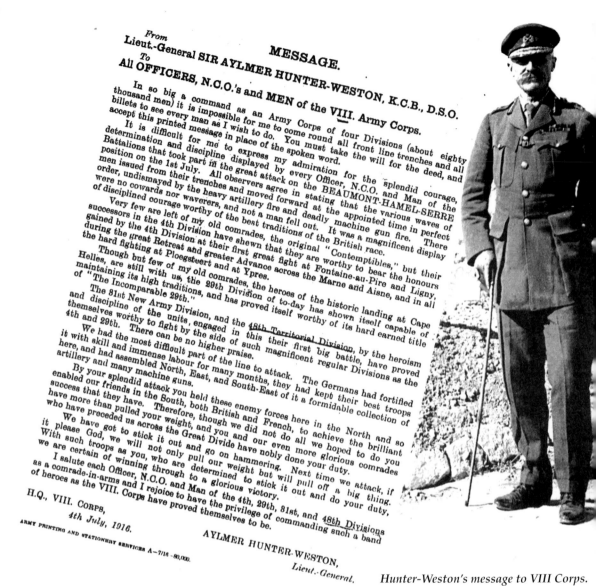

Hunter-Weston's message to VIII Corps.

… Brigadier came round, Brigadier Ingles. Said' You've done a good job chaps, you've done a very good job!', and one fellow said, 'We've hell as like!' He said, 'I beg your pardon? He said' We've hell as like, we've lost!' He said, 'Don't talk like that, lost, you mustn't speak like that, man!'

'Have we won then? 'Cos if we've won, God help us if we lose!' If we'd won that battle [where] we'd lost 600 men, I don't know how we should have got on if we'd lost.

15/471 Private Clifford Hollingworth, D Company[66]

The attack on Serre was a failure, on a day when there were few successes along the British front of assault. Serre was a particularly tough nut to crack, being the northern flank of the

ENING POST, WEDNESDAY, JULY 12, 1916.

OUR LOSSES ON THE SOMME.

FFRE CONGRATULATES THE BRITISH.

OF LEEDS AND BRADFORD.

"WE ARE PROUD OF THEM, BUT WE MISS THEM."

have just received a message from General e, saying that it was owing to the fight we p that successes were made all along the line. congratulations of General Joffre were, it seems, the brigade which includes the battalions of and Bradford Pals, on the big offensive of

The writer of the letter from which the above is made is Private F. W. Lennox, of the Leeds Battalion, who says, in writing from a rest n France: "What a life to be here after put- a big fight in the trenches, with its roar of d exploding shells. I am sat as peaceful as you within a beautiful orchard ed? Well, perhaps we are a bit—but we don't because we can breathe freely, and there is no There is certainly a sad tone keeps running the theme, bringing back memories of lads ve by now found their place and are resting. they will be wearing their laurels which they y deserved—the bravest of the brave, and we, mrades, who have been fighting side by side, them. We do not mourn; we are proud of ut we miss them."

stated yesterday through a misunderstanding . Whiteley Tolson, of Dalton, Huddersfield, had rom the War Office that his son, Second Lieut. Tolson, of the Leeds Pals Battalion, is wounded hospital. All the news at present received of Tolson is that he was wounded on July 1, and onfirmed by a letter from the battalion chaplain t. Tolson's wife, but his father has no news of reabouts, and is naturally very anxious.

ugh the War Office have reported Sec.-Lieut. Willey, of the Leeds Pals Battalion, as "miss- ll hope regarding his fate has unhappily to be ned upon the receipt of a telegram by his Alderman Arthur Willey, from the chaplain of talion, announcing, "Tom undoubtedly gone."

e indicated yesterday, the Leeds Rifles played ortant part in the fighting on July 1, though not advance from their trenches until the after- that day. The commanding officer of the 8th n Leeds Rifles (Lieut.-Colonel J. W. Alexander) uck on the arm by a stone thrown up by the n of the shell which killed Lieut. G. C. Ward. mmanding officer was not, fortunately, seriously

J. H. SIMPSON.

Lieut. R. D. ANDERSON. (Wounded and missing). Photo: Wilson, Wakefield.

d remained at the head of his men.

ave received a number of letters regarding s of the Pals Battalion from whom nothing has ard since the attack. It may be that letters from en or news of them will come through soon.

HE CASUALTIES IN THE LEEDS PALS.

FURTHER LIST OF NAMES.

casualties are reported among the Leeds Pals

Wilfred Sewell has died at Netley Hospital from wounds in the head and right thigh. He was of age, and son of the late Mr. Robert Sewell, let. His wife lives at 24, Newlaun Cottages. The body, which has been brought to Leeds, interred at Woodhouse Hill Cemetery, Hunslet. nd Mrs. T. Brook, of 14, Beckett Street, Leeds, ard that their son, Pte. Herbert Brook, has been He was 23 years old, enlisted in the Leeds Pals e battalion was formed, and was formerly em- by Mr. Pearson, joiner, Benson Street.

Rowland Poskitt has died of wounds in France. well-known in agricultural circles in the Whitley district. The eldest son of Mr. J. E. Poskitt, ngton, he was married a year ago to the eldest r of Mr. Thomas Beard, of Toxe Garth, Bur- nard, and leaves, besides his widow, a baby girl. te Clifford Hirst, who has died from wounds, oungest son of Mrs. Hirst, of the Crown Hotel, Road, Dewsbury. He was a member of the Heaton Cricket Club. He was wounded in s, and was lying in the trenches a considerable ore he was discovered. His age was 25 years. Alfred Moore, Thorndene, Crawshaw Avenue, would like to know the whereabouts of [illegible]

EVENING POST, THURSDAY, JULY 13, 1916.

MORE YORKSHIRE CASUALTIES.

MEN OF WHOM NOTHING HAS YET BEEN HEARD.

MANY ANXIOUS INQUIRIES.

YOUNG FELLOWS FROM ROUNDHAY IN THE THICK OF THE FIGHT.

We have received to-day further details as to the losses suffered by the Leeds Pals Battalion in the British offensive north of the Somme on July 1. Again the casualties are almost exclusively those relating to non-commissioned officers and men, who are wounded. It is probable that the full extent of the casualties to the officers is now known. "The Yorkshire Evening Post" has, indeed, published the names of fourteen officers who have been killed (including five killed before July 1), and fourteen who have been wounded. From the ranks we have published particulars of over 900 men who have been wounded, and from the anxious inquiries which are being made daily it is obvious that there are many men about whom, unfortunately, nothing has been heard since the big fight began.

One of a number of letters received to-day relates that "Dolphin, the Yorkshire cricketer, is all right," and mentions a number of young fellows from Roundhay who were "in the thick of the fight and enjoyed themselves immensely." One of them was George Dimery, one of the soldier-sons of Mr. Dimery, the headmaster of the Shadwell Industrial School. Dimery is described as "the first of six to get into the German trenches," and he came back without a scratch. Horace Beevers (a Leeds journalist), Jack Crossland, and "a number of other Roundhay boys" are reported to be quite safe, but "Mick" (otherwise Norman) Brown is in hospital near Manchester.

News is desired by the relatives regarding Private Norris Haigh, of the Leeds Pals, of 72, Pasture Road, Goole, who has been reported to have died of wounds; Corpl. Sidney Welton (reported missing), whose sister lives at 27, Gathorne Mount, Roundhay Road, Leeds; and Private W. Place, 10th West Yorkshires, of 1, Belle Isle Road, Hunslet Carr, who has been variously reported wounded and killed.

HUNS WHO SHOWED HUMANITY.

We have received letters to-day relating to two Leeds soldiers who acknowledge having received kindness even at the hands of the Germans. Private Harry Metcalf, whose mother lives at 31, Greenhow Walk, Burley, Leeds, was wounded in the thigh on July 1st, and was captured by the Germans. He was taken into one of their dug-outs, and was treated exceptionally well by his captors, who dressed his wound and gave him drink and smokes.

The following day the Germans themselves were captured, and Metcalf, who is in the West Yorkshires, was restored to his friends. He is now in the Essex County Hospital. Prior to the war he was a draper's assistant, employed by the Leeds Co-operative Society, in Albion Street. He has a brother, Private F. Metcalf, of the 10th Hussars, who is back in France after having been wounded.

Rifleman William Deacon, of the Leeds Rifles, also reports having been succoured by the enemy. He was wounded in the advance, and after lying nearly two days in the open, he was picked up and brought into our lines by a German who himself had been wounded. He and all his friends greatly appreciated this unexpected kindness. Rifleman Deacon, whose home is in Somers Street, off West Street, Leeds, is now in Fulham Hospital. His father, who is a member of the Leeds City Police Force, is also out at the front.

A GALLANT LAD OF 17.

Pte. Thomas Clarkson, of 30, Recreation Crescent, Holbeck, has died of wounds at St. Bartholomew's Hospital, London. He was only 17 years of age. Joining the Reserve Battalion of the Pals a year ago, he answered a call for volunteers to go abroad with the first battalion, and he was among the limited number accepted. His injury was a shrapnel wound in the head.

MORE OF THE PALS IN HOSPITAL.

The following further casualties are reported among the Leeds Pals to-day:—

Pte. J. W. Nicholson is in hospital at Birmingham seriously wounded. The youngest son of John Nicholson, Aselton Grange, Thorpe Stapleton, Knostrop, he is under 19 years of age. Before the war he was employed at Messrs. All Cooke's, Leeds.

Pte. Herbert Stephenson, aged 28, the youngest son of Mr. Isaac Stephenson, of The Avenue, Roundhay, received gunshot wounds in the right leg. He was at first reported dangerously ill, but a telegram received this morning from the casualty clearing station in France states that he is improving.

Signaller G. E. Todd (21), youngest son of Mr. and Mrs. Todd, Harehills, is in hospital at Weymouth, suffering from a shrapnel wound in the left foot.

Pte. Perry Gundill, wounded in the back by shrapnel, is 19 years of age, and youngest son of Mr. Henry Gundill, of Pontefract, and brother of Mr. Norman Gundill, solicitor.

Pte. H. Armitage, son of Mr. T. Armitage, Glebe Street, Pudsey, is in the Grange Hospital, Southport. Though he was buried for some time, his injuries are not very serious.

L.-Cpl. J. Willie Hinchliffe, only son of Mr. J. W. Hinchliffe, secretary of the Pudsey Conservative Club, is in hospital at Southampton wounded. He was a clerk at Messrs. All Cooke's, Leeds, and a promising young cricketer with the Pudsey St. [illegible]

EVENING POST, FRIDAY, JULY 14, 1916.

YORKSHIRE'S CASUALTY ROLL.

LARGE NUMBER OF DEATHS REPORTED TO-DAY.

THE LEEDS PALS' LOSSES.

MORE ABOUT THE PRICE OF OUR RECENT GAINS.

A further batch of casualties among members of the Leeds Pals and other local battalions has been notified to-day. Never has the city suffered so much personal bereavement and anxiety. Casualties to the Leeds Pals, Leeds Rifles, and other local battalions have been notified this week in hundreds, and, daily, anxious relatives ask us to publish the names of husbands and sons who are missing, in the hope that satisfactory tidings may be gleaned as to their welfare.

Among those of whom news is desired are Sec.-Lieut. M. H. Webster, of the Bradford Pals, whose father, Mr. R. Webster, of the Hollies, Wesley Road, Armley, has heard unofficially that he was killed in action. Relatives are seeking news of Pte. J. G. Brook (Leeds Pals), 48, Lower Oxford Street, Castleford; Pte. Ernest Hardy (10th West Yorkshires), 10, Cliff Road, Hyde Park, Leeds; Pte. Harold Wheatley (Leeds Pals), Holly Park, Calverley; Pte. Clifford Calderhead (Leeds Pals), 78, Reuben Street, Carlton Hill, Leeds; Corporal Edward Healy (Leeds Pals), 13, Norwood Road, Headingley; and Pte. J. D. Thompson (Leeds Pals), 8, Strathmore Avenue, Harehills; Pte. Herbert W. Sunderland (Leeds Pals), 14, Hyde Park Terrace, Leeds.

Lieut. M. H. Webster, mentioned above, gained his B.A. degree at the Leeds University. He enlisted as a private in the Highland Light Infantry a year ago, and served with that regiment in France about five months, when he received a commission. He returned to the front on the 15th of last month, being posted to the Bradford Pals. He was 22 years of age. His only brother, Willis Webster, is serving with the R.F.A.

HOW CITY EMPLOYEES FARED.

Mr. H. B. Rhodes, chief clerk in the Gas, Water, and Electric Light Department of the Leeds Corporation, has received a letter, to-day, from Lance-Corporal A. Hague, who is with the Pals in France, giving the following reported list of casualties among municipal employees in the battalion:

City Treasurer's Department:

- Corporal J. H. Wilkinson, wounded.
- [illegible]
- F. M. Walton, wounded.
- Slater, missing.

Gas, Water, and Electric Light Department:

- A. Meeson, killed.
- F. Rayner, killed.
- A. Cornforth, wounded.
- H. H. J. Mason, wounded.
- W. H. Briggs, wounded.
- G. W. Atkinson, wounded.
- N. Haddon, wounded.
- Lance-Corporal A. Hague, wounded.

Lance-Corporal Hague states in his letter that his

Sec.-Lieut. M. H. WEBSTER. (Killed.)

Sec.-Lieut. C. C. FRANK. (Missing.)

wrist watch was "smashed to smithereens" by a German bullet, and his clothing is punctured in several places.

"I am proud to say," he continues, "that the lads of the office stood their corner like heroes, and the battalion itself has made a name for itself that will never be forgotten. . . . The weather is fine and sunny, and it is good to be alive."

PALS WHO HAVE DIED.

Several more of the Pals have lost their lives as a result of the recent fighting. Mr. and Mrs. G. D. Lumb, of 31, Lyddon Terrace, Leeds, have suffered a second bereavement by the death of their second son, Private Wilfred Denison Lumb, who was wounded on July 1st, and died two days later in hospital in France. Private Lumb, who was 26 years of age, was educated at Leeds Grammar School, and was at the Leeds branch of the London City and Midland Bank. About a year ago his youngest brother, who was in the Yorkshire Hussars, was killed in action.

Two members of the Leeds Postal Department—Sergt. H. Hewitt and Corpl. J. Sharples—are reported to have fallen in action while serving with the Leeds Pals. Sergt. Hewitt was a married man, and lived at 39, Norman Street, Kirkstall. Corpl. Sharples was a single man, and his parents live at 1, Pasture Grove, Chapel-Allerton. Both were 33 years of age and ex-members of the branch committee.

Another of the Pals who has lost his life is Pte. T. Clarkson, of Recreation Crescent, Holbeck, who has died at St. Bartholomew's Hospital, London, from a shrapnel wound in the head. He was only 17 years old. He went out to the front from the reserve battalion.

Sergeant Clifford Brook, who joined the Pals Bat-

Sergt. W. BOOTH. (Killed).

Pte. E. R. STRANGEWAY. (Killed).

talion when it was formed, is reported killed. Twenty-four years of age, he was only married last November. In civil life he was employed by Messrs. George Mann and Co. (Limited), Hunslet Road, Leeds.

Private George Abbott, of 39, Whitcliffe Road, Cleckheaton, is reported to have died at the 2nd Canadian General Hospital, Le Treport. He was wounded in the thigh, which caused injury to the abdomen.

Official notification was received this morning of the death in hospital, in France, of Private John Ernest Dodgson, aged 21, only son of Mr. and Mrs. John T. Dodgson, of Uplands, Old Park Road, Roundhay, and grandson of the late Mr. Dixon Marshall, of Parkhurst, Headingley. Educated at Billaston School, Nantwich, Cheshire, which he left in 1912, the young man entered on a course of study at the Leeds University, which he was pursuing up to the time of his joining the Pals Battalion on its formation.

Private Harold Wheatley, of the Leeds Pals, is officially reported missing. He is 21 years of age, and the son of Mr. Sam Wheatley, Holly Park, Calverley. He joined the Pals a year ago, and was employed at the Lydgate Mills, Calverley.

The following other casualties are reported among the rank and file of the Pals:

Private Walter Berry, of Oulton, is in Whitchurch Metropolitan Hospital, near Cardiff, suffering from shell shock. Has since had rheumatic fever.

Private Sidney Lawlor, wounded in the leg, is the son of

offensive. Although there was a diversionary attack further north, at Gommecourt, it must have been obvious to the Germans that the mile-long sector of their line north of Serre was not about to be attacked. They could therefore concentrate all their considerable defensive efforts in that sector against the 93 and 94 Brigade attacks.

A few days before the attack, I pointed out to General Hunter-Weston that the assembly trenches stopped dead on the left of 94th Brigade and that not a spade had been put into the ground between me and the subsidiary attack at Gommecourt. Worse still, no effort at wire-cutting was made on that stretch either. A child could see where the flank of our attack lay, to within ten yards.

Brigadier-General H. C. Rees, GOC 94 Brigade[67]

What the British heavy artillery failed to do a direct hit on a German ammunition dump.

'ENING POST, SATURDAY, JULY 15, 1916.

E COST OF THE OFFENSIVE.

OOPS OF WHOM LEEDS IS JUSTLY PROUD.

E ABOUT THE ADVANCE.

LATOONS OF THE PALS FIRST "OVER THE LID."

de which all Leeds citizens feel in the gal-
gh costly part played by the city battalions,
and Rifles, in the first onset of the big
is shared by the troops at present stationed
y. Col L. G. F. Gordon, in command at
n Barracks, has addressed the following
the Lord Mayor of Leeds (Mr. Charles Lup-

writing on behalf of the officers and men
Reserve Brigade R.F.A., to express our
ion of the gallant manner in which our com-
om Leeds have behaved in the late severe
, and to express our deep sympathy with
tives of those who have fallen so gloriously.

details of the advance of the Pals against the
renches are furnished in a letter sent by Pte.
Hollings to his father, a member of the Leeds
cil. He writes that the honour of being first
lid" in the whole brigade belonged to the
13th platoons of the Pals Battalion. Lieut.
ey led the 13th platoon with the cry "Come
to them boil!"

Hollings says he owes his life to the fact that
tailed to bring up ammunition. He writes of
, steady way in which our lads climb over
es on to the parapet and made for their posi-
gular order. I have often read the phrase 'As if
I thought it rather ambiguous, but I am a
longer; I've seen it done. We felt inspired
out of the trenches watching them."

A LOSS TO THE LEEDS RIFLES.

eds Rifles who, in the neighbourhood of Thiep-
ripated in very heavy fighting, have suffered
rious loss in the death of Major Arthur Frank
, although only 31 years of age, had been con-
ith the Leeds Volunteers and Territorials for
We have previously reported him wounded,
s now died from his wounds at Queen Alexan-
pital for officers, in London. He was a director
Hess and Brother (Ltd.), oil manufacturers.

R. M. Pinder, of the West Riding Regiment,
pital in France suffering from a shrapnel
the head received on July 3. He is the
son of Dr. and Mrs. Pinder, Lee House, Hors-
was in the University of Leeds O.T.C.
R. D. Johnson, Sportsmen's Battalion, killed

H. BOTTOMLEY.
and Lancaster.
d)

Capt. R. D. JOHNSON,
Royal Fusiliers.
(Killed).

joined the Leeds Pals as a private on its
Before enlistment he was an inspect-
eer for the National Boiler and General
Company, and lived at 39, Ash Grove, Head-
He was 36 years of age and married.
ant Edwin H. Bottomley, York and Lancas-
ent, son of Mrs. M. Bottomley, Woodville,
was seriously wounded in the face and leg on
and is now in the hospital at St. Gabriel's Col-
berwell.

Audsley, of 117, Tong Road, Armley, whose
nd-Lieutenant E. C. Audsley, is unofficially re-
missing, has received a letter from a brother
ho expresses a belief that the young man,
eriously wounded, may have been picked up
some other unit.
informed that Lieut. Ellis (K.O.Y.L.I.), of
whose name appeared in the casualty list pub-
night, did not belong to the Mirfield Terri-
was stated.

HARROGATE OFFICER KILLED.

Lieut. Alfred Victor Ratcliffe, West York-
ment, aged 29, was killed in action on July
he third line German trench, near Fricourt,
he third son of Mrs. Brotherton Ratcliffe, of
oad, Harrogate, and nephew of Col. Brother-
oundhay, Leeds.
d at Dulwich and Sidney Sussex, Cambridge,
student of the Inner Temple, and joined the
the outbreak of war. On his next leave he
ave been married to Miss Pauline Benson
daughter of Mr Benson Clough, of the Inner
and Mrs. Benson Clough, Oxshott, Surrey,
ridge he was a friend of the late Rupert
nd had himself published many poems, which
favourably reviewed

'S ANXIOUSLY AWAITED.

S PALS OF WHOM RELATIVES HAVE NO TIDINGS.

s for further news continue to be received
tives of Pals, of whom no official news is yet
forthcoming. Mr. J. E. Wilson, 1, Thornville Grove, Cardigan Road, inquires after his son, Private N. Wilson, C Co.; Mr. and Mrs. Brown, 40, Congress Street, after Private Lawrence Brown, 10 Platoon, C Co., unofficially reported dead; Mrs. Bland, Clifford House, York Road, after her husband, Corporal B. C. W. Bland, B Co., unofficially reported killed; Mrs. Lake, Coach and Horses Hotel, Rothwell Haigh, after her husband, Private T. W. Lake, D Co., reported wounded; Mrs. Max Wissler, Kingston Grove, after her husband, Lce-Cpl. Max Wissler; Mr. A. Whitley, 9, Patti Street, Meanwood Road, after Private G. A. Whitley; Mr. Buxton, Gipton Council School, after Private S. L. Buxton, D Co., and Corporal P. Cook, A Co.; Mr. Taylor, after Private Fred W. Taylor, C Co., variously reported as dead and as wounded; Mr. P. Cawood, 32, Hall Grove, after Private Fred Cawood; and Mrs. Hunter, 80, Seaforth Road, Harehills, after Private J. H. Hunter, C Co.

Reports received to-day of Pals wounded, include:—

Private Reggie O. Smith, son of Mrs. John Smith, Glebeland House, South Parade, Pudsey, is in hospital in France, with gunshot wounds in the head.

Private F. H. Slater, who was yesterday reported missing by another member of the battalion, is now said to be in hospital at Whalley, Lancashire, with a bullet wound in the ankle, and shrapnel wounds in the left thigh and at the base of the back. He was employed in the City Treasurer's Office, and resided at 4, Grove Gardens, Headingley.

Private J. Arnold is in Hook Bank Hospital with three wounds. He lived with his parents at 2, Easton Mount, Holbeck.

Private T. H. Blackman, severely wounded in the chest, is in hospital in France. He is the son of Mr. and Mrs. H. Blackman, 54, Temple Street, Hull, and was manager of Sloane's Billiard Saloon, Kirkgate.

Private Thomas Clarkson, son of Mr. and Mrs. W. H. Clarkson, 30, Recreation Crescent, Holbeck, who has died from wounds, is to be buried at Holbeck Cemetery on Monday at 3.30 p.m. There will be a service in the Baptist Chapel, Cemetery Road, at 2.45.

TUESDAY, JULY 18, 1916.

Street, off Burley Road, Leeds, fell in action on July 2. He was 19 years of age, and prior to enlisting worked for Mr. H. J. Cryer, Kirkstall Road.

MORE INQUIRIES AFTER MISSING PALS.

It is to be feared that the full extent of the Leeds Pals' losses on July 1 are not even yet fully known. The names of dozens of Pals who are missing have been published in "The Yorkshire Evening Post" during the last few days. Still the list is being added to by the following requests for news from relatives of Pals of whom nothing has been heard:—Mr. Thomas Ingleson, of 21, Victoria Terrace, inquires after his son, Private Ernest Ingleson; Mr. T. H. Axe, 5, Bayswater View, after Private A. C. Axe; Mrs. J. F. Higginbottom, 12, Grant Row, Roundhay Road, after her husband, Pte. J. F. Higginbottom; Mrs. Chapman, 5, Sultan Street, Whingate, Armley, after her son, Pte. H. D. Chapman; Mrs. Herley, 13, Airlie Avenue, Harehills, after Pte. J. W. Herley, light mortar trench battery; Mr. John Crowther, Ridley House, Grassington, after her son, Pte. Maurice R. Crowther, C Co.; Mr. A. Hill, Toulston, near Tadcaster, after his son, Signaller C. Hill; Mr. and Mrs. B. Wood, Leeds, after their son, Pte. Ben F. Wood; Mr. A. J. P. Heaton, Lingfield, Oxenhope, Yorks., after his brother, Pte. T. H. Heaton; Mr. and Mrs. Bowman, 6, Broughton Terrace, Harehills, after Pte. D. Bowman; Mr. S. Newton, 60, Marlborough Street, Park Lane, after Pte. T. Newton; Mr. Hall, of 10, Beech Grove Terrace, Leeds, after his cousin, Private W. Hall, 1161, A Company, son of the late Vicar of North Grimston, near Malton, and living, before the war, at Blenheim Avenue, Leeds.

Others whose relatives would be grateful for any news from those who fought with them are Pte. W. P. Bennett, West Yorkshires, of 16, Craven Street, Woodhouse, Leeds; Lance-Corpl. W. White, "A" Co., Leeds

Pte. M. R. CROWTHER,
Leeds Pals (missing).
Photo: Bacon.

Pte. F. E. TUCKER,
Leeds Pals (killed).
Photo: Davy.

Pals, son of Mr. and Mrs. J. White, 28, Hilton Road, Headingley; and Pte. Holmes, Leeds Pals, son of Mr. and Mrs. Holmes, 1, Beulah View, Woodhouse.

News has been received, through the parent of a wounded comrade, of the death of Pte. Samuel Lawrence Buxton, aged 27. He was the son of Mr. Joseph Buxton, headmaster of the Gipton Council School, Harehills Road, Leeds. Before enlisting he was on the staff of the National Provincial Bank of England at West Hartlepool.

Pte. F. E. Tucker (27), of the Leeds Pals, is officially reported to have been killed in action. He was the son of Mr. and Mrs. C. W. H. Tucker, Glencairn, Park Avenue, Harrogate.

Pte. Frank Thompson (24) is in Rouen Hospital with a wound in the thigh. His mother lives at 24, Chapel Lane, Headingley, and he was employed by the Royal Insurance Co., Park Row, Leeds.

Pte. H. D. Myers, son of Mr. W. A. Myers, of Calverley, is in hospital at Birmingham, wounded. He was employed by Messrs. A. Walton and Sons, Lydgate Mills, Calverley.

Pte. Harold Shaw, son of Mr. and Mrs. Shaw, of Oak Royd, Glebe Street, Pudsey, is in a Lincoln hospital, in which is another Pudsey soldier, Pte. Sheffield, one of five brothers who have joined the colours. Sheffield, who is the son of an old soldier and a well-known Pudsey cricketer, has been shot through the larynx, and has lost his speech. It is a year to-day since Mr. and Mrs. Shaw lost a son who was with the Leeds Rifles at Ypres, Cpl. John H. Shaw.

A wounded member of the Leeds Pals Battalion—Sergt. "Jack" Sheard—sends an interesting acrostic

RE EVENING POST, MONDAY, JULY 24, 1916.

MANY YORKSHIREMEN KILLED.

HEAVY LOSSES AMONGST LEEDS BATTALIONS.

THE PALS' LONG DEATH-ROLL.

WELL-KNOWN HEADINGLEY DOCTOR'S SON DANGEROUSLY WOUNDED.

To-day's list of casualties, which is particularly distressing to Leeds by reason of the long catalogue of killed among the Leeds Pals, relates almost exclusively to casualties sustained in the Allies' great offensive on the Western front since July 1.

Another Leeds officer reported killed is Sec.-Lieut. Herbert Parsons, of the 2nd Royal Scots, who enlisted as a private at the beginning of the war. After attaining sergeant's rank, he obtained a commission and went out to France in September, 1915. He was wounded on December 5, and on returning to France, was killed on July 16. He was formerly a pupil of the Leeds Modern School, and gained an honours B.A. at London University, and was a well-known player of the Wakefield Rugby football club. His parents, Mr. and Mrs. Thomas Parsons, live at 298, Harehills Lane, Leeds.

Sec.-Lieut. C. A. WOOLER
West Yorks (killed).

Sec.-Lieut. H. PARSONS,
Royal Scots (killed).

Sec.-Lieut. Wm. Andrew Turnbull, Green Howards, a member of a well-known firm of Scarborough solicitors, was killed in action in France a week ago. He was 38 years of age.

Sec.-Lieut Arnold Nicholl, West Riding Regiment, whose mother lives at 2, Third Avenue, Manor Drive, Halifax, was killed in action on July 18. His commanding officer, in a sympathetic letter to Mrs. Nicholl, writes that the young officer—he was 25 years of age—was killed instantaneously by a shell which blew in the roof of his dug-out at midnight while he was asleep. Before the war, he was in the employ of Messrs. Frederick Smith and Sons, wire manufacturers, Halifax.

Sec.-Lieut. Godfrey Belasyse Smith, Machine Gun Corps, who has been dangerously wounded in the thigh is the second son of Dr. Archbold Smith, of Headingley. He was farming in Canada when the war broke out, but returned and obtained a commission in the York and Lancaster Regiment, with which he served until he was transferred to the Machine Gun Corps.

Sec.-Lieut. F. Baldwin, who has been wounded whilst commanding a trench mortar battery, was for many

Private B. JONES,
Leeds Pals (killed).

Private J. W. HERLEY,
Leeds Pals (killed).
Photo: Bacon.

years connected with the Leeds Rifles, with whom he went out to France, being subsequently given a commission in another battalion.

We give to-day a photograph of Sec.-Lieut. C. A. Wooler, whose death we have already recorded.

THE LEEDS PALS' LOSSES.

HEAVY ADDITIONS TO LIST OF MEN KILLED IN ACTION.

The following are brief particulars of members of the Leeds Pals' Battalion recorded to-day as dead:

Sergt. G. F. Easy, whose wife and two children live at 18, Otter Street, Kirkstall Road, was killed in action on July 1. At the age of 17 he enlisted in the 2nd W.Y.V.R. Engineers, and four years later became a sergeant. He served in the South African War, during which he was 16 weeks in hospital with enteric fever. For some time he was employed on the Leeds Corporation Tramways. He was 38 years of age.

Lance-Corporal A. Winch fell in the great attack. He formerly practised as an architect and surveyor at 62, Woodhouse Lane, and joined the Forces at the outbreak of war. He was 31 years of age.

L.-Cpl. Gerald Wilkinson, B Co., son of Mr. F. Wilkinson, stationmaster at Ulleskelf, was killed on July 1. He was a clerk in the booking office at Leeds New Station, N.E.R. A brother, Pte. Reginald Wilkinson, is reported to have been wounded on the same

Private J. C. DOUGHTY,
Leeds Pals (killed).

Private N. WILSON,
Leeds Pals (killed).

day, and is missing. He was a goods clerk at Crossgates.

Pte. J. W. Herley (23), Light Trench Mortar Battery, was killed by shrapnel whilst carrying a wounded comrade, Pte. W. Sowden, to safety. He was the only son of Mrs. Herley, 13, Airlie Avenue, Harehills.

Pte. J. G. Brook, C Co., was killed by a German machine gun on July 1, and is buried behind the lines. He was a clerk at the Prince of Wales Colliery, Pontefract, and his only and younger brother is a sergeant attached to the orderly room staff of the 2-5th K.O.Y.L.I. His parents live at 48, Lower Oxford Street, Castleford.

Pte. J. C. Doughty, only son of the late J. W. Doughty, of Farnley, and Mrs. Taylor, of 31, Cobden Road, Lower Wortley, is reported to have been killed. He was 22 years of age, and was a clerk with the Farnley Iron Company.

Pte. C. A. Hemingbrough, the only son of Mr. and Mrs. Hemingbrough, of 3, Camden Terrace, Woodhouse Lane, was killed in action on the 1st inst. He was 21

Private S. L. BUXTON,
Leeds Pals (killed).

Private A. HEMINGBROUGH
Leeds Pals (killed).

years of age, and was an assistant with Hyams and Co., Briggate.

Pte. J. H. Hunter, only son of the late Mr. Thomas Hunter and Mrs. Hunter, 80, Seaforth Road, Harehills, was killed in action on July 1. He was 27 years of age.

Pte. S. L. Buxton (27) is now officially reported to have been killed in action. His father is the headmaster of Gipton Council School, and he leaves a widow. He was 27 years of age, and was in the West Hartlepool branch of the National Provincial Bank.

Pte. Herbert Burnley (27) who is reported to have been killed in action by shell fire, was the youngest son of Mr. and Mrs. Walter Burnley, of Sisters Villas, Garforth. He was employed at the City Treasurer's Office, was an old Parish Church choir boy, and was educated at the Middle Class School. He was keenly interested in sport, being a member of the Garforth Golf Club. In a letter to his parents, a comrade says of Pte. Burnley:—"There was not a better soldier in the battalion, as, efficient himself, he did his best to get others to take a pride in their work. . . . He was second to none, not only in physique but as a soldier and bomber. . . . A true friend, he was always willing to do a good turn and help anyone who was down."

Mrs. Cawood, 9, Wilmington Grove, Leeds, has been informed by letter from the chaplain of the death of her husband, Private F. Cawood, machine-gun section. Previous to joining he was employed for many years by Messrs. J. Hepworth and Sons (Ltd.), clothiers, Clay Pit Lane, Leeds, as book-keeper. He leaves one son, aged 4 years, and was 34 years of age.

Information has now been received that Signaller R. W. Priestley, previously reported missing, was killed in action on July 1st. He joined the Pals Battalion on its formation, and previous to enlistment he was engaged at Messrs. Hyam and Co. (Ltd.), Briggate, Leeds. He was 23 years of age, and his relatives live at 7, Broomfield Road, Headingley.

Private ... Iles, who was only 18½ years old, was killed in action on July 1st. He belonged to D Company, and was the son of Mrs. Iles, 7, Spenceley Street, Woodhouse Lane. His father, the late Mr. William Iles, served through the Afghanistan campaign.

Official news has been received of the death of Pte. T. Herbert Heaton, Leeds Pals, on July 1st. He had been missing. He was the younger son of the late Mr. J. P. Heaton and Mrs. Heaton, Manorlands, Oxenhope, and a member of the firm of Messrs. J. P. Heaton and Co., Low Mills, Keighley.

Pte. Bert Wood, C Co., son of Mr. and Mrs. ...

The first day of the Battle of the Somme has been the subject of much discussion by generations of historians and soldiers, and there are many factors that are said to have contributed to the failure of most of the attacks: General Haig's policy of continuous aggression, which denied the British forces on the Western Front the opportunity of siting their trenches in positions of advantage, making use of natural features such as high ground, and which drove the Germans to fortify their lines, digging deep dugouts, especially in the chalk soil of the Somme, to protect them from British artillery fire. The Germans' superior tactical use of the

PENINSULAR & ORIENTAL STEAM
NAVIGATION COMPANY,

Mr. *Pte E. D. Longfield. 600.*
Berth No. *15th West Yorks Regt.*
Hospital Ship, "Egypt."
Havre to Southampton.
Date *4th July*. 1916.

A valuable document – Edric Longfield's ticket to Blighty.

machine gun which could, and did, stop whole brigades of attacking infantry, especially when they were attacking from a position of disadvantage, as at Serre. The British Army's blinkered reliance on its artillery being able to cut the barbed wire and kill the Germans before an infantry assault.

But perhaps an underestimated cause of the failure was inadequate counter-battery work by the British guns, which meant that an infantry attack, if stopped, would come under heavy artillery fire since the German guns were still in action.

While previous studies of the Pals battalions' attack at Serre[68] have, to their credit, placed great emphasis on locating the German machine guns and chronicling the

Private Edric Longfield, wounded.

Wounded soldiers at Portal Hospital, Cheshire, September 1916. Edric Longfield is third from left, back row.

German infantry's response to the assault, what is revealing when studying this attack, and particularly from the Leeds Pals' point of view, is the constant reference to the effects of the German artillery.

Of the seventy-five Leeds Pals whose wounds or cause of death were described in the casualty lists published between 7 and 31 July 1916 in the *Yorkshire Evening Post*, forty-three were attributed to shrapnel, six were buried or partially buried by shell-fire, five were shell-shocked and eight received both shrapnel and gunshot wounds. Only thirteen were listed as having gunshot wounds alone. This makes a total of sixty-two men, out of seventy-five, killed or injured by shell-fire, or about 82 per cent.

We have seen in this chapter how Morris Fleming described the ground that day as 'an upheaval', how Arthur Pearson and Charles Cryer had narrow escapes with pieces of shrapnel, how Morris Bickersteth was reported to have been killed by shrapnel and how the two men who saw him die were both buried by shells as they made their way back, one of them still carrying 'high-explosive' in his shoulder. We have also seen how Tom Willey was killed by a shell which took off his legs, and how Major Booth died from a shrapnel wound which pierced his heart. And so the list goes on …

Brigadier-General Rees, commander of the neighbouring 94 Brigade watched the attack from his headquarters that morning, and observed:

CASUALTIES OF YORKSHIRE REGIMENTS.

THE CASE OF THE MISSING.

LEEDS PALS' CHAPLAIN HOLDS OUT VERY LITTLE HOPE.

The price which has been, and is still being paid, for the great offensive on the Western front is once more reflected in the list of casualties to be published to-day.

Again Yorkshire and other North-Country regiments figure prominently in the lists. A not very encouraging message respecting the fate of the missing men of the Leeds Pals is contained in a letter from the battalion chaplain. "We hear," he writes, "that you think in Leeds that many have been taken prisoners, but we don't think here that this is to be relied on. They may have taken in five or six wounded men." From this one must regretfully conclude that the majority of those men posted as missing lost their lives in the great leap forward on July 1st.

That the older Leeds regiments, the two battalions of Rifles, have been equally in the thick of the fighting

Lieut. H. N. TURNER.   Capt. R. H. MURRAY.
West Yorks. (killed).   Yorks. Regt. (killed).
Photo: Wood, Darlington.

is shown by a letter from one of their officers. It appears that both battalions have been concerned in continuous fighting for over a fortnight. "Fortunately," he writes, "most of our casualties have been slightly wounded. We are still pushing all the time, and are going strong."

A Lewis officer in one of the West Yorkshire battalions, writing home, says: "No doubt you will have heard something about the wonderful German dugouts, but I wish you could see some of them about here. One we have been in is a most colossal affair, and without the slightest exaggeration I can say that it would not be an easy matter to put really a whole battalion in it. It is dug very deep, and is quite shell proof, containing dining rooms, kitchens, and bedrooms, in fact, everything that one can see in there, including handsome mirrors and electric bells. One of the passages is at least 50 yards long, and every portion of this underground mansion is boarded up.

CASUALTIES TO OFFICERS.

Lieutenant H. Norman Turner, West Yorkshire Regiment, eldest son of Mr. Arthur Turner, Dunollie, Headingley, near Leeds, was killed in action on July 14th, while leading his men. He was educated at the Leeds Grammar School, where he became a member of the O.T.C. After matriculating with first-class honours, he was articled with Messrs. H. H., and J. Blackburn, chartered accountants, East Parade, Leeds. Shortly after the outbreak of war, he joined the Leeds Pals as a private, and after a few months was given a commission. He was 22 years of age. His brother, Corporal

Pte. C. P. RYAL.   Sgt. H. HILL.   Pte. Trixer MASON.
Leeds Rifles   Signaller L.I.   Lincoler (killed).
(died of wounds).   (died of wounds).

Reginald Turner, is with the Cameron Highlanders in France.

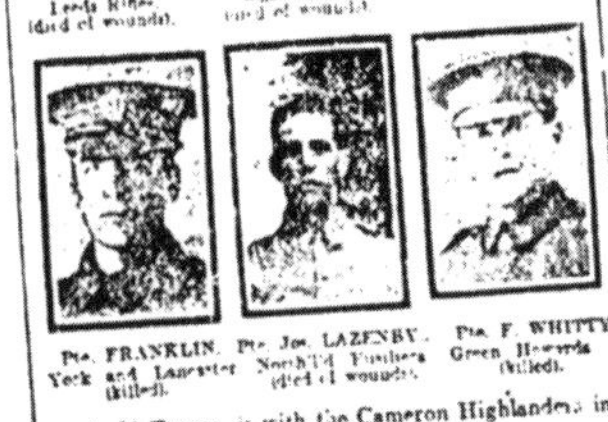

Captain R. H. Murray, Yorkshire Regiment (attached Royal Munster Fusiliers) was killed while attending to

a wounded man on the firing step of a trench. Captain Murray, the only son of Mr. and Mrs. R. Murray, of West House, Richmond, Yorkshire, was a Cambridge University man, and rowed in the Selwyn College boat at Henley Regatta just before the war.

Second-Lieutenant Richard Pearce Brown, Durham Light Infantry, killed on the 17th inst., was cashier at the Doncaster branch of the London Joint Stock Bank when the war broke out. His parents live at Whitebrook, Monmouth. Before receiving his commission he served in the ranks of the Coldstream Guards.

Captain Richard E. C. Ranson, East Yorkshire Regiment, who met his death on the 21st inst., was the nephew of Miss Ranson, Spring Bank, Hull.

Mr. C. E. Plackett, of Glenmore, Gledhow, Leeds, has received news from the colonel of his son's battalion that there is good ground for believing that Captain C. H. Plackett, officially reported as missing, is a prisoner.

Captain Bernard Louis Wilcher, of the West Yorkshire Regiment, wounded in the leg by shrapnel, was, before the war, in the insurance business in Leeds, and in the Headingley district. A keen Rugby football enthusiast, he has assisted his battalion in several matches.

A fellow officer of Captain Wilcher, and also a keen sportsman and athlete, Lieutenant William Henry Colbeck, has been wounded in the arm. A solicitor by profession, he was formerly with Messrs. Brook, Wade, Pari, and Lount-Walker, of Leeds, and he lives at Ben Rhydding.

Second-Lieutenant A. E. Mander, West Riding Regiment, who has been wounded, was an assistant master at the Crossley and Porter Orphanage, Halifax.

Second-Lieutenant J. H. Armstead, West Yorkshire Regiment, wounded, is one of several officer sons of Mr. Richard Armstead, surveyor and valuer, of Bradford. When war broke out he was reading for the Bar.

Another Bradford officer wounded (for the second time) is Second-Lieutenant H. C. Speight, West Yorkshire Regiment, the second son of Major Speight, the officer commanding at Bello Vue Barracks. He is going on all right.

Lieutenant Arthur Dickinson, Royal Field Artillery, who has returned to his duties since being wounded by shrapnel, is the husband of Mrs. Dickinson, of 97, Folkestone Street, Bradford Moor. He was in the retreat from Mons, and received a commission on the field.

THE LEEDS PALS.

A prominent member of the Leeds Pals who has been killed is Sergeant A. R. Greasley. He was 22 years of age, and was the son of the late Mr. T. H. Greasley, valuer and arbitrator, of Hull and Leeds, and Mrs. George Hendler, of 28, Stratford Terrace, Leeds. Educated at the Yorkshire Society's School in London,

Sgt. A. R. GREASLEY.   Sergt. CLAYTON.   Pte. B. WOOD.
Leeds Pals (killed).   Leeds Pals (killed).   Leeds Pals (missing).
Photo: Scrimshaw.

Lce.-Cpl. A. WINCH.   Pte. Horace ILES.   Pte. W. C. SHAW.
Leeds Pals (killed).   Leeds Pals (killed).   Leeds Pals (missing).

he was an all-round athlete, winning the boxing championship of his company at Colsterdale and coming in — and in the walking Marathon race at the Boulevard, Hull.

Sergeant Norman Jackson, youngest son of Mr. and Mrs. William Jackson, Chapel House, Tadcaster, was killed in action on July 1st. Before joining the Pals in September, 1914, he was in the offices of Messrs. John Smith's Brewery, Tadcaster.

Sergeant Frank Clayton, who was in partnership with his brother, Mr. William Clayton, incorporated accountant, Albion Street, Leeds, is reported missing. Sergeant Clayton, who is 40 years of age, enlisted in the battalion on its formation, and had served in Egypt and France. A Fellow of the Society of Accountants and Auditors, and a member of the Headingley Lodge of Freemasons, he is well known in business circles, and for some time was connected in its early days with the Leeds City Football Club.

In a letter received by his brother from the chaplain to the Battalion, little hope of Sergeant Clayton's safety is entertained. The letter states that careful inquiries have been made, "and though I cannot find anyone here ... who saw him, I can say with little doubt that your brother is amongst the killed. I am sorry to deprive you of hope, but it is better to know the truth than to hear the pain of uncertainty. We hear that you think in Leeds that many have been taken prisoners, but we don't think here that this is to be relied on. They may have taken in five or six wounded men."

The relatives of Pte. J. H. Hunter, of C Co., have received official intimation of his death in action on July 1. Formerly he was employed by the Leeds Sand and Gravel Co., and resided at 80, Seaforth Road, Harehills.

Miss L. Scawbord, 14, Wellington Terrace, Bramley, asks for news of her brother, Private Tom Scawbord, D Company.

Private G. Wilson, C Co. was wounded on July 1st, by bullet and shrapnel, in the right leg, right arm, and back, and is in Netley Hospital, Southampton. His wife lives at Quarry Lane, Brookroyd, Batley.

THE LEEDS PALS BATTALION.

Mr. W. Southward, of 44, Wilmington Terrace, Meanwood Road, Leeds, who asked in "The Yorkshire Evening Post" for news of his son, Pte. E. Southward, Leeds Pals Battalion, has received a letter from Pte. W. N. Brown, in hospital at West Didsbury, stating that Pte. Southward was killed on July 1. The shell which killed Southward inflicted the wounds from which Brown is suffering.

Pte. Ernest Ingleson (25), who joined the Pals on formation, is reported to have been killed. He was employed by Messrs. Ashworth, Brown and Co., Leeds, and his relatives live at 21, Victoria Terrace, Leeds.

Pte. R. Matthews, who was only 16 years of age last January, has been killed in action. He joined the Pals on formation, and was the son of Mr. R. Matthews, whose Leeds address is 17, Longroyd Terrace, Burton Road.

Pte. J. W. Milner, D Co., who is missing, is 36 years of age, and formerly worked for Messrs. Hodgson, Wetherby. His relatives live at 14, Ledbury Street, Kirkland Street, Beeston Hill, Leeds.

Pte. G. F. Stendell, C Co., was last seen on July 1 badly wounded. News of him is asked for by his rela-

Rfm. W. WILKINSON.   Pte. J. W. WEBSTER.   Pte. Burnett REYNER.
Leeds Rifles (killed).   West Yorks. (killed).   Leeds Pals (missing).

tives at 2, Morphet Grove, Claypit Lane, Leeds.

Pte. Norman Gough, A Co., last heard of on July 1, is inquired after by his wife, Mrs. Gough, of 5, Cobden Place, Claypit Lane, Leeds. He is 22 years of age, and worked at Keighley.

Nothing has been heard of Pte. J. R. A. Steel since June 24, and his wife and family, who reside in Strathmore Drive, Harehills, are anxious for news about him. He was employed by Messrs. A. W. Scarr and Sons, New York Street, Leeds.

Mr. J. J. Walker, 62, Caledonian Road, Leeds, asks for information about his nephew, Private J. H. Chambers (29), B Company. He was employed by Taylor Bros.

THE LEEDS RIFLES.

Mrs. Kendall, of 24, Weldon Place, Leeds, would be glad of information of her husband, Pte. J. Kendall. Word was received from a comrade that he had been wounded while stretcher bearing, but nothing has been heard of him since.

The name of Rifleman Harry Yarborough, son of Mr. W. H. Yarborough, 34, Bellbrooke Grove, Harehills, Leeds, killed in action, was unfortunately mis-spelt as Farborough in our issue of yesterday. Relatives sending in particulars of casualties are asked to write very clearly, especially names.

Rfm. A. E. Wood, Leeds Rifles, wounded in the left arm, on

Pte. J. W. MILNER.   Pte. N. GOUGH.   Cpl. E. J. STAMP.
Leeds Pals (missing).   Leeds Pals (missing).   Bdfd. Pals (missing).

July 20, is in hospital in England. His wife and two children live at 18, Claro Grove, Serria Road, Leeds.

Private John William Milner's grave in Serre Road No.3 Cemetery.

Pte. FRANKLIN.   Pte. Jos. LAZENBY.   Pte. F. WHITTY.
York and Lancaster   North'ld Fusiliers   Green Howards
(killed).   (died of wounds).   (killed).

Private Billy Lyons, wounded. He wore the identity bracelet on his wrist during the attack.

Private Arthur E. Fillingham, killed.

... *As our infantry advanced, down came a perfect wall of explosive along the front trenches of my brigade and the 93rd. It was the most frightful artillery display that I had seen up to that time and in some ways I think it was the heaviest barrage I have seen put down by the defence on any occasion*[69]

Lance Grocock, a journalist employed by the *Yorkshire Evening Post* who was wounded in the attack, and later invalided out of the army, recalled the German bombardment in an editorial a year later:

... *The Hun artillery was playing havoc with our line. Trench formations disappeared altogether under the deluge of high explosives, and many men fell before the infantry attack opened. Ere the hour of 'Zero' came our front line had become a mere maze of shell craters in which living and dead lay side by side.*[70]

A look at the War Diary of the German 169th Infantry Regiment reveals that a message was received at 4.30am (3.30am British Army time) that the attack was expected on 1 July, at 5.30am (4.30am). By 4.35am all the battalions had been warned of the imminent attack, and at 4.50am a message was received from Artillery Group 'South' that a strong surprise bombardment of the British front lines was to take place at 5.0am (4.0am).[71]

The War Diaries of the British divisional and corps artillery are also interesting in that they record how much effort was spent on wire-cutting and bombarding the German lines, but show how little counter-battery work there was in comparison. It must be admitted, however, that the appalling weather just before the attack made it very difficult for the Royal Flying Corps observers and the artillery observation officers to locate the German batteries, which, of course, were keeping silent for much of the time so that they would be ready to deal with the Somme offensive they knew to be imminent.[72]

The total number of Leeds Pals who went into the attack will probably never be known, nor will the precise number who were wounded or captured. Estimates of all the statistics vary widely, but perhaps the most reliable figures are '750 out of the 900 in the Battalion, and only 72 survivors' given by Private Bristow to Dr Samuel Bickersteth during his interview at Leeds Vicarage at some time in mid-July 1916, while Bristow was recovering from his wounds.[73]

A contemporary estimate of the casualties among the other ranks was 504, arrived at by adding the totals of fifty-six killed, 267 wounded and 181 missing. The officers' total of twenty-four, was made up of eleven killed, twelve wounded, and one missing. These figures were reported by Brigade Headquarters on the first day of the battle,[74] but may not include the men who were killed during the night. Morris Bickersteth, acting C Company Commander, is recorded as sending at least two casualty returns up to Battalion Headquarters before Zero hour.[75] An often-reported number of forty-seven unwounded survivors cannot be substantiated from any official sources,[76] and, as always when one is analysing statistics, the numbers of casualties and survivors do not add up to the estimated number of participants.

What we can be sure of, however, is the number of Leeds Pals killed and died of wounds as a result of the attack on 1 July. These are well documented in the lists of soldiers and officers who died in the First World War, published by HMSO,[77] and are all traceable through the records held by the Commonwealth War Graves Commission.[78] Thirteen officers were killed and two more died of wounds during or soon after the attack, and 209 other ranks were killed and twenty-four died of wounds.

It has often been argued that the Pals battalions lost their unique identity on 1 July 1916. While not in any way underestimating the tragedy of the losses, it is interesting to compare the list of men killed or died of wounds in the attack on Serre, with the lists of volunteers published in the *Yorkshire Post* in September 1914, and to compare the list of officers lost with the officers photographed soon after their arrival in Colsterdale in September 1914.[79]

Private John Parkinson, shell-shocked, and the notification his family received from the War Office.

Pv. ERNEST INGLESON 15th W.Y. KILLED IN ACTION JULY 1st 1916.

Pioneer Sergeant George F. Easy, killed.
(N. Hornby)

Of the 1,275 volunteers listed in the *Yorkshire Post* when the Pals were first recruited, 107 were killed or died of wounds during, or as a result of, the attack on Serre on 1 July 1916. This figure represents less than half the total number of members of the battalion who lost their lives that day, and less than 10 per cent of the original volunteers. Of the fifteen officers killed or died of wounds at Serre, only three

Corporal William Briggs, killed.

221

12. July 1916.

Mr. Hands,
    68 Gelderd Road,
        Leeds.

Dear Sir,

It was with much regret that Colonel Brotherton heard to-day that your Son had been wounded in Action, and I am desired to tender to you his sincere sympathy.

Should Pte. Hands be visiting Leeds in the near future it would give Colonel Brotherton much pleasure to see him.

Yours faithfully,

H. H....

Secretary.

No.
(If replying, please quote above No.)

Army Form B. 10

INFANTRY Record Of
YORK.
7th July, 191

Madam,

I regret to have to inform you that a report has this day received from the War Office to the effect that (No.) 15742
(Rank) Private (Name) W. F. Hands
(Regiment) WEST YORKSHIRE REGT.
was
wounded in action at Since taken to the S
on the General Hospital Rouen.
day of 191

I am at the same time to express the sympathy and regret of the Army Council.

Any further information received in this office as to his condition will be at once notified to you.

I am,

Madam,

Your obedient Servant,

F. D. Harrison Major

For Colonel ...
llc No. 2 Section
...in charge of Records.

Private Walter F. Hands, wounded.

were among the twenty-two officers who proudly posed for the first group photograph in 1914. Two other officers who lost their lives on 1 July 1916 had been commissioned from the ranks of the original volunteers, and so are included in the 107 mentioned above.[80] The men lost on 1 July 1916 were mourned long after the war had ended. Major Booth's sister kept a room for him in her cottage at Pudsey for nearly fifty years after his death, in the vain hope that he would return. He is also commemorated by a stained glass window in St Lawrence's Church, Pudsey.[81] Morris Bickersteth's father, Samuel, had a memorial plaque put up in the Lady Chapel in Leeds Parish Church, where Morris had received his last Communion in Britain. He also wrote a biography of his late son, which was published privately by the family as a Golden Wedding anniversary gift to Morris's parents in 1931.[82] Tom Willey's father published a memorial book containing photographs of his son and copies of the letters of condolence he received, and Tom is also commemorated on the family memorial in the cemetery of the Church of St John the Evangelist at Roundhay.[83] Private Wilfred Denison Lumb, and his younger brother, Corporal Thomas Denison Lumb, who was killed in action with the Yorkshire Hussars on 25 May 1915, are commemorated on the pulpit of Leeds Grammar School.[84]

Private Sydney M. Rayfield, killed.

222

MONDAY, JULY 31, 1916.

YORKSHIRE SOLDIERS IN THE CASUALTY LISTS.

LOSSES OF LEEDS BANTAMS.

MANY OF THE PALS NOW OFFICIALLY POSTED AS MISSING.

A heavy list of casualties is issued to-day by the War Office, and the number of Yorkshire soldiers killed or wounded of whom particulars have reached us is unusually large. There is a long roll of dead from the Leeds Rifles, and the names of three members of the Leeds Bantams killed in action are also reported. Many members of the Leeds Pals Battalion, about whom anxious inquiries have been made ever since the offensive began on July 1, are now officially posted as missing.

We have received for reproduction an exceedingly large number of photographs of men killed in action, from which we give a selection to-day. The remainder we hope to publish, as space and the pressure of work

THE LEEDS PALS.

Sergeant Albert Gutteridge, Leeds Pals, has died at Bethnal Green Hospital, following amputation of a leg. He was one of the best athletes in Yorkshire and first came into prominence in 1911, when he won the Yorkshire junior championship at Queen's Park, Castleford, beating a field of over 200 runners. Since then he had scored at Huddersfield, Brighouse, Malton, Bury, and Hellifield. He received five wounds in the recent fighting, when he was practically blown out of one shell hole into another. The funeral takes place at Lawnswood on Wednesday.

Mr. T. H. Axe, of 5, Bayswater View, Roundhay Road, Leeds, has received news that his brother, Private Arthur Cecil Axe, C Co., died in action on July 1st, while the War Office has just intimated that he is "missing." A comrade, Private H. Evans, who is in hospital in Hants, in a letter to Mr. Axe, says: "Your noble brother succumbed to a wound in the thigh. I went over the top along with him, and he was quite cool. We had got about 20 yards when Arthur received the wound. I tried to bandage his thigh, but I had to press on. A bullet broke my leg when I had got about ten yards from him. I crawled back to our line, and at night, with a great effort, I passed Arthur on the way back and saw that he was dead." Private Arthur Axe was educated at Archbishop Holgate's.

Pte. O. R. Walker, Leeds Pals (missing). Pte. H. Lowe, West Yorks (killed). Lce.-Cpl. A. Meeson, Leeds Pals (missing).

gate's School, York, and often officiated as organist at York Minster. Before joining the colours he was for nine years music master and organist at St. John's College, Hurstpierpoint, Sussex.

Several of the Pals are to-day officially reported missing, and their relatives would welcome any further news as to their fate.

Private H. Panther, who joined soon after the formation of the battalion, and who is now officially reported missing, was 21 years of age, and was the youngest son of Mr. Panther, undertaker, Holbeck. He worked for Messrs. R. Brown and Co., Boar Lane.

Private S. B. Fletcher is also officially reported missing as from July 1st. His relatives reside at Saxonholme, West Park Street, Dewsbury.

A third officially reported missing is Private H. S. Casson, C Co. He is 22 years of age, and was on the staff of the National Telephone Company for many years. He was the eldest son of the late Mr. N. H. Casson, aged of Mrs. Casson, 61, Richmond Avenue, Headingley.

Another in the same list is Lance-Corporal A. Meeson, B Co., who was employed in the City Treasurer's Office. He was 24 years of age, and his father lives at 89, Leopold Street, Leeds.

Private G. P. Townend, also officially reported missing, was a clerk in the Leeds offices of Beckett's Bank, and was the son of Mr. A. E. Townend, 191a, Girlington Road, Bradford.

Private W. F. Chapman, whose relatives live at 7, Elden Place, Woodhouse Lane, Leeds, has been officially reported as missing since July 1st.

Private Oliver Benson Walker, formerly employed at the Leeds G.P.O., has been missing since July 1st. His widow resides at 9, Broomfield Place, Headingley, Leeds.

Drummer S. B. Richardson, Leeds Pals (missing). Pte. C. Pickersgill, West Yorks (killed). Pte. A. Haigh, West Yorks (killed).

WEDNESDAY, AUGUST 2, 1916.

FEWER YORKSHIRE LOSSES REPORTED TO-DAY.

LETTER FROM PALS' CHAPLAIN.

WOUNDED MEN OF WHOM NOTHING HAS BEEN HEARD.

The casualties of which we have received news to-day are, happily, much fewer in number than some of the long lists which we have published recently.

THE LEEDS CITY BATTALION.

Mrs. Higginbottom, whose husband, Private J. F. Higginbottom, was in C Company, Leeds Pals, has received a letter from the chaplain to the battalion, who writes that Private Higginbottom was wounded in a trench, "but I fear that he was killed where he lay, like so many more, before he could be removed. . . ."

Cpl. W. GOODSON, Leeds Rifles (killed). Pt. J. F. HIGGINBOTTOM, Leeds Pals (killed). Pt. G. Y. MARSHALL, City Br. Rifles (died of wounds).

Many men were seen wounded, and then nothing at all was heard of them. Many were buried in the trenches owing to the shell fire, and I feel pretty sure that this happened to your poor husband. . . . Private Higginbottom was 28 years of age, and worked for 14 years for Messrs. Leighton, wholesale confectioners, Meanwood Road, Leeds. The widow lives with her husband's parents at 12, Grant Row, Roundhay Road. The last letter she received from him was dated June 26th, exactly a year after the day he enlisted with the Pals.

THURSDAY, AUGUST 3, 1916.

CASUALTIES TO YORKSHIREMEN IN VARIOUS UNITS.

THE WEST YORKSHIRES' LOSSES.

Private Tom Oyston (33), Leeds Pals, is reported missing. His relatives live at 12, Marshall Avenue, Crossgates, and he was employed as a cutter by Messrs. J. and F. Ibbotson (Ltd.), Park Place, Leeds.

Private P. H. Sherwin (27), Leeds Bantams, has been killed in action. His widow lives at 12, Scott Street, Woodhouse Street, Leeds, and he was employed by Messrs. J. B. Batley and Co., Leeds.

Mr. B. Lee, Ghyll Royd, Yeadon, has received official intimation that his son, Private B. Lee, B Company, Leeds Pals, is missing since July 1st. Any further information regarding him will be gratefully received by his father.

Lance-Corporal E. R. Whiteley, A Company, is now officially reported missing from July 1st, and a letter received by relatives (who live at 78, Pasture Lane, Chapel-Allerton) from the chaplain states that there is no hope of his being alive. He was employed by Messrs. James Hare (Ltd.), Wellington Street, Leeds, and he played for the North Leeds, Headingley, and Springfield Cricket Clubs.

Private Cyril Burrows (20), son of Mr. Walter Burrows, 4, First Court, Leeds, has been killed in action in France after only five months' service with the West Yorks. He was employed at the Copper Works, Leeds.

Official information has been received that Private Ernest Rhodes (20), K.O.Y.L.I., son of Mr. and Mrs. John Rhodes, of Grace Top, Pudsey, has been killed in action in France on July 1st. He has two brothers serving their country, one in the Navy and the other in the R.F.A.

Corporal W. Waters, R.F.A., killed in the Somme area, was the son of Mr. and Mrs. R. Waters, 65, Church Bank, Bradford.

L.-Cpl. S. HALL, W. Yorks (killed). Pte. J. HARDY, W. Yorks (missing). L.-Cpl. WHITELEY, Leeds Pals (missing).

He was well known in Stanningley, where he spent his youth, and was identified with various local athletic clubs. The captain in command of his battery, in a letter of condolence to his parents, says: "His loss is felt by every officer and man in the battery, where he was so very popular."

Signaller J. L. Mosby (24), R.F.A., has been missing

Lance-Corporal George Hollis, killed.

Corporal Harold Coggill, killed.

Lance-Corporal Percy Cook, killed.

Private Frank R. Sharp, killed.

Private A. Norman Summerscale, killed.

Private J. Stanley Summerscale, Norman's brother, killed.

Private Maurice R. Crowther, killed.

Private Tom Calverley, born in the USA, killed.

Private Tom Newton's Next of Kin Memorial Plaque.

Private Horace Iles' grave in Serre Road No.1 Cemetery.

225

NOTES

1. Author's recorded interview with Clifford Hollingworth, May 1988.
2. Diary of 15/1003 Private Edward Woffenden, 14 June 1916, in the possession of Bob Reed, York.
3. MS copy of the diary of George William Cosby, 15 June 1916.
4. Author's recorded interview with Cyril Charles Cryer, Devon, October 1989.
5. 93 Brigade War Diary, 19 June 1916, Public Record Office, London: W095/2359.
6. *Yorkshire Evening Post*, undated newscutting in the possession of Edna Bews (niece of 15/1784 Private Horace lies, killed in action 1 July 1916).
7. Woffenden, op.cit., 16 June 1916.
8. Hollingworth, op.cit.
9. *Yorkshire Evening Post*, 30 June 1917.
10. Hollingworth, op.cit.
11. 'Troops allotted to each bound will be distinguished by a piece of cloth of the same colour as the bound (shewn on map) tied to the right shoulder strap. Cloth will be provided by DADOS and will be 18" long by 3" wide. It is the duty of all ranks to see that no man belonging to a forward bound are allowed to stay in a trench behind the bound alloted to them.' 165 Brigade, Royal Field Artillery, War Diary, Public Record Office, London: W095/2349
12. Extract from a letter written by Burgon Bickersteth to his family, 29 June 1916, quoted in Morris Bickersteth 1891 – 1916 by the Rev. Samuel Bickersteth, DD, TD, privately published through the Cambridge University Press, 1931.
13. *Yorkshire Evening Post*, 25 September 1964. 15/451 Lance-Corporal Reginald Kilburn ('Peggy') Hewitt was discharged under paragraph 392 (XVI) King's Regulations, as no longer fit for war service, on 23 May 1917. West Yorkshire Regiment Medal Roll, Public Record Office, London: W0329/899.
14. Hollingworth, op.cit.
15. War Diary of the German 169th Infantry Regiment, Generallandesarchiv Karlsruhe, Germany. It is important to note that German time was one hour ahead of British time, and therefore the Pals' Zero hour (7.30am) was at 8.30am to the Germans.
16. Recorded interview with Morris Fleming by Peter Hawkins of BBC Radio Leeds, circa 1986.
17. Pearson, Arthur Valentine, *A Leeds Pal Looks Back*, unpublished manuscript in Leeds Reference Library, circa 1966.
18. *Yorkshire Evening Post*, 21 July 1916.
19. From an interview with 15/1244 Private Edmund Bristow at Leeds Vicarage, Bickersteth Family War Diary, op.cit., July 1916.
20. Hollingworth, op.cit.
21. 31st Division General Staff War Diary, Public Record Office, London: W095/2341
22. *Sec-Lieut. T.A.R.R.E. Willey. 15th West Yorks. Regt. (Leeds Pals) – 'Tribute' – Mort au champ d'honneur – July 1st 1916*, a memorial book privately published by Arthur Willey in the latter half of 1916, consisting of transcripts of a selection from the many letters of condolence he received, together with photographs of his late son.
23. Letter from 15/470 Private William Arthur Hollings to his father, 6 July 1916. It was reprinted anonymously in the above-mentioned tribute to Tom Willey, but is identified in the *Yorkshire Evening Post*, 15 July 1916.
24. Extract from a letter written by an unidentified soldier of No.10 Platoon, C Company, published in the *Yorkshire Weekly Post*, 29 July 1916.
25. Pearson, op.cit.
26. War Diary of the German 169th Infantry Regiment, op.cit. 27. 'The Story of Our Joe', written by his brother, Ernest Collinson, *Yorkshire Evening Post*, 9 November 1979.
28. War Diary of the German 169th Infantry Regiment, op.cit.
29. Woffenden, op.cit., 1 July 1916.

30. Cosby, op.cit., 1 July 1916.
31. Fleming, op.cit.
32. 93 Infantry Brigade Preliminary Instructions, 12 June 1916, 93rd Field Ambulance War Diary, Public Record Office, London: W095/2354.
33. *Yorkshire Evening Post*, 10 July 1916.
34. *Yorkshire Evening Post*, 11 July 1916.
35. Arthur Willey contacted some of the survivors of No. 13 Platoon in an effort to find out what had happened to his son, but it seems that neither he, nor the men who went to look for his body, discovered the truth. This account of Tom Willey's death was an annual reminiscence of Herbert Smith, as each anniversary of the attack on Serre brought back painful memories. It was recounted to the author by Jean Kennington, Herbert Smith's daughter.
36. Letter from Arthur Hutton, reproduced in Arthur Willey's Tribute memorial book, op.cit.
37. Vause was referring to his imminent promotion to Captain.
38. *Yorkshire Evening Post*, 11 July 1916.
39. Letter from Morris's brother Julian, transcript in the Bickersteth Family War Diary, op.cit.
40. Interview with Edmund Bristow at Leeds Vicarage, July 1916, Bickersteth Family War Diary, op.cit.
41. Published in Bickersteth, Morris Bickersteth 1891–1916, op.cit.
42. *Yorkshire Evening Post*, 11,12 and 22 July 1916, also Imperial (now Commonwealth) War Graves Commission Cemetery Registers.
43. Pearson, op.cit.
44. Cathrick's body was found; he is buried in Serre Road Cemetery No.3, Puisieux.
45. *Yorkshire Evening Post*, 9 November 1979.
46. *Yorkshire Evening Post*, 2 August 1916.
47. *Yorkshire Evening Post*, 31 July 1916.
48. Letter pasted into Fred Tucker's copy of Snapshots of the 15th Battalion The Prince of Wales's Own (West Yorkshire Regiment), Richard Jackson, Leeds, 1917.
49. Pearson, op.cit.
50. Cryer, op.cit.
51. Hollingworth, op.cit.
52. Lance-Corporal Hicks's letter to his wife published in the *Yorkshire Evening Post*, 11 August 1916.
53. Papers of 15/400 Private (later Sergeant) Harold Green, Department of Documents, Imperial War Museum, London.
54. Cryer, op.cit.
55. Mr Cyril Charles Cryer, of Topsham near Exeter, recognised the photograph of an unidentified Leeds Pal from his platoon, which had been lent to the author. He remembered helping to rescue this man, but could not remember his name. The author had an opportunity to appeal for help with his book on Yorkshire TV's *Calendar* programme on 10 November 1989, and within half an hour of the broadcast received a telephone call from Mr Arthur Dobson of Leeds, the man's nephew and namesake.
56. *Yorkshire Evening Post*, 14, 17 and 31 July 1916.
57. *Yorkshire Evening Post*, 8 July 1916.
58. Each time a British battalion went into the attack, 10 per cent, usually including the cooks and transport personnel, was left out of the line to provide a cadre from which to reform the unit in the event of heavy casualties, such as those suffered by the Leeds Pals on 1 July 1916.
59. Author's recorded interview with Arthur Dalby, May 1988.
60. Author's recorded interview with Mrs Grace Kemp (neé Newton). Tom Newton replaced his Leeds Pals cap-badge with that of the West Yorkshire Regiment when he went on leave in Leeds as there were taunts of 'Titty-bottle battalion' and 'Feather-bed battalion' in 1914 and 1915 after

criticism in the local press suggesting that the Pals were being 'molly-coddled'. See Chapter 1.

61. *Yorkshire Evening Post*, 11 and 14 July 1916.
62. Although it is possible that Private Howard reached the German lines, it is unlikely that he got into Serre, except under German escort as a prisoner of war.
63. Hollingworth, op.cit.
64. Cosby, op.cit.
65. Hollingworth, op.cit.
66. Ibid.
67. The papers of Brigadier-General H.C. Rees, DSO, Department of Documents, Imperial War Museum, London.
68. Cooksey, Jon, *Pals: The 13th and Nth (Service) Battalions (Barnsley), The York and Lancaster Regiment*, Wharncliffe Publishing, Barnsley, 1986; Gibson, Ralph, and Oldfield, Paul, *City: The 12th (Service) Battalion (Sheffield), The York and Lancaster Regiment*, Wharncliffe Publishing, Barnsley, 1988; Turner, William, *Pals: The 11th (Service) Battalion (Accrington), The East Lancashire Regiment*, Wharncliffe Publishing, Barnsley, 1987.
69. Rees, op.cit.
70. *Yorkshire Evening Post*, 1 July 1917.
71. War Diary of the 169th Infantry Regiment, op.cit.
72. See for instance: VII Corps Heavy Artillery War Diary, Public Record Office, London: W095/825, which records the following:
    24.6.1916 – Heavy rain showers interfered with registration, wire-cutting carried out with visual observation, no heavy Howitzers could be employed, observation impossible. (No sucessful attacks on enemy batteries recorded.)
    25.6.1916 – Heavy batteries wire-cutting. (No counter-battery work recorded.)
    26.6.1916 – Showers interfered with registration. Heavy batteries continued wire-cutting. One direct hit on an enemy gun recorded.
    27.6.1916 – Counter-battery work, wire-cutting and bombardment of enemy trenches. Heavy batteries engaged numerous hostile batteries, but light too bad for effective work – no hits recorded.
    28.6.1916 – Bombardment of hostile trenches and batteries. Six hits on gun emplacements and one on an ammunition dump. Germans appear to have reinforced their artillery.
    29.6.1916 – Two direct hits, conditions against accurate observation.
    30.6.1916 – Counter-battery work energetically continued, seven hits recorded.
    See also 31st Divisional Artillery War Diary, Public Record Office, London: W095/2345, which records that it was almost exclusively engaged on wire-cutting. Of the division's eighty guns only four 4.5-inch howitzers were allocated to counter-battery work.
73. Interview with Edmund Bristow, Bickersteth Family War Diary, op.cit.
74. 93 Brigade War Diary, op.cit.
75. Bickersteth War Diary, op.cit.
76. The earliest traceable use of this often-quoted number is in an article about the Leeds Pals, which appeared in the *Yorkshire Post*, 18 January 1919, the fourth in a series entitled 'Stories of North Country Troops'. It was repeated in Scott's *Leeds in the Great War* and in Arthur Pearson's unpublished account, *A Leeds Pal Looks Back*, and has been quoted in numerous articles published in the local press in Leeds on the anniversaries of 1 July 1916 and Armistice Day.
77. *Soldiers Died in the Great War 1914–1919*, Part 19, *The Prince of Wales' Own (West Yorkshire Regiment)*, HMSO, London, 1921; *Officers Died in the Great War 1914–1919*, Part 1, *Old and New Armies*, HMSO, London, 1919
78. Cemetery Registers of the Imperial (now Commonwealth) War Graves Commission.
79. See Chapter 2.

80. These were Tom Willey and Major Booth.
81. Woodhouse, Tony and Yeomans, Ron, *Yorkshire Cricket – A Pictorial Survey*, Dalesman Publishing Company, Clapham, North Yorkshire, 1974.
82. Bickersteth, *Morris Bickersteth 1891–1916*, op.cit.
83. I am grateful to Mrs Jean Kennington (nee Smith), daughter of the late (former 15/825 Private) Herbert Smith, for this information.
84. I am grateful to Mr John Davies, Head of the History Department of Leeds Grammar School, for pointing this out to me on a visit to the school in 1990.

Chapter Six

Hopeless Despair

It's a sort of soul sickness, the constant sordidness and never-ending return to the firing line unconsciously dulling the higher faculties and substituting a kind of dumb driven sheepish bearing. You will notice it in the facial expression of photos taken of chaps just out from the trenches, lack of sleep, constant nervous shock and uncertain food producing a look Of 'hopeless despair'.

15/470 Corporal W. Arthur Hollings, D Company[1]

FRANCE 1916–1917

The much-anticipated 'Big Push' had failed in its first moments and with it died the hopes for a swift decisive victory to end the war in 1916. The survivors were now faced with the prospect of a long, hard slog in the trenches of France and Flanders.

On 13 July 1916, 31st Division was transferred from VIII Corps of the Fourth Army to XI Corps of the First Army. On the 15th the Leeds Pals marched to Lestrem, where they stayed for ten days, during which time reinforcements were brought up, including fifteen officers. Major Hartley, who had joined the Pals on 29 June as second-in-command, was formally appointed commanding officer, and given the temporary rank of lieutenant-colonel, until Stuart Taylor had recovered from his wound.

At 3.15pm on 24 July the battalion was marched to billets at Vieille Chapelle in readiness for the next spell in the line. Three days later 93 Brigade took over the sector from 94 Brigade with the 2nd Bradford Pals (18th West Yorks) and 18th Durham Light Infantry in the trenches, and the Leeds Pals and 1st Bradfords (16th West Yorks) in Brigade Reserve.

At 9.30 that night the German artillery bombarded the brigade front, so the reserve battalions stood-to in readiness. At midnight the Leeds Pals sent off a party of eleven officers and 155 other ranks to reinforce the 2nd Bradfords in the trenches. Meanwhile, two parties of Germans attempted to get into the Bradfords' trench. They were driven back before the Leeds men arrived, however, leaving over fifty of their dead in no man's land. By 4am everything was quiet and the Pals were stood down.[2]

The Germans broke through and gave the Bradford Pals a shocking time, so our teams had to go up.

[One man said] 'They must have been getting round us for two hours, and all of a sudden they just plonked on us.' He said, 'Where they come from I don't know, it was a hell of a job, hand to hand, we got to fisticuffs.' He was a bit of a boxer and, he said, 'I knocked one fellow out. It lasted about twenty minutes, but,' he said, 'it was about two days to us!'

15/471 Lance-Corporal Clifford Hollingworth, D Company[3]

Later that morning a composite company from the battalion, consisting of four officers and seventy other ranks with four Lewis guns, was sent to support the 18th Durham Light Infantry in their sector of the line.

No.3 Lewis gun team, 1916. Front row, (left to right) Private J. Lund, Lance-Corporal Clifford Hollingworth, Private George Ferrand; back row, Privates Pickles, Smith and H. Hutchinson.

At midday on 4 August the men in the trenches were relieved by 94 Brigade, and on the 9th they moved up to Festubert to take over from 118 Brigade. When 93 Brigade went into the trenches in their new position on the next day, the Leeds Pals took over the second line from the 1/1st Hertfordshire Regiment, while the rest of the brigade went into the front line.

On 18 August it was the Pals' turn in the front lines, and they discovered at once that this sector was rather different from the trenches they had been used to further south.

The line now held by the Brigade is peculiar in some respects. The actual front line is not continuous throughout but consists of a number of 'Islands' – the ground being low-lying and very wet, the original continuous line of breastwork (sandbag) was found impossible to maintain and therefore in the past efforts were concentrated on keeping certain portions along the whole front in as good condition as possible, thus forming a series of posts. There is moreover practically no continuous support line; portions only being in existence. Viz on the left Richmond Terrace, in the centre Barnton Tee, on the right George Street. Behind the Islands on the left, there are some cover trenches which may be included as forming part of [the] front line, for if described as Support trenches it is difficult to understand the position of Richmond Terrace. The Reserve line of the front system is called the OBL or Old British Line. It is a strong continuous line of sandbag breastworks in good condition. The Village line, in rear of OBL, consists of a series of strongpoints manned by obligatory garrisons.

Communication trenches in the Festubert section are few and generally speaking indifferent, access to the centre and right of front line trenches being difficult during daylight for any but small bodies of troops. Forward of the OBL lateral communication is practically non-existent.

93 Brigade War Diary[4]

These were not ordinary trenches, the earth was too wet to dig, the water was too near the surface, so the posts were 'islands', separate posts with C Coy on the extreme left. The gap between our section and the East Yorks was patrolled at regular intervals by that regiment.

15/711 Lance-Corporal Arthur V. Pearson, C Company[5]

It was while they were manning these island trenches that the Pals were attacked.

Survivors talk of Sunday August 20th. After morning 'Stand Down', when the sentries were the only ones on lookout, everyone could try and get some sleep, Jerry began to drop a shell every minute, the first one up against our wire and gradually working back to his own lines. This went

Officers and NCO's of D Company, 1916. Front row (from second on the left), Sergeant-Major Drinkwater, Lieutenant Binnie, Captain Hunter, Lieutenant Brown and Sergeant Jackson. Clifford Hollingworth is immediately behind Sergeant Jackson.

on nearly all day and no one spotted what he was doing! He was ploughing three lines through his own wire, across No Man's Land and through our wire, three tracks for his raiding party.

It was just after evening 'Stand Down', I had just come off sentry and was sitting on a sandbag reading a Yorkshire Post which someone had received in a parcel from home, when 'Hell-fire' broke out. I dropped the paper, grabbed my rifle and rushed into the trench to see that Jerry was ringing each island with a box barrage that a mouse couldn't get through. Then the shelling suddenly stopped and his raiding troops came up the lanes the shells had dug, and up to our parapet, but as they climbed over our sandbags, our Lewis gun Corporal who had taken up a position down the trench with his No.2, mowed them down like ninepins.

On our island, Sgt Macauley and I were standing together under shelter of a sandbag bay. I had some Kenilworth cigarettes sent from a friend in Leeds, as I offered Sgt 'Mac' one, I remember saying, 'Have a cigarette, Sergeant, the next smoke we have will be in Berlin Town Hall or in Kingdom Come!'

Well, our Lewis gun Corporal smashed that raid of Jerry's, not a German penetrating our lines.

15/711 Lance-Corporal Arthur V. Pearson, C Company[6]

Lieutenant Binnie with his platoon. Sergeant Jackson is to his right (with hand on belt).

The German attack took place just before 10pm on 20 August and, as Arthur Pearson recalled, the Germans did not succeed in entering the battalion's front-line trenches. When they were clearing up, the Pals found a hatchet, wire-cutters, bridges for getting over obstacles, two land-mines, and a large quantity of bombs, all left behind by their assailants. Patrols were sent out to search for any signs of enemy wounded or dead in no man's land, but none were found. The Leeds Pals had suffered some casualties themselves, however. Second-Lieutenant Tom Applebee was killed, and Second-Lieutenants Lawrence and Cantell were wounded. Six other ranks lost their lives that day and seventeen were wounded. One of the wounded men, Private Horace Killen, who had lost his brother, John, on 1 July, died of his wounds on 30 August.

On 26 August the battalion was relieved, by which time the commanding officer, Lieutenant-Colonel Hartley, and Captain Gibson had been slightly wounded, although they remained with the battalion. (Gibson's wound was caused by a sniper's bullet, which grazed his nose as he looked over the parapet).[7] The Pals were due to go back into the line again on the 30th after only two days in Brigade Reserve, but the move was postponed because Captain F. Boardall had come down with suspected cerebro-spinal meningitis. This proved to be a false alarm, however, and on 1 September they returned to the front line.

The next day it was announced that 15/598 Corporal Cecil Lister had been tried by a Field General Court Martial and sentenced to be reduced to the ranks and to serve ten years' penal servitude for his cowardice on the night of 20 August, although he was not to be committed to prison until further notice.[8]

A German trench club picked up by
Alan Hey. (Bagshaw Museum)

233

The Pals were relieved again on the night of 3/4 September and, soon after they arrived in their billets, they learned that three men were to be decorated for their bravery during the German trench raid. These three were 15/1300 Private G. Robson, a signaller in No. 15 Platoon, D Company; 15/690 Private Harold R. Oddy, a bomber in No. II Platoon, C Company; and 15/195 Private Harold Child of No. 7 Platoon, B Company.[9]

On the 7th the battalion was paraded and Robson, Oddy and Child each had the ribbon of the Military Medal fastened to their tunics by Lieutenant-Colonel Hartley. This was to be Hartley's last battalion parade, for it was rumoured that Colonel Taylor would soon be back with his 'boys'.

They went back into the line on 11 September and were soon visited by a Stokes mortar battery, which sent a few salvoes over into the enemy trenches and then moved on, leaving the Pals to bear the brunt of the German retaliation. Sure enough, the Germans replied on the 14th with an artillery bombardment and heavy trench-mortaring, killing Second-Lieutenant Archibald P. Glenn, who had been with the battalion less than two months, and two of the men. 15/15 Lance-Corporal Albert

Sergeant Jackson, (left) with some of his fellow NCOs. (E. J. Jackson)

Althorpe, a 1914 volunteer, was killed outright, and 18/171 Private Frederick Wood, who had been transferred from the 2nd Bradford Pals, died of wounds. Eleven other ranks, were wounded, one of whom, 43110 Private Stanley Norton died of his wounds on 17 September.

As the battalion came out of the trenches on 16 September it was greeted by Lieutenant-Colonel Stuart Taylor, now recovered from his wound, who reassumed command. The three Military Medal winners were sent to Merville on the same day, to receive their awards from the Corps Commander.

During the rest of September and early October the Pals had three more spells in the trenches, as always with some casualties, and while out on rest they were hard at work.

On 7 October the 31st Division was transferred from XI Corps, First Army, to XIII Corps, Reserve Army (later renamed Fifth Army).[10]

The battalion then moved by train to Doullens and marched into billets at Famechon, and on 17 October moved into Brigade Reserve at Courcelles ready to take its turn in holding the line on Hebuterne Plain. Training commenced and reinforcements arrived, and on the 20th 102 of Colonel Taylor's 'Old Boys' were given good conduct stripes.

From 18 to 20 October working parties were sent into the trenches to carry up gas cylinders. These weighed approximately 180 pounds each, and each needed two men to carry it. On one occasion the working party was on duty for fifteen hours.

234

Billy Clark and Arthur Dalby with their good conduct stripes. (A. Dalby)

Harold Brown shows his good conduct stipe for the camera. (F. Groves)

The shutter from a billet in France with the painted badges of the Leeds and Bradford Pals. (Imperial War Museum)

October 22 1916

Dear Father, Isn't it somewhere about a year ago since I was home on leave last. I know it seems a very long time ago. Many things have happened in the meantime at this end and I suppose there have been many changes at that end. Nearly all the men about me are new as very few of the old lot are left, but it is surprising how many know me without my knowing them.

… I have not seen the papers lately but things are moving strongly here and you would think that the war was going on for several years yet by the work and preparation which is going on. Munitions of war of all kinds are pouring up towards the front line and we are having a full share in the final stages of its transport. The guns of all calibre are pounding away incessantly and Fritz must be having a rough time.

I wish you could just pop your head into our dugout now. We are having a 'bust up' tonight. We have a little log fire and it has taken the joint efforts of the seven of us who share the dugout to find the wood. At the moment of writing two billy-cans with their bubbling contents are on the fire. We have been lucky enough to get one onion, three carrots, two potatoes and one turnip, and these along with bully beef and army biscuits are going to provide us with a real feast. One chap is acting as cook and passes little morsels behind him for us to test. I have done my share of chopping wood, scraping carrots etc and have such confidence in the success of the supper that I am writing these few lines whilst we are waiting. It has been a keen frosty day, dry and clear atmosphere, but it is impossible for this part of the country to be anything else but muddy. The roads are very muddy, in spite of frequent working parties clearing them, and the other day I saw a London motor-bus stuck at the side of a road with axle and wheels buried in mud and they were thinking of sending divers down to put the jacks in position. Then a few days ago I saw a water-cart drawn by two horses, which in attempting to dodge the constant stream of traffic had toppled into a deep drainage ditch at the side of the road and one horse had gone over into a very bad position and great difficulty was being experienced in trying to extricate it. The thousand and one difficulties occurring every moment of day and night make up the soldier's life, not taking into consideration the dangerous side from the Boche's fire.

Well! I have very little else to say now. I usually think of a lot I might have said just after I have sent the letter. Love to all, Arthur

15/470 Corporal W. Arthur Hollings, D Company[11]

At about 9.30pm on 28 October the Pals sent out a raiding party. It was divided into four sections, each comprising ten men and an NCO, with the two-right hand sections under the command of Second-Lieutenant Absalom Parkin and the two on the left under Second-Lieutenant Marshall. At about 11pm Parkin's men discovered a gap in the enemy wire and, after passing over the Germans' parapet, found themselves in a mine crater some 12 feet in diameter and 6 feet deep. The trenches were almost unrecognisable as such, having been very badly battered by artillery, and there was no sign of any Germans, or even their dugouts. Marshall's two sections on the left managed to cross the first line of barbed wire by using a ladder as a bridge, and reached the German parapet.

Then a cloud of gas rolled over from the south and enveloped the raiders. The men started to cough and put on their anti-gas helmets, and it was then that they were spotted. Parkin's men were fired on with rifles by some Germans in the second line who sent up Very lights to illuminate the scene. Grenades and trench mortar bombs came over as the raiders advanced to another crater about 40 yards from the German second line, where they were faced by a massive tangle of barbed wire which, although damaged by artillery in places, was impassable, being some 20 feet deep. Meanwhile, Marshall's men also came under heavy fire from a detached post in the German front line. At 11.30pm suffering from the effects of the gas and by now under artillery fire, the two groups made their way back to the safety of their own trenches.[12]

Paraded in battle order and went to reserve trench along with some others. Awaiting orders. Colonel came up and told us we were going on a bombing raid. I am to be a bomber. Went over at 9.30pm. Was 2 yards from German trenches at 10.59pm. Got gassed by our own gas. Then spotted officer and man badly gassed and two men wounded. Had to retire, bombed and fired at by Germans.

15/1003 Private Edward Woffenden, C Company[12]

Since my last letter I have paid a visit to the Boches on a bombing raid, and here I have again to be very vague, lest I divulge what may be considered valuable information for Fritz. However I can only say that we went through gas.

We are a bit hardened to the dangerous side of these little dust ups with Old Fritz, and I cannot help thinking how ludicrous one would seem if only one could see oneself crawling, creeping or wriggling on the stomach across No Man's Land. We get plenty of time for thinking on these trips, as they are not rushed (that is, not until we have got within his wire) and it occurs to us a bit like hide and seek we used to play at. He's a tough customer yet is Fritz and likely to last a long time yet, but I think he had fairly 'got the wind up' as we never leave him alone. This meant putting on our gas-helmets in No Man's Land and, to whit! inside the Boche's wire.

I wish I was Bairnsfather, I'd give you a real sketch of us. To appreciate the position, I must ask you to take a piece of double flannelette, put two holes with glass in, and a tube for the mouth. Now go somewhere up Middleton on a pitch black night, enfold your head tightly in the flannelette and start to cross a ploughed field on hands and knees and then flat on the stomach. To make it more realistic sprinkle about lavishly a good supply of barbed wire, broken props etc etc and dig everywhere holes of every shape and size. This will be a step in your apprenticeship to the trade of a bombing raider. This does not take into consideration the transportation of all the impedimenta a bombing party must take, such as revolvers, rifles and bayonets, bombs, knob-kerries, wire cutters, electric torches, ladders etc etc and not mentioning the nasty habit Fritz has of endeavouring to break up your little visit by Whiz bangs, rifle grenades, bombs etc.

Have you ever let a squib or cannon off on the 5th Nov. If so the feeling of throwing one's first bomb is very similar to when you let off your first squib, the difference being that you don't wait until you see it fizz.

15/470 Corporal W. Arthur Hollings, D Company[14]

Second-Lieutenant Marshall was very badly gassed and was taken on a stretcher, semi-conscious, to an advanced aid post. Two of his men, 15/70 Private Calvert and 15/505 Private Jackson reported to the Medical Officer, and were sent to the Field Ambulance for treatment, and one other man had a slight shrapnel wound. At 4.30am the Brigade Medical Officer, Lieutenant A. McCowley, sent a report to HQ stating that in his opinion the gas was probably chlorine as the patients had been vomiting and suffering from giddiness and headaches. It was thought that the gas had originated from the British lines and a

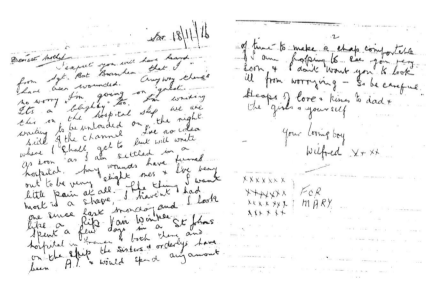

Wilfred Wainman's letter to his mother. Mary is his sister.

message was sent to the commanding officer of the Special Brigade, Royal Engineers, attached to V Corps, to enquire whether any gas had been released and to establish the direction of the wind that night.[15]

Early in November working parties were once again demanded, and being in range of the German artillery, they suffered some casualties.

> *Pouring with rain. Working party at 1.15. Marched to Hebuterne and drew shovels and pumps. Proceeded down Revel Trench between reserve and front line. Clearing out trench. Very bad condition. Hebuterne heavily shelled whilst we were in trench. Working from 5pm to 9pm. Arrived back about 12.45, muddied up.*
>
> *15/1003 Private Edward Woffenden, C Company*[16]

Training was briefly resumed until the men were called upon to go into the trenches again on 7 November, and while they were in the line a fighting patrol was caught in no man's land by the German artillery, resulting in more casualties. Before the battalion was relieved on 11 November, another officer, Second Lieutenant S. A. Day, had been killed.

The men who had been left out of the trenches were apparently not much safer – Wilf Wainman was among those wounded by the shells that regularly fell on Hebuterne.

After its relief the battalion had a short rest, and received the good news that leave was re-opened to the extent of fourteen men per week. All too soon, however, the Pals were back in the trenches with A and B Companies in the front line and C and D Companies in the support line. They were shelled almost constantly until they were relieved on 27 November, by which time the trenches were in such a terrible state that the men had to climb over the parados to complete the relief, which took six hours.[17]

On the next day the men were paraded and given a welcome opportunity to have a bath, but other creature comforts, such as canteens, were seemingly not available in their sector.

> *Do you know the word 'Canteen' has a magical sound for us, as we have been in the line and in villages where it was impossible to supplement your rations by even the simplest articles from a shop and when we know we are coming back to a village where there is a coffee bar, YMCA or Church Army hut we are absolutely fit up, but best of all is to get to a village where there is an Expeditionary Force Canteen. These are large barns converted into stores with shelves packed with all sorts of goods the soldiers need, chiefly eatables, and is the nearest approach we have out here to our home shops. These Canteens are run by men who have done their bit and many a time I wished I could get a similar job. I do not think you can appreciate what I really mean. After the eternal mud and filth and discomfort of the trenches, the life of opening packing cases, entering up accounts and moving about in a well lighted place is a vision of heaven itself.*
>
> *We are having some very wretched weather here and the water has nowhere to drain away to, therefore the whole country, roads and trenches are in a mobile muddy mess. We are seeing a lot of the trenches nowadays. We used to have hopes of someday going into a rest camp but I do not think such camps exist.*
>
> *15/470 Corporal W. Arthur Hollings, D Company*[18]

On 29 November the working parties were resumed requiring nearly every man in the battalion. During December the Pals had two more tours in the trenches, experiencing similar difficulty in carrying out the reliefs as the trenches were handed over from one unit to another. Meanwhile Hebuterne, where Battalion Headquarters was situated, was still being shelled intermittently.

On Christmas Day 1916 all work was stopped and they were given a Christmas dinner of Yorkshire Pudding, turkey and goose, beef potatoes and cabbage. Every NCO and man

William Radford as under gamekeeper to Charles Wilson, with his grandfather and father. He is second from right in the back row of the group photograph. He joined the Leeds Pals in 1915 to serve as Wilson's batman. In November 1916 he applied to join the Military Foot Police, and Wilson wrote him a letter of recommendation. Lance-Corporal Radford served with the MFP and survived being buried by a shell in 1918. After the war he joined Leeds City Police, but his health broke down and he suffered partial paralysis as a result of his traumatic experience during the war.

239

15th West Yorks. Regiment,
FRANCE.

IN THE STAR · SENT BEFORE THEM

With Best Wishes for a
Holy Christmas.
C. R. CHAPPELL, C.F.

Christmas, 1916.

HOLY COMMUNION

On *Sunday* | *Monday*

At *9 a.m & 6.30 p.m* | *Jan*
                        10 30 a.m

In *C of E Hut*

*The Christmas Communion card given
out by the Reverend Claude Chappell,
Battalion Chaplain.*

was also given a bottle of Bass beer, a tin of fifty Gold Flake cigarettes, an apple, an orange, and two candles. That night a concert was held in a Church Army hut at Authie.

Working parties were soon resumed, but good news followed – the number of men allowed home on leave was to be increased to twenty-three a week. Private Shaw, a bandsman, was among the lucky ones, although he didn't get away until early in the new year, and his visit to London on his return journey wasn't quite what he might have expected.

9 January – Came home on leave. Voyaged from Calais to Folkestone on HMS Onward. *21 January—Left Leeds 3.15am arrived Victoria 9.0am, was walking up Buckingham St and the Guards band came along with a guard behind. Being interested in the band forgot to salute. I was made to fall in and march with them to Palace, was then taken to Scotland Yard and put in a cell for hour then released.*

15/1951 Private John Jackson Shaw, Bandsman[19]

After the hard fighting of 1916, and the devastating outcome of the attack on Serre, the Leeds Pals now began their second year of trench warfare. But victory seemed no nearer.

*Private Arthur Houseago,
killed by artillery fire on 10
January 1917.*

The other day I had a letter from a pal of mine who was with the Battalion in the trenches and he says:

Each succeeding morning when I awake the day's labour has become more repugnant than the preceding one, I have not sung Perfect Day *for a long time – it is sacrilege, and I might say that a dull monotone seems to be settling on everyone.*

Probably you will not appreciate all that such a remark conveys, but as I have spent such a long time in the trenches I know exactly what kind of feeling he means. It's a sort of soul sickness, the constant sordidness and never-ending return to the firing line unconsciously dulling the higher faculties and substituting a kind of dumb driven sheepish bearing. You will notice it in the facial expression of photos taken of chaps just out from the trenches, lack of sleep, constant nervous shock and uncertain food producing a look of 'hopeless despair'. If only it was open warfare, it would be different, but the monotonous routine of trench warfare is depressing.

15/470 Corporal W. Arthur Hollings,
D Company[20]

On 5 January the battalion was paraded and each man was issued with a new 'small box respirator', which was more efficient, and certainly more comfortable, than their old 'PH' gas-helmets.

The Small Box Respirator introduced towards the end of 1916. It had a nose clip and mask so did not depend on a gas-tight fit around the wearer's face like the respirators carried by the Germans.

A working party.

On the following day they went into the trenches to relieve the 1st Bradford Pals. During their last two days in the line, German artillery caused the deaths of four men, with two more wounded, and a direct hit on a dugout as the battalion was being relieved caused four more casualties, three of them fatal.

Soon after the Pals returned from the trenches it was announced that the Quartermaster, Captain R. J. Anderson, and 15/1035 Sergeant Harry Jackman and 15/1320 Corporal H. Jackson had been mentioned in despatches, and former 15/790 Company Sergeant-Major Scholes, who had just rejoined from Officer Cadet School as a Temporary Second-Lieutenant, was awarded the Distinguished Conduct Medal.[21]

The rest of the month was spent in training, which optimistically placed great emphasis on open warfare, and early in February divisional and brigade sports were held.

> *During the whole period special stress was placed on getting the men fit. All men had to take a part in sports. Football, boxing, tug-of-war, cross-country runs were all indulged in.*
>
> *Battalion War Diary[22]*

Among the contestants running against the Pals in the Divisional 8-Mile Cross-Country Race was Lieutenant-Colonel the Hon Harold Alexander of the 2nd Irish Guards (later Field-Marshal the Earl Alexander of Tunis, one of the most distinguished British commanders of the Second World War).

Interviewed by the *Yorkshire Evening Post* some twenty-six years after the event, former 15/98 Private John Bywater was a little uncertain of the outcome of the race, but clearly recalled having Alexander pointed out to him as 'the bloke you have to beat', and thinking that his rival was big enough to eat him. Former 15/678 Private Percy Nettleton recalled that Alexander had reconnoitred the course on horseback the previous day, noting the places where there was barbed wire. These he nicely avoided in the race, leaving the others to find a way through it.

> *Johnny Bywater was about 50 yards behind Lt-Col. Alexander and the whole four of us were within 300 yards. I raced Alexander neck and neck for two miles but I had to let him go. But before that and before I got too winded, we spoke to each other about the going.*

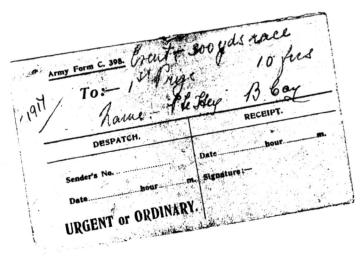

Alan Hey's prize envelope for the 300-yard race. It contained 10 francs. (Bagshaw Museum)

Almost at the start we had to barge through a thick thorn hedge and then followed a scramble almost on hands and knees, up a steep wood. I remarked to him that it was hard going and he agreed. In his running kit there was no palaver about him in regard to rank. He was just a friend who would slap you on the back and crack a joke with you.

15/436 Private Harold Hartley, HQ Stretcher-bearer[23]

Although Alexander was first in, the race was a team event so the Leeds Pals were the victors. Alexander told them afterwards that he could do with them in the Irish Guards, but they gratefully declined.

From about 20 February artillery observers began to notice that there were fires burning in the enemy lines, and by the 23rd it was noticed that German retaliation to the British bombardment of their trenches was less than usual.[24]

On 25 February the Pals returned to the trenches at Hebuterne and that night a patrol from C Company entered the German front line without meeting any opposition. On the next day they investigated further and found that the second and third lines were also empty. The enemy had withdrawn, and the fires the artillery observers had seen were the result of the Germans burning some of their dugouts before vacating the trenches. Although this withdrawal was celebrated as a victory by the Allies, it was a sensible strategy for the Germans, who had lost many men during 1916. They

Arthur Pearson in 1917, serving as a stretcher-bearer.

Lieutenant-Colonel the Hon. Harold Alexander in his Irish Guards uniform.

243

were not yet at breaking point, but their new, well-fortified 'Hindenburg Line' was shorter and easier to hold.

It was during one of our spells in that sector that Jerry evacuated his lines. Our intelligence must have got wind of something so our Company were ordered out of reserve trenches to go over and see whether Jerry had gone and we had to hold his first three lines of trenches.

Cold, chilly dawn, of course was the time for 'Zero', so over we went, Sergeant-Major Jones using his massive strength to pull off men caught in the wire. The SB [stretcher-bearers] followed on at the end of the advance as was their place. We climbed out of the trench and there on the ground in front of me was the 'white guide tape', which laid a trail from our trench to the 'terminus', but the tape was moving – the chap who was laying it out hadn't pegged it down securely and it was following him. I lost my jack knife that night as I had to use it to peg that tape down. The tape was a valuable guide for us SB as we carried our many casualties back to the First Aid Post. We could have wandered all over the place without that guide as all trenches look alike both by day and at night.

Our boys got safely into Jerries' lines, consolidated the position, explored his deep dugouts and very comfortable Jerry made himself, with wire beds, chairs and tables looted from the villages and even electric light.

Souvenirs galore – boxes of cigars and cheroots, caps and helmets, he had either got out in a hurry or was going a long way and had dumped his 'extras'. Now comes the tragic part of that advance. The Bradford Pals had been ordered to come through our Company and to probe deeper into the German line. At that time, those trenches were a wet, squelchy, sticky mess, mud was knee deep in the communication trench.

Consequently the Bradfords who should have gone over before daylight couldn't get through the mud so it was daylight when they climbed out to attack. Jerry had left a few machine-gun posts manned and the poor old Bradfords got the lot, they were cut down before they got far. There were not many unwounded survivors, and we SB were attending to their wounded and carrying them down to the First Aid Post. All night and every night this went on the whole time we were in the line.

15/711, Lance-Corporal Arthur V. Pearson, Stretcher-bearer[25]

Although the advance was costly, by 28 February the brigade was in control of Rossignol Wood, which had been the German fourth line, more a than a mile from the British line of 1 July 1916.

Now that the Germans had withdrawn and left Serre, the Pals took the opportunity to search their 1 July battlefield thoroughly, to see if they could identify any of their fallen comrades and give them decent burials. Among the officers they identified were Captain George C. Whitaker, Lieutenant Tolson, whose father had initially been told that he was in hospital in Britain recovering from his wounds, and Lieutenant Booth, the Yorkshire cricketer. Booth's remains were identified by a cigarette case given to him by

George Clifford Whitaker. His remains were discovered in no mans land when the Germans withdrew from Serre in spring 1917.

Lance-Corporal Arthur Hollings died of pneumonia at No.44 Casualty Clearing Station on 4 March 1917.

No 44 C.C. Station
B. E. F:
March 4th

Dear Mr Hollings

It is with very deep regret that I send you the sad news that your son passed away this morning at 8.25. For the last four days he has been terribly ill, yet I hoped against hope that he would take a turn for the better, but we can only conclude that his work on earth was done. If he was as good a son as he was a patient — then indeed you were to be congratulated on having such a son.

He will be buried in the little cemetery here & will have a little cross erected over his grave with his name & regiment engraved on it. I have taken from his belongings a handkerchief, sachet — an electric torch, a broken watch and his identity-disc & will send them on to you soon. I thought I would like to know you had those safely & I am sure you will value them. It is strictly against rules so please say nothing about it. His pay book, letters etc I had to hand in to the office & they will be sent to you in due course from the Base Office.

With deepest sympathy

Believe me
Yours sincerely
A Rawes
(Sister)

245

In British hands at last; soldiers pose in the German trenches at Serre, spring 1917.

the MCC when he took part in a tour of South Africa. The cigarette case was sent to his sister in Pudsey, but she did not cease her vigil.[26]

> *Months afterwards when he had abandoned Serre, a party of 'Old Boys' were sent up to the old sector we had attacked over and we identified several bodies. One was our Company Commander [Captain Whitaker]. We put what was left of him into a sandbag and carried him down to a cemetery. We had the Padre with us and he read the burial service as we buried him.*
>
> 15/711 Private Arthur V. Pearson, C Company[27]

The months of March and April were spent working, training and frequently moving from billet to billet. Throughout the year so far there had been a steady flow of reinforcements joining the battalion, some of them 'Old Boys' returning after recovering from wounds received on 1 July 1916.

Early in April a detachment was sent to Robecq to train reinforcements.

There were men come out from England who were trained so far, but they weren't trained by men who had been in the trenches, so when they got so far in their training, instead of keeping them in England, send them out to France to a Draft Training Depot where they were taught trench warfare by people who were experienced of trench warfare. When we got the first batch our commanding officer addressed them, and we were all stood behind him. 'Now these are your instructors and I want to tell you this much, you boys that have come from England. Every one of these men, every one, has been in battle. So what they're telling you is not canteen talk, it's real talk, every one has been in battle, thrown a bomb, they've advanced, they've had a raid, so therefore what they're teaching you is actually what they've seen and that will do you more good than stopping in England and [having] sergeants talking to you that don't know what they're talking about.'

They were eager fellows. We had proper trenches and barbed wire and everything, to practise on. I was teaching fellows Swedish Drill, put your arms up and they said they couldn't, I said 'Put your arms up!' One fellow says 'We can't do it Sergeant, our arms have been at plough all our lives, and they've got locked, we walk like that.' They didn't march like us, they walked like that, arms bent, they couldn't straighten them. I got hold of one and I tried to bring his elbows round and I couldn't, his muscles were fixed. When we were at baths once he showed us his muscles, tremendous muscles, but his arms, as he was stripped, was just like [a] gorilla's. He said when you've two horses and you're holding them, you're like that, that's why it's difficult to hold the rifle, they couldn't get that up and that underneath.

15/471 Lance Sergeant Clifford Hollingworth, D Company[28]

On 29 April the battalion was assembled in a field at Roclincourt and, at 6pm, took over the right sector of the line just north-east of Arras. Although they didn't know it, this was to be no ordinary tour in the trenches – the Leeds Pals were about to go over the top once more.

The Battle of Arras was essentially a diversion intended to draw the German reserves away from a French offensive further south. General Robert Nivelle, the French Commander-in-Chief, thought he had a plan that would win the war. A massive attack on the German lines along the River Aisne, using twenty-seven divisions, would break the trench deadlock on the Western Front once and for all.

The British offensive at Arras was to be mounted a week before Nivelle's attack. Theoretically it should have been a success. The Royal Artillery gunners were more experienced following the previous year's campaign on the Somme; infantry assault tactics had been improved; and an element of surprise would be gained by using the *boves* (the underground cellars of Arras) to conceal the troops massing for the assault, and by using specially constructed galleries to enable the men to enter the trenches unseen.

The opening attack on 9 April was a success, with the Canadians capturing Vimy Ridge and taking some 4,000 German prisoners. But the Germans had also drawn experience from the Somme and had refined their 'defence in depth' and their tactical use of the machine gun; as we have seen, they had also withdrawn to their new heavily fortified 'Hindenburg Line'. The initial success did not last. The British offensive soon degenerated into a series of local attacks on small objectives which Haig allowed to continue in order to take the pressure off the French.

Nivelle's offensive also floundered. An assault of such a size was difficult enough to keep secret in the first place, but the Germans had acquired a copy of the timetable for the attack, and they were ready. The first forty-eight hours were crucial but, despite some gains and some prisoners taken, the attack was a failure. Nivelle's use of colonial troops from North

Africa contributed to the failure, for they were not acclimatised and were therefore unable to press home an attack while suffering the effects of the unaccustomed cold weather.

Weary of being thrown into the line in one unsuccessful offensive after another, the French soldiers began to rebel.

A series of mutinies took place, varying in degree from refusal to attack to mass desertion. Nivelle's dream of winning the war was shattered and he was replaced by General Henri Petain, who took over as Commander-in-Chief on May 1917. It was to take him many months to rebuild his army's morale and revive the French soldiers' fighting spirit.

93 Brigade received the first intimation of its involvement in the Battle of Arras on 30 April 1917, in a 'Warning' Order from 31st Division HQ, which outlined the plan of attack and the objectives, but did not specify a date or time.

The Leeds Pals were to be on the division's right flank, with the 1st and 2nd Bradford Pals (16th and 18th Battalions, The West Yorkshire Regiment) on their left. Their objective was to capture the enemy first and second line trenches, construct strongpoints and position machine-guns to deal with any counter attacks.

The attack was to be made in four waves. The first wave would take the German front line and the second and third waves would press on to the second line. The fourth wave would then mop up any remaining Germans before joining their comrades holding the second line.[29]

Having entered the trenches on the night of 29/30 April the Pals were unaware of the impending attack, as final instructions were not issued until late the next night. The actual date and time of the attack were not revealed until 2 May when a secret memo was issued by Divisional HQ. Zero hour was to be 3.45am on 3 May 1917.

In bright moonlight under the watchful eyes of the Germans, who as usual held the high ground, the men gathered in the assembly trenches to await the signal to attack. By 2.40am the Leeds Pals were in position, and were joined a few minutes later by the Bradford Pals. At 3.44am the British barrage commenced, a minute early, and was described in a signal to Brigade HQ as 'Simply magnificent'.[30]

At 3.45am the Pals attacked, and despite casualties they managed to get into the German front line, driving the enemy back.

> On May 3rd 1917 at 3.40am my men of No. 7 Platoon 'B' Company were lined out at ten yards interval – 50 yards in front of our trench. We were the left platoon of 'B' Company and also left of Battalion.
>
> When I reached the German outpost… we entered a trench about 15 yards long, in good condition, and it seemed as if Germans had just left it. They had left rifles behind but no bayonets were fixed. I had ten men with me at the time with a Lewis gun and one magazine. Two men arrived later with the buckets [of magazines]. The Germans delivered a very small local counter-attack against us about two minutes after we entered post. This was easily repulsed and several of the dead lay in front of the trench killed by our bombs and rifle fire.
>
> Second-Lieutenant C. C. Davies, B Company[31]

Just before 4am the German artillery replied. Shells rained down onto the Pals, and the German guns began searching for the British artillery positions. By 4.30am communication between the Pals and Brigade HQ had been broken.

> [I remember] how easy it was to get into the German trenches and how big a mistake we all made, because the Germans had emptied their trenches and put their artillery on them within a yard or two and those that were wounded on that occasion were left in the German trenches to be prisoners. You see the Germans were too clever for us, I'll be quite truthful, their Generals were

The secret memo which revealed the
time and date of Zero hour.

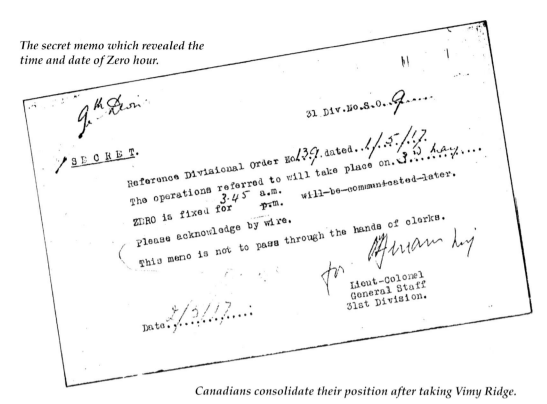

SECRET.

31 Div.No.S.O.

Reference Divisional Order No.139 dated 1/5/17.
The operations referred to will take place on 3 May.
ZERO is fixed for 3.45 a.m. p.m. will be communicated later.

Please acknowledge by wire.

This memo is not to pass through the hands of clerks.

Lieut-Colonel
General Staff
31st Division.

Date. 2/5/17

Canadians consolidate their position after taking Vimy Ridge.

Dear Mrs. Shaw,

    I sympathise most deeply with you and yours in the irreparable loss you have sustained through the death of your husband Private J.J. Shaw.   He was killed on May 2nd. 1917. near Gavrelle.   He died gallantly and doing his duty nobly.   For ourselves we mourn the loss of a good comrade and a brave soldier, and we feel for you the deepest sympathy in your great sorrow, but pray God to give you strength to bear it, and that it may be softened by the knowledge of your husband's noble sacrifice for you and his Country.

    With every wish for your comfort.

    Believe me,

      Yours sincerely,

23rd. May 1917.

Private John Jackson Shaw, killed by artillery fire as he took food up to Pals in the trenches during the night of 2/3 May 1917.

Lieutenant Anderson's letter of condolence to Shaw's family. (G. Cunningham)

15th West Yorks
B.E.F
France
17/5/17

Dear Mrs Shaw

I had hoped to write you a few days ago, but owing to pressure of work we did not get the opportunity until now. In the sad loss you have sustained, I deeply sympathise with you. Your husband was a good soldier, liked by all his comrades and we feel his loss tremendously. His death ... these ... incidents ... but don't happen very often, but when they do the results are disastrous. The Battalion was up in the fighting line and we had to take up Water + Rations to a certain point in that way all the Band were helping. When the carrying Party were leaving a certain point – a large Shell burst amongst them killing 3 or wounding 5 others. I deeply deplore the fact that your husband was amongst those killed. He was killed outright and suffered no pain. I knew him from the first day he joined us & it always was a pleasure to see how cheerfully he did his duty & bore the hardships which fall to the lot of we Soldiers. I pray that God in his mercy will give you strength to bear your sorrow + that in the midst of it all you will find comfort in the fact that he died as he lived doing his duty. If I can help you in all any thing I shall be glad to do so.

    Yours Sincerely
    R.J. Anderson
    Lieut & Quartermaster

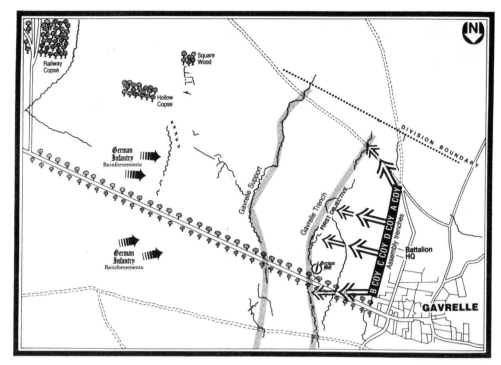

The Leeds Pals' attack at Gavrelle, 3 May 1917. This map has been turned round to line it up with the oblique aerial photograph.

better than our fellows, and they let us get across and they had vacated their trenches and then when we got in them they blew them to hell. They blew us as well. Seven of us came back out of twenty seven in my section.

15/259 Private Arthur Dalby, D Company[32]

Soon after 4.30, a German machine gun which had been missed in the smoke and fire of the advance enfiladed the captured trench. The second and third waves, pinned down, could not get to the German second line. As some of the wounded struggled back to the British trenches, it became clear to Colonel Taylor that the attack had lost momentum and that a determined counter-attack by the Germans could overrun the British lines.

Taylor gathered together eighty men from the detail left behind, and sent runners with all his papers back to Brigade HQ. He then took his men into an assembly trench to await the Germans. Because he had lost touch with the units on each side, both flanks of the trench were exposed so he ordered barricades to be erected and posted bombing parties at either end of the trench.

At this point the Germans realised how vulnerable the Pals were. Colonel Taylor, watching from his makeshift strongpoint, observed a group of about a dozen enemy prisoners being marched back to the British lines suddenly turn on their captors, wrenching the rifles from their grasp and taking them prisoner. Meanwhile two bodies of German infantry, each numbering about 400 men, were advancing in open order from behind their second lines. Taylor managed to get a telephone cable run back to Brigade HQ and was able to direct artillery fire onto the German troops, causing heavy casualties and dispersing the attack.

At 7am Taylor's group was reinforced by about 100 men of the 2nd Bradford Pals who had been driven back on the left flank, and he was therefore able to extend his frontage to

Private Frank Mills, killed.

Sergeant Herbert G. Pickles, killed.

Private Edward Woffenden, Killed.

Acting Corporal Bernard Gill (centre standing), wounded in the right hip, recovers in hospital.

the main part of Gavrelle village. He again contacted Brigade HQ to ask for further reinforcements, and at 8am a platoon of the Divisional Pioneers (12th Battalion, The King's Own Yorkshire Light Infantry) arrived. It had been the 12th KOYLI who had supported the Pals on 1 July 1916 when an enemy counter-attack seemed imminent.

At this time, Second-Lieutenant Davies's platoon were still holding on in the German trench. They had somehow survived the artillery bombardment, but they were about to be hard pressed.

It now became daylight, the Germans seemed to be wandering about in confusion. Sergeant Mackenzie sniped twelve and Corporal Birch did good execution with his Lewis gun. The Germans advanced in large groups down road leading from FRESNES to GAVRELLE. They ran back several times due to our sniping and Lewis gun fire.

The Germans were holding chalk trenches in front of the wood on our left. They had posts 30 to 40 yards on our right and left. They attacked us with bombs and rifle-grenades from both sides, and we were compelled to keep cover owing to frontal machine-gun fire. The enemy appeared strong on our right and advanced from trees in long half-moon lines. I sent two men back with news to battle headquarters, but both were severely wounded on the way and did not arrive.

There were eight German aeroplanes overhead.

We cut a small sap into a ditch on our left and crawled back to our own lines having held the post for four hours, and having run out of ammunition.

Second-Lieutenant C. C. Davies, B Company[33]

Shortly after the arrival of the KOYLI and the remnants of Davies's platoon, the Germans made another attack. Taylor again called down artillery fire onto them and, now equipped with two Lewis guns, his small force opened fire and once again dispersed the advancing German columns.

As the day wore on the Pals, watching from their trench, could see parties of Germans returning to man the front line they had abandoned during the initial assault, so they kept up a harassing fire with Lewis guns and rifles. Meanwhile, the Pals who had survived the attack made their way back to their own lines.

I came out, seven out of twenty-seven. We walked down Gavrelle Road and the Germans knew we used it. They used to put a shell every so far, now and again, and I came out. We walked a few together because if you get a lot together and one shell drops all are going to go. Anyway I was walking with a fellow called Schofield, [he] says 'What the hell are you walking for?' I said 'What would you do?' I said, 'I'm a fatalist, I'm neither running or going slow, I'm just walking normally,' I says, 'I don't know when the next shell's coming so you can please your bloody self!' He said, 'I'm off', and I found him oh, probably half a mile further on with a leg off. He ran into it!

15/259 Private Arthur Dalby, D Company[34]

Once again the battalion – and indeed the whole brigade – had suffered heavy losses. Estimates of the casualties among the Leeds Pals range from sixteen officers (four killed, four wounded and eight missing) and 396 other ranks (eighteen killed, ninety-nine wounded and 279 missing)[35] to twenty officers and 700 other ranks killed, wounded and missing.[36] We now know from official sources that ten officers[37] and 160 ORs were killed,[38] and four ORs died of wounds; it can also be ascertained that two officers and at least twenty-seven ORs were taken prisoner[39].

What also becomes apparent from a study of the Commonwealth War Graves Commission cemetery and memorial registers is that all but one of the officers' graves and all but thirteen of the soldier's graves were lost, and that many of them never had any known grave as their bodies were not recovered. Of the 164 ORs who lost their lives, seventeen were original 1914 volunteers, a further eighteen also had the '15' prefix to their regimental numbers, having joined the battalion during the 1915 recruiting campaign, and forty-six of the remainder had a direct connection with Leeds, either having been born there or been resident there when they joined the battalion.[40]

The survivors of the battle were relieved late on the night of 4 May, and at 2.40am the next morning the exhausted men arrived at St Catherine's, where they were met by field kitchens dispensing tea. They eventually arrived back at their camp at about 6am, where they spent the day resting and cleaning their battle-stained uniforms and equipment. That evening they were formed up again and marched up to the trenches to relieve the 12th York and Lancasters in Brigade Reserve. Although they were in the support trenches some distance from the front line, the battalion had suffered nine more casualties, including two killed and one died of wounds, by the time they were relieved once more on 13 May.

On the 16th, after a brief spell back at camp at St Catherine's, the Pals again went into the support lines in Brigade Reserve. They were relieved again on 19 May and marched to Ecurie, where they were reunited with the details left behind while they were in the trenches. From 23 to 27 May they were detailed to provide working parties to improve the trenches each night from 10pm to 2am. This was done at 'fighting strength'.[41] When this task was completed they were again called upon to provide a working party some 200-strong to build a firing range near St Eloy.

By the end of the month the Pals had received details of the awards to some members of the battalion, for their work during the attack on 3 May.

Colonel Taylor was Mentioned in Despatches, as also was Lance-Corporal G. M. Ferrand, who was still missing.[42]

Three men were awarded the Military Medal, Sergeant Mackenzie, who had been mentioned in Lieutenant Davies's report to Brigade Headquarters,[43] and stretcher-bearers 33686 Private Alfred P. Westerman and 33770 Private Henry Wrighton.

On 5 June further awards were announced. Second-Lieutenant William Hazzard, and Regimental Sergeant-Major William Wilson received the Military Cross, and Company

254

Men of 31st Division captured on 3 May at Gavrelle are marched away by their captors. (Imperial War Museum)

Sergeant-Major Joseph Edward Jones of B Company was awarded the Distinguished Conduct Medal.[44]

On 6 June Colonel Taylor went home to England for ten days' leave and some of the medal winners were sent to the First Army Rest Camp at Boulogne. Major Gibson took command and once again the battalion was called upon to provide working parties, this time for repairs to the roads at La Maison Blanche. The Pals went into the trenches at Gavrelle again on 9 June, but before they set off they were told that Colonel Taylor had been appointed to the Distinguished Service Order.[45]

George M. Ferrand, missing presumed dead.

The Pals were in the trenches until 15 June, and during that time C Company suffered seventeen casualties, including two men killed and four who died of wounds. The War Diary does not record the circumstances, but it seems likely that they were victims of the German artillery. The Pals then went into Brigade Reserve. Three days later a Divisional Horse Show was held, and once again the battalion showed its prowess, taking four first prizes and one second.

I was in the horse show. I was brought up with horses, I was a good rider, and I won. We had to ride a horse, without saddles, you got on by getting hold of the mane and pulled yourself on. You went over a three-foot-high jump, a three-foot trench, a three-foot-high jump, and you picked a dummy up, threw it over the withers, and then you mounted again, and brought it back over the three jumps. The first back got the prize, it was only a little cup. Oh, I got twenty francs as well, something like that.

15/259 Private Arthur Dalby, Transport Section[46]

The Pals went back into the line on 21 June, but this time it was relatively quiet and there were few casualties. After their relief on 28 June, they were called upon for working parties and these continued until 18 July. Brigade Sports were held at Mont St Eloy on the following day, and yet again the Leeds Pals came out on top, winning nine first prizes, five second prizes and six third prizes, and receiving the Championship cup from Brigadier-General Ingles.

The men went into the trenches near Neuville St Vaast on 21 July and remained there until the end of the month. For Percy Barlow, who had just arrived with a draft of reinforcements, it was a new and frightening experience.

If ever a place smelt of death it was that. They were there, the absent ones, sleeping there, only a light covering of soil, there, just over the top, just around the bend, gone, but still with us. The atmosphere was heavy with putrefaction, and we were not sorry to move though we knew we were for the front line. Accordingly we moved off again in the dusk, with a sickening feeling at the pit of our stomachs. The ardent militarism was evaporating fast, and being replaced by the primitive feeling of fear, but we knew we must go on, because it was certain death to refuse. A perfect brute of a shell landed in our rear, and we felt relieved. Afterwards we learnt that it had fallen amongst D Coy, who were lined up like us, and caused heavy casualties.

The night march proceeded. Tripping over wire, sliding into mud, sweating and swearing, on and on we went. At last we came to a deep trench, which we grew to know as 'Tired Alley', to be crossed at intervals by a sister trench known as 'Tommy Alley'. At intervals were signs abbreviated 'Tommy' & 'Tired'. After the last, someone had put a question mark, and scribbled underneath, 'No it's only a b....y rumour'. The rain fell steadily and we were soon wading in the dark trench. A sudden strafe arose. Without warning we came under heavy shellfire. A terrifying experience, the blast of the explosions, the whine of pieces of shrapnel, the **Major L. Baker.**

smell, acrid and pungent, of explosives. Pressing onwards, no loitering or lingering now, we came to our allotted section, occupied I think by the KOYLIs. In the meantime we were led to our posts. The sentries were on the fire step, looking out across No Man's Land, a word or two in quiet tones, the KOYLIs filed out, the new sentries posted and we were manning the trenches.

Just before stand-to (the critical time in the half-light), our guns opened up with a barrage on the enemy's trenches no great distance away. The shells came whizzing over our heads in a startling fashion. The Germans (anticipating attack), sent up rockets to their artillery, in fact the SOS.

256

Instantly their guns opened out onto our front line trench. It was truly terrifying. We had all to man the fire step, and to a man our knees were knocking. Suddenly a sickening crash just round the bay, the stench of explosive, then the plaintive cry of the wounded, 'Stretcher-bearers'.

20377 Private Percy Barlow, B Company[47]

Just before the relief the Pals were inspected by the Divisional Staff, who reported that the trenches were 'Exceptionally clean and well ordered'. The front line firebays were personally inspected by the Brigade Commander, who judged them for the award of prizes for the best three posts in each company.

It must have been at about this time that the Leeds Pals learnt that one of their longest-serving and most senior officers had left the battalion under very unfortunate circumstances. Canadian-born Major L. P. Baker, who had served for seven years in India before the war and had joined from the Reserve of Officers in February 1915, was 'Dismissed the Service' by sentence of a General Court Martial on 24 July 1917. He had been wounded in the head shortly before the attack on the Somme the previous year, but the battalion War Diary does not mention his return to France and it is not known whether he took part in the action at Gavrelle. It was rumoured that he, like Major Norman, had become a heavy drinker, and he was thought to have hit a subordinate while under the influence of alcohol and to have ended the war as a corporal in a Canadian regiment, although this cannot be confirmed from any available records.[48]

At the beginning of August the Pals were in reserve but still provided the inevitable working parties until their return to the trenches on the 16th. They moved into the support line on 24 August and remained there until 4 September, when they moved to Ecurie for two weeks where they were joined by reinforcements.

On 17 September the battalion went into the trenches again relieving the 12th East Yorkshires in the Arleux sector. Although this was probably the quietest period the men had spent in the line, with only two casualties, one of them, Private William Walker, a conscript from Leeds, took his own life.[49]

Lieutenant (later Captain) L. L. Binnie.

While his 'Boys' were in the line Colonel Taylor took over command of 93 Brigade and his place was taken temporarily by Major G. W. Tilley of the 18th Durham Light Infantry. The Pals were relieved on 25 September and moved into the support line to work on the trenches. On the 29th Lieutenant L. L. Binnie and Sergeant H. Thomas went up to the front line with a raiding party of twenty-six men, to attack a group of the enemy who were holding a shell crater. They got within a short distance of the German outpost but were seen in the moonlight, and were forced to withdraw under heavy fire. On their return it was found that one man was slightly wounded, and two others were missing.[50]

Binnie, he were a brave man because I remember him on one occasion, we'd been on a trench raid and we were coming back, and the Germans raided us as we were coming back. One of our fellows were left and he went forward did Binnie, and got hold and dragged him by the scruff of his neck, and he had his revolver, [was] using his revolver.

15/471 Sergeant Clifford Hollingworth, D Company[51]

257

A working-party carries duckboard up towards the front line at night. (Imperial War Museum)

When the battalion was relieved, Binnie was promoted captain and sent on leave. On 6 October Colonel Taylor resumed command, and the Pals proceeded to Ecoivres for training. They returned to the front-line trenches again on 13 October, and on the 19th went back into the support line for a week, during which time they spent their nights working on the trenches. After their return from the trenches on the 25th, they spent the rest of the month working, often under artillery fire, despite being behind the lines, and during this time the award of a belated Military Medal to 15/97 Sergeant Clifford Birch was announced, for 'the successful handling of his Platoon Lewis gun at Gavrelle, and consistent good work.'[52] The battalion moved to Ecurie and continued its training, but also continued to provide working parties.

258

When the Pals went back into the trenches on 9 November, it was for a spell in the support line before they took over the front line again on the 16th. After their relief on 27 November they went back into the support line, and on the 29th they took over from the 18th Durham Light infantry in 'close support'. There they stayed until they were relieved on 4 December and went into Brigade Support at Roclincourt Camp, having spent nearly a month in the trenches.

On the morning of 7 December the Leeds Pals were joined by the Leeds Bantams[53] (17th Battalion, The West Yorkshire Regiment). The Bantams had travelled from the Ypres Salient to billets at Acq where they bade farewell to Major J. H. Gill, DSO, their commanding officer, before marching to Le Pendu Camp to amalgamate with the Leeds Pals. The contingent consisted of seven officers, four sergeants, five corporals and 260 privates, including thirty transport men. They were greeted with hearty cheers and after they had been assigned to their companies, the whole battalion, now officially called the 15/17th Battalion, The Prince of Wales's Own (West Yorkshire Regiment), was addressed by Stuart Taylor, who welcomed

An engraved cigarette case was presented to every member of the battalion at Christmas in 1917; this one belonged to Bernard Gill.

the Bantams to his ranks, especially as they too were Leeds men. With the formal welcome over, they were issued with beer and then dismissed to get to know their new comrades.[54]

Three days later the battalion paraded again and was addressed by the GOC 31st Division, Major-General R Wanless O'Gowan, who presented Military Medals to six men for 'their devotion to duty repairing telephone wires under most dangerous conditions during heavy

Private William Boynton Butler, VC.

hostile bombardment and gas shelling East of Willerval on the night of 30 November and 1 December, 1917'. The six were:

15/1008 Sergeant A. E. Wood, C Company
15/1096 Corporal R. W. Sheppard, A Company
15/330 Lance-Corporal H. L. Firth, D Company
15/604 Lance-Corporal G. Meldrum, C Company
28197 Private W Dyson, D. Company
38058 Private L Young, C. Company[55]

On 20 December this distinguished group was joined by 17/1280 Private William B. Butler, a 23-year-old Bantam who had returned from leave in England, where he had been awarded the Victoria Cross by HM King George V.[56]

The next day the battalion received the news that two of its officers had been honoured, for Colonel Taylor and Major Gibson had been mentioned in Sir Douglas Haig's Despatches of 7 November. This was Taylor's second 'Mention'.

This period of good news and relative inactivity, which lasted nearly a month, was too good to last, and the Pals went back into the front line trenches at Arleux on 22 December, where they would spend Christmas. Although it was a comparatively quiet spell in the trenches, Second-Lieutenant George W. Davidson died of wounds on 27 December, the day before the battalion was relieved.

This was the Leeds Pals' first time in the trenches with their new additions from the 17th Battalion. Although the Bantams had been reinforced by some average-sized troops before joining the battalion, there was still a number of small men in the contingent, and the Pals soon found that they had to make some adjustments to accommodate their new comrades.

> *The Bantams were a nuisance. They couldn't help being little men, but the same time, when they stood on the firestep they couldn't see over! We filled a sandbag full of soil and let them stand on it. Not only that, when the Germans knew they were [in] they came over, because I think they took one or two as souvenirs.*
>
> *15/259 Private Arthur Dalby D Company*[57]

When the battalion returned from the trenches on 28 December it made its way to Ecurie Wood Camp where, on the following day, it was to enjoy a belated Christmas celebration. A marquee had been erected and a full day of festivities had been planned, starting at 7am with carol-singing and Christmas music from the band. From 12 noon until 4.15pm Christmas dinner

```
                              6
       (2nd SM ASHFORD)

                         20.12.17.
        THE PANTOMIME
           - of -
        "ALADDIN".
           - by -
  THE OWLS      --      15th West Yorks. Regt.
        -------

 ALADDIN          ----      C.S.M. Brinton.
 THE EMPEROR      ----      2nd Lt. ASHFORD.
 THE PRINCESS (his daughter)  Sgt. Hague.
 SLIM }                     Pte. Thompson.
 SLAM ) Policemen           Pte. Melia.
 Fairy Queen      ----      Pte. Gande.
 Genii of the Lamp ---      Pte. Walker.
 ABANAZAR         ----      Sgt. Hellewell.
 WIDOW TWANKEY    ----      Pte. Bunting.
        -------------------

     PROLOGUE.

 Scene 1. ---- The City of Pekin.
 Scene 2. ---- The Road to the Cave.
 Scene 3. ---- The Half Way House.
 Scene 4. ---- The Magic Cave.
 Scene 5. ---- The Road From the Cave.
 Scene 6. ---- The Emperor's Study.
 Scene 7. ---- The Road to the Palace.
 Scene 8. ---- The Emperor's Palace.
      Grand Floral Ballet.

        ----------
```

was served in three sittings, and at 5.30pm the pantomime *Aladdin* was performed by the 'Owls'.

At 8 o'clock that evening the whole battalion had supper in the marquee and everyone was given a present by the Colonel. The officers each received a whistle and cord and every man was given a silver-plated cigarette case engraved with a New Year message of good wishes signed by Stuart Taylor. The cigarette cases given to the battalion concert party were solid silver.

These gifts had been paid for by subscriptions raised in Leeds by Alderman Arthur Willey, who had lost his son, Tom, at Serre on 1 July 1916. In addition to those given to the men at the front, he made an appeal for extra money so that cigarette cases could be given to as many of the original volunteers as could be traced.[58]

> *We came out the day after Boxing Day, something like that. We were in that weekend, somebody has to be in. We had a grand do then, and another thing, we had a private do of our own. There was Stiffy Cooper, Joe Collinson and Bill Spence and one of them got a chicken, somebody got a lump of ham, and so we'd a right Christmas dinner. We got some paper, newspaper, and we made a big table-cloth of it, got all the enamel plates and we'd proper sandwiches and knives and forks and candles lit, we'd five bottles of champagne and some wine and we'd a right good do. A right good 'nosh up'. We sat down to this and we had a toast and a sing-song. We enjoyed ourselves to the best ability we could. Because we'd had some nasty moments.*
>
> *15/471 Sergeant Clifford Hollingworth, D Company*[59]

So ended the Pals' second year of trench warfare in France. Long gone were the optimistic days of Colsterdale when the men awoke to coffee and biscuits and looked forward to

The 'Owls', the battalion concert party, perform on a makeshift stage, 1917. (C. Hollingworth)

HE whom this scroll commemorates was numbered among those who, at the call of King and Country, left all that was dear to them, endured hardness, faced danger, and finally passed out of the sight of men by the path of duty and self-sacrifice, giving up their own lives that others might live in freedom. Let those who come after see to it that his name be not forgotten.

Pte. John Jackson Shaw
W. Yorkshire Regt.

The commemorative scroll sent to John Jackson Shaw's family after the war. He was killed on 2/3 May 1917.

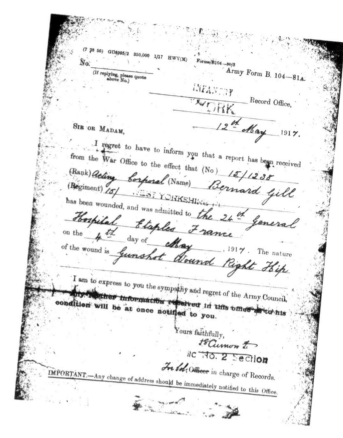

Notification from the War Office that Bernard Gill was wounded in the attack on Gavrelle, May 1917.

Bernard Gill's engraved cigarette case.

receiving their uniforms and rifles. The surviving few of Colonel Taylor's 'Old Boys' were now tough veterans of two major offensives, looked up to by the conscripts sent to replace the never-ending casualties. On their tunics the original volunteers now sported good conduct chevrons and wound stripes, and some of them, such as Harold Green, Clifford Hollingworth and Harold Jackson, were now full sergeants.

But the Allies seemed no nearer to victory. It would be almost another year before the Germans were defeated, and some of the bloodiest fighting was still to come, in the spring of 1918.

NOTES

1. Letter from Arthur Hollings to his sister, Margaret, 22 January 1917.
2. Battalion War Diary, 27 July 1916, Public Record Office, London: W095/2361.
3. Author's recorded interview with Clifford Holling-worth, May 1988.
4. 93 Brigade War Diary, 18 August 1916, Public Record Office, London: W095/2359.
5. Pearson, Arthur Valentine, *A Leeds Pal Looks Back* unpublished manuscript in Leeds Reference Library, circa 1966.
6. Ibid.
7. Battalion War Diary, op.cit., 27 August 1916, also Hollingworth, op.cit.
8. Battalion War Diary, op.cit., 2 September 1916. In October 1915 the 'Army Suspension of Sentences Act' was passed, to discourage men from committing custodial offences with the intention of avoiding front-line service. It is not known whether Lister served his sentence. He was given his full medal entitlement at the end of the war, but is listed in the medal roll as a private at the time of his discharge in April 1919. See Public Record Office, London: W0329/899.
9. Battalion War Diary, op.cit., 7 September 1916.
10. Ibid, 7 October 1916.
11. Letter from Arthur Hollings to his father, 22 October 1916.
12. Report in Battalion War Diary, op.cit.
13. Diary of 15/1003 Private Edward Woffenden, in the possession of Bob Reed, York.
14. Letter from Arthur Hollings to his father, 2 November 1916.
15. Report in Battalion War Diary, op.cit.
16. Woffenden, op.cit., 2 November 1916.
17. Battalion War Diary, op.cit., 27 November 1916. V Corps' Special Brigade RE records cannot now be traced.
18. Letter from Arthur Hollings to his father, 26 November 1916.
19. Diary of 15/1951 Private J.J. Shaw, 9 and 21 January 1917.
20. Letter from Arthur Hollings to his sister, Margaret, 22 January 1917.
21. See Appendix V for citation.
22. Battalion War Diary, op.cit.
23. *Yorkshire Evening Post* 8 February 1917, newscutting in Leeds Pals' Association Minute Book
24. Battalion War Diary, op.cit.
25. Pearson, op.cit.
26. Scott, W. H., *Leeds in the Great War 1914–1918*, Libraries and Arts Committee, Leeds, 1923. See also Woodhouse, T and Yeomans, R. *Yorkshire Cricket – A Pictorial Survey*, Dalesman Publishing Company, Clapham, North Yorkshire, 1974.
27. Pearson, op.cit.
28. Hollingworth, op.cit.
29. 31st Division Order No.139, 1 May 1917; Divisional War Diary, Public Record Office, London: W095/2342.
30. 93 Brigade War Diary, op.cit., – 'Diary of Information of May 3rd. as received in Advance Brigade Headquarters'.

31. Lieutenant Davies's Report, 93 Brigade War Diary, op.cit.
32. Author's recorded interview with Arthur Dalby, 1989.
33. Davies's Report, 93 Brigade War Diary, op.cit.
34. Dalby, op.cit. 15/788 Lance-Corporal Thomas Edward Schofield was discharged as unfit for War Service on 17 August 1917. See Regimental Medal Roll, Public Record Office, London: WO329/900.
35. 93 Brigade War Diary, op.cit.
36. Scott, op.cit.
37. *Officers Died in the Great War 1914–1919*, Part 1 *Old and New Armies*, HMSO, London, 1919.
38. *Soldiers Died in the Great War 1914–1919*, Part 19, *The Prince of Wales's Own (West Yorkshire Regiment)*, HMSO, London, 1921.
39. British Red Cross and Order of St John Enquiry List No.14, 1917, reprint by Sunset Militaria in conjunction with Ray Westlake Military Books, Gwent, South Wales, 1989.
40. *Soldiers Died in the Great War,* op.cit., records the birthplace and place of enlistment of each man who died on active service.
41. Battalion War Diary, op.cit., (ie less the 10 per cent 'details' that were usually left behind when the battalion went into action).
42. British Red Cross and Order of St John Enquiry List, op.cit. Ferrand was presumed dead in the Regimental Medal Roll, Public Record Office, London: W0329/899. See also Soldiers Died in the Great War, op.cit.
43. Battalion War Diary, op.cit.
44. Ibid.
45. Ibid.
46. Dalby, op.cit.
47. Barlow, Percy, unpublished MS memoir, circa 1919.
48. Author's conversations with Arthur Dalby and Clifford Hollingworth, 1988–1989. *The London Gazette*, 22 August 1917 records: 'Major L.P. Baker dismissed the service by sentence of a General Court Martial, 24 July 1917.'
49. Battalion War Diary, op.cit., and *Soldiers Died in the Great War,* op.cit.
50. Battalion War Diary, op.cit.
51. Hollingworth, op.cit.
52. Battalion War Diary, op.cit.
53. In October 1914 a Durham miner, who had walked to Birkenhead to enlist, was turned down for military service because he was considered too short. He offered to fight anyone in the room, and as a result Alfred Bigland, the Conservative MP for Birkenhead, obtained permission to recruit a Bantam battalion, composed of undersized men. Ultimately twenty-four Bantam battalions were raised, including the 17th Battalion, The West Yorkshire Regiment in Leeds. See Simkins, Peter, *Kitchener's Army; The Raising of the New Armies, 1914–16*, Manchester University Press, 1988; also Scott, op.cit.
54. Ibid.
55. Ibid.
56. See Appendix V for citation.
57. Dalby, op.cit.
58. *Yorkshire Post*, 15 December 1917; *Yorkshire Evening Post*, 18 December 1917; *Yorkshire Observer*, 22 December 1917.
59. Hollingworth, op.cit.

Chapter Seven

The Pantomime

1918? Oh, that was a pantomime that was!
15/471 Sergeant Clifford Hollingworth, D Company[1]

FRANCE 1918

With the dawning of the new year, a German offensive on the Western Front seemed a strong possibility. Both sides were weary from the prolonged battles of the previous years; Verdun, the Somme, Passchendaele, and the Nivelle offensive had all taken their toll. But Germany now had the potential to increase its army in the west by up to forty divisions, or nearly 30 per cent, for Russia's collapse in 1917 had released the German troops hitherto committed on the Eastern Front. The opening months of 1918 would provide the Germans with a last chance to strike a decisive blow on the Western Front.

The timing of such an attack was critical, however, as America had declared war on Germany[2] and 'the Yanks were coming' – the Allies would soon be joined by a vast army from the United States.

Over 10 million American men were registered as eligible for military service, and nearly 3 million would be in France by the end of 1918. And these were fresh troops, not worn down by years of debilitating trench fighting. If the Germans did not make their move before the Americans' arrival, defeat for Germany would surely follow.

The British Army on the Western Front was suffering a grave shortage of men at this time, due to a number of factors. First, a successful Austrian offensive on the Italian Front in 1917 had caused Britain to divert troops to support her Italian ally. Second, Lloyd George's Supreme War Council, which controlled manpower resources in Britain, had deliberately slowed the flow of men to the Western Front because of its distrust of Haig's tactics, which had already led to appalling losses, and to a lesser extent because a reserve of troops might be needed in the event of civil war in Ireland. Third, the demoralisation of the French Army after Nivelle's costly offensive in 1917, resulting in the soldiers agreeing to man the trenches

Clifford Hollingworth in 1918. This photograph was taken when he was on leave in Leeds, 8–23 February.
(C. Hollingworth)

American soldiers march along Piccadilly, having arrived in Britain en route to the Western Front.

but not to attack, caused pressure to be put on the British Army to take over even more of the line.[3]

The Germans, mounting their own offensive without having to rely on the co-operation of an ally, were in the unique position of having one completely unified command structure, unlike Britain and France whose attempts at a joint offensive had been continually complicated by dissent and disagreement between their respective senior commanders.

The German offensive, codenamed 'Michael', was the brainchild of General Erich Ludendorff, who had become gripped by the same mania as Haig and Nivelle that he too was going to win the war with a grand offensive. Realising that it must be mounted as soon as possible in order that the Germans might maintain their numerical advantage, the next question to be considered was 'where'? An attack against the French might be an easy option, but the British Army had to be fought and defeated sooner or later, and an attack on the British lines while the German fighting troops were still fresh and strong might dispose of a formidable opponent at the outset.

266

Field-Marshal von Hindenburg, the Kaiser and General Erich von Ludendorff. (Imperial War Museum)

It was finally decided that the attack should be directed towards the southern part of the British lines, where they joined those of the French. This would exploit any unwillingness among the French soldiers to take the offensive, and it would also take advantage of any weaknesses in the joint Anglo-French command structure.

In the event it proved to be a sound choice on the Germans' part, for this section of the line was held by the British Fifth Army, which was under strength – of all the British armies on the Western Front, the Fifth was suffering most from the shortage of men.

The new year started well for the Leeds Pals, with an allotment of leave passes for the men who had joined from the 17th Battalion, and the announcement of the brevet rank of lieutenant-colonel for Stuart Taylor, who had hitherto held that rank only temporarily. Captain Harold Smith, who had originally joined the battalion as a private in 1914, was awarded the Military Cross for his valuable service as Transport Officer and for the previous year's service as Adjutant, particularly during the attack on Gavrelle on 3 May 1917. Two of the men, 15/957

German soldiers march westwards. (Author's collection)

German reserves build up near the St Quentin Canal, 1918. (Author's collection)

Harold Smith MC. He was posthumously awarded a bar to his Military Cross after he died of wounds on 28 March 1918.

Sergeant N. F. Webster and 17/1226 Private C. E. Torr, were also decorated for their service, and mention was also made of Webster's work at Gavrelle.[4]

Two brief spells in the trenches followed in late January, and a thaw made conditions almost unbearable despite the issue of thigh-length gumboots. The tour of duty in the front and support lines was therefore reduced from six days to four.

Having taken in the contingent from the 17th Battalion, The West Yorkshire Regiment, towards the end of 1917, the men of the 15/17th Battalion, as it was now titled, were perhaps surprised to learn of further changes that were afoot. Because of the shortage of men, a major reorganisation of the British forces on the Western Front was under way. It was impossible to bring the existing units up to full strength, and it would have been inadvisable to appear to reduce the number of divisions deployed, so the obvious solution was to restructure the brigades so that they each consisted of three instead of four infantry battalions. This reorganisation was started on 10 January. One hundred and fifteen battalions were disbanded, and the troops thus released were used to bring those that remained up to strength; a further thirty-eight battalions were amalgamated with others. A condition of this reorganisation was that no Regular or first-line Territorial battalions were to be disbanded. Thus the cuts fell entirely on the New Army and the second-line Territorials raised after the outbreak of the war, such as those in the 31st Division.[5]

The 31st Division actually gained in some measure from its restructuring, for although six of its battalions were disbanded, and those which remained were condensed into two brigades, the division was joined by a new brigade formed of three battalions of Foot Guards which had been shed by the Guards Division in order to bring it into line with the new divisional organisation.

The changes to the 31st Division were completed by 17 February 1918, and from that date the composition of the three infantry brigades of the division were:[6]

4 Guards Brigade – 4th Battalion, The Grenadier Guards; 3rd Battalion, The Coldstream Guards; 2nd Battalion, The Irish Guards

92 Brigade – 10th Battalion, The East Yorkshire Regiment; 11th Battalion, The East Yorkshire Regiment; 11th Battalion, The East Lancashire Regiment

93 Brigade —15/17th Battalion, The West Yorkshire Regiment; 13th Battalion, The York and Lancaster Regiment; 18th Battalion, The Durham Light Infantry

The Leeds Pals spent February in billets or in support at Arleux, and on the 12th a contingent of two officers and 185 ORs arrived from the 16th West Yorkshires, which had been disbanded two days before. Among them were Sergeant-Major George Cussins and Private Walter Hare, who was to join his brother, Harold, in D Company.[7]

The rest of the month was spent in support and providing working parties for a Corps Defence Wiring Scheme near St Catherine. At the beginning of March 1918 the Pals were in GHQ Reserve at Caucourt undergoing a training programme, but liable to move to any part of the battlefront at twelve hours' notice. In anticipation of a German spring offensive, the leave allowance was reduced to four passes per brigade each day.

On 12 March a battalion sports meeting was held, which A Company won with 36 points, followed by B, C, and D Companies. Brigade sports were held over the next two days, and the Leeds Pals once again swept the board winning both the tug-of-war and the cross-country run at Frevillers, five of the first ten men in being original members of the battalion, carrying on the fine athletic tradition founded at Colsterdale in 1914–15.[8] On the 15th Colonel Taylor went to England on leave, and his place was taken temporarily by Lieutenant-Colonel Clifford C. H. Twiss, DSO, former commanding officer of the 13th Battalion, The East Yorkshire Regiment.[9] Then, on 17 March, continuing its sporting prowess, the battalion won the divisional cross-country race – this time, six out of the first ten men in were original Leeds Pals.[10]

In the early hours of the morning of 21 March 1918, the German artillery opened fire along the 50-mile front between Arras and La Fere. For five hours they pounded the British trenches with high explosive, shrapnel and poison gas. Mid-morning the German gunners relaid their weapons and the barrage crept forward.

Across no man's land behind the barrage came the first waves of the German infantry, lightly equipped

Alan Hay's 2nd prize rosette for the 300-yard race at the Battalion Sports Caucourt.

Stosstruppen (assault troops), some of them carrying the newly developed MP18 Bergmann submachine gun. They were supported by assault engineers who carried charges to destroy any barbed wire left intact by the artillery. The first waves were to rush the British front lines but, unlike their British counterparts on the Somme in 1916, they were not encumbered with extra equipment and they were not expected to walk at a steady pace towards the machine guns. They had the element of surprise, and their tactics were sound. Instead of attempting to break a wide gap in the front line and turn the flanks so that the cavalry could gallop through, the German *Stosstruppen* set out to penetrate the British lines anywhere they could, allowing the main force which followed to file through the gaps then spread out and encircle the British trenches along the whole 50-mile front. And in addition to their superior tactics, on this occasion the Germans had nature on their side, for their advance through the shell-torn British lines was cloaked by a mist, which helped to maintain the essential element of surprise.

On the morning of 21 March the Leeds Pals, in billets at Caucourt, sent a team to the Divisional Boxing Championship, where Private Meadow-croft won the featherweight competition and Private W. Lavine, a recently-joined Bantam from the 17th Battalion, was runner up in the lightweight competition.

That night, news of the German breakthrough came, and the 31st Division, in GHQ Reserve, was called upon to reinforce the line. It was intended to move 93 Brigade to the Pommier area, but the destination was changed en route and on the 22nd the Pals were taken by bus to Blairville. The German advance had been so swift that the Leeds men were sent into the

German assault troops advance through a smokescreen. (Author's collection)

trenches to relieve 101 Brigade of 34th Division, which had suffered heavy casualties as it was driven back.[11]

The Divisional front extended from the eastern side of Croisilles, westwards to about 1,000 yards east of Mory, with 4 Guards Brigade on the right and 93 Brigade on the left. The Leeds Pals were to take over the trenches from the 15th Royal Scots, on the brigade's right flank. This battalion had been in the line since 13 March, awaiting the German attack, but when it came they had been forced to withdraw in order to keep in touch with a unit on their right, which had been driven back.[12]

Early on the 22nd the 15th Royal Scots were still holding their second line, but heavy German machine-gun and rifle fire forced them back into a partially finished 'switch trench'. There they were spotted by a German aircraft, and were soon subjected to an artillery barrage which caused heavy casualties. Later that day they were ordered forward to support the 11th, Suffolks, who were clinging to a defensive line, but their commanding officer personally reported to Brigade that his men were too shaken and exhausted to go forward again. They were therefore told to stay where they were until the early hours of the 23rd when the Leeds Pals arrived to relieve them. By this time the 15th Royal Scots' casualties numbered fifteen officers and 381 other ranks, of whom two officers and thirty other ranks had been killed, and eight officers captured, among them Captain Brown, who had last been seen holding a trench block in order to allow the rest of his Company to escape.[13]

The Pals' battalion details were left at Blairville, and 625 other ranks and twenty-one officers went into the trenches. The 13th York and Lancasters were on their left with the 18th Durham Light Infantry in support. By 2am on 23 March the relief was complete and the Pals braced themselves for the expected German advance.[14]

> In the middle of the night, we runners were turned out as urgent messages had to be delivered to recall outlying detachments. Jerry had broken through our lines and was rapidly sweeping all before him. I was detailed to contact our boxing team and to lead them to a point where the whole battalion was to be picked up by buses and rushed to the line. We got into 'battle order', piled our packs in a field (we never saw them again, or our personal effects) and followed our guide across country to a line of old trenches which were held by the remnants of a battalion who had been badly cut up and had been retiring for days. We took over from them, stayed that night in those trenches, then, in daylight, we began to retire.
>
> 15/711 Lance-Corporal Arthur V. Pearson, C Company[15]

> We arrived, after a twelve-hour ride, at a lonely spot on the shell-scarred road, from which we could see several villages on fire, the ruddy glow lighting the blackness of the surrounding distance for miles. Here, after dumping all unnecessaries, we were collected together, the 10 per cent were detailed, and then we were quietly told that our task was to hold a trench one foot deep and to hold it at all costs.
>
> 20377 Private Percy Barlow, B Company[16]

The expected massive German attack did not come, probably because of a British artillery bombardment, which caught the Germans in the open in the early hours of the morning and forced them to take cover. An attack was launched against the 13th York and Lancasters holding the left of the brigade front, but that was quickly stopped by rifle and Lewis gun fire, and no further infantry attacks took place that day. That evening, when the divisional front was altered, the Pals were relieved by the Guards Division, and ordered to 'side-slip' towards St Leger and take up a new position near Judas Farm. Shortly after midnight the Germans shelled them in their trenches, but few casualties resulted.

At 7am on 24 March the Germans attacked the whole of 93 Brigade, but made no headway. The infantry attack continued until midday, when it lost momentum. It was resumed mid-afternoon, after an artillery and trench mortar bombardment, but was still unsuccessful. There was a danger of encirclement, however, due to the Germans making a successful advance in the 40th Division area further south. 4 Guards Brigade briefly came under fire from the rear when the Germans took Ervillers, but a counter-attack by 92 Brigade drove the enemy back. The situation now became confused, with both 92 Brigade, which was holding Ervillers in the 40th Divisional area, and 4 Guards Brigade coming under heavy artillery fire from the British lines, and even being bombed and shot at by the Royal Flying Corps.

During the night the Germans attacked again.

The 15th Battalion, The Royal Scots in their trenches early in 1918. They were holding the same sector line when they were attacked on 21 March. (Imperial War Museum)

They had no success against 4 Guards Brigade, but made progress to the south, reaching the western outskirts of Mory. An order was received from VI Corps HQ to swing the 31st Divisional line back to Ervillers, but the Guards Brigade commander pointed out that it was necessary to hold the high ground halfway between St Leger and Mory in order to protect the southern flank of the British line, since the Germans had driven a wedge between his Brigade and 40th Division. Later that night the Germans attacked Ervillers again, but were again driven out by 92 Brigade, with the consequence that 31st Division ended up holding a front of over 9,500 yards, with no contact with 40th Division on its right.[17]

On the 25th, 31st Division received orders to withdraw to a new line running from Moyenneville to Ablainzeville, where it would link up with 42nd Division, which had relieved the badly battered 40th Division. This withdrawal was completed in the early hours of 26 March. At about 11am the 31st Divisional Commander received some disturbing news from the Guards Division – two Battalions of 93 Brigade, the 13th York and Lancasters and the 18th Durham Light Infantry, had been seen marching further back to a new defensive line.

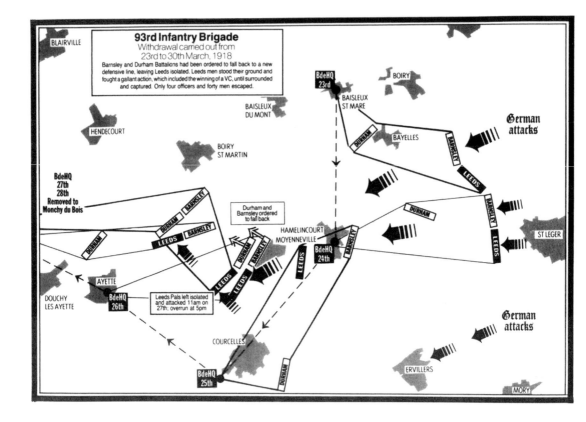

93rd Infantry Brigade
Withdrawal carried out from
23rd to 30th March, 1918

Barnsley and Durham Battalions had been ordered to fall back to a new
defensive line, leaving Leeds isolated. Leeds men stood their ground and
fought a gallant action, which included the winning of a VC, until surrounded
and captured. Only four officers and forty men escaped.

On making enquiries the Divisional Commander found out that the Acting Brigade Major, Captain R. V. Ramsden, had been blown from his horse by a the explosion of a shell, and had given the two battalions written orders to withdraw, but could not explain why.[18]

His action left the Leeds Pals completely isolated, with both flanks exposed. Meanwhile the Germans, meeting no opposition, had entered Moyenneville and established machine guns there to enfilade the British line, and had also gained control of the ridge south west of the town. After trying unsuccessfully to extend its flanks to link up with the unit on its right, the Leeds battalion counter-attacked. Two companies were sent up to take the ridge, while one platoon was sent into Moyenneville. The counter-attack was a great success. An entire German battalion was driven off the ridge, and then caught from the rear by fire from the platoon that had recaptured the town. After suffering heavy casualties the Germans laid down their arms and some thirty-five prisoners were taken. That afternoon a large German force mounted another attack on Moyenneville, which drove the Pals to the western outskirts of the town, where they held on tenaciously. A counter-attack was planned for 8.30 that evening, but the men were too exhausted and so were told to hold their positions for the night.[19]

Early morning saw us retreating in open order, across fields of growing corn, and hitherto prosperous villages were passed in that morning retreat. Throughout the past few days we were struck by the entire absence of our own aircraft, and this, with the disappearance of our own artillery, added to the gloom which hangs over the army compelled to retreat. The German observation balloon, which was up in record time, evidently spotted the move, for we were subjected to a harassing fire which made not a few gaps in our ranks. At last we came to a series of holes, some eight feet in length by about three feet deep. Here we stopped for a time, thinking these were our new positions. Such was not the case, for after waiting some four hours, till the Germans appeared, we again retreated to a sunken road just below. Here we were rapidly reorganised and attacked the slopes with such promtitude and vigour that the Germans were taken entirely by surprise, and driven a distance of about one mile. During this operation, thirty prisoners were taken, but we lost very heavily, particularly officers. During the evening Laverick, in my section, received a bullet in the head. As the stretcher bearers had all been killed, P. O'Hara and myself went in search of a stretcher. On our return we found the company had gone to attack the enemy's position on the ridge, leaving my pal (George Worrall) in charge of the wounded man. We took him down to the Dressing Station, but it was no light task, for only those who have carried wounded will know what it is to carry over ploughed ground for four miles, carrying at the same time our rifles and 170 rounds of ammunition. I believe I was walking asleep, during that walk, for I had had no sleep for five days.

On our arrival back, we found the attack on the enemy's position had failed owing to our chaps falling asleep during the waiting out, which precedes the signal to attack. They were utterly weary, as could be judged by their position on the sunken road. Officers and men were stretched out, intermingling in hopeless abandon, snatching the sleep which had been denied for five weary days. We were no exception, and were soon sleeping soundly, despite the fact of the Germans being no more than 150 yards away. I now believe that they were in a similar state for we were not disturbed that night.

20377 Private Percy Barlow, B Company[20]

On the 26th we were told to retire down to this cutting across. We drew that to save the Guards or something, cause they were being overpressed. Well when I got down, I said to the Sergeant-Major, 'This is all wrong, Sergeant-Major,' I said, 'we should either have stopped there or gone up there.' He said, 'What's it got to do with you? Mind your business, Sergeant!' But I was taught to be a soldier and never to retire into a valley. Always keep a hill behind you. Anyway, that's where we were and that's where they came over and that's when I was wounded.
15/471 Sergeant Clifford Hollingworth, D Company[21]

The morning of the 27th was beautiful and warm, and the first issue of rum (which I was unfortunate enough to miss) did much to cheer the chaps. The rations had appeared somehow and so we were like giants refreshed.

20377 Private Percy Barlow, B Company[22]

At about 11am on the 27th the Germans made a heavy attack on the whole divisional front. The brunt of the attack was borne by the Leeds Pals, the only battalion still in its correct position, but in spite of stout resistance the Germans steadily gained ground. The situation was rapidly beginning to deteriorate and the CO of B Company asked for volunteers to protect the Pals' exposed flank by holding the ridge against the advancing enemy. Sergeant Albert Mountain, a former member of the 17th Battalion, volunteered and, with ten men and a Lewis gun, succeeded in enfilading the German advanced patrol, killing about a hundred – the remainder fled. The main body of the enemy then appeared and Mountain and his men formed a defensive position in order to cover the retirement of his company, although by this time there were only four of the ten men left. They held the Germans off for half an hour

Alfred Holgate's medals and Next of Kin Memorial Plaque. (Author's Collection)

Sergeant Albert Mountain, VC.

before trying to get back to their comrades. Mountain was among the few who got out, but at least two of his remaining men, Percy Barlow and George Worrall, were captured. In June, Sergeant Albert Mountain was decorated with the Victoria Cross for his actions.[23]

The attention of our Company Commander was directed to a ridge on the left which was apparently unoccupied. He accordingly asked for ten volunteers, George [Worrall] and I being amongst them.

The first two set off at a gallop and were greeted with a perfect fusillade of machine-gun bullets. Things did not look very healthy, but George and I went casually along and curiously enough we were not fired on at all, and reached our destination to find one man holding a front of about forty yards. We were joined soon afterwards by Holgate, another of my section, and I think we were the only three to reach the far end of the position. The Germans were being reinforced by troops advancing in sectional rushes, and I could not but admire the skilful way in which they were handled. Immediately in front was a little knoll, over which Fritz was forced to run, and as he presented an excellent target, we soon got busy and continued so until after dinner, when Holgate stopped one with his head, the bullet passing out of the back of his head. He only sighed, and his blood formed pools in the little hole in which we were having such a struggle. My sleeve and hands were covered, as we found it necessary to move him. Before doing this we cut his ammunition

Looking towards Moyenneville from the sunken road. (W. Hare)

from around him, for we were getting very short. The day wore on, and four o'clock arrived with not a single round of ammunition left to spare, for we expected him to attack, and wanted a round or two for the last. The troops on our right were retreating, and so our flanks were now exposed, a fact which did not escape the eye of the Albatros aeroplane hovering above our heads.

20377 Private Percy Barlow, B Company[25]

By 4pm the Germans were back on the ridge and had worked around both flanks, and a machine gun opened up from a nearby farmhouse, enfilading D Company, which was taking cover along the sunken road.

At 5pm it was decided that the battalion would try to retire by platoons, but it was already too late. Only four officers and about forty men managed to get away. The rest of the Leeds Pals, including Colonel Twiss, the temporary Commanding Officer, were captured.[24]

Soon we saw the field greys [Germans, so-called from the colour of their uniforms] creeping round us so that we

Lieutenant W. S. Wharram, MC, DCM. His Military Cross was awarded for his flanking attack on the Germans who had been driven from the ridge by Albert Mountain's team, 26 March 1918.

The sunken road where the Pals were surrounded. The Germans opened fire with a machine gun from the farmhouse on the left. (W. Hare)

were in the centre of a half-moon. At this stage we noticed still further retirements, this time on our left, so we shouted to three of our chaps, about forty yards away, who volunteered to go to Headquarters and ascertain whether we should retire or not. They got about 15 yards away and were mown down by machine-gun fire from the flank. Their prostrate bodies were riddled through and through by the enemy. To retire in the face of such was suicide, so we decided to wait till nightfall. Soon after, however, a shrill whistle proclaimed that something unusual was about to happen and Germans sprang forward to the attack from three sides. As far as the eye could see, were perfect waves of the enemy. To resist was useless, for we were commanded to surrender from behind, and turning round we saw waves of men advancing on the Guards who were entrenched behind us.

20377 Private Percy Barlow, B Company[26]

There was a lull, and the Sergeant-Major ran, but I saw him go down in the field behind us so I decided to stay until it got a bit darker, but I was too late, we were surrounded and as I saw a German coming for me I put my hands up and dropped my rifle. I had been told that my brother who was in the same battalion had been killed two days before, so you can imagine my surprise when I saw him with about another forty of our men climb up the bank with their hands up.

37468 Private Walter Hare, D Company[27]

Private Walter Hare, who took part in the Gavrelle attack with the Bradford Pals and transferred to the Leeds Pals in February 1918. (W Hare)

278

A sniper got behind, he got a few of us, and on the 27th I was wounded, taken prisoner and after I had been taken prisoner I were gassed by our own shells.

We were all crouched in this embankment and this bullet went in my neck on the right and came out on the left and it hit the chap next to me on his tin hat.

I won't say I was … You know that feeling you have of What's happened?', and I coughed and I spat out to see if there was any blood. No blood, and [someone] said, 'What are you spitting for?' I said, 'You spit to see if there's any blood', he said, 'Well, its running down my face!' I said, 'Well see if it's coming from inside!' and he got a bullet wound through there and another chap, oh, he'd lost his ear altogether.

A sniper had got behind, he could see our heads and so of course we were taken prisoner, and [the] funny part about it, I'd taken my stuff, my gear off, to get my neck dressed. Of course when Colonel Twiss put his hands up to stop fighting, I stood up and I had my hands in my pockets, and Jerry was shoving his bayonet at me. So anyway someone says, 'Put your hands up, Jock!'

'Alright', I said. 'Ja gut, ja gut,' he'd got a bad temper, but he'd made a sergeant put his hands up.

They were funny, they were only sixteen-year-old lads. That's what hurt our pride more than anything else, we'd been out there since 1916, taken in 1918, two years after, and we were taken prisoner by school lads.

15/471 Sergeant Clifford Hollingworth, D Company[28]

One of the few who got away that day was Sergeant-Major George Cussins. As he ran he was fired upon and was seen to drop to the ground by Clifford Hollingworth and Walter Hare, who thought he had been hit. He got back to Brigade HQ unscathed, however, and later wrote to Walter and Harold Hare's parents to tell them their sons had been taken prisoner.[29]

Arthur Pearson was another of the men lucky enough to avoid capture. He was wounded, perhaps by the same sniper who shot Clifford Hollingworth, but he managed to make his way into Ayette.

Jerry had caught up with us during the night. As soon as the Adjutant spotted the enemy, he told me to go tell Captain Long to send up the SOS signal to the Artillery. I stepped out of the shelter of the roadside when 'Wallop!' I thought a row of houses had hit me. It turned out that the troops on the left of Battalion HQ had fallen back two fields behind the road, I was seen by the enemy who promptly took a pot shot at me. I got back to the roadside and thought that I had 'had my chips', as I was breathing through the hole in my back and spitting blood, I thought the bullet had gone through my chest. As I lay there, the Intelligence Officer crept up with two stretcher-bearers, he told them to attend to me. The SB took off my equipment, ripped open my tunic and shirt and when he saw the three bullet wounds across my shoulder, he said 'You've got a real Blighty one if only you can get away.'

Well, with that I began to sit up and take notice. I got my accessories (holdall with knife, fork, spoon and razor), stuffed them into a pocket and decided to try and make a break for it. I crawled

British prisoners captured during the March offensive. (Author's collection)

up the road, round the bend, past C Company who asked how I was and wished me luck, an A Company captain gave me a drink out of his flask, and I was on my way up that road. Some little distance higher up, the road petered out into an open field, so I had no option but to crawl along the open country in full sight of the Germans. I felt the whizz of bullets fly past my ear, but kept going over the brow of the hill where I was safe. I came across a crowd of wounded sitting waiting for ambulances, but I knew how near Jerry was so I kept moving. In the next village I was put in an ambulance convoy and taken to Doullens, where the field dressing was removed by an RAMC orderly who said 'My word, you have had a lucky escape. Another quarter of an inch and that bullet would have been through your spine!' The bullet had gone through the flesh over my shoulder, struck the brass buckle on my shoulder strap, penetrated lower down injuring the lung, breaking the ninth rib and coming out over the spine, one bullet made three wounds.

15/711 Lance-Corporal Arthur V. Pearson, C Company[30]
After nine gruelling days under heavy attack, the few surviving men of the 15/17th Battalion were relieved by the 11th (Londsale) Battalion, The Border Regiment.[31]

The casualties during these operations were estimated as being:

One officer died of wounds; two officers wounded and missing; seven officers wounded; nine officers missing; nineteen other ranks killed; seventy-seven other ranks wounded; 500 other ranks missing[32]

From official records we can confirm that during the period 21–30 March 1918 there were two officers and sixty-four other ranks killed and one officer and seven other ranks died of wounds.[33] The number of Pals wounded in those ten days is impossible to establish. Casualty returns in 1918 were published weekly, but there could be a delay of up to a month before a man's name appeared, and no mention was made of the date

Private Harold Hare, Walter's brother; they were captured on 27 March. (W. Hare)

on which he had received his wound. Furthermore, the local newspapers, which published extremely detailed lists of the killed and wounded after the Pals' attack on 1 July 1916, hardly mentioned this offensive. It seems that by 1918 the loss of over 500 men was either no longer considered newsworthy, or was perhaps subject to censorship.

With the help of surviving records we can also deduce that seven officers, including Lieutenant-Colonel Twiss, and at least 101 soldiers of the 15/17th West Yorkshire Regiment were taken prisoner when the battalion was finally surrounded on 27 March 1918.[34]

Although the Leeds battalion had borne the brunt of the fighting, the Diary of Operations for 93 Brigade records that, in the three battalions, a total of 1,074 other ranks were killed, wounded or missing, and that every commanding officer had become a casualty.[35]

All that remained of the Leeds Pals were moved into billets at Gaudiempre on 31 March, resuming their journey, on the next day and eventually ending up at Hermin on 2 April. They were joined by a new commanding officer, Major (Temporary Lieutenant-Colonel) C. W. Tilly,

Sergeant-Major Cussins, and his letter to Walter and Harold's family. Although he missed Walter very much, he was not familiar with his first name and called him Albert in this letter. (W. Hare)

Tues 9th April 1918.

Dear Mr & Mrs Hare,

Again I write you a few lines as promised, and as I told you in my note the other day am very sorry to say both your sons were captured in the hard fighting which took place about a fortnight ago, for six days we had been holding very superior numbers of the Enemy, and two days after we had held a position which had to be held at all cost, and we had succeeded in holding it until the 27th and of the second day 27th March, when owing to a mistake the Enemy surrounded us, not there on anyway Prisoners, two others and myself determined to chance our luck and get away, and we made a dash for it, but I was the only one to get through, one of the others was wounded, and the other I never saw again, your two sons were not far away from me but did not get the chance, not a slightest to escape, and as it was very very few who got clear owing to the terrible Machine Gun Fire, it was perhaps the best your two sons did not try, as the Germans were closing around them, and they would certainly have been shot a few minutes before I left I

saw them both, and they were near each other and quite alright, and as there was a lot more besides them I dont think the Germans would do anything to them We are now out for a rest and I miss Albert very very much, he was a good lad, and had been with me a long time, and had stuck with me all the hard fighting the previous seven days and we seemed to have exceptional good luck, when we left our other Batterions my last Colonel remarked to me what a clean lad he was. I hope both of you some little consolation to you to know that by our men holding on as they did they saved the situation, and the General said ours was the finest rear guard action that had been fought in this War. If I can get to know or if I hear anything of either of them I will let you know at once. Believe me to be,

Yours Sincerely,
George Cussins.
Sergt. Major

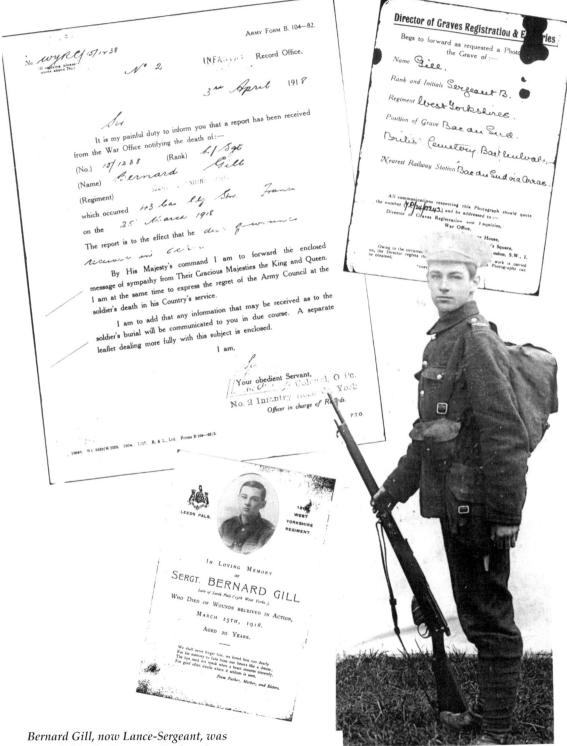

No. *wyRCf 15/1238*
(If replying, please quote above No.)

Nº 2

INFANTRY Record Office,

3rd April 1918

Sir

It is my painful duty to inform you that a report has been received from the War Office notifying the death of:—

(No.) 15/1238 (Rank) L/Sgt

(Name) Bernard Gill

(Regiment) West Yorkshire Regt.

which occurred 43 Cas Clg Stn France

on the 25 March 1918

The report is to the effect that he died of wounds received in action

By His Majesty's command I am to forward the enclosed message of sympathy from Their Gracious Majesties the King and Queen. I am at the same time to express the regret of the Army Council at the soldier's death in his Country's service.

I am to add that any information that may be received as to the soldier's burial will be communicated to you in due course. A separate leaflet dealing more fully with this subject is enclosed.

I am,
Sir,

Your obedient Servant,
Colonel, O. i/c.
No. 2 Infantry Record Office York
Officer in charge of Records.

P.T.O.

18840. Wt. 5629/M 2529. 150m. 7/17. R. & L., Ltd. Forms B 104—82/2.

Director of Graves Registration & Enquiries

Begs to forward as requested a Photo of the Grave of:—

Name Gill

Rank and Initials Sergeant B.

Regiment West Yorkshires.

Position of Grave Bac du Sud.

British Cemetery Bailleulval.

Nearest Railway Station Bac du Sud via Arras.

All communications respecting this Photograph should quote the number 1C94/12421 and be addressed to:—
Director of Graves Registration and Enquiries,
War Office,

Owing to the circumstances under which the work is carried on, the Director regrets that no copies of the Photographs can be obtained.

"copy..."

IN LOVING MEMORY
OF
SERGT. BERNARD GILL
Late of Leeds Pals (15th West Yorks.),
WHO DIED OF WOUNDS RECEIVED IN ACTION,
MARCH 25TH, 1918.
AGED 20 YEARS.

We shall never forget him, we loved him too dearly
For his memory to fade from our hearts like a dream;
The lips need not speak when a heart like a dream,
For grief often dwells where it seldom is seen.

From Father, Mother, and Sisters.

LEEDS PALS.
15TH WEST YORKSHIRE REGIMENT.

Bernard Gill, now Lance-Sergeant, was wounded in the German attack and succumbed to his wounds on 25 March.

Taylor's farewell letter to the battalion on his promotion to command of 93 Brigade, April 1918. 'Farewell letter to my comrades of the 15th Batt: West Yorkshire Regt. (1st Leeds) It was with deepest sorrow that on being appointed to the command of a Brigade, I have to take leave of my comrades of the 15th Battalion West Yorkshire Regiment (1st Leeds) – It is now close on three years since I took over command …'

on 4 April, and on the next day, by a new second-in-command, Major W. D. Coles from the 4th Entrenching Battalion. A draft of 503 other ranks who had just come from Britain also arrived to bring the battalion back up to strength.

They were inspected by their old colonel, Stuart Taylor, who had recently returned from leave. He addressed the men, congratulating the new arrivals on their smartness, and informing the few original members of the Leeds Pals that he would not be returning to command them as he had been promoted brigadier-general and given command of 93 Brigade.[36]

Eventually the battalion returned to the billets at Caucourt, where it had been in March when news of the German breakthrough came. Seven new officers from the 5th Reserve Battalion of the West Yorkshires joined on 9 April, and training recommenced.

At 4.15am on that same day the Germans mounted a second offensive, code-named 'Georgette', between Armentieres and the La Bassee Canal. The main force of the attack fell on the trenches around Neuve Chapelle, which were manned by Portuguese troops who fled in panic. Immediately to the north, 40th Division discovered that its right flank was exposed and, in the smoke drifting across the battlefield, the troops sent to fill the breach found it difficult to differentiate between the Portuguese in their grey uniforms, and the advancing Germans.[37]

At midday on the 10th urgent orders were once again received at the Pals' HQ – the battalion was to be ready to move by 2pm, to go into the line in support of IX Corps. This order was changed at the last minute, and at 2.30pm the men were marched in fighting order to Villers-Brulin, where they were met by a fleet of buses, which was to take them to La Motte, where they would support XV Corps. The troops embussed at 5pm but by 9pm they had received orders that their destination had once again been changed, and they were redirected

Wounded Portuguese soldiers are tended by a Sergeant-Major in the Royal Army Medical Corps, April 1918. (Imperial War Museum)

to Merris, which they reached at 5am having travelled for most of the night. They were taken to billets and told to rest as they would be needed as Brigade Reserve.[38]

On 11 April the battalion left its usual 10 per cent details at Brigade HQ and went into the reserve lines in support of the Barnsley Pals and the 18th Durham Light Infantry, who were attacking at La Becque in an attempt to link up with 40th Division.

By 8.15pm La Becque was in British hands and the two attacking battalions had linked up with 40th Division, taking about forty prisoners. That night it was quiet, and the men dug defensive positions until dawn. Next morning the Pals were brought up from their position in reserve to hold the left of the line, just east of La Becque, as the brigade frontage now extended for nearly 3,000 yards.

At this point the situation became even more confused. In accordance with a telegram from XV Corps, 40th Division was preparing to withdraw, having been relieved by 31st Division, but one brigade of the latter had been held up, with the result that the line became fragmented as the Germans pressed on with their offensive.

The Leeds Pals, left out of the line, formed a composite battalion with elements of the other units in 93 Brigade and under heavy fire, fell back to a defensive position at Merris. That night the Germans tried to get around their right flank, but were stopped by a composite company, while the rest of the men fell back further leaving Merris to the enemy. By the evening of 12 April they were dug in along the road between Meteren and Ballieul. In the meantime, the main body of the Leeds Pals once again became detached from the rest of the brigade and, after a hard fight, took up a defensive position with the 11th Battalion, The Suffolk Regiment, just north of Baillieul.

Ration parties from 31st Division HQ came up during the night, but were unable even to find out where the men were, let alone take them their food. On the 14th the battalion

The Germans advance.

lost another commanding officer when Tilly was killed by shell-fire; his second-in-command, Major Coles, took over, with the temporary rank of lieutenant-colonel.[39]

The composite battalion was relieved on 15 April and rejoined 93 Brigade HQ, by then at Hondeghem, while the main body held on in their position until 16 April and arrived at Hondeghem on the 17th, having first tried to find Brigade HQ in Borre. By this time two composite companies had been formed from the men who had returned on 15 April, and these had been sent to take up a defensive position in front of Hazebrouck.

During the five days in action, the Pals had again suffered heavy casualties. The battalion War Diary recorded that, besides the CO, two other officers were killed, six wounded and two missing, and casualties among the other ranks were estimated to be twenty-three killed, 153 wounded, and 143 missing.[40]

On 20 April the Pals went back to work, digging, and then manning, a defensive line. They were joined on the following day by a draft of 177 reinforcements and, during the next few days, by about thirty-five men who had lost touch during the recent fighting but had managed to find their way back. The work continued until 24 April, and the Pals stayed in the line until 27th. On the morning of their relief, Battalion HQ was bombarded with high-explosive and gas shells and so was temporarily moved to B Company HQ in the trench. During this bombardment, four men were killed, fourteen were wounded, and two more died of wounds.

Back in camp, the battalion received messages of congratulation from the Army, Corps, Divisional and Brigade Commanders, and the award of a number of decorations was announced.

G. 152. dated 18.4.18. To 31st Division.

'The following message received from Second Army timed 11.52 a.m. 17th inst. The Army Commander wishes to place on record his appreciation of the gallant conduct of the troops under your command in the present fighting. It is worthy of all praise and he wishes all ranks to be informed.' XV Corps

31st Division.

The Corps Commander wishes you to convey to the troops of your Division his appreciation of their courage and resolution during the period 12th to 14th April, when opposed to greatly superior numbers. The fine stand on the 13th April by your Brigades when much depleted, had an important bearing on the course of the operations.

To all ranks of the British Forces in France

Three weeks ago today the enemy began his terrific attacks against us on a 50 mile front. His objects are to separate us from the French, to take the Channel ports and destroy the British army.

In spite of throwing already 106 Divisions into the battle and enduring the most reckless sacrifice of human life, he has as yet made little progress towards his goals.

We owe this to the determined fighting & self sacrifice of our troops. Words fail me to express the admiration which I feel for the splendid resistance offered by all ranks of our army under the most trying circumstances.

Many amongst us now are tired. To those I would say that Victory will belong to the side which holds out the longest. The French army is moving rapidly & in great force to our support -----

There is no other course open to us but to fight it out! Every position must be held to the last man: there must be no retirement. With our backs to the wall, and believing in the justice of our cause each one of us must fight on to the end. The safety of our Homes and the Freedom of mankind alike depend upon the conduct of each one of us at this critical moment.

Thursday,
11 April 1918

D. Haig. F.M.

Haig's original draft of his 'backs to the wall' message, 11 April 1918. (Imperial War Museum)

286

A composite battalion composed of the details left behind when 93 Brigade went into the line, and some accumulated stragglers, man the railway line outside Merris, 12 April 1918. Within a few hours they were pushed back and Merris fell to the Germans. (Imperial War Museum)

XV Corps 17-4-18.
(Sgd) H. KNOX, Brigadier-General, G.S.

Headquarters,
93rd Infantry Brigade.
The Divisional Commander wishes to add his appreciation of the fine fighting spirit displayed by all ranks.
(Sgd) G.D. MELVILLE, Major, for Lieut-Colonel,
18-4-18 A.A. & Q.M.G. 31st Division.

The Brigade Commander also wishes to express his admiration of the excellent work done by all (Sgd) H.L.CHATFIELD, Captain,
18-4-18 Staff Captain 93rd Infantry Brigade.[41]

Wounded British soldiers make their way back after the heavy fighting in April 1918. (Imperial War Museum)

The month of May was mostly spent in training. The 31st Division was in Corps Reserve, and as such under orders to be ready to counter-attack or reinforce any part of the corps line. 93 Brigade had two brief spells in the trenches, but enemy activity was fairly slight, and there were no casualties although reconnaissance patrols from all three battalions were fired upon.

On 4 May notice was received that the division was to be disbanded, but by the 17th this had been rescinded. Eventually it was decided that 4 Guards Brigade was to be sent to GHQ Reserve and replaced by a new brigade composed of dismounted Yeomanry units transferred from Egypt. Thus 92 Brigade once again became the senior brigade in the division. The newly constituted 94 Brigade consisted of:[42]

12th (Norfolk Yeomanry) Battalion, The Norfolk Regiment
12th (Ayrshire and Lanarkshire Yeomanry) Battalion, The Royal Scots Fusiliers
24th (Denbighshire Yeomanry) Battalion, The Royal Welsh Fusiliers

On 3 June the whole division was paraded and inspected by the Army Commander, and also by the Divisional Commander who presented the following decorations to officers and men of the Leeds:

Military Cross
Captain and Adjutant D A F Needham
Captain J G Lee, RAMC (attached)
Lieutenant D T King
Lieutenant J W Buckley
Second-Lieutenant W S Wharram, DCM
Second-Lieutenant W Timson
Second-Lieutenant H Walker

288

The composite battalion marching along the railway near Merris, 12 March 1918. Some of the men appear to be under normal height – perhaps Bantams from the 17th Battalion who joined the Leeds Pals when the two battalions were amalgamated in 1917. (Imperial War Museum)

Second-Lieutenant G W Tiffany
3629 RSMf G Brennan

Bar to Military Cross
Captain W Peace MC
Captain and Adjtutant H Smith MC (Posthumous)

Distinguished Conduct Medal
3538 Sergeant H Wharfe 40183
Private J Warling

Military Medal
161819 Private C Berry
41555 Private A Hemingway

151490 Corporal H Hutchinson
1511321 Corporal H Jackson
161665 Private J Linford
28696 Private A Lord
151622 Private S Mason
24578 Private F Richardson
29387 Lance-Corporal H Slater
22253 Private P Stanton

Bar to Military Medal
151690 Corporal H R Oddy, MM[43]

Prize rosettes won by Alan Hey at the Battalion Sports, 19 August 1918.

Training continued throughout June, to ensure that the many reinforcements would be able to work efficiently alongside the more experienced men in forthcoming operations. Towards the end of the month the division was involved in 'Operation Borderland', an advance in conjunction with 5th Division further south. An attack was to be made by 92 and 93 Brigades on La Becque Farm on 28 June, and the front line advanced to the road west of the farm. It was preceded by the capture of Ankle Farm, to the north of La Becque, by units of 92 Brigade, on the 27th. Assembly trenches were dug during the night of the 27/28th by the 12th KOYLI, and at 2.30am the Leeds Pals arrived in their positions.

At Zero hour, 6am, the artillery and trench-mortars started their bombardments and the Pals attacked. The assault was a complete success. The Germans fled as the battalion advanced, and some of the Pals were even hit by the British artillery as they pursued the enemy. By 6.45am the objective had been taken and consolidation was underway. A report to Brigade Headquarters gives the enemy casualties as at least 135 dead, although there were some bodies that could not be recovered, and 122 captured, ninety-two of them by the Leeds Pals. Casualties among the Pals were estimated at the time to be twenty-two dead including one officer, and four died of wounds. Five officers and 138 men were listed as wounded, and one man was missing.[44] The officer, Second-Lieutenant George Hinchliffe, a former Leeds Pal in command of 93rd Trench Mortar Battery, was killed by a sniper at 3am, three hours before Zero. He had joined the Pals as a private in 1914, was wounded on 1 July 1916, and was commissioned into the battalion in 1917. He had been married on a recent leave.[45]

An expected German counter-attack did not materialise and the Pals spent July taking their turn in holding the new line which, on 19 July, was advanced to the stream east of La Becque Farm. Earlier while they had been out of the line, they were entertained by the Owls, and on 9 July they had been paraded and inspected by Stuart Taylor, their old colonel and now their Brigade Commander, who congratulated his 'Boys' on their recent success.

The enemy was unnaturally quiet, with little or no artillery fire, but aircraft patrolled the lines with increasing frequency and occasionally dropped bombs on the British trenches, although

George W. Hinchliffe marries Melicent Mary Frickely, 16 March 1918. Left to right: Miss Annie Stillings (bride's sister) Mr David W. Jones (best man, former 15/527, Private, medically discharged from Leeds Pals on 8 August 1918), the groom, the bride, Miss E. D. Hinchliffe (groom's sister), Mr Tom Stillings (bride's stepfather). (Author's collection)

without causing loss of life. At the end of the month the Pals went into the trenches once more, and during this tour, which lasted until 9 August, they were bombarded with gas shells, resulting in four officers and ninety other ranks needing hospital treatment. Apart from this isolated barrage, August too was generally quiet and when, on the 24th, the Pals took over the line in the Meteren area the CO Lieutenant-Colonel Coles, remarked in the War Diary:

This sector appears to be fairly quiet, and the general impression is still that the enemy has gone back leaving only a screen in front. Meteren itself is reduced to a heap of ashes.[46]

By the end of August the battalion had received intelligence reports that the enemy was retreating. Reconnaissance patrols were sent out but little or no opposition was encountered, and fires were found to be raging in the German trenches and dugouts. The Pals spent the first two weeks of September in camp training for open warfare, with particular emphasis on company attacks, and on the use of rifle-grenades. On the 13th they advanced through Bailleul and on the 18th, in conjunction with the 13th York and Lancasters, made a successful attack on Soyer Farm, in the Ploegsteert sector, capturing sixty Germans. They were then in camp just east of Bailleul, undergoing more training, until 28 September when they were called upon to form the advance guard of a brigade attack into Belgium through Neuve-Eglise, aimed at reaching the river at Warneton, south of the Ypres Salient. As they moved off, they were again caught by a barrage of gas shells.[47]

WITH THE W.A.A.C's
Harry (out since the beginning) "Lumme! There's the Angels of Mons"

(15th West Yorks (Leeds Pals))

H. C. Hornor 20-6-18

> I don't remember being put on a stretcher, I don't remember going to the railhead, I don't remember being put on a train. I came round and I opened my eyes and I couldn't see anything at all. I realised I was on wheels, and I put my hand out on the left and it was wood, and I got a weird idea I were being buried and I wasn't dead. I put my hand above my head and I couldn't feel anything there, I thought well, I can't be in a coffin, so I put my hand out to the right and there was nothing and then a voice said to me, 'Oh, you've come round, have you?' I said, 'Where am I?' He said 'You're in a train going to Paris Plage, you're going to hospital and you've got gas in your eyes.' He said, 'I don't think it's mustard gas, it's shell gas. It affects your brain a little bit as well.' So it must have put me to sleep.
>
> I'd been totally blind for three weeks, then I came round and my eyes got better and better. The war finished when I was in hospital, but I didn't think as my eyes were I should ever go back in the trenches.
>
> 15/259 Private Arthur Dalby, D Company[48]

The attack was making good progress when, on the morning of 1 October, Brigadier-General Stuart Taylor, on a tour of inspection of his battalions, was seriously wounded in the head and body by shell-fire, which killed Captain C Watts, the Brigade Major.[49] The advance continued despite German resistance, and by 3 October the Pals had reached the River Lys. A reconnaissance patrol established that the bridge had been destroyed, so the crossing was postponed for the time being and the men prepared

Arthur Dalby, blinded by gas on 28 September 1918.

a defensive line. On the 11th, Taylor died of his wounds, and was buried next day with full military honours at La Kreule Military Cemetery, near Hazebrouck, the scene of the Pals' gallant stand in April.

Meanwhile the battalion remained close to the west bank of the Lys. Training was resumed, and the men took the opportunity to clean their uniforms and equipment, while reconnaissance patrols were kept active along the river bank.

On 15 October the brigade was notified that information from prisoners indicated a general withdrawal by the Germans opposite the XV Corps front. Orders were therefore given to cross the Lys, and by the 18th 93 Brigade had entered Tourcoing, where it was enthusiastically welcomed by the inhabitants. The advance continued the next day across the canal at Roubaix, and on the night of 21/22 October an attempt was made to cross the River Escaut and establish posts on the east bank. This time, however, the division had caught up with the Germans, and came under machine-gun fire as the leading patrols attempted to cross. The divisional sector then came under artillery fire as a patrol of the 13th York and Lancasters crossed the river, but they were unable to maintain an outpost on the east bank under heavy trench-mortar and machine-gun fire. As they withdrew, the enemy fire intensified, and contact with Brigade Headquarters was lost. It was subsequently discovered that a 300-yard section of wire had been deliberately cut from the telephone line, and several civilians were arrested and handed over to the Belgian police as spies. The Germans then counter attacked and tried to cross the river, but were driven back with heavy casualties.[50]

On 24 October the Leeds Pals relieved the 13th York and Lancsasters in the front line along the river bank, and a patrol crossed at dusk to establish a picquet line on the east bank. This patrol, led by Second-Lieutenant G. G. Jenkins, soon came under heavy fire and was forced to withdraw. On the next night the Pals sent out another patrol in an attempt to capture one of the enemy, but they too were stopped by heavy machine-gun and rifle fire. Meanwhile, German reconnaissance aircraft were attempting to fly over the 31st Divisional sector, but were discouraged by anti-aircraft fire.

93 Brigade was relieved on 25 October by 121 Brigade of 40th Division, and went into billets at Mouscron, where it came under the tactical control of II Corps while in the latter's area. After spending a day cleaning up and resting, 93 Brigade moved to Staceghem, arriving by 2.30pm on the 28th. On 3 November it moved again, to Ronq, and on the 7th to Marcke.

At 11.45 on 9 November, the Leeds Pals received orders to continue the advance, as the enemy had retired from the River Escaut. The river was reached by 6.45 that evening, and the men spent the night at Orroir. On the next day they continued their pursuit, arriving in Rennaix during the afternoon. On 11 November 1918 at 9.45am, the battalion set off from Rennaix to march to Rigaudrue. At 11am, while the men were on the road, the Armistice came into operation. The war was over.[50]

1918 Peace and words are useless.

15/1082 Private Herbert Hargreaves, Giessen PoW Camp, Germany[51]

Apart from a ceremonial parade on the 19th, when the last gallantry awards were presented by the divisional commander, there was little in the way of celebration. Military training was soon replaced by vocational lectures, to prepare the men for demobilisation, by football matches, and by the still-inevitable working parties, carrying out such tasks as demolishing huts.

In February 1919, the battalion was disbanded in Belgium. There was to be no 'welcome home' parade through the city of Leeds to echo the enthusiastic scenes of 1914–15. Those who were able to quietly made their way to their homes. Clifford Hollingworth was repatriated from a prisoner-of-war camp near Hamburg and returned to Leeds to marry his beloved Blanche. Soon after the war he became seriously ill as a result of the poison gas he had inhaled, and for a time it seemed as though he would not survive. Arthur Dalby was in hospital in France when the war ended, gradually recovering his eyesight after being gassed. Arthur Pearson, in Newcastle on a signalling course but about to return to France, went absent without leave and rushed home to Leeds to attend a memorial service for his brother, who had been killed in action two weeks before the Armistice. Percy Barlow, served for almost another year after his repatriation from a prisoner-of-war camp and only narrowly avoided going off with a draft bound for India. Some 773 men would never return home. Many of them, including Stuart Taylor, Morris Bickersteth, and Arthur Hollings, lie in the cemeteries of France and Belgium. Others such as Edward Woffenden, who had no known grave, are commemorated on the massive memorials at Arras and Thiepval.

Those who survived would suffer for years. Not for them the counselling now offered to members of the armed forces and the emergency services to help them deal with post-traumatic

Clifford Hollingworth marries Blanche Beecham, his childhood sweetheart. (N Wallace)

stress. Instead, at least two former members of the battalion would lose their reason and end their days in mental institutions, and more than one would take his own life.

Bernard Gill's Next of Kin Memorial Plaque.
(Author's collection)

NOTES

1. Author's recorded interview with Clifford Hollingworth, July 1988.
2. The United States declared war on Germany on 6 April 1917, after President Wilson's commitment to maintaining America's neutrality was eroded by German provocation. This commenced with the loss of 128 US passengers when the British passenger liner *Lusitania* was sunk in May 1915. It continued with the Germans adopting a policy of unrestricted submarine warfare, also threatening US vessels, and culminated in the interception of a telegram from Arthur Zimmerman, German Foreign Secretary, promising Mexico territorial gains and seeking an alliance with that country if America entered the war.
3. See *Statistical Abstract of Information Regarding the Armies at Home and Abroad*, Part XXII, The *British Line in France*, War Office, London, June 1920.
4. Battalion War Diary, Public Record Office, London: W09572361.
5. Edmonds, Brigadier-General Sir J. E., *Military Operations: France and Belgium, 1918*, Volume 1, pp.51–55, Macmillan, London, 1935.
6. Becke, Major A. F., *History of the Great War: Order of Battle of Divisions*, HMSO, London, 1935–45.
7. Author's recorded interview with Walter Hare, 1990.
8. Battalion War Diary, op.cit.
9. Ibid.
10. Ibid.
11. 31st Division War Diary, Public Record Office, London: W095/2343.

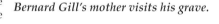

Bernard Gill's mother visits his grave.

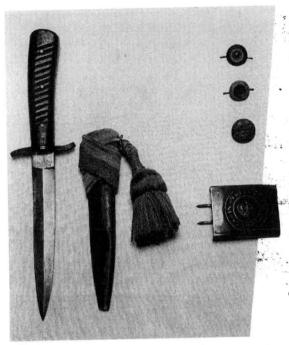

Some of Alan Hey's trophies: a German trench dagger, Bavarian cap cockades, a tunic button and a Bavarian belt buckle. (Bagshaw Museum)

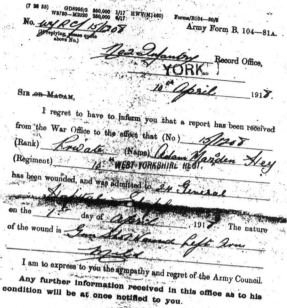

No. 44/RC/15/208 (If replying, please quote above No.)   Army Form B. 104—81A.

West Infantry Record Office,

YORK

10th April   1918

SIR or MADAM,

I regret to have to inform you that a report has been received from the War Office to the effect that (No) 15/208 (Rank) Private (Name) Adam Harden Hey (Regiment) 15 "WEST YORKSHIRE REGT" has been wounded, and was admitted to 24 General Hospital Etaples on the 1st day of April, 1918. The nature of the wound is Gun Shot Wound Left Arm Mild

I am to express to you the sympathy and regret of the Army Council.

Any further information received in this office as to his condition will be at once notified to you.

Yours faithfully,

Colonel, O. i/c
No. 2 Infantry Record Office, York.

IMPORTANT.—Any change of address should be immediately notified to this Office.

Notification from the War Office that Alan Hey was admitted to hospital. He was wounded on 27 March 1918.

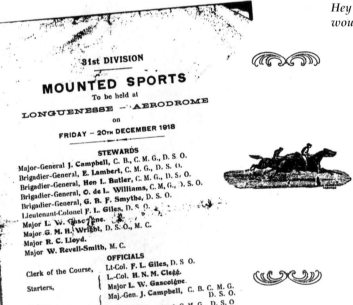

31st DIVISION

MOUNTED SPORTS

To be held at

LONGUENESSE - AERODROME

on

FRIDAY – 20th DECEMBER 1918

STEWARDS

Major-General J. Campbell, C. B., C. M. G., D. S. O.
Brigadier-General, E. Lambert, C. M. G., D. S. O.
Brigadier-General, Hon L. Butler, C. M. G., D. S. O.
Brigadier-General, O. de L. Williams, C. M. G., D. S. O.
Brigadier-General, G. B. F. Smythe, D. S. O.
Lieutenant-Colonel F. L. Giles, D. S. O.
Major L. W. Gascoigne.
Major G. M. H. Wright, D. S. O., M. C.
Major R. C. Lloyd.
Major W. Revell-Smith, M. C.

OFFICIALS

Clerk of the Course,   Lt-Col. F. L. Giles, D. S. O.
                        L.-Col. H. N. M. Clegg.

Starters,   Major L. W. Gascoigne.
             Maj.-Gen. J. Campbell, C. B. C. M. G. D. S. O.

Judges,   Br.-Gen. E. Lambert, C. M. G., D. S. O.
           Major L. Thorns, M. C.

Clerk of the Scales   Major L. Thorns, M. C.
Secretary & Treasurer,   Major R. C. Lloyd.

The Band of the 11th Battalion East Yorkshire Regiment will play, by kind permission of Lt-Col. S. H. FERRAND, M. C.

1st RACE

At 12.45.   **The Lys Sweepstakes.**

A flat race of about five furlongs : for horses under fifteen hands held to and to be ridden by regimental officers of R. E., Infantry, M.G.C., R.A.M.C., of 31st Division.

No.	Owner.		Horse.	Rider
1.	Lt-Col. G.P. Norton, 15 W. Yorks. R.	B. M.	Daisy.	Owner.
2.	Lt. J.W. Buckley, 15 W. Yorks. R.	B. M.	Betty.	"
3.	Major H.A. Birkbeck, 12 Norfolk R.	Bl. G.	Sambo	"
4.	Capt. R.W. Doherty, 12 Norfolk R.	B. M.	Fany	"
5.	Capt. C.G. Irvine, R.A.M.C.	B. M.	Katie.	"
6.	2/Lt. J.A. Belile, R.E.	Straw, Roan M.	Ermyntrude.	"
7.	Capt. G.W. Mayhew, 24 R.W. Fus.	B. G.	Dick.	"
8.	2/Lt. Tapper, 11 E. Lan. R.	Ch. G.	Billy I.	"
9.	Major King, 10 E. Yorks. R.	Ch. G.	Spotty.	"
10.	Capt. Naylor, 10 E. Yorks. R.	Ch. G.	Rat.	"
11.	2/Lt. Hutchinson, 10 E. Yorsh. R.	Br. G.	Tich.	"
12.	Major Pollock, 12 R.S. Fus.	Br. M.	Mayflower.	"
13.	Lt. Col. Ferrand, 14 E. Yorks. R.	B. M.	Bosche.	Lt. G.F. Hall.
14.	Capt. Bradley, 11 E. Yorks. R.	B. G.	Titch.	Lt. V.H. Jenkin.
15.	Capt. G.W. Bladen, 11 E. Yorks. R.	B. M.	Mollie.	2/Lt. W. Rumsay.
16.	Capt. Leonard, R.A.M.C.	B. G.	Bradford.	Owner.
17.	Lt. F.R. Burfield, R.E.	B G.	Charlie I.	"
18.	Major Wilson, M.G.C.	Dun M.	Peggy.	Lt. Duncan.
19.	Lt. Watkins, M.G.C.	Ch. G.	Bobby.	Lt. Wood.
20.	Lt. Williams, M.G.C.	B. M.	Southern Cross.	Owner.

Programme of the 31st Divisional Mounted Sports, December 1919.

Private Cyril N. Brown was wounded and taken prisoner – the date cannot be confirmed but it is likely to have been 3 May 1917. Because he needed specialised treatment for his wound, he was repatriated to Berne in Switzerland, where he was interned for the rest of the war. There he met Cecilia Schober, an Italian-Swiss girl who was working for the Red Cross collecting repatriated soldiers from the railway station. Cyril Brown had been a clerk in a solicitor's office before the war, so he was given a job as a clerk on the staff of Brigadier-General Hanbury Williams, British Attache. After the war Brown invited Cecilia to come to Leeds and they were married. He later confided in her that Hanbury Williams had been a member of the British Intelligence Service. Brigadier-General Hanbury Williams with his staff; Brown is fourth from right, middle row.

Cecilia Brown when the author met her in November 1989, at the age of 91.

297

Cyril Brown, seated, in a German prison camp before his repatriation.

Cecilia in 1922, shortly after her marriage to Cyril Brown.

12. 15th Battalion, The Royal Scots War Diary, Public Record Office, London: W095/2457.
13. Ibid.
14. Battalion War Diary, op.cit.
15. Pearson, Arthur Valentine, *A Leeds Pal looks Back*, unpublished manuscript in Leeds Reference Library, circa 1961.
16. Barlow, Percy, unpublished MS memoir, circa 1919.
17. 31st Division War Diary, op.cit.
18. 93 Brigade War Diary, Public Record Office, London: WO95/2360.
19. 31st Division and 93 Brigade War Diaries, op.cit.

20. Barlow, op.cit.
21. Hollingworth, op.cit.
22. Barlow, op.cit.
23. See Appendix V for full citation.
24. Barlow, op.cit.
25. 31st Division, 93 Brigade and Battalion War Diaries, op.cit.
26. Barlow, op.cit.
27. Hare, op.cit.
28. Hollingworth, op.cit.
29. 16/842 WO II George Cussins, DSO, was an original member of 16th (Service) Battalion (1st Bradford), The West Yorkshire Regiment. He transferred to the 15/17th Battalion in February 1918, and was discharged on 25 March 1919. After the war he joined the Police Force. West Yorkshire Regiment Medal Roll, Public Record Office, London: WO329/900; Hare, op.cit.
30. Pearson, op.cit.
31. Battalion War Diary, op.cit.
32. Ibid.
33. *Officers Died in the Great War 1914–1919*, Part 1, *Old and New Armies*, HMSO, London, 1919; *Soldiers Died in the Great War 1914–1919*, Part 19, *The Prince of Wales's Own (West Yorkshire Regiment)*, HMSO, London 1921.
34. *List of British officers taken prisoner in the various Theatres of War between August, 1914, and November, 1918*, compiled from records kept by Messrs Cox & Co's Enquiry Office at Harrington House, Craig's Court, Charing Cross, London SW1, privately published circa 1919. British Red Cross & St John Enquiry List, No. 17, 1st October 1918; British Red Cross & St John Enquiry List, No. 21, 1st December 1918; Prisoners of War, unpublished TS list in the West Yorkshire Regimental Archive, York.
35. 93 Brigade War Diary, op.cit.
36. Lieutenant-Colonel Stuart Taylor was promoted to Temporary Brigadier-General with effect from 6 April 1918. Quarterly Army List, July 1918; *Yorkshire Evening News*, 5 April 1918.
37. 40th Division War Diary, Public Record Office, London: W095/2593.
38. Battalion War Diary, op.cit.
39. Ibid.
40. 93rd Brigade War Diary, op.cit.
41. Ibid.
42. Becke, op.cit.
43. Battalion War Diary, op.cit.
44. 'Narrative of Operations 19 July 1918', Battalion War Diary, op.cit.
45. *Yorkshire Evening Post*, 16 March 1918; *Yorkshire Observer*, 18 March 1918; West Yorkshire Regiment Medal Roll, Public Record Office, London: WO329/900; 93 Brigade War Diary, op.cit.
46. Battalion War Diary, op.cit.
47. Ibid.
48. Dalby, op.cit.
49. 93 Brigade War Diary, op.cit.
50. Ibid.
51. 31st Division, 93 Brigade and Battalion War Diaries, op.cit.
52. Unpublished diary of Herbert Hargreaves, 1916.

Epilogue

On 21 May 1919, Colonel Sir Edward Brotherton gave a dinner at Leeds Town Hall, for the surviving members of the Leeds Pals. Although it was the Pals' first reunion, it would not be their last. As early as 1916, after their terrible losses on the Somme, some of the survivors had already begun making plans for a Battalion Association to be formed after the war.

The precise details of the formation of this association can no longer be found, for the earliest surviving minutes date from April 1942. Nor is it now possible to establish the original qualifications for membership. It is variously thought that only those who joined in 1914 were eligible, or perhaps only those who held the 1914–15 Star, having served in Egypt. Whatever criterion was applied, there is no doubt that the Leeds Pals Association, an organisation founded on the bonds of friendship forged at Colsterdale and at Suez, and on the battlefields of France, was of immense help to its members in coming to terms with their experiences and memories of the war.

Apart from the visits to the battlefields of the Western Front, which took place during the late 1920s and early 1930s, three annual pilgrimages became an essential part of the Pals' calendar, and continued to be observed, whenever possible, until Arthur Dalby's death in 1992.

A memorial erected by the Association in the Lady Chapel of Leeds Parish Church was dedicated on 1 July 1931 to the memory of the Pals who had fallen during the First World War. Every year thereafter, on the Friday nearest to 1 July, the surviving Leeds Pals attended a memorial service in the chapel and laid a wreath.

On 28 September 1935 a memorial cairn was unveiled by Walter Stead at Colsterdale. It was erected at the side of the road and marked the site of the Pals' old camp. On 25 September each year, the anniversary of the Pals leaving Leeds in 1914 to begin their training, the association returned to Colsterdale and a service was held at the cairn, where the previous year's wreath from the Parish Church was laid.

Each year on what used to be called Armistice Day, 11 November – not Remembrance Sunday but on the actual day whenever it fell – the Leeds Pals laid a wreath on the Leeds Cenotaph.

The badge of office of the Chairman of the Leeds Pals Association. The last Chairman was Clifford Hollingworth who died in November 1989.

Leeds Cenotaph soon after the unveiling in City Square, November 1922. The message on the back of this postcard reads: **Leeds 6 November 1922 I thought you would like one of these. They are the first I have seen. The 'crown' is the wreath the Lady Mayoress put on from L M and Corporation. There were some lovely flowers on when I saw it on the Wed. after the unveiling ceremony. Hope you are well. Love from Emily.** *(Jean Kennington Collection)*

There were, of course, social functions as well as commemorative ones, and an important part of the association's business was to take care of its less fortunate members, particularly those who had been disabled during the war.

From 1923 the association was run by a committee elected from its members, irrespective of their former rank, although the first three holders of the office of President had been more figureheads than active members of the committee. Arthur Dalby, the last president, had served for two and a half years as chairman before his election, and had been a committee member from the beginning.

I will say this, I never met a finer body of fellows in my life, and I've always been proud to have been on the committee and chairman and president of the Leeds Pals, because they were such a grand lot of fellows. In the whole of the four years that I was in the army with them I never had a wrong word with any one of them. They were really good friends. Even in latter life, when we all came home and got married, all our friends were Leeds Pals and their wives.

We tried in business to help each other, as well. I mean to say, I had a business I took over from my father. I gave all my insurance to a Leeds Pal, I gave all my printing to a Leeds Pal, and everything I could possibly do, I did do, and we all helped each other in a way. Every business was represented so to speak, there were lots of solicitors …

I've had more to do with them since the war was over really, you know, with being on the committee since the beginning. I've been chairman three – well, two and a half times, twice on my own and once a fellow was poorly and I took his other half, and I've been now President for twenty years.

Our first president was Sir Charles Wilson, 'Cheeky Charlie' he was known as, but he was taken ill. Harry Jackman, Captain Atkinson, Reddyhoff and myself went to see him and Lady … his wife, showed us up to the bedroom, you see, and you have to say something when you're leaving, I went and shook hands with him and I says 'Well, don't be so long, Sir Charles, before you are back amongst us.' So he kept hold of my hand and he pulled me round, he says 'Dalby,

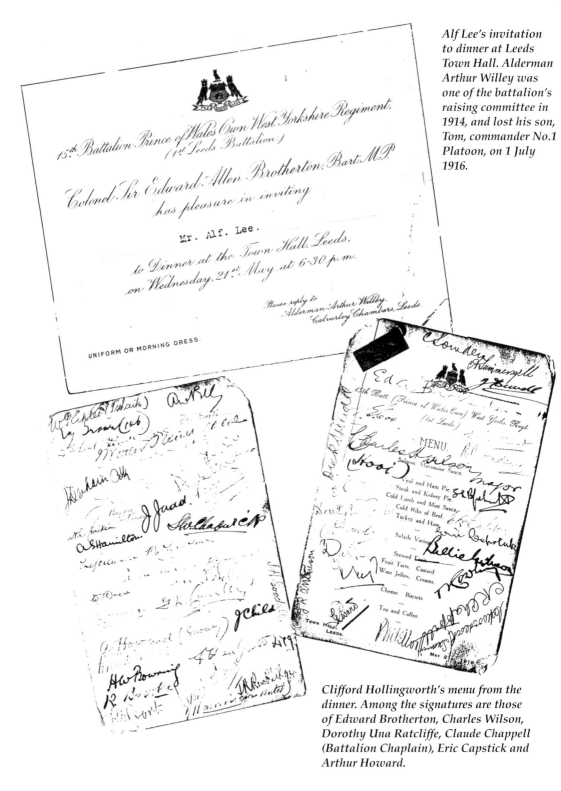

Alf Lee's invitation to dinner at Leeds Town Hall. Alderman Arthur Willey was one of the battalion's raising committee in 1914, and lost his son, Tom, commander No.1 Platoon, on 1 July 1916.

15th Battalion Prince of Wales Own West Yorkshire Regiment. (1st Leeds Battalion.)

Colonel Sir Edward Allen Brotherton, Bart. M.P.
has pleasure in inviting

Mr. Alf. Lee.

to Dinner at the Town Hall, Leeds,
on Wednesday, 21st May at 6-30 p.m.

Please reply to
Alderman Arthur Willey,
Calverley Chambers, Leeds.

UNIFORM OR MORNING DRESS.

MENU

Salmon. Mayonaise Sauce.

Veal and Ham Pie.
Steak and Kidney Pie.
Cold Lamb and Mint Sauce.
Cold Ribs of Beef.
Turkey and Ham.

Salads Various.

Stewed
Fruit Tarts. Custard
Wine Jellies. Creams.

Cheese. Biscuits.

Tea and Coffee.

TOWN HALL LEEDS

Clifford Hollingworth's menu from the dinner. Among the signatures are those of Edward Brotherton, Charles Wilson, Dorothy Una Ratcliffe, Claude Chappell (Battalion Chaplain), Eric Capstick and Arthur Howard.

don't you try and kid me, when I go out of this room I go out feet first, I've cancer!' He put me back in my place.

The next president was Colonel Stead. I will say that Colonel Stead only came to the memorial service and things like that, he never visited anybody, I never saw him at any funeral, they were dying soon after the war. The only thing that Colonel Stead did for us was he left us a thousand quid … a thousand pounds in his will to the Benevolent Fund and it was put in the paper.

Well, if there's any money going, there's always somebody … My office was in Holbeck and a fellow came in my office and he said 'Would you be chairman of the Leeds Pals?' I said, 'Well, I am Benevolent Secretary at present.' 'I have been told to come to you to be helped out with some of my debts, from some of this money that our colonel left us.' So I looked at him, I thought, 'You weren't born – when we went to war you weren't even born!' So I said, 'Which company was you in?' He said, 'A Company'. I said, 'Who was your commanding officer?' He said, 'I don't know, it just slipped my mind.' I thought, 'Slipped his mind, it never slipped in'. So I said, 'Did you go to Gallipoli with us?' He says, 'Yes!' I said, 'You went by yourself because we went to Egypt.' I says, 'Hop it!' and he were really hard-faced because he said 'There's nowt got wi'out trying!' He had the war debt with him, electricity, gas, he brought everything!

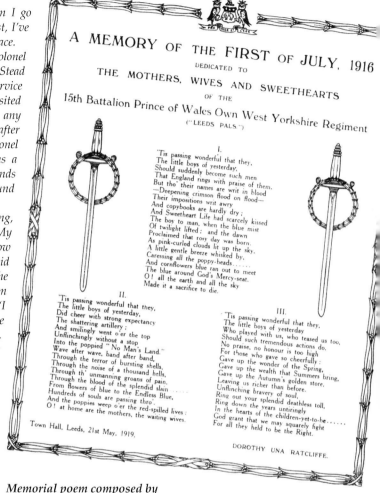

Memorial poem composed by
Dorothy Una Ratcliffe and recited by her at the Pals' dinner at Leeds Town Hall on 21 May 1919. Mrs Ratcliffe was Edward Brotherton's niece, and served as Lady Mayoress in 1914 when the battalion was raised. (Harvey Hirst)

Then Sir Maxwell Ramsden [elected 31 January 1947] he was the next president. He were a private to start, mind you he were a well-educated man, a solicitor. I think he got to be Colonel of the Leeds Rifles, but he was still a Leeds Pal, at the beginning, and he took his commission from the Leeds Pals. But he came to the meeting at the Parish Church every year on July 1st. [Sir

The pilgrims and their well-wishers met at Leeds Station on 5 April 1928. In the foreground holding a wreath is George Cosby, to his left (wearing a bowler hat) is Alan Fenton, who lost a leg on 1 July 1916. (G. Fenton)
A souvenir brochure compiled by George Cosby, illustrated with photographs of the pilgrimage. (Gerry Lyons)
Serre in 1928 – the debris of war, including barded-wire piquets and shell cases are dumped by the roadside. (Arthir Dalby)

Maxwell Ramsden was succeeded by Harry Jackman, elected 16 February 1959, then by Clifford Lawrence, on 13 February 1961, and by Major T. G. Gibson, on 14 February 1963.]

When I was put up for president [circa 1970] Roland Barrett said 'I'm putting your name forward as president, Arthur, you've worked as well as anybody for the association.' He said 'I'll tell you who's going to put his name up, used to be Lord Mayor of Leeds, Bretherick.' He were a Leeds Pal as well, but he'd never taken on any work in the association, he'd never been on the committee, he'd never been anything at all except he'd come to the dinners, he'd come to Colsterdale with us a couple of times. Anyway, I got every vote, every vote. I felt proud of it, really.

Arthur Dalby[1]

Committee meetings were held regularly at the Guildford Hotel in Leeds, itself managed by a former Leeds Pal, and they were well attended, with most of the committee members taking a turn as chairman, a daunting task if the person elected was not used to public speaking.

I can't see well and every Chairman of the Leeds Pals at our Memorial Service in the Parish Church read the lessons. And the Vicar told me – I asked the Vicar ten days before – what are the lessons for that day, and he told me and I went home and I got a Bible out, and I wrote it out in good … and I memorised it. When the Verger came to take me across to read it, when the Choir's looking up and all the Leeds Pals were looking up and the congregation were looking up, the Vicar said to me, 'Don't start, Mr Dalby, until they stop shuffling.' I believe I waited a bit too long because they thought I'd forgotten the opening chorus, but I might tell you I'd the wind up, and I don't mind admitting it. Because memorising things from a Bible, ten verses, is difficult. There's too much biblical words to remember. But you can be just as frightened in civil life as you are in the trench.

Arthur Dalby[2]

The Pals at Serre No.1 Cemetery, 7 April 1928. (Trevor Cosby)

Back in the trenches, the Pals in a preserved trench at Vimy Ridge. This remains almost unchanged today. (Gerry Lyons)

As the years passed, they took their toll. Almost every Annual General Meeting of the Association brought news that another member had died, and of course the battalion would be represented at the funeral.

> *The comradeship continued long after the war, and he [Fred Naylor] always attended the annual outing to Colsterdale, and the remembrance service at Leeds Parish Church where the Pals' Memorial is. The real meaning of that comradeship was brought home to me when Grandpa died in 1974 at the grand old age of eighty-two. At his funeral I was surprised and touched to see a contingent of Pals (by then in their eighties) stood to attention outside the crematorium. They then did a smart right turn and marched in to pay their last respects. This really was a 'Pals' Battalion in the true sense of the word.*
>
> Margaret Sudol[3]

NOTES
1. Author's recorded interviews and conversations with Arthur Dalby, 1988–1990.
2. Ibid
3. Letter from Margaret Sudol, granddaughter of Fred Naylor, to the author 4 May 1988.

Order of service for unveiling of Pals the Memorial in the Lady Chapel in Leeds Parish Church, 1 July 1931, fifteenth anniversary of the Pals' attack at Serre. (Harvey Hirst)

LEEDS PARISH CHURCH.
ORDER OF SERVICE
to be used on the
1st Day of July, 1931, at 7-30 p.m.
at the
DEDICATION OF THE MEMORIAL
erected by
THE LEEDS "PALS" ASSOCIATION
to the memory of the Officers, Non-Commissioned Officers
and men, of the
LEEDS "PALS" BATTALION (15th West Yorkshire Regt.)
who fell in the war, 1914-1918.

EGYPT 1915-16
SOMME 1916
ANCRE 1916
GAVRELLE 1917

SCARPE 1918
ARRAS 1918
YPRES 1918
HAZEBROUCK 1918

TO THE GLORY OF GOD AND IN MEMORY OF THOSE OF THE LEEDS PALS BATTALION (15TH WEST YORKSHIRE REGIMENT) WHO DIED IN THE GREAT WAR, 1914-1918.

The pals' commemoration dinner at Leeds Town Hall, October 1934.

THE LEEDS MERCURY, TUESDAY, OCTOBER 9, 1934.

Reunion of Leeds "Pals" || The Princess Royal at York

ALL TOGETHER AGAIN.
Some of the Leeds "Pals" their commemoration dinner the Leeds Town Hall last nig
The Earl of Harewood was guest of honour. A report the dinner is printed in Page
(By a "Mercury" photographe

A GREAT COMRADESHIP COMMEMORATED.

Lt.-Col. J. W. Stead (third on the left), who unveiled the Memorial Cairn of the Leeds Pals, with the Rev. C. R. Chappell (Padre—first on left), the Lord Mayor of Leeds and the Lady Mayoress (Alderman and Mrs. W. Hemingway), with officers of the Leeds Pals Association at Colsterdale yesterday.

The Order of Service for the unveiling and dedication of the Leeds Pals Cairn at Colsterdale. The Cairn was designed and built by former Leeds Pals, and paid for by the Battalion Association. It stands on consecrated ground and the ashes of more then twenty of the Pals as well as wives and families have been scattered there. (Harvey Hirst)

A SOLEMN MOMENT.—Lt.-Col. J. W. Stead unveiling the Memorial Cairn erected to the memory of the Leeds Pals at Colsterdale.

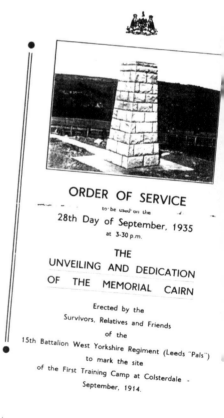

ORDER OF SERVICE

to be used on the

28th Day of September, 1935

at 3-30 p.m.

THE
UNVEILING AND DEDICATION
OF THE MEMORIAL CAIRN

Erected by the
Survivors, Relatives and Friends
of the
15th Battalion West Yorkshire Regiment (Leeds "Pals")
to mark the site
of the First Training Camp at Colsterdale .
September, 1914.

The Leeds Pals at the Cairn in the 1970s; the numbers are dwindling.

Clifford Hollingworth and Arthur Dalby are interviewed by Yorkshire Television at Colsterdale, September 1989.

A Note on the Appendixes

The appendixes, published here for the first time, have been compiled as far as possible from surviving official records, augmented where appropriate by newspaper reports and, to a lesser extent, by the reminiscences of surviving members of the battalion, and by documents kept by the relatives of former members. They are as complete as sources will allow some seventy years after the last medal roll was compiled. Authors, and indeed official records, are fallible. If anyone can add to, or correct, any of the information in the following appendixes, the author will be delighted to hear from them, via the publisher, so that the copies in the regimental archive can be updated.

Appendix I

Nominal Roll

This lists the men who enlisted between September 1914 and July 1915, and includes details of men killed and died of wounds.

To attempt to list every man who served with the battalion up to the end of the war would take several volumes and, indeed, many more years of research. This list therefore covers only the men who joined the battalion up to the closure of recruiting for the Leeds Pals on 5 July 1915. They were given the prefix '15' to their regimental numbers, which started at 1 and went up to 1956. There is a rough alphabetical sequence to the numbers from 15/1 up to and including 15/1024, which suggests that that may have marked the end of the 1914 intake. It is interesting to note that the number of names listed in the local press when the 1914 contingent was first raised was 1025.

When recruiting was resumed in December 1914, it proceeded in fits and starts until July 1915, so there was little possibility of assigning the men their serial numbers in anything approaching an alphabetical order.

Men recruited between July 1915 and September 1916 were given the prefix '19' because they were recruited into the 19th Battalion, an amalgamation of the depot companies of the Leeds Pals and Leeds Bantams. On 1 September 1916 the 19th Battalion was redesignated the 88th Training Reserve Battalion. The men's serial numbers were then given out regimentally, throughout the entire West Yorkshire Regiment, and had five and later six digits.

Three main sources have been used for this appendix:
1. A Nominal Roll published towards the end of 1915, just before the battalion went to Egypt.
2. The Regimental Medal Rolls for the 1915 Star, the British War and Victory Medals and the Silver War Badge (Public Record Office, London: W0329).
3. A microfiche copy of the Army Medal Office index to the First World War Medal Rolls (Public Record Office, London).

The nature of the records used to compile this roll has, to a great extent, determined the type and amount of information that can be included. For instance, because the Medal Rolls list only the men who completed their service in the ranks with the regiment, this list includes men who received commissions as they were 'discharged to commission', likewise it includes men who were killed, died of wounds, or were presumed dead.

What it does not list is the men who transferred to other regiments during their service in the ranks, nor does it list those men who did not serve overseas. The former can sometimes be picked out of the card index if a name can be found from another source, but no dates are given for the transfer. The latter can sometimes be extracted from the Silver War Badge lists, but entail a massive search as these lists were bound together in apparently random order by the Infantry Office that issued the badge.

Where the word 'discharged' appears after a man's name, this was his normal discharge at the end of hostilities, although in Army parlance he normally went on to the Z Reserve (sometimes referred to as Class Z), unless his conduct or his age were such that his services were no longer required, a rare occurrence. Z Reserve effectively meant that he had no further obligation but the army could recall him in the unlikely event of the Armistice being broken and hostilities resumed. Where 'discharged 392 (XVI)' follows a man's name, this refers to a discharge under that paragraph of the King's Regulations, for soldiers who were 'no longer fit for war service' either through wounds or illness. Where service with another battalion of The West Yorkshire Regiment is mentioned, it can be taken to mean that this man never served overseas with the Leeds Pals.

15/1 ABDY, Lance-Corporal Charles William discharged 392 (XVI) 3.11.1917
15/2 ABRAMS, Private Fred discharged 392 (XVI) 29.6.1917
15/3 ABRAMS, Private George transferred to Royal Defence Corps
15/4 ADAMS, Private John H. transferred to Northumberland Fusiliers
15/5 ADAIR, Private Thomas Reginald commissioned RFC 25.9.1917
15/6 ADAMS, Lance-Corporal Wilmot transferred to Lancs Fusiliers, then Labour Corps
15/7 AGUTTER, Private Frank discharged 2.4.1919
15/8 AGUTTER, Lance-Corporal Douglas discharged 392 (XVI) 6.7.1917
15/9 AIREY, Sergeant Jas. Henry killed in action 3.5.1917
15/10
15/11
15/12 ALLISON, Acting Corporal John transferred to Labour Corps
15/13
15/14 ALLSOP, Private Jack discharged 15.1.1919
15/15 ALTHORPE, Lance-Corporal Albert killed in action 14.9.1916
15/16 ANDERSON, Private Eric Bryant discharged 15.3.199
15/17
15/18 ANDREW, Acting WO II Stanley discharged 9.4.1919
15/19 APPLEYARD, Acting Lance-Corporal Herbert commissioned West Yorks 27.11.1917
15/20 ARGILE, Lance-Corporal Charles commissioned West Yorks 25.4.1917
15/21
15/22 ARMITAGE, Sergeant George discharged 5.6.1919
15/23
15/24 ARMITAGE, Corporal Harold discharged 13.3.1919
15/25
15/26
15/27
15/28 ARNOLD, Private Thomas Reginald transferred to MGC
15/29 ARNOTT, Acting Sergeant Charles Edward Stuart discharged 19.3.1919
15/30 APPLEYARD, Lance-Corporal Ernest M. commissioned Yorks Regt 25.4.1917
15/31 APPLEYARD, Private Leonard Everett commissioned 3rd Suffolk 29.1.1918
15/32 ASHWORTH, Sergeant Walter discharged 392 (XVI) 19.11.1917
15/33
15/34 ASPINALL, Private John Franklin died of wounds home 15.7.1916
15/35 ASTLE, Lance-Corporal Walter discharged 392 (XVI) 21.5.1919

15/36 ASTON, Private E.G. transferred to RAF

15/37

15/38

15/39 ATKINSON, Corporal Ernest M. transferred to Labour Corps, discharged 392 (XVI) 3.1.1918

15/40

15/41 ATKINSON, Private Thomas A. transferred to York & Lancs, discharged 10.4.1919

15/42

15/43

15/44 AYRTON, Private William commissioned 52nd West Yorks 28.5.1918

15/45 BALDWIN, Private Leonard discharged 392 (XVI) 9.1.1918

15/46 BEVERLEY, Private Bernard presumed dead 1.7.1916

15/47 BERRY, Private Allison B. discharged 392 (XVI) 7.6.1917

15/48

15/49 BRITTON, Acting Lance-Corporal George Harold discharged 392 (XVI) 4.4.1918

15/50 BROADHEAD, Lance-Corporal Charles Roy discharged 10.4.1919

15/51

15/52 BOND, Private Ernest discharged 392 (XVI) 16.11.1917

15/53 BOOTHE, Private Lawrence Gordon discharged 17.3.1919

15/54

15/55

15/56

15/57 BULLIMORE, Corporal James William killed in action 1.7.1916

15/58 BURCH, Private Reginald discharged 28.2.1919

15/59

15/60

15/61 BUTCHER, Acting RSM Emanuel did not go overseas, discharged 392 (XVI) 28.4.1916

15/62

15/63 BEAUMONT, Private Reginald commissioned Indian Army Reserve 22.5.1918

15/64 BURNISTON, Private Harry killed in action 1.7.1916

15/65 BROWN, Lance-Corporal John discharged 15.2.1919

15/66

15/67

15/68 BROWNING, Lance-Corporal Harold discharged 23.2.1919

15/69 BARNES, Private Laurence Fairbank commissioned 25.4.1917

15/70 BROOKE, Sergeant Clarence transferred to 88 TR Bn, commissioned 1/4 E Yorks 31.3.1918

15/71

15/72

15/73

15/74 BYGOTT, Corporal Frank killed in action 30.3.1916

15/75

15/76 BOWMAN, Private David C. killed in action 1.7.1916

15/77

15/78

15/79 BRAY, Corporal Louis discharged 392 (XVI) 5.9.1917

15/80 BARUXAKI, Private Leonard Allan transferred to MGC, commissioned 25 Bn Tank Corps 8.10.1918

15/81 BROWN, Cyril Nicholas discharged 28.5.1919

15/82 BRIGGS, Lance-Corporal F. transferred to MGC, commissioned MGC 26.3.1917

15/83 BLECKSLEY, Sergeant Francis Gilbert killed in action 1.7.1916

15/84 BRECKIN, Sergeant Edward Foster discharged 6.3.1919

15/85

15/86

15/87

15/88

15/89 BURRAS, Private George transferred to East Yorks Regt

15/90

15/91 BEARD, Private Harold killed in action 28.4.1916

15/92

15/93 BLAND, Corporal Benjamin Clifford Wadsworth presumed dead 1.7.1916

15/94 BRYANT, Private Charles discharged 23.2.1919

15/95

15/96

15/97 BIRCH, Private C.

15/98 BYWATER, Private John discharged 392 (XVI) 11.2.1919

15/99 BARRETT, Private Rowland discharged 1.7.1919

15/100 BUNTING, Private James discharged 7.3.1919

15/101 BROWN, Corporal Bromner commissioned 18.5.1917

15/102

15/103 BROOKE, Private H.

15/104

15/105 BARNES, Acting Colour-Sergeant William Lane discharged 18.2.1919

15/106 BROWN, Private Roy discharged 13.3.1919

15/107 BOOTH, Sergeant William Herbert discharged 1.3.1919

15/108 BRIGGS, Private Rowland discharged 10.1.1919

15/109 BOLTON, Private Charles no overseas service, discharged 392 (XVI) 21.4.1916

15/110

15/111 BIRCH, Lance-Corporal William commissioned in Yorkshire Regt 29.5.1917

15/112 BURNELL, Private Roland transferred to RDC, deceased 19.10.1918

15/113 BURTON, Private Herbert transferred to Y & L, commissioned 115 Y & L 26.6.1917

15/114 BROOKE, Private John James killed in action 1.7.1916

15/115

15/116

15/117 BARKER, Sergeant Joseph commissioned RE 18.3.1917

15/118

15/119

15/120 BROWN, Private Harry discharged 12.2.1919

15/121 BOWRING, Private Horace discharged 23.2.1919

15/122 BOWMAN, Private R.

15/123 BYGATE, Lance-Corporal William Anthony

15/124

15/125
15/126 BATTY, Private Samuel Thomas Duncan presumed dead 1.7.1916
15/127 BROWN, Acting Sergeant John William commissioned YorksRegt25.4.1917
15/128 BROOMHEAD, Private Robert presumed dead 1.7.1916
15 BEETHAM, Private Joseph Henry discharged 27.3.1919
15/130
15/131 BUTTERFIELD, Sergeant O.J., DCM re-enlisted in RGA 10.1.1919
15/132 BROOM, Sergeant Thomas discharged 3.6.1919
15/133 BEEVERS, WO II Horace Wilfred discharged 1.7.1919
15/134
15/135
15/136
15/137
15/138 BINNS, Private Arthur discharged 28.2.1919
15/139 BRIGGS, Corporal William Henry presumed dead 1.7.1916
15/140 BURTON, Private Arthur Stanley discharged 7.3.1919
15/141 BERRY, Private Walker discharged 392 (XVI) 17.10.1916
15/142
15/143 BLACKMAN, Private Harold discharged 5.2.1919
15/144
15/145 BROOK, Private Herbert killed in action 1.7.1916
15/146 BRENNAN, Private F.T.
15/147
15/148
15/149 BURNHILL, Sergeant Jas. Horner discharged 2.3.1919
15/150 BANNISTER, Private Charles died of wounds 4.7.1919
15/151
15/152 BASTOW, Sergeant John discharged 392 (XVI) 2.9.1916
15/153
15/154
15/155
15/156 BUTTERFIELD, Private Zenas discharged 392 (XVI) 20.2.1917
15/157
15/158 BELL, Private Harry also served in R Scots, discharged 22.3.1919
15/159 BOND, Private Percy Gilson killed in action 1.7.1916
15/160 BURNLEY, Lance-Corporal Herbert killed in action 1.7.1916
15/161
15/162 BROTHERTON, Private Alan discharged 392 (XVI) 3.9.1917
15/163 BROOKE, Sergeant Clifford killed in action 1.7.1916
15/164 BROWN, Lance-Corporal W.N.
15/165 BATTY, Privates.
15/166 BAINES, Private John Reginald discharged 392 (XVI) 10.1.1918
15/167 BEESTON, Private J.
15/168 BOWER, Corporal John Alfred discharged 2.3.1919
15/169 BOOTH, Private William
15/170 CALVERT, Private Harry killed in action 24.3.1918

15/171 CALVERT, Private John William discharged 392 (XVI) 26.7.1916

15/172 CAPSTICK, Private Eric discharged 392 (XVI) 23.12.1916

15/173 CARNES, Corporal George presumed dead 3.5.1917

15/174 CARR, Private G.W.

15/175

15/176 CARTER, Private Harold discharged 392 (XVI) 14.7.1917

15/177 CARTER, Company-Sergeant-Major R.

15/178 CARTER, Sergeant William Shaul discharged 6.3.1919

15/179

15/180 CASSON, Private Henry Stuart presumed dead 1.7.1916

15/181 CATHRICK, Private Harry Raine killed in action 1.7.1916

15/182 CATON, Lance-Corporal Thomas discharged 22.3.1919

15/183 CAYGILL, Lance-Corporal Leonard Edward discharged 23.3.1919

15/184 CHADWICK, Sergeant Samuel Wilkinson discharged 9.3.1919

15/185 CHADWICK, Private W.

15/186 CHAMBERS, Sergeant Bernard Douglas discharged 26.2.1919

15/187 CHAMBERS, Private John Herbert presumed dead 1.7.1916

15/188 CHAPMAN, Sergeant Brian discharged

15/189 CHAPMAN, Sergeant Edgar commissioned 3 W Yorks 29.1.1918

15/190 CHAPMAN, Corporal Harry discharged

15/191 CHAPMAN, Private Herbert presumed dead 1.7.1916

15/192 CHAPMAN, Private William Foster presumed dead 1.7.1916

15/193 CHANDLER, Private A.

15/194

15/195 CHILD, Lance-Corporal Harold MM commissioned 3 Yorks Regt 25.4.1917

15/196 CHILD, Private J.

15/197 CHILD, Private W.

15/198 CHIVERS, Private Herbert discharged 392 (XVI) 9.1.1918

15/199 CLAPHAM, Private Harry Bernard discharged 392 (XVI) 28.11.1918

15/200 CLARKE, Private Archibald Thomson died of wounds 23.4.1918

15/201

15/202 CLARKE, Private Frank died of wounds 8.6.1917

15/203 CLARK, Lance-Corporal Charles Hope discharged 12.3.1919

15/204 CLARK, Lance-Corporal Joseph, MM commissioned Northumberland Fusiliers 27.3.1917

15/205 CLARK, Private L.

15/206 CLARK, Private William discharged 7.3.1919

15/207 CLARKSON, Private J.

15/208

15/209 CLAYTON, Sergeant Frank killed in action 1.7.1916

15/210 CLAYTON, Private George Edward, MM discharged 392 (XVI) 18.10.1918

15/211 CLAYTON, Private H.

15/212

15/213 COCKERILL, Private Sam discharged 17.3.1919

15/214 COCKRAM, Acting Sergeant Harry discharged 17.3.1919

15/215 COGGILL, Corporal Harold killed in action 1.7.1916

15/216

15/217 COLLINSON, Acting Corporal Joseph William, MM killed in action (with 9th Bn) 5.11.1918

15/218 COLQUHOUN, Acting WOI Frank discharged 3.4.1919

15/219 COLQUHOUN, Corporal William Campbell killed in action 1.7.1916

15/220

15/221

15/222 CONYERS, Lance-Sergeant William presumed dead 1.7.1916

15/223

15/224

15/225 COOPE, Lance-Sergeant Samuel Wainwright discharged 4.4.1919

15/226 COOPER, Lance-Corporal George Alfred discharged 5.4.1919

15/227 COOPER, Private George William discharged 17.3.1919

15/228 COOPER, Private H.A.

15/229

15/230 CORNFORTH, Private Allan transferred to ASC

15/231 COSBY, Private George Wm transferred to MGC, commissioned Tank Corps 29.9.1917

15/232

15/233 COULTAS, Private Percy suicide 31.1.1919

15/234 COULTATE, Private Herbert no overseas service, discharged 392 (XVI) 23.11.1915

15/235

15/236 COWLING, Lance-Corporal Thomas Varvill discharged 10.2.1919

15/237 COX, Lance-Corporal Charles Francis Alexander killed in action 1.7.1916

15/238

15/239 COX, Sergeant Thomas Eyke discharged 6.3.1919

15/240 CRABTREE, Lance-Sergeant Robert Miles commissioned West Yorks 28.3.1917

15/241 CRANSWICK, Acting Corporal John Wilkinson discharged 392 (XVI) 25.1.1919

15/242 CRAVEN, Private Ernest killed in action 1.7.1916

15/243

15/244

15/245 CROSSLAND, Acting Corporal Charles Wemyss discharged 24.4.1919

15/246 CROSSLAND, Acting Corporal John Burgess discharged 18.3.1919

15/247 CROSSLEY, Sergeant Frank Hainsworth commissioned 29.2.1917

15/248 CROSSLAND, Private Robert deceased 18.11.1918

15/249 CROSSLEY, Private Wilfred presumed dead 1.7.1916

15/250

15/251

15/252 CROWTHER, Private Maurice Robinson presumed dead 1.7.1916

15/253 CROWTHER, Sergeant Tom transferred to Labour Corps

15/254 CUDMORE, Acting Colour-Sergeant Hadley John discharged 21.2.1919

15/255 CURPHY, Private Albert Edward killed in action 1.7.1916

15/256

15/257

15/258

15/259 DALBY, Private Fewster Arthur discharged 16.3.1919

15/260

15/261 DALES, Sergeant Richard killed in action 3.10.1918
15/262 DALES, Private Wm. Handsley commissioned KOYLI 17.12.1917
15/263
15/264
15/265 DANKS, Lance-Corporal Thomas discharged 9.8.1919
15/266
15/267 DAVIS, Private Wm. Creswell presumed dead 1.7.1916
15/268
15/269 DAWSON, Private Henry Stanley discharged 392 (XVI) 21.5.1918
15/270
15/271
15/272
15/273
15/274 DENTON, Private John Henry discharged 1.7.1919
15/275
15/276 DERHAM, WO II James discharged 16.2.1919
15/277 DICKINSON, Private Sydney presumed dead 3.5.1917
15/278 DIMERY, Sergeant George Wentworth commissioned 9.1.1917
15/279 DIMERY, Acting Sergeant Joseph Edwin commissioned KOYLI 25.9.1917
15/280
15/281 DOBSON, Private Arthur Spencer died of wounds 1.7.1916
15/282 DOCKRAY, Lance-Corporal Frank Myers commissioned 3rd R Sussex 17.12.1917
15/283 DODGESON, Private John Ernest deceased 9.7.1916
15/284
15/285 DONNELLY, Private Stephen killed in action 1.7.1916
15/286 DOUGHTY, Private John Cecil killed in action 1.7.1916
15/287 DREWRY, Private George killed in action 10.6.1916
15/288 DREWRY, Private Robert killed in action 1.7.1916
15/289
15/290 DRURY, Private Harry discharged 16.1.1919
15/291 DUCKETT, Private Frank commissioned 26.5.1917
15/292
15/293 DUNN, Private Charles Edward discharged 392 (XVI) 10.1.1918
15/294 DUNWELL, Private Clifford presumed dead 3.5.1917
15/295
15/296 DUXBURY, Private Donald discharged 20.2.1919
15/297
15/298 DYSON, Private Wm. Gladstone no overseas service, discharged 392 (XVI) 8.3.1915
15/299
15/300 EARNSHAW, Corporal Percival H. transferred to Labour Corps
15/301
15/302 EASY, Sergeant George Fison killed in action 1.7.1916
15/303
15/304
15/305 EDWARDS, Lance-Corporal Frank A. transferred to Labour Corps
15/306 EDWARDS, Private Irvin discharged 392 (XVI) 6.1.1918

15/307
15/308 ELLIS, Private Rowland C. transferred to Labour Corps
15/309
15/310
15/311
15/312 ESCHLE, Private Arthur Bertrand, MM presumed dead 1.7.1916
15/313
15/315 EWART, Corporal John Sydney killed in action 20.8.1916
15/316 EXLEY, Private Claude discharged 392 (XVI) 16.10.1916
15/316
15/317 FAIRBURN HART, Corporal George Stanley died of wounds 27.4.1916
15/318
15/319 FARNDALE, Lance-Corporal George killed in action 3.5.1917
15/320 FAWBERT, Lance-Corporal Russell discharged 10.1.1919
15/321 FAWCWETT, Private H.
15/322 FAWCETT, Acting Sergeant Thomas Constantine commissioned KOYLI 13.4.1917
15/323 FENTON, Private Alan James discharged 392 (XVI) 31.7.1917
15/321 FENTON, Lance-Corporal Joe discharged 392 (XVI) 8.9.1916
15/325 FERRAND, Lance-Corporal George Major presumed dead 3.5.1917
15/326 FIELDING, Private A. B.
15/327 FILLINGHAM, Private Arthur Edwin killed in action 1.7.1916
15/328
15/329
15/330 FIRTH, Lance-Corporal Harry Leslie, MM discharged 15.3.1919
15/331 FIRTH, Private Norman discharged 16.2.1919
15/332
15/333
15/334
15/335 FITZPATRICK, Private Bernard discharged 11.4.1919, re-enlisted RASC 25.11.1919
15/336 FLANNAG AN, Sergeant J Arthur discharged 2.3.1919
15/337 FLANNAGAN, Private J.
15/338
15/339 FLEMING, Private W. Morris commissioned West Yorks 7.6.1917
15/340 FLINT, Private John presumed dead 1.7.1916
15/341 FLOCKTON, Private Fred presumed dead 1.7.1916
15/342 FLYNN, Private Thomas James discharged 4.3.1919
15/343
15/344 FOSTER, Lance-Corporal Eric B. transferred to RE, discharged 18.2.1919
15/345 FOSTER, Private James discharged 392 (XVI) 21.3.1917
15/346
15/347
15/348 FOX, Private Harold discharged 12.3.1919
15/349 FOXCROFT, Private John killed in action 1.7.1916
15/350 FOXTON, Lance-Corporal Herbert killed in action with 2nd Bn 31.7.1917
15/351 FRANKLIN, Sergeant Frederick W. transferred to Labour Corps, discharged 20.3.1919
15/352

15/353 FRIEDER, Acting Sergeant Sydney discharged 19.2.1919
15/354 FROST, Private Charles discharged 26.2.1919
15/355 GAMBLE, Private Donald R. transferred to E Yorks Regt
15/356 GANDE, Private Arthur Sydney discharged 23.2.1919
15/357 GARBUTT, Private John William killed in action 9.6.1916
15/358 GARDINER, Private Herbert transferred to MGC, discharged 19.2.1919
15/359 GARLICK, Acting Corporal George Wilfred discharged 29.3.1919
15/360 GARNER, Private Walter discharged 392 (XVI) 17.4.1918
15/361 GARNETT, Private Egerton deceased 6.11.1918
15/362
15/363
15/364
15/365
15/366
15/367
15/368
15/369
15/370 GIBS0N, Private Wm. Henry commissioned West Yorks 28.3.1917
15/371 GREASLEY, Lance-Sergeant Alfred Reginald killed in action 1.7.1916
15/372
15/373
15/374 GILL, WO II Harry died of wounds 3.7.1916
15/375 GILLATT, Lance-Sergeant Gordon Basil commissioned MGC 29.10.1918
15/376
15/377
15/378 GLADDERS, Sergeant William Edgar killed in action 3.5.1917
15/379
15/380
15/381 GODSON, Private Arthur died of wounds serving with 16 Bn 4.11.1918
15/382 GODRICH, Lance-Corporal James Arthur discharged 10.3.1919
15/383 GOODALL, Private Sidney Herbert discharged 7.3.1919
15/384 GOODFELLOW, Private Joseph Herbert discharged 392 (XVI) 22.8.1917
15/385
15/386 GOTT, Private Howard died of wounds 14.7.1916
15/387 GOWTHORPE, Lance-Corporal Eric George Cecil discharged 392 (XVI) 30.3.1918
15/388 GRAHAM, Private Frank H. transferred to Yorks Regt
15/389 GRAHAM, Colour-Sergeant Percy Joseph discharged 1.7.1919
15/390 GRAHAM, Private R. transferred to RFC
15/391
15/392
15/393
15/394 GRAY, Lance-Corporal Alfred Ambrose died of wounds 20.8.1917
15/395
15/396 GRAY, Sergeant James commissioned N Fusiliers 17.12.1917
15/397 GRAY, Sergeant Robert commissioned West Yorks 28.5.1918
15/398 GRAYSHON, Private Matthew Burnett discharged 10.2.1919

15/399 GREEN, Sergeant Ernest Alfred, MM discharged 392 (XVI) 12.12.1916
15/400 GREEN, Sergeant Harold discharged 5.3.1919
15/401 GREEN, Sergeant John Walter commissioned 3.2.1919
15/402
15/403 GREENWOOD, Private Arthur discharged 5.3.1919
15/404
15/405 GURMIN, Sergeant George Thomas killed in action 1.7.1916
15/406
15/407 GUTTRIDGE, Lance-Sergeant Albert died of wounds 30.7.1916
15/408 HADDON, Private Norman J transferred to E Yorks Regt
15/409 HATFIELD, Private James Gilbert served with 2nd & 9th Bns, discharged 20.3.1919
15/410 HAGUE, Sergeant Arthur discharged 23.3.1919
15/411
15/412 HAIST, Sergeant John killed in action 3.5.1917
15/413 HALE, Sergeant Frank Russell discharged 392 (XVI) 15.2.1918
15/414 HALL, Acting Corporal James Thomson commissioned KOYLI 2.4.1917
15/415
15/416 HALLIDAY, Private Herbert discharged 392 (XVI) 11.1.1918
15/417
15/418
15/419 HAMILTON, Private Gavin Park killed in action 1.7.1916
15/420 HAMMOND, Private Willie transferred to Y & L Regt, killed in action 15.11.1916
15/421 HAMPSHIRE, Private Joe killed in action 1.7.1916
15/422 HANCOCK, Lance-Corporal Geoffrey killed in action 9.6.1916
15/423
15/424 HANDS, Private Walter F. transferred to Labour Corps, discharged 20.5.1919
15/425 HANLON, Private Frank died of wounds 31.3.1918
15/426 HANSON, Private E.
15/427
15/428 HARDY, Private Frank presumed dead 1.7.1916
15/429 HARE, Sergeant Herbert Edgar discharged 7.3.1919
15/430 HARGRAVE, Private Horace transferred to Y & L Regt, killed in action 15.11.1916
15/431 HARGREAVES, Private John transferred to Northumberland Fus, discharged 4.2.1919
15/432 HARLOW, Private Edward Cecil presumed dead 1.7.1916
15/433 HARRALL, Private Ernest no overseas service, discharged 5.5.1915
15/434 HARRIS, Private Sydney Wm commissioned West Yorks 27.11.1917
15/435
15/436 HARTLEY, Private Harold discharged 7.3.1919
15/437
15/438
15/439 HAXBY, Private Richard discharged 392 (XVI) 18.1.1918
15/440 HAYNES, Sergeant Harry Edgar presumed dead 3.5.1917
15/441 HEATON, Sergeant Thomas Herbert killed in action 1.7.1916
15/442 HEALEY, Corporal Edward presumed dead 1.7.1916
15/443 HELLEWELL, Sergeant Walter discharged 20.3.1919
15/444 HEMINGBROUGH, Private Charles Arthur killed in action 1.7.1916

15/445 HEPWORTH, Private George A. transferred to Labour Corps, discharged 22.4.1919
15/446
15/447 HERLEY, Private John William killed in action 1.7.1916
15/448 HESLINGTON, Lance-Corporal William Henry discharged 3.7.1919
15/449 HEWITT, Lance Sergeant Herbert killed in action 1.7.1916
15/450 HEWITT, Private Herbert Henry discharged 1.7.1919
15/451 HEWITT, Private Reginald Kilburn discharged 392 (XVI) 23.5.1917
15/452 HEWSON, Private Frank discharged 22.2.1919
15/453
15/454 HEY, Lance-Corporal Charles Edward discharged 12.3.1919
15/455 HEY, Corporal William Andrew transferred to Labour Corps, commissioned 14.5.1917
15/456 HICKS, Lance-Corporal Sidney Clifford discharged 392 (XVI) 14.1.1918
15/457 HICKSON, Private Laurence killed in action 1.7.1916
15/458 HIGGINS, Corporal Clifford John commissioned 25.4.1917
15/459 HILL, Private Charles presumed dead 1.7.1916
15/460 HILL, Private Claude Scott died of wounds 24.10.1916
15/461 HINDS, Private George Devonport commissioned West Yorks 25.5.1917
15/462 HIRD, Private Thomas A. transferred to E Yorks Regt, then R Munster Fusiliers
15/463
15/464 HIRST, Private Lewis discharged 392 (XVI) 16.11.1917
15/465 HIRST, Private Oswald killed in action 1.7.1916
15/466
15/467 HODGSON, Private Arthur transferred to Y & L Regt, discharged 24.4.1919
15/468 HOGG, Sergeant John Louis presumed dead 3.5.1917
15/469
15/470 HOLLINGS, Lance-Corporal Wm. Arthur died 4.3.1917
15/471 HOLLINGWORTH, Sergeant Clifford discharged 2.3.1919
15/472 HOLDS, Lance-Corporal George Worthington presumed dead 1.7.1916
15/473 HOLTON, Private A.
15/474
15/475 HOPKIN, Private Edward died of wounds 29.5.1916
15/476 HORNE, Private E.
15/477 HORTON, Sergeant Reginald Wm. deceased 12.11.1918
15/478
15/479
15/480 HOWARD, Private Alfred discharged 27.2.1919
15/481 HOWARTH, Private Norman commissioned Yorks Regt 28.8.1917
15/482 HOWELLS, Lance-Corporal Courtney commissioned 3rd Yorks Regt 28.9.1917
15/483 HUDSON, Sergeant A.O.
15/484
15/485 HULLAH, Sergeant James Albert commissioned 29.12.1916
15/486
15/487
15/488 HUNTER, Private John Henry killed in action 1.7.1916
15/489 HURST, Private James Forrestno overseas service, discharged 392 (XVI) 5.5.1915
15/490 HUTCHINSON, Corporal Harry MM discharged 21.2.1919

15/491

15/492 HUTTON, Private George Arthur killed in action 9.6.1916

15/493

15/494

15/495 IBBOTSON, Private John served with 12th Bn, killed in action 14.7.1916

15/496 IBBOTSON, Company-Sergeant-Major Alfred discharged 392 (XVI) 16.4.1918

15/497 IBBOTSON, Private Arthur discharged 392 (XVI) 3.7.1917

15/498

15/499

15/500 INGLE, Sergeant Alfred Ernest discharged 1.2.1919

15/501 INGLESON, Private Ernest killed in action 1.7.1916

15/502

15/503 JACKSON, Corporal Arthur died of wounds 20.7.1916

15/504 JACKSON, Corporal Arthur discharged 392 (XVI) 6.10.1917

15/505 JACKSON, Private Clarence commissioned 4th Lancs Fusiliers 10.9.1918

15/506

15/507 JACKSON, Lance-Corporal Henry Stead presumed dead 3.5.1917

15/508 JACKSON, Private J.E.

15/509 JACKSON, Sergeant Norman killed in action 1.7.1916

15/510

15/511

15/512 JACKSON, Corporal William Homsby discharged 27.2.1919

15/513 JAMES, Private Frank Burton discharged 392 (XVI) 26.11.1916

15/514 JAMES, Sergeant Thomas Galloway killed in action 1.7.16

15/515 JAMES, Private William killed in action 20.8.1917

15/516 JEFFREY, Private E.R.

15/517

15/518 JENKYNS, WO II Eric Carew, MM discharged 4.5.1919

15/519

15/520 JENKINSON, Private Harold discharged 392 (XVI) 12.5.1917

15/521 JENKINSON, Private Ronald discharged 24.3.1919

15/522 JENKINSON, Private Sydney killed in action 1.7.1916

15/523

15/524 JOHNSON, Lance-Corporal Charles discharged 2.4.1919

15/525 JOHNSON, Corporal Ernest Boyes discharged 10.1.1919

15/526

15/527 JONES, Private David William discharged 392 (XVI) 8.8.1917

15/528

15/529 JONES, Lance-Corporal Ernest Mason discharged 20.2.1919

15/530

15/531 JONES, WO II Joseph Elliott, DCM discharged 19.2.1919

15/532 JONES, Corporal Percy Harold discharged 6.3.1919

15/533 JONES, Private Reginald killed in action 1.7.1916

15/534 JOY, Private Wilfred killed in action 3.5.1917

15/535 JUDD, Lance-Corporal Joe discharged 19.2.19

15/536 AITCHISON, Lance-Corporal Gilbert discharged 13.2.1919

15/537 HENRY, Private Joseph presumed dead 3.5.1917

15/538 KAY, Private Charles Henry discharged 31.1.1919

15/539 KAYE, Private Joseph discharged 3.4.1919

15/540 KEIGHLEY, Lance-Corporal Emest commissioned West Yorks 30.10.1917

15/541 KEIGHLEY, Private T.L.

15/542

15/543

15/544

15/545

15/546 KERSHAW, Private James Thomas discharged 10.3.1919, re-enlisted RASC 29.10.1919

15/547 KERTON, Private H.

15/548 KERTON, Sergeant Sydney killed in action 22.5.1916

15/549 KILLEN, Private Horace Hugh killed in action 30.8.1916

15/550 KILLEN, Private John killed in action 1.7.1916

15/551 KILLERBY, Lance-Sergeant James Frederick presumed dead 26.3.1918

15/552 KILNER, Lance-Corporal Roy 15/553 KING, Sergeant Benjamin discharged 18.2.1919

15/554 KING, WO II Stanley Hurst Lister commissioned 3rd West Yorks 27.11.1917

15/555 KITCHEN, Private Richard presumed dead 3.5.1917

15/556

15/557 KIRK, Lance-Corporal Alfred Edward Morgan killed in action 1.7.1916

15/558 KIRK, Private Fred discharged 20.3.1919

15/559

15/560 KIRKM AN, Lance-Corporal E.

15/561 KIRKMAN, Private Frank no overseas service, discharged 392 (XVI) 26.7.1915

15/562

15/563

15/564

15/565 LAKE, Private Thomas Wm. killed in action 1.7.1916

15/566 LAMBERT, Private W.M.

15/567 LANCASTER, Private Frederick died of wounds 21.8.1916

15/568 LANDER, Private Leopold Huber discharged 392 (XVI) 8.8.1917

15/569 LANE, Lance-Corporal S.G.

15/570 LAWRENCE, Acting Sergeant Louis commissioned 18th Manchester 19.2.1917

15/571 LAWRENCE, Corporal Louis discharged 392 (XVI) 20.5.1916

15/572 GLEW, Private Frank presumed dead 1.7.1916 15/573

15/574 LAWSON, Lance-Sergeant Harry Hudson discharged 21.2.1919

15/575

15/576

15/577

15/578

15/579 LAYCOCK, Private Harold Riley commissioned 3rd York & Lancs 27.3.1917

15/580

15/581

15/582 LEE, Private Albert presumed dead 1.7.1916

15/583

15/584

15/585

15/586 LENNOX, Private F.W.

15/587 LEWIS, Frederick Richard died of wounds 5.7.1916

15/588

15/589

15/590

15/591

15/592 LINDOW, Private Wm. James commissioned R Lancs 26.6.1917

15/593 LINFOOT, Private James Wm. discharged 392 (XVI) 27.12.1917

15/594

15/595

15/596

15/597

15/598 LISTER, Corporal Cecil discharged 24.4.1919

15/599

15/600 LONGFIELD, Private Edric D. transferred to RE

15/601 LONGLEY, Private Ernest killed in action 1.7.1916

15/602 LONSDALE, Private Fred discharged 392 (XVI) 13.11.1917

15/603 LUMB, Private Wilfred Denison died of wounds 3.7.1916

15/604

15/605

15/606 LYONS, Private William

15/607

15/608 MACAULAY, Sergeant Wm. Hope killed in action 29.4.1917

15/609 MACKAY, Private James discharged 16.3.1919

15/610 MAHON, Acting Sergeant John Sykes discharged 5.8.1919

15/611

15/612 MARCHANT, Lance-Sergeant William killed in action 3.5.1917

15/613

15/614 MARSDEN, Private H.

15/615

15/616

15/617

15/618

15/619

15/620

15/621 MASON, Lance-Corporal Herbert Harry Jagger presumed dead 1.7.1916

15/622 MASON, Corporal Sydney, MM discharged 1.3.1919

15/623 MASON, Private R.

15/624

15/625 MATTHEWS, Private Harry discharged 22.3.1919

15/626 MATTHEWS, Sergeant Ernest Edward commissioned 2.2.1919

15/627 MAWSON, Private Gerald commissioned 3rd West Yorks 10.9.1918

15/628 McCULLAGH, Corporal Frank served with 21st Bn, killed in action 28.3.1918

15/629 McEWAN, Private Robert Watt presumed dead 1.7.1916

15/630

15/631 McKENZIE, Acting WO II William commissioned KOYLI 29.1.1918
15/632 McNEIL, Private W.C.
15/633 MEESON, Lance-Corporal Arthur presumed dead 1.7.1916
15/634 MELDRUM, Private G.
15/635
15/636
15/637 MERRITT, Private C.
15/638 METCALFE, Private Clifford presumed dead 3.5,1917
15/639 METCALFE, Private James Henry discharged 392 (XVI) 20.9.1916
15/640 METCALFE, Acting Sergeant John Clarence discharged 27.3.1919
15/641 METCALFE, Private S.
15/642 METCALFE, Private Walter died of wounds 9.7.1916
15/643 MIDDLETON, Private J.B.
15/644
15/645
15/646
15/647 MILLER, Lance-Corporal John Anderson presumed dead 1.7.1916
15/648
15/649 MILNER, Lance-Corporal Frank discharged 13.4.1919
15/650 MILNER, Private Ralph discharged 5.4.1919
15/651 MILNES, Private Fred presumed dead 1.7.1916
15/652
15/653 MITCHELL, Private E.
15/654 MOORHOUSE, Sergeant Walter commissioned West Yorks 28.3.1917
15/655 MORCAMBE, Private E.
15/656 MORTIMER, Private Arthur discharged 12.3.1919
15/657 MORTIMER, Private George Francis Beaumont killed in action 1.7.1916
15/658 MORTIMER, Private George Harold presumed dead 1.7.1916
15/659
15/660
15/661
15/662
15/663 MOORE, Acting Lance-Corporal Edgar killed in action 1.7.1916
15/664 MORTON, Corporal John Stewart killed in action 1.7.1916
15/665 MOSS, Private G.B.
15/666 MUSCHAMP, Private Rhoderick Harold discharged 16.3.1919
15/667 MUSGRAVE, Private Joe presumed dead 1.7.1916
15/668
15/669
15/670 NALLEY, Private George Wilfred discharged 392 (XVI) 7.5.1917
15/671 NAYLOR, Private Frank presumed dead 1.7.1916
15/672 NAYLOR, Lance-Sergeant Fred commissioned DLI 30.10.1917
15/673
15/674 NAYLOR, Lance-Corporal Tom discharged 22.3.1919
15/675 NEEDHAM, Private Clifford discharged 392 (XVI) 14.4.1917
15/676

15/677
15/678 NETTLETON, Acting Lance-Corporal Percy discharged 22.3.1919
15/679 NEWBORN, Sergeant Percy George died of wounds 23.5.1916
15/680 NEWELL, Lance-Corporal Sam died of wounds 12.11.1916
15/681
15/682 NEWTON, Acting WO I Montague discharged 15.4.1919
15/683 NICOL, Private J.
15/684 NICOL, Acting WO I Percy, DCM discharged 14.3.1919
15/685
15/686 NIXON, Private Fred discharged 27.3.1919
15/687 NOBLE, Private Thomas Thorold discharged 392 (XVI) 10.11.1916
15/688 NOTTINGHAM, Private John discharged 27.3.1919
15/689 ODDIE, Lance-Corporal Stanley discharged 392 (XVI) 16.12.1918
15/690 ODDY, Sergeant Harold Reynolds, MM discharged 7.3.1919
15/691 ODGERS, Sergeant Hugh Bearns killed in action 1.7.1916
15/692 OLIVER, Private Albert discharged 392 (XVI) 31.8.1916
15/693
15/694 ORTON, Private Walter discharged 392 (XVI) 4.9.1918
15/695
15/696 PALLISER, Private Arnold presumed dead 1.7.191
15/697
15/698 PAPE, Sergeant Ernest discharged 7.3.1919
15/699 PAPE, Private James killed in action 21.9.1916
15/700 PAPE, Private R.B.
15/701 PARK, Private John Francis Chalmers commissioned Yorks Regt 28.8.1917
15/702 PARKER, Private W.D.
15/703 PARKER, Private H
15/704
15/705
15/706 PARKINSON, Private John commissioned 6th West Yorks 28.5.1918
15/707 PATTISON, Private Malcolm commissioned Yorks Regt 28.8.1917
15/708 PAUL, Private Alfred killed in action 24.7.1916
15/709
15/710 PEACOCK, Private H.
15/711 PEARSON, Lance-Corporal Arthur Valentine discharged 18.2.1919
15/712 PEARSON, Private H.
15/713
15/714
15/715
15/716 PENF0LD, Lance-Corporal Edwin commissioned 6th Rifle Bde 28.8.1917
15/717
15/718
15/719
15/720
15/721 PICKLES, Sergeant Herbert Gladstone presumed dead 3.5.1917
15/722 PICKLES, Private William discharged 29.3.1919

15/723

15/724 PLATT, Corporal William Alexander discharged 7.3.1919

15/725 POLL, Private Alexander William transferred to MGC, discharged 26.2.1919

15/726 PONTEFRACT, Private Frank L. transferred to RDC

15/727

15/728 PORTER, Private Leslie Groves discharged 392 (XVI) 21.12.1918

15/729 POTTER, Private Victor Jones discharged 25.2.1919

15/730

15/731 POTTS, Corporal Robert Gowland commissioned 3rd York & Lancs 20.3.1918

15/732 POWER, Private Alan Maynard killed in action 28.4.1916

15/733 PRATT, Corporal James discharged 392 (XVI) 19.1.1918

15/734 PREECE, Lance-Corporal John Llewellyn discharged 7.12.1919

15/735 PRIESTLY, Private Wm. Robert presumed dead 1.7.1916

15/736 PRINCE, Sergeant Joseph transferred to Labour Corps, discharged 17.5.1919

15/737 PROCTOR, Lance-Corporal Ralph Victor killed in action 1.7.1916

15/738 PULLAM, Private Harry Lowther discharged 25.2.1919

15/739 PURCHON, Sergeant Samuel Rowling discharged 26.3.1919

15/740

15/741

15/742 RANSOM, Acting Colour-Sergeant William

15/743 RATCLIFFE, Private John Ellis discharged 392 (XVI) 29.9.1917

15/744 RAWNSLEY, Private Bernard discharged 24.2.1919

15/745 RAYFIELD, Private Sydney Marshall killed in action 1.7.1916

15/746 RAYNER, Private Frederick killed in action 1.7.1916

15/747 REDDYHOF, WO II Fred commissioned 3rd York & Lanes 28.8.1917

15/748 REDFERN, Acting Lance-Corporal Harry killed in action 1.7.1916

15/749 REDSHAW, Acting Lance-Corporal Leonard killed in action 25.9.1916

15/750 REDSHAW, Private Sidney transferred to RE, York & Lanes, then back to RE

15/751 REED, Sergeant Bernard commissioned West Yorks 30.10.1917

15/752 RENNISON, Acting Corporal Wm. Edward discharged 27.5.1919

15/753

15/754 REYNER, Private Burnett presumed dead 1.7.1916

15/755 REYNOLDS, Private Herbert discharged 392 (XVI)

15/756 RHODES, Private Henry F. transferred to York & Lanes, discharged 2.3.1919

15/757 RHODES, Corporal Herbert Walker killed in action 22.5.1916

15/758 RICHARDSON, Sergeant Albert Victor commissioned 3rd West Riding 29.10.1918

15/759 RICHARDSON, Private Eddie discharged 392 (XVI) 21.1.1918

15/760 RICHARDSON, Private Sidney Brown presumed dead 1.7.1916

15/761 RICMOND, Sergeant William discharged 18.3.1919

15/762

15/763

15/764 RILEY, Lance-Corporal Walter discharged 1.5.1919

15/765 RIMMER, Private George Charles discharged 392 (XVI) 2.6.1917

15/766

15/767 ROBERTSON, Corporal Henry discharged 392 (XVI) 21.3.1919

15/768 ROBINSON, Private Clarence no overseas service, discharged 392 (XVI) 26.7.1915

15/769 ROBINSON, Private Ernest Leslie presumed dead 1.7.1916
15/770 ROBINSON, Sergeant Marmaduke commissioned MGC 26.6.1917
15/771 ROBINSON, Lance-Corporal R. B.
15/772 ROGERS, Private Arthur Denton presumed dead 1.7.1916
15/773
15/774 ROPER, Private F.
15/775
15/776 ROUSE, Corporal Ernest presumed dead 12.4.1918
15/777 ROWLING, Private S.
15/778 RUCKUDGE, Private John Richard discharged 392 (XVI) 16.11.1917
15/779 RYAN, Sergeant Frederick died of wounds 16.6.1917
15/780 MORLEY, Private Wm. Foster presumed dead 1.7.1916
15/781 SANDERS, Private Kenneth Charles discharged 14.3.1919
15/782
15/783
15/784 SAXBY, Private Frank killed in action 20.8.1916
15/785
15/786
15/787 SCHOON, Lance-Corporal Walter commissioned West Riding 28.12.1918
15/788 SCHOFIELD, Lance-Corporal Thomas Edward discharged 392 (XVI) 17.8.1917
15/789 SCHOFIELD, Private William Arthur discharged 392 (XVI) 4.9.1919
15/790 SCHOLES, WO II Frederick W. DCM commissioned West Yorks 25.12.1916
15/791 SCOTT, Corporal Arthur discharged 392 (XVI) 21.7.1917
15/792 SCOTT, Private Fred killed in action 1.7.1916
15/793 SELBY, Private Charles Ernest presumed dead 1.7.1916
15/794
15/795 SEN, Private Jogendra killed in action 22.5.1916
15/796 SENIOR, Private Clifford discharged 392 (XVI) 20.4.1917
15/797
15/798 SEWELL, Lance-Corporal John commissioned King's (Liverpool) Regt 28.5.1918
15/799
15/800 SEWELL, Sergeant Wilfrid died of wounds 8.7.1916
15/801
15/802 SHARMAN, Lance-Corporal Edward Percy commissioned HLI 10.3.1917
15/803
15/804 SHARPLES, Corporal James presumed dead 1.7.1916
15/805
15/806 SHAW, Private Walter Clifford presumed dead1.7.1916
15/807 SHEARD, Sergeant Cyril commissioned Y & L 28.8.1917
15/808 SHEARD, Sergeant John discharged 392 (XVI) 2.2.1918
15/809 SHEARD, Private John Linley died of wounds 26.5.1916
15/810 SHELLEY, Sergeant C.H.
15/811 SHIPP, Lance-Corporal W.
15/812 SIMPSON, Private Horace Cumberland presumed dead 1.7.1916
15/813 SIMPSON, Corporal Edward Hargreaves discharged 11.3.1919
15/814

15/815 SIMPSON, Corporal Reginald discharged 18.3.1919
15/816 SISSONS, Private T.
15/817
15/818 SUCER, Private Norman discharged 392 (XVI) 6.9.1917
15/819
15/820 SMITH, Private Benjamin Arthur discharged 24.4.1919
15/821 SMITH, Corporal C.
15/822 SMITH, Private E.
15/823 SMITH, Private H.
15/824
15/825 SMITH, Private H.
15/826
15/827 SMITH, Corporal J.
15/828 SMITH, Private J.
15/829 SMITH, Private Robert Edward discharged 12.3.1919
15/830 SMITHSON, Private T.H.
15/831
15/832
15/833 SOKELL, Lance-Corporal Harry commissioned 3rd West Yorks 26.2.1918
15/834 SOUTHWARD, Private Edward presumed dead 1.7.1916
15/835
15/836
15/837 SOWDEN, Acting Lance-Corporal Walter Andrew discharged 14.5.1919
15/838 SPENCE, Private W.
15/839 SPENCER, Private Harold discharged 4.3.1919 15/840
15/841 SPIVEY Sergeant Arnold discharged 22.2.1919
15/842 STANDISH, Private, C.E.
15/843 STANSFIELD, Corporal Harold commissioned West Yorks 25.9.1918
15/844 STEAD, Private Albert Harold discharged 392 (XVI) 24.4.1919
15/845
15/846 STEEL, Private Charles discharged 1.7.1919
15/847 STEELE, Private A.
15/848 STENDELL, Colour-Sergeant Richard Harold discharged 16.3.1919
15/849 STEPHENSON, Private Herbert discharged 392 (XVI) 2.6.1917
15/850 STEPHENSON, Private John William discharged 2.3.1919
15/851 STEPHENSON, Private Percy killed in action 1.7.1916
15/852 STEPHENSON, Private H.G.
15/853
15/854 STOCKS, Private A.
15/855 STOCKOE, Private Crawford presumed dead 1.7.1916
15/856 STOREY, Private B.B.
15/857
15/858
15/859
15/860 SUMMERSCALE, Private Frank commissioned Yorks Regt 28.8.1917
15/861 SUMMERSCALE, Private Norman presumed dead 1.7.1916

15/862 SUMMERSCALE, Private Stanley presumed dead 1.7.1916
15/863 SUMMERSGILL, Sergeant Arthur discharged 12.2.1919
15/864 SUNDERLAND, Private Herbert William presumed dead 1.7.1916
15/365 SUTCLIFFE, Private Fred presumed dead 1.7.1916
15/866 SUTCLIFFE, Private Harold transferred to HLI
15/867 SUTCLIFFE, Private William N. discharged
15/868 SWIFT, Private Alan Whitty killed in action with 2/5 West Yorks 20.7.1918
15/869
15/870
15/871
15/872
15/873
15/874 TATTERSFIELD, Private H.
15/875 TAYLOR, Private A.H.
15/876 TAYLOR, Lance-Corporal Bertie died of wounds 27.10.1918
15/877 TAYLOR, Private E.
15/878 TAYLOR, Private Frederick William presumed dead 1.7.1916
15/879 TAYLOR, Corporal Reginald Charles discharged 12.3.1919
15/880 TAYLOR, Sergeant William discharged 17.3.1919
15/881 TENNANT, Private Percy Herbert died of wounds 28.7.1916
15/882
15/883 THACKER, Private George discharged 16.3.1919
15/884 THOMAS, Private Arthur discharged 26.2.1919
15/885 THOMPSON, Private Arthur Norman killed in action 1.7.1916
15/886 THOMPSON, Private Charles Henry deceased 21.3.1917
15/887 THOMPSON, Lance-Corporal Harry discharged 17.3.1919
15/888 THOMPSON, Private J.
15/889 THOMPSON, Private James discharged 15.2.1919
15/890 THOMPSON, Private James Donald killed in action 1.7.1916
15/891 THORNES, Private H.
15/892 THORNTON, Private Cecil commissioned West Yorks 28.3.1917
15/893
15/894
15/895 THORNTON, Private Percy commissioned RFC 11.1.1918
15/896 THURLOW, Sergeant Harry discharged 1.5.1919
15/897 TILLOTSON, Private Thomas Weeks killed in action 1.7.1916
15/898
15/899 TIMMS, Private Robert Evans killed in action 22.5.1916
15/900
15/901 TODD, Private George Edwin discharged 392 (XVI) 23.11.1917
15/902 TODD, Private Sydney killed in action 28.8.1917
15/903 TOMALIN, Private Harry commissioned 3rd West Yorks 28.8.1917, later KOYU
15/904 TOMLINSON, Private Cecil discharged 13.6.1919
15/905
15/906 TOPHAM, Corporal Arthur Pollard discharged 1.7.1919
15/907 TOWERS, Sergeant William commissioned 3rd E Kent 29.1.1918

15/908 TOWLER, Private Frank attached RAF
15/909
15/910
15/911 TOWNEND, Private George Priestley killed in action 1.7.1916
15/912
15/913
15/914 TURKINGT0N, Private John Williamson discharged 11.4.1919
15/915
15/916 TURNOCK, Sergeant Thomas Berkeley discharged 15.2.1919
15/917
15/918 VINCE, WO I Walker William killed in action 1.7.1916
15/919 VICKERS, Private Arthur Edwin discharged 392 (XVI) 20.7.1917
15/920 VAULKHARD, Acting Lance-Corporal Norman Garnett discharged 21.2.1919
15/921 VICKERS, Temporary Colour-Sergeant Frederick discharged 12.1.1920
15/922 VERO, Corporal W.
15/923
15/924
15/925 WALCH, Private Harold discharged 10.1.1919
15/926
15/927
15/928 WALKER, Private Albert Edward presumed dead 27.3.1918
15/929
15/930 WALKER, Private Ernest killed in action 22.5.1916
15/931
15/932 WALKER, Private John Adlington discharged 19.4.1919
15/933 WALKER, Private Norman discharged 17.3.1919
15/934
15/935 WALKER, Private Watson Midgely discharged 11.3.1919
15/936 WARD, Private Joseph Rhodes discharged 28.4.1919
15/937 WARD, Lance-Sergeant John Edward commissioned W Riding 31.7.1917
15/938 WARD, Private John James commissioned W Yorks 29.1.1918
15/939
15/940
15/941 WARD, Corporal Samuel Clifford discharged 18.3.1919
15/942 WARING, Private Horace killed in action 1.7.1916
15/943 WARD, Lance-Corporal Alec commissioned West Yorks 6.3.1917
15/944 WAINMAN, Private W.B.
15/945 WARRINGTON, Private Arthur discharged 392 (XVI) 7.8.1917
15/946 WATSON, Colour-Sergeant Henry James discharged 392 (XVI) 6.6.1918
15/947 WALTON, Private F.M.
15/948 WALTON, Corporal Sidney killed in action 1.7.1916
15/949 WATS0N, Lance-Corporal Harry killed in action 22.5.1916
15/950
15/951 WATSON, Corporal H.
15/952
15/953

15/954 WATTS, Private Harry Martlieu discharged 9.3.1919
15/955 WEBB, Private C.E.
15/956
15/957 WEBSTER, Sergeant Norman Fothergill discharged 5.3.1919
15/958 WEBSTER, Private George Robert discharged 392 (XVI) 13.11.1918
15/959 WHITE, Acting Corporal Walker killed in action 1.7.1916
15/960 WHITEHEAD, Private Sydney presumed dead 1.7.1916
15/961 WHITEHEAD, Private Arthur no overseas service, discharged 392 (XVI) 5.5.1915
15/962
15/963
15/964
15/965 WEST, Lance-Corporal Norman Frederick presumed dead 1.7.1916
15/966
15/967 WHARTON, Lance-Corporal J.
15/968 WHEELER, Private Oswald Percy discharged 22.2.1919
15/969
15/970 WHITAKER, Sergeant John discharged 16.3.1919
15/971 WHIT AKER, Sergeant Samuel killed in action 3.5.1917
15/972 WHITAKER, Private Ralph discharged 5.3.1919
15/973 WHITELEY, Private John Ramsden commissioned W Riding 26.3.1918
15/974 WHITEHEAD, Private A.
15/975 WHITELEY, Lance-Corporal Leonard Ratcliffe presumed dead 1.7.1916
15/976 WHITAKER, Private Norman no overseas service, discharged 392 (XVI) 28.10.1915
15/977
15/978 WHITWORTH, Private George Stewart served with 9th & 1st Bns, discharged 6.3.1919
15/979 WICE, Private Herbert George served with 1 /6th Bn, discharged 24.1.1919
15/980 WILKINSON, Corporal Edgar discharged 9.2.1919
15/981
15/982 WILKINSON, Lance-Corporal Gerald killed in action 1.7.1916
15/983 WILKINSON, Acting Corporal Joseph Henry discharged 13.3.1919
15/984 WILKINSON, Private Reginald presumed dead 1.7.1916
15/985
15/986
15/987 WILLIAMS, Private E.O.
15/988 WILSON, Private Frank Norman Emmett killed in action 1.7.1916
15/989 WILSON, Private F.
15/990 WILSON, Private George deceased 30.9.1917
15/991 WILSON, Private George Arthur discharged 392 (XVI) 5.12.1917
15/992 WILSON, Private Herbert killed in action 22.5.1916
15/993 WILSON, Private John discharged 392 (XVI) 30.7.1916
15/994
15/995 WILSON, WO I William, MC discharged 13.2.1919
15/996 WILTON, Private Edward discharged 3.4.1919
15/997 WINCH, Lance-Corporal Arthur killed in action 1.7.1916
15/998
15/999 WINTLE, Private Edward Collingwood accidentally killed 9.2.1916

15/1000 WISSLER, Lance-Corporal Max Taylor presumed dead 1.7.1916

15/1001 WITHELL, Private Walter discharged 392 (XVI) 25.11.1916

15/1002 WITNEY, Acting WO II Harry commissioned West Yorks 25.6.1918

15/1003 WOFFENDEN, Private Edward killed in action 3.5.1917

15/1004 WORBOYS, Private James discharged 392 (XVI) 21.3.1917

15/1005 WORBOYS, Private Stanley discharged 392 (XVI) 6.11.1917

15/1006

15/1007

15/1008 WOOD, Sergeant Arthur Edward died of wounds 15.4.1918

15/1009 WOOD, Private Bertram killed in action 1.7.1916

15/1010

15/1011 WOOD, Private Benjamin Frederick presumed dead 1.7.1916

15/1012

15/1013 WOOD, Private Frederick William killed in action 1.7.1916

15/1014

15/1015 WOOD, Corporal John Arthur discharged 392 (XVI) 26.4.1918

15/1016 WOOD, Lance-Corporal M.

15/1017 WOOD, Private Robert died of wounds 2.7.1916

15/1018 WOODCOCK, Lance-Corporal Crossley Ainsworth discharged 25.1.1919

15/1019

15/1020

15/1021 WRIGHT, Private Frank discharged 392 (XVI) 14.8.1916

15/1022

15/1023

15/1024 YEADON, Private John transferred to RAMC

15/1025 EDDISON, Private James served with 11th Bn, died of wounds 13.7.1916

15/1026 CRANAGE, Sergeant Frank no overseas service, discharged 392 (XVI) 12.5.1916

15/1027 MOSSOP, Sergeant Matthew Hudson, MM killed in action 1.7.1916

15/1028

15/1029 BRUERTON, Sergeant Harry discharged 15.2.1919

15/1030

15/1031

15/1032 PRESTON, Private Harold discharged 6.4.1919

15/1033

15/1034

15/1035 JACKMAN, WO II Harry commissioned RE 17.11.1917

15/1036

15/1037

15/1038 JONES, Private Thomas Evans discharged 2.3.1919

15/1039 SHARPE, Private Frank presumed dead 1.7.1916

15/1040 JACKSON, Sergeant Harold commissioned W Yorks 28.5.1918

15/1041

15/1042

15/1043

15/1044 BRIGGS, Private A.

15/1045 BLAND, Acting Sergeant Robert killed in action 1.7.1916

15/1046

15/1047

15/1048 HEMINGWAY, Colour-Sergeant Harold discharged 22.2.1919

15/1049

15/1050 JONES, Lance-Corporal David John presumed dead 3.5.1917

15/1051

15/1052

15/1053 BRIGGS, Private R.

15/1054 BEECROFT, Lance-Corporal Thomas discharged 392 (XVI)7.3.1917

15/1055 ARMITAGE, Private Wm. Arthur commissioned 3rd W Yorks 28.2.1917

15/1056

15/1057 WEST, Private V.

15/1058 JOHNSON, Private Charles Howard presumed dead 1.7.1916

15/1059 ATKINSON, Lance-Corporal George Wm killed in action 1.7.1916

15/1060 WOOD, Private C.

15/1061 CULLINGWORTH, Private Harold commissioned R Lancs 28.8.1917

15/1062 WALDEGRAVE, Lance-Corporal Wm Henry no overseas service, discharged 392 (XVI) 14.1.1916

15/1063 PARK, Private James Chalmers commissioned W Yorks 29.5.1917

15/1064 TUCKER, Private Frederick Edmundson killed in action 1.7.1916

15/1065

15/1066 TINSDALE, Private Fred discharged 392 (XVI) 28.11.1917

15/1067 HOLT, Lance-Corporal William presumed dead 3.5.1917

15/1068

15/1069

15/1070 SCOTT, Lance-Corporal John Edwin killed inaction 1.7.1916

15/1071 PRESTON, WOI Henry killed in action 1.7.1916

15/1072 HINCHLIFFE, Lance-Corporal George Wm. commissioned W Yorks 28.3.1917, died of wounds 26.6.1918

15/1073 WOOD, Private Godfrey commissioned RE 2.11.1918

15/1074

15/1075 CHEESBROUGH, Acting Lance-Corporal Harold commissioned 52 W Yorks 29.1.1918

15/1076

15/1077 CUNDILL, Private Robert Percy commissioned N Fusiliers 25.4.1917

15/1078 ROSS, Private John Popham discharged 392 (XVI) 15.1.1918

15/1079

15/1080 ATACK, Lance-Corporal James discharged 392 (XVI) 11.5.1918

15/1081 SUMMERSGILL, Private A. E.

15/1082 HARGREAVES, Private Herbert discharged 28.2.1919

15/1083 NELSON, Sergeant Arthur Lumley died of wounds 28.7.1918

15/1084

15/1085 TUKE, Private Harold discharged 23.7.1919

15/1086 CALVERLEY, Private Tom presumed dead 1.7.1916

15/1087

15/1088 HIRST, Private Clifford died of wounds 8.7.1916

15/1089 WEALTHALL, Acting Colour-Sergeant Alfred discharged 15.2.1919

15/1090 MANN, Private A.

15/1091 PICKARD, Private Joseph Raymond commissioned 3 Y&L 28.3.1917

15/1092 DYSON, Private H.A.

15/1093 BALME, Private John Edwin died of wounds 8.7.1916

15/1094 PICKUP, Private Fred Herbert discharged 392 (XVI) 7.11.1917, re-enlisted RASC 25.8.1919

15/1095 HARRISON, Private Eric John commissioned Yorks Regt 29.5.1917

15/1096 SHEPPARD, Corporal Robert Wickham, MM presumed dead 27.3.1918

15/1097 MOUNTAIN, Private Hubert discharged 27.3.1919

15/1098 FOX, Private Arthur Fitton commissioned N Fusiliers 4.10.1918

15/1099 WILD, Private F.

15/1100 BOOTH, Private Harry Dawson discharged 392 (XVI) 13.10.1917

15/1101 PLACE, Lance-Corporal Thomas Hinsley discharged 13.1.1919

15/1102 RAMSDEN, Private Harold killed in action 20.8.1916

15/1103 GAUNT, Private Edgar discharged 27.3.1919

15/1104 MELLOR, Sergeant Harry presumed dead 3.5.1917

15/1105 HUGHES, Private Sydney Noel commissioned in W Yorks 28.3.1917

15/1106 QUIGLEY, Corporal Isaac killed in action 1.7.1916

15/1107 POSKITT, Private John Rowland died of wounds 16.7.1916

15/1108 SMITH, Private Sidney Arthur discharged 31.3.1919

15/1109 WAINMAN, Private John discharged 31.3.1919

15/1110 CRYER, Private Cyril Charles

15/1111 BENSON, Private C.H.

15/1112 THOMPSON, Private George discharged 12.3.1919

15/1113 OYSTON, Private Tom presumed dead 1.7.1916

15/1114 SPENCER, Private G.

15/1115 PANTHER, Private Horace presumed dead 1.7.1916

15/1116

15/1117 MOORBY, Private Robert presumed dead 3.5.1917

15/1118

15/1119

15/1120 BROOK, Private H.W.

15/1121 CAWOOD, Private Fred killed in action 1.7.1916

15/1122 HOLMES, Private Rennard Leuty presumed dead 1.7.1916

15/1123 MARSTON, Private C.

15/1124

15/1125 LAWLOR, Private S.

15/1126 ATKINSON, Private Clifford discharged 392 (XVI) 18.10.1918

15/1127

15/1128 HODGSON, Lance-Corporal Harold discharged 15.3.1919

15/1129 LEEMING, Private John Wm. discharged 22.3.1919

15/1130 WIGGLESWORTH, Private Walter commissioned MGC 28.5.1917

15/1131

15/1132 HARPER, Lance-Corporal Frederick Wm. commissioned R Irish Fus 28.8.1917

15/1133 TURNER, Private R.

15/1134

15/1135

15/1136 MOSS, Private W.H

15/1137 BINNS, Private Arthur, MM discharged 26.2.1919

15/1138 BINNS, Private T.W.

15/1139 BROWN, Lance-Corporal Harold presumed dead 3.5.1917

15/1140 THOMPSON, Private Gibson discharged 13.3.1919

15/1141 COOK, Corporal Percy killed in action 1.7.1916

15/1142 SANDLAND, Sergeant Harry discharged 14.2.1919

15/1143 CONYERS, Private Joseph discharged 25.1.1919

15/1144 GITTUS, Private William died of wounds 11.7.1916

15/1145

15/1146 SCOTT, Private Clyde discharged 17.3.1919

15/1147 MEADOWS, Private Sydney Robert discharged 14.2.1919

15/1148 MINSHULL, Private George Henry discharged 392 (XVI) 7.12.1916

15/1149 WATSON, Private W.

15/1150 SLATER, Private Francis served with 5th Bn, discharged 392 (XVI) 23.6.1917

15/1151 HAIGH, Private N.

15/1152

15/1153 BOWRAN, Private Alfred discharged 392 (XVI) 17.10.1917

15/1154 BRIGGS, Private James Kitson discharged 8.4.1919

15/1155 BROOKSBANK, Private James Clifton discharged 7.3.1919

15/1156 BROOKSBANK, Private Vincent discharged 27.3.1919

15/1157 BYWOOD, Private Gabriel discharged 7.3.1919

15/1158 CARTER, Private Wm. Alfred discharged 12.2.1919

15/1159 DAVIDSON, Private Arthur Jones discharged 392 (XVI) 30.11.1917

15/1160 FLOWER, Private Percie no overseas service, discharged 392 (XVI) 28.4.1916

15/1161 HALL, Private William killed in action 1.7.1916

15/1162 INGHAM, Private Ernest discharged 392 (XVI) 27.6.1917

15/1163 IRWIN, Private A.

15/1164 JOHNSON, Acting Sergeant Percy Samson, MM discharged 15.3.1919

15/1165 MILNER, Lance-Corporal George commissioned Y &L 26.2.1918

15/1166 MYERS, Private H.D.

15/1167 POLLARD, Private Walter Bayldon discharged 392 (XVI) 27.10.1916

15/1168 RATHBONE, Lance-Corporal John Henry Hart discharged 1.5.1919

15/1169

15/1170 SOAR, Private H.

15/1171 STOCKWELL, Private Albert Edward presumed dead 1.7.1916

15/1172 STRINGER, Private O.

15/1173 SWABEY, Private Edmund Charles commissioned W Yorks 4.2.1919

15/1174 SUTTON, Private Reginald discharged 17.3.1919

15/1175 THOMPSON, Private Herbert discharged 10.4.1919

15/1176 GILL, Private John Henry killed in action with 9th Bn, 28.8.1917

15/1177 ELLA, Private Stanley discharged 28.3.1919

15/1178 BLACKBURN, Private Joseph no overseas service, discharged 392 (XVI) 7.6.1916

15/1179 JOHNSTONE, Lance-Corporal Ernest discharged 20.3.1919

15/1180 CLARKE, Private Robert Little presumed dead 1.7.1916

15/1181 STEEL, Private John Robert Arthur presumed dead 1.7.1916
15/1182
15/1183 CURTIS, Private G.E.
15/1184 COWLING, Private William killed in action 1.7.1916
15/1185 COLE, Private George Clifford presumed dead 1.7.1916
15/1186 ATKINSON, Private Sydney commissioned W Yorks 25.4.1917
15/1187 WALTON, Private A.H.
15/1188 MELLOR, Corporal Joseph Cecil discharged 6.3.1919
15/1189 WEBSTER, Lance-Corporal George Edward commissioned W Riding 30.4.1918
15/1190
15/1191 HIRST, Private D.G.
15/1192 ACKROYD, Private J.W.
15/1193 HARKER, Private J.N.
15/1194 WILKINSON, Lance-Corporal William died of wounds 22.5.1916
15/1195 WILKINSON, Lance-Corporal Cecil discharged 17.4.1919
15/1196 ROBERTS, Private Arthur commissioned DLI 30.10.1917
15/1197 SPENCE, Private Ernest discharged 392 (XVI) 26.12.1917
15/1198 WRIGHT, Private J.
15/1199
15/1200 JONES, Corporal Henry Roland discharged 27.3.1919
15/1201 BENNETT, Private Frederick George killed in action 1.7.1916
15/1202 ALLAN, Private H.
15/1203 SMITH, Private C.W.
15/1204 JACKSON, Private Fred killed in action 1.7.1916
15/1205 NICHOLSON, Private James Wilfred discharged 392 (XVI) 15.9.1917
15/1206
15/1207 DRINKWATER, Sergeant Harry commissioned 3 Yorks 28.8.1917
15/1208 HEY, Private Alan Marsden discharged 27.3.1919
15/1209 ODDY, Corporal George Edward discharged 5.2.1919
15/1210 PARKER, Private Ben Thornton presumed dead 1.7.1916
15/1211
15/1212 NELSON, Private Arthur discharged 392 (XVI) 26.12.1917
15/1213 BLACKBURN, Private Charles Hodgson discharged 392 (XVI) 28.8.1917
15/1214 WAIT, Private Thomas killed in action 21.7.1916
15/1215 KLOUMAN, Private Gerhard Arnulf killed in action 1.7.1916
15/1216 WILSON, Lance-Corporal Charles Arthur discharged 12.3.1919
15/1217 EVANS, Acting Corporal Clifford discharged 25.4.1919
15/1218 BATESON, Private G.
15/1219 BATEMAN, Private S.
15/1220 GRANT, Private Horace discharged 7.2.1919
15/1221 RHODES, Private Harry discharged 392 (XVI) 30.4.1918
15/1222 NAPPER, Private Oswald John discharged 392 (XVI) 19.11.1916
15/1223 ROCHFORD, Lance-Corporal John discharged 14.2.1919
15/1224 APPLEBY, Private Wm. Albert discharged 12.3.1919
15/1225 STILLWELL, Private Clifford killed in action 6.6.1916
15/1226 TODD, Lance-Corporal John Edward, MM discharged 1.4.1919

15/1227 DALGOUTTE, Private Victor Douglas commissioned 25.9.1917

15/1228 RAYNER, Private H.

15/1229 GOTT, Acting Corporal Wilfred discharged 7.2.1919

15/1230 SEWELL, Private William discharged 392 (XVI) 25.8.1917

15/1231 SHAW, Private Harold commissioned W Yorks 25.4.1917

15/1232 BODDY, Acting Corporal Richard Henry discharged 13.3.1919

15/1233 BELL, Private Robert Norman transferred to Royal Flying Corps

15/1234 LARGE, Private Albert discharged 12.2.1919

15/1235 GREAVES, Lance-Corporal George Edward Spencer commissioned RE 30.9.1917

15/1236 BARKER, Private Sidney presumed dead 1.7.1916

15/1237 LANGSTAFF, Private Clifford presumed dead 1.7.1916

15/1238 GILL, Lance-Sergeant Bernard died of wounds 25.3.1918

15/1239 WORSNOP, Private C.

15/1240 FOXCROFT, Private Harold discharged 13.6.1919

15/1241

15/1242 BENN, Private Alan discharged 29.3.1919

15/1243 KIRK, Private John Robert presumed dead 3.5.1917

15/1244 BRISTOW WO II, Edmund presumed dead 12.4.1918

15/1245

15/1246 MAGUIRE, Private Philip discharged 392 (XVI) 11.4.1919

15/1247 FIRTH, Private William discharged 392 (XVI) 11.3.1919

15/1248 STEAD, Private Fred discharged 392 (XVI) 14.6.1917

15/1249 FOX, Private A.

15/1250 LINSLEY, Private Douglas Gascoine presumed dead 3.5.1917

15/1251 POPPLETON, Lance-Corporal Burton deceased 14.8.1918

15/1252 DOLPHIN, Private Arthur discharged 27.3.1919

15/1253 BELL, Corporal Robert Norman commissioned RFC 25.9.1917

15/1254 HALL, Corporal Robert George discharged 392 (XVI) 12.10.1918

15/1255 HILL, Private J.H.

15/1256

15/1257 NESBITT, Private J.J.

15/1258 CLARKSON, Private G.W.

15/1259 BOOTH, Acting Corporal Leonard Holgate discharged 5.2.1919

15/1260 CLARKE, Private Cyril discharged 392 (XVI) 17.6.1918

15/1261 WOODS, Private Hugh killed in action 1.7.1916

15/1262

15/1263 KITCHING, Private William discharged 17.3.1919

15/1264 HUTCHINSON, Private Tom presumed dead 1.7.1916

15/1265 LACY, Private G.W.

15/1266 EWINGTON, Private Robert discharged 13.4.1919

15/1267 ANDREW, Private Wm. Frederick discharged 392 (XVI) 2.1.1917

15/1268 RADFORD, Private William H. transferred to Military Foot Police

15/1269 HARDWICK, Lance-Corporal Wm. Cyril served with 11,10 & 18Bns, killed in action 3.5.1917

15/1270 STENDELL, Private George Frederick presumed dead 1.7.1916

15/1271 BROOK, Private John George killed in action 1.7.1916

15/1272 VAILE, WO II Joseph died of wounds5.7.1916
15/1273 PHILLIPS, Private George Geoffrey presumed dead 1.7.1916
15/1274
15/1275 FLETCHER, Private Stanley Pickup presumed dead 1.7.1916
15/1276 GROCOCK, Private Lance discharged 392 (XVI) 6.11.1917
15/1277 WESTERMAN, Private Burnett presumed dead 3.5.1917
15/1278 SWINDELLS, Private Thomas presumed dead 1.7.1916
15/1279 HIRST, Lance-Sergeant Thomas Lodge discharged 29.1.1919
15/1280
15/1281 HAYHURST, Private John killed in action 22.5.1916
15/1282 AXE, Private Arthur Cecil killed in action 1.7.1916
15/1283
15/1284 EVANS, Private H.
15/1285
15/1298 FENBY, Private Thomas Paul served with 1st Bn, killed in action 16.5.1916
15/1299 LANE, Private George Edward discharged 27.3.1919
15/1300 ROBSON, Private George MM killed in action 23.11.1916
15/1301
15/1302 HIRST, Private Albert Victor deceased 13.5.1917
15/1303
15/1304 MONGER, Private Jack discharged 392 (XVI) 10.3.1917
15/1305 MYERS, Private W.
15/1306 SHAW, Private William presumed dead 1.7.1916
15/1307 SLOAN, Private Alexander discharged 392 (XVI) 27.6.1917
15/1308 HORNSEY, Sergeant John Alfred killed in action 18.5.1917
15/1309 PEEL, Lance-Corporal Clifford presumed dead 1.7.1916
15/1310
15/1311 GIBSON, Private Norman killed in action 22.4.1918
15/1312 WATMOUGH, Private William discharged 392 (XVI) 6.10.1916
15/1313 ASHWORTH, Private Herbert presumed dead 1.7.1916
15/1314 AVEYARD, Private Charles William discharged 392 (XVI) 6.11.1917
15/1315 BASTOW, Private Sydney no overseas service, discharged 392 (XVI) 8.1.1916
15/1316 BATEMAN, Acting Lance-Sergeant Edward discharged 15.2.1919
15/1317 BURROW, Private Wilfred presumed dead 1.7.1916
15/1318
15/1319 ECCLES, Private Charles no overseas service, discharged 392 (XVI) 21.4.1916
15/1320 FEWSTER, Private Gordon discharged 21.2.1919
15/1321 JACKSON, Acting Sergeant Herbert, MM
15/1322
15/1323 LOUGHTON, Private George Wm. killed in action 1.7.1916
15/1324 NAYLOR, Private J.F.
15/1325 ROGERSON, Private William discharged 1.7.1919
15/1326 SHAW, Private Horatio killed in action 1.7.1916
15/1327 STEWART, Private William presumed dead 1.7.1916
15/1328 WOOD, Private Percy presumed dead 1.7.1916
15/1329

15/1330 BETTS, Acting Corporal Herbert discharged 392 (XVI) 2.4.1919
15/1331 CAMPLEMAN, Private Charles presumed dead 1.7.1916
15/1332 GOLDSBROUGH, Private Wilfred killed in action 1.7.1916
15/1333 GOWER, Private Sidney presumed dead 1.7.1916
15/1334 MANN, Private H.
15/1335 WALKER, Private W.
15/1336 WHEATLEY, Private Harold killed in action 1.7.1916
15/1337 BUXTON, Private Samuel Laurence killed in action 1.7.1916
15/1338 BEAUMONT, Private T.
15/1339
15/1340 McCORMACK, Corporal Gerald discharged 27.3.1919
15/1341 McGREGOR, Private Charles killed in action 9.10.1917
15/1342
15/1343
15/1344
15/1345
15/1346
15/1347 TEMPERTON, Private W.
15/1348 TAYLOR, Private Herbert served with 12th Bn, discharged 392 (XVI) 5.8.1917
15/1349 SWETMAN, Lance-Corporal Arthur Henry discharged 15.3.1919
15/1350 SHAW, Private William discharged 12.3.1919
15/1351 SAYNOR, Lance-Corporal William killed in action 1.7.1916
15/1352 RAWLING, Private Fred discharged 10.4.1919
15/1353
15/1354 PICKLES, Private W.B.
15/1355 PAYNE, Private James Victor killed in action 1.9.1916
15/1356 PARKIN, Private C.
15/1357
15/1358
15/1359 RAMSDEN, Private Walter S. discharged 392 (XVI)
15/1360 FOWLER, Lance-Corporal Herbert killed in action 19.7.1918
15/1361 PANNETT, Private Arthur presumed dead 3.5.1917
15/1362 LUMB, Private Norman discharged 10.4.1919
15/1363 DUNN, Private Ernest discharged 392 (XVI) 1.1.1917
15/1364
15/1365
15/1366 JOHNSON, Private Vernon killed in action 1.7.1916
15/1367
15/1368
15/1369 HEPWORTH, Private Alfred discharged 24.3.1919
15/1370 HEMMINGWAY, Acting Sergeant Arthur killed in action 28.6.1918
15/1371
15/1372 HARDCASTLE, Private John Thomas died of wounds 26.5.1916
15/1373
15/1374 DENNI SON, Private Austin Wm. killed in action 5.12.1916
15/1375

15/1376 CRAWSHAW, Sergeant Percy served with 12, 1 & 10Bns, discharged 14.3.1919
15/1377
15/1378 COCKBURN, Private Henry Andrew discharged 392 (XVI)10.1.1918
15/1379 BURTON, Corporal Charles Richard discharged 392 (XVI)4.1.1917
15/1380 BROWNING, Private John Haydn discharged 18.3.1919
15/1381 BROWNING, Corporal Harry Percival discharged 20.3.1919
15/1382 BOOT, Private Charles no overseas service, discharged 392 (XVI) 21.4.1916
15/1383 BENNETT, Corporal John commissioned 5 W Yorks 29.1.1918
15/1384 APPLEYARD, Private P.
15/1385 ABBOTT, Private George deceased 9.7.1916
15/1386 MASON, Private John Eugene Joseph discharged 10.4.1919
15/1387 BEST, Corporal Clifford, MM served with 1st Bn, discharged 26.4.1919
15/1388
15/1389 BULLOCH, Lance-Sergeant Alexander served with 1st Bn, commissioned 3 W Yorks 29.1.1918
15/1390 BYROM, Private John Edmund discharged 392 (XVI) 9.1.1918
15/1391
15/1392
15/1393 SMITH, Private L.
15/1394
15/1395
15/1396
15/1397
15/1398 BADER, Private Leonard discharged 6.3.1919
15/1399 BATLEY, Acting Lance-Corporal George Clifford presumed dead 3.5.1917
15/1400
15/1401 BUTLER, Private Harry presumed dead 2.5.1917
15/1402 CRONE, Private John no overseas service, discharged 392 (XVI) 9.5.1917
15/1403 HOLDSWORTH, Corporal Charles discharged 3.4.1919
15/1404
15/1405 MOODY, Private C.
15/1406 MORTIMER, Sergeant Albert Victor discharged 15.2.1919
15/1407
15/1408 NOWELL, Private Harold served with 1st Bn, discharged 392 (XVI) 29.12.1917
15/1409
15/1410
15/1411
15/1412
15/1413
15/1414 WOOD, Private Godfrey killed in action 1.7.1916
15/1415 HARRISON, Private Evelyn Clifford killed in action 22.5.1916
15/1416
15/1417 ALNWICK, Private George killed in action 1.7.1916
15/1418
15/1419 BOOKER, Private Henry discharged 16.3.1919
15/1420

15/1421 BULLIVANT, Private Harry discharged 20.3.1919
15/1422
15/1423 ELLIOT, Private Harry no overseas service, discharged 392 (XVI) 19.2.1916
15/1424
15/1425 GRIFFITHS, Private Harold killed in action 20.8.1916
15/1426
15/1427 LINDLEY, Private Ernest discharged 22.2.1919
15/1428 PANNETT, Lance-Corporal Arthur served with 1st Bn, killed in action 12.10.1916
15/1429
15/1430 PINNINGTON, Private James served with 9 & 1st Bns, discharged 392 (XVI) 13.6.1919
15/1431 WALKER, Private Frederick discharged 25.3.1919
15/1432 WALTER, Corporal Maurice served with 1st Bn, deceased21.12.1918
15/1433
15/1434
15/1435
15/1436
15/1437 JULIAN, Sergeant William discharged 14.3.1919
15/1438 CAMMIDGE, Private Harry discharged 392 (XVI) 22.8.1917
15/1439
15/1440 WILKES, Private Fred presumed dead 1.7.1916
15/1441 BONNER, Private Albert discharged 392 (XVI) 12.7.1917
15/1442
15/1443 BROOKE, Sergeant Richard discharged 21.2.1919
15/1444 BROWN, Private Lawrence killed in action 1.7.1916
15/1445
15/1446 CAPES, Acting Corporal Harry discharged 3.2.1919
15/1447
15/1448
15/1449 DOCKRAY, Private Leonard served with 1st Bn, discharged 19.6.1919
15/1450
15/1451
15/1452 FISHER, Private Robert Mitchell served with 1st Bn, discharged 392 (XVI) 8.8.1917
15/1453 GALL, Private John William served with 1 & 11 Bns, discharged 13.3.1919
15/1454 GOMERSAL, Sergeant George discharged 14.3.1919
15/1455 GOODER, Private Byron discharged 16.3.1919
15/1456 GOODER, Private George drafted to 1st Bn then 15th, discharged 10.4.1919
15/1457
15/1458
15/1459 HEYWOOD, Private Edwin discharged 392 (XVI) 11.1.1918
15/1460
15/1461 JOHNSON, Private Alfred discharged 392 (XVI) 6.9.1919
15/1462
15/1463
15/1464
15/1465
15/1466 PHILLIPS, Private Wm. Henry served with 11th bn, presumed dead 7.10.1916

15/1467
15/1468
15/1469 RAMSDEN, Private John Clark no overseas service, discharged 392 (XVI) 5.5.1916
15/1470
15/1471 ROBINSON, Private A.
15/1472 SAUNDERS, Private Harold Macleod commissioned E Lancs 25.4.1917
15/1473 SENIOR, Lance-Corporal Harry Vincent served with 1st Bn. discharged 16.4.1919
15/1474 TAYLOR, Private Lawrence served with 11 then 15/17Bn, deceased 11.8.1918
15/1475 THOMPSON, Private Frank Hodgson served with 11Bn, discharged 392 (XVI) 22.6.1917
15/1476
15/1477
15/1478 TOMLINSON, Private Harry served with 11 & 10 Bns, discharged 24.1.1919
15/1479
15/1480 WEST, Private Tom no overseas service, discharged 392 (XVI) 5.5.1916
15/1481
15/1482
15/1483 WILLIAMS, Sergeant John Richard, MM served with 1st Bn. discharged 10.4.1919
15/1484
15/1485
15/1486
15/1487
15/1488
15/1489 HILL, Lance-Corporal Herbert Archer died of wounds 24.9.1916
15/1490 HIRST, Private George presumed dead 1.7.1916
15/1491
15/1492
15/1493 WHITLEY, Private George Arthur presumed dead 1.7.1916
15/1494 JONES, Private Sidney served with 1st Bn. discharged 392 (XVI) 17.9.1917
15/1495
15/1496 HILL, Private Alfred presumed dead 3.5.1917
15/1497 LANGSTAFF, Private Francis
15/1498
15/1499 SUTTON, Private L. killed in action 1.7.1916
15/1500
15/1501
15/1502
15/1503
15/1504
15/1505
15/1506
15/1507
15/1508
15/1509
15/1510
15/1511

15/1512
15/1513
15/1514
15/1515
15/1516
15/1517
15/1518
15/1519
15/1520
15/1521
15/1522
15/1523
15/1524
15/1525
15/1526
15/1527
15/1528
15/1529
15/1530
15/1531 LEE, Private Lawrence discharged 3.4.1919
15/1532
15/1533 LONG, Private Harry discharged 3.4.1919
15/1534
15/1535 MANN, Private John no overseas service, discharged 392 (XVI) 28.4.1916
15/1536 MARSHALL, Sergeant Harold, DCM served with 11th Bn,discharged 6.5.1919
15/1537
15/1538 MORRIS, Private Thomas Milner served with 11th Bn, killed in action 19.9.1917
15/1539
15/1540 PLOWMAN, Private Arthur presumed dead 1.7.1916
15/1541 POTTER, Private Samuel discharged 28.3.1919
15/1542
15/1543 REDHEAD, Private Robert served with 11th Bn, killed in action 4.7.1916
15/1544
15/1545 SCAWBORD, Private Tom killed in action 1.7.1916
15/1546
15/1547 STONES, Private Leonard served with 11th Bn, discharged 392 (XVI) 4.9.1917
15/1548
15/1549 THOMAS, Private Harold served with 1st Bn, killed in action 27.5.1916
15/1550 UNDERWOOD, Private Harry discharged 26.3.1919
15/1551 VARLEY, Private Joseph Worsnop served with 1st Bn, discharged 27.2.1919
15/1552 GARSIDE, Private Clarence discharged 392 (XVI)
15/1553 WILCOCK, Private Julius discharged 392 (XVI) 30.8.1918
15/1554
15/1555
15/1556
15/1557

15/1558
15/1559
15/1560 DOBSON, Private Tom served with 1st Bn, discharged 10.4.1919
15/1561
15/1562
15/1563 PRESTON, Private Arthur killed in action 21.9.1916
15/1564
15/1565
15/1566
15/1567
15/1568 SHAW, Private Alfred Houlden presumed dead 1.7.1916
15/1569 YOUHILL, Sergeant Herbert discharged 392 (XVI) 15.3.1918
15/1570 ALLEN, Private Harold killed in action 1.7.1916
15/1571 ASQUITH, Private
15/1572
15/1573
15/1574
15/1575
15/1576
15/1577
15/1578
15/1579
15/1580
15/1581
15/1582 CULPAN, Lance-Corporal Benjamin presumed dead 3.5.1917
15/1583 COLLIER, Corporal Edward killed in action 26.10.1916
15/1584 CALDERHEAD, Private Clifford killed in action 1.7.1916
15/1585
15/1586
15/1587
15/1588
15/1589 CROOK, Private Harry served with 1st Bn, presumed dead 21.3.1916
15/1590
15/1591 CHARLESWORTH, Private Edmund no overseas service, discharged 392 (XVI) 21.4.1916
15/1592 DAVISON, Private Christopher killed in action 1.7.1916
15/1593 DENT, Private William deceased 9.7.1916
15/1594
15/1595
15/1596
15/1597
15/1598
15/1599
15/1600
15/1601 GREAVES, Private Charles Galloway killed in action 1.7.1916
15/1602 GALLOWAY, Private Alfred served with 16th Bn, discharged 19.3.1919

15/1603
15/1604
15/1605 GREEN, Private Joseph Wood discharged 392 (XVI) 5.1.1918
15/1606
15/1607
15/1608
15/1609
15/1610 HUTCHINSON, Private Leonard served with 18th & 1st Bns, discharged 2.4.19
15/1611
15/1612 JUBB, Private Joseph Sheard died of wounds 2.8.1916
15/1613
15/1614 KNOWLES, Private Albert served with 1st, 10th & 11th Bns, died of wounds 18.7.1917
15/1615
15/1616 LEUCHTERS, Private Douglas served with 11th Bn, killed in action 10.7.1916
15/1617
15/1618
15/1619 MEEGAN, Private William Arthur no overseas service, discharged 392 (XVI) 25.1.1916
15/1620 MATTHEWS, Private Richard killed in action 1.7.1916
15/1621
15/1622 PAWSON, Private Reginald, MM served with 1/6th Bn, discharged 23.2.1919
15/1623 PEAKMAN, Private Sydney discharged 25.2.1919
15/1624 PARKIN, Private William presumed dead 3.5.1917
15/1625
15/1626
15/1627
15/1628 SHARP, Private Norman Henry no overseas service, discharged 392 (XVI) 21.4.1916
15/1629 SUGDEN, Private William Octavius discharged 13.6.1919
15/1630
15/1631
15/1632 SMITH, Private William no overseas service, discharged 392 (XVI) 21.6.1915
15/1633
15/1634
15/1635
15/1636
15/1637
15/1638
15/1639
15/1640 WILKINSON, Private Norman Benjamin discharged 392 (XVI) 8.10.1917
15/1641
15/1642
15/1643 WILCOCK, Private Harry no overseas service, discharged 392 (XVI) 6.8.1915
15/1644
15/1645 WEBSTER, Private James discharged 392 (XVI) 13.12.1917
15/1646
15/1647 ARMATAGE, Private Walter drafted to 1st Bn, then 15th, presumed dead 3.5.1917
15/1648

15/1649
15/1650
15/1651 ARNOLD, Corporal Harold served with 12th Bn, killed in action 28.9.1917
15/1652 ATKINSON, Private Edwin Darley deceased 30.11.1918
15/1653
15/1654 BRAYSHAW, Private Sam served with 1st Bn, discharged 7.3.1919
15/1655 PICKARD, Private E.
15/1656 TRUEMAN, Private Cyril deceased 1.7.1916
15/1657
15/1658 EALAND, Private James served with 16 & 2 Bns, killed in action 26.10.1916
15/1659 MASSEY, Private Joseph served with 1 & 9 Bns, discharged 7.3.1919
15/1660
15/1661
15/1662
15/1663
15/1664 MYERS, Corporal Edwin Fox served with 2/7 & 10 Bns, disch 392 (XVI) 14.6.1919
15/1665 LETCHFORD, Private John discharged 9.2.1919
15/1666
15/1667
15/1668
15/1669
15/1670 SYKES, Private Harry served with 1/8th Bn, resisted 19.1.1919
15/1671 GRASSBY, Private Wm. Henry presumed dead 1.7.1916
15/1672
15/1673 GAUNT, Private Charles Edward discharged 392 (XVI) 28.8.1916
15/1674 BECKTON, Private John killed in action 22.5.1916
15/1675 RICHARDSON, Private H.
15/1676
15/1677
15/1678
15/1679
15/1680 BYWOOD, Lance-Corporal Samuel served with 1st Bn, discharged 10.3.1919
15/1681 HEATON, Private Joseph Copley served with 12th Bn, killed in action 11.7.1916
15/1682
15/1683
15/1684
15/1685
15/1686 RAMSDEN, Private William served with 1st, 15/17, 2/7 & 1/7 Bns, discharged 392
      (XVI) 17.2.1919
15/1687
15/1688
15/1689
15/1690
15/1691
15/1692 OXLEY, Private Fred served with 1st Bn, discharged 7.2.1919
15/1693 STAINFORTH, Private Sydney died of wounds 11.6.1916

15/1694
15/1695
15/1696
15/1697 COULSON, Private Leonard served with 11th, 1st & 10 Bns, discharged 30.3.1919
15/1698
15/1699
15/1700
15/1701 RUDKIN, Private Willie served with 1st, 17 & 2/8 Bns, presumed dead 9.10.1917
15/1702 FOSSEY, Private Robert served with 1st Bn, died of wounds 22.5.1916
15/1703
15/1704 PERKINS, Private George Willie served with 1st, 2 & 10 Bns, disch 392 (XVI) 20.5.1918
15/1705
15/1706 HARDWICK, Acting Sergeant Sydney Prince discharged 1.3.1919
15/1707
15/1708
15/1709
15/1710
15/1711
15/1712
15/1713 THOMSON, Lance-Corporal James commissioned West Yorks 30.10.1917
15/1714 COATES, Private Gilbert discharged 392 (XVI) 27.2.1919
15/1715
15/1716 HUGHES, Lance-Corporal Thomas discharged 4.3.1919
15/1717
15/1718
15/1719
15/1720 AINSWORTH, Private J.
15/1721 BIRKS, Private Joseph discharged 392 (XVI) 29.12.1916
15/1722
15/1723
15/1724
15/1725 LACEY, Private Willie served with 1st, 17, 12 & 2/8 Bns, killed in action 27.11.1917
15/1726 TINDALL, Acting Sergeant Eric served with 16 & 15/17 Bns, discharged 27.3.1919
15/1727
15/1728
15/1729
15/1730
15/1731
15/1732
15/1733
15/1734
15/1735
15/1736
15/1737 RACE, Private William served with 11, 2/7, 1 & 1/5 Bns, killed in action 12.10.1918
15/1738
15/1739

15/1740
15/1741 HODGSON, Private Edwin served with 1 & 10 Bns, discharged 7.3.1919
15/1742 WHINCUP, Lance-Corporal John Henry served with 1 & 21 Bns, discharged 392 (XVI) 8.11.1917
15/1743 ISON, Private Edwin served with 1st Bn, commissioned W Riding 31.7.1917
15/1744 WEST, Acting Sergeant William Bruce, MM served with 2/7 & 1/8 Bns, discharged 16.3.1919
15/1745
15/1746
15/1747
15/1748
15/1749
15/1750 SUTCLIFFE, Private George served with 9th Bn, discharged 392 (XVI) 31.1.1919
15/1751
15/1752 DOBSON, Private Hamlet discharged 392 (XVI) 18.9.1918
15/1753
15/1754 HARRISON, Private Charles Wm. presumed dead 1.7.1916
15/1755 WHITLEY, Corporal John James served with 11th Bn, discharged 392 (XVI) 23.10.1919
15/1756
15/1757 PAUL, Private Thomas served with 1st Bn, died of wounds 22.9.1916
15/1758 TALBOT, Corporal Leonard served with 11th Bn, discharged 6.5.1919
15/1759 DUNHILL, Private Thomas served with 1st, 11 & 9 Bns, discharged 4.8.1919
15/1760
15/1761
15/1762
15/1763
15/1764
15/1765 SANDERS, Private James served with 1st Bn, killed inaction 13.10.1916
15/1766
15/1767 DEARDEN, Private Frank served with 11th & 2/8 Bns, killed in action 20.7.1918
15/1768
15/1769
15/1770
15/1771
15/1772 HITCHEN, Private Geoge Henry presumed dead 1.7.1916
15/1773 THOMPSON, Francis William served with 1st Bn, discharged 392 (XVI) 27.8.1916
15/1774
15/1775
15/1776 PADGETT, Private John Simpson served with 11th Bn, discharged 24.3.1919
15/1777
15/1778
15/1779 CAWOOD, Private Clifford Holdsworth served with 1st Bn, discharged 6.3.1919
15/1780 MURGATROYD, Private Frank served with 1st Bn, discharged 392 (XVI) 17.3.1919
15/1781
15/1782
15/1783 BARRETT, Lance-Corporal Herbert no overseas service, discharged 392 (XVI) 21.4.1916

15/1784 ILES, Private Horace killed in action 1.7.1916

15/1785 MILNER, Private John William presumed dead 1.7.1916

15/1786 FROBISHER, Corporal Albert died of wounds 22.8.1916

15/1787 ALDERSON, Private Cyril Laverack served with 1st Bn, killed in action 12.10.1916

15/1788

15/1789 DEMAINE, Sergeant William, MM discharged 31.3.1919

15/1790 TURNER, Private Bert presumed dead 1.7.1916

15/1791

15/1792

15/1793 WALKER, Private Frank served with 11th & 1/7 Bns, discharged 392 (XVI) 24.10.1918

15/1794 JOY, Private Walter served with 1st Bn, died of wounds 16.4.1917

15/1795 ROME, Private William served with 1/5th Bn, discharged 5.4.1919

15/1796 CROXFORD, Private Harry re-enlisted 13.1.1919

15/1797

15/1798

15/1799

15/1800 PINK, Private Harold served with 1st, 2/7 & 8 Bns, discharged 9.5.1919

15/1801 STANHOPE, Sergeant Clarence, DCM served with 1st Bn, discharged 5.4.1919

15/1802 GOUGH, Private Norman presumed dead 1.7.1916

15/1803 WOOD, Private Harry discharged 392 (XVI) 8.2.1918

15/1804

15/1805 HIGGINBOTTOM, Private Joseph Frederick killed in action 1.7.1916

15/1806

15/1807 ATKINSON, Private Albert served with 11th Bn, killed in action 10.7.1916

15/1808

15/1809

15/1810 WIGGLESWORTH, Lance-Corporal Esmond Arthur discharged 392 (XVI) 30.4.1919

15/1811

15/1812

15/1813 SMITH, Private G.M.

15/1814

15/1815 GRAY, Private Christopher served with 9th & 1 Bns, discharged 392 (XVI) 7.3.1919

15/1816

15/1817

15/1818 WALKER, Sergeant Adolphus served with 11th Bn, commissioned W Riding 3.7.1917

15/1819 FOSTER, Private John discharged 392 (XVI) 7.11.1917

15/1820 STOKES, Private Ernest no overseas service, discharged 392 (XVI) 21.4.1916

15/1821

15/1822 DAVEY, Lance-Corporal Percy attached 9 Cheshire & 2/7 W York, discharged 6.3.1919

15/1823

15/1824

15/1825

15/1826

15/1827 WILSON, Private Thomas Arthur discharged 392 (XVI) 12.10.1918

15/1828

15/1829 SKIRROW, Corporal William served with 1st Bn, discharged 392 (XVI) 29.6.1917

15/1830

15/1831
15/1832
15/1833
15/1834
15/1835
15/1836
15/1837 BIELBY, Corporal Percy served with 1st Bn, discharged 392 (XVI) 29.6.1917
15/1838 SWALLOW, Private Harold served with 1st Bn, discharged 392 (XVI) 4.12.1917
15/1839
15/1840
15/1841 WORSNOP, Acting Corporal Harry served with 16th & 11th Bns, discharged 3.5.1919
15/1842 STANSFIELD, Private Allen Firth presumed dead 1.7.1916
15/1843 GELDEART, Corporal Albert discharged 392 (XVI) 29.3.1917
15/1844
15/1845 HOLMES, Private Walter discharged 12.2.1919
15/1846
15/1847
15/1848
15/1849 SMITH, Private Stanley deceased 3.5.1917
15/1850
15/1851
15/1852
15/1853
15/1854
15/1855
15/1856 WILSON, Acting Corporal Norman commissioned 29.10.1918
15/1857 WARREN, Private Arthur presumed dead 1.7.1916
15/1858
15/1859 CHAMBERLAIN, Private Charles served with 11th Bn, discharged 392 (XVI) 7.5.1917
15/1860 WALKER, Private Oliver Benson presumed dead 1.7.1916
15/1861
15/1862 SLATER, Private Ben served with 1st Bn, discharged 29.4.1919
15/1863
15/1864
15/1865
15/1866
15/1867
15/1868 GARSIDE, Sergeant James discharged 392 (XVI) 17.1.1918
15/1869
15/1870
15/1871 ELLIOTT, Sergeant Joe discharged 392 (XVI) 25.2.1919
15/1872
15/1873
15/1874
15/1875
15/1876 REEKIE, Private Alexander served with 1st Bn, discharged 18.3.1919

15/1877 AMBLER, Private Charles attached 93rd Bde, discharged 26.6.1919
15/1878
15/1879 CROWTHER, Corporal Albert killed in action 19.7.1918
15/1880
15/1881 MELLARD, Acting Sergeant Richard Lawrence presumed dead 1.7.1916
15/1882
15/1883
15/1884 McDOWALL, Private Ivor discharged 15.3.1919
15/1885 RICHARDSON, Private David Wm. served with 1st Bn, discharged 392 (XVI) 15.1.1918
15/1886
15/1887 BLACK WELL, Private Harry served with 1st & 16th Bns, discharged 392 (XVI) 4.4.1917
15/1888
15/1889
15/1890
15/1891
15/1892
15/1893
15/1894
15/1895
15/1896
15/1897 MOORE, Private Clifford presumed dead 1.7.1916
15/1898 CLARKSON, Private Thomas died of wounds 12.7.1916
15/1899
15/1900 BLAKEY, Acting Sergeant Robert discharged 14.2.1919
15/1901 RHODES, Private Walter served with 1st, 2/7 & 11th Bns, died of wounds 4.11.1918
15/1902
15/1903
15/1904 SMITH, Sergeant Leighton commissioned 3rd York & Lancs 28.5.1918
15/1905
15/1906 NEWTON, Private Thomas presumed dead 1.7.1916
15/1907
15/1908 MANN, Private William Hodgson discharged 21.3.1919
15/1909
15/1910 MARSHALL, Lance-Corporal Charles Victor discharged 6.3.1919
15/1911
15/1912 PEACE, Private Harry discharged 3.4.1919
15/1913 GILBERT, Corporal James discharged 18.3.1919
15/1914 TAYLOR, Private Joseph Frederick discharged 392 (XVI) 12.10.1916
15/1915 WISE, Private George Ernest discharged 27.3.1919
15/1916 BONNER, Private Clifford Arthur discharged 19.3.1919
15/1917 ROSINDALE, Private Charles discharged 27.3.1919
15/1918 WILD, Private Walter
15/1919 SPINLE, Private John William discharged 14.2.1919
15/1920 GATEHOUSE, Private Harold discharged 3.4.1919

15/1921
15/1922
15/1923
15/1924 BURTON, Private Alfred discharged 28.3.1919
15/1925
15/1926
15/1927
15/1928
15/1929 STONES, Private Arthur served with 1st Bn, presumed dead 16.4.1917
15/1930 MAUDE, Private Donald Charles killed in action 1.7.1916
15/1931
15/1932
15/1933 PILKINGTON, Private A.
15/1934 HOLLAND, Private J.H.
15/1935 WILSON, Private Herbert discharged 392 (XVI) 5.10.1916
15/1936 SLATER, Private W.
15/1937
15/1938
15/1939 TEBAY, Private Ernest served with 1st Bn, discharged 392 (XVI) 29.12.1916
15/1940 SUNLEY, Private John discharged 392 (XVI) 20.12.1918
15/1941 MARKS, Private W.B.
15/1942
15/1943 FRIEDER, Private Percy discharged 392 (XVI) 10.11.1917
15/1944
15/1945 ELLIS, Private John presumed dead 3.5.1917
15/1946
15/1947 PICKARD, Private Private F.
15/1948 KYLE, Private Joseph discharged 23.3.1919
15/1949 HAYWARD, Private Walter discharged 3.4.1919
15/1950 HARDY, Sergeant Lawrence commissioned West Yorks 30.10.1917
15/1951 SHAW, Private John Jackson killed in action 2.5.1917
15/1952
15/1953 PILKINGTON, Private Arthur discharged 23.2.1919
15/1954 WOOD, Private Warrie Fawcett discharged 12.2.1919
15/1955 WHITELOCK, Private Percy Jarvis discharged 392 (XVI) 16.1.1918
15/1956 SEVILLE, Lance-Corporal Norman discharged 7.4.1919

Roll of Honour

This lists those men killed or died of wounds who joined the battalion after July 1915 and therefore did not have the '15' prefix regimental number. The men who enlisted before July 1915, and were killed or died of wounds, are listed in the Nominal Roll (Appendix I).

34185 ABRAHAMS, Corporal Myers killed in action 3.8.1917
59183 ACKROYD, Private Douglas killed in action 17.9.1918
41630 ACKROYD, Private Henry died 9.10.1918
60111 ADCOCK, Private Charles died of wounds 13.8.1918
62009 AGER, Private Walter killed in action 13.4.1918
24964 AINLEY, Private Harold died 26.5.1917
36818 ALDOUS, Private Frederick killed in action 16.6.1917
17/931 ALLEN, Lance-Corporal Willie killed in action 19.7.1918
49891 ANDERSON, Private Alfred died 27.9.1918
61584 ANDERSON, Private Frederick R. killed in action 12.4.1918
53367 ANTHONY, Private Harold killed in action 28.6.1918
33041 ARMITAGE, Private Ernest killed in action 8.11.1916
28779 ARMITAGE, Corporal George killed in action 27.3.1918
17/799 ARMITAGE, Private Robson died 22.4.1918
53826 ARMSTRONG, Private Harold died of wounds 30.8.1918
57878 ARROWSMITH, Private John W. died of wounds 7.10.1918
18/1238 ASTLE, Corporal William killed in action 19.7.1918
38831 ATKINSON, Private Stanley killed in action 15.10.1918
26286 ATKINSON, Private William A. killed in action 20.8.1916
62012 ATTY, Private James killed in action 12.4.1918
36941 AUDIN, Private Alfred killed in action 3.5.1917
53369 BAINES, Private Sydney killed in action 12.4.1918
12783 BAKER, Private John killed in action 24.3.1918
60708 BAKER, Private Norman killed in action 20.10.1918
40144 BARDSALL, Lance-Sergeant Thomas Z. died of wounds 23.10.1917
40524 BARRACLOUGH, Private Haydn killed in action 3.5.1917 3
3760 BATTY, Private Edgar killed in action 3.5.1917
61591 BAXENDALE, Private Philip killed in action 29.6.1918
41661 BEATTIE, Private Arthur B. died of wounds 26.10.1918
62020 BEATTIE, Private William killed in action 28.6.1918
41461 BEAUMONT, Private Ernest died 14.7.1918
40349 BEDDOW, Private George R.G. killed in action 3.5.1917

34450 BEDFORD, Private Alfred killed in action 3.5.1917
29199 BENN, Private James killed in action 3.5.1917
39660 BENNETT, Private William killed in action 23.5.1918
72561 BENTLEY, Private Joseph H. killed in action 19.7.1918
60646 BERNARD, Private William P. killed in action 17.9.1918
16/819 BERRY, Private Charles died of wounds 30.9.1918
41412 BERRY, Corporal Harry killed in action 29.3.1918
17/1565 BEST, Corporal Thomas E. killed in action 12.4.1918
62042 BETTS, Private Harry killed in action 12.4.1918
53354 BEXON, Private Alfred died of wounds 23.4.1918
28771 BICKERDIKE, Private John killed in action 29.9.1918
62039 BIRCH, Private Harry killed in action 12.4.1918
72562 BIRKENSHAW, Private Luke killed in action 28.6.1918
37786 BLACKER, Private Edward A. died 5.11.1918
27368 BLAZE, Private William killed in action 3.5.1917
42998 BLETCHER, Private John T. killed in action 27.3.1918
59025 BLUNT, Private Frederick killed in action 28.6.1918
38563 BODDY, Private James H.B. killed in action 3.5.1917
32180 BOLTON, Private Squire died of wounds 1.4.1918
40347 BOOKER, Private Charles A. killed in action 3.5.1917
40141 BOOTH, Lance-Corporal Walter killed in action 3.5.1917
236358 BOOTHBY, Private William L. killed in action 31.8.1918
62040 BOOTHMAN, Private Harry killed in action 12.4.1918
43355 BOWERS, Lance-Corporal Wilfred died of wounds 11.7.1918
61601 BOX, Private John S. killed in action 12.4.1918
42999 BOX, Private Matthew killed in action 29.9.1918
22121 BOYES, Private Walter died of wounds 24.6.1918
61776 BRAY, Corporal Henry A. killed in action 12.4.1918
62023 BRIDGETT, Private Samuel killed in action 12.4.1918
61605 BRIDGEWATER, Private William A. killed in action 19.7.1918
53379 BROUGH, Private Samuel killed in action 28.6.1918
38194 BROWN, Private Alfred killed in action 3.5.1917
61606 BROWN, Private Frederick killed in action 12.4.1918
53879 BROWN, Private George died 6.11.1918
25961 BROWN, Private William died of wounds 13.4.1918
25334 BRUINES, Private Bertie killed in action 3.5.1917
16/238 BRUNDRETT, Private Frank died of wounds 12.5.1918
53380 BUCKLEY, Private Edgar killed in action 12.4.1918
53382 BURGESS, Private Cyril R. died of wounds 14.8.1918
62015 BURNS, Private Frank killed in action 12.4.1918
18/1221 BUSH, Private John killed in action 12.4.1918
61609 BUTTON, Private Charles killed in action 12.4.1918
23234 CAISLEY, Private John W. killed in action 3.5.1917
300126 CALLABY, Lance Corporal John L. died of wounds 26.6.1918
40254 CALVERLY, Sergeant George H. DCM, MM died of wounds 12.8.1918
35623 CARR, Private Walter killed in action 3.5.1917

61613 CARROTT, Private Eric A. killed in action 24.4.1918

36833 CARTER, Private Charles killed in action 16.6.1917

53968 CARTER, Private Ernest W.S. died of wounds 13.8.1918

62051 CARTLEDGE, Private Herbert killed in action 12.4.1918

38262 CARTLICK, Private Stanley killed in action 3.5.1917

61614 CARVER, Private Henry H. killed in action 12.4.1918

20/334 CASEY,Private Harry killed in action 14.5.1918

24225 CASLING, Private Stanley killed in action 21.9.1916

24853 CATTON, Private Alfred died of wounds 16.6.1917

28022 CHADWICK, Private Fred killed in action 3.5.1917

36865 CHADWICK, Private Frederick W. died of wounds 26.6.1917

18/1315 CHADWICK, Private Herbert died 12.6.1918

19/173 CHAFFER, Private Fred killed in action 28.6.1918

57930 CHAPMAN, Private John W. killed in action 29.9.1918

60965 CHEETHAM, Private Ernest died of wounds 11.8.1918

37482 CHILD, Lance-Corporal William killed in action 19.7.1918

32015 CHISHOLM, Lance-Corporal Robert killed in action 3.5.1917

204287 CLARKE, Corporal George killed in action 19.7.1918

32333 CLARKE, Private William H. killed in action 3.5.1917

40527 CLAYTON, Private Edwin killed in action 3.11.1916

47146 CLEMMET, Private Robert H. killed in action 28.6.1918

201519 CLEVELAND, Lance-Corporal Harry died of wounds 8.4.1918

27317 CLIFF, Private Arthur killed in action 3.5.1917

36346 CLOUGH, Private Harold killed in action 3.5.1917

53378 COLDWELL, Private William B. killed in action 28.6.1918

38049 COLLINS, Private David killed in action 12.4.1918

61621 COLVIN, Private Frederick J. killed in action 12.4.1918

61623 COOPER, Private Rupert R. killed in action 12.4.1918

60813 COOPER, Private William killed in action 28.4.1918

17/340 COULTATE, Private Thomas killed in action 28.6.1918

21207 COWAN, Private John W. died of wounds 13.5.1918

33480 COWGILL, Private George killed in action 3.5.1917

18/514 COWGILL, Lance-Corporal Harold, DCM died of wounds 2.7.1918

62047 COWLISHAW, Lance-Corporal Henry W. killed in action 28.6.1918

60976 COX, Private Arthur killed in action 28.6.1918

53389 COX, Private John W. killed in action 12.4.1918

53890 CRADDOCK, Private John J. died 26.10.1918

40512 CRANE, Private Anthony killed in action 20.8.1917

33368 CRAVEN, Private Ernest died of wounds 27.10.1916

60660 CRAWFORD, Private James died of wounds 1.7.1918

38430 CRAWSHAW, Private Harry died of wounds 18.6.1917

20945 CRISP, Private Arthur S. killed in action 27.3.1918

17/710 CROSSLEY, Private Herbert died 3.6.1918

41625 CROWTHER, Private Irving killed in action 27.3.1918

36799 CROWTHER, Private Willie died 13.3.1917

61627 CUFFLEY, Private Albert A. killed in action 28.6.1918

17/45 CUMMINGS, Private James H. killed in action 13.4.1918
16/1180 CURE, Corporal Edward killed in action 12.4.1918
36864 DALBY, Private Arthur killed in action 3.5.1917
27859 DALBY, Corporal George H. killed in action 3.5.1917
265262 DALE, Private Gosnay killed in action 30.9.1918
325265 DALTON, Private John W. died 22.6.1918
17/818 DARBYSHIRE, Private Clifford killed in action 26.3.1918
62067 DARWEN, Private William S. died of wounds 11.8.1918
40465 DAVIES, Private Denel died 2.2.1919
61629 DAVIS, Private Joseph J. killed in action 12.4.1918
53390 DAVISON, Private John killed in action 12.4.1918
13093 DAVY, Sergeant Edgar, MM killed in action 19.7.1918
17/259 DAWE, Private Robert died of wounds 10.5.1918
53392 DAWSON, Private William killed in action 19.7.1918
40357 DECAMPS, Private Charles F. died 20.2.1918
28561 DELANEY, Private George died of wounds 20.6.1917
32818 DENISON, Private Henry killed in action 3.5.1917
61631 DENISON, Private Leonard killed in action 12.4.1918
17/1596 DENNIS, Private Walter killed in action 19.7.1918
36376 DENTON, Private Ernest killed in action 27.3.1918
12225 DEVANEY, Corporal John died of wounds 31.3.1918
36674 DIBB, Corporal Fred died of wounds 23.7.1917
33429 DICKINSON, Private Edward killed in action 3.5.1917
41445 DIMBLEBY, Private Richard killed in action 27.3.1918
61076 DIXON, Private Sidney killed in action 1.10.1918
27877 DOBSON, Private George E. died 4.5.1918
3/10376 DOLBEN, Private John A. died of wounds 22.8.1916
62062 DONNISON, Private James killed in action 19.7.1918
4/8651 DOUGLAS, Private James killed in action 3.5.1917
53397 DOWD, Private George killed in action 12.4.1918
16/243 DRAKE, Private Bertram, MSM died 15.7.1918
62061 DUCK, Private John killed in action 12.4.1918
40151 DYKES, Private Harry died of wounds 5.12.1916
32655 DYSON, Private James killed in action 3.5.1917
62070 DYSON, Private Leonard killed in action 12.4.1918
29964 EARY, Private Sidney killed in action 3.5.1917
62071 ECCLES, Private James died of wounds 14.4.1918
27345 EDWARDS, Private Arthur L. killed in action 3.5.1917
62265 EDWARDS, Private Frederick killed in action 12.4.1918
9143 ELLERINGTON, Lance Corporal Reginald R. died of wounds 30.6.1918
23981 ELLIFF, Lance-Corporal Charles killed in action 3.5.1917
53402 ELLIS, Private Jackson died of wounds 29.9.1918
53908 ELLIS, Private Joseph died of wounds 22.4.1918
33747 ELLIS, Private Thomas killed in action 3.5.1917
23483 ELSEGOOD, Sergeant Stanley F. died of wounds 21.9.1916
38232 ENGLAND, Private Jonathan killed in action 3.5.1917

25472 ENGLISH, Private Robert W. killed in action 27.3.1918
28422 FAIRBANK, Private William killed in action 18.5.1917
28331 FARMERY, Private John W. killed in action 28.6.1918
18/1623 FAWCETT, Private Gilbert died of wounds 7.5.1918
38269 FENWICK, Private George W. killed in action 3.5.1917
53843 FINLOW, Private John C. killed in action 19.7.1918
241465 FIRTH, Corporal Leonard killed in action 28.9.1918
61641 FISH, Private William H. killed in action 12.4.1918
40253 FLATLEY, Sergeant John killed in action 26.3.1918
61644 FLETT, Private Andrew N. killed in action 4.7.1918
61775 FLINT, Corporal William M. killed in action 12.4.1918
28777 FORD, Private Charles H. killed in action 26.10.1916
62083 FORSTER, Private James killed in action 13.4.1918
62082 FOSTER, Private Francis J. died of wounds 11.8.1918
36774 FOTHERBY, Private Alfred killed in action 16.12.1916
64106 FOX, Private George killed in action 17.9.1918
41585 FRANCE, Private Robert H. died 25.9.1918
55011 FRANCE, Private Joseph W. killed in action 24.8.1918
59169 FRANK, Lance-Corporal John F. killed in action 29.9.1918
37484 FRANKLIN, Private Norman W. killed in action 27.3.1918
42980 FREARSON, Private Eric H. killed in action 29.8.1918
33014 FREEMAN, Private Harry killed in action 27.3.1918
4/8539 GALLAGHER, Private James killed in action 3.5.1917
17/1446 GAMBLES, Private William killed in action 24.3.1918
62101 GAUNT, Private Frederick A. died of wounds 26.4.1918
20/313 GEARY, Private Alfred died of wounds 19.7.1918
60392 GEARY, Private Leonard killed in action 17.9.1918
61651 GIBBINS, Private James killed in action 12.4.1918
62096 GILL, Private William killed in action 12.4.1918
29768 GILMORE, Private Arthur H. died of wounds 6.5.1917
38410 GLEDHILL, Private Otis killed in action 3.5.1917
43642 GOODGER, Sergeant Walter B. killed in action 27.3.1918
19/181 GRAY, Private Edwin killed in action 3.5.1917
32961 GREAVES, Private Albert V. killed in action 3.5.1917
62090 GREAVES, Private Henry G. killed in action 12.4.1918
64107 GREEN, Private Harvey killed in action 18.9.1918
53915 GREEN, Private Willie killed in action 28.6.1918
62102 GREENWOOD, Private Frederick died of wounds 28.4.1918
62092 GRIFFIN, Private Cyril B. killed in action 24.5.1918
53414 GRIMES, Private John R. died of wounds 31.7.1918
62100 GRINDLEY, Private Edward killed in action 12.4.1918
25913 GROGAN, Private James killed in action 3.5.1917
38268 GUDGEON, Corporal Albert killed in action 29.9.1918
61658 HAGGERTY, Private Sidney killed in action 12.4.1918
17/1306 HAGUE, Private Isiah killed in action 28.6.1918
54072 HALDEN, Private Ernest J. died of wounds 12.8.1918

36859 HALEY, Private John killed in action 3.5.1917

33077 HALL, Private George W. killed in action 3.5.1917

59454 HALL, Private John killed in action 23.5.1918

53920 HALL, Private Manney killed in action 19.7.1918

60580 HALLARD, Private Lewis killed in action 29.9.1918

36999 HALSTEAD, Private Albert killed in action 3.5.1917

38454 HALSTEAD, Private George killed in action 3.5.1917

42137 HAMILTON, Private Harry E. killed in action 20.8.1917

60222 HANCOCKS, Private William died of wounds 11.8.1918

40361 HARBY, Private William killed in action 3.5.1917

5682 HARDY, Private Cyril killed in action 19.7.1918

42139 HARNESS, Lance-Corporal John killed in action 27.3.1918

36846 HARPER, Private Ezra killed in action 3.5.1917

40157 HARRISON, Private Maurice killed in action 3.5.1917

61662 HARRISON, Private Thomas killed in action 28.6.1918

32630 HARRISON, Private Thomas W.B. killed in action 3.5.1917

61663 HARRISON, Private William H. killed in action 12.4.1918

53422 HASTINGS, Private Patrick died of wounds 30.6.1918

62126 HAVERON, Private Thomas died 9.7.1918

38239 HAYHURST, Private Samuel killed in action 3.5.1917

36357 HEALD, Private Harold killed in action 3.5.1917

41570 HELME, Private Harry died of wounds 27.7.1918

36753 HEMINGWAY, Private Harry B. killed in action 3.5.1917

59446 HENDERSON, Private Joseph killed in action 20.10.1918

19704 HENDERSON, Private Robert killed in action 30.6.1916

10929 HEPBURN, Corporal Robert killed in action 27.3.1918

62109 HEPWORTH, Private Joseph A. killed in action 12.4.1918

21044 HERSON, Private George W. killed in action 1.7.1916

40263 HEWITSON, Private Fred killed in action 27.3.1918

34826 HILL, Private Fred killed in action 3.5.1917

35279 HILL, Private Ernest killed in action 3.5.1917

53428 HILL, Private Irving killed in action 12.4.1918

16/1310 HILL, Private John died 26.3.1918

17/1154 HILL, Private Robert killed in action 24.3.1918

16/386 HINSLEY, Private William killed in action 25.3.1918

41669 HIRST, Private Joseph died 2.7.1918

60398 HIRST, Private Thomas killed in action 14.5.1918

53429 HIRST, Private Willie killed in action 12.4.1918

53430 HOBSON, Private William killed in action 28.6.1918

42967 HODGSON, Private Charles E. died 22.5.1918

42142 HODGSON, Private Francis G. killed in action 23.7.1917

62115 HODGSON, Private Fred killed in action 19.7.1918

40178 HODGSON, Private John killed in action 27.3.1918

61671 HODGSON, Private William P. killed in action 12.4.1918

32360 HOLDSWORTH, Private William died 5.11.1918

41516 HOLGATE, Private Alfred killed in action 27.3.1918

41557 HOLGATE, Private Walter killed in action 12.4.1918
61674 HOLLIDAY, Private Norman J. killed in action 12.4.1918
61887 HOLLINGS, Private Albert E. died of wounds 14.8.1918
61675 HOLROYD, Private John E. killed in action 26.8.1918
62127 HOPKINSON, Private Clarence died of wounds 28.6.1918
41715 HOPKINSON, Private Harold killed in action 27.3.1918
20247 HORNBY, Private John F. killed in action 3.5.1917
55518 HOULDEN, Private Arthur killed in action 19.7.1918
33000 HOUSEAGO, Private Arthur killed in action 10.1.1917
53435 HOWARD, Private Frederick W. killed in action 19.7.1918
53848 HOWE, Private John killed in action 29.6.1918
36956 HOWE, Private John C. died 5.1.1917
53433 HOYLE, Private Albert killed in action 23.5.1918
34769 HOYLE, Private George died of wounds 18.6.1917
34164 HUBY, Private Herbert killed in action 3.5.1917
28686 HUDSON, Private Walter killed in action 3.5.1917
32025 HUDSON, Private William killed in action 3.5.1917
40162 HUGHES, Private John J. killed in action 3.5.1917
20/324 HUNT, Private Frederick J. killed in action 24.8.1918
201695 HUTCHINSON, Private Henry killed in action 29.9.1918
27872 HUTCHINSON, Private Sydney killed in action 3.5.1917
62135 I'ANSON, Private Harold killed in action 5.5.1918
18285 ILEY, Private Charles killed in action 1.7.1916
62135 ILIFFE, Private George died of wounds 14.4.1918
77463 IRELAND, Private William died of wounds 22.10.1918
40167 JACKMAN, Private Ingham killed in action 3.5.1917
32022 JACKSON, Private Bertie killed in action 3.5.1917
40395 JACKSON, Private Ernest died 22.3.1918
43013 JAGGER, Private Luther died of wounds 14.4.1918
41426 JANNEY, Private Harold killed in action 27.3.1918
18/1006 JARMAN, Lance-Corporal Harry died 16.2.1919
39460 JENKINSON, Private John W. killed in action 27.3.1918
37004 JENNISON, Private Thomas W. killed in action 20.6.1917
305597 JILLINGS, Private William A. killed in action 18.9.1918
24842 JOHNSON, Private Ernest killed in action 3.5.1917
60422 JONES, Private John died of wounds 26.6.1918
77411 JONES, Private William killed in action 20.10.1918
18/1428 JOWETT, Sergeant Albert killed in action 18.9.1918
55654 JOWETT, Private George killed in action 19.7.1918
28312 JOYCE, Private John E., MM killed in action 27.3.1918
53443 KEARNS, Private Arthur killed in action 28.6.1918
18/203 KEIGHLEY, Lance-Corporal Snowdon killed in action 12.4.1918
25312 KELSEY, Private Herbert killed in action 3.5.1917
51316 KEMP, Private George died 15.5.1918
18/267 KENDALL, Private George killed in action 27.3.1918
22882 KENNEDY, Corporal Patrick killed in action 23.3.1918

21345 KINGDON, Corporal Robert killed in action 29.9.1918
38236 KIRBY, Private Arthur killed in action 3.5.1917
29193 KITCHEN, Private Tom killed in action 3.5.1917
53447 KITELY, Private Albert died 21.10.1918
53448 KITSON, Private William H. died of wounds 2.5.1918
53450 KNOCKTON, Private George killed in action 12.4.1918
24818 LACY, Private James killed in action 10.1.1917
18/729 LACEY, Private Ernest killed in action 27.3.1918
40514 LAMPLOUGH, Private Fred C. killed in action 3.5.1917
60821 LAW, Private Henry killed in action 19.7.1918
27357 LAWRENCE, Private Reginald killed in action 12.4.1918
41637 LAWSON, Corporal Ernest killed in action 24.3.1918
32413 LAWSON, Private John E. killed in action 3.5.1917
61696 LAYBURN, Private Edward killed in action 12.4.1918
25075 LAYFIELD, Private Harry killed in action 29.6.1918
38251 LEA, Private George R. killed in action 27.3.1918
62150 LEAFE, Private Thomas E. killed in action 12.4.1918
16/772 LEE, Corporal Allen died 21.7.1918
16/493 LEE, Private Wilfred died 2.10.1918
33688 LEFFLEY, Lance-Corporal Leonard killed in action 24.3.1918
19780 LETBY, Private Robert killed in action 3.5.1917
53356 LEVERINGTON, Lance-Corporal Arthur killed in action 19.7.1918
62152 LEWIS, Private John T. killed in action 13.4.1918
60967 LINLEY, Private Ernest killed in action 19.7.1918
38122 LINNECOR, Private Leonard L. killed in action 3.5.1917
62154 LINNEY, Private Joseph killed in action 12.4.1918
62151 LISTER, Private Benjamin killed in action 12.4.1918
32882 LISTER, Private Lawrence killed in action 3.5.1917
16/1091 LISTER, Sergeant Sam, MM killed in action 22.9.1918
57153 LITTLE, Private David died of wounds 18.9.1918
62153 LLOYD, Private David died of wounds 18.4.1918
60395 LLOYD, Private Harold killed in action 19.7.1918
32048 LOCK, Private George W. killed in action 16.10.1917
60846 LODGE, Private Cyril killed in action 19.7.1918
40232 LUXFORD, Private Fred killed in action 3.5.1917
53853 LYNN, Private Walter C. killed in action 19.7.1918
38094 MALLINSON, Private Albert died 23.2.1917
25277 MANN, Corporal James A. killed in action 3.5.1917
23790 MANN, Private Herbert died of wounds 1.5.1918
59007 MANNING, Private Frederick J. died of wounds 27.3.1918
25992 MARSHALL, Private Walter G. killed in action 3.5.1917
10930 MASON, Private Leonard killed in action 27.3.1918
18899 MEADES, Private James E. killed in action 10.6.1916
33762 MEEKS, Private Walter E. killed in action 3.5.1917
4/8386 MEEKS, Lance-Corporal John died of wounds 5.12.1916
33978 MEDD, Private Albert killed in action 3.5.1917

60858 MERRITT, Private Edgar died of wounds 28.7.1918
62157 MERRITT, Private Freddied3.11.1918
33078 METCALFE, Private Joseph killed in action 3.5.1917
260114 MIDGLEY, Private Fred killed in action 19.7.1918
14966 MILLER, Lance-Corporal Mark killed in action 22.5.1916
40365 MILLNS, Private Harold died of wounds 15.12.1916
40l74 MILNES,Private George died of wounds 21.11.1916
38545 MILLS, Private Frank killed in action 3.5.1917
42163 MILLS, Private Joseph killed in action 27.3.1918
32906 MITCHELL, Private John E. killed in action 3.5.1917
62169 MITCHELSON, Private Bryan died of wounds 29.5.1918
28333 MOORE, Private Albert killed in action 3.5.1917
38210 MORELAND, Private Thomas W. killed in action 24.3.1918
32995 MORLEY, Private Fred killed in action 3.5.1917
55641MORRISS, Private Lawrence killed in action 20.10.1918
40184 MORTIMER, Private William died of wounds 26.11.1916
43729 MUDD, Private Archie H. killed in action 28.6.1918
18/1564 MURGATROYD, Private Albert killed in action 27.3.1918
40508 McKILL, Private Henry died 24.12.1916
61704 McTIERNAN, Private John killed in action 14.4.1918
25181 NAYLOR, Lance-Corporal Charles killed in action 24.3.1918
38434 NAYLOR, Private Guy killed in action 3.5.1917
24845 NAYLOR, Private Thomas C. killed in action 27.3.1918
72703 NELSON, Private Harold G. killed in action 28.8.1917
40534 NEWMAN, Private George killed in action 3.5.1917
23849 NEWTON, Private Harold killed in action 3.5.1917
40529 NICHOLSON, Private Arthur killed in action 5.3.1917
38078 NICHOLSON, Private Walter killed in action 3.5.1917
62175 NIGHTINGALE, Private Ephraim A. died of wounds 18.7.1918
56723 NORTHCOTE, Private Percival L. killed in action 28.7.1918
43110 NORTON, Private Stanley died 17.9.1918
38487 NUTTER, Private Wilfred E. died 12.8.1918
38227 OATES, Private Gilbert killed in action 11.5.1917
24986 O'GRADY, Lance-Corporal Thomas died of wounds 26.6.1917
16/1565 OLDFIELD, Private Robert killed in action 17.9.1918
51327 OLIVER, Private George killed in action 27.3.1918
32905 O'NEILL, Private Patrick killed in action 17.6.1917
62184 PAGE, Private Richard killed in action 19.7.1918
31984 PAGE, Private Wilfred killed in action 3.5.1917
17/237 PALEY, Private Lawrence killed in action 27.3.1918
60847 PAPE, Private Charles B. killed in action 19.7.1918
32399 PARKER, Private Alfred L. died of wounds 30.3.1918
25732 PARKER, Private William B. killed in action 3.5.1917
325250 PATERSON, Private Wallace L. died 10.8.1918
40180 PEARSON, Private Ernest killed in action 18.9.1918
3/8657 PEARSON, Corporal Joseph killed in action 20.8.1917

18/491 PEEL, Acting-Corporal Harold killed in action 29.9.1918
62192 PERCIVAL, Private Enoch killed in action 19.7.1918
40374 PERKINS, Private Frederick B. died of wounds 12.11.1916
27306 PERKS, Private Alfred died of wounds 21.11.1917
40376 PERRY, Private John C. killed in action 3.5.1917
19188 PHILP, Corporal Frederick G. killed in action 18.9.1918
32367 PICKLES, Private Walter killed in action 27.3.1918
62193 PIERCY, Private George W. died 21.12.1918
41401 PILLING, Private Horace killed in action 27.3.1918
38055 POLLARD, Private William C. killed in action 3.5.1917
60274 POWELL, Private Charles W. died of wounds 4.7.1918
37125 PRATT, Private Lister killed in action 12.4.1918
40177 PROCTER, Private Ernest died of wounds 8.4.1918
16/841 PROCTOR, Private Willie killed in action 25.3.1918
62209 RANDALL, Private Harry C.L. killed in action 19.7.1918
53975 RANSON, Private Clifford killed in action 28.6.1918
8748 READ, Corporal William T. killed in action 24.3.1918
62206 REDHEAD, Private Laurence E. killed in action 12.4.1918
42215 REED, Private Joseph S. killed in action 20.8.1917
33097 REUBEN, Private Morris killed in action 3.5.1917
61725 REVILL, Private Charles H. died of wounds 13.4.1918
61726 REWCASTLE, Private John G. killed in action 12.4.1918
33943 REYNER, Private Percival killed in action 13.11.1916
38252 RHODES, Private Fred killed in action 27.3.1918
40378 RICHARDSON, Private Edwin killed in action 5.11.1916
33758 RICHARDSON, Corporal Fred L. killed in action 3.5.1917
32831 RICHARDSON, Private Lewis T. died 10.9.1918
43635 RICHARDSON, Corporal William died 13.4.1918
37976 ROBERTS, Private Fred killed in action 3.5.1917
60478 ROBINSON, Private Frank killed in action 19.7.1918
37892 RODER, Private Frederick W. killed in action 12.4.1918
21456 RODGERS, Private James killed in action 3.5.1917
17/409 RODLEY, Private Hedley killed in action 27.3.1918
16/1236 ROE, Private Harry killed in action 27.3.1918
33094 ROSS, Private Alfred H. died 5.7.1918
62199 ROTHERY, Private Vincent killed in action 3.5.1918
38054 ROTHERFORTH, Private Charles H. killed in action 3.5.1917
62207 ROWLEY, Private Charley killed in action 12.4.1918
38089 RUSBY, Private Joe killed in action 3.5.1917
61731 RUMBLE, Private George H. died of wounds 7.8.1918
42173 RUSSELL, Private James G. died 3.11.1918
60492 SALT, Private James died of wounds 22.4.1918
59638 SALTER, Private Francis H.S. killed in action 12.4.1918
14515 SALVIN, Private Charles W. killed in action 20.8.1916
37937 SAMPSON, Private Ernest O.G died 10.5.1917
37816 SAMPSON, Private John E.G. died 23.7.1918

61733 SANDERSON, Private Charles P. killed in action 12.4.1918
23970 SANDERSON, Private Frank died of wounds 12.5.1917
62222 SAULT, Private Wilfred killed in action 3.5.1917
9701 SHARLOTTE, Private William killed in action 3.5.1917
40384 SHARPE, Private John T. killed in action 8.11.1916
62216 SHAW, Private Seth killed in action 12.4.1918
40382 SHELLEY, Private John T. killed in action 3.5.1917
33748 SHEPHERD, Private James killed in action 3.5.1917
51336 SHEPHERD, Private Samuel killed in action 22.4.1918
40383 SHORTER, Private John W. killed in action 3.5.1917
54071 SILLS, Private Herbert S. killed in action 19.7.1918
38270 SIMPSON, Private Ernest, DCM killed in action 19.7.1918
62212 SIMPS0N, Private Joseph died of wounds 12.8.1918
265767 SIMS, Private Alexandra killed in action 29.9.1918
60957 SKIDMORE, Corporal Edward killed in action 19.7.1918
33785 SKINGLEY, Private Samuel killed in action 3.5.1917
29105 SLACK, Private John A. died of wounds 16.6.1917
325257 SLATER, Private William G. died 25.4.1918
62225 SLATER, Private Earl D. killed in action 12.4.1918
62228 SMITH, Private Charles killed in action 12.4.1918
28983 SMITH, Private David killed in action 19.7.1918
62215 SMITH, Private Dennis killed in action 12.4.1918
33170 SMITH, Private Edward killed in action 8.11.1916
40389 SMITH, Private George killed in action 18.6.1917
40387 SMITH, Private Harry E. killed in action 3.5.1917
64026 SMITH, Private Reginald P. killed in action 20.10.1918
62223 SMITH, Private Thomas killed in action 12.4.1918
61741 SMITH, Private Thomas E. killed in action 29.9.1918
61740 SMITH, Private Walter killed in action 12.4.1918
15639 SOWERY, Private Arthur killed in action 9.1.1917
33488 SPACEY, Private Ernest died of wounds 24.3.1918
27364 SPENCER, Private Percy killed in action 3.5.1917
24867 SPURR, Lance Corporal Samuel F. died 28.12.1918
55479 STAFFORD, Private James G. killed in action 19.7.1918
27518 STALEY, Private Arthur G. died 20.7.1918
33085 STEEL, Private George died of wounds 28.6.1917
32611 STEPHENSON, Private George R. killed in action 3.5.1917
19/61 STEWART, Private James killed in action 24.3.1918
55860 STONEHAM, Private Albert died of wounds 7.10.1918
27338 STOPPARD, Private Walter killed in action 3.5.1917
60797 STRETTON, Private Chris died of wounds 5.10.1918
24404 SUTCLIFFE, Private Ernest killed in action 3.5.1917
60825 SUTCLIFFE, Private George E. killed in action 20.10.1918
54902 SUTCLIFFE, Private Joe killed in action 27.3.1918
60964 SUTCLIFFE, Private Orlando killed in action 28.6.1918
38814 SWIFT, Private William H. killed in action 19.7.1918

19/164 SYKES, Lance Corporal William C. killed in action 3.5.1917
18/1566 TATTERSFIELD, Private Ernest killed inaction 12.4.1918
64317 TAYLOR, Private Arton R.F. died 26.10.1918
20/311 TAYLOR, Sergeant Cedric H. killed in action 24.8.1918
17/1390 TAYLOR, Lance Corporal Cyril killed in action 27.3.1918
33474 TAYLOR, Private Edwin killed in action 3.5.1917
325259 TAYLOR, Private Ernest killed in action 24.3.1918
42180 TAYLOR, Private George H. killed in action 27.3.1918
40393 TAYLOR, Private George H. killed in action 10.1.1917
236350 TAYLOR, Private Joseph died of wounds 28.8.1918
14174 TAYLOR, Private Lawrence died of wounds 11.8.1918
40143 TAYLOR, Private William killed in action 3.5.1917
33691 TEALE, Private James A. killed in action 3.5.1917
286236 TEDDER, Private Alex H. killed in action 24.3.1918
20/217 TETLEY, Private Sydney killed in action 19.7.1918
16/320 TETLEY, Lance Corporal Walter G died 11.5.1918
46205 THEAKSTONE, Private Walter F. died 10.11.1918
55058 THOMPSON, Private Frank G. died 1.11.1918
38272 THOMPSON, Private James killed in action 3.5.1917
36628 THOMPSON, Private Thomas E. killed in action 27.3.1918
37912 THOMPSON, Private Walter G. died 26.4.1918
9575 THORN, Private George A. killed in action 3.5.1917
18/932 THROP, Private Thomas killed in action 12.4.1918
62244 TIBBETTS, Private Benjamin killed in action 19.7.1918
53360 TILSTONE, Private George killed in action 19.7.1918
62241 TINLING, Private George died of wounds 20.5.1918
40397 TITCHENER, Private Charles killed in action 13.11.1916
32188 TOMMIS, Private Squire killed in action 3.5.1917
60799 TOULSON, Private Alfred G. killed in action 22.4.1918
32924 TOWNSLEY, Private Ernest killed in action 3.5.1917
42182 TURNBULL, Private Robert died of wounds 14.4.1918
60800 TWITCHETT, Private Walter killed in action 22.4.1918
33717 VAREY, Private John H. killed in action 3.5.1917
25712 WADDINGTON, Private Rowland killed in action 12.4.1918
62261 WADE, Private Arthur killed in action 19.7.1918
38093 WADE, Private Tom killed in action 27.3.1918
31724 WAINWRIGHT, Private John killed in action 27.3.1918
38197 WALKER, Private Albert killed in action 3.5.1917
25569 WALKER, Private Francis killed in action 3.5.1917
204293 WALKER, Private Fred killed in action 14.5.1918
38442 WALKER, Private John killed in action 3.5.1917
36156 WALKER, Private Stephen died of wounds 16.6.1917
48627 WALKER, Private William G. died 20.9.1917
62259 WALTON, Private Francis killed in action 28.6.1918
41477 WALSH, Private James, MM killed in action 27.3.1918
21300 WALSH, Private Michael died of wounds 25.8.1918

62256 WARD, Private Edward C. killed in action 12.4.1918

17/1402 WARD, Private William H. killed in action 23.3.1918

64324 WARNER, Private John G. killed in action 18.9.1918

40131 WARREN, Private Thomas killed in action 3.5.1917

40149 WASNIDGE, Private Harry killed in action 10.5.1917

62250 WATERS, Private Robert killed in action 30.7.1918

32896 WATKINSON, Private Harold killed in action 11.5.1917

62254 WATSON, Private William Harrison killed in action 12.4.1918

33458 WEBSTER, Private Herbert killed in action 3.5.1917

62257 WEBSTER, Private James W. killed in action 12.4.1918

38061 WEST, Private Arthur killed in action 3.5.1917

16/61 WHARTON, Private Timothy died of wounds 29.7.1918

25148 WHITE, Private Charles G. died 30.8.1917

62262 WHITELAM, Private William H. killed in action 19.7.1918

64329 WHITELEY, Private Frederick R. killed in action 18.9.1918

38261 WHITELOW, Private Harry killed in action 3.5.1917

42221 WIDDOWSON, Private William died of wounds 28.6.1918

32624 WIDER, Private Albert E. killed in action 25.3.1918

60611 WILES, Private Charles W. killed in action 25.10.1918

36S10 WILKINSON, Lance Corporal Edward C. killed in action 3.5.1917

32626 WILKINSON, Private Felix killed in action 3.5.1917

48695 WILKINSON, Private Walter killed in action 27.3.1918

62263 WILLIAMSON, Private Fred killed in action 12.4.1918

384S6 WILLIAMSON, Private George killed in action 3.5.1917

55754 WILLOCK, Private George E. killed in action 18.9.1918

64333 WINDROSS, Private Joss killed in action 29.9.1918

37772 WOOD, Private Albert F. died 17.11.1918

28325 WOOD, Private Frank died of wounds 23.5.1917

18/471 WOOD, Private Frederick died of wounds 14.9.1916

60845 WOOD, Private Stanley killed in action 19.7.1918

52426 WORTLEY, Private Bernard died of wounds 12.7.1918

64338 WYETT, Private Edward killed in action 29.9.1918

38229 WROE, Private Thomas killed in action 3.5.1917

40519 WRIGHT, Private Fred died of wounds 15.5.1917

43542 WRIGHT, Private John G. died of wounds 12.8.1918

33379 YATES, Private Charles T. killed in action 27.3.1918

204109 YOUNG, Private Albert J. killed in action 29.9.1918

Appendix III

Officers Killed or Died of Wounds

Because of the high turnover of officers in the battalion, only the officers who lost their lives while actually serving with the Leeds Pals are listed.

APPLEBEE, Second-Lieutenant Thomas killed in action 20.8.1916
BICKERSTETH, Lieutenant Stanley M. killed in action 1.7.1916
BLEASE, Captain Richard M.S. killed in action 3.5.1917
BOOTH, Second-Lieutenant Major William killed in action 1.7.1916
BURBRIDGE, Second-Lieutenant Frederick died of wounds 28.8.1918
DAVIDSON, Second-Lieutenant George W. died of wounds 27.12.1917
DAY, Captain Francis T.P. died of wounds 25.3.1918
DEVERELL, Second-Lieutenant Richard S. died 4.11.1916
DE PLEDGE, Captain Edward K.M. killed in action 3.6.1916
DIMERY, Second-Lieutenant George W. died 4.4.1917
EVANS, Lieutenant Frederick H. killed in action 9.10.1917
EVERITT, Second-Lieutenant John P. killed in action 1.7.1916
FOSTER, Second-Lieutenant Leonard died of wounds 13.8.1916
GLENN, Second-Lieutenant Archibald P. killed in action 14.9.1916
GRIFFITH, Second-Lieutenant John H. killed in action 27.3.1918
HAZZARD, Second-Lieutenant William. MC died of wounds 28.3.1918
HUMPHRIES, Second-Lieutenant Thomas killed in action 1.7.1916
JACKSON, Second-Lieutenant William H. killed in action 3.5.1917
JAMES, Second-Lieutenant Clement W. killed in action 1.7.1916
JENNISON, Second-Lieutenant James L. killed in action 3.5.1917
KING, Captain Gilbert S. killed in action 3.5.1917
LINTOTT, Lieutenant Evelyn H. killed in action 1.7.1916
LISLE, Second-Lieutenant John W. killed in action3.5.1917
LIVERSIDGE, Second-Lieutenant Albert died of wounds 2.7.1916
LONG, Captain Cyril Edwin A. killed in action 27.3.1918
MARSHALL, Lieutenant John killed in action 18.9.1918
NEIL, Captain Stanley T.A. killed in action 1.7.1916
OLAND, Second-Lieutenant Valentine, MC killed in action 1.7.1916
PARKIN, Second-Lieutenant Absalom S. killed in action 3.5.1917
PEEK, Second-Lieutenant Alfred T. killed in action 3.5.1917
RAYNER, Lieutenant Roy B.H. died of wounds 24.5.1916
REED, Lieutenant Bernard killed in action 12.4.1918
REED, Lieutenant Bertram killed in action 12.4.1918

ROBINSON, Lieutenant Donald killed in action 3.5.1917
SAUNDERS, Second-Lieutenant Charles killed in action 1.7.1916
SCHOLES, Second-Lieutenant Frederick W. killed in action 3.5.1917
SMITH, Captain Harold, MC died of wounds 28.3.1918
THOMAS, Second-Lieutenant James S. killed in action 3.5.1917
TOLSON, Second-Lieutenant Robert H. killed in action 1.7.1916
VAUSE, Lieutenant John G. killed in action 1.7.1916
WARD, Second-Lieutenant Albert killed in action 28.6.1918
WARD, Second Lieutenant Alec killed in action 28.6.1918
WARDLE, Lieutenant James K. died of wounds 30.4.1916
WHITAKER, Captain George C. killed in action 1.7.1916
WILLEY, Second Lieutenant Thomas A.R.R.E. killed in action 1.7.1916

Appendix IV

Prisoners of War

Probably the least complete of the appendices is the list of prisoners of war. This has been compiled from records kept by Cox and Company, and by comparing the Enquiry Lists of the British Red Cross and Order of St John, published in 1917 and 1918, which listed men who were missing, with a regimental list of prisoners of war kept in the West Yorkshire Regimental Archive in York. The fact that a man was captured was unfortunately not recorded in the Medal Rolls or on the Army Medal Office index, as it had no bearing on his entitlement to campaign medals.

LEEDS PALS CAPTURED OFFICERS
(Name and rank, date captured, date repatriated)
RILEY, Lieutenant A.H. 3.5.1917, 23.2.1918
TATE, Second-Lieutenant R.S. 3.5.1917, 14.12.1918
TWISS, Lt-Colonel C.C.S. 27.3.1918, 25.12.1918
WILLEY, Second-Lieutenant, B. 27.3.1918, 13.12.1918
KIEGHLEY, Second-Lieutenant E. 27.3.1918, 23.12.1918
PEDLEY, Second-Lieutenant J.G. 27.3.1918, 25.12.1918
ROBERTS, Second-Lieutenant A.W. 27.3.1918, died 18.12.18
STEVENS, Second-Lieutenant E.G. 27.3.1918, 11.12.1918
SMITH, Second-Lieutenant R.H. 27.3.1918, 11.12.1918
CLEGG, Second-Lieutenant J.H. 12.4.1918, 13.12.1918
STRONG, Second-Lieutenant W. 27.4.1918, 31.12.1918
WEATHERILL, Second-Lieutenant G. 18.9.1918, 29.11.1918

OTHER RANKS:
(Number, name and date captured)
15/1082 HARGREAVES, Private Herbert 20.5.1916
15/452 HEWSON, Private Frank 20.5.1916
15/744 RAWNSLEY, Private Bernard 20.5.1916
27376 ARROWSMITH, Private W. 3.5.1917
37041 BACKHOUSE, Private John T. 3.5.1917
36186 BEST, Private F. 3.5.1917
32943 CONNELL, Private Thomas 3.5.1917
38492 CULPAN, Private Arthur 3.5.1917
32962 ELLIS, Private E. 3.5.1917
37042 FORD, Private W. 3.5.191
15/1456 GOODER, Private George 3.5.1917

32994 HALLIDAY, Private Herbert E. 3.5.1917
28618 HIGGINS, Private John J. 3.5.1917
32997 HORNSEY, Private H.P. 3.5.1917
1197 JOHNSTON, Lance-Corporal Ernest 3.5.1917
40140 JONES, Private R.W. 3.5.1917
32411 KAYE, Private G. 3.5.1917
29527 LEVI, Private H. 3.5.1917
37961 OLIVANT, Private L. 3.5.1917
27371 PHILIPS, Private William 3.5.1917
15/722 PICKLES, Private William 3.5.1917
28707 PORTER, Private D.(J.) 3.5.1917
15/1541 POTTER, Private Samuel 3.5.1917
15/1032 PRESTON, Private Harold 3.5.1917
37661 ROBINSON, Private Alfred 3.5.1917
24275 STEPHENSON, Private A. 3.5.1917
34270 TAYLOR, Private Hubert 3.5.1917
34994 TRENDALL, Private Harry 3.5.1917
38459 WHITE, Private Harry 3.5.1917
33073 SHAW, Private Thomas 3.5.1917
15572 BROWN, Sergeant George W. 21.3.1918
42196 CARNEY, Private T. 21.3.1918
59635 TULLEY, Private E. George 25.3.1918
38348 AIRSTONE, Private Edgar 27.3.1918
325183 ALLEN, Private Alfred Robert 27.3.1918
43513 AUTEY, Private E. 27.3.1918
240704 BAKER, Private W. 27.3.1918
41576 BARKER, Private A. 27.3.1918
20377 BARLOW, Private Percy 27.3.1918
41573 BATTYE, Private A. 27.3.1918
40164 BEECROFT, Private H. 27.3.1918
43004 BLACKBURN, Private Arthur 27.3.1918
40173 BLAKEY, Private Alfred W. 27.3.1918
41508 BODDY, Private J. 27.3.1918
39175 BOTTERILL, Private John 27.3.1918
57370 BOWLER, Private Walter 27.3.1918
42124 BRASS, Private Jos N. 27.3.1918
16/1680 BROWN, Private Alt E. 27.3.1918
17/1135 BUCKTON, Private Tom 27.3.1918
19/109 BUTTERS, Lance-Corporal Harry 27.3.1918
2394 CHAMBERLAIN, Corporal S. 27.3.1918
33436 CHEESBOROUGH, Private H. 27.3.1918
10601CLOUGHTON, Private John V. 27.3.1918
46490 COLES, Private Arthur 27.3.1918
43831 COLLINS, Private Roy F. 27.3.1918
16/1365 COOK, Private Harry 27.3.1918
15/1671 COWAN, Private William T. 27.3.1918

42199 CRAIG, Private A.G. 27.3.1918
42205 CROSS, Corporal Robert A. 27.3.1918
38638 DARBYSHIRE, Private Harry 27.3.1918
42188 DOUGLAS, Private William 27.3.1918
41535 DYSON, Private J. 27.3.1918
28738 FEATHER, Private G. Harry 27.3.1918
25983 FIRTH, Private Arthur 27.3.1918
15/330 FIRTH, Lance-Corporal Harry L. MM 27.3.1918
15/354 FROST, Private Charles 27.3.1918
15/1602 GALLOWAY, Private Alfred 27.3.1918
43546 GARRY, Private Philip 27.3.1918
32880 GRASBY, Private William C. 27.3.1918
40422 GREENFIELD, Private T. 27.3.1918
40160 HAGUE, Corporal Chas W. 27.3.1918
300110 HALLIDAY, Private Walter 27.3.1918
41680 HARGREAVES, Private Hubert 27.3.1918
29394 HARE, Private Harold 27.3.1918
37468 HARE, Private Walter 27.3.1918
42202 HARRISON, Private R.L.T. 27.3.1918
42191 HARRISON, Privates. Robert 27.3.1918
325240 HARVEY, Private Albert S. 27.3.1918
19/65 HICK, Private J.W. 27.3.1918
15/471 HOLLINGWORTH, Sergeant Clifford 27.3.1918
18/354 HOYLE, Private James A. 27.3.1918
15/1716 HUGHES, Lance-Corporal Thomas 27.3.1918
23889 JACKSON, Lance-Corporal J.W. 27.3.1918
59115 JACKSON, Private T. 27.3.1918
31706 JEFF, Private J.27.3.1918
15/1461 JOHNSON, Private F. Alfred 27.3.1918
15/524 JOHNSON, Lance-Corporal C. 27.3.1918
42208 JOHNSON, Private S. 27.3.1918
17/983 JONES, Corporal Arthur 27.3.1918
15/532 JONES, Corporal Percy H. 27.3.1918
15/535 JUDD, Lance-Corporal Joe 27.3.1918
41419 KEAN, Lance-Corporal Albert 27.3.1918
59629 KELLY, Private D.R. 27.3.1918
37899 LAMBERT, Private C.H. 27.3.1918
32370 LANG, Private P. 27.3.1918
18/185 LAWSON, Private Arthur 27.3.1918
35406 LICKARD, Private Ernest 27.3.1918
300020 LILLYWHITE, Private James 27.3.1918
29525 LONGLEY, Private W. 27.3.1918
42209 LONGTHORNE, Private John 27.3.1918
17/41443 MALKIN, Lance-Corporal F. 27.3.1918
40367 MARSHALL, Sergeant Abraham Chas. 27.3.1918
38338 MORTIMER, Private Willie 27.3.1918

42164 NICHOL, Private William 27.3.1918
26018 NICHOLL, Private John 27.3.1918
37376 NOTTINGHAM, Private Cyril 27.3.1918
18338 PARKHOUSE, Private Robert 27.3.1918
41469 PROCTOR, Private Frank 27.3.1918
39237 ROBINSON, Private Stanley 27.3.1918
57114 RODGERS, Private Alfred 27.3.1918
38431 ROTHERA, Lance-Corporal J. 27.3.1918
27488 ROTHERAM, Private Albert 27.3.1918
16/845 SEEKINS, Private H. 27.3.1918
40088 SLATER, Private Ernest 27.3.1918
17/533 SMITH, Private Albert 27.3.1918
235242 SMITH, Private Percy 27.3.1918
39599 SMITH, Private R.A. 27.3.1918
47134 TAYLOR, Private Alfred N. 27.3.1918
42180 TAYLOR, Private G.H. 27.3.1918
12591 THORPE, Private Harold 27.3.1918
17/789 TRELLER, Private R. 27.3.1918
16/325 UNDERWOOD, Corporal George F. 27.3.1918
42183 WALKER, Private A. 27.3.1918
S1348 WALLEY, Private Edgar C. 27.3.1918
28327 WARD, Corporal Sam 27.3.1918
23987 WILKS, Corporal H. 27.3.1918
41572 WOOD, Private Albert 27.3.1918
40136 WOOD, Lance-Corporal Jas W. 27.3.1918
42185 WOOD, Private William E. 27.3.1918
31708 WORRALL, Lance-Corporal George 27.3.1918
17/592 WRIGHT, Corporal Horace V.27.3.1918
325264 YOUNG, Private W.W.H. 27.3.1918
61593 BEETHAM, Private Chas 12.4.1918
62027 BENNETT, Private C. 12.4 1918
53376 BLAKEY, Private Ebenezer 12.4.1918
62104 BRIGGS, Private George 12.4.1918
18/1370 BRIGHTON, Private Ernest 12.4.1918
62043 BROGDEN, Private Harold 12.4.1918
61781 CORNEY, Corporal J.H. 12.4.1918
62063 DYSON, Private B. 12.4.1918
32336 GODFREY, Private J. 12.4.1918
61659 HALL, Private C.E. 12 4.1918
53423 HAWKER, Private G.H. 12.4.1918
16/846 HEATON, Private W. 12.4.1918
62134 HOLLEY, Private A.W. 12.4.1918
62180 NEILL, Private G. 12.4.1918
16/853 RAWNSLEY, Private F. 12.4.1918
24568 RICHARDSON, Private R.F. 12.4.1918
53361 WARD, Private Richard 12.4.1918

62253 WATSON, Private E. 12.4.1918
61718 PILKINGTON, Private Edward 13.4.1918
240059 GRACE, Sergeant Frank 14.4.1918
21553 FLEMING, Private Frank 19.7.1918
60591TOONE, Private Frank 31.7.1918
53855 MOORE, Private G.S. 15.9.1918
203005 DOUGHERTY, Private John 17.9.1918
51938 EDWARDS, Private G.E. 18.9.1918

The following men are known to have been taken prisoner while serving with the 15th or 15/17th Battalion, The West Yorkshire Regiment, but their dates of capture cannot be confirmed from available documentary sources:

15/81 BROWN, Lance-Corporal Cyril N.
15/1330 BETTS, Acting Corporal Herbert
15/1137 BINNS, Private Arthur, MM
15/138 BINNS, Private Arthur
15/1232 BODDY, Acting Corporal Richard H.
15/1916 BONNER, Private Clifford A.
15/106 BROWN, Private Roy 15/178 CARTER, Lance-Corporal William S.
15/1779 CAWOOD, Private Clifford H.
15/186 CHAMBERS, Sergeant Bernard D.
15/1514 COLLEY, Private Tom W.
15/225 COOKE, Lance-Sergeant Samuel W.
15/248 CROSSLAND, Private Robert
18/1122 EMSLEY, Private Benjamin
15/1247 FIRTH, Private William
15/335 FITZPATRICK, Private Bernard
15/382 GODRICH, Lance-Corporal James A.
15/429 HARE, Sergeant Herbert E.
15/480 HOWARD, Private Arthur
15/1610 HUTCHINSON, Private Leonard
15/1437 JULIAN, Sergeant William
15/546 KERSHAW, Private James T.
187185 LAWSON, Private Arthur
15/1427 UNDLEY, Private Ernest
15/598 LISTER, Private Cecil
15/724 PLATT, Private William A.
15/781 SANDERS, Private Kenneth C.
15/1473 SENIOR, Lance-Corporal Harry V.
15/815 SIMPSON, Corporal Reginald
15/1349 SWETMAN, Lance-Corporal Arthur H
15/914 TURKINGTON, Private John W.
15/1551 VARLEY, Private Joseph W.
15/966 WHALLEY, Private R E.

The accounts of their imprisonment by three of the men captured when the battalion was surrounded on 27 March 1918 are published here for the first time. Although they were from the same company and were captured on the same day, they did not share a common experience while in captivity. Their stories illustrate not only the diversity of their experiences, but also the privations and dangers faced by British prisoners taken in the desperate fighting during the German spring offensive of 1918.

CLIFFORD HOLLINGWORTH

One of the original Leeds Pals who signed on at Leeds Town Hall in September 1914, Clifford had been with the battalion from the beginning. He was slightly wounded on 1 July 1916, by a shell splinter that cut the bridge of his nose. When the Pals took part in the offensive at Gavrelle, he was on attachment to a Draft Training Depot, and on his return he was promoted to sergeant. On 27 March 1918, Clifford was wounded by a sniper's bullet that passed through his neck, miraculously without hitting anything vital, and taken behind the German lines where, having lost his respirator, he was gassed by a British shell.

On the 27th I was wounded, taken prisoner and after I had been taken prisoner I were gassed by our own shells. When we got behind German lines and I got into hospital and got comfortable, we were talking and I said to one fellow, I said, 'Well, you know how many times we've said we've lost the war,' I said, 'by gosh, the Germans have lost theirs'. All you could see were rickety old carts. Oh, they hadn't the transport like us. Then when I got into hospital all bandages was taken off and washed because they were short of bandages. Even the field dressing was taken from my neck, one at each side. That was taken away to be washed, and they put a paper bandage round, two pads of wood wool, it was a kind of wood pulp, and put a pad of that on and a paper bandage around my neck and thats what I got. I got an inoculation in my chest and I was there about two or three weeks, had a nice rest, then of course I had to come out and go up and meet the lads in the camps, and then I finished up at Langforden near Hamburg. Springhirsch Lager. There were lots of Pals there, all sergeants. You see if you were a corporal, sergeant or sergeant-major you didn't work, but other ranks had to work. We were told not to work, because if you work you release a man for the front line.

You got your breakfast at seven o'clock, and your ration for the day, so much bread. We got a loaf of bread like that [a small loaf] for twelve, black bread. Coffee was made out of barley, burnt barley, there was nothing then until four o'clock in the afternoon when you got your evening meal and that could be meal soup, anything like that you know, but no more bread, and I lost four stone. I went down from thirteen-and-a-half stone down to under nine.

I'm glad the Armistice came, when I look back I wouldn't have liked to have winter in that camp! Oh, do you know, I'm not

Clifford Hollingworth in prisoner-of-war uniform. He is wearing a borrowed cap with a 6th Battalion shoulder title as a badge. His sergeant's stripes were made from garter tab scrounged from a Highlander. (C. Hollingworth)

Clifford's postcard to his father.

joking, it was that flat you could see a flea walking on the horizon miles away! One morning when we were lining up for our coffee a German said 'Regen kommen' – rain, and we could see the storm in the sky, flash of lightning and thunder, and it hit our camp at about half-past five in the evening and in seconds we'd that much depth of hailstones as big as eggs. We were flooded out in our hut, we'd to climb up, we were just round the door, we'd to get out because the water come in. Well that was a position, but it cleared next morning.

The Feldwebel, he was a marvellous man, but we had an interpreter, he was a little swine. Oh yes, if you looked at him, you daren't look at him because, you see, he'd have you up for all sorts of silly things you know, and he'd put you in the jug for a month, bread and water. Made no difference, what you got outside was bread and water, but you restricted your movements you see.

When we went down to fetch the parcel wagon from the station at Langforden, we'd no horses, we'd to push the van. There were men in rags and tatters working on the roadside cleaning ditches and one thing and another. They never lifted their heads up or anything, they just went on working. So anyway, we got friendly with the Posten [sentry] and we said, 'What's all these fellows?' He told us they were conscientious objectors. Now then in Germany, in our war, this is what they did. You're a conscientious objector, they tried and tried to turn your head. No, you're a conscientious objector, right-oh, come on, go to the prison, find a man that's got a twenty-year sentence to do for murder, will he volunteer for the front if he's freed? 'Certainly sir, I will!'

376

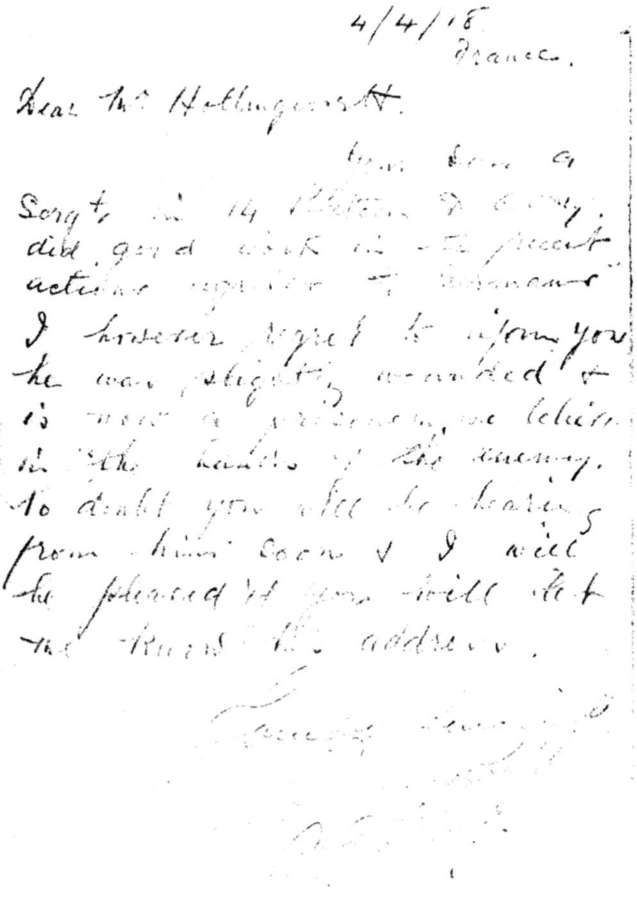

4/4/18
France.

Dear Mr Hollingworth.

Your son a Sergt in 14 Platoon D Coy, did good work in the recent actions against the Germans. I however regret to inform you he was slightly wounded & is now a prisoner, we believe, in the hands of the enemy. No doubt you will be hearing from him soon & I will be pleased if you will let me know the address.

Letter sent by one of the officers informing Clifford's father that he had been wounded and captured.

You went and you did his twenty years. Mind you these fellows were all sent to the front, it wasn't long till they were killed, but that's how they treated their conscientious objectors. They must have been brave, must them people. Oh, he said they were half-fed, half-starved, none of them would survive the war and they'll die afterwards, consumption, no, no, they were in a very bad way.

I got a suit from [the British Red Cross in] Berne, pair of boots, pants, vest and a cap, and then I got an overcoat and then when I got all rigged up like that we heard rumours about the advance. Now then, before the advance, when the Germans came to the gate with the red flag, the revolution, they opened the gates and said we were free to go if we want, the revolution's taking over you can go if you want. So Sergeant-Major Cook, he was a Regimental Sergeant-Major, he'd been taken since 1914, a right Regular soldier, he said, 'Hey, steady on, where are you going? Who's going to look after you when you get through these gates? Now then think, the war's finishing, it isn't finished yet, stay put.' 'Course it were good sound advice, 'cause once you get outside there, the crowd might spend their venom on you.

So of course, it was official, the Armistice was signed, the flags were raised and bands played. One of the [German] officers had shot himself and the guards had just simply disappeared and they'd taken their rifles with them. Nobody on duty, and we were told to stay where we were, till the camp committee had made sure that everything was alright. Well [they] went into the village and saw the Burgomeister, Lord Mayor, [who] said, 'As far as we're concerned the war is finished, thank the Lord.'

So we decided we'd have a trip into Hamburg. You could sell a bit of chocolate [out of a Red Cross parcel] for money, so we went into Hamburg and we just sat in a cafe with our prisoner-of-war uniforms. There were five of us and of course people were having jubilation because the war was over. 'The war is over – now schnapps, schnapps all round', so of course we drank full of schnapps and we were walking down the Alster singing 'Rule Britannia'.

A game of football at Springhirsch Lager near Hamburg.

The German hospital admission form filled in when Clifford was captured.

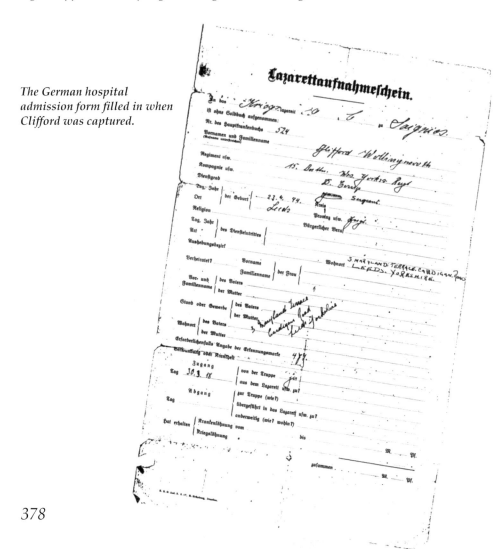

Anyway after that we got notification we'd to move and we'd to go to Hamburg. We went to Langforden. We got on the train into Denmark and we went to a place called Lazaretten van Helden Hospital [in Viborg]. Then we went to Arhus, round the top of Denmark through the Kattegat and Skagerrak across to Leith in Scotland. Then we came from Leith to Ripon Camp. We were examined and when I showed the officer my wound he said 'You should be dead, man.' I said 'That's what the German doctor said,' I said, and the sister there said, 'Am I talking to a ghost?' I said, 'No you're talking to a hundred per cent man!'

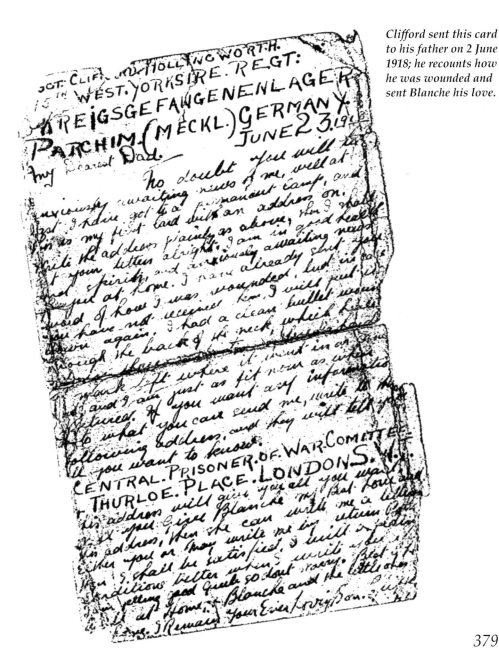

Clifford sent this card to his father on 2 June 1918; he recounts how he was wounded and sent Blanche his love.

PERCY BARLOW

Percy Barlow attested for Army service in December 1915 under the Derby Scheme and joined the West Riding Regiment in January 1916. After training in the notorious 'Bullring' at Etaples, in July 1917 he was sent with a draft of reinforcements to the 15/17th Battalion, The West Yorkshire Regiment. Early in 1918 he returned to Britain on leave and, soon after he rejoined his unit, the German March offensive began and he was taken prisoner

In common with many of the prisoners, Percy Barlow was detailed to help carry a wounded German soldier to the rear.

We found shelter in an advanced dressing station where we obtained a drink of water. Here we saw some awful sights, and were not sorry to be detailed off to carry a German to the dressing station on a door.

Percy Barlow when he was with the Duke of Wellington's Regiment in 1916.

After a long and difficult journey, Percy and his comrades arrived at the dressing station with their burden and were sent to join a group of some 1,300 prisoners, and were kept waiting for several hours. They eventually moved off and marched most of that night.

On arrival at their destination they were given 'a drop of black liquid, we afterwards identified as coffee, made from acorns burnt and ground like coffee beans'.

The men were put into a large cage without any kind of shelter, where they slept for a couple of hours until they were woken up by the sentries who relieved them of razors, knives and any letters or documents they were carrying.

The following night it rained heavily, and the next day, 'dirty, bedraggled and downhearted,' they were taken to another cage, at Villers, which had at least one hut. Six hundred of the 1,300 men, Percy Barlow among them, managed to crowd into the hut, and attempted to sleep, while the remaining 700 tried to make themselves comfortable on the sodden ground.

At four in the morning they were roused by the sentries, given some ersatz coffee, and marched off to work on the roads for twelve hours. Returning to their cage late in the afternoon they received their first meal since their capture, some barley soup, a piece of horse meat and a small piece of bread.

Despite rumours that they were to move to Germany, Percy Barlow was among a group of 700 prisoners sent to work closer to the front lines at Ecoust-St-Mein. The only hut in the compound was taken over by the NCOs, so Percy and his

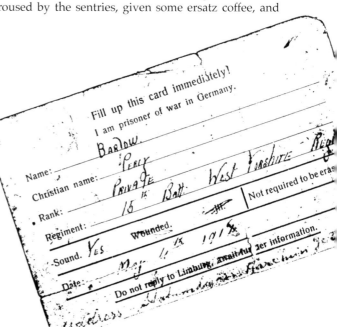

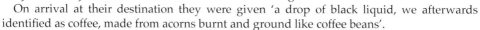

Fill up this card immediately!
I am prisoner of war in Germany.

Name: Barlow
Christian name: Percy
Rank: Private 15 Batt. West Yorkshire Regt.
Regiment: 15 *Not required to be erased*
Sound. Yes   Wounded.   9 1918
   May 1 ...information.
Date: Do not reply to Limburg, await further ...

Notification that Percy has been captured, dated 4 May 1918, but not received until late June.

380

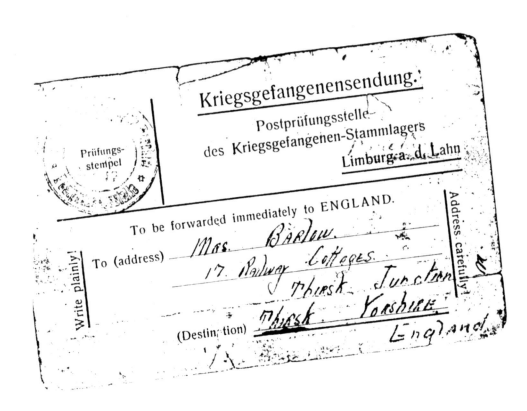

Percy's postcard home, 8 June 1918.

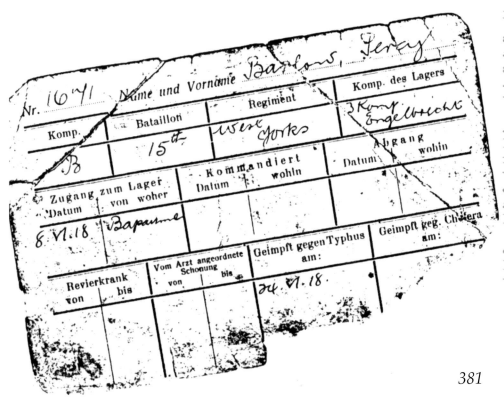

comrades dug holes, which they partially roofed over with anything they could find. They were set to work in the village, filling in holes with bricks in the pouring rain, which flooded their shelters, but here was an added danger to their well being, for they were in range of the British guns, which frequently shelled the village and their camp, causing many casualties.

The severe shortage of food prompted some of the men to risk eating slices cut from dead horses on the roadside, which led to an outbreak of dysentery and some deaths. Although Percy fortunately managed to avoid illness, his condition was not improved when

> working near the hospital [I] had occasion to walk over a heap of charcoal. I picked a piece up, intending to make a fire in our little hole that night. I was seen, as it happened, by a sentry, who caught me by the neck and thrashed me mercilessly with a steel machine-gun rod. He was a man of about six feet in height, and knew how to lay it on, and I was in a very weak state when he desisted.

After about eleven days the men were returned to Villers to improved accommodation, including tents and wire beds with fresh straw to sleep on. On 27 April they were again moved. Percy was among a hundred men picked for a working party. They marched off at 6.15am without any food, and at 3.30pm, after covering some 18 miles, they arrived in Bapaume and were set to work immediately, clearing a space in a dump of captured equipment in order to build themselves a shelter for the night. When this was completed they received their first food of the day – coffee and bread – and then turned in.

The next morning the contingent was divided in two; half began loading captured British trench pumps on a train bound for Germany, while the others erected huts for their living quarters. Always on the lookout for ways to improve their diet, Percy and his comrades had already tried to exchange their meagre possessions for food, and were pleased to find that the rate for bartered goods was better at Bapaume.

> For my watch I received a piece [of bread] weighing no more than seven ounces. Dealing with the Germans at Bapaume, however, I got a whole loaf for my braces, and a piece of cheese for my puttees.

Although probably out of range of the artillery, Bapaume was often bombed by British aircraft, so the men were made to unload trains bringing in heavy timbers and corrugated iron for the German dugouts. After about a fortnight, Percy was one of several men picked to go to the next village, Favreuil, to help dig a sump. Conditions were slightly better there, and they were able to scrounge some potato peelings to supplement their rations; their English-speaking sentry also let them have his cigar butts.

Still subjected to air-raids, they were in the vicinity when a horse was killed by a bomb fragment, and were given permission to help themselves.

> The whole hundred of us were soon hacking, cutting, slashing to our hearts' content. What an orgy of flesh that night, for we had it grilled, boiled and frizzled, it being fresh and fairly tender.

At last, on 19 May, they were to be formally registered as prisoners of war, some nine weeks after their capture. By now all the men had beards and were crawling with lice – many had sores on their bodies. Percy Barlow's right leg was 'one mass of matter'.

Their stay at Favreuil was brought to an abrupt end after a German railway gun was briefly sited there while bombarding Arras. The British retaliation was devastating and, after spending a day cowering in a slit-trench, Percy and his comrades were taken to Ecourt-St-Quentin, where they were bathed and deloused before joining another contingent of prisoners.

... Here I saw the chaps as they really were, and I have not yet seen anything so pitiful. Hollow cheeks could always be seen, but the poor half-nourished bodies were camouflaged by clothes. Deprived of these, it was easy to see what the past three months of starvation had done, for shoulder-blades protruded like wings, ribs appearing as though covered by skin alone. It was wonderful to see the expressions on the men's faces as they stood under the hot shower, and for the first time since capture they broke out into song.

In their new camp, although discipline was strictly maintained by a German sergeant-major who had 'the disposition of a snake', work was better regulated, being limited to eight-hour shifts, and because of the large number of prisoners it was sometimes possible to dodge a shift. The men were also allowed to write home, but their letters were subject to the utmost scrutiny, and anything approaching criticism of their captors or conditions was censored.

At this time many rumours were circulating, among them that the Royal Navy had mutinied, King George had abdicated, Lloyd George had resigned, and London was in ruins. One rumour, which turned out to be true, however, was that a conference had been held in a neutral country and an agreement reached on the distance from the ' line in which prisoners could be employed.

This resulted, on 9 July, in Percy and his comrades boarding a train, which took them to Blaton, just across the Belgian border, after more than twenty-four hours' travel through rural France. After a week of unaccustomed rest, billeted in a disused veterinary hospital where there was an outbreak of fever resulting in more deaths, the men were moved south to Blanc Misseron, soon re-christened 'Blank Misery'.

Quartered in a ruined factory and an empty house, Percy and his comrades, now numbering about fifty, were under the control of a German NCO. The village had been devastated by a British air-raid and a large number of the French population killed. Those who had survived were living in abject poverty in the ruined buildings, so the prospect of scrounging any additional food here looked bleak. The men were soon set to work again, starting at 7am and working until 1pm without a break either for food or rest. At 2.30pm they received their soup ration.

While on their way to work they passed another column of prisoners who had been captured at Cambrai in 1917 and who were slightly better off for food. Each day as they passed, the Cambrai contingent dropped little packages at a level-crossing where their paths coincided. This caused jealousy and arguments at first as the men scrambled to be among those who got a package, until it was made clear that unless the food was shared equally no more would be given.

On 16 August the first mail arrived from Britain and Percy was among the lucky ones. He heard that he had not been registered as a prisoner of war until 23 June, so it would be some time before he could expect a Red Cross parcel. The monotony of their existence, and the constant quest for food, were becoming unbearable, until one of the British prisoners offered them some spiritual comfort.

Amongst us was a schoolteacher who started the idea of holding service amongst ourselves on Sunday morning. He was assisted whole heartedly by the German sergeant-major who was very keen on promoting a religious feeling amongst us. A battered hymn-book appeared, a few hymns were selected, and these were practised assiduously by a now-enthusiastic choir.

The following Sunday we held our first service, conducted by the schoolteacher who read the scripture appointed with great expression, and together we sang the hymns, bare-headed in the open air. We held a service each Sunday afterwards and this was the one thing to look forward to.

The men were moved from their billet into the Station Hotel, which was 'wired-in, back and front', and were joined by a large contingent from Conde.

Percy and his comrades, now about thirty in number, were working in Onnaing on the French side of the border, and were occasionally able to acquire odd scraps of food. The rest of the men were sent into Quievrain in Belgium, a garrison town heavily populated with German troops who 'strutted along the main streets in insolent pomposity', and who prevented the prisoners from scrounging food from the subdued civilian inhabitants.

The Sunday services continued and on 6 October the men were addressed by an unexpected guest speaker,

> a German officer wearing a huge Red Cross on each arm. He chose a well-known passage of scripture for his text, and he pronounced thus. 'It vos goot for you, that you haf been afflicted!' The civilians seemed wildly excited, and we found out this was caused by the rapid advance of the British armies at Cambrai.

A week later when the men paraded for work, they were told to 'stand fast'. A move was afoot, and Percy and his comrades watched the procession of refugees from Valenciennes struggle by with their worldly goods loaded on little wagons. Then came

BUCKINGHAM PALACE

1918.

The Queen joins me in welcoming you on your release from the miseries & hardships, which you have endured with so much patience & courage.

During these many months of trial, the early rescue of our gallant Officers & Men from the cruelties of their captivity has been uppermost in our thoughts.

We are thankful that this longed for day has arrived, & that back in the old Country you will be able once more to enjoy the happiness of a home & to see good days among those who anxiously look for your return.

George R.I.

Every returned prisoner-of-war received a letter from the King. This one was sent to Percy Barlow.

the order to move and the prisoners and their captors joined the traffic jam on the road to the east. Eventually they came to the outskirts of Mons, and were billeted in a disused gendarmerie at Frameries, a fairly wealthy suburb. There prisoners of war were a novelty, and attracted the attention of the civilians who did all they could to supply Percy and his comrades with food.

> Each evening, there were brought in fresh vegetables and soup, in addition to a fair amount of French bread, by the kindly civilians. As each sentry received a portion of whatever was brought in, we soon found out that they were not against the practice, but on the contrary looked forward to it with almost as much eagerness as ourselves. For our Unteroffizier [German NCO] who graciously allowed this I have nothing but praise, for he did all he could to alleviate the sufferings and better the conditions of the prisoners.

Soon, one of the men noticed that a part of the wall was lower than the rest, and led to a garden from where they could get out into a dark alley. A party of three went out the first night, and returned two hours later laden with as much food as they could carry. Percy and one of his pals ventured out the following night and caught the attention of a small boy, who

Percy Barlow in 1986.

took them to the back door of an estaminet where they were given a meal and some beer. Perhaps emboldened by the drink, they decided to try their luck again, and this time met a Belgian man who took them home where they were again fed, and this time invited to fill their haversacks. After narrowly avoiding two Germans as they returned to their billet, Percy and his friend were horrified to find the sentry just below the wall, smoking his pipe, ten minutes before the early morning roll call. Fortunately he ambled off with five minutes to spare, and the two scavengers made roll call just in time.

On the next night some fifty men assembled in the dark near the corner of the wall that could be scaled. All got out safely and Percy was taken to the Bugomeister's house, where he was again well fed and given provisions to take back with him. As an added bonus, he was shown a secret map on which the Burgomeister had been plotting the Allies' advance. This was the first reliable war news he had received since his capture, and he was encouraged to see how much progress had been made.

Still more men gathered the next night, and again all got out and returned safely, having satisfied their appetites, but on the following day the interpreter warned them that the Germans knew what was going on, and that it would have to stop.

Percy and his comrades decided to heed the warning and stayed in, but some foolhardy men went out as usual.

> They had been out the usual time, and we were expecting them any minute, when we were startled by a disturbance at the front gate. Several shots rang out, and the sentries were rushing about wildly excited. A party of Germans, billeted in the town, brought two of our chaps in by the front gate. This was the signal for a general round-up, and soon all of the seventeen who had ventured out were reposing in durance vile down the coal cellar, where they passed the night, by order of the officer. The next morning he paraded the seventeen, begrimed and miserable. He had decided not to bring the matter before the Colonel, but to punish the whole of us, by stopping the Belgians from bringing the food, which came every evening. Proving as good as his word, that night we received only the German issue, which meant no breakfast the following morning, and we were in consequence very miserable.

Next day the men were taken from their billets and set to work loading military supplies on a train bound for Germany because, as one of their sentries explained, 'Tommy come!' Very soon Percy and his comrades were on the road east again. This time their destination was Liege, about 75 miles away. They halted at Binche, a large town roughly halfway between Mons and Charleroi, where they put their recently acquired skill at scrounging food and tobacco to good use, and again they received news, this time that the Allies had reached Bruges.

Their journey continued for the next five days, until they arrived at Jauche, another town used as a garrison by the Germans. Some of the men tried to resume the nocturnal search for food, with almost tragic results as it turned out.

Three of the chaps, not content with the food they were receiving, went through a window into the village. They never made a bigger mistake, for Jauche was a garrison headquarters, besides being a training depot for young soldiers. The alarm was raised twenty minutes after their departure and soon a whole battalion of young soldiers were scouring the village. The prisoners were soon caught, after narrowly escaping being shot, for the recruits were having a pot at any opportunity. After receiving a severe drubbing at the hands of their captors, the civilian food they had obtained was confiscated, and they were compelled to stand before a blank wall for fourteen hours without moving.

The first intimation of the end of the war came to Percy and his comrades when, on the afternoon of 11 November, a rumour (true as it happened) was circulated that the Kaiser had abdicated.

We could not credit this, but shortly afterwards our sergeants called us together, and told us we were free men once more. That night the Germans packed their kit in readiness for the tramp to Deutschland on the morrow. As they had no rations, one German killed one of the farmer's pigs with his bayonet, carrying it off and cutting it up with sheer callousness.

Percy and his comrades took to the road again next day, this time marching west, and pulling a cart containing two men who were not well enough to make the journey on foot. As they arrived at Wavre they were passed by a long column of Germans on their way home.

The Germans were in great spirits, singing, laughing and exchanging jokes with us as we passed by. Each man wore in his coat the red ribbon of revolution, and the transports were draped with red.

By the early hours of Sunday 17 November the Pals had reached Nivelles, and at 11 o'clock that morning there was a celebration in the town.

The freedom from German rule was celebrated. The last German had left the city. There was a procession of the councillors, city fathers, etc., and citizens to the Cathedral. When the service was over the band struck up a lively tune and the people, as one, joined hands and danced around the Cathedral, good-naturedly compelling us to join them, shouting with all their might 'Vive les Anglais, Vive les Anglais!'

On the following day the Pals were on the road once more, where they met.

… the English cavalry, well-groomed, spurs and buckles gleaming in the sun. They were very good to us, giving us cigarettes and food, bandaging our feet and giving each [man] a pair of socks.

The men travelled on by tram and train until they got to Mons, where they spent the night in the cavalry barracks in company with thousands of other prisoners. Next day they were taken to Valenciennes by lorry, and there they boarded a Red Cross train to Calais.

Percy's story does not end here, however. After two months on leave, by which time he had recovered his health, he was ordered to report to Fulford Barracks in York, and told his name was on a draft bound for India! It seems that a number of the men on this draft were ex-prisoners of war awaiting demobilization, and a deputation went to see the Lord Mayor of York. Strings were pulled and Percy's name was removed from the list, but he was sent to Salisbury Plain to join the Motor Transport section of the Royal Army Service Corps, and was not released from the Army until October 1919, almost a year after the war had ended.

WALTER HARE

Walter Hare enlisted in May 1916 at the age of 18. He had hoped to join his brother Harold in the Leeds Pals, but after his training he was sent with a draft to the 1st Bradford Pals (16th [Service] Battalion, The West Yorkshire Regiment). When the British Army was reorganised early in 1918, the two battalions of Bradford Pals were disbanded and Walter was one of the contingent posted to the Leeds Pals. He joined the battalion in mid-February and was captured on 27 March.

> *Now my first thought was how am I going to get back to my own side? That was all I was concerned about, I wanted to back with our lads again.*
>
> *They told me two days before that my brother had been killed and I wasn't at all surprised because we'd a lot of casualties but he hadn't been. I saw him coming in and I couldn't believe it. I waved at him and after that we were always 'Zwei Bruder – the two brothers.*

Walter Hare.

> *We were ordered to keep moving and after passing through never-ending waves of advancing German troops were finally lined up in an old quarry just over the brow of the hill. A short discussion took place between a German officer and NCO and I wondered if they were debating whether to shoot us then or some time later. We had certainly caused them a lot of casualties.*
>
> *We were relieved of our field dressings of which the German Army was desperately short. Then we were moved on and finally found ourselves in a wire cage together with a varied assortment of men from other units.*
>
> *It was raining, the ground was muddy both inside and outside the wire cage, but that was our home for the next six weeks. We slept out on the wet ground in this camp [Villers]. I think we were captured either three or four days before they gave us anything to eat, then they gave us some soup; well they called it soup, it were cabbage water. After that we got a small piece of bread about as big as your fist. We went to work during the day on a railway they were repairing at Romacourt.*
>
> *We used to try to keep together to keep warm at night and some of the chaps died of exposure. The Germans used to come of a morning, look around and pick the dead ones and take them out. One night I put my hand out to my brother who were next to me and his arm fell down like that, it were dead cold. I thought, 'Oh my goodness, he's died'. When it got a bit light I looked and it wasn't him, he'd moved during the night and somebody else had come and laid down by side of me. Poor lad had died anyway.*
>
> *One day they took us down to Romacourt and put us in the cattle trucks and we set off on our way to Germany. We stopped somewhere for baths, in beer barrels cut in*

Harold Hare.

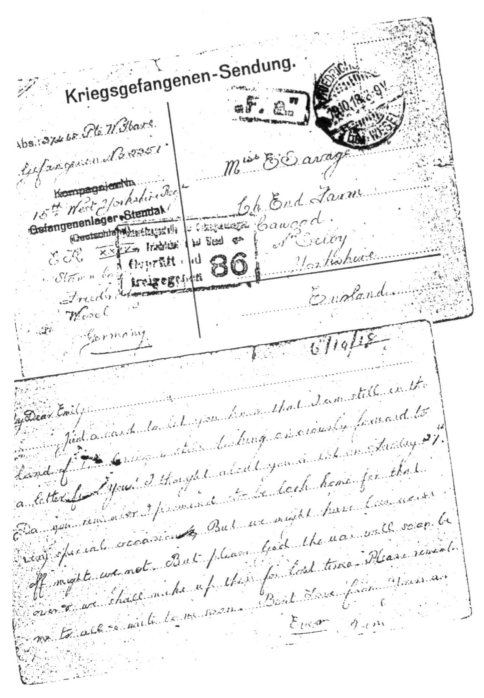

*Walter's card to his girlfriend Emily Savage. She wrote back but her letter was returned by
the German authorities.*

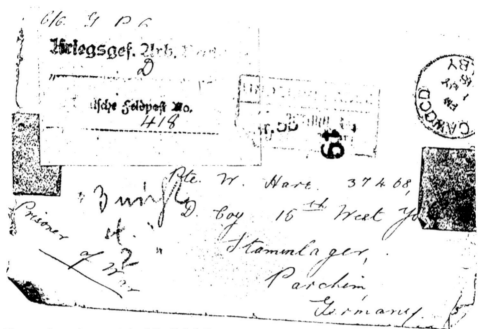

The envelope that contained Emily's letter.

INSER TOP OF MISSING
SCAN – PAGE 271

BROTHERS MISSING.–Pte. H. Hare (on left) and Pte. W. Hare, sons of Mrs. Hare, of The Poplars, Cawood, Selby. News wanted. Both of the West Yorkshire Regiment.

MISSING. – Pioneer J. A. Binks, Highfield View, Tingley, Leeds, News wanted.

Private Ernest 'Bob' Lickard.

two and filled with cold water. They took our clothes and put them in a fumigator. No soap or anything like that, we just washed, you see, and we got our clothes and put them on while they were still warm. That was the first bath we had. The first time we had been warm for a while.

We never got any parcels or letters. We'd no contact with the outside world at all.

Eventually they stopped at Strasbourg and they took us out and marched us round the streets. It was so humiliating to be shown round the streets as prisoners just captured; we weren't, we'd been there for weeks sleeping in this mud.

Anyway we got on the train again, we stayed the night at Freiburg in a hospital and the next day we got on the train to a place called Emmendingen, near the Swiss border. It was a nice camp. There were huts and we'd a wash house and a blanket and wire beds. There were sixty of us in two huts and we worked eight-hour shifts in a factory quite near. I think this place had been built specially for working in this factory. There was a big high wall around the factory and there were armed guards on duty all the time, and armed guards to march us across and back of course, and in charge of each room in that factory there were army personnel.

Now what they were making I just don't know, I worked on what they called a 'Schneider' machine. The raw material was straw, and it was cut very small and went up the chute into another place. What happened after that I don't know, I don't think the people who worked in the factory there knew what the final product was. It might have been something towards some explosive they were making.

They were short of everything, and particularly oil and grease and we used to do a bit of sabotage. There was a German corporal in charge of five or six machines and I got sort of friendly with him and he used to let me help him to oil the machines. Each shift used to stop halfway through to cool the machines down because they got running hot with being short of grease. They had a tin of grease and they kept it locked in a cupboard, and the corporal used to get his key out, open up and get his tin of grease out, and he let me do it. Well he'd walk off somewhere and I used to put a little bit round the top of the little caps where they put the grease, in and rub some into my boots, and after a while the machine ran dry again and they never twigged what it was.

At Emmendingen they used to take us down to Freiburg about once a fortnight for baths, so we were better looked after there. If we'd had letters or parcels or something like that we wouldn't have been too bad.

They never took our name or number or anything like that. When we eventually got a [prisoner-of-war post] card each, my brother said, 'I'll send my card home, you write to your girlfriend, and then next time I'll send [mine] to my girlfriend and you send it home,' so we did that. But we only had the two cards, we never got any more. When I sent my card home they wrote to me but I never got it. They sent it back, 'untraceable', so that upset them because they thought I must have died; same thing happened to my brother.

One morning we thought they were taking us down to the station for baths but they didn't. They put us on the cattle trucks, it would have been early November, I think, and moved us all day, and towards evening they got us out and marched us over a bridge across a huge river, about another mile, and then put us into an old school room, with walls around it and guards. There was about a hundred and twenty of us. They let us out each day for a bit of exercise in the yard, but that was all.

There was a church just across the square and one Sunday after the morning service the population came and gathered round the school gates and shouted, 'Die Krieg fertig, Die Krieg fertig' – 'The war is over, the war is finished'. So of course we rushed to see what it was all about but the guards got us back inside quickly and shoved the people away. In the tumult I jumped over the school wall. I wanted to get away. We didn't know where we were in Germany but I wanted to get away. I got to the river side and I thought, shall I try and see if anybody will give me something to eat? While I was wondering whether to risk it, a German soldier on horse back saw me, asked me where I came from and he made me get back. He rode on his horse and made me walk. I got back to the [school], the guards shouted and swore at me and pushed me inside again. After a bit, a German officer came and he was swearing at me, 'Englander Schweinhund [pig-dog]' and so on, and I said to him, 'You can't do that, the war's over!'. I didn't know if it was, but I'd heard these people shout, and he whipped his revolver out. I thought I'd had it, he pointed it straight at me and he carried on shouting. I stood perfectly still and never said another word, and at the finish he spun round and off he went.

That was 11 November 1918, Armistice Day.

Anyway the next morning the people came and gathered around again and shouted that the war was over so we said there must be some truth in it. Well, we talked about it and we said, 'If it is, we've had it, we've lost', because they were advancing so fast when we were taken prisoner we thought all of France would have been occupied in no time. I said to my brother, 'I think they'll either shoot us or send us to a work camp.' He said 'Well I hope they don't shoot us.'

Towards evening they lined us up on the road outside with armed guards at either side. They marched us about four miles into an old unoccupied barracks and they put us into a room and locked us in – no light, of course, and we felt around and there were wire beds so we decided we'd try and get a bit of rest. We knew we wouldn't sleep because we didn't know what tomorrow would bring.

The next morning when it got daylight somebody tried the door and it opened. I said, 'Be careful.' I think I was the youngest, but I think I was the fittest of the lot. We'd been short of food all that time, we got even less than the Germans. I got down to seven stone. Anyway we opened it a little bit, a little bit further, and still nothing happened. We knew they'd shot some of our chaps who'd tried to escape and I said, 'They'll shoot us one at a time as we come out and say we were trying to escape'. But we pulled the door wide open and nothing happened. So at the finish I volunteered with another chap to go out and have a look, and I ran out into the barrack yard expecting to hear a shot from somewhere, but nothing happened, and I looked around and there was nobody there, no guards, they'd left us, high and dry. So we talked a bit and said, 'We can't stop here, we've no money and we've no food and we don't know where we are.' There were about a hundred of us, I suppose. Bob Lickard from York [35406 Private Ernest Lickard], he was with us.

I saw a priest walking down the village street so I went across and asked him the only thing I could think of, 'Which is the way to France?' I didn't know if we were near to France, you see. I spoke a little bit of German and he spoke a little bit of English. [He said] 'How do you mean to get there?' I said, 'Walk'. 'Walk?' he said, 'A hundred and fifty kilometres – over a hundred miles!' [actually about 94 miles] I said, 'Yes, which is the way?' and he pointed down the road, he said, 'West'. So I went back into the barrack square to my brother, this Bob Lickard and this Jack we had with us, and I told them what had happened. It was down this road, west.

We walked all that day, slept in a hedge at night, that was on the Tuesday. Walked all the next day. On the Thursday it rained, it was raining very badly and Jack wasn't very well at all. We'd gone maybe a mile or two and he said 'I feel very ill, you go on', so we said, 'We'll have a rest on the side of the road for a bit', so we sat down and rested maybe half-an-hour. My brother went to have a look at him, he said 'Jack's gone'. He died on the roadside. All we knew was his name was Jack. We had to leave him, we couldn't do anything with him.

German prisoner-of-war money. It was worthless, for there was nothing to buy.

So we set off again with very heavy hearts. It rained most of the day. We thought 'We'll have to find somewhere to shelter tonight,' then we saw a huge quarry, and there was ladders down the side and a hut at the bottom, and we said if we can get in that hut it will be alright. There might be a bit of food there, maybe some of the workmen will have left something. We got down but there was no food. We slept there that night, but by Jove we'd a job to get out the next day up them ladders, because we were so weak.

I tore the sleeves off my shirt – my socks had all gone, of course – and wrapped them round my feet to make it a bit easier for walking. The next day, it would be the Friday, I think, we heard a band, it was coming gradually nearer, there was a bank at the roadside, and we got up the bank and got behind the hedge and waited. It was a German battalion marching down the road from the direction we were going, so we knew we were going the right way. The band was playing and they all seemed jolly so we thought well, we've lost, we'll have to be very careful now. Anyway we let them get past and then we set off. We didn't want to be captured again.

We'd no food, we'd plenty of water and we ate nettles, you can eat nettles, you know. We tried grass but you couldn't eat grass, but nettles kept us going. On Saturday afternoon we came to maybe half-a-dozen houses, just one street and there was nobody in them, they were all empty. So we had a look to see if there was any food and one was a German quartermaster store. There was all sorts of stuff in there, binoculars and things like that, and we said we'd stay the night here and set off early the next morning, so we decided to stay in one of the houses, we had a look all over to see if there was any food but of course there wasn't. There were three of us, Bob Lickard, my brother and me, and we sat down and after we'd been sat there a bit, my brother said, 'Has anybody looked in that cupboard under the stairs?', so we said, 'No'. He said, 'Oh, I'll have a look', and it wasn't a cupboard it was a cellar. He went down and came back in a few minutes with two bottles of wine, lifesavers! There was a little mug on the mantelpiece so we poured some in and then I remembered when the Germans had pulled back to the Hindenburg Line, they'd left bottles of poisoned wine and some of our chaps drunk it and that was the end of them. I said they've very likely left that poisoned wine, don't drink it. So we sat down for a bit and we kept looking at this wine and we decided somebody would have a little sip and see what happened. Well I don't know who took the first drink, it wasn't me, but I remember watching and looking to see if he collapsed, but nothing happened so eventually we drank those two bottles of wine.

We set off early the next morning, and suddenly we saw in front of us trenches. We got past all this trench system, barbed wire, and crossed no man's land and we got over the wire at the other side and we said, 'We're home'. But it was completely devastated, the whole area. We looked around and there was some French equipment laying about, well we knew we'd got to a place where the French had been, you see, but ahead of us was this huge forest and that was a bit upsetting 'cause getting through a forest that you know is a bit difficult, but we kept going forward.

We got to the edge of the wood and I said, 'Look, I'll tell you what we ought to do, we ought to walk up the side of the wood until we come to a roadway leading through,' and so we did. We set off, and we'd gone perhaps half a mile when my brother flopped down, he said, 'I can't go on, you go, you might find somebody to help us.' I said, 'We're not leaving you, we've stuck together, we'll stay.' Then Bob flopped down as well. I said, 'I'll tell you what, we'll have five or ten minutes' rest, then we'll all get up and move on,' and I lay down to die.

I knew I wasn't going to get up, I'd no strength, I'd no will power, I just laid there, and I thought if they ever do find us, I wonder if they'll know we're British soldiers on our way home from a German prisoner-of-war camp. We may be in such a mess they won't even know.

I don't know now whether we laid there minutes, hours or how long we laid there, it was getting dusk and suddenly we heard the whistle of a railway engine from somewhere across the wood and all three of us were up on our feet like a shot, and it came again, that life-saving whistle. Without thinking we plunged into the wood. We knew that somebody there might be able to help us. Eventually we found a road, we turned down this road and we'd gone maybe half a mile, we saw two figures in uniform ahead of us. It was getting quite dark now, and I said, 'Look, it's the moment, we can't go any further, we'll have to give ourselves up and hope for the best.'

When we got up to them, they were two French soldiers in uniform, but they couldn't believe we were prisoners of war by the condition we were in. But I said look at my back, my prisoner-of-war number was painted on my back. They took us back to a little hut they had at the edge of the wood, but they hadn't any food for us. They said they'd have to take us to their billeting quarters at Luneville about a couple of miles away. 'Well', we said, 'We can't walk'. 'Oh', they said, 'We'll help you. There was about a couple of dozen of them and they all turned out, and they almost carried us down there.

We got there about midnight and met the orderly sergeant and he got the cooks out and told them to give us something to eat. They gave us a mug of proper coffee, not the 'Ersatz' muck that we'd been having. We'd two cold sausages each and that's all they had till the next morning's rations. That was the first food I had, eatable, for eight months, two sausages and a mug of coffee. Well, the next day they got a French officer, an interpreter, and he spoke very good English. He was awfully upset that we'd walked all that way. He said that the Armistice terms said you had to be handed over, they had to find transport. We said, 'They just left us, we don't even know there was an Armistice.' 'Well', these lads said, 'We've won'. We said, 'Won?' They said 'Yes, you've walked right through Alsace-Lorraine from Saarbrucken!'

Gallantry Awards

Compiling a complete list of the awards received by members of a battalion is by no means as simple as one might expect. No central record appears to have been kept that would enable a researcher to extract the names of recipients of gallantry awards made to members of a particular regiment or battalion. Such records that survive are indexed by soldier's name, so without a complete nominal roll one cannot trace every gallantry award to a battalion. A further complication is the transfer of men from one battalion to another, as mentioned above, which means that it is not always possible to determine which battalion a man was serving with when he received his award.

The Military Cross Distinguished Conduct Medal and campaign star and medals awarded to Second-Lieutenant W. S. Wharram. (Author's collection)

VICTORIA CROSS:
17/1280 Private (later Sergeant) William Boynton Butler (17th Battalion serving with 106th Trench Mortar Battery)

For most conspicuous bravery when in charge of a Stokes gun in trenches which were being heavily shelled. Suddenly one of the fly off levers of a Stokes shell came off and fired the shell in the emplacement. Private Butler picked up the shell and jumped to the entrance of the emplacement, which at that moment a party of infantry were passing. He shouted to them to hurry past as the shell was going off, and turning round, placed himself between the party of men and the live shell and so held it till they were out of danger. He then threw the shell on to the parados, and took cover in the bottom of the trench. The shell exploded almost on leaving his hand, greatly damaging the trench. By extremely good luck, Private Butler was contused only. Undoubtedly his great presence of mind and disregard for his own life saved the lives of the officer and men in the emplacement and the party which was passing at the time.

London Gazette 17 October 1917

The action for which Sergeant Butler was awarded the VC took place on 6 August 1917. He was invested with the Victoria Cross at Buckingham Palace on 5 December 1917.

19/11 Sergeant Albert Mountain (15/17th Battalion)

For most conspicuous bravery and devotion to duty during an enemy attack, when his company was in an exposed position on a sunken road, having hastily dug themselves in. Owing to the intense artillery fire, they were obliged to vacate the road and fall back. The enemy in the meantime was advancing in mass, preceded by an advanced patrol about two hundred strong. The situation was critical and volunteers for a counter-attack were called for. Sergeant Mountain immediately stepped forward, and his party of ten men followed him. He then advanced on the flank with a Lewis gun and brought enfilade fire to bear on the enemy patrol, killing about one hundred. In the meantime the remainder of the company made a frontal attack, and the entire enemy patrol was cut up and thirty prisoners were taken.

At this time the enemy main body appeared and the men, who were numerically many times weaker than the enemy, began to waver. Sergeant Mountain rallied and organised his party and formed a defensive position from which to cover the retirement of the company and the prisoners. With this party of one non-commissioned officer and four men, he sucessfully held at bay six hundred of the enemy for half an hour, eventually retiring and rejoining his company. He then took command of the flank post of the Battalion which was 'in the air', and held on there for twenty seven hours until finally surrounded by the enemy. Sergeant Mountain was one of the few who managed to fight their way back. His supreme fearlessness and initiative undoubtedly saved the whole situation.

London Gazette 4 June 1918

Sergeant Mountain was invested with the ribbon of the Victoria Cross in France on 10 June 1918.

DISTINGUISHED SERVICE ORDER:
Lieutenant-Colonel Stuart Campbell Taylor

For conspicuous gallantry when in command of the right of an infantry attack. The attacking troops having been compelled to fall back, he collected the remnants of his battalion and about 100 men of other units, and, regardless of a heavy fire, he organized these in defence of a position, and by his fine example of courage and skill he successfully resisted three counter-attacks, and thus saved a critical situation.

London Gazette 18 July 1917

DISTINGUISHED SERVICE ORDER AND BAR:
Major (Temporary Lieutenant-Colonel) A. V. Nutt

London Gazette 1 January 1918 (DSO) London Gazette (Bar)

MILITARY CROSS:
Captain and Quartermaster Robert J. Anderson

London Gazette

Captain Richard Burnie Armistead

This officer was in command of a company which captured an important fortified position of the enemy. He personally directed the advance of the leading wave, ensuring touch with the flanks being maintained. When the objective was reached he went forward to the most advanced posts to superintend the work of consolidation, and he inspired all ranks with cheerful confidence, which enabled them to withstand the heavy shelling. During the whole operation his behaviour was a fine example to everyone in the battalion.

London Gazette 15 October 1918

Lieutenant George Emil Jowett Brooksbank

For conspicuous gallantry and devotion to duty. When in command of a raiding party he displayed very capable leadership, and it was due to his skill and previous careful reconnaissances of the enemy front that the raid was successfully carried out in exact accordance with orders. This officer was the first to enter the enemy front trench, and the success of the operation was largely due to his intimate knowledge of this portion of the enemy's line.

London Gazette 18 March 1918

Lieutenant John Wall Buckley

For conspicuous gallantry and devotion to duty. During eight days' continuous fighting, as Battalion Transport Officer, he made daring reconnaissances of roads by day and night, and never failed to deliver full supplies of rations and ammunition.

London Gazette 26 July 1918

Second-Lieutenant William Hazzard

Acting as an intelligence officer with the Battalion at Gavrelle on May 3rd 1917, 2 Lieut Hazzard reconnoitred under heavy machine gun and shell fire to gain information. After the attack was held up by machine-gun fire he assisted in consolidating and strengthening a line of defence, and organised the defenders from the remnants of several units.

Battalion War Diary 5 June 1917

For conspicuous gallantry and devotion to duty. During an infantry attack he reconnoitred under heavy fire to gain information. After the attack was held up he assisted in consolidating and strengthening a line of defence, and in organising the defenders from the remnants of several units. The security of the defence was largely due to his coolness and courage.

London Gazette 18 July 1918

Second-Lieutenant E. W. Hewland

London Gazette

Second-Lieutenant Fred Sidney Hollingworth

For conspicuous gallantry and devotion to duty. During the night this officer successfully placed three guns with their ammunition in an unreconnoitred position. Against a subsequent attack he worked one of the guns himself until it was blown up.

London Gazette 26 July 1918

Lieutenant Daniel Thomas King

For conspicuous gallantry and devotion to duty. Though suffering from a severe bruise on the knee from a shell splinter he volunteered to make, and successfully carried out, a reconnaissance under very heavy machine-gun and shell fire, which was of value at a critical moment. He has shown a fine example to all in conducting many valuable reconnaissances and in collecting men under heavy shell fire.

London Gazette 16 September 1918

Captain John Gagon Lee, MB (Royal Army Medical Corps, attached to 15/17th Battalion)

For conspicuous gallantry and devotion to duty in attending to casualties under very heavy machine-gun and shell fire continuously for four days. He was wounded on the second day, but remained at duty. He had his dressing stations blown up twice. Each time new stations were reorganised very quickly. He behaved splendidly, and his conduct was a very fine example to all.

London Gazette 16 September 1918

Captain and Adjutant Desmond Annesley Fraser Needham, (Royal Fusiliers, attached to 15/17th Battalion)

For conspicuous gallantry and devotion to duty. During an enemy attack this officer displayed great coolness and gallantry, personally organising and supervising the defence and encouraging the men under very heavy machine-gun fire. When forced to retire, as the enemy had broken through on a flank, he rallied stragglers from different battalions and personally organised and led a counter-attack which resulted in a substantial advance of our line. On another occasion, when the men, wearied with prolonged fighting, were being hardly tried by an exceptionally severe bombardment, his great coolness and cheerfulness did much to keep up their spirits. During the whole time his energy was untiring and his disregard of personal safety conspicuous. His conduct of the operations saved a very critical situation.

London Gazette 16 September 1918

Lieutenant Valentine Oland (14th Battalion, attached 15th Bn – posthumous award, killed in action 1 July 1916)

For conspicuous courage. When attacked by a hostile raiding party, 2nd-Lt Oland jumped on the parapet, rallied our wiring party who had been bombed, and finally drove off the enemy, who were superior in numbers.

London Gazette 27 July 1916

Second-Lieutenant George William Tiffany

For conspicuous gallantry and devotion to duty. This officer led his platoon to attack a farm which the enemy had occupied. Twice he attacked and had to fall back under a withering fire, the third time he succeeded in surrounding the farm.

London Gazette 16 September 1918

Second-Lieutenant W. Timson

For conspicuous gallantry and devotion to duty throughout a week of the enemy attack. During the whole time he set a splendid example of coolness and determination, and on one occasion when the enemy by sheer force of numbers penetrated the line his company resisted to the last, saving a critical situation.

London Gazette 26 July 1918

Second-Lieutenant Harry Walker

For conspicuous gallantry and devotion to duty. This officer led his platoon against a farm which the enemy had captured. By excellent tactics he got within 50 yards of his objective over open ground swept by machine gun fire, with only six casualties. Here he was shot through the arms and leg but controlled the situation until he was carried away by the stretcher-bearers.

London Gazette 16 September 1918

Lieutenant (Acting Captain) Wilfrid Clement Septimus Weighill

London Gazette

Second-Lieutenant William Stephen Wharram, DCM

For conspicuous gallantry and devotion to duty. After our front had retired he took out his platoon and enfiladed the advance of the enemy, directing a very effective fire against them. When the enemy took up fresh positions he again enfiladed them, enabling a frontal attack to be made which led to the capture of 35 prisoners.

London Gazette 26 July 1918

Regimental-Sergeant-Major John Gordon Brennan

For conspicuous gallantry and devotion to duty. When a retirement was ordered he showed great coolness and judgement in rallying many of his battalion's right flank. This held the enemy in check and allowed the remainder of the battalion to take up its position.

London Gazette 16 September 1918

Regimental-Sergeant-Major William Wilson

At Gavrelle on May 3rd 1917 when the enemy were counter attacking RSM Wison assisted in organising a force from several Battalions, and posting them for defence, also served out ammunition and bombs.

Battalion War Diary 5 June 1917

For conspicuous gallantry and devotion to duty. During an enemy counter-attack he assisted in organising and posting a force for defence from several battalions. In the absence of officers he took charge of fire orders, and was greatly instrumental in correct fire being directed upon the advancing enemy. His courage and cheerfulness under critical circumstances were invaluable.

London Gazette 8 July 1917

MILITARY CROSS AND BAR

Major Walter Peace:

Military Cross:

For conspicuous gallantry and devotion to duty in attack. Although twice wounded in the early morning, he still held on to a portion of our front line trench with a small party of men for the rest of the day, being completely isolated.

London Gazette 20 October 1916

Bar

For conspicuous gallantry and devotion to duty. When the enemy had penetrated the right flank of his company he brought up two platoons and counter-attacked with success. Although slightly wounded in the head, he remained with his men, and by his example encouraged them to hold on in a critical situation.

London Gazette 16 September 1918

Captain Harold Smith

London Gazette 1918 (Military Cross)
London Gazette 1918 (Bar – awarded posthumously, died of wounds 28 March 1918)

DISTINGUISHED CONDUCT MEDAL

15/131 Sergeant O. J. Butterfield

For conspicuous gallantry and devotion to duty. He personally attacked and captured an enemy machine gun and its detachment during our advance. He showed the greatest energy and determination when the final objective had been reached, in consolidating the position, cheering and encouraging his men under the intense shell fire of the enemy. During the whole day and the following night he was continually moving about from post to post quite regardless of his own safety, showing a fine example of tireless devotion to duty and conspicuous gallantry to his men.

London Gazette 30 October 1918

40254 Acting Warrant Officer II G. H. Calverley, MM

For conspicuous gallantry and devotion to duty. This NCO was in command of a platoon in the leading wave of an attack. He displayed fine qualities of leadership, and by his courage and initiative enabled his platoon to capture an enemy machine gun and two trench mortars. On reaching the final objective he pursued the enemy across the stream, and inflicted severe casualties on him as he retreated. On his return he exercised excellent judgement in the measures he took to secure his position against a possible counter-attack. Up to the time he was severely wounded in the face shoulder and hand by shrapnel, his idefatigable coolness inspired his men with the greatest confidence.

London Gazette 30 October 1918

38S23 Private (acting Lance-Corporal) Harold Stanley Child, MM

From 25th February 1918, to 16th September 1918. For continuous devotion to duty and absolute disregard for his own personal safety during the past year, particularly during the period under review. He has proved himself to be absolutely reliable during operations and in the presence of the enemy. His cheerfulness at all times has been most marked and a great encouragement to the gun teams.

London Gazette 3 September 1919

18/1514 Lance-Corporal H Cowgill

For conspicuous gallantry and devotion to duty. This NCO displayed great gallantry and initiative during our attack. At one moment an enemy machine-gun was about to open fire, when with the utmost promptitude, he rushed the gun, killing the gunner and scattering the detatchment, who were subsequently made prisoners. The advance then progressed. The next day, though very severely wounded by a shell in the chest and legs he continued to command his section until he became unconscious. His cool courage and fine leadership contributed largely to the rapidity and success of the advance.

London Gazette 30 October 1918

16/637 Corporal (later Sergeant) C Farrar

For conspicuous gallantry and devotion to duty. He has performed consistent good work throughout, and has at all times set a splendid example.

London Gazette 13 February 1917

15/531 Company-Sergeant-Major Joseph Edward Jones

At Gavrelle on May 3rd 1917, CSM Jones attacked with his Company and reached the first German line. He killed several Germans with his bayonet, and drove out the remainder from his section of trench, which he proceeded to consolidate and hold with the few men he gathered together. He was wounded altogether 5 times.

Battalion War Diary 5 June 1917

For conspicuous gallantry and devotion to duty. He attacked with his Company and drove the enemy from his section of the trench, which he at once consolidated and held. Though five times wounded he held on, and repulsed local counter-attacks, setting a splendid example of courage and resolution to his men.

London Gazette 18 July 1917

15/1536 Sergeant H. Marshall

For conspicuous gallantry and devotion to duty. He took command of half a company and captured fifty prisoners. Later he established communication with the battalion on his left and thus enabled the whole objective to be consolidated.

London Gazette 25 August 1917

15/684 Acting Warrant Officer II P. Nichol

For constant devotion to duty during the last nine months. He has proved himself to be very capable and thoroughly conscientious. He has shown conspicuous gallantry in active operations. On several occasions he has been called upon to act as platoon commander, and has always justified the confidence placed in him.

London Gazette 3 September 1919

37805 Private A. Richelieu

For conspicuous gallantry and devotion to duty. Immediately after our objective in an attack had been reached, he went out in charge of a patrol. He was severely wounded in the leg shortly after starting, but refused to have his wound dressed until he had completed his reconnaissance, during which he captured two prisoners and obtained valuable information.

He showed a conspicuous example of soldierly endurance and devotion to duty.

London Gazette 30 October 1918

15/790 Company Sergeant-Major (later Second-Lieutenant) F. Scholes

For conspicuous gallantry and devotion to duty. He rendered most valuable assistance in reorganising the battalion after the attack. He has performed consistent good work throughout.

London Gazette 13 February 1917

38270 Private E. Simpson

For conspicuous gallantry and devotion to duty. While Pte Simpson was engaged in cutting a gap in the enemy wire, which was checking the progress of his section during our advance, he was attacked by an enemy officer, who fired at him at point blank range. Pte Simpson, who was untouched, desisted from his task and killed his assailant, and then resumed his work cutting the wire, eventually making a way for his section to advance. Subsequently, when the enemy threw several stick grenades at his section, with rare promptitude and courage he picked up the grenades before they exploded and threw them back, undoubtedly saving many casualties. During the whole operation his conduct was distinguished by fine courage and disregard of danger.

London Gazette 30 October 1918

15/1801 Sergeant C Stanhope (did not serve overseas with 15th Battalion, DCM awarded with 1st Battalion)

17/1226 Private C. E. Torr (DCM awarded for service with 17th Battalion, after he had joined the 15/17th Battalion)

For conspicuous gallantry and devotion to duty. He carried messages under heavy fire during several engagements, and showed the greatest coolness, courage and determination during a long period.

London Gazette 17 April 1918

For showing great bravery and devotion to duty in carrying messages from the Headquarters of the Trench Mortar Battery in Guillemont Farm Sector to the gun under heavy shell fire. Towards the end of the attack only one gun was left in the Battery, which was without ammunition. Pte Torr located an emplacement which had been blown up, dug up the ammunition and carried to the effective gun.

Battalion War Diary 1 January 1918

3/8538 Sergeant H. Wharfe

For conspicuous gallantry and devotion to duty. During the whole time the enemy were attacking he showed fine qualities as a leader, keeping his men together and controlling their fire. When surrounded by six of the enemy and ordered to surrender he fought his way out with clubbed rifle and regained the line.

London Gazette 3 September 1918

16/1068 Private (later Second-Lieutenant) William Stephen Wharram (DCM while serving with the 11th Battalion, on 7 October 1916)
For conspicuous gallantry in action. In the company of one officer he bombed down an enemy trench and assisted in the capture of over 100 prisoners.

London Gazette 25 November 1916

Captain and Quartermaster A. Barker (DCM for service with The King's Own Yorkshire Light Infantry)

MILITARY MEDAL
15035 Private James Arthur Allsop
At Gavrelle on 3rd May 1917 was a Headquarters runner. He went through enemy barrage and intensive machine gun fire to obtain information as to the situation of the forward companies. The information gained was most important, and cleared up the situation.

Battalion War Diary 24 May 1917
London Gazette 9 July 1917

15/30 Private E. Appleyard

London Gazette 11 November 1916

16/819 Private Charles Berry

London Gazette 6 August 1918

16/1137 Private Arthur Binns
Advanced with his platoon to attack the German positions East of Gavrelle. He gained the first objective where he established a bombing post. He repulsed a local counter-attack, and drove the enemy down the trench with bombs. The enemy afterwards fired a rifle grenade into the post which Private Binns was holding. Private Binns picked it up and threw it over the parapet where it exploded without any damage. Re Binns undoubtedly by his courage and coolness saved his comrades from being killed or wounded.

Battalion War Diary 24 May 1917
London Gazette 9 July 1917

15/97 Sergeant C. Birch

London Gazette 28 January 1918

15/84 Sergeant Edward Foster Breckin (MM for service with the 11th Battalion)

15/164 Lance-Corporal William N. Brown

London Gazette 11 November 1916

40254 Acting Warrant Officer II G H Calveriey (also DCM with 18th Battalion)

London Gazette 18 January 1918

15/195 Private (later Lance-Corporal) Harold Child

London Gazette 21 October 1916

38523 Private Harold Stanley Child (see also DCM)

London Gazette 14 May 1919

15/204 Lance-Corporal Joseph Clark (awarded for gallant action on the night of 22 May 1916)

London Gazette 10 August 1916

15/210 Private George E. Clayton

A Battalion runner, when no information could be received from the attacking companies, went out at Gavrelle on May 3rd 1917 under a heavy barrage of fire and succeeded in obtaining information which allowed preparations to be made to meet counter attacks. He was badly wounded in both legs.

Battalion War Diary 24 May 1917
London Gazette 9 July 1917

15/217 Acting Corporal Joseph W. Collinson (MM awarded for service with 9th Battalion)

13093 Sergeant E. Davy

28197 Private W. Dyson

London Gazette 23 February 1918

15/312 Private A. B. Eschle (posthumous award, killed in action 1 July 1916)

London Gazette 28 June 1917

15/330 Lance-Corporal Harry Leslie Firth

London Gazette 23 February 1918

15/399 Sergeant Ernest A. Green

London Gazette 11 November 1916

41555 Private A. Hemingway

London Gazette 16 July 1918

15/490 Corporal Harry Hutchinson

London Gazette

15/1321 Acting Sergeant Herbert Jackson

London Gazette 6 August 1918

15/518 Warrant Officer II Eric Carew Jenkyns

London Gazette 11 November 1916

Acting Sergeant Percy Samson Johnson

London Gazette

28312 Private J. E. Joyce (awarded for service with 18th Battalion).

33688 Lance-Corporal L. Leffley (awarded for service with 16th Battalion).

16/1091 Sergeant S. Lister (posthumous award, killed in action 22 September 1918)
London Gazette 13 November 1918

28696 Private A. Lord
London Gazette 16 July 1918

15/631 Sergeant William Mackenzie
Was with the leading wave of his company at Gavrelle, and succeeded in reaching his objective, and consolidating the position. He repulsed the counter-attacks coming from Fresnes and held on to his position for 4 hours until his ammunition failed.
Battalion War Diary 24 May 1917

15/662 Private (later Corporal) Sydney Mason
London Gazette 6 August 1918

15/634 Private George A. Meldrum
London Gazette 23 February 1918

15/1027 Acting Sergeant Matthew H. Mossop (posthumous award, killed in action 1 July 1916)
London Gazette 28 July 1917

15/690 Private Harold Reynolds Oddy (MM and Bar)
London Gazette 21 October 1916 (MM) London Gazette 16 July 1918 (Bar)

15/1622 Private Reginald Pawson (MM for service with l/6th Battalion)

57883 Private George William Poulter
London Gazette 14 May 1919

24568 Private F. Richardson
London Gazette 6 August 1918

15/1300 Private George Robson
London Gazette 21 October 1916

15/1096 Corporal Robert Wickham Sheppard (posthumous award, killed in action 27 March 1918)
London Gazette 23 December 1918

29387 Lance-Corporal H. Slater
London Gazette 16 July 1918

22255 Private P. Stanton

London Gazette 6 August 1918

15/879 Corporal Reginald Charles Taylor

London Gazette 14 May 1919

15/1226 Private (later Lance-Corporal) John Edward Todd (MM for service with the 2/8th Battalion)

41477 Private J. Walsh (for service with 17th Battalion, later killed in action with 15/17th Battalion)

London Gazette 26 May 1917

15/1744 Acting Corporal William Bruce West (for service with 2/8th Battalion)

33686 Private Alfred P. Westerman
A stretcher bearer at Gavrelle on May 3rd 1917, went out into the open during the action and tended wounded men under heavy bombardment. He was shot in the eye.

Battalion War Diary 30 May 1917 London Gazette No. 58

3/8538 Sergeant Harry Wharfe (see also DCM)

London Gazette No.58

15/1483 Sergeant John Richard Williams (for service with 1st Battalion)

33770 Private Henry Wrighton
A stretcher bearer at Gavrelle remained in the open under heavy machine-gun and shell fire. He brought in No. 33686 Private A. P. Westerman when he was wounded and then returned to the open for 24 hours dressing the wounded and searching the shell holes for other cases.

Battalion War Diary 30 May 1917 London Gazette 18 July 1917

15/1008 Sergeant Arthur Edward Wood (postumous award, died of wounds 15 April 1918)

London Gazette 23 December 1918

MERITORIOUS SERVICE MEDAL
15/536 Acting Lance-Corporal Gilbert Aitchinson

London Gazette No.60

15/1029 Sergeant Harry Bruerton

London Gazette No.60

15/218 Acting Regimental Sergeant-Major Frank Colquhoun

Peace Gazette

16/243 Private B Drake

London Gazette 17 June 1918

15/336 Sergeant Arthur Flannaghan

London Gazette No.60

15/1101 Lance-Corporal Thomas H. Place

London Gazette 17 June 1918

15/848 Colour-Sergeant Richard Harold Stendell

London Gazette No.60

15/957 Sergeant Norman Fothergill Webster

London Gazette 1 January 1918

MENTIONED IN DESPATCHES
Temporary Quartermaster and Hon-Lieutenant R. J. Anderson

London Gazette 4 July 1917

15/325 Lance-Corporal George M. Ferrand (posthumous, missing presumed dead 3 May 1917)

London Gazette 22 May 1917

15/1035 Sergeant Harry Jackman

London Gazette 4 January 1917

15/1321 Corporal Herbert Jackson

London Gazette 4 January 1917

Lieutenant W. D. Gray (5th Bn attached)

16 March 1919

Lieutenant-Colonel Stuart Campbell Taylor (mentioned twice)

London Gazette 22 May 1917 London Gazette 11 December 1917

FORIEGN AWARDS
Croix de Guerre – Belgium
16/320 Lance-Corporal Walter Tetley, 19 January 1918

Croix de Guerre – France
Captain Richard Burnie Armistead (6th Battalion, attached to 15/17th Battalion, see also MC), 4 September 1919
15/1311 Private Norman Gibson (posthumous, killed in action 22.4.1918), 30 April 1918

Headquarters,
93rd Infantry Brigade.
——————————

Reference your S.C.1094 dated 189.18.   Herewith list
giving numbers of Honours gained by the Battalion during the
present War.

V.C.   2 O.Rs.
D.S.O.   1 Officer.
Bar to D.S.O.   1 Officer.
M.C.   21 Officers.   2 O.Rs.
Bar to M.C.   2 Officers.   14 O.Rs.
D.C.M.   2 Officers.
M.M.   64 O.Rs.
Bar to M.M.   1 O.R.
M.S.M.   5 O.Rs.
Belgian Croix de Guerre.}   2 O.Rs.
Mentions in Despatches. }   4 Officers (1 Off. twice mentioned.)
                            3 O.Rs.

                                        Lieut-Colonel,
                        Commanding 15/17th West Yorks. Regt.

15th/17
W.Y...

3.9.18.

The War of 1914-1918.

West Yorkshire Regiment

Lt. W. D. Gray, 5th Bn. (T.F.) attd. 15/17th Bn.

was mentioned in a Despatch from

Field Marshal Sir Douglas Haig, K.T. G.C.B. O.M. G.C.V.O. K.C.I.E.

dated 16th March 1919

for gallant and distinguished services in the Field.

I have it in command from the King to record His Majesty's

high appreciation of the services rendered.

War Office
Whitehall, S.W.
1st July 1919.
                        Secretary of State for War.

Appendix VI

Campaign Medals and Badges

Every soldier who served overseas during the First World War was entitled to at least one campaign medal, and his entitlement was calculated from the moment that he entered a recognised theatre of war. Members of the Leeds Pals qualified for the following:

CAMPAIGN MEDALS

1914–15 Star – Instituted by King George V under Army Order 20 of 1919, this bronze star was awarded for service in a theatre of war between 5 August 1914 and 31 December 1915 (provided the recipient had not qualified for the 1914 Star). Thus the Leeds Pals who arrived in Egypt on 6 or 22 December 1915 just qualified for the 1914–15 Star.

British War Medal – This silver medal was instituted by King George V under Army Order 266 of 1919. It was 'granted to record the bringing of the war to a successful conclusion, and the arduous services rendered by His Majesty's Forces', and was given to every serviceman who served overseas.

Victory Medal – This bronze medal was instituted by King George V under Army Order 301 of 1919, to 'obviate the interchange of Allied Commemorative war medals'. Each of the Allies issued a similar medal with the winged figure of Victory on the obverse, and hung on the familiar rainbow-coloured ribbon. This too was given to every serviceman who served overseas. If a man was 'Mentioned in Despatches' he wore a bronze oak-leaf spray on the ribbon of the Victory medal.

The three medals came to be known as 'Pip, Squeak and Wilfred' after the cartoon characters.

BADGES WORN ON UNIFORM

From the time they first received their uniforms, towards the end of 1914, up to their disbandment in 1919, the Leeds Pals wore the coat of arms of the City of Leeds as a cap-badge. The other ranks' cap-badges were in gilded brass, although the gilt was soon polished off in the interests of 'military bull'. Those worn by officers were silver in 1914, and dull bronze thereafter.

On the shoulder straps, the men wore a brass title, 'Leeds – W Yorks', and tunic buttons for the rank-and-file were the usual General Service pattern bearing the Royal Arms. Officers wore the normal West Yorkshire Regiment collar badges, a running horse in bronze, and regimental buttons on their tunics.

Brigade and battalion recognition signs were added to the Pals' uniforms when they joined 93 Brigade at Ripon in 1915. The brigade sign consisted of a square patch of red and white flannel, representing the colours of the roses of York and Lancaster, divided diagonally, worn on the back immediately below the collar. The battalion sign was a single red flannel bar worn at the top of the sleeve, just below the seam of the shoulder strap. This indicated that the Leeds

Cap-badge, shoulder title and battalion signs worn by Alan Hey. (Bagshaw Museum)

Alfred Johnson and his War Badge certificate. (Bob Reed Collection)

Pals were the senior battalion in the brigade, the 1st and 2nd Bradford Pals wearing two and three bars, respectively.

While the Pals were in Egypt they wore the brigade sign as a puggaree badge, as well as wearing it on the back of the tunic. Some officers and men also wore the cap-badge on the front of the pith helmet; those worn by the men were blackened.

15 February 1916 – Served out with new shirts and pair of socks. Had my badge blackened and fastened same in my helmet.

15/1024 Private John Yeadon, B Company

From about July 1918, officers and men of 31st Division who had been recommended for a gallantry award, whether or not it was confirmed, were entered in the Divisional Honour Book, and were entitled to wear the Divisional Honour Badge on the right sleeve, about 2 inches from the shoulder. This, in gilt and enamel, consisted of the white and red roses of York and Lancaster respectively, surrounded by a laurel wrath.

SILVER WAR BADGE

Worn on the lapel in civilian clothes, this silver badge was instituted by King George V under Army Order 316 of 1916. As the war progressed and the number of men eligible to receive it increased, the conditions governing its issue were amended and clarified by Army Orders 50 of 1917, 291 of 1918 and 29 of 1919. Thus the final conditions were:

… The badge will, subject in every case to the approval of the Army Council, be awarded to all officers and men who, having served with the Colours for at least 7 consecutive days subsequent to the 4th August, 1914, have, on account of wounds or sickness caused otherwise than by misconduct, or on attaining the age of 51 years, retired, resigned or relinquished their commissions, or been discharged from the military forces.